COMMONWEALTH CARIBBEAN BUSINESS LAW

Third Edition

Now in its third edition, *Commonwealth Caribbean Business Law* continues to break away from the traditional English approach of treating business law primarily as the law of contract and agency.

Taking a panoramic view, it explores the foundation of various legal systems before examining areas of legal liability that affect business activities. These include areas such as contract law, tort law, criminal law, agency and internet law which present significant challenges confronting the business sector. The book primarily targets the development of business law principles in several Caribbean Commonwealth jurisdictions but, where appropriate, also embraces the jurisprudence of other Commonwealth nations, such as the United Kingdom, Canada and Australia. It also explores the United States as a non-Commonwealth jurisdiction, given the increasing importance in the Caribbean of judicial pronouncements relating to internet law from this territory.

Using excerpts from key judgments, the book allows students, particularly those with a non-legal background, to understand key legal principles for business as presented by the judiciary and draws parallels between legal theory and business practice.

Natalie Persadie is an Assistant Professor in the Design and Manufacturing Engineering Unit, University of Trinidad and Tobago, Trinidad.

Rajendra Ramlogan is a Professor of Commercial and Environmental Law in the Department of Management Studies, University of the West Indies, St. Augustine, Trinidad.

COMMONWEALTH CARIBBEAN LAW SERIES

The Commonwealth Caribbean Law Series is the only series of law books that covers the jurisdiction of the English-speaking Caribbean nations. The titles in the series were first published in 1995 to acclaim from academics, practitioners and the judiciary in the region. Several editions followed, and they have now become essential reading for those learning and practising Caribbean law.

This must-have series is required holdings for any law library specialising in Caribbean legal information.

Titles in this series include:

Alternative Dispute Resolution
Albert Fiadjoe

Commonwealth Caribbean Business Law 2/e
Rajendra Ramlogan and Natalie Persadie

Commonwealth Caribbean Company Law
Andrew Burgess

Commonwealth Caribbean Civil Procedure 3/e
Gilbert Kodilinye and Vanessa Kodilinye

Commonwealth Caribbean Constitutional Law
Sir Fred Phillips

Commonwealth Caribbean Land Law
Sampson Owusu

Commonwealth Caribbean Law and Legal Systems 2/e
Rose-Marie Belle Antoine

Commonwealth Caribbean Public Law 3/e
Albert Fiadjoe

Commonwealth Caribbean Tort Law 4/e
Gilbert Kodilinye

Commonwealth Caribbean Law of Trusts 3/e
Gilbert Kodilinye and Trevor Carmichael

Judicial Review in the Commonwealth Caribbean
Rajendra Ramlogan

Commonwealth Caribbean Administrative Law
Eddy Ventose

Commonwealth Caribbean Contract Law
Gilbert Kodilinye and Maria Kodilinye

Commonwealth Caribbean Practice and Procedure 4/e
Dana S. Seetahal

Commonwealth Caribbean Employment and Labour Law
Natalie Corthésy and Carla–Anne Harris-Roper

Commonwealth Caribbean Tort Law 5/e
Gilbert Kodilinye

Commonwealth Caribbean Property Law 4/e
Gilbert Kodilinye

Commonwealth Caribbean Business Law 3/e
Natalie Persadie and Rajendra Ramlogan

Forthcoming titles:

Commonwealth Caribbean Land Law 2/e
Sampson Owusu

Commonwealth Caribbean Intellectual Property Law
Eddy Ventose

Commonwealth Caribbean Civil Procedure 4/e
Gilbert Kodilinye and Vanessa Kodilinye

COMMONWEALTH CARIBBEAN BUSINESS LAW

Third Edition

Natalie Persadie and Rajendra Ramlogan

Routledge
Taylor & Francis Group
LONDON AND NEW YORK

Third edition published 2016
by Routledge
2 Park Square, Milton Park, Abingdon, Oxon, OX14 4RN

and by Routledge
711 Third Avenue, New York, NY 10017

Routledge is an imprint of the Taylor & Francis Group, an informa business

First edition published 2004 by Cavendish Publishing Ltd
Second edition published 2010 by Routledge-Cavendish

British Library Cataloguing in Publication Data
A catalogue record for this book is available from the British Library

Library of Congress Cataloging-in-Publication Data
A catalog record for this title has been requested
Ramlogan, Rajendra.
Commonwealth Caribbean business law / Natalie Persadie, Rajendra Ramlogan. — Third edition.
pages cm. — (Commonwealth Caribbean law series)
Includes bibliographical references and index.
1. Commercial law—West Indies, British. 2. Business enterprises—Law and legislation—West Indies, British. I. Persadie, Natalie Renée. II. Title.
KGL5231.R36 2015
346.72907—dc23
2015007049

ISBN: 978-1-138-02427-4 (hbk)
ISBN: 978-1-138-02426-7 (pbk)
ISBN: 978-1-315-77587-6 (ebk)

Typeset in Baskerville by
Apex CoVantage, LLC

For

Rajendra

Faith. Hope. Courage.

CONTENTS

Table of cases xiv
Acknowledgements xx
Country name abbreviations xxi

1 INTRODUCTION TO LEGAL SYSTEMS **1**

THE RULE OF LAW 1

LEGAL TRADITIONS OR FAMILIES 3
- Civil law 4
- Common law 5
- Socialist law 5
- Religious law 6
- Customary law 8
- Mixed legal system 8

SUBJECTS OF LAW IN COMMON LAW JURISDICTIONS 9
- Constitution 9
- Legislation 10
- Case law 12
- Books of authority 19
- Equity 20

STATUTORY INTERPRETATION 20
- Literal rule 21
- Golden rule 23
- Mischief rule 26
- Purposive approach 30

SEPARATION OF POWERS 33
- Parliamentary sovereignty 33
- Role of the executive 33
- Judicial independence 34

2 LAW OF OBLIGATIONS: MAKING THE CONTRACT **36**

CONTRACT 36

CONTRACTUAL INTERPRETATION 40

OFFER 45

INVITATION TO TREAT 49
Advertisements 50
Tenders 52

UNILATERAL CONTRACTS 70

ACCEPTANCE 73
Definition 73
By post/telegram 75
By telex 76
By email 78
By facsimile transmission 79
By telephone/video conference 80
By conduct 83

INTENTION TO CREATE LEGAL RELATIONS 85
Commercial agreements 85
Domestic agreements 87

CERTAINTY OF CONTRACT 89

COUNTER-OFFERS 91
Battle of the forms 92

CONSIDERATION 94
Meaning 94
The bargain 96
Nature of the consideration 97
Forbearance and compromise 99
Past consideration 104
Performance of duty under existing contract 107
Duty under law 109
Duty under contract in favour of third party 110

TERMS 111
Express terms 113
Incorporation by express reference 116
Implied terms 118
Conditions 140
Warranties 143
Exemption clauses 145

3 LAW OF OBLIGATIONS: ATTACKING THE CONTRACT 149

CAPACITY 149
- Legal ability 149
- Taking advantage 160

MISTAKE 174
- Mutual mistakes 176
- Unilateral mistakes 183

MISREPRESENTATION 187
- Materiality 192
- Ambiguity 193
- Inducement 195
- Reliance 197
- Damage 198
- Knowledge of representee 198

FRUSTRATION 201
- Early developments 201
- Contemporary formulation 202

ILLEGAL CONTRACTS 207
- Restraint of trade 208
- Contracts contrary to public policy 218
- Contract to commit a crime 220

PRIVITY 221

REMEDIES FOR BREACH OF CONTRACT 224
- Damages 224
- Specific performance 234

4 LAW OF OBLIGATIONS: TORTS 237

THE LAW OF TORTS 237

NEGLIGENCE-GENERATED TORTS 238
- General principles of negligence 238

SPECIFIC ASPECTS OF NEGLIGENCE: TORT-BASED LIABILITY AS PART OF BUSINESS ACTIVITIES 267
- Product liability 267
- Negligent misstatement/misrepresentation 278

Occupiers' liability 286
Employers' liability 293
Vicarious liability 303

TORTS OF INTERFERENCE WITH USE AND ENJOYMENT OF PROPERTY 310
Nuisance 310
Rule in *Rylands v Fletcher* 312

ENGAGING IN UNFAIR TORTIOUS BUSINESS PRACTICES 317
Passing off 317
Conspiracy 325
Deceit 330
Injurious/malicious falsehood 334
Unlawful interference with trade 337
Inducement to breach of contract 338

CONCURRENT LIABILITY IN TORT AND CONTRACT 345

5 CRIMINALISING BUSINESS ACTIVITIES 348

ACTUS REUS 349

MENS REA 350
Intention 350
Recklessness 351
Negligence 353

DEFENCES 354
Mistake as to facts 354
Ignorance of the law 356

CORPORATE CRIMINAL LIABILITY 357
Vicarious liability 357
Individual liability for breach of a statutory duty 357
Liability on the basis of the 'directing mind' principle 360

CRIMINAL LIABILITY FOR ACTS IN PURSUANCE OF COMMERCIAL ACTIVITIES 369

SENTENCING CORPORATIONS 370

6 THE LAW OF AGENCY 374

WHAT IS AGENCY? 374

AUTHORITY OF AN AGENT 376
Express actual authority 376
Implied actual authority 381
Apparent/ostensible authority 382
Usual authority 387

AGENCY OF NECESSITY 389

RATIFICATION OF ACTS DONE WITHOUT AUTHORITY 394

DUTIES OF THE AGENT TO THE PRINCIPAL 396

PRINCIPAL'S DUTIES TO THE AGENT; AGENT'S RIGHTS AGAINST THE PRINCIPAL 403

7 INTERNET LAW AND BUSINESS 417

CONTRACTING IN THE DIGITAL MARKETPLACE 418
Shrink-wrap agreements 419
Click-wrap agreements 422
Browse-wrap agreements 425

ISSUES ARISING OUT OF INTERNET CONTRACTS 429
Jurisdiction 429
Forum selection clause and venue 435
Choice of law 439
Taxation 442

Bibliography 447
Index 451

TABLE OF CASES

Aaron Krohn (Claimant) v Jose Tun (First Defendant), Ali Safa (Second Defendant) and Walid Jundi (Third Defendant); The Attorney General and The Comptroller of Customs (Interested Parties) Claim No. 78 of 2011 (BZ) ... 143
A, B, C, D v E (2011) HCVAP 2011/001 (AI) ... 12
Adnan Mkhoul v Keith Henry and Etola Richards HC Civil Claim No. 121 of 2008 (SVG) ... 90
Aho v Kelly 1998 CanLII 6616 (BCSC) (CA) ... 16
Airline Freight Services Ltd. v Rosalind Morris and Exhibition & Building Contractors Ltd. (2005) CA No. 25 of 1997 (BB) ... 289
Allied Protection Limited (Claimant) v John Barnes and John Barnes v Donald Williams [2013] JMCC Comm. 12 (JA) ... 216
Althea Mitchell (Claimant) v Cheryl Stewart (Defendant) [2014] JMSC Civ 92 (JM) ... 332
Amazon.com LLC and Amazon Services LLC v New York State Department of Taxation and Finance and The State of New York No. 60124708 (New York Sup Ct 2008) ... 429, 443
Anderton v Rodgers [1981] Crim LR 404, DC (GB) ... 357
Andre Alexander (Claimant) v St Lucia Golf Resort & Country Club Limited (Defendant) (2011) SLUHCV2007/0715 (LC) ... 315
Andrene Brown (Claimant) v Insurance Company of the West Indies (Defendant) (2011) Claim No. HCV 04439 of 2007 (JM) ... 192, 195
Andy Bhagwandeen (Claimant) v The Attorney General of Trinidad and Tobago (First Defendant), Deonarine Mahadeo and Sasenarine Deonarine (T/A Deonarine Mahadeo and Son) (Second Defendant), and The Chairman, Alderman, Councillors and Electors of the Region of Princes Town (Third Defendant) (2012) Claim No. CV2010–03421 (TT) ... 266
Ann Marie Redman (Claimant) v Hillary Samuel (Defendant) (2009) Claim No. CV2007–02664 (TT) ... 300
Anthony Francois (Claimant) v Maritime Preservation Limited (Defendant) (2011) CV2008–00055 (TT) ... 294
Anthony Walrond (Appellant) v National Assistance Board (Respondent) (2010) Civil Appeal No. 16 of 2008 (BB) ... 286
Apple Corps Limited v Apple Computer, Incorporated [2004] EWHC 768 (Ch) (GB) ... 80
Arthur Belisle (Appellant) v Anna Crawford (Respondent) Civil Appeal No. 30 of 2009 (BZ) ... 291
Asha Charan v Omar Mohammed (2011) CV2008–00683 (TT) ... 187
Audrey Baratt (Claimant) v Hawksbill Limited (Defendant) (2012) Claim No. ANUHCV 2009/0343 (AG) ... 287
Australian Woollen Mills Pty Ltd. v The Commonwealth (1954) 92 CLR 424 (AU) ... 96

Baby Nagessar v Xavier Goodridge (2011) Claim No. CV2009–00771 (TT) ... 13, 15, 18
Bariki International Limited et al v Jamaican Treat Limited Claim No. HCV-00545 of 2004 (JM) ... 114
Barnett v Chelsea and Kensington Hospital Management Committee [1969] 1 QB 428 (GB) ... 244
Barrack Construction Ltd v National Housing Corporation No. 1320 of 2001 (BB) ... 116
Benton Brooks (Appellant/Plaintiff) v Syne Contractors Limited (Respondent/Defendant) (2012) Cv App No. 195 of 2003 (TT) ... 301
BFi Optilas v Blyth & Others [2002] EWHC 2693 QBD (GB) ... 211
Birse Construction Limited v St David Limited No. 1998 TCC No 419 (GB) ... 38
Bisnath Boodram v The Bank of Nova Scotia Trinidad and Tobago and Leelawatie Boodram (1990) HCA S-1301 and S-1438 of 1986 (TT) ... 393
Blomley v Ryan (1956) 99 CLR 362 (AU) ... 156
Bougainville Investment Corp. v Semple 2013 BCSC 1919 (CA) ... 73
Branwhite v Worcester Works Finance Ltd [1969] 1 AC 522 (GB) ... 375
Brentwood Plastics Inc. v Topsyn Flexible Packaging Ltd 2014 MBQB 97 (CA) ... 92
Brinkibon Ltd v Stahag Stahl und Stahlwarenhandelsgesellschaft M.B.H. [1982] 1 Lloyd's Rep. 217 (HL) (GB) ... 76
Bromley v Smith [1909] 2 KB 235 KBD (GB) ... 153
Broome v Cassell [1972] AC 1027 (GB) ... 17
Brown (Uriah) v R (2005) 66 WIR 238 (PC) (JM) ... 353
Brown's Bay Resort Limited (Appellant) v Luca Possoni (Respondent) (2014) ANUHCVAP2010/0033 (AG) ... 233
Burnie Port Authority v General Jones Pty Limited (1994) 120 ALR 42 (AU) ... 313
Bushell and Another v Port Authority of Trinidad and Tobago and Others (1998) 56 WIR 460 ... 14

Canada v Glengarry Bingo Assn. (1999–0305) FCA A-502–95 (CA) ... 374
Canadian Dredge & Dock Co. v The Queen [1985] 1 SCR 662 (CA) ... 362
Canadian National Railway Co. v Norsk Pacific Steamship Co. [1992] 1 SCR 1021 (CA) ... 254
Canadian Pacific Hotels Ltd v Bank of Montreal [1987] 1 SCR 71 (CA) ... 129

Caparo Industries Plc. v Dickman and Others [1990] 2 AC 605 (GB) 279
Carlill v Carbolic Smoke Ball Company [1893] 1 QB 256 (GB) 70
Carmel Smith v Statutory Authorities Service Commission (2007) HCA S-95 of 2004 (TT) 422, 423
Cathryn Harris v Blockbuster Inc. No. 3:09-cv-217-M (15 April 2009) 422, 423
Chaplin v Leslie Frewin (Publishers) Ltd. and Others [1966] Ch 71 (GB) 154
Chappell & Co. Ltd. and Another v Nestle Co. Ltd. and Another [1960] AC 87 (HL) (UK) 98
China Pacific SA v Food Corporation of India [1982] AC 939 (GB) 390
Chloé v Queen Bee of Beverly Hill, LLC 616 F.3d 158 (2010) 430
Citibank NA v Blue Chateau Limited SC Civil Appeal No. 90/99, Suit No. 1998/E248 (JM) 100
Clacken and Clacken v Causwell and Causwell et al (2010) 2008 HCV 01834 (JM) 40
Classic Maritime Inc v Lion Diversified Holdings & Anor [2009] EWHC 1142 (Comm) (21 May 2009) (GB) 104
Claudette Edwards v Quest Security Services Ltd. (2005) Claim No. 2005 HCV 01124 (JM) 221
Clive Morris (Plaintiff) v Francis Furniture Limited (Defendant) (2010) No. 735 of 2006 (BB) 265, 293
Clotelle Holder-Delves (First Plaintiff), Patrick Delves (Second Plaintiff) and Renaldo Springer (Third Plaintiff) [suing by his mother and next friend Rhonda Holder] v BS&T Motors (Defendant) No. 1724 of 2002 (BB) 194
CMF Projects P/L v Riggall & Anor [2014] QDC 90 (AU) 13
Coles v Clarenville Drydock Ltd. 1998 CanLII 13306 (NL SCTD) (CA) 145
Colgate-Palmolive Limited and Another v K. F. Pattron [1978] RPC 635 PC (TT) 318
Commissioner of Metropolitan Police v Caldwell [1982] AC 341 (GB) 352
Crown Corke de Guatemala SA (Claimant) v Carlo Products Limited (1st Defendant), Carlys Dahlia Hughes (Executrix of the Estate of David Henry Hughes, Deceased) (2nd Defendant) (2009) Claim No. CLC – 324 of 1999 (JM) 381, 389
Crown Paving v Her Majesty The Queen 2009 NLCA 5 (CA) 64
Curlon Orlando Lawrence Claimant v Channus Block And Marl Defendant/Ancillary Claimant Quarry Limited And Owen Bailey Ancillary Defendant [2013] JMSC Civ 6 (JM) 307
Curtis Arthurs (Claimant) v James Jackson (Trading as Negril Tree House Resort) (Defendant) (2010) Claim No. CL 1999/A0–42 (JM) 305

Dairy Distributors Ltd. v Nestle Trinidad and Tobago Limited [2005] HCA 528 of 2003 (TT) 325
Dammer v Wallace and Others (1993) 45 WIR 161 (AI) 181
Dave Lopez and Versatile Investment Trust Limited v The Bank of Nova Scotia Trust Company of Trinidad and Tobago Limited and Constantine Mendez (2001) HCA No. 3418 of 1986 (TT) 197, 198
David Walcott (Appellant) v The Royal Bank of Trinidad and Tobago (Defendant) (2010) Civ App #158/2006 (TT) 346
David Wong Ken and Others (Claimants) v National Investment Bank Jamaica Limited and Others (Defendants) [2012] JMSC Civ 32 (JM) 327
Devon Ltd Claimant v Cap Juluca Properties Ltd. (Doing Business As Cap Juluca Resort) Defendant (2012) Claim No. AXAHCV 0041/2009 (AI) 204
Director of Personnel Administration and the Police Service Commission v Eusebio Cooper and Others, Civil Appeal No. 10 of 2004 (TT) 35
Donoghue v Stevenson [1932] AC 562 (GB) 239, 267
Donsland Ltd v Nicholas Van Hoogstraten, Barnhill Investments Ltd, Selective Management Ltd [2002] EWCA Civ 253 (GB) 381
Doucette v Marin 2008 CanLII 66625 (ON SC) (CA) 108
Dr James Boyce (Appellant) v Corine Lorde and Stephen Lorde (Respondents) (2011) Civil Appeal No. 20 of 2008 (BB) 245
Dr P Samuels v Lakeland Farms Limited [2003] JMCA 8 (31 July 2003) (JM) 125, 388
Dranez Anstalt and Others v Zamir Hayek and Others [2002] EWCA Civ 1729 (GB) 210
Dunlop Pneumatic Tyre Co. Ltd v New Garage and Motor Co. Ltd [1915] AC 79 (GB) 232

Eastern Canada Coal Gas Venture Ltd. (Venture) v Cape Breton Development Corp. (Devco) 2001 (NSCC) 196 (CA) 177
Eastern Power Limited v Azienda Communale Energia and Ambiente 1999 CanLII 3785 (ON CA) (CA) 79
Eaton Baker and Another v R (1975) 23 WIR 463 (Privy Council) (JM) 15
Erven Warnink BV v J Townend & Sons (Hull) Ltd. [1979] 2 All ER 927 (GB) 317
Essa v Laing Ltd. [2004] EWCA Civ 2 (GB) 256
Esso Petroleum Co. Ltd. v Harper's Garage (Stourport) Ltd. [1968] AC 279 (GB) 209

Fazal v Annamanthadoo (1991) 48 WIR 150 (GY) 404
Fazal Ghany (Regimental No. 12853 CPL) (Appellant) v The Compensation Committee and the Attorney General of Trinidad and Tobago (Respondents) (2011) Civil Appeal No. 197 of 2008; G-13 No. 26 of 2007 (TT) 31
Fernkiln Pty Ltd. v Australian Building Industries Pty Ltd. [1999] QCA 179 (AU) 73

First Charter Financial Corp. Ltd. v Musclow 49 DLR (3d) 138 1974 (BCSC) (CA) 150
Firth v Staines [1897] 2 QB 70 (GB) 394
Fiser v Dell Computer Corp., No. 30,424 (SC NM, 2008) 439
Fitch v Dewes [1921] 2 AC 158 (GB) 215
Foster (Trevor) and Williams (Cedric) v R. (2007) 70 WIR 60 (PC) (BB) 352
Floral Fantasy v Bethel Brackin HC Claim No. 17 of 2012 (SVG) 21

Gator.com Corp. v LL Bean, Inc. 341 F.3d 1072 (9th Cir. 2003), 366 F.3d 789 (9th Cir. 2004) 429
George Burchell v Desmond Tomlinson HCV 03126/2006 (JM) 285
Gerard Kraakman DBA 'The Woodshop' v Donna Sterling (2011) HCVAP 2010/12 (VG) 140
Glasbrook v Glamorgan County Council [1925] AC 270 (GB) 109
Gloria Wilson (Appellant/Opposer) v Wigvon Cadogan and Selby Renetta Ross (Respondents/Petitioners) (2010) Appeal No. 3 of 2008 (GY) 375
Graham Barclay Oysters Pty Ltd v Ryan 211 CLR 540 (2003) (AU) 275
Great Peace Shipping Limited v Tsavliris (International) Limited 'Great Peace'/'Cape Providence' [2002] EWCA Civ No. 1407 CA (GB) 175
Greater Manchester Police v Wigan Athletic AFC Ltd. [2008] EWCA Civ 1449 (19 December 2008) (GB) 109
Greater Vancouver Water District v North American Pipe & Steel Ltd. 2011 BCSC 30 (CA) 55
G S Dale & Ors v P C I Jeffrey and Anor [2008] NZHC 147 (19 February 2008) (NZ) 78

Harvela Investments Ltd. v Royal Trust Company of Canada (C.I.) Ltd. and Others [1986] AC 207 (CA) 53
Haseldine v Daw and Son Limited (1941) 2 KB 343 (GB) 268
Hawkins v Coulsdon and Purley UDC [1954] 1 QB 319 (GB) 273
Henthorn v Fraser [1892] 2 Ch 27 (GB) 75
Hilda Elisabeth Stoutt (By Her Guardians and Next Friends Peggy Stoutt-Harewood and Preston Stoutt), Peggy Stoutt-Harewood, Preston Stoutt Appellants v Firstbank Puerto Rico Respondent (2011) HCVAP 2010/016 (VG) 159
Hines v Overstock.com Inc., 668 F. Supp. 2d 362 (EDNY 2009) 425
Holt v P.P.G. Industries Canada Ltd. (1983) 25 CCLT 253 (CA) 269
Howmet Ltd v Economy Devices Ltd & Ors [2014] EWHC 3933 (TCC) (GB) 273
Hubbuck & Sons, Limited v Wilkinson, Heywood & Clark, Limited [1899] 1 QB 86 CA (GB) 336
Hughes v Lord Advocate [1963] AC 837 (GB) 250

Ian Hoyte v Toyota Trinidad and Tobago Limited (2013) CV2012–02049 (TT) 138
Idameneo (No 123) Pty Ltd v Dr Teresa Angel-Honnibal [2002] NSWSC 1214 (AU) 212
Iman Abouzaid v Mothercare (UK) Ltd [2000] EWCA Civ 348 (GB) 271
In the Matter of the Estate of Raphael Williams, Deceased, Cliff Williams and Aggie Williams v The Moorings Limited (2010) BVICV2009/0083 (BVI) 86

Jamaica Carpet Mills Ltd v First Valley Bank (1986) 45 WIR 278 (JM) 17
Jane Craig (Claimant) v LJ Williams (Defendant) (2012) Claim No. CV2009–01023 (TT) 292
Jasmat Ramanand and Shyam Ramanand (Plaintiffs) v Ramcharran Singh and Shiva Woodworking Establishment Limited (Defendants) (2010) No 213-W (GY) 304
Javier Arthurton BNF, Sandra Arthurton, Claimant v Winston Skeete, First Defendant and Wesk Limited, Second Defendant (2012) Claim No. NEVHCV2007/0024 (KN) 241
Jimmy Robinson (Claimant) v Prinselsio Rivero (Defendant) Claim No. 311 of 2012 (BZ) 174
Joe Douglas v Talk America Inc. No. 06–75424 (9th Cir. 2007) 423
Jorge Raizman (Plaintiff) [As Principal Agent for a Business T/A Ride N' Style] v Aftabay Raja (Defendant) CV 1526 of 2006 (BB) 121
Joseph Henry v Tobago Plantations Limited (2009) Claim No. CV2007–03427 (TT) 229

Kay Mart Ltd., Steve Khemlani and Raju Khemlani v K-Mart Corporation (Plaintiff/Respondent) CA No. 85 of 1997 (JM) 318
Kelly v Cooper and Another [1992] 41 WIR 80 (BM) 399
Kings Beach Hotels Limited and JGL Hotels Limited (Appellants) v Johanna Kesmin Marks (Respondent) (2011) Civil Appeal No. 23 of 2006 (BB) 208
Kiyo Itakura Investments v Bentall Properties Ltd. 1993 CanLII 289 BCSC (CA) 49
Kleinwort Benson Ltd. v Lincoln City Council [1999] 2 AC 349 (GB) 181

Lennox Linton v The Attorney General of Antigua and Barbuda (2009) Claim No. ANUHCV2007/0354 (AG) 24
Leona Francis (Claimant) v Daven Joseph (Defendant) (2013) Claim No. ANUHCV2011/0573 (AG) 413
Lloyd Michael Pommells Claimant v EW Lewis Investments & Finance Ltd Defendant [2013] JMCC Comm 10 (JM) 380
Lonrho Plc. v Fayed and Others [1991] 3 WLR 188 (GB) 326

M.A. Mortenson Co. v Timberline Software Corp., et al. Docket No. 67796–4 (Wash, 2000) 420
Maclean-Beaudet v Belanger 2012 CanLII 97365 (ON SCSM) (CA) 206
Mandraj and Mandraj v Texaco Trinidad Inc (1969) 15 WIR 251 (TT) 316
Marc Rich & Co. AG v Bishop Rock Marine Co. Limited [1996] AC 211 (GB) 239
Marie Egger v Herbert Egger (2004) Civ App 17 of 2002 (LC) 378
Marilyn Spencer and Ors v The Attorney General of Antigua and Barbuda Claim No. ANUHCV 2008/0226 (AG) 23
Martin Devaux (Claimant) v (1) Theresa Goddard (2) Mark Goddard (3) Roebuck Properties (St. Lucia) Ltd. Defendants (2010) Claim No. SlUHCV2008/0405 (LC) 414
Marubeni Hong Kong and South China Limited v Ministry of Finance of Mongolia [2004] EWHC 472 (Comm) (GB) 377
Masontech Inc. v Aaffinity Contracting and Environmental Ltd. 2014 NSSC 164 (CA) 84
Matthews v Baxter (1872–73) LR 8 Ex 132 Ex Ct (GB) 158
McDonald's Corporation v McDonald's Corporation Ltd. and Another (1996) 55 WIR 226 (JM) 323
McFarlane and Another v Tayside Health Board [2002] 2 AC 59 (GB) 252
Meretz Investments NV and another v ACP Ltd. and others [2008] Ch 244 (GB) 341
Mid Island Poultry Ltd. (Claimant) v Electrical Rewind Services Ltd (1st Defendant) and John Salter (2nd Defendant) [2012] JMSC Civ 175 (JM) 253
Miller v Edelweiss International Franchise Corp. 1996 BCSC C914895 (CA) 199
M.J.B. Enterprises Ltd. v Defence Construction (1951) [1999] 1 SCR 619 (CA) 61
Mohamed Ali v Guyana Teachers' Union (1991) 50 WIR 203 (GY) 224
Mont (J.A.) UK Limited v Mills [1993] FSR 577 (GB) 214
Mustapha v Culligan of Canada Ltd. 2008 SCC 27 (CA) 259

Nadine Nabie and Michelle Mayers Appellants / Interested Parties v Law Association of Trinidad and Tobago First Respondent / Claimant, The Attorney General Of Trinidad And Tobago Second Respondent / Defendant Claim No. Cv 2012–00892; Civil Appeal No. 72 of 2012 (TT) 21
National Carriers Ltd. v Panalpina (Northern) Ltd. [1981] AC 675 HL (GB) 202
National Insurance Board (Appellant) v [1] Ann Marie Duncan-Mason [2] Peter Mason (Respondents) HCVAP 2009/002 (GD) 95
Natural Resources Conservation Authority v Seafood and Ting International Ltd; Natural Resources Conservation Authority v DYC Fishing Ltd (1999) 58 WIR 269 (JM) 337
Nelson Pierre, Claimant v Millennium Holdings Ltd. (MHL) and Frederick Sahadeo, Defendants (2013) Claim No. MNIHCV2009/0025 (MS) 203
New Falmouth Resort Limited v International Hotels Jamaica Limited [2013] UKPC 11 (GB) 394
New Zealand Shipping Co. Ltd. v A.M. Satterthwaite & Co. Ltd. [1975] AC 154 (PC) (GB) 110
Nguyen v Barnes & Noble Inc., No 12–56628 DC No 8:12-cv-00812-JST-RNB (9th Cir. 2014) 426
Niedermeyer v Charlton 2014 BCCA 165 (CanLII) (CA) 218
Norman Aviation Flight Training Academy Inc. Claimant/Respondent v Leroy Smith, Dulani Smith Defendants/Applicants (2014) Claim No. ANUHCV 2013/0523 (AG) 151

OBG v Allan [2008] 1 AC 1 (GB) 338
Omar Maraj (Appellant) v The Public Service Appeal Board (Respondents) (2009) Civil Appeal No. 100 of 2006 (TT) 31
Orchard v Lee [2009] EWCA Civ 295 (GB) 242
Overseas Tankship (U.K.) Ltd. v Morts Dock & Engineering Co. Ltd. [1961] UKPC 1 (18 January 1961) (AU) 248
Overstock.com, Inc., Appellant, v New York State Department of Taxation and Finance, et al., Respondents. No. 33 and Amazon.com, LLC, et al., Appellants, v New York State Department of Taxation and Finance, et al., Respondents. No. 34 (NY Ct App, 2013) 445

Page v Smith [1996] AC 310 (GB) 258
Palace Amusement Company Ltd (1921) v CD Alexander Company Realty Ltd (2005) SC Civ App No. 34/2003 (JM) 410

Pebble Beach Co. v Caddy No. 04–15577 DC No. CV-03–04550-PJH, 453 F.3d 1151 (9th Cir. 2006)............429
Persaud and Another v Neal and Massy Enterprises Limited (2001) 63 WIR 122 (GY)............385
Pomerleau Inc. v Newfoundland and Labrador (Transportation and Works) 2014 NLTD (G) 19 (CA)............57
Pouderoyen Village Council v Singh; Pouderoyen Village Council v Samuels, Jahoor, Deonaraine And Others (1961) 3 WIR 178 (GY)............356
Powercor Australia Ltd v Pacific Power [1999] VSC 110 (AU)............235
Premnath Jaikaran (Plaintiff) v Saiscon Limited (Defendant) (2011) CV2007–2813 (TT)............295
Presidential Security Services of Australia Pty Ltd v Brilley [2008] NSWCA 204 (AU)............361
ProCD Incorporated v Matthew Zeidenberg and Silken Mountain Web Services Inc. 86 F.3d 1447 (7th Cir. 1996), No. 96–1139............420

Quill Corp. v North Dakota 504 U 298 (1992)............443

R v Cunningham [1957] 2 All ER 412 (GB)............351
R v Derek Penney Electrical Ltd., 2013 NLTD (G) 177 (CA)............67
R v F (M.B.) 2003 ABQB 368 (CA)............27
R v G [2003] 1 AC 1034 (GB)............352
R v General Scrap Iron & Metals Ltd [2003] ABQB 22 (CA)............371
R v Hinchey [1996] 3 SCR 1128 (CA)............369
R v Mohan [1976] QB 1 (GB)............350
R v Patterson 2002 NSPC 14 (CA)............358
Ramsay v Walker [1962] 4 WIR 539 (JM)............395
Rasheed Mohammed Claimant v Dheerajie Benny Defendant (2010) Claim No. CV 2007–00205 (TT)............165
RBTT Bank Jamaica Limited v YP Seaton, Earthcrane Haulage Limited and YP Seaton and Associates Claim No. [2014] JMSC Civ 34 (JM)............131
RBTT (Claimant) v Almon Nisbett (Respondent) and Almon Nisbett (Claimant) v RBTT (Respondent) (2012) Consolidated Claims Nos. NEVHCVI996/0 177 & NEVHCV200110113 (KN)............183
RBTT Merchant Bank Limited, RBTT Bank Limited, RBC Financial (Caribbean) Limited, (Claimants) v Reed Monza (Trinidad) Limited (In Receivership), James W. Sneddon Limited, Eugene Robert Gransaull (Defendants) (2012) CV2010–03699 (TT)............334
Redmond v Dainton [1920] 2 KB 256 (GB)............201
Register.com v Verio, Inc. Docket No. 00–9596 (2nd Cir. 2004)............425
Rembert Thomas Claimant v 1. Quarry Products Limited 2. Kernie Emmanuel Defendants (2011) Claim No. SLUHCV 2009/0693 (LC)............383
Roback v UBC 2007 BCSC 334 (CA)............51
Robyn Rihanna Fenty, Roraj Trade LLC, Combermere Entertainment Properties, LLC Claimants/Respondents v Arcadia Group Brands Limited Topshop/Topman Limited Defendants/Appellants [2015] EWCA Civ 3 (GB)............320
Roger Rahamut and National Insurance Property Development Company Limited v Airport Authority of Trinidad and Tobago HCA No. S-732 of 1995 (TT)............147
Ronicles Limited Claimant v 1. DCG Properties Ltd. 2. Stewart Title Eastern Caribbean Ltd. Defendants Claim No. SLUHCV2011/0547 (LC)............119
Roxborough v Rothmans of Pall Mall Australia Pty Ltd. [2001] HCA 68 (6 December 2001) (AU)............123
Russell Scarcella v America Online Inc. 2004 NY Slip Op 51021(U); 4 Misc 3d 1024 A (NY Civ Ct 2004)............422, 435
Rust v Abbey Life Assurance Co. Ltd. and Another [1978] 2 Lloyd's Rep 386 (GB)............83
Rylands v Fletcher (1866) LR 1 Exch. 265 (GB)............312, 313

Saffron Limited (Claimant) v Angel Estates Limited (Defendant) (2012) Claim No. ANUHCV2008/0641 (AG)............227
Saskatchewan Government Insurance v Medynski (Lakeland Towing) 2012 SKQB 157 (CanLII) (CA)............71
Schroeder Music Publishing Co. v Macaulay (formerly Instone) [1974] 1 WLR 1308 (GB)............167
Select Properties v Texaco (Trinidad) Limited and Nealco Properties Limited (2009) HCA No. S-765 of 2003 (TT)............47
Singh v Chung 1995 CanLII 914 BCCA (CA)............91
Smith v Mottley (1993) 48 WIR 20 (BB)............87
Spyglass v McCabe 2010 SKPC 164 (CanLII) (CA)............220
Starry Benjamin Claimant v Caribbean Commercial Bank (Anguilla) Limited Defendant Claim No. AXAHCV2013/0079 (AI)............135

Stennett v Hancock and Peters [1939] 2 All ER 578 (GB)....272
Stewart v Superior Canadian Livestock Auction Ltd. 2014 SKQB 394 (CA)....99
Storer v Manchester City Council [1974] 1 WLR 1403 (GB)....46
Sunset Crest Property Owners Inc v Peter Grannum Suit No. 1940 of 2007 (BB)....112
Swimwear Etc. v Raymark Xpert Business Systems Inc. 2006 ABQB 82....436
Sylvan Lashley (First Plaintiff) and Gloria Lashley (Second Plaintiff) v Azul Dacosta Lashley (Defendant) (2011) No CV 1996 of 2006 (BB)....190
Sylvia Steens (Claimant) v National Commercial Bank of Jamaica Limited (Defendant) [2013] JMSC CIV 104 (JM)....280, 303

Tajo Beharry v BWIA International Airways Limited (2006) Civ. App. No. 27 of 2003 (TT)....298
Tanya Susanne Phillips Applicant v RBC Royal Bank (Jamaica) Limited Respondent [2014] JMCC Comm. 2 (JM)....161
Taylor (Respondent/Claimant) v A Novo (Appellant/Defendant) (UK) Ltd [2013] EWCA Civ 194 (GB)....261
Tercon Contractors Ltd. v British Colombia (Transportation and Highways) 2010 SCC 4 (CA)....62
Tesco Supermarkets Ltd. v Nattrass [1971] AC 153 (GB)....366
The Attorney General v The Barbuda Council Civil Appeal No. 7 of 2001 (AG)....28
The Constituency Boundaries Commission and the Attorney-General of the Commonwealth of Dominica v Urban Baron Civil Appeal No. 12 of 1998 (DM)....35
The Imperial Loan Company, Limited v Stone [1892] 1 QB 599 CA (GB)....158
The Moorcock (1889) 14 PD 68 (GB)....131
Toojays Limited (Appellant) v Westhaven Limited (Respondent) Civil Appeal No. 14 of 2008 (BB)....89
Topp v London Country Bus (South West) Ltd. [1993] 1 WLR 976 (GB)....246
Transco Plc v Stockport Metropolitan Borough Council [2004] 2 AC 1 (GB)....313
Tricome v eBay, NO. 09–2492 (ED Pa, 2009)....436

Verona Robinson (Claimant) v Marcia Robinson (Defendant) [2014] JMSC Civ 19 (JM)....200
Visual Arts Production Limited v Marcus Jean Baptiste (2011) CV2008–01020 (TT)....37
Vraj Pankhania, Joshna Pankhania v The London Borough of Hackney, The Receiver for the Metropolitan Police District (2002) WL 1876382 (GB)....189

Walt Disney Productions v Fantasyland Hotel Inc. [1996] 6 WWR 403 (CA)....319
Watteau v Fenwick [1893] 1 QB 346 (GB)....388
Wayne Camps (Claimant) v Angela Attong (Defendant) (2010) CV2007–00840 (TT)....407
William Derry, J. C. Wakefield, M. M. Moore, J. Pethick, and S. J. Wilde v Sir Henry William Peek, Baronet (1889) LR 14 App.Cas. 337 HL (GB)....331
Williams (Hubert) v The State (1995) 48 WIR 328 (TT)....355
Williams v Murraine (1987) 40 WIR 160 (MS)....314
Wilton Innis (Plaintiff) v Guyana Telephone & Telegraph Company Limited (Defendant) (2012) 1998 No. 392/W (GY)....310
Winston Padmore Claimant v James Morgan First Defendant, Roderick A. Thomas Second Defendant, Yacoob Ali Third Defendant (2009) CV2006–277 (TT)....397
Winston Walters v Jose Cartellore Construcciones Civiles S.A. (2009) HCV No. 05597 of 2008 (JM)....225
Woodhouse v Walsall Metropolitan Borough Council [1994] Env LR 30 QBD (GB)....359
Wright v Davidson (1992–02–07) BCCA CA011480 (CA)....249

Yahoo!, Inc. v La Ligue Contre Le Racisme et L'Antisémitisme 433 F.3d 1199 (9th Cir. 2006)....439
Yambou Development Co Ltd. v Kauser (2000) 59 WIR 141 (VC)....186
Yassim Ali, substituted on behalf of the Estate Of Dean Mohammed Ali (pursuant to the order of the Honourable Justice Jones dated 8th July, 2009) v Salesh Ramnarine [CV 2008–01471] Salesh Ramnarine; St. Augustine Gas Station Limited v Yassim Ali, substituted on behalf of the Estate of Dean Mohammed Ali [2010] Claim No. CV 2009–00958 (TT)....169
Yeomans v Wilkins 2011 NBQB 85 (CanLII) (CA)....282
Ying v Song [2009] SWSC 1344 (3 December 2009) (AU)....16

Zephyr Services Limited (Claimant) v Ministry of Forestry Fisheries and Sustainable Development (First Defendant) and the Attorney General (Second Defendant) Claim No. 69 of 2013 (BZ)....54
Zippo Mfg. Co. v Zippo Dot Com, Inc. 952 F.Supp 1119 (WD Pa 1997)....429, 430

ACKNOWLEDGEMENTS

The authors wish to thank the following creators and publishers for allowing us to reproduce their cartoons: Stu's Views for their images relating to law (Chapter 1), contract law (Chapter 2), criminal business activities (Chapter 5), agency (Chapter 6), and internet law (Chapter 7); and CartoonStock for their images relating to contract law (Chapter 3) and tort law (Chapter 4).

Special thanks also go to the Registrar of the Court of Guyana as well as the librarians at the Court library who were all very helpful.

The authors wish to thank Jonathan Jagessar for his research assistance.

COUNTRY NAME ABBREVIATIONS

Anguilla	AI
Antigua and Barbuca	AG
Australia	AU
Barbados	BB
Bermuda	BM
Canada	CA
Dominica	DM
Great Britain	GB
Grenada	GD
Guyana	GY
Jamaica	JM
Montserrat	MS
New Zealand	NZ
St Kitts and Nevis	KN
St Lucia	LC
St Vincent and the Grenadines	VC
Trinidad and Tobago	TT
United Kingdom	GB
Virgin Islands, British	VG

CHAPTER 1

INTRODUCTION TO LEGAL SYSTEMS

Reproduced with the permission of Stu's Views

THE RULE OF LAW

Law is a social phenomenon. It has grown into an essential principle of social organisation in Western civilisations as a result of the historicity of those societies.[1] Law functions as the formal machinery for creating and maintaining social order, as seen in the Western world. All societies possess some degree of order which allows for sustained social interaction within a period of time. The form of order which exists depends on the particular society and the perceived needs of that society. Political, historical and moral characteristics of a society also assist in shaping that form of order. According to Sinha, law is a composite of three components: rules of law (mental), attitudes (psychological) and external aspects (behaviour). It is these three components which shape law in any given society; however, the question begs itself, how *does* law maintain social order? Law prescribes what acceptable social conduct for any given society

1 Sinha, SP, *What is Law?: The Differing Theories of Jurisprudence*, 1989, New York: Paragon House, p 218.

is and punishes deviant behaviour which results in conflict or disorder. There are established institutions and procedures through which the law operates in civil and criminal issues to return a society to its status quo of social normalcy.

The constitutional and administrative law of the United Kingdom has long respected a number of values, many of which are encapsulated in the concept of the rule of law: checks against arbitrary power; democracy through universal suffrage and regular elections; representative and accountable government; individual freedom; fair procedures; and judicial independence.[2] The intricately woven interrelationship between government and the law is reflected in the concepts postulated by the rule of law. The notion itself is fluid and lends itself to a wide range of interpretations. Despite the inability to propose a concrete definition for the concept, it is accepted that central to the general idea of the rule of law is the specific proposition that it involves the rule of *law* as opposed to the rule of *people* to control the exercise of arbitrary power. It can be said that it is usually intended to imply that the powers exercised by politicians and officials must be based on authority conferred by law and that the law should conform to certain minimum standards of justice, both procedural and substantive.[3] This is why the actions and decisions of those whose authority is conferred by law can be subject to judicial review proceedings. Politicians and government officials should, therefore, ordinarily be minded not to abuse the discretionary powers associated with the office that they hold.

The concept of the rule of law versus the rule of people is most significantly reflected in the stated role of judges. Their position is such that they are expected to deliver completely impartial judgments through a strict application (and sometimes interpretation) of the law without fear or favour; neither are they expected to allow personal preferences or beliefs to influence decisions taken.

Legal philosophers on the topic of the rule of law abound. At this juncture, three shall be highlighted: AV Dicey, EP Thompson and Joseph Raz.[4]

Dicey was a theorist on the right of the political spectrum and was of the view that the rule of law constituted a key distinguishing feature of the English constitution, where this was absent in the constitutions of continental Europe. For Dicey, there were three elements which comprised the rule of law:

- An absence of arbitrary power exercised by the state. The discretionary powers exercised by the state were subject to the boundaries set by laws which sought to control the abuse of such powers.
- Equality before the law. No one was above the law, regardless of social class or rank.
- Supremacy of ordinary law. This is based on the fact that the English constitution was the result of the ordinary law of the land and based on the provision of remedies by the court as opposed to a declaration of rights in the form of a written constitution.

Dicey wrote from a historico-political period where the maintenance of individual property and individual freedom to use that property was vital. Following from this, he believed that everyone should be treated as possessors of abstract rights and duties in the eyes of the law and the state, despite their wealth or power.

---

2 Bridge, J, 'Values, Principles and Standards in the Public Law of the United Kingdom'. Delivered at Newcastle Law School Staff Seminar, 23 May 2000.

3 See De Smith, S and Brazier, R, *Constitutional and Administrative Law*, 1998, London: Penguin Books, p 17.

4 See generally Slapper, G and Kelly, D, *The English Legal System*, 2000, London: Cavendish Publishing Limited, pp 14–19.

EP Thompson, a Marxist historian on the left of the political spectrum, saw the rule of law as protection against, as well as being under attack from, the encroaching power of the modern state. Thompson believed that the state used its control over the legislative process in order to undermine civil liberties in the pursuit of what it considered to be the public interest. He argued that the core meaning of the rule of law is not simply procedural propriety but also the manner and extent to which it limits the exercise of state power.

Joseph Raz suggested that the pursuit of social goals practically required the enactment of general laws as well as particular laws. This goes against the German notion of *Rechtsstaat* where the state is subordinate to the law and, as such, is required only to institute general laws and cannot make laws aimed at particular people. According to Raz, the wider idea of the rule of law emerges from the requirement that the law must be capable of guiding the individual's behaviour. From this general idea, the most important principles for Raz are as follows:

- Laws should be prospective rather than retroactive. People cannot be guided by or expected to obey laws which have not as yet been introduced. Laws should also be open and clear to enable people to understand them and guide their actions in line with them.
- Laws should be stable and should not be changed too frequently, as this might lead to confusion as to what was actually covered by the law.
- There should be clear rules and procedures for making law.
- The independence of the judiciary has to be guaranteed to ensure that it is free to decide cases in line with the law and not in response to any external pressure.
- The principles of natural justice should be observed, requiring an open and fair hearing to be given to all parties to proceedings.
- The courts should have the power to review the way in which the other principles are implemented to ensure that they are being operated as demanded by the rule of law.
- The courts should be easily accessible as they remain at the heart of the idea of making discretion subject to legal control.
- The discretion of the crime-preventing agencies should not be allowed to pervert the law.[5]

LEGAL TRADITIONS OR FAMILIES

Textbooks on legal traditions generally cite the existence of three highly influential legal traditions: civil law, common law and socialist law. Such traditions are not necessarily mutually exclusive. They are of particular interest as they came from some of the most powerful and technologically advanced nations of the world and have been adopted, to a greater or lesser extent, in other regions of the world. From these varying types, legal systems evolved, which include religious law, customary law and mixed law systems.

It is necessary to differentiate between the term 'legal tradition' and 'legal system'. While these terms are sometimes used interchangeably, they are most certainly not synonymous. A legal tradition refers to a set of deeply rooted, historically conditioned attitudes about the nature of law; the role that law plays in society; the proper organisation and operation of a legal system; and the way that law is or should be made, applied, studied and taught. The style of a legal tradition is influenced by factors such as its historical development and background; predominant and characteristic mode of thought in legal matters, especially distinctive institutions; acknowledged legal sources; and ideological epistemologies. The legal tradition puts the legal system into

5 Slapper and Kelly, *The English Legal System*, pp 18–19.

cultural perspective.[6] According to Merryman, a legal system is an operating set of legal institutions, procedures and rules borne of a legal tradition. As an example, there are many nations which share the commonality of civil law tradition, such as France, Germany, Italy, Switzerland, Argentina, Brazil and Chile, but there exist great differences in each respective operating legal system as they each have quite different legal rules, legal procedures and legal institutions.

Civil law

The civil law tradition is characterised by a particular interaction in its early formative period among Roman law, Germanic and local customs, canon law, the international law merchant and, later on, by a distinctive response to the break with feudalism and the rise of nation states.[7] It is the oldest and most widely distributed of all legal traditions and is said to date back to 450 BC. It remains as the dominant legal tradition in most of Western Europe, all of Central and South America, many parts of Asia and Africa and can even be found in a few enclaves in countries practising common law, such as in Louisiana (USA), Québec (Canada), the Philippines and Puerto Rico. Civil law was the dominant legal tradition of countries which practise socialist law and continues to exercise great influence on socialist legal systems.

A common misconception is that codification is peculiar to civil law. The state of California has more codes than a civil law nation, but it is not a civil law jurisdiction.[8] What distinguishes the system found in California from the concept of codification in civil law nations is the underlying ideology. The notion of what a code is and the functions it should perform in the legal process make the ideology of codification in the civil law world entirely different to that which obtains in California.

The Scandinavian countries introduced codification in the seventeenth and eighteenth centuries; however, it was the French Civil Code of 1804 and, to a much lesser extent due to its highly technical and scientific nature, the German Civil Code of 1896, which have served as models for most other modern civil codes. One of the main features of codification was the emphasis on the separation of powers (see 'Subjects of law in common law jurisdictions' below). It advocated the need for disparate functions of the judiciary and the legislature, as legislative skills and judicial skills are indeed distinct. Judges are, therefore, only expected to apply and interpret laws through wise and reasoned application and not to make laws themselves, while legislators are expected to discover the principles in each area which are most conducive to the common good. The code, a codified body of general abstract principles, must, of necessity, be complete, coherent, unambiguous and clear, so that judges would not be in a position where they might need to exercise their discretion in any given matter, thereby making law.

Some civil law political entities have hybrid legal traditions which have survived in uncodified form but have, to varying degrees, retained an adequate number of elements of Roman law in written form to permit their inclusion in the civil law tradition. Such is the case of Scotland and South Africa where the hybrid involves common law in the former and common law and Dutch law in the latter. Other political entities less influenced by Roman law, whether codified or not, founded on a perception of the role of statute law, are considered to be of a 'pure' civilian tradition, such as the Nordic legal tradition.

6 Merryman, J, *The Civil Law Tradition: An Introduction to the Legal Systems of Western Europe and Latin America*, 1985, Stanford, CA: Stanford University Press, p 2.

7 Glendon, M *et al*, *Comparative Legal Traditions in a Nutshell*, 1999, St Paul, MN: West Group, p 16.

8 Merryman, *The Civil Law Tradition*, p 26.

Common law

Common law was born at the end of the Norman Conquest in 1066 AD. The identifying character of this tradition, unlike civil law where, typically, principles and ideas are formally recorded, is its reliance on precedents and judge-made law. Judicial discretion finds expression in common law countries where new law emerges frequently to deal with changing times and needs. It is devoted to the careful and realistic discussion of live problems and makes it quicker to deal with matters in concrete and historical terms, rather than having to think systematically or in the abstract, or to analyse problems and fit them into the existing system, as is required in civil law.[9]

Like civil law, common law has taken on a variety of cultural forms worldwide, due in large part to colonialism and the imposition of the legal tradition on member countries of the British Empire. These include Australia, Canada, New Zealand, Fiji, India, Hong Kong, the United States, some West African countries and most of the English-speaking Caribbean. Common and civil law exist in geo-politically contiguous zones, such as Québec in Canada and, to a lesser degree, Louisiana in the Southern United States. It also exists as a more complex common-civil law hybrid, as typified in the unique case of South Africa.

Common law countries include political units whose law is, in the main, based on English common law concepts and legal organisational methods which place great emphasis on case law, as opposed to statutory law, as the general means of expressing general law. Countries that do not necessarily have close ties to the English tradition and possess an abundance of codes, legislation and non-jurisprudential normative instruments may maintain common law jurisprudence as their basic law, as seen in California.

Socialist law

Socialist law was born in the former Union of Soviet Socialist Republics at the end of the Bolshevik Revolution of October 1917. It saw the introduction of a radically new socio-economic and political system. As with the other legal traditions, socialist states assume a variety of forms and do not adhere to any standardised political form, as is generally believed. Socialist law spread to many countries in the Slavic region as well as to China and even to the Caribbean countries of Grenada and Cuba.

Socialist law, the legal foundation of communist countries, is based on the civil law system with a Marxist-Leninist ideological twist. The most important of the radical reforms included property relations (the substitution of social property for private capitalist and landed property), labour relations (banning of exploitation), political relations (transfer of power to the working people, 'the proletariat'), national relations (establishment of complete equality of the peoples oppressed by tsarism) and family relations (the abolition of the unequal status of women).[10]

One of the most significant aspects of civil law that figures as a central institution of socialist ideology is the right to personal property. Such law protects the right of citizens to own, as their personal property, income and savings derived from work, a dwelling house, a small personal farm, and a household and personal effects.[11] Two major misconceptions arising out of

9 For a comprehensive exposition on comparative law, see Zweigert, K and Kötz, H, *An Introduction to Comparative Law*, trans. T Weir, 1998, Oxford: Oxford University Press.

10 Chkhikvadze, VM (ed), *The Soviet State and the Law*, trans. Y Sdobnikov, 2000, Honolulu: University Press of the Pacific, pp 214–15.

11 Chkhikvadze (ed), *The Soviet State and the Law*, p 204.

this form of law is that all property, including individual property, has been abolished and that personal property can be equated with the capitalist notion of private property.

At the end of the Cold War, combined with the collapse of communism in most countries and the close similarity of socialist law to civil law, socialist law has lost its consideration as one of the most influential legal traditions. In the remaining communist countries, there is a movement away from the distinctively command market economy features of the legal foundation toward the free market economy model. Such is the case of China, which underwent fundamental legal reform in the 1980s and 1990s. This legal reform took place within the context of a specific tradition of socialist law which took China through 'the preliminary stage of socialism'. That 'preliminary stage' was to allow for a substantial commodity economy and an open-door economic policy. The market economy, justified by that formula, demanded forms of legal regulation unknown in the old planned and closed economy in which public ownership dominated.[12]

Religious law

Islamic

Shari'ah, Arabic for Islamic law, is a complex of divinely revealed rules which the faithful Muslim must observe if he seeks to perform the duties of religion.[13] Islamic law is uniquely valid by the fact that it is the manifested will of the Almighty and is not dependent on the authority of any earthly legislator. It is, however, also rooted in customary Arabic law, where the Prophet Muhammad modified only that which he believed to be inadequate or which went counter to his political goal of replacing the old Arab tribalism with a community of men bound together by belief in Allah.[14] Theoretically, therefore, Islamic law is immutable, for it is the law as revealed by God and reflects the will of Allah. *Shari'ah* covers all aspects of life and not simply those which are of interest to state or society.

Islamic legal theory, *usul al-fiqh*, is said to have four roots. The first root and primary source of law is, of course, the *Qur'an*, for which, it is believed, the legal instructions for the completion of the text were revealed in the context of particular affairs over a period of 23 years.[15] The second root is the *Sunnah* of the Prophet, the sum total of the inspired practice of the Prophet, so important for interpreting and clarifying the rules of the *Qur'an*. Juristically, *Sunnah* refers to the normative practice set up by the Prophet of Islam as a model: his sayings, doings and tacit approvals which were later established as legally binding precedents in addition to the law established by the *Qur'an*. The basis of the *Sunnah* is derived from *Hadith*, the orally transmitted traditions containing the teachings of the Prophet. It is the normative activity of the Messenger of Allah, Muhammad, who was the prime interpreter of the divine revelation of the *Qur'an*.[16] The third root is *Ijma'*, the consensus reached by the entire Islamic community, laymen as well as lawyers, on any question of the doctrine of the duties of the faithful. The last root of Islamic law is *qiya* (analogical deduction) or *aql* (reason) which is the application to new and similar

12 Lo, CW-H, 'Socialist Legal Theory in Deng Xiao-Ping's China', (1997), 11 *Columbia of Journal of Asian Law* 469.

13 Zweigert and Kötz, *An Introduction to Comparative Law*, p 303.

14 Zweigert and Kötz, *An Introduction to Comparative Law*, p 305.

15 Mumisa, M, *Islamic Law: Theory and Interpretation*, 2002, Beltsville, MD: Amana Publications, p 22.

16 Mumisa, *Islamic Law*, pp 56–7.

cases of rules established by the *Qur'an*, the *Sunnah*, or *Ijma'*.[17] This last root of law depends on a concept of divine motive or the intent of the law. In order to perform *qiya* the community must have in mind what a particular law was meant to achieve and only then can this motive or intent be applied to a similar situation.[18]

This classical system of the four roots of *Shari'ah* actually comprises three different notions, namely, the two sources of Islamic law (*Qur'an* and *Sunnah*), a method (the use of *qiya*) and a judgment (*Ijma'*). This means that the agreed judgment of scholars has the critical role, for they alone can ultimately decide, with or without the use of *qiya*, what valid rule of law can be extracted from the *Qur'an* or the *Sunnah*.

Islam spread from the Middle East to North and East Africa, South-Eastern Europe in the Slavic regions and even to Asia in Pakistan and Indonesia. *Shari'ah*, however, is most popular in the Middle East and in many African countries. It consists, in large part, of principles of proper ethical behaviour and regulates the rituals of prayer, fasting and pilgrimage. It is too imprecise to have a strictly legal perspective. The *Qur'an* frowns upon usury and gambling and states that in business dealings the good Muslim must act in good faith and must not bribe judges, but does not specify legal consequences for disregarding these rules.

Judaic

Halakhah, or Jewish law, is extremely similar to Islamic law in form and content. It provides a code of ethics by which Jews are expected to abide and perform religious duties. Judaism is a comprehensive way of life, filled with rules and practices that affect every aspect of life: what to do when one wakes up in the morning, what to eat or not eat, what to wear, how to groom one's self, how to conduct business, whom to marry, how to observe the holidays and *Shabbat*, and perhaps most importantly, how to treat God, other people and animals. This set of rules and practices is known as *halakhah*.[19] *Halakhah* was born in Jewish communities where laws, ideas and norms were established with a view to governing the people. Many of these established traditions were recorded and became part of Jewish religious law.

The principal source of law is the *Torah* or the Law of Moses, where Moses received the *Torah* on Mount Sinai from Jehovah. This law was recorded in the Old Testament in the books of Genesis, Exodus, Deuteronomy, Numbers and Leviticus.[20] The second notable source is the oral law or the oral traditions. This law explained the manner in which the written law was to be observed. This is known as the *Talmud* – a record of the oral law in practice. In this record is found the means by which to apply the law in a changing world. The *Talmud* comprises two books: the *Mishna* and the *Gemara*. The *Mishna* is a collection of notions forming the basis of the *Talmud* and which embodies Jewish oral law; the *Gemara* is the rabbinical commentary of the *Mishna* and forms the second part of the *Talmud*. The third important aspect of *Halakhah* is the *Responsa*. This comprises a collection of Jewish literature that contains segments on Jewish theology, philosophy, history and folklore. The greatest worth of the *Responsa* is that they are an indispensable source of the application of Jewish common law. They record how great Jewish jurists decided cases by the application of *Talmudic* law. They include cases from every field of law from the course of

17 Zweigert and Kötz, *An Introduction to Comparative Law*, p 308.

18 See Mumisa, *Islamic Law*, p 15.

19 Rich, T [online], 'Halakhah: Jewish Law' [accessed 30 December 2014]. Available at: http://www.jewfaq.org/halakhah.htm.

20 Call, J [online], 'The Halakhah and its Role in Modern Israeli Law', p 2 [accessed 27 May 2003]. Available at http://www.law2.byu.edu/lwb/papers/Call-Halakhah_FINAL.PDF [link no longer active; copy available with the author].

everyday life to commerce. It is said that the answers to legal questions found in the *Responsa* are 'recognized as definitive statements of the law in various areas, represent persuasive legal precedents and are as crucial a factor in a lively and productive Jewish law as the *Talmud*'.[21]

Orthodox Jews are of the belief that, like Islamic law, Jewish law is static and immutable as the Revelation on Mount Sinai was a one-time event valid for all generations and because 'these are the laws, rules, and instructions that the Lord established, through Moses on Mount Sinai, between Himself and the Israelite people'.[22] The attitude toward *halakhic* authority is based on a fundamentalist conception of the essence and significance of divine revelation. It would appear, however, that *Halakhah* is more open to change than *Shari'ah* and that a historical review of Jewish law would in fact reveal substantive changes in the realm of family law with particular reference to the treatment of women.

Unlike other legal traditions discussed, Jewish law is particular to Israel. The State of Israel would like to cultivate a close relationship with the Jews of the Diaspora, but given the intimate relationship between state and religion, those of the Diaspora who live in secular societies are in a quandary as to the application of Judaic law in such a society.[23]

Customary law

Customary law consists of customs accepted by members of a community as binding among them. It may be said that there is no political entity that is guided solely by customary law and that it is found in mixed legal systems; however, it does form an integral part of the legal systems of many African countries as well as of the laws of China and India, albeit under very different circumstances. The establishment of customary law requires proof of its uninterrupted existence for a long period of time and that it existed through common consent rather than through the use of force. It must be consistent with other customs, contain certainty and be accepted as mandatory, and be of significant importance.[24] After proof of existence, customary law must undergo and pass the 'repugnancy' test. To be enforceable, customary law was not to be repugnant to natural justice, equity and good conscience.[25] In Nigeria, for example, the legal system is influenced by English common law, Islamic law and customary law which all coexisted, at times, under military governance. The legal system in Swaziland is partly based on Roman–Dutch law, as applied in English organised courts, and traditional Swazi law and customs, as applied in Swazi National Courts.[26]

Mixed legal system

As the term implies, this category includes political entities where two or more traditions apply together or are juxtaposed with each other. There are jurisdictions where civil and common

21 Call, 'The Halakhah and its Role in Modern Israeli Law', p 5.

22 Zemer, M, *Evolving Halakhah: A Progressive Approach to Traditional Jewish Law*, 1999, Woodstock, VT: Jewish Lights Publishing, p 41.

23 Call, 'The Halakhah and its Role in Modern Israeli Law', p 14.

24 Glendon *et al*, *Comparative Legal Traditions in a Nutshell*, p 270.

25 Kuruk, P [online], 'Customary Water Laws and Practices: Nigeria' (n.d.), pp 7–8 [accessed 30 December 2014]. Available at: http://www.fao.org/fileadmin/templates/legal/docs/CaseStudy_Nigeria.pdf.

26 See Dube, B and Magagula, A [online], 'The Law and Legal Research in Swaziland', *Hauser Global Law School Program, New York University School of Law*, September / October 2007 [accessed 30 December 2014]. Available at: http://www.nyulawglobal.org/globalex/swaziland.htm#_Swazi_National_Courts.

law have come to coexist. One rather peculiar case is that of South Africa. South Africa had a strong civil law persuasion when it was under Dutch governance. It was later incorporated into the British Empire and English procedure and statutes were juxtaposed with the pre-existing Dutch law. In cases of uncertainty, reliance by the English-trained South African jurists tended towards English case law. On political independence, there was a restoration of Dutch legal scholarship. Today South African law possesses Roman–Dutch law substantive elements and aspects of English law procedural methodology and structure.[27]

SUBJECTS OF LAW IN COMMON LAW JURISDICTIONS

Constitution

Every independent Commonwealth country has a written constitution with the exception of Britain itself. Constitutions are primarily about political authority and power – the location, conferment, distribution, exercise and limitation of authority and power among the organs of a state.[28] Constitutions generally also include explicit guarantees of the rights and freedom of an individual.

A constitution may be defined as 'any document, series of documents, and or customary rules which are either formally designated as enjoying a higher authority than other rules of the politico-legal order . . . or which deal with the basic structure and function of the state . . . [and are] stable and effective frameworks within which legal and governmental processes habitually take place'.[29] In other words, it may be said to describe the whole system of government of a country and the collection of rules which establish and regulate or govern the government. These rules are both legal and customary, where the latter takes the form of usages, understandings, customs or conventions and are as effective as law strictly construed.[30]

In most countries, the constitution is generally the supreme law of the land. Section 2 of the Constitution of the Republic of Trinidad and Tobago, Ch. 1:01 states, 'This Constitution is the supreme law of Trinidad and Tobago, and any other law that is inconsistent with this Constitution is void to the extent of that inconsistency.'[31] It is from this supreme law that laws dealing with the establishment, composition and functions of Parliament are derived. It establishes the highest political office of the land, the office of the President, and governs his behaviour and his election to office. The Constitution also provides for the regulation of electoral activities. It governs the executive powers to be exercised by all ministers of cabinet as well as the functions, appointment and behaviour of other public officers. Financial provisions are an important part of the Constitution as it provides for the establishment and use of the Consolidated Fund which comprises monies to be used as government expenditure. The legal basis for the establishment and functioning of the judicature is also to be found in the Constitution. The Constitution is, therefore, an important source of law with respect to the establishment and regulation of government.

---

27 Zweigert and Kötz, *An Introduction to Comparative Law*, pp 231–5.
28 De Smith and Brazier, *Constitutional and Administrative Law*, p 6.
29 Wolf-Phillips, L, *Constitutions of Modern States*, 1967, London: Pall Mall, p x.
30 See Wheare, KC, *Modern Constitutions*, 1966, London: Oxford University Press, p 1.
31 Section 2, The Constitution of the Republic of Trinidad and Tobago, Ch. 1:01 (Revised Laws of Trinidad and Tobago, 2013).

Legislation

The Constitution provides Parliament with the power to make laws for the peace, order and good governance of Trinidad and Tobago.[32] Parliament may enact, revoke or alter such and any law as it sees fit (within the constraints of the Constitution, of course). Coupled with this wide power is the convention that no one Parliament can bind its successors in such a way as to limit their absolute legislative powers.[33] While the legal system of the Commonwealth is based on common law and the courts play an important role in the interpretation of statutes, legislation has become the predominant means of law-making in contemporary times. It is for this reason that background knowledge of the legislative process is necessary.

The legislative process

Parliament in Trinidad and Tobago consists of three distinct elements: the House of Representatives, the Senate and the President. Before any legislative proposal, known at that stage as a Bill, can become an Act of Parliament, it must proceed through and be approved by both Houses of Parliament (the House of Representatives and the Senate) and must receive presidential assent. Sometimes, the Bill is preceded by a Green or White Paper which sets out the government's plans in advance. White Papers announce firm government policy for implementation; Green Papers announce tentative proposals for discussion.[34] An Act of Parliament only comes into effect on the date of the presidential assent, unless there is any provision to the contrary in the Act itself.

Drafting legislation

Criticisms on the quality of drafting commonly make mention of the obscure and complex language used; the often illogical and convoluted grammatical structure of individual clauses; and the lack of clear connection between various Acts bearing on related subjects which make it difficult to ascertain the current state of law on any given matter. The parliamentary draftsman does, indeed, have a difficult task to face. Francis Bennion, in an article entitled 'Statute Law Obscurity and Drafting Parameters', identified nine parameters within which the draftsman must work.

- **Legal effectiveness**. The draftsman must be able to express the government's intention in such a way that the statute will have the desired effect.
- **Procedural legitimacy**. The Bill must comply with the procedural requirements of the House of Representatives as well as the Senate. Parliamentary procedure governs the form of the Bill. A Bill must have a long title, be divided into clauses, may have a preamble and Schedules but no other type of formulation or it will not be considered by Parliament.
- **Timeliness**. Legislation must be drafted within particularly pressing time constraints. This has the effect of the production of poorly drafted and defective provisions.
- **Certainty**. It is extremely important that the law be clearly enunciated so that individuals can know its scope and effect. This may sometimes result in rather long-winded provisions with limiting and refining sub-clauses which increase the obscurity of the intended meaning.

32 Section 53.

33 Slapper and Kelly, *The English Legal System*, p 33.

34 Zander, M, *The Law-Making Process*, 1999, London: Butterworths, p 8.

- **Comprehensibility**. Most statute-users are lawyers or experts, but most politicians lack the legal framework to understand statute. It is expected that the law be comprehensible to all who read it. Given the complex nature of legislative drafting, however, this ideal is most certainly unattainable in practice.
- **Acceptability**. Legislation is expected to be couched in non-contentious language and use a traditional prose style.
- **Brevity**. Legislative provisions should be as short as is compatible with the attainment of the intent of the clause. Brevity can, however, lead to conflicts in the attainment of certainty and acceptability of the language used.
- **Debatability**. It is expected that legislative clauses be structured to allow the members of the Parliament to debate it and the policy that lies behind it.
- **Legal compatibility**. When a Bill is enacted, it should fit as well as possible with existing law. New provisions are also expected to fit in with the rest of the Act when an Act is amended. Where the provision alters or repeals existing provisions, such effect should be clearly stated.[35]

Types of legislation

Legislation can be categorised in several ways. Differences can be drawn among public acts, private acts, consolidating legislation and codifying legislation.

- Public Acts refer to matters affecting the general public. A further sub-division can be made into either government Bills or Private Member's Bills. Ordinarily, Bills are introduced by government ministers; however, each year a certain amount of time is reserved for the introduction of Bills by private members of Parliament who are not ministers.[36]
- The original conception of a Private Act may be described as one that altered the general law in relation to a particular institution or individual. It is possible for such an Act to have effect on the general public. Today, Private Acts tend to deal with nationalised industries, local authorities, universities, commercial undertakings and other institutions.
- The effect of consolidating legislation is to bring together provisions previously contained in a number of different Acts without altering the provisions themselves. In the Occupational Safety and Health Act of Trinidad and Tobago, Parliament purported to consolidate several pieces of legislation (the Factories Ordinance 1948; the Employment of Women (Night Work) Act, Ch. 88:12; and the Gas Cylinders (Use, Conveyance and Storage) Act, Ch. 35:52) into one statutory instrument.
- Codifying legislation does not only seek to consolidate laws, but gives statutory expression to common law rules. Examples of this include the English Partnership Act of 1890 and the Sale of Goods Act 1893, now 1979,[37] which enacted that certain terms were to be implied into contracts.[38]

---

35 See Zander, *The Law-Making Process*, pp 18–19 and Slapper and Kelly, *The English Legal System*, pp 38–9.

36 Zander, *The Law-Making Process*, p 67.

37 Slapper and Kelly, *The English Legal System*, pp 39–40.

38 Kreling, P [online], 'In Praise of Common Law and Equity and Against Statute Law', 1991, London: Libertarian Alliance [accessed 30 December 2014]. Available at: http://www.libertarian.co.uk/lapubs/legan/legan013.pdf. This also applies to TT.

Case law

Case law refers to the creation and refinement of law in the decision-making process of judges in the courts. While statutory legislation has become extremely important as a source of law, most countries of the Commonwealth predominantly follow common law principles. The importance and effectiveness of judicial decisions and common law principles and practices cannot be underestimated.

Precedent

Stare decisis, or the doctrine of binding precedent, is an important aspect of all legal traditions. A fundamental characteristic of law is the objective that like cases should be treated alike – this is even the case in religious legal systems. This doctrine refers to the fact that within the hierarchical structure of the courts in the common law tradition the decision of a higher court will be binding on a lower court where the facts of the case appear to be similar. Common law system precedents are not simply models to be imitated. Where the precedent is set by a court of higher or equal status, the judge should ordinarily follow the rule of law established in the earlier case. Where the precedent is set in a lower court, the judge in the higher court is not obliged to follow the decision but will most certainly consider it. It should be noted that judicial decisions are of immediate effect. Precedent is not set by everything stated in a reported decision. The report can be divided into two theoretical categories: *ratio decidendi* and *obiter dictum*. The fact of being bound is actually a function of three different elements. The precedents must have been pronounced by a court that stands in the hierarchy in a position to bind the present court, the statement of law must have formed the *ratio* of that decision and it must be relevant to the facts of the present case.[39]

> *A, B, C, D v E* (2011) HCVAP 2011/001 (AI)
>
> **Facts:** This is a procedural matter concerning whether the appellants should have first applied for leave to proceed in the High Court for permission to force the respondent to disclose certain information so that they would be able to put forward their case. The request was granted on appeal.
>
> **Held:** Rawlins, CJ; Edwards, JA; Pereira, JA
> This doctrine [*stare decisis*] is to the effect that, save in exceptional circumstances, this court is bound to follow previous decisions of its own. The objective is to ensure certainty or finality in the law. This doctrine, as indicated, gives way, as enunciated in the said decision, to notable exceptions: the doctrine and the principles engaged in applying the exceptions were recently addressed and restated in *Brandwood and Others v Bakewell Management Ltd.* another decision of the English Court of Appeal given in 2003. These principles for present purposes . . . may be summarised as follows:
>
> (1) This Court is bound to follow previous decisions of its own save only in exceptional circumstances.
>
> (2) Such exceptions are where:
>
> (a) the court is confronted with two conflicting decisions of its own, then it may decide which of the two decisions it will follow;

39 Zander, *The Law-Making Process*, p 263.

(b) a decision of its own, though not expressly overruled, cannot in its opinion stand with a decision of a higher court (in this case the Privy Council) which is binding;

(c) the court is satisfied that its prior decision was given *per incuriam* [through lack of care].

. . . It is firmly established that authorities of the English courts are of persuasive force only in our courts whereas decisions of the Privy Council, as our final appellate court, are binding and therefore of authoritative force.

Baby Nagessar v Xavier Goodridge (2011) Claim No. CV 2009–00771 (TT)

Facts: The claimant in this matter has brought these proceedings for possession of 2 parcels of land which she claims to own. The defendant, on the other hand, claims to have been on the said parcels for more than 16 years and claims title by adverse possession.

Held: Rampersad, J

> The use of precedent is an indispensable foundation upon which to decide what is the law and its application to individual cases; it provides at least some degree of certainty upon which individuals can rely in the conduct of their affairs, as well as a basis for orderly development of legal rules . . . What constitutes binding precedent is the ratio decidendi, and this is almost always to be ascertained by an analysis of the material facts of the case, for a judicial decision is often reached by a process of reasoning involving a major premise consisting of a pre-existing rule of law, either statutory or judge-made, and a minor premise consisting of the material facts of the case under immediate consideration.

Faced with this principle, this court must consider the authority which is applicable in this matter. In *Bakewell Management Limited v Roland Brandwood and Others* [2002] EWHC 472 (Ch), Mr Justice Park said at paragraph 15 that: 'In my judgment a High Court judge ought not to regard himself as able to depart from an applicable Court of Appeal decision on the basis that a new argument, not presented to the Court of Appeal, is presented to him.' This approach was endorsed by the House of Lords when that matter reached before that court. Eventually, the House of Lords overruled the Court of Appeal decision which Mr Justice Park found himself bound by even though he had found that that Court of Appeal decision may not have been correct. 64. In *Lane v Willis; Lane v Beach (Executor of estate of George William Willis (deceased))* [1972] 1 All ER 430 at page 436 DAVIES LJ. said: 'It is unusual and, I am bound to say, undesirable, in my opinion, for a judge sitting at first instance—indeed, in that case in chambers—to express the opinion, although accepting that he is bound by it, that a decision, and a fairly recent decision, of this court was wrong.' . . . Conclusion on the title issue 67. Fortified by this declaration from such a distinguished Caribbean jurist and the unchallenged Privy Council declaration in *Bakshuwen*, this court feels obligated to follow the Privy Council's binding authority on this point of law applicable to 1969 Bahamas which is the same as still applies in our current jurisdiction.

CMF Projects P/L v Riggall & Anor [2014] QDC 90 (AU)

Facts: The plaintiff is a builder. The defendants are home owners. The home owners requested that the plaintiff renovate their house. The builder and the home owners reached an agreement which was a 'cost plus contract' within the meaning of the Domestic Building Contracts Act 2000 ('the DBCA'). The agreement was also a 'regulated contract' as that term is defined in the DBCA and it was not signed by the home owners and it did not itself contain any estimate of the amount which the builder was likely to receive under the agreement. A consequence of that is that the builder 'can not enforce the contract against the' home owners. The builder maintains that its amended statement of claim does not seek to enforce the contract, (the amended statement of claim does seek to enforce the contract) that it has pleaded a claim in debt (it has not). The builder pleaded an alternative claim in quantum meruit and argues that it may do so in this court notwithstanding the wording of DBCA s 55 (3) and (4). [It may not.]

Held: Andrews, SC DCJ
The doctrine of stare decisis takes its name from the Latin phrase 'stare decisis et non quieta movere' which translates as 'stand by the thing decided and do not disturb the calm'. It is a doctrine based on policy. The rationale for the doctrine can be grouped into four categories: certainty, equality, efficiency and the appearance of justice. *Stare decisis* promotes certainty because the law is then able to furnish a clear guide for the conduct of individuals. Citizens are able to arrange their affairs with confidence knowing that the law that will be applied to them in future will be the same as is currently applied. The doctrine achieves equality by treating like cases alike. *Stare decisis* promotes efficiency. Once a court has determined an issue, subsequent courts need not expend the time and resources to reconsider it. Finally, *stare decisis* promotes the appearance of justice by creating impartial rules of law not dependent upon the personal views or biases of a particular judge. It achieves this result by impersonal and reasoned judgments.

In an interesting decision of the Trinidad and Tobago Court of Appeal, Chief Justice Michael De la Bastide, as he then was, warned of the need for care in following precedents that may have been established under different conditions. *Bushell and Another v Port Authority of Trinidad and Tobago and Others* (1998) 56 WIR 460: 'It may be that we are too prone in jurisprudential and constitutional matters to transport from England and transplant in Trinidad and Tobago conventions, concepts and constructs without critically examining whether the soil conditions in which they have grown and flourished in their native land are, or can be, replicated in this country.'

Ratio decidendi

It is important to note that the precedent is not set by the actual decision of the case but by the rule of law upon which the decision is made. The *ratio decidendi* of a case can be said to be the proposition of law applied in deciding the legal problem(s) raised by the accepted facts of the case. Simply stated, the *ratio decidendi* is a ruling on a point of law that a judge provides because he conceives it to be necessary to the justification of his particular decision. It can be the rule of law laid down in a precedent or the rule of law that others regard as having binding authority. 'The *ratio decidendi* of a case is any rule of law expressly or implicitly treated by the judge as a necessary step in reaching his conclusion, having regard to the line of reasoning adopted by him, or as a necessary part of his direction to the jury.'[40] The *ratio decidendi* of a decision of the Board of the Judicial Committee of the Privy Council in an appeal from any jurisdiction for which it is the final court of appeal must be strictly followed by the lower courts of the respective jurisdiction. An exception, however, arises where the *rationes decidendi* of two decisions of the Board conflict with one another and the later decision does not purport to overrule the earlier. In such an instance, the judges

40 Blackwell [online], 'Ratio Decidendi', 2004 [accessed 30 December 2014]. Available at: http://www.blackwellreference.com/public/tocnode?id=g9781405106795_chunk_g978140510679519_ss1-11.

may choose which *ratio decidendi* they will follow and, in doing so, they may act on their own opinion as to which is the more convincing, as per *Eaton Baker* below.

Eaton Baker and Another v R (1975) 23 WIR 463 (Privy Council) (JM)

Facts: On 26 November 1969 the appellants committed murder. Both were then under the age of eighteen years – they were actually seventeen and a half. By the date of their conviction on 3 March 1971, both had attained the age of eighteen years. They were sentenced to death. They appealed against their sentences to the Court of Appeal for Jamaica. Sentence of death for murder is mandatory in Jamaica; but there is a statutory exception in the case of a person under the age of eighteen years. The only question in this appeal was whether the relevant date for ascertaining whether a convicted murderer falls within the exception is the date on which the murder was committed or the date on which the sentence is pronounced. This depends upon the true construction of s 29(1) of the Juveniles Law and ss 20(7) and 26(8) of the Constitution of Jamaica. There is a conflict of judicial authority as to the effect of these two provisions of the Constitution on s 29(1) of the Juveniles Law.

Held: Lord Diplock
Although the Judicial Committee is not itself strictly bound by the *ratio decidendi* of its own previous decisions, courts in Jamaica are bound as a general rule to follow every part of the *ratio decidendi* of a decision of this Board in an appeal from Jamaica that bears the authority of the Board itself To this general rule there is an obvious exception, viz where the *rationes decidendi* of two decisions of the Board conflict with one another and the later decision does not purport to overrule the earlier. Here the Jamaican courts may choose which *ratio decidendi* they will follow and in doing so they may act on their own opinion as to which is the more convincing . . . For these reasons the Court of Appeal for Jamaica were not bound to follow the decision of this Board in *Maloney Gordon v R* as to the effect of s 20(7) of the Constitution on s 29(1) of the Juveniles Law. Their decisions in *R v Wright* ((1972) 18 WIR 302) and in the instant case were correct. Their Lordships will accordingly humbly advise Her Majesty that this appeal should be dismissed.

Baby Nagessar v Xavier Goodridge (2011) Claim No. CV 2009–00771 (TT)[41]

Held: Rampersad, J

> . . . What constitutes binding precedent is the ratio decidendi, and this is almost always to be ascertained by an analysis of the material facts of the case, for a judicial decision is often reached by a process of reasoning involving a major premise consisting of a pre-existing rule of law, either statutory or judge-made, and a minor premise consisting of the material facts of the case under immediate consideration.

Obiter dictum

This refers to any statement of law that is not an integral part of the *ratio decidendi*. It refers to statements said 'by the way' as, strictly construed, any statement not a part of the *ratio* is

41 See case brief above.

unnecessary. While *obiter dicta* (plural) pronouncements do not form part of the binding precedent, weighty *obiter* pronouncements from the higher courts are persuasive authority and are likely to be followed, and will certainly be considered, but there is no obligation on the judge to follow them. Nevertheless, in *Ying v Song* [2009] NSWSC 1344 (3 December 2009) (AU), the court held that 'the weight accorded to obiter dicta will vary depending on the circumstances in which those dicta fell and that considered dicta of appellate courts, though not strictly binding on courts in a lower or equal position within the judicial hierarchy, must be afforded great weight and should be departed from only with the greatest of caution'.

Aho v Kelly 1998 CanLIII 6616 (BCSC) (CA)

Facts: The petitioner and Aaro Aho married in 1974. In 1975 lands comprising 342 acres were purchased and registered in the name of Mr Aho. They were operated as a farm. In 1977 Mr Aho was killed in a farming accident; he died intestate. Title to the lands, therefore, was in the names of the petitioner and the respondents. The respondents were the children of a previous marriage of the petitioner's deceased husband. Each of the parties held an undivided one-third interest in the lands as a tenant in common. They took title pursuant to the Estate Administration Act, RSBC 1996, c. 114, on the deceased's intestacy. Mrs Aho was entitled, on the intestacy, to the sum of CAN$20,000, a one-third interest in the estate, and the right to occupy the matrimonial home under what is now s 96(2)(a). Legal proceedings affecting the estate were protracted. A final resolution was achieved in 1995. Those proceedings included an issue that was tried before Mr Justice Wood in 1988. That issue concerned the petitioner's claim that she was entitled to be compensated, in the circumstances then pertaining, for the capitalised value of her s 96 interest in the matrimonial home which was then the subject of a proposed sale.

Held: Bauman, J
The view that Mr Justice Wood's conclusion, that the widow's s 96 [then s 108(2)(a)] right was only possessory, was in fact *obiter dictum*, is undoubtedly correct . . . This follows inevitably from the conclusion that Mr Justice Wood's general observation was *obiter dictum*, that is: 'Words of an opinion entirely unnecessary for the decision of the case . . . a remark made, or opinion expressed, by a judge, in his decision upon a cause, "by the way", that is, incidentally or collaterally, and not directly upon the question before him, or upon a point not necessarily involved in the determination of the cause.' *Black's Law Dictionary*, Sixth Edition.

Hierarchy of the courts

The House of Lords reigns at the top of the English hierarchical court structure as well as of some Commonwealth Caribbean countries in the form of the Board of the Judicial Committee of the Privy Council and its decisions are binding on all courts below it. In the past, the House of Lords also regarded itself as bound by its own previous decisions. This changed in 1966 when Lord Gardiner indicated in a Practice Statement of that year that the House of Lords would in future regard itself as free to depart from its previous decisions when it appeared right to do so.[42] This is, of course, not a discretion that the House of Lords uses lightly due to the potentially destabilising legal effect that may ensue.

42 Slapper and Kelly, *The English Legal System*, p 46.

The Court of Appeal is generally bound by earlier decisions of the House of Lords in civil cases. On several occasions, the Court of Appeal, under the aegis of Lord Denning, tried to escape the constrictions of *stare decisis*, but the House of Lords repeatedly and forcefully reasserted the binding nature of the decisions of the House of Lords on the Court of Appeal and the fact that 'in the hierarchical system of courts which exists in this country, it is necessary for each lower tier, including the Court of Appeal, to accept loyally the decisions of the higher tiers'.[43]

The Court of Appeal is generally also bound by its own previous decisions with exceptions where:

- there is a conflict between two previous decisions of the Court of Appeal;
- a previous decision of the Court of Appeal has been overruled, either expressly or impliedly, by the House of Lords;
- the previous decision was given *per incuriam* or given in ignorance of some authority, either statutory or case law, that would have resulted in a different decision.

The High Court is also bound by the decisions of the higher courts. The decisions made by High Court judges are binding on inferior courts, but not on other High Court judges, although they are of strong persuasive authority and tend to be followed in practice.[44]

Jamaica Carpet Mills Ltd v First Valley Bank (1986) 45 WIR 278 (JM)

Facts: By specially-indorsed writ issuing out of the Supreme Court, the respondent claimed against the appellant, as debt due by the appellant, the sum of US$201,166.60 with interest thereon at 10 per cent from January 1979 to 31 August 1983 amounting to US$93,877.74, making the total claim US$295,044.34. The US currency was converted into the Jamaican currency at the parallel market rate then existing at JM$2.60 to US$1 and the resulting sum was JM$767,115.28.

Vicart Inc of Pennsylvania, USA was, in the 1970s, an associated trading partner of the appellant. Attempts at unscrambling the several business relationships between these two parties foundered and led to a suit being filed by Vicart Inc against the appellant in the Supreme Court which proceeded as far as the defence and was not further prosecuted. Vicart Inc had previously obtained judgment against the appellant in Pennsylvania, USA in the sum of US$201,166.60 and it appears that this judgment was the basis of the Jamaican action.

On 13 April 1983 Vicart Inc assigned to First Valley Bank (the respondent) 'all the rights, interest and privileges, (a) which assignor had and may have in the accounts (as the term is defined in the Pennsylvania Uniform Commercial Code (UCC) now existing or hereafter made) arising out of goods sold or services performed to, or for the benefit of Jamaica Carpet Mills [the appellant] of Spanish Town, Jamaica.' On the basis of this assignment, the present action was brought.

Held: Rowe, P
Mr Chin See argued that the courts in Jamaica are bound by the decision in the *United Railways of Havana* case and the decision of the Privy Council in *Khoury v Khayat* and that the statutory provisions referred to above indicate that the Parliament of Jamaica adopted the breach date rule as the one applicable to Jamaica . . .

43 *Broome v Cassell* [1972] AC 1027 at 1054.
44 Slapper and Kelly, *The English Legal System*, p 49.

I have to consider briefly the relationship between the courts in Jamaica on the one hand and the Judicial Committee of the Privy Council on the other hand. In *Baker v R* (1975) 23 WIR 463, Lord Diplock, in delivering the decision of the majority of the Board, said (at page 471): 'Although the Judicial Committee is not itself strictly bound by the *ratio decidendi* of its own previous decisions, courts in Jamaica are bound as a general rule to follow every part of the *ratio decidendi* of a decision of this Board in an appeal from Jamaica that bears the authority of the Board itself.' It has been argued before us that the binding authority of the decisions of the Privy Council on courts of Jamaica only applies to decisions in appeals from Jamaica and the authority for such a proposition is said to be *Baker v R* (above). I do not share that view. I was a member of the court in *R v Commissioner of Police, ex parte Cephas (No 2)* (1976) 24 WIR 500, in which Henry J, in delivering the judgment of the Full Court, referred to the decision of the Privy Council, *Eshugbayi Eleko v Nigeria Government Officer Administering* [1928] AC 459, and said (at page 502): 'That judgment is binding on this court because although it was given in a case coming from another territory the issue of law in both cases is the same.' . . .

I am, therefore, of the view that the Privy Council would now decide that the decision in *Syndic in Bankruptcy of Salim Nasrallah Khoury v Khayat* [1943] AC 507 ought not to be followed in the light of the decision of the House of Lords in the *Miliangos* case [1975] 3 All ER 801 and that it is open to this court to adopt the decision and reasoning of the House of Lords in the *Miliangos* case and to apply that decision to the instant appeal. It was for these reasons that I concurred in the decision to dismiss the appeal.

Baby Nagessar v Xavier Goodridge (2011) Claim No. CV 2009–00771 (TT)[45]

Held: Rampersad, J
In those circumstances, faced with two Court of Appeal decisions endorsing a more absolute approach using the principles described in the provisions of the Conveyancing and Law of Property Act on either side of a Bahamian Privy Council decision which endorsed a relative approach to the proof of title, this court has to consider what is the binding authority it must follow. 66. The resolution, to my mind, originates from the words of Rowe P. JA in *Jamaica Carpet Mills Ltd v First Valley Bank* (1986) 45 WIR 278 where he said at page 287:

> It has been argued before us that the binding authority of the decisions of the Privy Council on courts of Jamaica only applies to decisions in appeals from Jamaica and the authority for such a proposition is said to be Baker v R (above). I do not share that view. I was a member of the court in R v Commissioner of Police, ex parte Cephas (No 2) (1976) 24 WIR 500, in which Henry J in delivering the judgment of the Full Court referred to the decision of the Privy Council, Eshugbayi Eleko v Nigeria Government Officer Administering [1928] AC 459, and said (at page 502): 'That judgment is binding on this court because although it was given in a case coming from another territory the issue of law in both cases is the same.' And he relied upon Fatuma Binti Mohammed Bin Salim Bakhshuwen v Mohammed Bin Salim Bakhshuwen [1952] AC 1. It was decided in that case that on the assumption that the rights of the parties were to be determined without reference to any Ordinance dealing specifically with wakfs, that the interpretation of Mohamedan law given by the Judicial Committee of the Privy Council in a series of cases was not confined to that law as applied or administered in India and that decisions of the Board given in appeals which came from India were binding on the Court of Appeal for Eastern Africa in appeals to that court from the Supreme Court of Kenya.

45 See case brief above.

Advantages and disadvantages of case law

There are many apparent advantages to using and conforming to the doctrine of *stare decisis*:[46]

- **Consistency**. Cases are decided on the basis of similarity of facts and therefore remove the unnecessary exercise of discretion of the individual judge in making his decision.
- **Certainty**. This is a necessary result of the consistent character of the doctrine. This makes it easier for legal practitioners to predict the likely outcome of a particular legal question in light of previous judicial decisions.
- **Efficiency**. The judiciary is saved time because cases do not have to be reargued. It is also cost-efficient for litigants because their lawyers can guide them on how their case will be decided on the basis of previous judgments made on similar points of fact.
- **Flexibility**. Under the common law tradition, judges are provided with the means to develop law in particular areas without waiting for Parliament to enact legislation. Flexibility also allows judges to overrule, distinguish or modify the effective scope of a precedent. This gives judges much greater freedom and discretion than is initially evident in the traditional perspective of *stare decisis*.

  There are two main means by which a judge may alter or avoid a precedent:

- **Overruling**. A court higher up in the hierarchy may set aside the legal ruling established in a previous case. This is reluctantly used but the courts will overrule authorities where they see them as no longer reflecting an appropriate statement of law.
- **Distinguishing**. This is the more popular means of avoiding binding precedents. The court may decide that the facts of the case before it are significantly different from the facts of the precedent before them and, as a result, will not consider itself bound by the previous decision.

The advantage of flexibility has the effect of potentially contradicting the advantage of certainty. There are other disadvantages to the doctrine of *stare decisis* which should also be considered:

- **Uncertainty**. Despite the fact that the doctrine itself is based on binding precedent, the fact that judges have the discretion to distinguish cases on the basis of factual differences undermines the degree of certainty that should ordinarily be associated with the doctrine, as established principles may be set aside for the court to do what it feels to be right for any particular case before it.
- **Fixity**. When a higher court, such as the Court of Appeal or the House of Lords, has decided a point, it tends to remain the law regardless of its applicability to a situation. In other cases, an unjust precedent may have the consequence of perpetuating previous injustices. The possibility of rape within marriage, for example, has only been recently recognised by the court despite the long history of this practice.

Books of authority

Authoritative legal works are generally given consideration when a precise or analogous precedent cannot be found. Strictly speaking, only certain literary sources are considered appropriate

46 See Slapper and Kelly, *The English Legal System*, pp 52–4.

in this regard. Bracton, Glanvil, Littleton, Coke, Hale and Blackstone are the most significant writers of authoritative sources of textbook law. These sources date as far back as the twelfth century and it must be borne in mind that situations have changed a great deal since then and such law may no longer be applicable. It was generally held that the author must be dead before he could be cited as authority.[47] Zander argues (albeit jokingly) that on that basis no living judge ought to have been cited either. Lawyers have been able to circumvent this impractical rule by saying that they are adopting the views of a living author as part of their arguments. The courts are also open to the idea of accepting eminent works produced by accepted experts in the field in order to assist them in determining a particular point of law.

Equity

Equity refers to a particular set of remedies and associated procedures in law. These equitable doctrines and procedures are distinguished from 'legal' ones that are strictly construed. Equitable relief is generally available only when a legal remedy is insufficient or inadequate in some way. This could be when a claim involves a particular piece of real estate, or if specific performance is the relief requested by the plaintiff.[48] Remedies borne out of equity, and now an integral part of common law, include specific performance of contracts (law provided only monetary compensation), injunction, rectification, rescission and estoppel.[49]

The distinction arose in England where there were separate courts of common law and of equity. Where the common law failed those with worthy cases, they found recourse with the king's chaplain, also known as the chancellor, who was the 'keeper of the king's conscience'. By the early sixteenth century, a fairly well-defined jurisdiction was exercised by the Court of Chancery in rivalry with the common law. In the seventeenth century, it was definitely established that the Court of Chancery would decide any claim to jurisdiction that the courts of common law disputed. The coexistence of different systems of justice and delays in the Court of Chancery came to present such great procedural difficulties that in England the Judicature Act was adopted (1873) to amalgamate law and equity, so that the same court that may fashion a legal remedy has the power to prescribe an equitable one.[50]

It should be noted that common law remedies are available as of right; remedies in equity are discretionary and the court will not award an equitable remedy where it considers the conduct of the party seeking such an award as undeserving.[51]

STATUTORY INTERPRETATION

Judicial discretion is sometimes necessary when legal reasoning requires that judges interpret statutes. This arises from the sheer and inherent difficulty of statutory draftsmanship, as discussed above. When the Interpretation Act does not provide the answer, statutory interpretation must be derived elsewhere. It must be noted, however, that the judiciary is not permitted to write statute, but simply give effect to the provisions:

47 Zander, *The Law-Making Process*, p 388.

48 Legal Information Institute [online], 'Equity: An Overview' [accessed 30 December 2014]. Available at: http://www.law.cornell.edu/topics/equity.html.

49 See generally Farlex [online], 'The Free Dictionary: Equity', 2014 [accessed 30 December 2014]. Available at: http://legal-dictionary.thefreedictionary.com/equity.

50 Factmonster [online], 'Equity' [Columbia University Press, 2012] [accessed 30 December 2014]. Available at: http://www.factmonster.com/ce6/society/A0817541.html.

51 Slapper and Kelly, *The English Legal System*, p 5.

> . . . the main principle of statutory interpretation is that Parliament makes the laws and the Court interprets the laws[] that have been made by Parliament. If there is a situation that Parliament has not covered, then it is for Parliament to mend the situation. If the legislation is unambiguous then the court must carry out that in[t]ention expressed unambiguously, no matter how harsh it may be. If the intention, as expressed in the phrasing of the legislation[,] is not clear then the court's aid is enlisted. The court gives the interpretation to the statute that carries out the intention of Parliament as phrased in the legislative provisions.[52]

As a result of this difficulty, there has been the development of three rules of statutory interpretation: the literal rule, the golden rule and the mischief rule. The purposive approach, a more modern take on statutory interpretation, seeks to give effect where applying the literal meaning of the statute would lead to results which clearly defeat the purpose of the Act by reviewing the purpose of the legislation before interpreting the meaning of the words.

Literal rule

The literal rule requires the court to consider what the legislation actually says rather than try to infer what Parliament might have meant by it. It is expected that the judge should look at the words of the legislation in their literal meaning and that the words be construed in their natural and grammatical meanings, even if this results in a complete absurdity. Why? It is presumed that words are used in an Act of Parliament correctly and exactly. An Indian writer has suggested that even though words are to be taken in their literal meaning, reliance should be had on the context in which the words are used as opposed to a pure dictionary meaning which may offer several permutations:

> The words of a statute are first understood in their natural, ordinary or popular sense and phrases and sentences are construed according to their grammatical meaning . . . The true way is to take the words as the legislature has given them, and to take the meaning which the words given naturally imply, unless where the construction of those words is either by the preamble or by the context of the words in question, controlled or altered. If commercial words are used, the words are to be construed in the sense the commercial house understands them. Similarly words of popular use are to be understood in their popular meaning if the text so demands. Similarly, technical words used are to be understood in the technical meaning and not according to the dictionary meaning . . .[53]

Nadine Nabie and Michelle Mayers Appellants / Interested Parties v Law Association of Trinidad and Tobago First Respondent / Claimant, The Attorney General Of Trinidad And Tobago Second Respondent / Defendant Claim No. Cv 2012–00892; Civil Appeal No. 72 of 2012 (TT)

Facts: This appeal involves the interpretation of certain provisions of the Legal Profession Act (LPA) Chap. 90:03. By a fixed date claim form filed on 5th March 2012, the Law Association of Trinidad and Tobago (LATT) applied to the High Court for a determination of the following issues: 1. Whether, according to the provisions of the LPA, 'law officers' as defined by Section 26 thereof are entitled to (i) attend and vote at a general meeting of the Association or at an election of the Association; or (ii) be elected to the Council of the Association, without paying fees under the Act.

52 Per Joseph, J in *Floral Fantasy v Bethel Brackin* HC Claim No. 17 of 2012 (SVG), at 3–4.

53 Patil, VH [online], 'General Rules of Statutory Interpretation', *I.T. Review*, July 2001, p 5 [accessed 7 December 2009] [link no longer active; copy available with the author].

Held: Mendonça, Narine, Smith, JJA
Section 9 provides as follows: 9(2) Only practitioner members who pay their annual subscription to the Law Association are eligible – (a) to attend and vote at a general meeting or at an election of members of the Council; or (b) to be elected to the Council. Section 26 (1) defines 'law officer' as follows: (i) An Attorney-at-Law who holds office in the Judicial and Legal Service established by the Judicial and Legal Service Act, which office is declared by Order of the Minister to be a law office; or (ii) A legal officer employed by the State on contract. Section 26 (2) provides that a law officer shall be deemed to be the holder of a valid practising certificate. Section 27 provides that subject to subsection 9(2) a law officer is exempt from paying an annual subscription to the Law Association and an annual contribution to the Compensation Fund. The Principles of Statutory Interpretation. The presumption in favour of a literal interpretation of the words of a statute are set out in Bennion on Statutory Interpretation . . .

Section 285 Presumption that literal meaning to be followed. '*Prima facie, the meaning of an enactment which was intended by the legislator (in other words its legal meaning) is taken to be that which corresponds to the literal meaning.*' In seeking to ascertain the intention of Parliament as expressed in the language it employed, it must be borne in mind that the intention of Parliament is an objective concept. The task of the court in finding the intention of Parliament from the language of an enactment was articulated by Lord Nicholls of Birkenhead in the House of Lords decision in *R v Secretary of State for the Environment, Transport and the Regions, Ex-parte Spath Holme Ltd.* (2001) 2 AC 349 at 396 F – 397-B. 'Statutory interpretation is an exercise which requires the court to identify the meaning borne by the words in question in the particular context. The task of the court is often said to be to ascertain the intention of Parliament expressed in the language under consideration . . . In identifying the meaning of the words used, the courts employ accepted principles of interpretation as useful guides. For instance, an appropriate starting point is that language is to be taken to bear its ordinary meaning in the general context of the statute.' It is desirable that parliament should express its intention in clear and unambiguous language so that ordinary citizens and their advisors are able to understand their meaning. This aspect of the rule of law, and the need for legal certainty was expressed by Lord Diplock in *Fothergill v Monarch Airlines Ltd.* (1981) AC 251 at 279–280, and cited by Lord Nicholls in *R v Secretary of State for the Environment, Transport and the Regions, Ex-parte Spath Holme Ltd.* (supra.) at 397 H to 398 B: 'The source to which Parliament must have intended the citizen to refer is the language of the Act itself. These are the words which Parliament has itself approved as accurately expressing its intentions. If the meaning of those words is clear and unambiguous and does not lead to a result that is manifestly absurd or unreasonable, it would be a confidence trick by Parliament and destructive of all legal certainty if the private citizen could not rely upon that meaning but was required to search through all that had happened before and in the course of the legislative process in order to see whether there was anything to be found from which it could be inferred that Parliament's real intention had not been accurately expressed by the actual words that Parliament had adopted to communicate it to those affected by the legislation.'

Applying the Literal Approach. The issue to be decided in this case is whether, on a proper interpretation of the relevant provisions of the LPA, the judge was correct in coming to her decision. I will now consider the relevant provisions of the Act, construing those provisions in order to find the intention of Parliament by presuming that the words used were intended to convey their literal and ordinary meaning in the context of the statute . . .

Section 26 defines 'law officer' and provides that a law officer 'shall be deemed to be the holder of a valid practising certificate and to be a practitioner member.' Section 27 exempts a law officer from paying an annual subscription to the LATT or an annual contribution to the Compensation Fund. This section as noted earlier is, however, subject to section 9(2).

> Section 9(1) provides that subject to this section and section 10, all members of the LATT have the same rights and privileges. However, section 9(2) expressly states that only practitioner members who pay their annual subscription to the LATT are eligible (a) to attend and vote at a general meeting or at an election of members of the Council; or (b) to be elected to the Council. It follows from the plain and ordinary meaning of the words of the provisions referred to above, that law officers are deemed to be practitioner members of the LATT. They are expressly exempted from the payment of an annual subscription to the LATT or contribution to the Compensation Fund by section 27. However, section 27 is made expressly subject to section 9(2), which makes it clear that only practitioner members who pay their annual subscription to the LATT, are eligible to attend and vote at a general meeting or at an election of members of the Council or to be elected to the Council. In my view, on a reading of the provisions, giving the words used by Parliament their plain and ordinary meaning, the intention of Parliament is clear. It was intended that law officers should fall into the category or class of practitioner members, and are deemed to hold practising certificates which entitle them to practise law. It is clear from the words used that they are not required to pay an annual subscription or a contribution to the Compensation Fund, subject to section 9(2), which makes it compulsory for them to pay their annual subscription to the LATT in order to exercise the privileges contained in section 9(2)(a) and 9(2)(b). The trial judge concluded as I do that on a literal interpretation of the relevant sections there is no ambiguity or absurdity which requires the court to apply any other rule of statutory interpretation, or any external aid, such as parliamentary statements . . . This is sufficient to dispose of this appeal.

Golden rule

The golden rule is generally considered to be an extension of the literal rule. This rule is given preference when the application of the literal rule is likely to result in a manifest absurdity. The golden rule is said to have two versions: the narrow interpretation and the wider interpretation.

Narrow meaning

When the use of a particular word with two apparently contradictory meanings or a provision is ambiguous in its effect, the golden rule operates to ensure that preference is given to the meaning which does not result in making the provision an absurdity.

> *Marilyn Spencer and Ors v The Attorney General of Antigua and Barbuda* Claim No. ANUHCV 2008/0226 (AG)
>
> **Facts:** The claimants, who were the executive committee of the church Hallelujah Square Harvest Tabernacle, submitted to the Attorney General for his approval the Articles of Incorporation for the proposed 'Hallelujah Square Harvest Tabernacle Inc.' to be incorporated as a non-profit company for religious purposes. They also submitted to the Attorney General the intended articles of association. The Attorney General responded and stated that he was unable to accede to the claimants' request for approval to register the church as a non-profit company. The Attorney General outlined the reason for his decision as being based on his interpretation of sections 3, 328(1) and 329 of the Companies Act 1995 Laws of Antigua and Barbuda that a non-profit company must be a commercial enterprise, which is to be carried out without pecuniary gain to its members. Subsequently, the claimants, through their Attorneys-at-Law, responded to the Honourable Attorney General, stating

that the Companies Act does not require non-profit companies to be commercial enterprises, but instead, section 328(2) of the Companies Act restricts a non-profit company's operations by listing a number of 'useful' non-commercial objects, including specifically that 'a non-profit company shall restrict its business to one that is of religious object'.

Held: Blenman, J
Section 328(1) makes it mandatory to obtain the Attorney General's approval in order for a non-profit company to file articles. I am satisfied that section 328(2) of the Companies Act must be given its literal meaning. Indeed, the literal rule of interpretation states that in construing or interpreting a statute, if the words are precise and unambiguous, then no more can be necessary than to expound those words in their natural and ordinary sense. *Sussex Peerage* (1844) 11 CIF 85. There is no reason for reading any other words into section 328(2) of the Act . . .

Even though in common parlance the word 'company' is used to refer to persons who associate for economic gain, this is not the exclusive purpose of a company. Further, it need not be the purpose at all of a company. Companies can be charitable in nature. These types of companies are limited by guarantee instead of shares. This is recognised by section 326(1) of the Companies Act which acknowledges that companies without a share capital can be incorporated as a non-profit company . . .

Even though most companies are incorporated for 'business purposes' which is used here interchangeably with 'commercial purposes', I do not hold the view that 'business' as used in section 328(2) of the Act is confined to commercial transactions. I am more attracted to the meaning as advocated by Mr John, namely purposeful activities, functions, affairs, matters, commercial, personal activities. Accordingly, I am afraid that I am unable to accept the interpretation of the above sections as urged by the learned Attorney General. That is too restrictive. It is my respectful view that the word 'business' as used in [] section 328(2) is wider in scope than commercial business and includes one's concerns or affairs, matters, purposeful activities. Section 328(2) of the Act enables persons to associate themselves and form a company for religious or charitable purposes, once it is non-profit . . . With respect, I am afraid that I am unable to agree with the learned Attorney General, that in order to obtain approval for incorporation a non-profit company must be a commercial enterprise.

Wide meaning

In the wider meaning, when a provision has only one possible meaning and the court believes that adopting such a literal meaning will result in an absurdity, the golden rule is used to give the words a meaning that would not result in an absurdity.

Lennox Linton v The Attorney General of Antigua and Barbuda (2009) Claim No. ANUHCV2007/0354 (AG)

Facts: Mr. Lennox Linton, a national of the Commonwealth of Dominica, has filed judicial review proceedings against the Attorney General as the representative of the State of Antigua and Barbuda. The proceedings are in respect of certain rights which, Mr. Linton claims, he enjoys by virtue of the Caribbean Community Single Market and Economy (CSME). Mr. Linton says that he came to Antigua and Barbuda in order to seek employment based on the legitimate expectation which he held as a result of statements made by

Government Officials. The statements were to the effect that qualified skilled CARICOM nationals, and Mr. Linton is a CARICOM national, would be entitled to come to Antigua and Barbuda to work. He calls in his aid the RTC [Revised Treaty of Chaguaramas]. He contends that he possessed a Caribbean Community Skilled Certificate issued to him by the Government of the Commonwealth of Dominica, which certifies him to be a media worker. He says he presented the Certificate to the then Chief Immigration Officer and was given permission to remain in Antigua for six months. Before the time granted to him had expired, the permission was unlawfully revoked and he was placed on a flight back to the Commonwealth of Dominica. He also says that this was in clear breach of his rights which are granted to skilled CARICOM nationals, pursuant to the 4 RTC. He further complains that the Immigration Authorities' conduct was in clear breach of law, namely the CARICOM Skilled Nationals Act Cap No. 3 of 1997 Laws of Antigua and Barbuda and the Immigration and Passport Act Cap 208 Laws of Antigua and Barbuda (IP Act).

Held: Blenman, J
In determining what Mr. Linton's obligation was, it brings into sharp focus section 5 of the Caricom Skilled Nationals Act No. 3 of 1997. It is prudent to recite section 5(1) and (2) which state: '**5**. (**1**) Notwithstanding the provisions of any other law, an immigration officer shall, subject to section[s] 14 and 16, permit a person to whom this subsection applies, to enter Antigua and Barbuda for a period of six months. (**2**) This section applies to the holder of a passport issue[d] by a qualifying Caribbean Community state who – (a) was born in the state issuing the passport or in another qualifying Caribbean Community state; and (b) present[s] on entry to Antigua and Barbuda a certificate issued by the Government of a qualifying Caribbean Community state in that state's equivalent form to the form in Schedule II certifying that the holder of the passport is recognised by the Government of that qualifying Caribbean Community state as holding qualifications which satisfy the conditions for recognition of Caribbean Community skills qualification. Section 5(2) (b) of the Act is of great significance since the Attorney General, as stated earlier, maintains that Mr. Linton did not act in compliance with this section. The Attorney General in effect has asked the court to give a literal interpretation of the Act. This suggests that a CARICOM national who falls within the stipulated categories of persons must present the Caricom Skilled Certificate (from a qualifying Caricom State) on *entering* Antigua and Barbuda. As alluded to earlier, in the case at bar, this did not occur. In fact, it is clear that Mr. Linton presented his Certificate to the Immigration Authorities some four weeks after entry into Antigua and Barbuda. In order to determine this issue, the court must seek to interpret section 5(2) (b) of the Act. In so doing, the court must ensure that it ascertains what the intention of the legislature was at the time of the enactment. In so doing, the court usually has regard to the Literal rule of interpretation which requires, in the interpreting or construing an Act of Parliament, acceptance of words which are precise and unambiguous. See *Sussex Peerage Case* [1844] 1 CI&F 85. However, where the literal interpretation of the statutory provision leads to an absurdity or yields unjust results, the courts have, from time to time, utilised the alternative rules of interpretation. The Golden . . . Rule of interpretation is frequently utilized. This enables the court to ascertain the meaning of words in order to avoid repugnance or absurdity. See *Grey v Pearson* (1857) 6 HLC 61. It is the general principle of statutory interpretation that every clause or Act must be construed in the context of and with reference to the other clauses or sections of that statute. The court must seek to determine the legislative intention. Indeed, the learned Professor V.C.R.A.C Crabbe in his enlightening treatise 'Understanding Statutes' at p 87 states as follows: 'In *The Duke of Buccleuch* (1889) 15 PD 86 AT P 96, Lord Lindley said that: You are not so to construe the Act of Parliament as

to reduce it to rank absurdity. You are not to attribute to general language used by the Legislature in this case, any more than in any other case, a meaning which would not carry out its object, but produce consequences which to the ordinary intelligence, are absurd. You must give it such a meaning as will carry out its objects.' In *Gartside v IRC* [1968] AC 553 at p 612, Lord Reid said that: 'It is always proper to construe an ambiguous word or phrase in light of the mischief which the provision is obviously designed to prevent, and in the light of the reasonableness of the consequences which follow from giving it a particular construction.' All these authorities raise one fundamental problem: what is the test to be applied? In *River Wear Commissioners v Anderson* (1877) 2 AC 743 at pp 764–765 Lord Blackman stated: 'We are to take the whole statute together, and construe it all together, giving the words their ordinary signification, unless when so applied they produce an inconsistency, or an absurdity or inconvenience so great as to convince the court that the intention could not have been to use them in their ordinary signification, and to justify the court in putting on them some other signification, though less proper, is one which the court thinks the words will bear. That, then, is the test. The departure from the grammatical or ordinary sense of the words must of necessity relate to the Act read as a whole, and to a consideration of the objective or scheme of the Act.' Guided by the above principles, it is clear to me that an examination must be taken of the whole of the legislation and its context in interpreting section 5(2). The court must ensure that the intention of the Legislature is the foremost consideration. Having done so, the court is unable to agree with the contention of the learned Deputy Solicitor General as to the meaning of section 5(2) (b). To accord section 5(2) (b) the meaning urged by Ms. DeFreitas-Rait would yield absurd results and would run counter to the clear intention of Parliament. If Ms. DeFreitas-Rait is correct, it would mean that a skilled Caricom national who is qualified under the Act and is a visitor to Antigua and Barbuda, and who subsequently receives the requisite certificate from his home country, would have to leave Antigua and Barbuda and return for the sole purpose of being able to present the certificate *on entry*. It is not in the interest of justice to give the section such a rigid interpretation, which would yield to absurdity and which would, with the greatest of respect, be contrary to the intention of the Legislature. It is clear to the court that a purposive approach must be given to the interpretation of section 5(2) (b). I am fortified in this view since there is nothing in the scheme of the legislation that will support the court giving the section such a narrow and restrictive interpretation. By way of emphasis, the court is of the considered view that the case at bar requires the application of the Golden Rule of Interpretation. With the greatest of respect, I reiterate that if the court was to apply the literal interpretation to the section it would yield results that are repugnant to both the intention of the Legislature and to common sense.

Mischief rule

The mischief rule is the most flexible of the three rules of interpretation but is still limited to the extent that reference can only be made to previous common law rules on the subject matter. In cases of ambiguous constructions, recourse is had to the rules laid down in the classic statement given in *Heyden's* case. The rule enables consideration of four matters in constructing an Act:

(i) what was the common law before the making of the Act;
(ii) what was the mischief or defect for which the common law did not provide;

(iii) what remedy for that mischief had Parliament intended to provide; and
(iv) what is the reason for the remedy?[54]

Adversaries of the mischief rule often decry its application as being akin to judges seeking to project a parliamentary role onto themselves. It is, however, generally the case that the mischief rule is rarely used and, when it is, there is an element of public interest involved.

R v F (M.B.) 2003 ABQB 368 (CA)

Facts: On 23 September 2002 the appellant was convicted of Section 253(a), having the care and control of a motor vehicle while his ability to operate it was impaired by alcohol or a drug. The Court heard that on 9 March 2002 Constable Bourgeois was dispatched to 10123–73 Street and arrived at 1:01 am. He spoke with a witness and was directed to a 1986 Ford Ranger motor vehicle. The appellant was found in the vehicle. Constable Bourgeois saw the appellant sitting on the driver's seat, with his upper body lying towards the passenger seat, and his feet and legs on the floor of the driver's side of the vehicle. The appellant was sleeping and 'with a little bit of persistence' Constable Bourgeois woke up the appellant. It was evident that the appellant's ability to operate a motor vehicle was impaired by alcohol. The officer formed an opinion to this effect and the appellant, in his evidence, admitted this. The Constable stated that the motor vehicle was not running, but the keys were in the ignition. The Constable agreed that the appellant was resting his upper body and head on property he had piled up on the passenger seat and was using the property as a pillow. This was consistent with the appellant being asleep.

The appellant identified several photographs that were made exhibits that described the layout of the vehicle. Briefly, the appellant described the vehicle as a truck-type vehicle with a manual transmission. The transmission required that a clutch be used in order to put the vehicle into gear and into motion. In order to start the vehicle the appellant stated that the vehicle had to have the keys in the ignition, the clutch would have to be depressed, the gears would have to be checked and the accelerator would have to be activated. The appellant had driven the vehicle earlier, but at the relevant time had made the decision not to drive. The appellant was sleeping and had decided that only when he was sober would he operate the vehicle.

Held: Lee, J
In coming to his decision, the trial judge stated that the critical issue was the location of the keys, and this was the main issue on the question of care and control: The appellant submits that there was insufficient evidence to support a finding that the appellant was able to place the vehicle in motion . . . However, the Supreme Court of Canada was clear that the absence of an intention to drive does not constitute a complete defence to the charge of impaired care and control . . .

The mischief sought to be prohibited by the section as expressed by the wording is that an intoxicated person who is in the immediate presence of a motor vehicle with the means of controlling it or setting it in motion is or may be a danger to the public. *Even if he has no immediate intention of setting it in motion he can at any instant determine to do so, because his judgment may be so impaired that he cannot foresee the possible consequences of his actions* . . . While evidence of

54 See Patil, 'General Rules of Statutory Interpretation', p 6.

the physical manipulation of the systems of the vehicle was minimal in this case, other circumstances such as the location of the vehicle in the parking lot of a hotel outside licensed premises, as well as the continued consumption of drugs in the vehicle, lends support to the finding made that the Appellant had care or control and that the Appellant constituted a danger to the public.

The Attorney General v The Barbuda Council Civil Appeal No. 7 of 2001 (AG)

Facts: In the early 1990s representatives of Unicorn Development Limited approached the respondent to obtain its approval for a hotel development project in Barbuda. These representatives were Barbudans who had been living in England. The Council approved the project and a hotel site at Palmetto Point. On 16 August 1996, at a meeting of the Council, Mr Brillheart James applied, on behalf of Unicorn, to change the location of the project site to Spanish Point, because of damage caused by Hurricane Luis to Palmetto Point. The Council approved the change of location in principle and its secretary issued documents to that effect. Almost immediately after, the representatives of Unicorn appeared before the Cabinet of Antigua and Barbuda with their proposal. On 21 August 1996 the Cabinet made a decision approving the proposal. On 12 March 1997 the Cabinet approved the terms of a lease to Unicorn, and on 13 August 1997 the Cabinet made a correction in respect of the area of land from 25 to 35 acres. On 22 November 1997 His Excellency the Governor-General executed the lease.

Party politics intervened. One of the witnesses in the trial was Mr Hilbourne Frank, the leader of the Barbuda Peoples Movement. He indicated that in August 1996 the majority of the Council were sympathetic to the Antigua Labour Party Government. He was a member of the Council but his party was in the minority. He testified that he voted in favour of the project at that meeting. There were Barbuda Council elections in March 1997 and control of the Council reverted to the Barbuda Peoples Movement. The newly constituted Council initially decided to affirm its approval of the project, but the political climate changed. The evidence indicated that since 1989 the Council had passed resolutions about making a conservation area on Spanish Point, and concerns about this resurfaced.

This was not a live issue on appeal because the respondents conceded that the Council did not have the constitutional authority to establish a conservation area without the sanction and authority of the Cabinet, which was neither sought nor obtained. But at the time it was an emotive issue. The evidence indicated that there was a public perception that there was overlapping of the area so earmarked and the area of land contained in the lease granted to Unicorn. Mr Frank testified that in his opinion the area designated in the lease exceeded the area which the Council had approved. There were also public meetings that were held on this issue. The dispute included the contention that the lease was issued without the consent of the Council and was therefore illegal. In addition to the public meetings, there were interventions through judicial proceedings by way of applications for injunctive relief.

Eventually, Unicorn entered on its lease and began to undertake work on the site. These proceedings sought relief aimed at stopping the development on that site. The pleadings were extensive. The writ initiating the claim applied for declarations of the rights to which inhabitants of Barbuda were entitled under The Barbuda Ordinance 1904 as amended and the Barbuda Local Government Act 1976 as amended and for ancillary relief. The notice of appeal listed some 18 grounds. These were summarised in the written skeleton argument of the appellant as raising three issues:

(a) whether the Crown has the authority and power to grant, including the power to lease, lands on the island of Barbuda;

(b) whether the Crown is obliged to first obtain the consent or approval of the respondent; and

(c) whether the lease in this case was inconsistent with any alleged right of the respondent and therefore unlawful.

Held: Byron, CJ

This case is therefore to be resolved on the meaning to be attached to the relevant provisions of the two statutes, the Barbuda Act as amended, and the Local Government Act 1976 as amended. It is necessary to remind ourselves of the principles which a court should apply in order to adjudicate on the meaning and effect of a statute. I would adopt the expression of the principle stated by Sir Vincent Floissac, CJ in the Dominica case of *Charles Savarin v John Williams* Civil Appeal 3 of 1995:

In order to resolve the fundamental issue in this appeal, I start with the basic principle that the interpretation of every word or phrase of a statutory provision is derived from the legislative intention in regard to the meaning which that word or phrase should bear. That legislative intention is an inference drawn from the primary meaning of the word or phrase with such modifications to that meaning as may be necessary to make it concordant with the statutory context. In this regard, the statutory context comprises every other word or phrase used in the statute, all implications therefrom and all relevant surrounding circumstances which may properly be regarded as indications of the legislative intention.

The Mischief Rule, when properly applied, involves the use of an aspect of the statutory context to indicate the statutory intention. It is of ancient vintage. It was succinctly explained by Lindley MR in the case of *Bartlette v MayFair Property Company* [1898] 2 Ch 28 at 35:

> In order properly to interpret any statute it is as necessary now as it was when Lord Cooke reported Heydon's Case to consider how the law stood when the statute to be construed was passed, what the mischief was for which the old law did not provide, and the remedy provided by the statute to cure that mischief.

The Mischief Rule is an important aid to construction when there is lack of clarity or ambiguity in the language in which the statute is expressed. But if the words of the statute are clear and unambiguous there is a real danger that in applying the mischief rule subjective perceptions on the mischief and the remedy may influence the interpretation to be applied by substituting a perceived remedy for the meaning which the legislature intended.

A properly drafted statute is capable of conveying its meaning through the actual words used in the statute. It is obvious that in many cases the perception of the mischief, the relevant historical context and what constitutes a desirable solution or remedy is capable of wide variance. And this case was no exception to that concept. In the case of *Universal Caribbean Establisment v James Harrison* Civil Appeal 21 of 1993, Antigua, the court was faced with interpreting the jurisdiction section of the Industrial Court Act 1976, an act which was generally agreed to have been poorly drafted. In considering the approach to be adopted I had to remind myself, and I do so again, of the following principle:

The first principle to affirm is to recognise the separation of power between the Legislature and the Judiciary. It is the province of Parliament to make the law and for the Court to interpret, without basing its construction of the Statute on a perception of its wisdom or propriety or a view of what Parliament ought to have done. The dominant purpose in construing a Statute is to ascertain the intention of the legislature as expressed in the Statute, considering it as a whole and in its context. It is only where the words of the Statute are not clear and unambiguous that it is necessary to enlist aids for interpretation . . .

The Plain Meaning. As I embark on the exercise in this case I should indicate that I do not find that the drafting is ambiguous. The language seems quite simple, clear and straightforward. In my view the legislative intention could be derived from the primary meaning of the words in the Statute . . .

The issues which were relevant to this case were the following provisions: Section 5 – [In the original version of the act this was section 13]. The amendments are contained in the introduction of the new subsections [2]–[8]:

[1] All persons inhabiting the Island of Barbuda shall be and are hereby declared to be tenants of the Crown; and such persons shall neither hold nor deal with any land situate within the said island save and except as hereinafter appears by the provisions of this Act and subject to any by-law made by the council in that behalf.

[2] Nothing in this section shall be construed as precluding the grant by the Crown of any interest in or over any piece of land within Barbuda to any person whether or not that person is an inhabitant of Barbuda.

[3] Notwithstanding the provisions of any other law, no person shall acquire the ownership of any piece or parcel of Crown land within Barbuda by prescription.

[4] If any inhabitant of Barbuda can show to the satisfaction of the Crown that a grant by the Crown to any other person of any interest in or over any piece or parcel of land within Barbuda has caused him any material loss in respect of any use that he has been making of that piece or parcel of land by virtue of the provisions of subsection [1] of this section, that inhabitant shall be entitled to fair compensation in respect of that loss within a reasonable time . . .

In my view the new section 5[2] did not change the law. It merely declared it. As I have explained earlier the 1904 legislation did not preclude the Crown from granting any interest in or over any piece of land in Barbuda . . . I assess that the statutory intent was to clarify the existing law . . .

I would now summarise my answers to the issues raised on this appeal. The law is that the Crown as the owner of land has the power to grant, including the power to lease, lands on the island of Barbuda. The laws in my view are equally clear that the Council has no role in the transfer of title. There is no requirement in the Barbuda Act, nor the Local Government Act nor in any other Act requiring the Crown to first obtain the consent or approval of the Barbuda Council before exercising its powers to grant any land. The Council had no legal or other interest in the land contained in the grant of the lease to Unicorn. Neither did the Council have any legal or constitutional status in the process of granting an interest in land to anyone. The legislation, as I have shown, does not preclude the Crown from behaving as a universal and absolute owner and in that capacity granting an interest in land. The evidence indicates that the proper processes required by law were observed and the lease was properly issued by His Excellency the Governor General. In my view the granting of the lease was not unlawful.

Purposive approach

The purposive approach is a more modern take on statutory interpretation and might even be said to be an updated version of the mischief rule. It allows for still more flexibility than the mischief rule, as judges may decide what they think Parliament intended to say rather than what the Act actually says.[55] This approach seeks to give effect where applying the literal meaning of the statute would lead to results which clearly defeat the purpose of the act. Here, the court's task, within permissible bounds of interpretation, is to give effect to Parliament's purpose. In this way, the controversial provisions should be read in the context of the statute as a whole, and the statute as a whole should be read in the historical context of the situation which led to its enactment (Archie, CJ; Hamel-Smith, JA; Jamadar, JA in *Omar Maraj (Appellant) v The Public Service Appeal Board (Respondents)* (2009) Civil Appeal No. 100 of 2006 (TT)). As with any other interpretative approach, it must be used judiciously, as the notion of Parliament's intention can be subjective. This approach is not without its criticisms, as it allows judges to develop the law in line with Parliament's intentions thereby blurring the line between the Judiciary and the Legislature.[56]

Fazal Ghany (Regimental No. 12858 CPL) (Appellant) v The Compensation Committee and the Attorney General of Trinidad and Tobago (Respondents) (2011) Civil Appeal No. 197 of 2008; G-13 No. 26 of 2007 (TT)

Facts: The appeal is from the decision of The Compensation Committee ('the Committee') established under the Protective Services (Compensation) Act Chap. 23:60 ('the Act') that it had no jurisdiction to award compensation to the Appellant for the injury he had suffered. It is to be noted at the outset that there is no contention that Mr. Ghany suffered the injury complained of and that the injury was suffered in the course of his duty. The outcome of the appeal turns on two issues: first, the correct principles to be applied when interpreting a statute; and second, whether the Appellant has discharged the burden on him.

Held: Kangaloo, Stollmeyer and Smith, JJA

The Purposive Approach
It was long held that it was not '. . . competent for a judge to modify the language of an act of parliament in order to bring it in accordance with his views as to what is right and reasonable.' Several authorities thereafter upheld this proposition, the 'literal approach', until the decision of Lord Denning in *Seaford Court Estates v Asher* [1949] 2 KB 481. In that case it was held that the court must '. . . set to work on the constructive task of finding the intention of Parliament . . .' and '. . . supplement the written word so as to give 'force and life' to the intention of the legislature.' Lord Simmons in *Magor & St. Mellons Rural District Council v Newport* [1950] 2 All ER 1226 condemned Lord Denning's approach as 'a naked usurpation of the legislative function under the thin disguise of interpretation, and it is the less justifiable when it is guesswork with what material the legislature would, if it had discovered the gap, have filled it in. If a gap is disclosed, the remedy lies in an amending Act.' This continued to represent the law. Subsequently, Lord Diplock in an apparently singular opinion (the other members of the House do not appear to have agreed with him) opined in *Jones v. Wrotham Park Settled Estates and Anor* [1979] 1 All ER 286 (at page 289) that a purposive construction should be adopted where applying the literal meaning of the legislative language used would lead to results which would clearly defeat the purposes

55 Hussain, 'Notes on Statutory Interpretations'.

56 Colleg Gwent, [online], 'Statutory Interpretation: Purposive Approach' [PPT Presentation], [accessed 05 January 2015]. Available at: http://learn.coleggwent.ac.uk/mod/resource/view.php?id=144939.

of an act. He then set out three conditions which would need to be satisfied to allow that approach to succeed:

> First, it was possible to determine from a consideration of the provisions of the Act read as a whole precisely what the mischief was that it was the purpose of the Act to remedy; secondly, it was apparent that the draftsman and Parliament had by inadvertence overlooked, and so omitted to deal with, an eventuality that required to be dealt with if the purpose of the Act was to be achieved; and thirdly, it was possible to state with certainty what were the additional words that would have been inserted by the draftsman and approved by Parliament had their attention been drawn to the omission before the Bill passed into law.

His view subsequently found favour in *Inco Europe Ltd. and Ors. v. First Choice Distribution (a firm) and Others* in both the Court of Appeal ([1999] 1 All ER 20) and the House of Lords ([2000] 2 All ER 109). In the latter, Lord Nicholls reiterated those three conditions but also pointed out the need for 'considerable caution' when deciding whether words should be added or omitted from a statute. What he says there bears repetition:

> . . . It has long been established that the role of the courts in construing legislation is not confined to resolving ambiguities in statutory language. The court must be able to correct obvious drafting errors. In suitable cases, in discharging its interpretative function the court will add words, or omit words or substitute words. Some notable instances are given in Professor Sir Rupert Cross' admirable opuscule, *Statutory Interpretation*, 3rd edn., (1995) pp. 93–105. He comments, at page 103: 'In omitting or inserting words the judge is not really engaged in a hypothetical reconstruction of the intentions of the drafter or the legislature, but is simply making as much sense as he can of the text of the statutory provision read in its appropriate context and within the limits of the judicial role.' This power is confined to plain cases of drafting mistakes. The courts are ever mindful that their constitutional role in this field is interpretative. They must abstain from any course which might have the appearance of judicial legislation. A statute is expressed in language approved and enacted by the legislature. So the courts exercise considerable caution before adding or omitting or substituting words. Before interpreting a statute in this way the court must be abundantly sure of three matters: (1) the intended purpose of the statute or provision in question. (2) that by inadvertence the draftsman and Parliament failed to give effect to that purpose in the provision in question: and (3) the substance of the provision Parliament would have made, although not necessarily the precise words Parliament would have used, had the error in the Bill been noticed. The third of these conditions is of crucial importance. Otherwise any attempt to determine the meaning of the enactment would cross the boundary between construction and legislation: see Lord Diplock in *Jones v Wrotham Park Settled Estates* [1979] 1 All ER 286 at 289, [1980] AC 74 at 105–106. In the present case these three conditions are fulfilled. Sometimes, even when these conditions are met, the court may find itself inhibited from interpreting the statutory provision in accordance with what it is satisfied was the underlying intention of Parliament. The alteration in language may be too far-reaching. In *Western Bank Ltd. v Schindler* [1976] 2 All ER 393 at 404, [1977] Ch. 1 at 18. Scarman LJ observed that the insertion must not be too big, or too much at variance with the language used by the legislature. Or the subject matter may call for a strict interpretation of the statutory language, as in penal legislation. None of these considerations apply in the present case. Here, the court is able to give effect to a construction of the statute which accords with the intention of the legislature . . .

If Parliament's intention was to provide for the injury suffered by the Appellant, or for injuries not specified or listed in the Second Schedule to the WCA, then it can amend the Act appropriately. Indeed, Parliament delegated certain powers to the Minister at Section 21 of the Act: 'The Minister may by Order amend the First and Second Schedules by adding to them any other Service or benefits as the case may be'. It is not for the court to declare what injuries attract compensation, much less prescribe a formula for the calculation of such compensation. The court must be cautious because it cannot appear to be ignoring the supremacy of Parliament, and cannot cross the great divide from construction into legislation. The gap or void in the instant case is one that should be properly filled by the Minister or by an amending act.

SEPARATION OF POWERS

Separation of powers is the doctrine that:

- there are three main classes of governmental functions: the legislative, the executive and the judicial;
- there are (or should be) three main organs of government in a state: the legislature, the executive and the judiciary;
- to concentrate more than one class of function in any one person or organ of government is a threat to individual liberty.[57]

This is the doctrine as espoused by the French philosopher Montesquieu and found in countries practising common law. The basic purpose of keeping these elements separated is to prevent the centralisation and abuse of powers. The legislative branch has the power to make laws, such as the declaration of what acts are to be regarded as criminal. The executive branch has the authority to administer the law, primarily by bringing lawbreakers to trial, and to appoint officials and oversee the administration of government responsibilities. The judicial branch has the power to try cases brought to court and to interpret the meaning of laws under which the trials are conducted.

Parliamentary sovereignty

The doctrine of parliamentary sovereignty was born out of the English revolutionary struggles of the seventeenth century, when Parliament became the sovereign power of the land. English philosopher, John Locke, emphasised the centrality of the independence of judges and the legal system from direct control or interference of the state as an integral component of the Social Contract, whereby the people would consent to a government to which they would give up their right to punish violators of the natural law in exchange for an impartial legal and political system that would secure their natural rights and would ensure their safety and general welfare.[58] The doctrine of parliamentary sovereignty effectively means that Parliament, as the ultimate source of law, can make such laws as it determines necessary[59] for the peace, order and good governance of the land.

Role of the executive

The executive branch of government in Trinidad and Tobago consists of the chief of state (President), the head of government (prime minister) and the cabinet as appointed from among the Members of Parliament. The President is the repository of all executive authority. Executive

57 De Smith and Brazier, *Constitutional and Administrative Law*, pp 18–19.

58 McGraw, B, 'Introduction: Church and State in Context'. In A Duncan and S Jones (eds), *Church-State Issues in America Today: Religion and Government*, 2007, Santa Barbara, CA: Praeger Publishers, pp 9–10.

59 Slapper and Kelly, *The English Legal System*, p 10.

responsibilities in relation to the administration of justice are delegated by the prime minister to members of his cabinet. This executive body has the administrative role of controlling the affairs of the nation.

In Commonwealth nations such as this, with politically appointed Attorney Generals, the Director of Public Prosecutions is given judicial security of tenure by the Constitution and is vested with an exclusive independent responsibility for decision to take over, continue or discontinue prosecutions.[60] Under section 90 of the Constitution of the Republic of Trinidad and Tobago, the Director of Public Prosecutions may institute criminal proceedings against any person before any court in respect of any offence against the law of Trinidad and Tobago and may also do so against the President.[61] It is expected that he will not act under the direction of any other person, so emphasising the importance of maintaining public confidence in the process of prosecution and the precarious delicacy of the balance achieved by habits of political self-restraint.[62]

Judicial independence

In TT, the judicial branch is comprised of the Supreme Court of Judicature, which consists of the High Court of Justice and the Court of Appeals. The highest Court of Appeal is the Privy Council in London. Independence of the judiciary necessary implies that justice will be dispensed fairly in the courts and that the general public can feel confident that it will be executed in an impartial manner, as embodied in the Rule of Law as stated above.

The issue of the practice of the doctrine of separation of powers as applied to the independence of the judiciary is debatable, as can be seen in the example of what obtains in TT. Although some believe in the independence of the judiciary given its supposed immunity from the executive (read: political pressure) through the buffer provided by the Judicial and Legal Services Commission, the various appointments to the Judicial and Legal Services Commission illustrate the basis for questioning the notion of the independence of the judiciary.[63] Members of the Judicial and Legal Services Commission are all appointed by the President; therefore, it is important to examine how the President is appointed. The Electoral College is the unit that is responsible for appointing the President. What constitutes the Electoral College? According to section 28(1) of the Constitution, the Electoral College is a unicameral body consisting of all the Members of both Houses of Parliament: 31 Senators in the Upper House and 36[64] Members of Parliament in the Lower House. The President appoints all 31 Senators;[65] however, 16 are appointed on the Prime Minister's recommendations, six are appointed on the advice of the Leader of the Opposition, and nine 'Independent Senators' are appointed at the President's

60 De Smith and Brazier, *Constitutional and Administrative Law*, pp 386–7.

61 See section 38.

62 De Smith and Brazier, *Constitutional and Administrative Law*, p 387.

63 See for example Selwyn Ryan, *The Judiciary and Governance in the Caribbean*, 2001, St. Augustine, Trinidad: Sir Arthur Lewis Institute of Social and Economic Studies, UWI, pp 7–11.

64 The 2010 national elections saw the election into office of 41 members. Such a change in number is permitted under section 46(2) of the Constitution.

65 See section 40 of the Constitution.

discretion. As for the Members of Parliament, it is generally the ruling party that has more members.[66] In any event, it is clear that the majority of the Members of Parliament are affiliated with the ruling party and it is these Members that make up the Electoral College which appoints the President. It should be clear from this that the appointment of President is in fact a political appointment and that any appointments made by the President may arguably have political overtones.[67]

As mentioned above, all members of the Judicial and Legal Services Commission are appointed by the President (section 110). The Chief Justice and the Chairman of the Public Service Commission are constitutionally designated as members of the Judicial and Legal Services Commission and they are appointed directly by the President after consultation with the leaders of the governing party and the opposition.[68] The three other members of the Judicial and Legal Services Commission are appointed in the same manner as the Chief Justice and the Chairman of the Public Services Commission. The Chief Justice is President of the Court of Appeal and Chairman of the Judicial and Legal Services Commission. He is also, *ex officio*, a judge of the High Court. Effectively, therefore, the Executive is ever present in these appointments, causing the notion of a separation of powers to be somewhat questionable.

66 Except in cases of deadlock, where the President has the discretion to choose which party shall govern.

67 In *Director of Personnel Administration and the Police Service Commission v Eusebio Cooper and Others*, Civil Appeal No. 10 of 2004 (TT), Chief Justice Sharma also outlined the relationship among the Executive, Legislature and the Judiciary asking 'What can be more political than that?' at paragraph 34, stating at the same time, however, that there must be a presumed integrity of holders of high office or the Constitution would be rendered unworkable. See paragraphs 33–39. In Kangaloo JA's judgment of the same case, he admits at paragraph 20 that 'the potential for interference must exist once there is the overlap of powers' but emphasises that the real issue is the *degree of influence or interference that is permissible* in any given situation. Similarly, in the Dominican case of *The Constituency Boundaries Commission and the Attorney-General of the Commonwealth of Dominica v Urban Baron*, Civil Appeal No. 12 of 1998 (DM), Singh JA believes that Commissions borne from the Constitution 'will lean more towards political loyalty than constitutional integrity' due to the same political relationship existing among the three bodies.

68 See sections 102 and 120 of the Constitution respectively.

CHAPTER 2

LAW OF OBLIGATIONS: MAKING THE CONTRACT

Reproduced with the permission of Stu's Views

At the heart of any business agreement can be found the contract. Whether oral or written, it is the contract that regulates the transaction between the parties. Contracts identify the legal obligations of the parties involved and may often include clauses that allow for third-party resolution of differences of opinion and penalties for non-performance. In the business world contracts regulate employment, sale of goods, carriage, shipping, agency, provision of services, leases, guarantees and loans, among many other business relationships.

CONTRACT

More specifically, a contract is an agreement, either written or oral, by which two or more parties having legal capacity agree with sufficient certainty in accordance with terms and conditions that are express or implied to perform certain obligations (either for a benefit or a detriment) that are not contrary to law or public policy.

Since the law of contracts is at the heart of most business dealings, it is one of the three or four most significant areas of legal concern and can involve variations on circumstances and complexities. The existence of a contract requires finding the following factual elements:

(a) an offer;
(b) an acceptance of that offer which results in a meeting of the minds;
(c) a promise to perform;
(d) a valuable consideration (which can be a promise or payment in some form).

Terms and conditions of the contract usually include the following:

(a) a time or event when performance must be made (meet commitments);
(b) terms and conditions for performance, including fulfilling promises;
(c) performance, if the contract is 'unilateral'.[1]

While it is expected that contracts will contain all relevant information, it often happens that some of the necessary terms and conditions may not have been specifically documented. In such cases, the court will objectively assess whether or not a contract was made between two or more parties on the basis of the facts presented.

Visual Arts Production Limited v Marcus Jean Baptiste (2011) CV2008–01020 (TT)

Facts: The Claimant was a tenant of premises located at Taylor Street, Woodbrook but vacated the premises in April, 2007, leaving behind an air conditioning unit, an air conditioning duct, a water tank and a water pump ('the disputed items'). Thereafter, the Defendant took possession of the rented premises sometime in June, 2007 and entered into negotiations with the Claimant, through its agent, Naushad Khan, for the purchase of the disputed items for the sum of ten thousand dollars ($10,000.00). After the Defendant took possession of the premises, the Claimant, through its said agent, orally demanded payment in the agreed sum on several occasions or, in the alternative, that the Defendant deliver up the disputed items. However, the Defendant has failed and/or refused to pay the agreed sum or deliver up the disputed items.

Held: Charles, J
It is trite law that to formulate a contract, there must be an offer, acceptance of that offer and consideration. The evidence before the Court is sketchy at best; the Claimant contends that there were negotiations between its agent, Naushad Khan, and the Defendant whereby the latter agreed to purchase the disputed items. However, Thomas Mora, the Chief Executive Officer of the Claimant Company, conceded in cross examination that the negotiations did not result in a purchase price being agreed. Rather the Defendant was to be later contacted by the Claimant's accountant with a price. There was no further evidence on whether contact was ever made with the Defendant by the Claimant's accountant. While . . . the Defendant denied that any such discussions ever took place. The Court does not accept that there was acceptance in these circumstances by the Defendant to purchase the disputed items. An acceptance is a final and unqualified expression of assent to the terms of an offer; a mere acknowledgment of an offer would not be an acceptance, nor would a person to whom an offer to sell goods had been made accept it merely by replying it was his 'intention to place an order' or by asking for an invoice. The Court finds that there may have been some discussions by the Claimant and Defendant regarding the disputed items that were on the rented premises; items which may have been too arduous to remove after being on the premises for over six years. In these circumstances, it is easy to understand how the Claimant would assume that the Defendant would want to purchase them and why the Claimant did not insist on a written contract for the items. When the Defendant took possession of the rented premises, however, and admittedly started using

1 Law.com Dictionary [online], 'Contract', n.d. [accessed 25 January 2015]. Available at: http://dictionary.law.com/Default.aspx?selected=337.

the disputed items, the Court finds that this was acceptance by conduct for the purchase of the items. An offer may be accepted by conduct where an offer to sell goods, made by sending them to the offeree, can be accepted by using them. However, conduct will amount to acceptance only if it is clear that the offeree did the act of alleged acceptance with the intention of accepting the offer. It is clear that the Defendant knew that the disputed items were not part of the rented premises, as it is commonplace when renting premises to ascertain the amenities. Further, that the Defendant knew that the disputed items belonged to the Claimant and they either were to be paid for, or returned to the Claimant. Therefore, the Court holds that by utilising, instead of returning, the disputed items the Defendant agreed to purchase them. The Court therefore holds that there was acceptance of the oral contract to purchase the disputed items . . .

Birse Construction Limited v St David Limited No. 1998 TCC No 419 (GB)

Facts: The claimant, Birse Construction Limited (Birse), carried out certain work required by the defendant, St David Limited (St David), for the construction of luxury apartments at Adventurers' Quay, Cardiff Bay. By a Writ issued on 8 September 1998 and a Statement of Claim served on 12 October 1998, Birse sought to recover payment for the work upon a *Quantum Meruit*. Birse contended that by 11 August 1998 – the date upon which it left site – it had executed works to the value of and/or for which a fair commercial price was £6,759,608.21. St David had paid £5,745,518.65 in respect of the works, leaving an outstanding balance of £1,014,089.56 which was the sum claimed in these proceedings. Birse accepted that there were extensive negotiations with St David with a view to making a contract, but it contended that no contract was made prior to its leaving site in August 1998. St David took a different view. It contended that a contract, incorporating JCT Conditions (Private Without Quantities, 1980 Edition) and containing an arbitration clause, was made.

Held: Reese, J
In my judgment, the most helpful statements of the general principles which need to be considered and applied in this case are to be found in the judgment of Bingham J (as he then was) and Lloyd LJ in *Pagnan* (*supra*). At pp 610–11 of the report Bingham J said this:

> B. The law . . . The Court's task is to review what the parties said and did and from that material to infer whether the parties' objective intentions as expressed to each other were to enter into a mutually binding contract. The Court is not of course concerned with what the parties may subjectively have intended. As Lord Denning MR put it in *Storer v Manchester City Council* [1974] 1 WLR 1403, at p 1408H:
>
> > In contracts you do not look into the actual intent in a man's mind. You look to see what he said and did. A contract is formed when there is, to all outward appearances, a contract. A man cannot get out of the contract by saying, 'I did not intend to contract' if by his words he has done so. His intention is to be found only in the outward expression which his letters convey. If they show a concluded contract, that is enough.
>
> It is furthermore clear that where exchanges between parties have continued over a period, the Court must consider all these exchanges in context and not seize upon one episode in isolation in order to conclude that a contract has been made . . . The parties may by their words and conduct make it clear that they do intend to be bound even though there are other terms yet to be agreed, even terms which may often or usually be agreed before a binding contract is made; see *Love and Stewart sup.*, per Lord Loreburn LC at p 476 . . . The parties are to be regarded as masters of their contractual fate. It is their intentions which matter and to which the Court must strive to give effect . . . That is, I think, the result of *Brogden v*

Metropolitan Raiwway Co. (1877) App Cas 666 and *Hussey v Horne-Payne* (1874) 4 App Cas 311. But the Court's task remains essentially the same: to discern and give effect to the objective intention of the parties.

. . . At p 619 of the report Lloyd LJ said this:

As to the law, the principles to be derived from the authorities, some of which I have already mentioned, can be summarised as follows:

(1) In order to determine whether a contract has been concluded in the course of correspondence, one must first look at the correspondence as a whole (see *Hussey v Horne-Payne*).

(2) Even if the parties have reached agreement on all the terms of the proposed contract, nevertheless they may intend that the contract shall not become binding until some further condition has been fulfilled. That is the ordinary 'subject to contract' case.

(3) Alternatively, they may intend that the contract shall not become binding until some further term or terms have been agreed; see *Love and Stewart v Instone*, where the parties failed to agree the intended strike clause, and *Hussey v Horne-Payne*, where Lord Selborne said, at p 323: '. . . The observation has often been made that, a contract established by letters may sometimes bind parties who, when they wrote those letters, did not imagine they were finally settling the terms of the agreement by which they were to be bound; and it appears to me that no such contract ought to be held established, even by letters which would otherwise be sufficient for the purpose, if it is clear, upon the facts, that there were other conditions of the intended contract, beyond and besides those expressed in the letters, which were still in a state of negotiation only, and without the settlement of which the parties had no idea of concluding any agreement . . .'

(4) Conversely, the parties may intend to be bound forthwith even though there are further terms still be agreed or some further formality to be fulfilled (see *Love and Stewart v Instone* per Lord Loreburn at p 476).

(5) If the parties fail to reach agreement on such further terms, the existing contract is not invalidated unless the failure to reach agreement on such further terms renders the contract as a whole unworkable or void for uncertainty.

(6) It is sometimes said that the parties must agree on the essential terms and that it is only matters of detail which can be left over. This may be misleading, since the word 'essential' in that context is ambiguous. If by 'essential' one means a term without which the contract cannot be enforced then the statement is true; the law cannot enforce an incomplete contract. If by 'essential' one means a term which the parties have agreed to be essential for the formation of a binding contract, then the statement is tautologous. If by 'essential' one means only a term which the Court regards as important as opposed to a term which the Court regards as less important or a matter of detail, the statement is untrue. It is for the parties to decide whether they wish to be bound and, if so, by what terms, whether important or unimportant. It is the parties who are, in the memorable phrase coined by the Judge, 'the masters of their contractual fate'. Of course, the more important the term is, the less likely it is that the parties will have left it for future decision. But there is no legal obstacle which stands in the way of the parties agreeing to be bound now while deferring important matters to be agreed later. It happens every day when the parties enter into so-called 'heads of agreement' . . .

In my judgment it is the second and sixth of Lloyd LJ's principles that fall to be considered and applied in this case. This is not one of the ordinary 'subject to contract cases', but it is necessary to consider whether, even if it could be said that all essential terms were agreed between the designated negotiators, the parties intended that they should only become contractually bound when the putative agreement had been scrutinised and approved by the directors of the respective companies and/or when documents formally recording the approved agreement had been duly signed or executed. In those circumstances, the issue falls to be determined in favour of Birse and accordingly the application for a stay must be dismissed.

CONTRACTUAL INTERPRETATION

Much like statute, contractual provisions are also open to interpretation. The United Kingdom seems to have adopted the purposive approach to contractual interpretation by reviewing the background and context within which the agreement was drafted to assist in interpreting any given clause. Ashurst notes:[2]

> In all cases where a court is required to construe a contract in a dispute, first the judge will look at the express terms. English law takes a purposive and commercial approach to the construction of contracts as per the approach set down in the leading authority on contractual interpretation: the House of Lords decision in *Investors Compensation Scheme v West Bromwich Building Society* (ICS). As a starting point, the meaning of the document is to be found in the document itself, so the court tries to find the 'ordinary and natural meaning' of the words as they are written down. This is because the courts 'do not easily accept that people have made linguistic mistakes, particularly in formal documents'. However, the wording must make sense in the relevant commercial setting and so the court will investigate the full background circumstances to the contract. The judge will take an objective approach to ascertaining the meaning of the words in question . . . The court looks, therefore, at the contract as a whole and considers all of the surrounding facts and circumstances of the particular transaction. It then examines the express wording against this background. It asks itself what would the reasonable commercial parties, using these words in those circumstances, reasonably have understood them to mean? In other words, does it make business common sense?

This approach is not without its criticisms, as the court must be very careful to not be seen as rewriting any terms of the contract. Moreover, the choice of which aspect of the context should predominate is not always easily discernible.

Clacken and Clacken v Causwell and Causwell et al (2010) 2008 HCV 01834 (JM)

Facts: Equipment Maintenance Limited (EML) was incorporated on January 31, 1978. At that time, the only shareholders were the Clackens. Shortly after its incorporation, the Causwells, cousins of Mr. Dwight Clacken, were made part of the company with each holding 33.33% with the Clackens holding 16.66% each. The company was operated as a family company for nearly twenty three years. By 2001, the relationship between the Clackens and the Causwells had deteriorated so badly that October 5, 2001 saw a petition to wind up the company being filed. It was this petition that led ultimately to the agreement that the Causwells would purchase the shares of the Clackens. This agreement was embodied in the order of Anderson, J on May 29, 2002. It is accepted that this order is a contract which the claimants seek declarations that it is now frustrated and based on a common or mutual mistake. The declarations are refused.

2 Ashurst, *Interpretation of Contracts under English Law*, 2012, London: Ashurst, p 1.

Held: Sykes, J

The principles of contractual interpretation

The Court of Appeal of Jamaica has firmly committed itself to the exposition of the principles enunciated by Lord Hoffmann in the important case of *Investor Compensation Scheme Ltd v West Bromwich Building Society* [1998] 1 All ER 98. Morrison JA in *Goblin Hill Hotels Ltd v John Thompson* SCCA No. 57/2007 (delivered December 19, 2008) and Smith JA in *Clacken v Causwell* SCCA 111/2008 (delivered October 2, 2009) expressly adopted the formulation of Lord Hoffmann without reservation or qualification. It can now be taken as settled law in Jamaica that Lord Hoffmann's propositions are now the law of Jamaica and are to be applied to the construction of contracts. Morrison JA, in particular, approved Lord Hoffmann's further refinement in *BCCI v Ali* [2002] 1 AC 251, where his Lordship (Lord Hoffmann) said that background, for the purposes of interpreting a contract, included the law and proved common assumptions regardless of whether those assumptions were accurate or not (see Morrison JA at para. 36 of *Goblin Hill*). Lord Hoffmann also added that admissible background included anything that a reasonable man would regard as relevant. Lord Hoffmann's principles can now be set out. His Lordship stated in *Investor Compensation* at pages 114–115

> My Lords, I will say at once that I prefer the approach of the judge. But I think I should preface my explanation of my reasons with some general remarks about the principles by which contractual documents are nowadays construed . . . The result has been, subject to one important exception, to assimilate the way in which such documents are interpreted by judges to the common sense principles by which any serious utterance would be interpreted in ordinary life. Almost all the old intellectual baggage of 'legal' interpretation has been discarded. The principles may be summarised as follows.
>
> (1) Interpretation is the ascertainment of the meaning which the document would convey to a reasonable person having all the background knowledge which would reasonably have been available to the parties in the situation in which they were at the time of the contract.
>
> (2) The background was famously referred to by Lord Wilberforce as the 'matrix of fact,' but this phrase is, if anything, an understated description of what the background may include. Subject to the requirement that it should have been reasonably available to the parties and to the exception to be mentioned next, it includes absolutely anything which would have affected the way in which the language of the document would have been understood by a reasonable man.
>
> (3) The law excludes from the admissible background the previous negotiations of the parties and their declarations of subjective intent. They are admissible only in an action for rectification. The law makes this distinction for reasons of practical policy and, in this respect only, legal interpretation differs from the way we would interpret utterances in ordinary life. The boundaries of this exception are in some respects unclear. But this is not the occasion on which to explore them.
>
> (4) The meaning which a document (or any other utterance) would convey to a reasonable man is not the same thing as the meaning of its words. The meaning of words is a matter of dictionaries and grammars; the meaning of the document is what the parties using those words against the relevant background would reasonably have been understood to mean. The background may not merely enable the reasonable man to choose between the possible meanings of words which are ambiguous but even (as occasionally happens in ordinary life) to conclude that the parties must, for whatever reason, have used the wrong words or syntax . . .
>
> (5) The 'rule' that words should be given their 'natural and ordinary meaning' reflects the common sense proposition that we do not easily accept that people have made linguistic

> mistakes, particularly in formal documents. On the other hand, if one would nevertheless conclude from the background that something must have gone wrong with the language, the law does not require judges to attribute to the parties an intention which they plainly could not have had.

This passage, as refined in *BCCI*, leads to the following observations. Lord Hoffmann insists that the meaning of a document is not necessarily determined by the dictionary meaning of the words in the document. This is a necessary corollary of the proposition that a document must be construed against the context and background in which it originated. Given the breadth of Lord Hoffmann's propositions, including his Lordship's refinement, it follows that it is entirely possible that when the interpreter, in this case the court, reads the entire document, in its context and background, it may be that the normally understood or conventional meaning of a word or words used in the document may have to yield to another meaning that would not be immediately obvious.

Arden, LJ, in the case of *Static Control Components (Europe) v Egan* [2004] 2 Lloyd's Rep 429, has reaffirmed the ultimate logic of Lord Hoffmann's reasoning in *Investor Compensation*. Her Ladyship was confronted with this submission from counsel. Learned counsel submitted that 'the factual background to the execution of the guarantee is admissible, but . . . it cannot be used to alter or qualify the plain meaning of the guarantee on its face' (para. 23). Her Ladyship rejected this submission as being contrary to authority. 'This was indeed a very remarkable submission from counsel because the very thing he submitted could not be done was in fact done in *Investor Compensation*, namely, that the natural and ordinary meaning was rejected because the background and context, when taken into account, made it plain (according to the majority) that the natural and ordinary meaning of the words was not the correct meaning. Thus Arden LJ, in *Static Control* was able to say that 'in principle, all contracts must be construed in the light of their factual background, that background being ascertained on an objective basis. Accordingly, the fact that a document appears to have a clear meaning on the face of it does not prevent, or indeed excuse, the Court from looking at the background' (para. 27). The purpose of this examination of context and background must be for the purpose of determining whether the 'clear meaning' of the document must yield to another meaning when the background and context are examined.

Another implication of Lord Hoffmann's approach was highlighted by Lord Steyn in *R (on the application of Westminster City Council) v National Asylum Support Services* [2002] 4 All ER 654. His Lordship said, reasoning by analogy in the context of statutory interpretation, that, 'in his important judgment in *Investors Compensation Scheme Ltd v West Bromwich Building Society* [1998] 1 WLR 896, 912–913 Lord Hoffmann made crystal clear that an ambiguity need not be established before the surrounding circumstances may be taken into account. The same applies to statutory construction.'

Miss Catherine Mitchell in her book *Interpretation of Contracts (Current Controversies in Law)* (2007) highlights some problems with Lord Hoffmann's approach. This court agrees with her and summarises her views. She points out that one is never quite sure, in the new approach, which of two persons is given the lead in interpreting a contract. Is it the pedantic lawyer (as in *Investor Compensation*) or is it the reasonable man (as in *Mannai Investment Co Ltd v Eagle Star Life Assurance Company* [1997] AC 749)? A number of cases from the House of Lords, including *Investor Compensation* have brought home this difficulty with Lord Hoffmann's approach in quite a striking manner. In *Investor Compensation*, the majority gave the pedantic lawyer pride of place because, according to Lord Hoffmann, the document in that case was designed to be read by lawyers. In *Malik v BCCI* [1998] AC 20, a former employee not only received redundancy payment but an additional payment on the signing of a release 'in full and final settlement of all or any claims . . . of whatsoever nature that exist or may exist'. At the time of signing the release the House of Lords had not yet decided that an employee could claim 'stigma damages' if they had difficulty in seeking employment because of the stigma attached to them because they worked with the previous employer. However, despite the apparently clear wording of the release, the majority in the House of Lords held that stigma damages were not covered by the release. Ironically, Lord Hoffmann dissented on the basis that the majority had not given sufficient weight to the actual wording of the document. Lord Hoffmann's position was that the wording of the release was clear enough; in other words, having looked at the background, there was no reason to give the clear words of the release any other meaning. In the case of *Mannai Investment Co Ltd v Eagle Star Life Assurance Company* [1997] AC 749, the reasonable man, by a majority, trumped the pedantic lawyer when a notice to terminate a lease had the wrong date but was saved from invalidity by the majority who held that it was clear that an error had been made and the notice was to be read as if the correct date was in fact present. In the case of *The Starsin* [2004] 1 AC 715, the reasonable man triumphed in the House of Lords when the issue before the court was who was the contracting party in a bill of lading.

On reading Lord Hoffmann's fourth and fifth principles, it seems that there is some tension between the two. If it is the case that the meaning of words is a matter of dictionaries and grammar while the meaning of a document is that which the parties using the words against the relevant background would have been reasonably understood to mean, it would seem that it is difficult to speak of the natural and ordinary meaning of the words, unless one means by 'natural and ordinary meaning' the initial prima facie meaning which the words convey in and of themselves without reference to context and background. Unless this is so, the process of construction cannot even begin. When one speaks of natural and ordinary meaning, it must be that the speaker means the conventional prima facie meaning one arrives at just by reading the document, as in *Malik*. Unless this is so, one could not even begin to construe the document.

Thus dictionaries and grammar are not entirely useless in the process of construction because when one reads the words of a document, the dictionary meaning is where the reader starts. The reason for examining the background and context even after one understands the document by relying on the natural and ordinary meaning is to see whether the natural and ordinary meaning holds at the end of the process of construction or whether it is displaced.

For communication to take place, the parties to the exchange must have an agreed lexicon of the words used if they are to have any meaningful dialogue. It would seem that the conventional meaning is the natural and ordinary meaning which ought to be adopted unless there is something which may yield a different meaning after the background and context are taken into account or maintain their conventional meaning.

It would seem to the court that in arriving at the proper construction of the document, the court must limit itself by determining whether the rival interpretations put forward by the contending parties are within the semantic range of the word or words in issue, unless it is clear that the parties have their own dictionary or the trade or business in which the contract is made has developed a particular understanding of certain words and expressions. That is whether the words used are capable of bearing the meaning being attributed to them. If the meaning sought to be placed on the words are beyond the accepted or usual semantic range then that is usually a very strong indication that, unless the parties have a very unusual vocabulary, that meaning is not the one intended. As the former President of the Israeli Supreme Court, writing extra judicially, puts it, 'The language of a text sets its interpretive limits: giving it a meaning it cannot support semantically is not interpretive activity but rather the creation of a new text' (Barak, Aharon, *Purposive Interpretation in Law*, (2005) Princeton University Press, 57).

What this means is that one begins with the actual words used by the parties but in light of Lord Hoffmann's approach the interpreter is not confined by those words. As Lord Bingham said in *BCCI* 'the court reads the terms of the contract as a whole, giving the words used their natural and ordinary meaning in the context of the agreement, the parties' relationship and all the relevant facts surrounding the transaction so far as known to the parties.' However, despite the breadth of Lord Bingham's views, barring a special type of vocabulary used by the parties, it is the court's view that the ultimate interpretation must fall within the semantic range of the words used. If this is not so, then the court is rewriting the agreement of the parties – a role it cannot have (in the absence of a claim for rectification) since it is not the author of the agreement. Dictionaries and grammars can assist in determining the semantic range of words. To this extent dictionaries and grammars still have a place in spite of the apparent insistence of Lord Hoffmann to the contrary.

Before leaving this point, I wish to refer to a recent decision of the House of Lords. In *Chartbrook Ltd v Persimmon House* [2010] 1 All ER (Comm) 365, Lord Hoffmann not only reaffirmed his position in *Investor Compensation* but confirmed the suspicion that much of the work of rectification has now been taken over by the task of construction. His Lordship said at paragraph 25:

> What is clear from these cases is that there is not, so to speak, a limit to the amount of red ink or verbal rearrangement or correction which the court is allowed All that is required is that it should be clear that something has gone wrong with the language and that it should be clear what a reasonable person would have understood the parties to have meant.

This passage appears to be giving the court much power to rewrite agreements – a power not easily reconcilable with the understanding that the courts in interpreting contracts give way to party autonomy which means that the parties are at liberty to state the terms governing their contractual relationship. To be fair, Lord Hoffmann insists, in spite of the just cited passage, that this was not the case when he said 'that "correction of mistakes by construction" is not a separate branch of the law, a summary version of an action for rectification' (para. 23). However the question arises: at what point does correction of mistakes cross over and becomes in fact, though not in name, rectification masquerading as construction of the agreement?

In interpreting this consent order, the court has to start with the words actually used in the order. The words are the product of lawyers. They advised their clients. This does not mean that one cannot find errors in language but where lawyers are intimately involved in drafting a contract one does not lightly conclude that something has gone wrong with the language. The court starts with the proposition that the parties intended the words to have their conventional meaning.

If the words used have a range of meaning, then the court has to identify the range of meanings which they can bear semantically. The meaning intended, on an objective view, is arrived at by an examination of the context and background. Under the current understanding, the court does not have to identify any ambiguity before it can look at the context and background. The context and background is now part and parcel of the construction of a contract. If *Mannai* is correctly decided, the context and background may even permit the court to substitute a date for the one actually used by the parties.

Even this exercise of context and background is not without its problems since there can be a dispute over which aspect of the context and background should predominate since, according to Lord Hoffmann, background, conceptually includes anything that a reasonable man would consider relevant. This can range from the state of law (statutes, regulations and case law) to the commercial objective that the parties wanted to achieve. The decision of the Court of Appeal in *Goblin Hill* is a classic demonstration of the commercial objective determining the proper interpretation. The case of *The Starsin* illustrates how problematic choice of background can be. As Lord Bingham observed at page 747:

> Taking advantage of their knowledge of the way in which the market works two commercial judges – Colman J [at first instance] and Rix LJ in the Court of Appeal – adopted the mercantile view. The majority in the Court of Appeal – Sir Andrew Morritt V-C and Chadwick LJ – in effect gave preponderant effect to the boilerplate clauses on the back of the bill. In my view it would have an adverse effect on international trade if the latter approach prevails.
>
> What this passage shows is that while all four judges (one at first instance and three in the Court of Appeal) who heard the case before it arrived in the House of Lords agreed that context and background were important and should be examined, they differed on which context and which background should predominate. Two favoured the mercantile background and context while two favoured giving the actual text greater preeminence.
>
> The point being made is that despite the fact that the Jamaican Court of Appeal have adopted Lord Hoffmann's scheme, there is still the possibility of great uncertainty in contractual interpretation especially where the context and background is like a montage. And then having selected which part of the montage is given greater prominence, the interpreter has a further choice of whether he is looking through the eyes of the pedantic lawyer or a reasonable non-lawyer. It was Lord Steyn in *Mannai* who said the 'real question is what evidence of surrounding circumstances may ultimately be allowed to influence the question of interpretation' (page 768).

OFFER

An offer is an expression of willingness to contract, on specified terms, made with the intention that it shall become binding on the person making it as soon as it is accepted by the person to whom it is addressed.[3] The person making the offer must intend to be bound without further negotiation. The offer must be clear, complete and final and it must be communicated to the offeree.[4] It is a principle of law that a person who has made an offer must be considered as continuously making it until he has brought to the knowledge of the person to whom it was made that it is withdrawn. Accordingly, in conducting its operations and in dealings with other persons or entities, businesses need to ensure that they distinguish when they are making an offer to be bound or merely engaging in negotiations. Once an offer is accepted, contractual obligations arise between the party making the offer and the party accepting the offer. Such obligations are enforceable in a court of law.

It is a general principle that an offer may be withdrawn at any time prior to acceptance, even where the offeror has promised to keep the offer open for a specified time.[5] Where an offer is withdrawn but communication of this takes place after the offeree has communicated his acceptance to the offeror, then the offer is held to be valid. An offer may be withdrawn expressly or by conduct, but in either case it must be communicated to the offeree. Such communication

3 The Common Law Library, *Chitty on Contracts, Volume 1, General Principles*, 1999, London: Sweet & Maxwell, para 2–002, p 90.
4 Salzedo, S *et al*, *Briefcase on Contract Law*, 2004, London: Cavendish Publishing, p 2.
5 *Chitty on Contracts*, para 2–080, p 125.

need not come directly from the offeror; it may also be given by a reliable source.[6] An offer may be terminated by conduct where the offeror acts in a way that is inconsistent with the continuing existence of the offer – such as deciding to sell to a third party instead – and the offeree knows of that fact.

Storer v Manchester City Council [1974] 1 WLR 1403 (GB)

Facts: The plaintiff was a tenant of a council house. On 15 November 1970 he filled in a request for information asking for the price and the details of any mortgage. On 14 January 1971 he received a reply from the corporation that it might be prepared to sell the house. The letter also indicated a sum that might be payable if a mortgage were granted but also stated that it was not a firm offer of a mortgage. On 11 February 1971 the plaintiff filled in an application form to buy the council house. On 9 March 1971 he received a letter concerning terms of a loan and on the said date received another letter stating that if he signed the enclosed purchase agreement, then he would receive a copy of the agreement signed by the corporation. The plaintiff filled in the form and returned it on 20 March 1971. There was an election and the control of the corporation changed prior to the execution by the corporation. In July 1971 the corporation, under new control, decided that there would be no more sales of council houses. The plaintiff claimed that there was a binding contract even though there was no exchange of contracts.

Held: Lord Denning
Where parties arrange for a sale 'subject to contract' that means, as a rule, that there is no binding contract until the contracts of sale have been formally exchanged . . . But where there is no agreement 'subject to contract' the only question is whether a contract has been concluded . . .

The corporation put forward to the tenant a simple form of agreement. The very object was to dispense with legal formalities. One of the formalities – exchange of contract – was quite unnecessary. The contract was concluded by offer and acceptance. The offer was contained in the letter of 9 March in which the town clerk said: 'I enclose the agreement for sale. If you will sign the agreement and return it to me I will send you the agreement signed on behalf of the corporation in exchange.' The acceptance was made when Mr Storer did sign it, as he did, and return it, as he did on 20 March. It was then that a contract was concluded. The town clerk was then bound to send back the agreement signed on behalf of the corporation. The agreement was concluded on Mr Storer's acceptance. It was not dependent on the subsequent exchange . . .

The final point was this: Mr Francis said that the town clerk did not intend to be bound by the letter of 9 March 1971. He intended that the corporation should not be bound except on exchange. There is nothing in this point. In contracts you do not look into the actual intent in a man's mind. You look at what he said and did. A contract is formed when there is, to all outward appearances, a contract. A man cannot get out of a contract by saying: 'I did not intend to contract' if by his words he has done so. His intention is to be found only in the outward expression which his letters convey. If they show a concluded contract, that is enough. It seems to me that the judge was quite right in holding that there was a binding contract in this case, even though there was no exchange. It is a proper case for specific performance; and I would dismiss the appeal.

6 *Chitty on Contracts*, para 2–082, p 126.

Select Properties v Texaco (Trinidad) Limited and Nealco Properties Limited (2009) HCA No. S-765 of 2003 (TT)

Facts: There was little dispute on the facts of this action. The plaintiff, Select Properties Limited (SPL), the first defendant, Texaco (Trinidad) Limited (TEXACO) and the second defendant, NEALCO Properties Limited (NEALCO) were all companies incorporated under the laws of the Republic of Trinidad and Tobago. TEXACO was the lessee of property at Gulf View, San Fernando (the Gulf View Property) described in the schedule to deed of assignment registered as No. 9278 of 1999, for the remainder of a term of 999 years from 7 July 1981. NEALCO was a real estate broker which often acted as a real estate agency.

By a letter dated 24 March 2003 from Amit Mirhai, one of NEALCO's sales representatives acting on NEALCO's behalf, to Vishnu Maharaj, SPL's director, NEALCO informed Vishnu Maharaj that they were writing on TEXACO's behalf as its exclusive agent to offer him their sites for sale including the Gulf View property at the price of TT$4,500,000.00. Vishnu Maharaj, together with Amit Mirhai, visited the Gulf View property that same afternoon. By letter dated 25 March 2003 Vishnu Maharaj informed Amit Mirhai of his acceptance of Mirhai's offer in respect of the Gulf View property at the asking price of TT$4,500.000.00. The letter further stated: 'we hereby tender a deposit of ten percent and will complete payment in 90 days. This acceptance is based on your representation that the property is freehold and there are no restrictive covenants.'

On 27 March 2003 Amit Mirhai informed Vishnu Maharaj that another party had paid TEXACO a deposit on the Gulf View property as a result whereof NEALCO returned Vishnu Maharaj's cheque to him. By letter of the same date, Vishnu Maharaj wrote to Sharon Inglefield, director of NEALCO, informing her, *inter alia*, that since NEALCO made an offer which he accepted and for which he tendered the required deposit, there was a binding contract and that he intended to pursue his full legal rights in respect of that transaction. SPL's attorneys, by letter dated 28 March 2003, called upon NEALCO to give an unequivocal assurance that the Gulf View property would be sold to their clients upon the payment of the balance of the purchase price within 90 days from 28 March 2003, and should NEALCO fail to do so on or before 1 April, 2003, they were instructed to commence legal proceedings against TEXACO and NEALCO. By letter dated 3 April 2003, TEXACO's attorneys informed SPL's attorneys that TEXACO was willing to discuss this matter with SPL to determine whether a mutually acceptable written agreement for the sale of the Gulf View property might be achieved and enclosed a draft agreement for their consideration. By letter dated 14 April 2003, SPL's attorneys informed TEXACO's attorneys that their clients were agreeable to the draft agreement but requested that the agreement should be between TEXACO and SPL instead of TEXACO and Vishnu Maharaj. A further draft agreement was sent by TEXACO's attorneys to SPL's attorneys under cover of a letter dated 13 May 2003, by which time SPL had already commenced this action. SPL claims, *inter alia*, damages for breach of contract.

Held: Alexander, J (Ag)
The next issue for consideration is whether there was an agreement for sale between NEALCO and SPL. It is contended on behalf of SPL that the evidence as a whole and, in particular, the evidence of Inglefield support a strategy adopted by NEALCO that would result in both NEALCO and TEXACO emerging unscathed from this action. With all due respect to SPL's attorneys, I reject this contention without reservation. There is no evidence to support that view which was never an issue in this action. Both Mr Walker and Mr Reid, on the other hand, have submitted that in order to find an agreement between NEALCO

and SPL, it must first be determined whether NEALCO's letter of the 24 March 2003 to Vishnu Maharaj was an offer or an invitation to treat. They both consider that letter to be an invitation to treat. Both counsel are relying on the approach of the courts, that the mere use of the word offer in the letter is not conclusive of an offer having been made.

In *Clifton v Palumbo* [1944] 2 All ER 497 it was held that a letter written by the plaintiff to R stating 'I am prepared to offer you my estate for £600,000 . . .' in all the circumstances did not amount to an offer to sell. Lord Green MR at p 499 B explained:

> Anyone who has had experience of transactions in relation to the purchase of land can recall letters written by vendors saying that they agree to sell at a named price, or that purchasers agree to purchase at a named price. The use of the word 'agree' in such a context may or may not involve a contractual result. On the other hand, if you say that the price has been agreed when the contract is being negotiated, you do not use the word 'agree' in the sense that any binding contract has been entered into. All you mean is that particular element in the contract which you are negotiating has been decided. You are agreeing that is the figure which will be put into the contract and then you go on to debate the other matters which fall for discussion. Therefore, words like 'agree', 'offer', 'accept', when used in relation to price are not to be read necessarily as indicating an intention to make, then and there, a contract or an offer as the case maybe. Whether they do or do not must depend entirely on the construction of the particular document.

Mr Walker also referred me to *Bigg & Anor v Boyd Gibbins Limited* (1971) 1 WLR 913 and *Harvey v Facey* (1893) AC 552. In *Harvey v Facey* the appellants telegraphed 'Will you sell us B.H.P.? Telegraph lowest cash price', and the respondent telegraphed in reply 'Lowest price for B.H.P. £900'. And then the appellants telegraphed, 'We agree to buy B.H.P. for £900 asked by you. Please send us your title-deed in order that we may get early possession', but received no reply. It was held that there was no contract. The final telegram was not the acceptance of an offer to sell for none had been made. It was itself an offer to buy, the acceptance to which must be expressed and could not be implied. Lord Morris reasoned at p 555:

> The contract could only be completed if L.M. Facey had accepted the appellant's last telegram. It has been contended for the appellants that L.M. Facey's telegram should be read as saying 'yes' to the first question put in the appellant's telegram, but there is nothing to support that contention. L.M. Facey's telegram gives a precise answer to a precise question, viz: the price. The contract must appear by the telegrams, whereas the appellants are obliged to contend that an acceptance of the first question is to be implied. Their Lordships are of the opinion that the mere statement of the lowest price at which the vendor would sell contains no implied contract to sell at that price to the persons making the inquiry.

In *Bigg v Boyd Gibbins Ltd* the court ordered specific performance after finding a binding agreement formed from letters exchanged between the parties starting with the plaintiff's letter which stated for a quick sale I would accept £26,000. The defendants replied accepting the offer, with the third letter from the plaintiff informing the defendants that the plaintiff and his wife are both pleased that you are purchasing the property. Russell LJ found that these letters and the plain impression conveyed to his mind was that the language used was intended to and did achieve the formation of an open contract.

It is submitted on SPL's behalf that the fundamental distinguishing factor between an offer and an invitation to treat is that the former displays a contractual intent while the latter is merely an indication that the party is open to negotiation. In support thereof, the following cases were cited: *Gibson v Manchester City Council* (1979) 1 WLR 294; *Storer v Manchester City Council* (1974) 1 WLR 1403; *Bigg & Anor v Boyd Gibbing Ltd* (1971) 1 WLR 913.

In *Gibson v Manchester City Council* the court did not find a concluded agreement where the respondent filled out an application form for the purchase of a council house as advised by the city treasurer's letter to him which stated 'if you would like to make formal application to buy your council house, please complete the enclosed application form and return it to me as soon as possible . . .'. The Court found the letter as one setting out the financial terms on which it may be the council will be prepared to consider a sale and purchase in due course. In *Storer v Manchester City Council,* on the other hand, the Court found an agreement for sale where the council forwarded a form of agreement for sale to the tenant which he should sign as an indication of his acceptance. The Court held that an offer was contained in the town clerk's letter which included the agreement and the acceptance was made when Storer did sign and return it as he did.

The cases cited demonstrate that a Court should only find a binding contract for sale when there is offer and acceptance; whether there is, depends on the construction of the documents. In this action, I do not find that there was a binding contract between NEALCO and Vishnu Maharaj or indeed between NEALCO and SPL. NEALCO's letter to Vishnu Maharaj dated 24 March 2003, in my opinion, was not an offer to sell, it was an invitation to Vishnu Maharaj to make an offer to purchase; it was an indication of the price at which TEXACO was prepared to sell; the other matters to be included in the contract were to be discussed if Vishnu Maharaj were in agreement with the price quoted. In the absence of further evidence, it is difficult to find an offer in Mirhai's letter.

INVITATION TO TREAT

Where a party is invited to make an offer, this is commonly known as an invitation to treat. As opposed to an offer, an invitation to treat is not made with the intention that it is to become binding as soon as the person to whom it is addressed simply communicates his agreement with the terms,[7] although it is not always simple to differentiate between the two. The court will determine whether a statement is an offer or an invitation to treat based primarily on the intention with which it was made. It follows from the nature of an offer that a statement is not an offer if it in terms negatives the maker's intention to be bound on acceptance.

Kiyo Itakura Investments v Bentall Properties Ltd. 1993 CanLII 289 BCSC (CA)

Facts: The plaintiff, Kiyo Itakura, was the sole shareholder and director of the plaintiff company Kiyo Itakura Investments Ltd. He entered into a lease agreement to open a restaurant with the defendant, Bentall Property Management Inc. (BPMI) on 16 March 1987. By March 1988 the plaintiff could not make the rent based on poor sales and sought to renegotiate the lease. The agreement was amended to reflect a reduction in the base rent. When the business eventually became profitable, the plaintiff attempted to negotiate the lease again to a five-year lease. By letter dated 22 December 1989 BPMI sent an 'agreement to lease' to the representative of the plaintiff requesting that it be executed and returned in quadruplicate for execution by the defendants. The executed document was never returned to the defendants. Mr Itakura eventually signed the agreement to lease document on 5 September 1991, which reached the office of BPMI on 12 September 1991. While negotiations were proceeding, the premises were offered for lease to another party

7 *Chitty on Contracts*, para 2–007, p 93.

and the defendants accepted this offer on 24 September 1991. The plaintiff did not vacate the premises, and on the night of 2 January 1992 the defendants re-entered the premises and changed the locks. This lawsuit resulted.

Held: Smith, J
I must determine the intent of the parties from an objective reading of the document as a whole. Parol evidence is not admissible to vary or contradict the document, but I am entitled to take into account the surrounding circumstances to determine the commercial purpose, the genesis, the background, and the context of the document . . .

While the document was entitled 'Agreement to Lease', it would not become an agreement until executed and delivered by the defendants; until then it was an offer by the tenant. The plaintiff submitted that the delivery of the documents by the defendants' agent constituted an invitation to treat. The law on this point is summarised in *The Law of Contract*, 8th edn, 1991 by GH Treitel at pp 8, 10, and 11: 'An offer is an expression of willingness to contract on certain terms, made with the intention that it shall become binding as soon as it is accepted by the person to whom it is addressed.' The question whether a statement is an offer or an invitation to treat depends primarily on the intention with which it was made. It follows from the nature of an offer as described above that a statement is not an offer if it in terms negatives the maker's intention to be bound on acceptance: for example, if it expressly provides that he is *not* to be bound merely by the other party's notification of assent, but only when he himself has signed the document in which the statement is contained.

I think this document can fairly be described as an invitation to treat. It was prepared not by the defendants but by the defendants' agent. There was no negotiation between the two contracting parties, nor any invitation to negotiate, prior to the plaintiff's receiving the document. As a result, once signed and delivered by the plaintiff, the document constituted no more than an offer. The express words of the document make it clear beyond question that the defendants did not intend to be bound until they should execute the document. It was clearly intended to be an offer by Mr Itakura which the defendants were free to accept or reject.

Advertisements

While an advertisement may be classified as either an invitation to treat or an offer, depending on its nature, it is generally held that advertisements are an invitation to treat. This is due in large part to the fact that the parties may wish to engage in further bargaining or negotiations, especially where the sale of an expensive item is involved. Advertisements for the sale of goods or job positions are intended to be invitations to treat where the interested party responds by making a purchase or submitting an application for consideration which may be accepted or rejected.[8] The rule is also necessary to protect the interest of the seller since to hold otherwise would mean that every advertiser and catalogue publisher is obliged to sell to every person who responds, regardless of their capacity or level of supply. Similarly, if employment notices were offers, then the advertising employer would be obliged to hire every appropriately qualified candidate who applied for the position. Display items, for example, are simply placed in a position to attract an offer and are not by their mere display offers that would only require acceptance to form a binding contract. If they were offers, should a person place an item in his shopping basket, he would immediately lose his entitlement to switch products if he changed his mind.

8 See *Chitty on Contracts*, paras 2–014 to 2–015, pp 96–7.

In certain circumstances, an advertisement may be considered as meeting the requirements of an offer and therefore be binding on the offeror. If the advertiser makes it clear that he is prepared to be bound in certain circumstances, an advertisement may be construed as an offer. This is akin to a unilateral contract, where a person who complies with the terms of an advertisement that was issued without limitation can establish a contractual duty on the part of the person placing the advertisement.[9] This has the potential for the imposition of extensive liability on the part of the offeror if there are many replies to the advertisement.[10] This reasoning also applies to offers of rewards for the return of lost or stolen property and creates similar issues concerning liability.

Roback v UBC 2007 BCSC 334 (CA)

Facts: This was a hearing pursuant to Rule 34 of the Rules of Court for the determination of specific points of law which arose from the pleadings of the parties. One of the four points of law is whether a contract between the plaintiff and defendant arose from the plaintiff's application for the position of Assistant Professor in the defendant's Creative Writing Department of the Faculty of Arts (the position). The conclusion was that on the undisputed facts of this case, and having particular regard to the advertisement for the position published by the University of British Columbia, no contract arose between the plaintiff and the defendant at any time with respect to the publishing of the invitation to apply for the position by UBC and the application for it by the plaintiff.

The advertisement in question stated:

> CREATIVE WRITING UNIVERSITY OF BRITISH COLUMBIA – Faculty of Arts. The Department of Creative Writing invites applications for a tenure-track appointment at the Assistant Professor rank commencing July 1, 1995. Appointment may be considered at a higher rank for a woman with exceptional qualifications. M.F.A., or equivalent, preferred. Salary commensurate with qualifications and experience. This position is subject to final budgetary approval. The successful candidate's primary roles will be as a teacher of screenwriting to graduate students and senior undergraduates, and as an active, energetic liaison with the Film Division of the Theatre Department, in particular to help get student work produced. The candidate should also have writing experience in another genre and should have had work in that genre published or produced. Candidates should have worked with and expanded opportunities for student writers, as well as having had experience in the teaching of workshops and tutorials. Candidates should have a strong screenwriting credits and some production knowledge.

The plaintiff commenced this proceeding against the defendant UBC in relation to a hiring competition conducted by the University in the summer and autumn of 1994 and 1995. The plaintiff submitted an application for the position. The plaintiff was an unsuccessful applicant. The plaintiff advanced claims in contract and tort against the University arising from his reply to the advertisement and said that by submitting his application for the position and not being selected for the position, there was a breach of his contractual rights and a tort committed against him. The claims are essentially based on the facts that the successful candidate did not have any post-secondary academic degrees. The plaintiff, on the other hand, has six academic qualifications including two MFAs and a PhD in fields specifically related to the qualifications mentioned in the advertisement.

9 See 'Unilateral contracts' below.

10 *Chitty on Contracts*, para 2–016, p 97.

Held: Koenigsberg, J

Breach of Contract. Simply put, the plaintiff alleges that he entered into a contract with the University when, in response to the advertisement, he submitted an application for the position. The plaintiff relies on the law relating to unilateral contracts and specifically he relies on the leading case on this subject, *Carlill v Carbolic Smoke Ball Co.* [1893] 1 QB 256 (CA). The plaintiff further alleges that the University breached the contract by hiring a person who allegedly failed to meet the selection criteria for the position, which the plaintiff alleges are set out expressly or impliedly in the advertisement.

The University's defence, in part, is that the University did not enter into a contract with the plaintiff when the plaintiff submitted his application for the position. The University says that, by causing the advertisement to be published, it did not intend to enter into contractual relations with any person who may have viewed the advertisement and submitted a résumé to be considered for the position. The University submits that, at most, the advertisement was an invitation to treat or an announcement of the position. The advertisement merely called for individuals to identify themselves as potential candidates for consideration for the position. The advertisement contained no offer or statement that the position would be awarded to an individual submitting an application in response to the advertisement, nor that the candidate with the highest post-secondary degree or degrees would be hired. In fact, the advertisement states 'M.F.A., or equivalent, preferred'.

The plaintiff submits that the advertisement constitutes a 'promise' or an offer to hire a candidate on 'merit' defined, says Dr Roback, by the achievement of academic credentials of an MFA or equivalent. This then constitutes a form of unilateral contract upon the candidate submitting his résumé. However, the facts in this case are distinguishable from those in *Carlill v Carbolic Smoke Ball Co.* and the unilateral contract line of cases in which the court enforces a promise (or an offer of a reward) that is made to the general public to induce performance. In the present case, the advertisement was not meant to induce specific performance such as reward cases do. Nowhere in the advertisement does the University promise anything or make any representations relating to the hiring process. The clear purpose of the advertisement was to invite applications: 'The Department of Creative Writing invites applications for a tenure track appointment at the Assistant Professor rank commencing July 1, 1995.' The advertisement was an invitation for expressions of interest. Unlike *Carlill v Carbolic Smoke Ball Co.*, the advertisement does not provide a sufficient basis to ascertain the essential terms of a contract . . . While other material differences are apparent, the two cardinal ones, in my view, are the following: first, there is no promise to hire anyone, and, second, there are no specific requirements which candidates have to meet . . .

There is no basis whatsoever to analogise the published invitation by the University to potentially qualified candidates to unilateral contractual situations . . . Thus, there is no basis for finding a contract or an intention to be legally bound to anything by the publishing of the advertisement.

Tenders

Tenders are generally placed in the category of invitation to treat, where a party is only being invited to make a bid which constitutes the offer and the party issuing the invitation is merely seeking offers. Typically, the party issuing the invitation for tenders is not bound to accept any submitted tender, unless the invitation for tenders indicates very clearly that the party seeking the tender binds himself to accept a particular offer, such as the highest offer to buy or the lowest offer to sell. In such cases, the invitation for tenders may be regarded either as an offer or as an invitation to submit offers coupled with an undertaking to accept the highest or lowest offer; the contract is concluded upon communication of the relevant offer.[11]

Harvela Investments Ltd. v Royal Trust Company of Canada (C.I.) Ltd. and Others [1986] AC 207 (CA)

Facts: By telex messages (the invitation) despatched on 15 September 1981 the respondent vendors, the Royal Trust Company of Canada (C.I.) Ltd, invited the appellants, Harvela Investments Ltd (Harvela) and Sir Leonard Outerbridge (Sir Leonard), to make offers to purchase the vendors' shares in A. Harvey & Co. Ltd (the shares). The invitation stipulated that offers must be made by sealed tender or confidential telex which would not be divulged by the vendors before the invitation expired at 3.00 pm on 16 September 1981 when the vendors would accept 'the highest offer'. Completion of the purchase was to take place within 30 days of 16 September 1981 in Canadian dollars. Harvela offered CAN$2,175,000. Sir Leonard offered CAN$2,100,000 'or CAN$101,000 in excess of any other offer which you may receive which is expressed as a fixed monetary amount, whichever is the higher.' The issued share capital of A. Harvey & Co. Ltd (the company) was held as to 43 per cent by the Harvey family, represented by Harvela, 40 per cent by the Outerbridge family, represented by Sir Leonard, and 12 per cent by the vendors. Acquisition of the shares by Harvela or by Sir Leonard would confer control of the company on the purchaser. Having received two offers under different terms and conditions, the full terms of the invitation were revised. Having obtained an injunction preventing the first defendant from accepting the referential bid, the plaintiff claimed a right to enforce a contract against the first defendant for the purchase of the shares.

Held: Waller, J
Only two of the terms in the telex are important for the decision of this part of the case. The first is: 'Tenders are to be submitted on the following terms: 1. That tenders are a single offer for all shares held by us.' Then later in the telex: 'We confirm that if any offer made by you is the highest offer received by us we bind ourselves to accept such offer provided that such offer complies with the terms of this telex.' This court has to consider whether this telex was an invitation to treat or a binding offer to enter into a contract with the highest bidder or an offer which the bidder who was highest could accept.

In my judgment the clause confirming that the trustees bound themselves to accept the highest offer received by them made it clear that it was not a mere invitation to treat. It emphasised that if the offer complied with the terms of the telex, the trustees would accept the highest offer and therefore it was either an offer which when the highest bid was received completed a contract of sale or at least completed a contract to enter into a contract of sale: see, e.g., *Carlill v Carbolic Smoke Ball Co.* [1893] 1 QB 256. The question of whether it would be a complete contract of sale or a contract to enter into a contract of sale, as it seems to me, is purely a question of words; the effect is a contract of sale. I find support for this view in the speech of Lord Wright in *Hillas and Co. Ltd v Arcos Ltd.* (1932) 147 LT 503, 515 where he says:

> A contract *de praesenti* to enter into what, in law, is an enforceable contract, is simply that enforceable contract, and no more and no less; and if what may not very accurately be called the second contract is not to take effect till some future date but is otherwise an enforceable

11 *Chitty on Contracts*, para 2–019, pp 98–9.

> contract, the position is as in the preceding illustration, save that the operation of the contract is postponed. But in each case there is *eo instanti* a complete obligation.

If it were not for the words 'we bind ourselves to accept', this would have been a mere invitation to treat but those words, in my opinion, make it an offer which the bidder being highest accepted.

Zephyr Services Limited (Claimant) v Ministry of Forestry Fisheries and Sustainable Development (First Defendant) and the Attorney General (Second Defendant) Claim No. 69 of 2013 (BZ)

Facts: Belize has abundant natural resources with respect to biodiversity as well as its water, land and sea physical environment. These resources have to be managed, which the Government of Belize has been attempting to do under a system called 'National Protected Areas System'. This claim in public law has been brought by a private company, ('the Claimant') against the First Defendant being a public authority or body within Belize charged with the responsibility of managing its National Protected Areas System ('the Defendant') being undertaken in 2012 under a project entitled 'Strengthening National Capacities for the Operationalization, Consolidation and Sustainability of Belize's Protected Areas System' ('the Project'). In furtherance of the Project consultants were encouraged in 2012 to tender for an advertised consultancy which was budgeted at $200,000.00 to develop business plans in relation to the protected areas and specifically the Project and for which the Claimant put in a bid of $221,054.00. The Claimant's bid undeniably attracted the highest score under the agreed bidding process and the Defendant declared to the claimant, in writing, the Defendant's 'intention to contract' the Claimant for the consultancy on certain term(s) and/or conditions. Following (a) pre-contract meeting, and despite the Claimant having considered that it had not only addressed, but had acceded to, all but one of the Defendant's demands, on the 28th of November, 2012 the Claimant received a letter from the Defendant informing it that: 'A meeting was convened on November 21, 2012 amongst members of the Project Board and personnel from the Ministry of Forestry, Fisheries and Sustainable Development to review the status of the status of the various consultancies under the "strengthening National Capacities" Project, including the consultancy to develop business plans. After much deliberation, a decision was made that the contract for the said consultancy would not be issued to your firm. The process will now be closed until alternate arrangements can be made . . .'

Held: Abel, J
The terms of a tendering process is governed by the so-called private law area of the law of contractual obligations, by which the courts will enforce concluded Agreements relating to the terms of such process as well as any concluded agreement which results from such process. In the tendering process, like the case of ordinary agreements, the contractual process can be analyzed into an offer, being made by the person submitting the tender, and the acceptance, made by the person accepting the tender. This has been summarized by Gallen J in the case of *Pratt contractors Ltd v Palmerston North City Council* 1 NZLR 469 as follows: 'As Bingham LJ pointed out, the commercial reality is that a tenderer is obliged to expend substantial amounts of time and money in preparing a complex tender and is frequently required also to deposit substantial . . . money in order to establish bona fides. Tenderers will normally be prepared to accept such obligations where they do so in light of obligations which the body seeking the tender indicated it accepts and which relate to the consideration which ultimately is to be given to the tender submitted. To such circumstances it is at least possible to formulate the relationship in terms of offer and acceptance

and it is in commercial and practical terms, appropriate to be categorized as contractual in nature.' . . . The terms of reference (TOR) provided detailed instructions on the submissions of proposals, the procedure which would be adopted in the evaluation of such proposals and the criteria to be satisfied for any submitted proposals. The TOR, the forms provided and used by the Claimant for submission of proposals (which was not bound to be accepted by the Defendant) and a price schedule, constituted agreed contractual documentation in the case. It was agreed by the parties that the bid would be evaluated using the Cumulative analysis procedure in two stages comprising the technical aspects of the proposal and its price with scores and procedures applying to each. There was, in the circumstances of the present case, a clear representation or promise made by the Defendant that the contract would be awarded to the proposal that received the highest score after the results of the technical proposal and the price proposal had been combined but with the right being reserved to the Defendant to accept or reject any proposal and to annul the solicitation process and reject all proposals at any time prior to an award of contract. . . . This has [led] this court to conclude that good administration requires that the Defendant, as a public authority, ought to be given an opportunity to be held to its promises, representations, procedures and processes by awarding the contract to the Claimant or alternatively be penalized in damages for failure to do so. Furthermore, that public confidence may be undermined in the Defendant, as a public authority, if it were not held to such a reasonable standard of conduct. The court has determined therefore, the Defendant should not be so penalized as to warrant the payment of damages without getting some value for its money; and so it has determined that the Defendant should be given the option to make the award of the Contract to the Claimant which the Claimant was reasonably led to expect from the Defendant.

Greater Vancouver Water District v North American Pipe & Steel Ltd. 2011 BCSC 30 (CA)

Facts: The Greater Vancouver Water District (the 'GVWD') entered into a contract with North American Pipe & Steel Ltd. ('NAP') for the supply of water pipes for two large water projects in December 2005 (the 'Supply Agreement'). This was pursuant to a successful public tender submitted by NAP. Moody International Ltd. ('Moody') was retained by the GVWD in January 2006 to provide inspection services during the manufacture of the water pipes, which took place in Korea. The GVWD alleges that both NAP and Moody breached their contracts because the coal tar enamel (the 'CTE') coating on the pipes supplied by NAP was defective and did not meet the specifications in the Supply Agreement. NAP and Moody take the position that the CTE coating was manufactured and inspected in accordance with the specifications in the Supply Agreement, and any defects in the CTE coating were caused by the specifications. NAP alleges that GVWD is in breach of the Supply Agreement because it has not paid NAP's invoices. NAP has counterclaimed for the amount the GVWD owes under the Supply Agreement. NAP also counterclaims for damages NAP alleges it has incurred as the result of the GVWD's failure to take delivery of the pipe in accordance with the Supply Agreement.

Held: Gerow, J
The following is one of the questions that arose in this case. Does Moody have any liability for any of the deficiencies as a result of failing to provide adequate inspection services during the manufacture of the pipes?

The first issue to be addressed is what documents, and in particular whether the RFP [request for proposals], forms the contract between the GVWD and Moody.

An RFP is different from a request to tender. The determination of whether a particular invitation constitutes an invitation to tender or an RFP focuses on the intentions between the respective parties. Accordingly, the analysis that the courts employ to determine the contractual relationship between tendering parties is also applicable within the context of an RFP.

The Supreme Court of Canada discussed when a contract was formed in the context of a tender in *M.J.B. Enterprises Ltd. v Defence Construction (1951) Ltd.*, [1999] 1 SCR 619, and stated at para. 37: A tender, in addition to responding to an invitation for tenders, is also an offer to perform the work outlined in the plans and specifications for a particular price. The invitation for tenders is therefore an invitation for offers to enter into Contract B on the terms specified by the owner and for a price specified by the contractor. The goal for contractors is to make their bid as competitive as possible while still complying with the plans and specifications outlined in the tender documents.

The Court held it is not always the case that a contract A arises upon the submission of a tender. In order to determine whether a contract A arises, it is necessary to determine whether the parties intended to initiate contractual relations upon the submission of a bid in response to the invitation to tender. If the parties did intend to enter into a contractual arrangement, then the request to tender would constitute nothing more than an invitation to treat. Consistent with the traditional common law approach, the request to tender would not form part of any contract established between the parties.

Moody has cited a number of cases in which courts have determined whether a RFP forms part of the contract . . .

In considering whether a RFP forms part of a contract, the courts have looked at the overall dealing between the parties to determine if they intended to establish contractual relations upon the submission of a bid. No single factor is determinative. Some of the factors courts have considered include:

- Whether further negotiations are required after the submission of a bid. Where negotiations are necessary, it is likely the court will find that no contractual relationship has been established.
- Whether the owner has the discretion to reject any and all bids. Where the owner is afforded such discretion, it is likely that the process will be something other than a formal tendering process.
- The nature and scope of the selection criteria. Where the selection criterion is limited to that of cost, a court is more likely to equate the bid submission framework with a formal tendering process. Where the price consideration is secondary to qualitative and/or other considerations, it is more likely a court will equate the process with an RFP.
- Established timelines for the opening of proposals, provisions that proposals are irrevocable and/or requirements that a deposit be submitted with a bid are indicia of a formal tendering process.

The evidence does not support the GVWD's submission that it intended to establish a contractual relationship with Moody at the time that it issued its RFP. First, the RFP stipulates that GVWD reserves the right to reject any and all proposals. Second, cost appears to be a secondary consideration with respect to the proposal evaluation. The evidence is that the GVWD gave equal, if not greater weight, to considerations such as the bidders' ability to deliver the service, and the bidders' familiarity with technical issues associated the quality service inspection work. Third, the RFP contained no irrevocability provision. Fourth, no deposit was required. Finally, the RFP allows for further negotiation, thereby indicating that the terms of any contract were not finalized by virtue of the RFP. Moreover, Mr. Meldrum admitted that the GVWD did not intend to establish a contractual relationship with Moody at the time it issued the RFP.

The wording of the RFP and Mr. Meldrum's admission are inconsistent with a formal tendering process It follows that no contractual relationship was entered into at the time that Moody submitted its proposal to the GVWD. In my view, the RFP was tantamount to an invitation to treat. As such, the RFP, without more, does not form part of the contract documents between the parties . . . As a result, none of the conditions contained in the RFP, including the requirement of a NACE Certified inspector, form part of the contract between the GVWD and Moody . . . I have concluded that the GVWD has not established that Moody has any liability for the deficiencies for failing to provide adequate inspection services during the manufacture of the pipes.

Contract A and Contract B

While the party inviting tenders is not bound to accept any submitted tender unless it is specifically stated, there are circumstances under which a submitted tender must be considered by the party inviting the tenders. Where tenders are to be submitted by a stated deadline, the person submitting the tender has the contractual right to have the tender considered, even if it is not accepted. This is so as the submission of the tender is deemed to be an acceptance of a tender process and the person inviting (offering) the tenders is contractually bound to consider the bid. The Canadian courts term this contract 'Contract A'. Moreover, a person inviting tenders may not be permitted to accept a non-compliant bid and a person whose bid was rejected in favour of a non-compliant bid may take action against the person inviting the tenders who accepted the non-compliant bid. Contract A, also known as the process contract, is the contract that arises between the tenderer and the party inviting tenders upon submission of a compliant bid. Contract A is not, however, automatic; it only arises where the parties intended to initiate contractual relations by submission of a bid. Whether Contract A is formed depends on the precise language and intention of the tender call. The court will look only to the substance of the transaction in the context of the procurement documents in order to determine whether the parties intended to enter into contractual relations. The courts have recognised several factors or terms indicative of an intent to form Contract A, principal among them being the irrevocability of the bid. The corollary term is the obligation of both parties to enter into a contract (Contract B) upon the acceptance of the tender.

Moreover, the party inviting tenders is expected to treat all bids in accordance with the request for tender documents and not to make decisions contrary to such documents. Parties inviting tenders are required to act fairly and in good faith. The emphasis is on the notion that awards should be made with compliant bids and that compliant bids should be assessed based on representations made in the invitation to tender and during the process contract phase. Contract B is the ultimate contract entered into with the successful bidder upon acceptance of the bid.

Pomerleau Inc. v Newfoundland and Labrador (Transportation and Works) 2014 NLTD (G) 19 (CA)

Facts: The plaintiff (hereinafter referred to as 'Pomerleau') is a construction company. The defendant (hereinafter referred to as 'the government') is the department of the government of Newfoundland and Labrador responsible for the construction of the Royal

Newfoundland Constabulary ('RNC') campus building and associated work at St. John's pursuant to a tender identified as number 180819002 redevelopment of RNC campus, C.P.2 (the 'project'). Pomerleau submitted a bid for the construction of the project which was disqualified by the government as being incomplete and thus non-compliant with the tender call. Pomerleau sued for damages.

Held: Adams, J
The Instructions to Bidders contained a number of provisions particularly relevant to these proceedings:

2. TENDER DOCUMENTS
   (a) The Tender Documents consist of the Instructions to Bidders, Tender Form, Agreement, Drawings, Specifications, and any Amendments to the Contract Documents issued during the tender period.
4. COMPLETION OF TENDER FORM
   (a) The Tender Form is to be completed in its entirety . . .
5. UNACCEPTABLE TENDERS
   (d) Incomplete Tenders will be rejected.
   (g) Incorrectly prepared tenders may be rejected.
10. ACCEPTANCE OF TENDER
   (a) The Owner will not necessarily accept the lowest or any tender.

Analysis
Ontario v Ron Engineering & Construction (Eastern) Ltd., [1981] 1 SCR 111 established the now familiar Contract A/Contract B analysis for resolving disputes arising out of the tendering process. This seminal case has been subsequently considered and further explained in three more recent Supreme Court of Canada decisions: *M.J.B. Enterprises Ltd. v Defence Construction (1951) Ltd.*, [1999] 1 SCR 619, *Martel Building Limited v R.*, 2000 SCC 60, 2 SCR 860 and *Double N. Earthmovers Ltd. v Edmonton (City)*, 2007 SCC 3, 1 SCR 116.

These four cases and the main points for which they stand were recently helpfully reviewed by G.R. Strathy J in *North American Construction (1993) Ltd. v York (Municipality)*, 84 CLR (3d) 89, 2009 Carswell Ont 511 (Ont. Sup. Ct. J.). I adopt his interpretation of those cases. At paragraph 30 Strathy J affirmed the need to maintain the integrity of the tendering process, particularly 'in the tendering of contracts by public bodies'. Then at paragraphs 31 to 37 he reviewed the above authorities:

> 31 The analytical path for the resolution of disputes of this kind has been paved by a quartet of decisions in the Supreme Court of Canada, beginning with the seminal case of *Ontario v Ron Engineering & Construction (Eastern) Ltd.*, [1981] 1 SCR 111, [1981] SCJ No. 13 [*Ron Engineering*]. In that case, Estey J developed the 'Contract A/Contract B' analysis for the tendering process. He held that an owner's invitation to tender constitutes an offer to potential bidders. Contract A comes into existence when a contractor submits a compliant tender in response to that offer. Submission of a compliant bid amounts to acceptance of the owner's offer. The terms and conditions of Contract A are governed by the terms and conditions of the call for tenders, which usually include a provision that if the owner accepts the contractor's bid, the contractor will be obliged to enter the construction contract ('Contract B'). Contract A can impose other obligations on the parties, apart from the obligations relating to the construction contract. The nature and extent of those obligations is determined by examining the terms and conditions of the call for tenders.
>
> 32 The next case is *M.J.B. Enterprises Ltd. v Defence Construction (1951) Ltd.*, [1999] 1 SCR 619, [1999] SCJ No. 17 [*MJB*]. In that case, the Supreme Court considered the extent of the

> owner's obligations under Contract A. Reviewing the terms of the tender documents, including the 'privilege clause,' the court held that it was reasonable to imply a term that only a compliant bid would be accepted by the owner. While the privilege clause provided that '[t]he lowest or any tender shall not necessarily be accepted', the Supreme Court said that this was only one term of Contract A and it must be read in harmony with the rest of the tender documents. The Supreme Court acknowledged that an owner could, by clear words, reserve to itself the right to accept non-compliant bids. The court held, however, that the 'privilege clause' in question did not give the owner the right to accept a bid that was non-compliant. The court held that the unsuccessful bidder was entitled to damages for breach of Contract A as its bid, which was the lowest valid bid, would likely have been accepted.
>
> 33 In *Martel Building Ltd. v Canada*, [2000] 2 SCR 860, [2000] SCJ No. 60 [*Martel*], the Supreme Court confirmed that Contract A includes an implied term that the owner will treat all bidders fairly and equally in the assessment of bids, having regard to the terms of the call for tenders. Iacobucci and Major JJ., giving the judgment of the court at para 88 stated:
>
> > In the circumstances of this case, we believe that implying a term to be fair and consistent in the assessment of the tender bids is justified based on the presumed intentions of the parties. Such implication is necessary to give business efficacy to the tendering process . . . in light of the costs and effort associated with preparing and submitting a bid, we find it difficult to believe that the respondent in this case, or any of the other three tenderers, would have submitted a bid unless it was understood by those involved that all bidders would be treated fairly and equally . . . Implying an obligation to treat all bidders fairly and equally is consistent with the goal of protecting and promoting the integrity of the bidding process, and benefits all participants involved. Without this implied term, tenderers, whose fate could be predetermined by some undisclosed standards, would either incur significant expenses in preparing futile bids or ultimately avoid participating in the tender process.
>
> 34 The Supreme Court acknowledged, however, at para 89, that the owner could reserve certain privileges to itself, provided that the implied duty of fair treatment was not breached. The analysis of whether the owner had made such a reservation, and the scope of that reservation, requires an examination of the tender documents: A privilege clause reserving the right not to accept the lowest or any bids does not exclude the obligation to treat all bidders fairly. Nevertheless, the tender documents must be examined closely to determine the full extent of the obligation of fair and equal treatment. In order to respect the parties' intentions and reasonable expectations, such a duty must be defined with due consideration to the express contractual terms of the tender. A tendering authority has 'the right to include stipulations and restrictions and to reserve privileges to itself in the tender documents' *(Colautti Brothers*, [*Colautti Brothers Marble Tile & Carpet (1985) Inc. v Windsor (City)* (1996), 36 MPLR (2d) 258] supra, at para. 6).
>
> 35 These authorities were further discussed and applied by the Supreme Court of Canada in the last case of the four, *Double N Earthmovers Ltd. v Edmonton (City)*, [2007] 1 SCR 116, [2007] SCJ No. 3. The majority held that, on the facts of the case and the tender documents, the owner was entitled to waive compliance of an 'informality' – that is, something that did not materially affect the price of performance of Contract B. In waiving the informality pursuant to a clause that reserved its right to do so, the owner did not breach Contract A with the other bidder . . .

In *Health Care Developers Inc. v Newfoundland* (1996), 141 Nfld & PEIR 34, 136 DLR (4th) 609 (Nfld. C.A.) Cameron, JA spoke for our Court of Appeal respecting the *Ron Engineering* analysis, where she stated at paragraph 33:

> 33 It is, however, possible to discern certain generally accepted principles from the cases decided since Ron Engineering. The trial judge adopted those enumerated by Jenkins J of the Prince Edward Island Supreme Court, in *Murphy v. Alberton (Town)* (1993), 114 Nfld & PEIR 34 at 43. Jenkins J stated:
>
> > . . . upon contract A coming into being:

a. there arises at law rights and obligations of the parties that are consistent with the protection and promotion of the integrity of the bidding system where under the law of contracts it is possible to do so.

b. the owner owes a general duty to treat all bidders fairly.

c. an owner has the right to include in the tender documents stipulations and restrictions on the rights of bidders and to reserve privileges to the owner.

d. an owner does not have the right on consideration of competing bids to rely upon undisclosed terms and conditions.

e. 'Lowest or any tender not necessarily accepted' reserves conditionally to the owner the privilege to decide not to proceed with the work at all, but does not allow the owner to (i) choose comparatively among the bidders based on criteria that has not been disclosed to the bidders; or (ii) to award to another bidder or another person something other than contract B.

f. general custom in bidding, and particular local customs, can result in implied contractual rights.

g. an owner does not have the right to pass over properly filed bids and enter into contract B with a bidder whose bid is informal, or invalid.

h. where there is a breach of contract A, the measure of damages can include (i) the cost of preparation of the bid; and (ii) upon the low bidder proving he would have obtained the contract, the estimated loss of profit on the work.

I, too, would adopt the summary of Jenkins J of principles enunciated by the cases since *Ron Engineering* . . .

In the case at bar, the tender documents did not include 'a discretion clause' whereby the government could waive any irregularity or accept an incomplete tender. As stated in the Supreme Court of Canada cases referred to above, Contract A is governed by the terms of the tender documents. I therefore conclude that the standard to be applied in this case is strict compliance, not substantial compliance. This was a stipulated price contract with a unit price component. The government was entitled to set the terms of the tender provided it applied to all bidders fairly and did not give the government the opportunity to award the contract on an undisclosed preference . . .

While in the case at bar there is no 'clear statement' that the failure to include a unit price would constitute an incomplete bid and automatically lead to rejection of the bid, in my view, in the circumstances the inclusion of such a provision is not necessary, although it may have been desirable for greater certainty. The Instructions to Bidders in the case at bar are clear that incomplete tenders 'will be rejected'. Nothing more was required in the absence of a discretion clause.

By failing to complete one of the appendices to the tender form Pomerleau submitted a non-compliant bid for the construction of the RNC Campus. The government disqualified the bid. In the absence of a discretion clause permitting it to waive Pomerleau's failure to submit a complete bid, the government was required to reject it and award the contract to Olympic. To have done otherwise would have been a breach of the government's duty of fairness to Olympic, the only other bidder, which had submitted a fully compliant bid.

The privilege clause

In the tendering process, the party inviting others to submit a tender might choose to include a privilege clause in the call for tenders. This clause simply reserves the right of the party inviting the tenders to not accept the lowest or any bid at all or even to cancel the call for tenders altogether. Nevertheless, the inclusion of such a clause does not permit the party inviting tenders to accept a non-compliant bid. All bidders are to be treated fairly. While including such a clause reserves conditionally to the party inviting the tender to decide not to proceed with the work at all, it does not allow the party inviting the tender to: '(i) choose comparatively among the bidders based on criteria that has not been disclosed to the bidders; or (ii) to award to another bidder or another person something other than contract B'.[12]

M.J.B. Enterprises Ltd v Defence Construction (1951) [1999] 1 SCR 619 (CA)

Facts: The respondent invited tenders and awarded the contract to the lowest tenderer of the four received notwithstanding the fact that the bid did not comply with the tender specifications. The tender documents included a 'privilege clause' that stated that the lowest or any tender would not necessarily be accepted. The winning bid included a handwritten note outlining a schedule of final costs even though amendments to the tender documents required tenderers to submit only one price. The other tenderers complained that this note constituted a qualification that invalidated the tender. The respondent nevertheless determined that the note was merely a clarification and accepted the bid. The appellant, who had submitted the second lowest tender, brought an action for breach of contract claiming that the winning tender should have been disqualified and that its tender should have been accepted as the lowest valid bid. The parties agreed on damages prior to trial, subject to the determination of liability. The trial judge found that the note was a qualification but held that, given the presence of the privilege clause, the respondent was under no obligation to award the contract to the appellant as the next lowest bidder. The Alberta Court of Appeal dismissed the appeal. At issue here was whether the inclusion of a 'privilege clause' in the tender documents allows the respondent to disregard the lowest bid in favour of any other tender, including a non-compliant one.

Held: Lamer CJ and Cory, McLachlin, Iacobucci, Major, Bastarache, Binnie, JJA
It is the contention of M.J.B. Enterprises Ltd (the appellant) that in the circumstances of this case Defence Construction (1951) Limited (the respondent) was obligated to accept the lowest valid tender. The respondent argues that the privilege clause precludes the finding of such an obligation . . .

What is important, therefore, is that the submission of a tender in response to an invitation to tender may give rise to contractual obligations, quite apart from the obligations associated with the construction contract to be entered into upon the acceptance of a tender, depending upon whether the parties intend to initiate contractual relations by the submission of a bid. If such a contract arises, its terms are governed by the terms and conditions of the tender call. I note that the jurisprudence in other common law jurisdictions supports the approach that, depending upon the intentions of the parties, an invitation to tender can give rise to contractual obligations upon the submission of a bid . . .

At a minimum, the respondent offered, in inviting tenders through a formal tendering process involving complex documentation and terms, to consider bids for Contract B. In submitting its tender, the appellant accepted this offer. The submission of the tender is good consideration for the respondent's promise, as the tender was a benefit to the respondent, prepared at a not insignificant cost to the appellant, and accompanied by the Bid Security. The question to be answered next is the precise nature of the respondent's contractual obligations . . .

12 *Murphy v Alberton (Town)* (1993), 114 Nfld & PEIR 34 at 43.

I find it difficult to accept that the appellant, or any of the other contractors, would have submitted a tender unless it was understood by all involved that only a compliant tender would be accepted. However, I find no support for the proposition that, in the face of a privilege clause such as the one at issue in this case, the *lowest* compliant tender was to be accepted. A review of the tender documents, including the privilege clause, and the testimony of the respondent's witnesses at trial, indicates that, on the basis of the presumed intentions of the parties, it is reasonable to find an implied obligation to accept only a compliant tender . . .

I find that the respondent was under no contractual obligation to award the contract to the appellant, who the parties agree was the lowest compliant bid. However, this does not mean that Contract A was not breached. In awarding the contract to Sorochan, the non-compliant bidder, the respondent breached its obligation to the appellant and the other tenderers that it would accept only a compliant tender. I would allow the appeal.

Duty to act fairly

The duty to act fairly in the tender process is an emerging doctrine in contract law. Recent decisions suggest that there is an implied duty to act fairly in treating with all tenderers. The integrity of the tendering process depends upon no competitive advantage being given to any tenderer. As a result, there is an implied duty of fairness upon those calling for tenders in relation to their dealings with tenderers which calls for the reasonable expectation of the parties involved in the bidding process to be respected. In other words, the duty to act fairly means that all compliant tenders or bids should be treated equally. It is expected by tenderers that all submissions will be closely evaluated and that only compliant or valid bids will be accepted for consideration with respect to Contract B. This is particularly important for tenders requested by the government which could be subject to judicial review if it acts in bad faith.

Tercon Contractors Ltd v British Colombia (Transportation and Highways) 2010 SCC 4 (CA)

Facts: The Province of British Columbia issued a request for expressions of interest ('RFEI') for the design and construction of a highway. Six teams responded with submissions including Tercon and Brentwood. A few months later, the Province informed the six proponents that it now intended to design the highway itself and issued a request for proposals ('RFP') for its construction. The RFP set out a specifically defined project and contemplated that proposals would be evaluated according to specific criteria. Under its terms, only the six original proponents were eligible to submit a proposal; those received from any other party would not be considered. The RFP also included an exclusion of liability clause which provided: 'Except as expressly and specifically permitted in these Instructions to Proponents, no Proponent shall have any claim for compensation of any kind whatsoever, as a result of participating in this RFP, and by submitting a Proposal each Proponent shall be deemed to have agreed that it has no claim.' As it lacked expertise in drilling and blasting, Brentwood entered into a pre-bidding agreement with another construction company ('EAC'), which was not a qualified bidder, to undertake the work as a joint venture. This arrangement allowed Brentwood to prepare a more competitive proposal. Ultimately, Brentwood submitted a bid in its own name with EAC listed as a 'major member' of the team. Brentwood and Tercon were the two short-listed proponents and the Province selected Brentwood for the project. Tercon successfully brought an action in damages against the Province. The trial judge found that the Brentwood bid was, in fact, submitted by a joint venture of Brentwood and EAC and that the Province, which was aware of the situation, breached the express provisions of the tendering contract with Tercon by considering a bid from an ineligible bidder and by awarding it the work. She also held that, as a matter of construction, the exclusion clause did not bar recovery for the breaches she had found. The clause was ambiguous and she resolved this ambiguity in Tercon's favour. She held that the Province's breach was fundamental and that it was not fair or reasonable to enforce the exclusion clause in light of the Province's breach. The Court of Appeal set aside the decision, holding that the exclusion clause was clear and unambiguous and barred compensation for all defaults.

Held: LeBel, Deschamps, Fish, Charron, Cromwell, JJA
The Province breached the express provisions of the tendering contract with Tercon by accepting a bid from a party who should not even have been permitted to participate in the tender process and by ultimately awarding the work to that ineligible bidder. This egregious conduct by the Province also breached the implied duty of fairness to bidders. The exclusion clause, which barred claims for compensation 'as a result of participating' in the tendering process, did not, when properly interpreted, exclude Tercon's claim for damages. By considering a bid from an ineligible bidder, the Province not only acted in a way that breached the express and implied terms of the contract, it did so in a manner that was an affront to the integrity and business efficacy of the tendering process.

Submitting a compliant bid in response to a tender call *may* give rise to a contract – called Contract A – between the bidder and the owner, the express terms of which are found in the tender documents. The contract may also have implied terms according to the principles set out in *Canadian Pacific Hotels Ltd. v Bank of Montreal*, [1987] 1 SCR 711; see also *M.J.B. Enterprises Ltd. v Defence Construction (1951) Ltd.*, [1999] 1 SCR 619, and *Martel Building Ltd. v Canada*, 2000 SCC 60, [2000] 2 SCR 860. The key word, however, is 'may'. The Contract A/Contract B framework is one that arises, if at all, from the dealings between the parties. It is not an artificial construct imposed by the courts, but a description of the legal consequences of the parties' actual dealings. The Court emphasized in *M.J.B.* that whether Contract A arises and if it does, what its terms are, depend on the express and implied terms and conditions of the tender call in each case. As Iacobucci J put it, at para. 19: 'What is important . . . is that the submission of a tender in response to an invitation to tender may give rise to contractual obligations, quite apart from the obligations associated with the construction contract to be entered into upon the acceptance of a tender, *depending upon whether the parties intend to initiate contractual relations by the submission of a bid.* If such a contract arises, its terms are governed by the terms and conditions of the tender call.' [Emphasis added.] . . .

Here, there is no basis to interfere with the trial judge's findings that there was an intent to create contractual obligations upon submission of a compliant bid and that only the six original proponents that qualified through the RFEI process were eligible to submit a response to the RFP. The tender documents and the required ministerial approval of the process stated expressly that the Province was contractually bound to accept bids only from eligible bidders. Contract A therefore could not arise by the submission of a bid from any other party. The trial judge found that the joint venture of Brentwood and EAC was not eligible to bid as they had not simply changed the composition of their team but, in effect, had created a new bidder. The Province fully understood this and would not consider a bid from or award the work to that joint venture. The trial judge did not err in finding that in fact, if not in form, Brentwood's bid was on behalf of a joint venture between itself and EAC. The joint venture provided Brentwood with a competitive advantage in the bidding process and was a material consideration in favour of the Brentwood bid during the

Province's evaluation process. Moreover, the Province took active steps to obfuscate the reality of the true nature of the Brentwood bid. The bid by the joint venture constituted 'material non-compliance' with the tendering contract and breached both the express eligibility provisions of the tender documents, and the implied duty to act fairly towards all bidders.

When the exclusion clause is interpreted in harmony with the rest of the RFP and in light of the commercial context of the tendering process, it did not exclude a damages claim resulting from the Province unfairly permitting an ineligible bidder to participate in the tendering process. The closed list of bidders was the foundation of this RFP and the parties should, at the very least, be confident that their initial bids will not be skewed by some underlying advantage in the drafting of the call for tenders conferred only upon one potential bidder. The requirement that only compliant bids be considered and the implied obligation to treat bidders fairly are factors that contribute to the integrity and business efficacy of the tendering process. The parties did not intend, through the words found in this exclusion clause, to waive compensation for conduct, like that of the Province in this case, that strikes at the heart of the tendering process. Clear language would be necessary to exclude liability for breach of the implied obligation, particularly in the case of public procurement where transparency is essential. Furthermore, the restriction on eligibility of bidders was a key element of the alternative process approved by the Minister. When the statutory provisions which governed the tendering process in this case are considered, it seems unlikely that the parties intended through this exclusion clause to effectively gut a key aspect of the approved process. The text of the exclusion clause in the RFP addresses claims that result from 'participating in this RFP'. Central to 'participating in this RFP' was participating in a contest among those eligible to participate. A process involving other bidders – the process followed by the Province – is not the process called for by 'this RFP' and being part of that other process is not in any meaningful sense 'participating in this RFP'.

Bid shopping

A sub-component of the duty to act fairly is the duty to not engage in bid shopping. This is 'the practice of soliciting a bid from a contractor, with whom one has no intention of dealing, and then disclosing or using that in an attempt to drive prices down amongst contractors with whom one does intend to deal'.[13]

Crown Paving v Her Majesty The Queen 2009 NLCA 5 (CA)

Facts: Two companies submitted bids in response to a call for tenders for the maintenance of a portion of highway in southern Labrador. The bids were substantially higher than anticipated by government. In the result, the call for tenders was cancelled. Prior to that cancellation, but after the bids had been opened, government entered into a contract purporting to extend the existing maintenance contract held by Glenn Corporation, one of the two companies that had submitted bids. Crown Paving, having been identified as the preferred bidder, brought an action seeking damages for breach of contract. The trial judge dismissed that action. Crown Paving now appeals.

13 *Naylor Group Inc. v Ellis-Don Construction Ltd.* [2001] 2 SCR 943, 2001 SCC 58, at para. 9.

Coram: Welsh, Rowe, Barry, JJA

The Law

The courts have also discussed the requirement for the tendering authority to act in 'good faith'. The principle is referenced in *Health Care Developers Inc. v Newfoundland* (1996), 141 Nfld. & PEIR 34 (NLCA). Cameron JA, for the Court, wrote:

> [43] . . . While one can logically conclude that good faith performance of contractual obligations should be imposed on all contracts, the necessity for its application to Government tendering to 'protect the integrity of the bidding system' was expressed in *Kencor* [*Holdings Ltd. v Saskatchewan*, [1991] 6 WWR 717 (SKQB)] and I need not state the principle more broadly than that it is a part of the law of tendering for Government contracts. As to the standard of conduct demanded by good faith, at a minimum, it would require that a party not act in bad faith. In my view, it would be acting in bad faith to award something other than contract B, to fail to reject tenders not in compliance with the call or to award contract B on the basis of an undisclosed preference.

With respect to the duty to act in good faith, Iacobucci J, in M.J.B. Enterprises, cautioned:

> [54] The respondent's argument of good faith in considering the Sorochan Bid to be compliant is no defence to a claim for breach of contract: it amounts to an argument that, because it thought it had interpreted the contract properly, it cannot be in breach. Acting in good faith or thinking that one has interpreted the contract correctly are not valid defences to an action for breach of contract . . .

However, the availability of other options is not determinative of whether the Department acted fairly and in good faith. The privilege clause in the tendering documents specifies that the Department 'will not necessarily accept . . . any tender'. As noted above, this language has been interpreted to mean that the tender may be cancelled and the contract not awarded provided the tendering authority acted fairly and in good faith. Accordingly, a bidder knows from the outset that the costs and effort expended in submitting a bid may come to naught if no tender is accepted. In the case before this Court, Crown Paving had obtained the required security in the form of a bid bond, and had 'secured all necessary equipment to be used and required to complete the contract' (Affidavit of Paul O'Keefe, on behalf of Crown Paving, at paragraph 4). Obligations such as these, being imposed on a bidder, while working in favour of the authority calling for tenders, are common in the tendering process (paragraph 21, above).

However, when a tender is cancelled, and a contract for the work is nonetheless awarded, the question of whether the tendering authority was acting unfairly arises. An example of unfairness is 'bid shopping'. This term is discussed in *Double N Earthmovers Ltd. v Edmonton* (City), [2007] 1 SCR 116. Abella and Rothstein JJ, for the majority, wrote:

> [56] In *Naylor Group Inc. v Ellis-Don Construction Ltd.*, [2001] 2 SCR 943, 2001 SCC 58, at para. 9, the Court quoted a definition of bid shopping that described the practice as follows: . . . 'the practice of soliciting a bid from a contractor, with whom one has no intention of dealing, and then disclosing or using that in an attempt to drive prices down amongst contractors with whom one does intend to deal' . . . Other courts have described bid shopping somewhat more broadly, as 'conduct where a tendering authority uses the bids submitted to it as a negotiating tool, whether expressly or in a more clandestine way, before the construction contract has been awarded': [authorities cited].

Crown Paving submitted that the Department had engaged in bid shopping because the extension of the Glenn Corporation contract was negotiated after the tenders had been opened and before the tender was cancelled. This, submitted counsel, 'effectively gave Glenn the opportunity to re-bid the highway maintenance with the knowledge that it had not been the lowest bidder', gave Glenn Corporation the ability 'to undercut' Crown Paving's bid, and allowed the Department to use Crown Paving's bid as a bargaining tool to obtain a better price for the maintenance of the road. I do not accept this submission. In the circumstances, it could not be said that the Department engaged in bid shopping.

The bids from both companies were approximately double the cost estimated by the Department. The contract for three years, to be extended an additional two years at the instance of the Department, was never awarded. While the Department did obtain a contract for maintenance of the road for an additional year at the same unit prices as in the three previous years, there is no indication the Department issued the call for tenders for the purpose of driving down the cost of maintaining the road, or that the bids were used for the purpose of obtaining an extension of the contract at existing unit prices.

Further, the facts do not support the conclusion that the tender was used for the purpose of negotiating a lower price for a portion of the work. The Department was faced with bids significantly higher than the amounts which had been budgeted for work that could not be postponed. The option chosen to deal with that situation was to request the current contract holder to extend the contract for a period of time to permit a reassessment. The contract extension provided a necessary bridging period. In my view, it cannot be said that the Department used the bids submitted to it as a negotiating tool, either expressly or in a clandestine way, to obtain a portion of the tendered work at the existing unit price rate. Crown Paving has not established that the Department engaged in bid shopping.

Dissenting: Rowe, J
As regards the second issue, duty of fairness, while I am in accord with the general statements of the law set out by Justice Welsh, I respectfully disagree with her conclusion; in my view, the Department breached its duty of fairness toward Crown Paving.

It seems to me inescapable that the Department was involved in a form of bid shopping when it held in one hand the irrevocable bid by Crown Paving and with the other hand negotiated a contract extension (albeit including certain price increases) with Glenn.

While this conduct would not come within the definition given to bid shopping by the Supreme Court of Canada in *Naylor Group Inc. v Ellis-Den Construction Ltd.*, [2001] 2 SCR 943 at para. 9, it does come within the further definition of bid shopping referred to by the Supreme Court of Canada in *Double N. Earthmovers Ltd. v Edmonton (City)*, [2007] 1 SCR 116, para. 56, being: 'conduct where a tendering authority uses the bids submitted to it as a negotiating tool . . . before the . . . contract has been awarded.'

It seems to me that is exactly what the Department did here. By requesting that time be extended for accepting Crown Paving's bid, the Department maneuvered itself into a position where it could either accept Crown Paving's bid or come to terms with Glenn for a contract extension . . .

As well, if bid shopping is permitted, then the efficacy of tendering will be degraded, as potential bidders would seek to hedge their bets in what would be a mixed process of competition and negotiation.

If the Department wanted to negotiate an extension with Glenn, in order to comply with the duty of fairness it should first have ended the tender in which Crown Paving was the low bidder. To both keep that tender open and negotiate an extension with Glenn was bid shopping.

In the result, I would have set aside the Trial Judge's decision on the issue of duty of fairness, remitted the matter back to the Trial Division for an assessment of damages, and awarded Crown Paving its costs on a party and party basis in this Court and the Trial Division.

Substantial compliance

A tender which is submitted that is not in compliance with fundamental terms and conditions of the invitation to tender (for example, not submitted on time, is conditional, deficient) is non-compliant and does not give rise to the process contract. The test applied by the Canadian courts to determine whether a bid is compliant with the terms and conditions of an invitation to tender is one of 'substantial' compliance. A bid will be in substantial compliance when all material terms and conditions of the tender have been complied with, determined on an objective basis by the court. Price is an essential part of a tender. Where this had been omitted or is uncertain, this will result in a non-compliant tender and cannot form the basis of a binding contractual relationship (in the form of Contract A). Mere technical or grammatical deficiencies which do not give rise to uncertainty may not operate to invalidate a tender.

R v Derek Penney Electrical Ltd., 2013 NLTD (G) 177 (CA)

Facts: On 17 April 2012, the government, represented by the Department of Transportation and Works (hereinafter the 'Department'), issued a tender call for the upgrade of exterior lighting at the Marine Institute and the College of the North Atlantic on Ridge Road in St. John's known as 'Ridge Road Exterior Lighting Upgrade Project No. 111105112'. The tender call was later advertised to the public on 13 October 2012 with a closing on 25 October. Prior to the closing date, Penney Electrical along with seven other contractors, submitted a tender for the project on the proper form. Initially, all bids were considered to be compliant and Penney Electrical's tender was the lowest price. However, upon a secondary review of the tenders it was discovered that six of the eight bids, including that of Penney Electrical, had not enclosed in the tender package certain material set out in the specification contained in the tender call. All six bids which did not include the information, including that of Penney Electrical, were then declared non-compliant and disqualified. The contract was then awarded to the lowest bidder which had included the material. On 31 October 2012, the government advised Penney Electrical that its bid had been disqualified along with the five others which had not included the material in its tender package. The government and Penney Electrical then engaged in a series of emails in which Penney Electrical objected to the disqualification of its bid on various grounds. The government maintained its position. It is worthy of note that Penney Electrical does not rely on the initial information that its bid was compliant to ground this application.

Held: Adams, J
In the Queen in Right of *Ontario v Ron Engineering & Construction (Eastern) Ltd.*, [1981] 1 SCR 111, Estey, J introduced the now familiar Contract A/Contract B formulation into the law of public tendering. A Contract A arises when a bidder submits a compliant bid in response to the owner's tender call. This contract carries with it certain obligations for the owner, including to treat all bidders fairly. Contract B is the formal contract entered into between the successful bidder and the owner to carry out the terms of the tender call. Contract A may also carry with it implied terms. The test is substantial compliance with the call for tenders.

The process is well explained in *Double N Earthmovers Ltd. v Edmonton (City)*, 2007 SCC 3, [2007] 1 SCR 116, at paragraphs 104–107 and 109–110, per Charron, J:

> 104 This is the cautionary tale of a tendering process gone badly wrong. Although in some business contexts parties might decide to turn a blind eye to contractual inaccuracies and ambiguities, the tendering process is different. It is a process in which fairness and integrity are of paramount importance. Owners spend large amounts of money composing and issuing tenders, and bidders spend large amounts of money formulating and submitting bids . . .
>
> 109 The test for compliance in the tendering process is 'substantial' rather than strict. Estey J's remark [page151] in *Ron Engineering* that it would be 'anomalous indeed if the march forward to a construction contract could be halted by a simple omission' (p. 127) is often cited in support of the substantial compliance test: for example, see *British Columbia v SCI Engineers & Constructors Inc.* (1993), 22 B.C.A.C. 89. Although Estey J made this remark in reference to the Contract B stage of the tendering process, there is no reason to doubt that these same considerations apply to the Contract A stage as well. It would make tendering unworkable if an owner and bidder were prevented from entering into Contract B based on an unchecked box.
>
> 110 Substantial compliance requires that all material conditions of a tender, determined on an objective standard, be complied with: *Silex Restorations Ltd. v Strata Plan VR 2096* (2004), 35 BCLR (4th) 387, 2004 BCCA 376, at paras. 24 and 29; *Graham Industrial Services Ltd. v Greater Vancouver Water District* (2004), 25 BCLR (4th) 214, 2004 BCCA 5, at para 15. A bid is substantially compliant if any departures from the tender call concern mere irregularities.

The mere submission of a tender does not necessarily mean that a Contract A has been formed. It is always possible in the public tendering process that Contract A never arises as all the terms and conditions, express and implied, of the tender call have not been met: *M.J.B. Enterprises Ltd. v Defence Construction (1951) Ltd.*, [1999] 1 SCR 619 paragraph 17.

Application of Law to the Facts

It is therefore necessary to carefully review the terms of the tender and Penney Electrical's bid in response to it in order to determine if a Contract A arose giving rise to the duty of fairness referred to in the authorities. The Instructions to Bidders state in relevant part:

2. TENDER DOCUMENTS

   (a) The Tender Documents consist of the Instructions to Bidders, Tender Form, Agreement, Drawings, Specifications, and any Amendments to the Contract Documents issued during the tender period . . .

4. COMPLETION OF TENDER FORM

   (a) The Tender Form is to be completed in its entirety and submitted in the envelopes provided . . .

   (e) Spaces or Appendices will be provided with the Tender Form if required for a list of sub-contractors, use of bid depository, contractor's experience, list of equipment. All such spaces and appendices must be completed in their entirety legibly by typewriter or by printing in ink.

5. UNACCEPTABLE TENDERS

. . .

   (d) Incomplete Tenders will be rejected. . . .

   (f) Tenders containing qualification or additional clauses to the Tender Form will be rejected. . . .

10. ACCEPTANCE OF TENDER . . .

   (c) The Contractor shall, within 14 days of receipt of the letter of intent, submit to the Owner a breakdown of the bid to the satisfaction of the Owner.

. . .

[15] Section 26 50 00 – Lighting of the specifications states in relevant part:

2.10 PROVIDE THE FOLLOWING INFORMATION WITH THE BID PROPOSAL.

1. Literature.
2. Detailed Manufacturer's Specifications.
3. IES photometric file based on Independent Lab Photometric Test Report, tested in accordance with LM-79.
4. Lighting design in the form of a computer printout as per par 1.3 submittals

Penney Electrical relied on section 4(e) of the Instructions to Bidders to argue that the tender form did not contain any spaces or appendices for a list of equipment so it was impossible for it to comply in respect of specification 26 50 00–2.10. However, I agree with counsel for the government that the material listed in specification 26 50 00–2.10 is not a list of equipment as contemplated in section 4(e) of the Instructions to Bidders. Section 4(e) is general in nature in reference to a 'list of equipment' and, in any event, the section says that a space will be provided for a list of equipment, among other things, 'if required'. No space was provided on the tender form and thus I conclude that the government did not feel that any space or list of equipment was necessary at the time of submission of the tender.

On the other hand, specification 26 50 00–2.10 is clear and unambiguous that the Manufacturers Specifications and Literature as defined therein were to be included in the tender envelope just as was the bond. Section 5(d) of the Instructions to Bidder is also clear that incomplete tenders will be rejected.

Secondly, the inclusion of the Manufacturer's Specifications and Literature cannot be considered a qualification or additional clause to the tender as it was specifically required by the specifications (an integral part of the tender documents) to be included with the bid proposal.

Thirdly, I find that it was not necessary to have had some reference to specification 26 50 00 included in some check list on the envelope to remind a tenderer that the required information should be included. The government was entitled to rely on the bidders to read the documents thoroughly and comply with the requirements. For example, it was also a requirement to include a bond (which Penney Electrical included) but there was no checklist or box to tick to confirm that the bond was included. It was simply required to be included and its omission would have rendered the bid non-compliant.

Fourthly, the fact that the government had the right to request similar information (Section 01 61 00–1.4.4 Common Product Requirements) at a later stage after the formation of Contract B or even for that matter prior to the formation of Contract A does not negate the clear obligation of a tenderer at the Contract A stage to provide the information set out in specification 26 50 00–2.10 with the tender form in the supplied envelope. This is particularly the case in my view, when other bidders have enclosed the required information and complied fully with the tender call.

This case is similar to *Starco Enterprises Ltd. v Stephenville Airport Corp.*, 2005 NLTD 63, 246 Nfld & PEIR 140. In that case, the airport authority issued a tender call for the supply of a front end loader, among other things, for use at the airport. The specifications stated in section 2.6, '. . . Published literature is to be supplied to indicate the actual capacities of the equipment being offered.' Toromont Cat submitted a bid but did not include the required literature. Nevertheless, the airport authority awarded the contract to Toromont as the lowest bidder.

Seaborn, J concluded that the failure to include the literature rendered Toromont's bid non-compliant and the airport authority breached its duty of fairness to other bidders in accepting the tender. Seaborn, J stated at paragraph 58 (referring to the Health Care Developers case):

> 58 The Airport Corporation set the mandatory requirements in the tender specifications and entered into Contract A with the bidders. The following comments of Sue Arrowsmith in the text, Government Procurement and Judicial Review, Carswell (1988), at p. 99, were approved by Cameron JA in *Health Care Developers Inc. v. Newfoundland* (1996), 141 Nfld. & PEIR 34 (NLCA) at paragraph 40, and are applicable in this matter. 'Another practice required by the fair treatment concept is that of rejecting bids which are not responsive to the specifications, or do not comply with other mandatory requirements of the tender call. If this is not done other bidders may be unfairly prejudiced by their own reliance on the terms as originally set out.' . . .

Penney Electrical's bid was substantially and actually non-compliant in not including the Manufacturers Specifications and Literature in its bid as required by specification 26 50 00–2.10. The government was justified, and indeed required, pursuant to its duty of fairness to all bidders to disqualify Penney Electrical's bid as it was non-compliant. There was no Contract A formed with Penney Electrical giving rise to it to the duty of fairness in the public tendering process.

UNILATERAL CONTRACTS

A unilateral contract arises where only one party undertakes an obligation, such as where the promisor makes an offer to pay another party (the promisee) in return for the performance or forbearance of an act, and the promisee gives his assent by performing or forbearing the said act. A reward offered for the return of lost property or for providing certain information is a unilateral contract.[14] The contract is formed on the return of the property or provision of the information, as this constitutes the offeree's acceptance of the offer and the furnishing of consideration for the creation of the contract.[15]

Where there is an offer to pay for the performance of a certain task, part performance can produce a contract under which that offer cannot be withdrawn. That should be the more so where there has not only been part performance but there is a real benefit being accepted by the offeror from that part performance. In such a case, the court should be reluctant to find that the offeror has reserved a right to withdraw the offer after part performance.

Carlill v Carbolic Smoke Ball Company [1893] 1 QB 256 (GB)

Facts: The defendants, who were the proprietors and vendors of a medical preparation called 'The Carbolic Smoke Ball', inserted in the newspapers an advertisement stating that a reward would be paid by the Carbolic Smoke Ball Company to any person who contracted influenza (which was becoming epidemic at that time), colds or any disease caused by taking cold, after having used the ball three times daily for two weeks according to the printed directions supplied with each ball. The plaintiff, a lady, on the faith of this

14 BusinessDictionary.com [online], 'Unilateral Contract', 2009 [accessed 27 August 2009]. Available at: http://www.businessdictionary.com/definition/unilateral-contract.html.

15 *Chitty on Contracts*, para 1–036, pp 21–2.

advertisement, bought one of the balls at a chemist's, and used it as directed, three times a day, from 20 November 1891 to 17 January 1892, when she was attacked by influenza.

Held: Bowne, Lindley, Smith, LLJ
The first observation I will make is that we are not dealing with any inference of fact. We are dealing with an express promise to pay £100 in certain events. Read the advertisement how you will, and twist it about as you will, here is a distinct promise expressed in language which is perfectly unmistakable – '£100 reward will be paid by the Carbolic Smoke Ball Company to any person who contracts the influenza after having used the ball three times daily for two weeks according to the printed directions supplied with each ball.' We must first consider whether this was intended to be a promise at all, or whether it was a mere puff which meant nothing. Was it a mere puff?

My answer to that question is No, and I base my answer upon this passage: '£1,000 is deposited with the Alliance Bank, shewing our sincerity in the matter.' Now, for what was that money deposited or that statement made except to negative the suggestion that this was a mere puff and meant nothing at all? The deposit is called in aid by the advertiser as proof of his sincerity in the matter – that is, the sincerity of his promise to pay this £100 in the event which he has specified. I say this for the purpose of giving point to the observation that we are not inferring a promise; there is the promise, as plain as words can make it.

Then it is contended that it is not binding. In the first place, it is said that it is not made with anybody in particular. Now that point is common to the words of this advertisement and to the words of all other advertisements offering rewards. They are offers to anybody who performs the conditions named in the advertisement, and anybody who does perform the condition accepts the offer. In point of law this advertisement is an offer to pay £100 to anybody who will perform these conditions, and the performance of the conditions is the acceptance of the offer.

Saskatchewan Government Insurance v Medynski (Lakeland Towing) 2012 SKQB 157 (CanLII) (CA)

Facts: The defendants are tow truck operators in the Prince Albert district of Saskatchewan. The plaintiff, Saskatchewan Government Insurance ('SGI') is a significant user of tow truck services throughout Saskatchewan, including the Prince Albert district. For many years SGI and the defendants operated on the basis that SGI would tender an offer to the tow truck universe in the Prince Albert district. It would do so by publishing the rates it would pay for towing and related services. Tow truck operators, including the defendants, would, from time to time, provide those tow services and then be entitled to payment as per the published rates.

In 2005, the defendants repudiated the arrangement. They complained that SGI's schedule of fees was not realistic and was forcing them into penury. They advised SGI that they would charge what they regarded as reasonable rates. This included a flat fee which was variously called an administrative fee or an MVA (motor vehicle accident) fee. In addition, the defendants reserved the right to charge rates that may be in excess of the SGI schedule for towing and incidental services. SGI took steps to avoid using the defendants, but the nature of towing services is that it is the owner of the vehicle and/or the police, not SGI, that engage the services of the tow truck operator. SGI becomes involved only if the vehicle is insured, in which case, a part of the insurance provided, SGI indemnifies the owner by paying for the tow service fee.

In this instance, if the defendants were called to provide a towing service, SGI would be presented with the insured's vehicle hooked up to one of the defendants' tow trucks. The defendants, because of the dispute, would then exact payment in full (including the administrative or MVA fee) before it would release the vehicle to SGI for repair or salvage. SGI paid what it regarded as the excess fees under protest. The defendants concede they knew such payments were made under protest. SGI commenced the claim in April, 2005 to recover what it asserts are excess and unreasonable fees. The defendants join issue and assert their fees were reasonable and, in addition, they claim against SGI for wrongs they assert it has done to them.

Held: Smith, J
In my view, prior to the dispute in 2005, the contractual construct between SGI and tow truck operators generally was that of a unilateral contract. The genesis of the unilateral contract arises from a seminal decision in England in 1892. Students of the common law, beyond counting, have examined and analysed the decision in *Carlill v Carbolic Smoke Ball Co.*, [1892] 2 QB 484. In *Carlill*, the defendant company had advertised that they would pay anyone 100 pounds if he or she caught influenza despite having used its product for a particular period of time. The company had even deposited money in a bank for the express purpose of paying any such person. The Court concluded that the plaintiff, by purchasing the defendant's product and using it as directed, had accepted its offer – even though she did not communicate her acceptance to the defendant. When she eventually caught influenza, the defendant was obliged to uphold its end of the bargain: it had to pay the plaintiff the money it had promised. This was the birth of the unilateral contract. The Court reasoned that because Ms. Carlill was enticed to purchase the defendant's carbolic smoke ball by its advertisement guaranteeing its effectiveness, and because she used the product according to its instructions and still caught influenza, she was entitled to the money that the defendant promised to any of the product's users who nonetheless contracted influenza.

Unilateral contracts are different from the normal contractual paradigm which involves an exchange of promises, i.e., a bilateral contract. Unilateral contracts are unique and valuable in that they provide a mechanism by which promises made to the general public, or a group of individuals (like tow truck operators), can be enforced when relied upon by the offeree who accepts by performance. However, they can only be enforced according to the express terms offered by the offeror. The offeree cannot accept the unilateral contract, while simultaneously changing the terms of that contract.

As explained by Bastarache J, in *Sail Labrador Ltd. v Challenge One* 1999] 1 SCR 265, at para. 33:

> 33 . . . a unilateral contract is one in which a party makes a promise in return for the performance or forbearance of an act. There is no counter-promise to perform this act or forbearance. In this way, a unilateral contract is a contract in which only one party undertakes a promise. This promise takes the form of an offer which can only be accepted by performance of the required act or forbearance. Such performance provides the other party's consideration, allowing it to enforce the original promise (*Treitel* [Treitel, G.H. *The Law of Contract*, 9th ed. London: Sweet & Maxwell, 1995], at pp. 35–36; *Waddams* [Waddams, S.M. *The Law of Contracts*, 3rd ed. Toronto: Canada Law Book, 1993], at p. 111; *United Dominions Trust (Commercial), Ltd. v Eagle Aircraft Services, Ltd.*, [1968] 1 All ER 104 (CA)).

Accordingly, in those years where the defendants were compliant with the SGI Fee Schedule, there was clarity and certainty within the contractual construct of a unilateral contract. The tow truck operators knew what they would be paid if they performed the service detailed in the SGI Fee Schedule.

The situation becomes problematic when the tow truck operators reject the SGI Fee Schedule but still perform the service. The defendants argue that they are hired by the owner of the vehicle (or the police acting on behalf of the owner) and that they are entitled to charge a reasonable fee. They have made no promise to SGI as to the amount that is to be charged. If SGI is obligated to indemnify the vehicle owner in an amount beyond the SGI Fee Schedule, then that is not the problem of the defendants.

Accordingly, in the face of the defendants' repudiation of the SGI Fee Schedule, we are met with a fact circumstance where the defendant tow operators have performed a service but there is no agreement as to price . . . I conclude that SGI is entitled to recover from the defendants those charges made by the defendants for towing and other related services that were greater than 15% above the SGI Fee Schedule. In sum, I conclude that the reasonable range is within 15% of the SGI Fee Schedule.

ACCEPTANCE

Definition

An acceptance is a final and unqualified expression of assent to the terms of the offer.[16] Acceptance must be unequivocal; that is, the language used must be such as would convey to a reasonable person in the position of the offeror a clear and definite decision by the offeree to be bound by the terms of the offer leaving nothing further to be negotiated.

An acceptance must be communicated to the offeror orally or in writing.[17] Acceptance may also be inferred by conduct; for example, an offer contained in a request for services can be accepted by beginning to render them.[18] Apart from actual communication of the acceptance, a general rule of contract law is that a contract is made in the location where the offeror receives notification of the offeree's acceptance.

Another principle of the law of contracts is that there is no obligation posed on the offeror until the offer has been accepted according to the terms in which the offer was made. Any qualification of, or departure from, those terms, invalidates the offer unless agreed to by the offeror and may constitute a counter-offer. To be valid, therefore, an acceptance must precisely conform to the terms required in the offer if a contract is to result.[19]

Bougainville Investment Corp. v Semple 2013 BCSC 1919 (CA)

Facts: The defendant Lindsay Semple is a former director, president and chief executive officer of the plaintiff Bougainville Investment Corp., whose former name was Invincible Resources Corp., during the relevant time frame. Since Bougainville is an actual place that figures in this narrative, I will refer to the plaintiff as 'Invincible'. The background of this dispute involves business operations of Invincible in Papua New Guinea ('PNG') and an island called Bougainville, which is an autonomous region in PNG. Invincible was

16 *Chitty on Contracts*, para 2–025, p 100.
17 *Chitty on Contracts*, para 2–041, p 109.
18 *Chitty on Contracts*, para 2–027, pp 101–2.
19 See Pincus J in *Fernkln Pty Ltd v Australian Building Industries Pty Ltd* [1999] QCA 179 (AU).

conducting business in PNG and Bougainville in the hopes of securing certain mining interests in Bougainville. While a director and officer of Invincible, Mr. Semple arranged for certain expenditures relating to a cattle project in Bougainville. Those expenditures ultimately amounted to approximately $175,000. . . . Invincible claims recovery based on certain statements of Mr. Semple whereby it is alleged that he agreed to pay $175,000 to Invincible. Mr. Semple denies that he entered into a binding agreement to pay these funds to Invincible.

Held: Fitzpatrick, J
To create an enforceable contract there must be agreement between the parties or consensus ad idem, an offer, acceptance and consideration . . . As Fridman states at p. 25, the mechanism of agreement is contained in the notion of offer and acceptance, without which there is no contract: If either or both is missing, there is no proof that the parties were ever ad idem, that is, had reached a stage in their negotiations in respect of which it could be said that they had shown not only an intent to be bound together, but the nature, extent, and manner of their being bound so as to give rise to a legally recognizable and enforceable contract . . . Even if Mr. Semple's comments could be construed as an offer capable of being construed as an intention to contract, his second line of defence is that there was no acceptance by any representative of Invincible. The only person on the call with that capacity was Mr. Parry. As such, Mr. Semple says that no binding contract was formed.

Acceptance is discussed in *Chitty on Contracts* at para. 2–027:

> An acceptance is a final and unqualified expression of assent to the terms of an offer. The objective test of agreement applies to an acceptance no less than to an offer. On this test, a mere acknowledgement of an offer would not be an acceptance; nor would a person to whom an offer to sell goods had been made accept it merely by replying that it was his 'intention to place an order' . . .

In determining whether an acceptance has occurred, the Court in *Marehard v Ridgway*, 2002 BCCA 405 (CanLII) at para. 27 stated that 'acceptance must be one which a reasonable person comprised of the circumstances could confidently understand to be an acceptance of the offer.'

Acceptance is generally subject to a requirement that it be communicated to the offeror. The general rule is that an acceptance has no legal effect until it is communicated to the offeror. For an acceptance to be 'communicated' it must normally be brought to the notice of the offeror: *Chitty on Contracts* at paras. 2–045–2–046.

During the conference call, at no time did Mr. Parry communicate any acceptance of Mr. Semple's 'offer'. His evidence was to the effect that he said nothing in response as he was simply 'happy' to hear Mr. Semple's offer. Nor did any later communication occur from Mr. Parry or anyone else at Invincible to the effect that the 'offer' was accepted. Mr. Parry agreed the only communication to Mr. Semple about the alleged offer after the call was the demand for payment of $175,000 in July 2010. Certain offers may expressly or impliedly waive the requirement of communication of acceptance, and allow acceptance by conduct. In the case of unilateral contracts, performance of the required act or abstention may suffice without the need for a previous acceptance. *Chitty on Contracts* at paras. 2–047 and 2–030 notes: An offer may be accepted by conduct. For example, an offer to buy goods can be accepted by supplying them; an offer to sell goods, made by sending them to the offeree, can be accepted by using them, and an offer contained in a request for services can be accepted by beginning to render them . . . conduct will amount to acceptance only if it is clear that the offeree did the act of alleged acceptance with the intention (ascertained in accordance with the objective principle) of accepting the offer . . .

In this case, Invincible does not allege that the offer was accepted by any conduct, as allegedly invited by the terms of Mr. Semple's offer. While reference is made to the agreement not to sue Mr. Semple, any such agreement of forbearance did not arise at all in the discussions on the conference call, either expressly or impliedly. In these circumstances, it cannot be contended that Mr. Semple imposed a unilateral contract on those terms. I conclude that even if Mr. Semple did make an offer, Invincible did not accept that offer and therefore, no contract was entered into.

By post/telegram

It is usually considered that an acceptance by post or telegram takes place at the time of the posting of the letter of acceptance or transmission of the telegram. This is the exception to the general rule that a contract is made in the location where the offeror receives notification of the offeree's acceptance. The reasoning behind the exception is commercial expediency where there is bound to be a substantial interval between the time when the acceptance is sent and the time when it is received. The most notable application of the acceptance by post rule is that a person who has made an offer must be considered as continuously making it until he has brought to the knowledge of the person to whom it was made that it is withdrawn; therefore, should B post notice of his acceptance to A, notice of A's withdrawal of the offer will be of no effect if it did not reach B before B posted his acceptance. This rule only applies when, implied or expressly, post is contemplated by the parties as the mechanism for acceptance.

Henthorn v Fraser [1892] 2 Ch 27 (GB)

Facts: On 7 July 1891, the secretary of the building society, whom the defendants represented, handed to the plaintiff, in the office of the society at Liverpool, a letter containing an offer for the plaintiff to purchase a property for £750. The plaintiff resided in Birkenhead, and he took away with him to that town the letter of 7 July containing the offer of the society. On 8 July a letter was posted in Birkenhead at 3.50 pm, written by his solicitor, accepting on his behalf the offer to sell the property. This letter was not received at the defendants' office until 8.30 pm, after office hours, the office being closed at 6 pm. On the same day a letter was addressed to the plaintiff by the secretary of the building society revoking the offer. This letter was posted in Liverpool between 12 pm and 1 pm, and was received in Birkenhead at 5.30 pm. It was received before the plaintiff's letter of acceptance had reached Liverpool, but after it had been posted. On 8 July the secretary of the building society sold the same premises to Mr Miller for the sum of £760.

Held: Lord Herschell
If the acceptance by the plaintiff of the defendants' offer is to be treated as complete at the time the letter containing it was posted, I can entertain no doubt that the society's attempted revocation of the offer was wholly ineffectual. I think that a person who has made an offer must be considered as continuously making it until he has brought to the knowledge of the person to whom it was made that it is withdrawn . . .

But it is contended on behalf of the defendants that the acceptance was complete only when received by them and not on the letter being posted. It cannot, of course, be denied . . . that, where an offer has been made through the medium of the post, the contract is complete as soon as the acceptance of the offer is posted, but that decision is said to be inapplicable here, inasmuch as the letter containing the offer was not sent by post to Birkenhead, but handed to the plaintiff in the defendants' office at Liverpool. The question therefore arises in what circumstances the acceptance of an offer is to be regarded as complete as soon as it is posted . . .

I should prefer to state the rule thus: where the circumstances are such that it must have been within the contemplation of the parties that, according to the ordinary usages of mankind, the post might be used as a means of communicating the acceptance of an offer, the acceptance is complete as soon as it is posted . . . For the reasons I have given, I think the judgment must be reversed and the usual decree for specific performance made.

See *Brinkibon Ltd. v Stahag Stahl und Stahlwarenhandelsgesellschaft MBH* [1982] 1 Lloyd's Rep 217 (HL) (GB) for an exposition of the law dealing with telegrams where they were treated in the same manner as acceptance by post.

By telex

Telexes are considered as forms of instantaneous communications and they are treated in accordance with the general rule of acceptance, which is that a contract is formed at the place where acceptance is communicated to the offeror.

Brinkibon Ltd. v Stahag Stahl und Stahlwarenhandelsgesellschaft M.B.H. [1982] 1 Lloyd's Rep 217 (HL) (GB)

Facts: The appellant buyers in England, by a telex dated 26 April 1979, offered to buy from the respondent sellers in Austria 20,000 metric tonnes of mild steel bars c & f liner out of Alexandria. Delivery was to be by five roughly equal shipments in June, July, August, September and October 1979. Payment was to be in Vienna by irrevocable letter of credit in the sum of US$1,412,000. By a telex dated 3 May 1979 the sellers accepted the buyers' offer subject to certain amendments. In particular, the sellers were only prepared to supply a performance bond of 3 per cent instead of the 5 per cent proposed by the buyers and, in addition, the sellers stipulated that if freight rates rose for shipments in September and October, the price would be increased accordingly. The sellers requested the buyers to open a letter of credit by which the sellers could derive payment through their bank, the Zentralsparkasse Der Gemeinde. The aforesaid terms and conditions of the contract were contained in and evidenced by a telex from the appellants to the respondents dated 26 April 1979 offering to purchase on those terms and an acceptance by the respondents to sell to the appellants on those terms by telex dated 3 May 1979. Pursuant to the aforesaid agreement and in performance thereof, the appellants caused to be opened, through the Bank of Credit and Commerce International SA, 100 Leadenhall Street, London EC3, a revolving irrevocable letter of credit in the sum of US$1,412,000 payable against the aforesaid documents to the respondents in Vienna through their bank, the Zentralsparkasse Der Gemeinde, on 4 May 1979. By telex dated 9 May 1979 the respondents alleged that the letter of credit was unworkable and, despite requests by the appellants by telex, they declined to state how or why or in what way the said letter of credit was unworkable, and by a further telex dated 21 May 1979 the respondents purported to withdraw from the contract with effect from that date. In breach of the aforesaid agreement the respondents did not open a performance bond and did not deliver any steel.

Held: Lord Wilberforce
In the present case it seems that if there was a contract (a question which can only be decided at the trial), it was preceded by and possibly formed by a number of telephone

conversations and telexes between London and Vienna, and there are a number of possible combinations upon which reliance can be placed. At this stage we must take the alternatives which provide reasonable evidence of a contract in order to see if the test is satisfied. There are two:

(i) A telex dated 3 May 1979, from the respondents in Vienna, said to amount to a counter-offer, followed by a telex from the appellants in London to the respondents in Vienna dated 4 May 1979, said to amount to an acceptance.
(ii) The above telex dated 3 May 1979, from the respondents followed by action, by way of opening a letter of credit, said to have amounted to an acceptance by conduct.

The first of these alternatives neatly raises the question whether an acceptance by telex sent from London but received in Vienna causes a contract to be made in London, or in Vienna. If the acceptance had been sent by post, or by telegram, then, on existing authorities, it would have been complete when put into the hands of the post office – in London. If on the other hand it had been telephoned, it would have been complete when heard by the offeror – in Vienna. So in which category is a telex communication to be placed?

Existing authority of the Court of Appeal decides in favour of the latter category, that is, a telex is to be assimilated to other methods of instantaneous communication – see *Entores Ltd v Miles Far East Corporation* [1955] 1 Lloyd's Rep 511. The appellants ask that this case, which has stood for 30 years, should now be reviewed. Now such review as is necessary must be made against the background of the law as to the making of contracts. The general rule, it is hardly necessary to state, is that a contract is formed *when* acceptance of an offer is communicated by the offeree to the offeror and if it is necessary to determine *where* a contract is formed (as to which I have already commented), it appears logical that this should be at the place where acceptance is communicated to the offeror.

In the common case of contracts, whether oral or in writing *inter praesentes*, there is no difficulty; and again logic demands that even where there is not mutual presence at the same place and at the same time, if communication is instantaneous, for example by telephone or radio communication, the same result should follow. How should communications by telex be categorised? In *Entores*, the Court of Appeal classified them with instantaneous communications. Their ruling, which has passed into the textbooks, including *Williston on Contracts*, appears not to have caused either adverse comment, or any difficulty to businessmen. I would accept it as a general rule. Where the condition of simultaneity is met, and where it appears to be within the mutual intention of the parties that contractual exchanges should take place in this way, I think it a sound rule, but not necessarily a universal rule. Since 1955, the use of telex communication has been greatly expanded, and there are many variants on it. The senders and recipients may not be the principals to the contemplated contract. They may be servants or agents with limited authority. The message may not reach, or be intended to reach, the designated recipient immediately: messages may be sent out of office hours, or at night, with the intention, or upon the assumption, that they will be read at a later time. There may be some error or default at the recipient's end which prevents receipt at the time contemplated and believed in by the sender. The message may have been sent and/or received through machines operated by third persons and many other variations may occur. No universal rule can cover all such cases: they must be resolved by reference to the intentions of the parties, by sound business practice and in some cases by a judgment where the risks should lie (see *Household Fire and Carriage Accident Insurance Co. Ltd. v Grant* (*sup.*) p 227 per Lord Justice Baggallay and *Henthorn v Fraser* [1982] 2 Ch 27 per Lord Herschell).

The present case is, as *Entores* itself, the simple case of instantaneous communication between principals, and, in accordance with the general rule, involves that the contract (if any) was made when and where the acceptance was received. This was on 3 May 1979, in Vienna.

By email

Acceptance by email, problems of proof aside, is clearly binding, even though no handwritten signature is in evidence. As a form of instantaneous communication, emails are considered in like manner as telexes and, when employed as a mechanism for transmitting an acceptance, the contract is formed at the place where acceptance is communicated to the offeror.

G S Dale & Ors v P C I Jeffrey and Anor [2008] NZHC 147 (19 February 2008) (NZ)

Facts: The defendants applied pursuant to r 477 and the Court's inherent jurisdiction, for an order staying or dismissing this proceeding, on the grounds that New Zealand was *forum non conveniens*. They said that the proceeding ought to have been brought in Spain. The parties were related in that the second-named first plaintiff, the first-named second plaintiff, and the second-named defendant were siblings. The defendants (Paul and Madonna) were partners. In the 1990s, they developed an Australasian business which involved the sale of a product known as Anti-Flamme, an anti-inflammatory cream. That business flourished and was sold to Ebos Group Ltd in 2002. A condition of the sale was that Paul and Madonna were not to compete within Australasia in respect of such products for a period of five years. Subsequently, Paul formulated a plan to incorporate a Spanish company which would distribute a product similar to Anti-Flamme in Europe. The new product was to be called Fisio Crem. They decided to run their business from Spain where they already had other interests, but their intention was that ultimately the business would extend throughout Europe and beyond. In February–March 2003 Paul and Madonna discussed their plans with the plaintiffs, who were offered an opportunity to invest in the new project. They did eventually participate, with the result that on 29 April 2003 a company, Casa Pronat, was incorporated in Spain. Paul Jeffrey, Geoff Dale and Frank Gilchrist were the initial shareholders. Over time a dispute had arisen between the parties as to whether the business of the company and the exploitation of the Fisio Crem product had been conducted in accordance with what the plaintiffs said was the initial agreement between the parties.

Held: Allan, J
On or around 19 February 2003, the first and second plaintiffs entered into a partly oral and partly written agreement (agreement) with the defendants . . . An oral offer was made on the above terms to the first and second plaintiffs at a meeting with the first- and second-named defendants in or about early February 2003 and was accepted by the first and second plaintiffs by way of email to the first-named defendant on or around 19 February 2003 . . .

The plaintiffs' case is that the joint venture agreement came into existence no later than 19 February 2003, by virtue of the acceptance by email from Frank Gilchrist of an earlier offer from Paul Jeffrey. In an email of 18 February 2003, Mr Jeffrey advised Mr Gilchrist that he (Mr Jeffrey) was 'heading to Dubai on Friday [21 February 2003] and all according to plan I will go to Spain early March'. It is a reasonable inference that Mr Jeffrey was in New Zealand at the time of receipt of Frank Gilchrist's email of 19 February, to which I have referred earlier in this judgment. Paul Jeffrey says nothing to the contrary in his extensive affidavits. That being so, it is not in dispute that the agreement (if it exists) was made in New Zealand, and that in the absence of other considerations, New Zealand law must apply to it.

By facsimile transmission

Acceptance by facsimile transmission, another form of instantaneous communication, is treated in accordance with the general rule of place of acceptance – the contract is formed at the place where acceptance is communicated to the offeror.

Eastern Power Limited v Azienda Communale Energia and Ambiente 1999 CanLII 3785 (ON CA) (CA)

Facts: The appellant, Eastern Power Limited (EP), was a corporation organised under the laws of Ontario with its principal place of business in Toronto. Its business was the generation of power from non-conventional sources of energy such as landfill gas. Azienda Communale Energia and Ambiente (ACEA) was a corporation under the laws of Italy with its principal place of business in Rome. ACEA provided power to the City of Rome. ACEA generated some of its own power; however, it also purchased power from other sources. In December 1994 EP met with ACEA in Italy. The parties drafted a Co-Operation Agreement. ACEA signed the agreement on 9 December and faxed it to EP in Ontario. EP signed the agreement in Ontario and faxed it to ACEA in Rome on 21 December. It was an express term of the agreement that the two companies would co-operate and use their best efforts to enter into a project agreement. This agreement, relating to the implementation of the alternative energy project, would be based on proposals to be developed by EP and submitted to ACEA for approval. The project was described as 'an electricity generating plant fuelled by landfill gas, sewage sludge and fossil fuel(s) located near Rome, Italy'.

On 29 January 1996 ACEA signed a Letter of Intent relating to the project. The Letter of Intent was faxed by ACEA to EP in Ontario. On 14 February EP accepted and signed the Letter of Intent in Ontario and faxed it back to ACEA in Rome. The Letter of Intent indicated that the parties wanted to proceed with the project and set out how EP would structure itself in order to be permitted to carry out its work in Italy. The parties worked to conclude a Joint Venture Agreement. Many drafts were prepared; however, none was ever signed. During these further negotiations EP was concerned that ACEA was not diligently pursuing the important CIP 6 subsidy. On 14 February 1997 ACEA wrote to EP and effectively terminated their relationship.

The contract which formed the basis of EP's action in contract and tort against ACEA was the Co-operation Agreement. The motions judge found that the Co-operation Agreement was made in Italy because 'acceptance was communicated to Italy'. Since EP's acceptance was communicated by facsimile transmission, this raised the interesting question of the legal relationship between a faxed acceptance of an offer and the place where a contract is formed.

Held: Abella, Laskin, MacPherson, JJA
The general rule of contract law is that a contract is made in the location where the offeror receives notification of the offeree's acceptance: see Fridman, *The Law of Contract in Canada*,

3rd edn, (1994), at p 65; and *Re Viscount Supply Co.* [1963] 1 OR 640 (SC). However, there is an exception to this general rule. It is the postal acceptance rule. As expressed by Ritchie J in *Imperial Life Assurance Co. of Canada v Colmenares* [1967] SCR 443 at 447: 'It has long been recognized that when contracts are to be concluded by post the place of mailing the acceptance is to be treated as the place where the contract was made.' EP contends that the rule with respect to facsimile transmissions should follow the postal acceptance exception.

With respect, I disagree. EP has cited no authority in support of its position. There is, however, case authority for the proposition that acceptance by facsimile transmission should follow the general rule, which would mean that a contract is formed when and where acceptance is received by the offeror. In *Brinkibon Ltd. v Stahag Stahl G.m.b.H.* [1983] 2 AC 34 (HL), a contract was concluded when the buyer in London transmitted its acceptance to the seller in Vienna. The mode of acceptance was a message sent by telex, a form of instantaneous communication like the telephone. The law lords were unanimous in concluding that the contract was formed in Vienna where the acceptance was received by the offeror . . .

The cases on acceptance by letter and telegram constitute an exception to the general principle of the law of contract stated above. The reason for the exception is commercial expediency: see, for example, *Imperial Land Co. of Marseilles In re (Harris' Case)* (1872) LR 7 Ch. App. 587, 692 per Mellish LJ. That reason of commercial expediency applies to cases where there is bound to be a substantial interval between the time when the acceptance is sent and the time when it is received. In such cases, the exception to the general rule is more convenient, and makes on the whole for greater fairness, than the general rule itself would do. In my opinion, however, that reason of commercial expediency does not have any application when the means of communication employed between the offeror and the offeree is instantaneous in nature, as is the case when either the telephone or telex is used. In such cases the general principle relating to the formation of contracts remains applicable, with the result that the contract is made where and when the telex of acceptance is received by the offeror. In my view, this analysis is equally applicable to facsimile transmissions, another form of instantaneous communication . . .

In my view, the present appeal is also 'the simple case'. The acceptance was faxed by the principals of EP in Ontario to the principals of ACEA in Italy. There is nothing to suggest that the communication between these principals was not instantaneous. Hence, applying the general rule, the contract was formed in Italy.

By telephone/video conference

Contracts made over the telephone follow the general principle that the contract is formed in the location where the offeror receives notification of the offeree's acceptance. Communications technology developments, however, require flexibility in the application of this rule. It has been accepted that where a contract is made over a telephone and where the parties so intend, it is possible for the contract to be held to be simultaneously formed in two or more places. This rule would also apply to contracts negotiated and accepted via video conferencing.

Apple Corps Limited v Apple Computer, Incorporated [2004] EWHC 768 (Ch) (GB)

Facts: The defendant, Apple Computer Inc (Apple Computer), is the well-known producer of computers and software. The claimant (Apple Corps) is the well-known record company formed by the Beatles. The basis of the claim made against Computer is that

that corporation had broken, and intended to break, an agreement made between the two companies in October 1991 which regulated the use of their respective marks in respect of various areas of activity or proposed activity. The defendant brought an application on the grounds that the claimants did not have a good arguable case, as the contract was not made in England. On 9 October 1991 a telephone conversation took place between Mr Zeffman of Apple Corps (who was in the United Kingdom) and Mr Lagod of Apple Computer (who was in the United States) as a result of which completion (or closure) of the agreement took place. During the telephone conversation (at around 11.45 pm), it was agreed to close the negotiations on the basis that both agreements would have 9 October typed in as the relevant date, even though Apple Computer had not signed their part of the agreement. Nevertheless, the parties would close the agreement on the basis that (a) Apple Corp had by then signed both the agreements and that (b) Apple Corp had by then received the funds. The issue arose as to where the contract was made.

Held: Mann, J

I confess that I can detect no conceptual barriers to the notion of a contract being treated as having been made in two places, and some not inconsiderable attractions. In a case where the two parties to a contract are not in the same location at the time of contracting, the notion of where the contract is made is essentially a lawyer's construct. It seldom matters of course, but where it does matter (principally for the purposes of jurisdiction under English law) the law has to provide some answers where an application of the experience of everyday life does not enable one to provide them. Hence the rule in *Entores* and *Brinkibon* to the effect that in the case of instantaneous communications (in those cases telex), the contract is made where acceptance is received. That form of approach assumes that one can analyse the formation of a contract in offer and acceptance terms, and in *Brinkibon* Lord Wilberforce indicated that, difficult though the exercise may be, the courts have to do their best with the evidence in order to work out, sometimes in situations of some difficulty, how the offer and acceptance analysis pans out. However, in the post-*Brinkibon* world, where oral telephone communications are even more common, and where such communications can involve three or more participants in three or more different jurisdictions, and where parties might even conclude a written contract by each signing, and observing each other signing, over a video-link, the law may have to move on and to recognise that there is nothing inherently wrong or heretical in allowing the notion of a contract made in two (or more) jurisdictions at the same time. This is not merely a way of avoiding an unfortunate, and perhaps difficult, evidential enquiry. It may well reflect the reality of the situation. Take the case of three parties who each agree to complete a written agreement by signing simultaneously over a three-way video link – where is that contract made? The natural answer is that it is made in all three jurisdictions. Such a conclusion does not necessarily create practical difficulties. If one of those jurisdictions is England, then one of the foundations for the English courts to assume jurisdiction is present, but it does not necessarily follow that jurisdiction will be assumed, because a claimant who seeks to sue here would still have to establish that it is the most appropriate jurisdiction in which to sue. Jurisdiction would then be dealt with on the basis of a mature *forum conveniens* doctrine rather than what might otherwise be a very forced and artificial analysis of trying to establish in which single jurisdiction the contract was made.

Such an analysis also has the merit of reflecting the fact that it is simply not always possible to analyse a contract in offer and acceptance terms. As Lord Diplock observed in *Gibson v Manchester CC* [1979] 1 WLR 294 at page 297: 'My Lords, there may be certain types of contract, although I think they are exceptional, which do not fit easily into the normal analysis of a contract as being constituted by offer and acceptance.' Where such a contract is brought into existence, *a fortiori* it will not be possible to find out where the contract is made by applying the *Brinkibon* test. Of course, in most cases there will be no problem, but I do not see why, in the exceptional case, the answer should not be that a contract is made in two places (or conceivably in more than two places) if the facts admit of that result and drive one to that conclusion . . .

There is therefore no authority which directly supports the proposition. Is there any authority which gainsays it? Unless it is implicit in *Brinkibon* then it does not seem to me that there is. *Brinkibon* was a case in which the House of Lords had to consider a contract reached by means of a telex machine. The effect of the decision was to apply the rule as to instantaneous communications which appeared in *Entores*. Despite the recorded submission of Mr Thompson that a contract can be made in two places at once, the debate in the judgments is really as to the applicability of the instantaneous communication rule. True it is that Lord Wilberforce at page 40 anticipates that an offer and acceptance analysis will be appropriate, but I do not read him as saying that it would be appropriate if it cannot be done or if it is utterly artificial or inappropriate to do it. At page 42D, he observed that many variations might occur in relation to the communication and receipt of a telex and that: 'No universal rule can cover all such cases: they must be resolved by reference to the intentions of the parties, by sound business practice and in some cases by a judgment where the risk should lie.' While that does not suggest that he was supporting the notion that in some cases it might be possible to find that a contract is made in two places at once, he is certainly pointing against any general rule applicable to all circumstances, and I think it is fair to say that it recognises the need to be appropriately flexible in reflecting the needs and practices of commerce. Both Lord Fraser and Lord Brandon (at pages 44 and 50 respectively) expressed the view that the general rule would have to give way to particular circumstances. In the circumstances, and while *Brinkibon* clearly lays down a general rule which is very helpful and desirable in terms of creating certainty, I do not take it as inevitably standing in the way of the concept that a contract can be made in two places at once in the sense that it forces a court always to find a single jurisdiction in which the contract should be taken to have been made.

So far as it is necessary for me to do so, therefore, I am prepared to consider this matter on the footing that it is possible, as a matter of principle, for a contract to be made in two places at once so that if one of those two places is England the requirement of CPR 6.20(5)(a) is made out. It is therefore necessary to consider whether, on the facts of this case, there is a good arguable case for saying that that is the appropriate analysis. In my view, Mr Vos has succeeded. It seems to me that this sort of case is very arguably one of the class contemplated by Lord Diplock in which an analysis in terms of offer and acceptance is not appropriate. The parties had, by a long process of negotiation, arrived at agreed forms of agreement which were not to be made binding until both parties indicated that they were. If both parties had met in order to sign and complete in the same place, it might well have been extremely difficult to find anything amounting to an offer and acceptance. Where completion takes place at a distance over the telephone, it might well be possible to construct an offer and acceptance analysis (indeed, each party has sought to do so in this case) but it might equally be thought that that analysis is extremely forced and introduces a highly random element. The offer and acceptance may well depend on who speaks first and who speaks second, which is likely to be largely a matter of chance in closing an agreement of this sort. It is very arguably a much more satisfactory analysis to say that the contract was made in both places at the same time. On the facts of this particular case, that would coincide with the clearly expressed intentions of the parties that neither wished to give the other an advantage in terms of governing law and jurisdiction, and although introducing the somewhat random element of offer and acceptance into the concept might be said in one sense to coincide with their respective wishes, and although their expressed wishes did not go so far as to encompass the place of contracting, it seems to me that there is a good arguable case for saying that a dual place of contracting coincides rather more closely with the intentions of the parties. I therefore conclude that as a matter of principle, and on the facts of this case, [Apple] Corps has a good arguable case for saying that the contract was made in both England and California.

By conduct

It may be the case that a person in receipt of an offer can be deemed to have accepted the offer and created a binding legal relationship on the basis of his conduct subsequent to the receipt of the offer. The essence of the principle is that an offer may be accepted by an offeree's conduct which a reasonable person, viewing the matter objectively, would interpret as acceptance.

Rust v Abbey Life Assurance Co. Ltd. and Another [1978] 2 Lloyd's Rep 386 (GB)

Facts: The plaintiff in this action, Mrs Christine Agnes Rust, determined to sell her hotel called 'The Georgian House' in Gloucester Place in 1973. She had some idea of creating a trust in favour of her daughter with the proceeds of sale. When she received the purchase moneys, about £75,000, she paid them into her current account at the National Westminster Bank in Baker Street. Her account with this addition stood at a sum in excess of £90,000. She decided to invest most of the money in this account until she had made up her mind how to deal with it definitively. She spoke to an acquaintance who recommended her to put the money in Abbey Life Property Bonds. As a result she met the second defendant on at least three occasions in 1973 and finally paid over a cheque for £91,600 to the first defendants accompanied by an application form for Abbey Property Bonds. Subsequently she said that this act was a mistake, that she never intended to make a long-term investment with the first defendants but rather a short-term deposit with the similarly named Abbey National Building Society. She said she was misled by the second defendant as to the nature and purpose of property bonds, that he exercised undue influence to procure her application to the first defendants for property bonds, and that in any case no binding contract was ever concluded between her and the first defendants. She claimed the return of her money and damages for misrepresentation and negligence. The defendants denied that the plaintiff was entitled to relief on any of these grounds.

Held: Clothier, J
It is said on behalf of the plaintiff that the material terms of the alleged contract between the parties had not been agreed upon when the policy was delivered to the plaintiff by post. Therefore, it is said, the policy could be no more than a counter-offer to the plaintiff which she could not have accepted by mere silence. Therefore, the argument continues, there is no evidence of a concluded agreement between the parties, and the plaintiff is entitled to the return of her money in full with interest from the date when she first asked for it . . .

I was pressed to find in certain statements of the plaintiff and written correspondence evidence of her affirmation of the policy in accordance with its terms. Although on several occasions she speaks of 'my investment with Abbey Life' and 'my reason for investing in property bonds', I think that to fix her with acceptance of the policy on the basis of isolated phrases incautiously uttered would be as aridly technical and unjust as the point she now takes against the defendants. However, I see great difficulty in the practical transaction of insurance business if persons who have solicited policies of insurance by means of a descriptive title the meaning of which has been explained to them may later say that the tendering of a policy containing detailed terms is only a counter-offer as to which they may remain silent until they choose expressly to accept or reject it. This is the effect of the argument on behalf of the plaintiff, and I do not accept it.

In my judgment the plaintiff, having applied for a single premium bond policy, was obliged when she received the policy to reject it expressly if it or any part of it was not what she required or had been led to expect. She was not entitled to remain silent while the defendants held and invested her premium on terms which they honestly thought were acceptable to her and her advisers and then much later after a fall in value of the fund in which her money was invested, to tell them that the entire policy was unacceptable to her. In my judgment she was in the particular circumstances obliged within a reasonable time of receipt of the policy to say if she objected to it or any of it. Until that time had elapsed she would be entitled to the return of her money in its entirety if the policy was not in accordance with her wishes. But if as I find she delayed unreasonably in declaring her rejection, she must be held to the agreement.

Masontech Inc. v Aaffinity Contracting and Environmental Ltd. 2014 NSSC 164 (CA)

Facts: This proceeding arises out of a construction contract. Defence Construction Canada (DCC) contracted Aaffinity, as general contractor, to conduct repairs to the drainage system, foundation and retaining walls of the Halifax Armoury. DCC manages the real property of the Department of National Defence on behalf of the federal Crown. Aaffinity retained Masontech as a subcontractor. This proceeding arises out of a disagreement between Aaffinity and Masontech respecting the amount due under the subcontract. Masontech's scope of work included dismantling and rebuilding the Armoury's north and south retaining walls. The original contract was priced partly as a lump sum, for amounts that could be priced in advance, and partly as by unit pricing, with amounts due to be determined as the work was carried out. The lump sum price was $330,000.00 plus HST. This included $115,500.00 as the original price for Masontech's work on dismantling and rebuilding the south retaining wall. Due to unforeseen changes in circumstances, it was necessary to revise the contract value downward . . . Aaffinity subsequently sought change orders from DCC. DCC approved a change order dated November 24, 2011, indicating an increase in the expenditure for the retaining wall of $129,964.32. There is no evidence suggesting that this change order was seen by anyone at Masontech. Masontech maintains that over the next several months it carried out the work in accordance with its quote on November 4, 2011 (original contract), invoicing Aaffinity by way of monthly progress claims based on the winter price and being paid . . . Aaffinity claims that it never agreed to the November 4 figures.

Held: LeBlanc, J

Masontech argues that since Aaffinity paid earlier progress claims, it accepted the total contract prices for the relevant items, and is therefore responsible for the payment of the later progress claims. There is no dispute that Aaffinity paid those invoices, nor is there any dispute that Aaffinity paid the progress claims without any protest or concern being raised as to their terms. Masontech's says it completed the work on the expectation of payment, and would not have continued the work otherwise.

Masontech submits that the concepts of acceptance through conduct and estoppel by conduct provide such a foundation. Masontech relies, first, on the principle of acceptance through conduct, citing *Saint John Tug Boat Co. Ltd. v Irving Refining Ltd.*, [1964] SCR 614, where Ritchie J said, for the court: 'It must be appreciated that mere failure to disown responsibility to pay compensation for services rendered is not of itself always enough to bind the person who has had the benefit of those services. The circumstances must be such as to give rise to an inference that the alleged acceptor has consented to the work being done on the terms upon which it was offered before binding contract will be implied.'

Masontech further relies on *Nicholas v Pictou Landing Band Council* (2000), 189 NSR (2d) 64, affirmed at 2001 NSCA 60, where the defendant's continued payment under the terms of an apparently expired contract led to the conclusion that there was continued acceptance of the terms. In *Irving Oil Limited v Incan Ships Limited* (1979), 26 NBR (2d) 512, [1979] NBJ No. 169 (NBQB), the trial judge held that the defendant, being aware of a potential retroactive adjustment to oil prices, accepted that possibility by continuing to pay for oil. The decision was reversed on appeal: 30 NBR (2d) 319, [1980] NBJ No. 120 (NBCA), but Hughes CJNB agreed with the trial judge that the continued payment constituted acceptance by conduct, based on the reasoning in *Saint John Tugboat*; there could be, he stated, 'no doubt that Incan's conduct in making further purchases of fuel oil at domestic prices was evidence that it consented to the terms proposed by Irving' (para. 50) . . .

Masontech argues that it could only infer from Aaffinity's payment of the progress invoices that Aaffinity had accepted the prices set out therein. Aaffinity, however, says the cases relied on by Masontech are distinguishable. The acquiescence in *Saint John Tug Boat* and *Nicholas*, it is submitted, concerned the renewal or extension of pre-existing contracts, rather than a change or amendment. In *Saint John Tug Boat* it was held that each invoice constituted a new offer, and that payment of the invoices constituted acceptance. This was not the case here, where Masontech takes the position, in effect, that the progress claims were increments of an existing single contract. Aaffinity contends that these cases do not establish that paying progress invoices amounts to accepting their terms . . . I am satisfied that Aaffinity could accept the winter price terms by conduct.

INTENTION TO CREATE LEGAL RELATIONS

Commercial agreements

In commercial agreements there is a rebuttable presumption that parties intend to create legal relations and conclude a contract. The establishment of the intention to create legal relations will be determined by the court on the basis of facts and may be established by evidence. The burden of rebutting the presumption of legal relations in commercial agreements rests with the party seeking to deny the contract.[20]

It is a common practice in commercial transactions that businesses engaging in negotiations will often exchange detailed drafts of the proposed agreement. They may be marked 'Subject to Contract' or 'Letter of Intent'. Where parties exchange letters of intent or agreements subject to contract and act before the preparation of the formal contract, the court will be required to examine all documentation and oral evidence very carefully to determine whether there existed an intention between the parties to create legal relations. Some jurisdictions, notably England

20 Articlesbase [online], 'The Need for the Intention to Create Legal Relations in Contract Law', posted 8 April 2008 [accessed 21 January 2015]. Available at: http://www.articlesbase.com/law-articles/the-need-for-intention-to-create-legal-relations-in-contract-law-381745.html.

and Canada, have, understandably, tended to treat letters of intent or subject to contract agreements as mere agreements to negotiate not resulting in concluded binding agreements, on the premise that they are too uncertain to have any binding force. Nevertheless, where, on examination of all evidence, it appears to the court that the parties came to a consensus on all the essential aspects of the bargain, it will be inclined to conclude that there was an intention to create legal relations and will hold that a contract was formed and is binding on the parties.

In the Matter of the Estate of Raphael Williams, Deceased, Cliff Williams and Aggie Williams v The Moorings Limited (2010) BVICV2009/0083 (BVI)

Facts: The claimants, in their capacity as administrators for the estate of the deceased, instituted these proceedings against the defendant claiming damages in the amount of $420,693.95 for works done by the deceased at the defendant's facility. Subsequently, the parties met and reached an agreement on a sum to be paid in full and final settlement of debts due to the estate. A week after the meeting, the claimants refused to accept the cheque of the agreed amount stating that the sum agreed upon was greater than initially thought. They sought a further meeting to review additional documents and receipts which had come to their attention. The defendant refused to enter into further negotiations, contending that an agreement had already been reached and that the claimants cannot unilaterally vary the binding agreement.

Held: Hariprashad-Charles, J
The issues which arise for determination are (1) whether the oral agreement reached by the parties on 19 March 2008 constitutes a binding contract or whether it was an agreement in principle only; and (2) if it was a binding contract, whether the claimants can unilaterally vary it?

For convenience, I will start with some general principles of contract law. In the ordinary case, the law does not require a contract to be made in any particular form, nor according to any particular formalities. It is sufficient that there be a simple contract. Such a contract may be validly made either orally or in writing, or partly orally and partly in writing.

To constitute a binding contract there must be a concluded bargain, and a concluded contract is one which settles everything that is necessary to be settled and leaves nothing to be settled by agreement between the parties. This requirement may be expressed by way of a general rule that for the parties to be bound they must have finished reaching an agreement, so that it is possible to infer an intention on the part of both of them to be bound immediately.

According to the learned authors of *Chitty on Contracts*

> The question whether the parties have reached a complete agreement frequently arises where there has been an agreement in general terms but the parties have stipulated for the execution of some further formal document. The problem then is whether the agreement is too general to be valid in itself and is dependent on the making of a formal contract, or whether the parties have in fact completed their agreement so that the execution of a further formal contract is intended only as a solemn record of the already completed agreement. This is a question of construction for the court. In the words of Parker J in *Von Hatzfeldt-Wildenburg v Alexander* [1912] 1 Ch 284, 288–89: 'It appears to be well settled by the authorities that if the documents or letters relied on as constituting a contract contemplate the execution of a further contract between the parties, it is a question of construction whether the execution of the further contract is a condition or term of the bargain or whether it is a mere expression of the desire of the parties as to the manner in which the transaction already agreed to will in fact go through. In the former case there is no enforceable contract either because the condition is unfulfilled or because the law does not recognize a contract to enter into a

contract. In the latter case there is a binding contract and the reference to the more formal document may be ignored.'

. . . The issue of whether or not there was a binding agreement between the parties is a question of construction for the court. I am satisfied that on the facts and the applicable legal principles, a binding contract was reached between the parties on 19 March 2008. This was an agreement reached by the parties which settles everything. It was to be followed up with the payment of a cheque in the agreed amount and the claimants signing the release. These were ancillary to the fact that the parties have finished reaching an agreement. This was not an agreement in principle only. It was the duty of the claimants to carry out all due diligence before reaching an agreement.

In my opinion the execution of the written release cannot be equated to an agreement in principle where the only proper inference to be drawn is that the parties have not yet finished agreement. For instance, where they make their agreement conditional, or subject to contract, or where so many important matters are left uncertain that their agreement is incomplete. This is a clear case of where the parties reached a binding agreement and subsequently, the claimants may have found more invoices and now seek . . . to vary that agreement unilaterally. This cannot the done. The law is that the parties to a contract may effect a variation of the contract by modifying or altering its terms by mutual agreement. A mere unilateral notification by one party to the other, in the absence of any agreement, cannot constitute a variation of the contract.

In the premises, I will hold that a binding contract was reached between the parties on 19 March 2008 and the claimants cannot unilaterally vary it because they have now found new invoices.

Domestic agreements

In domestic agreements, in contrast, there is a rebuttable presumption that the parties do not have an intention to create legal relations. In agreements between family members or friends, there is no intention to create legal relations and no intention that the agreement should be subject to litigation. Familial relationships or friendships, however, do not preclude the formation of a binding contract, though to create contractual relations, there must be a clear intention on either party to be bound.[21] The presence or absence of an intention to create legal relations depends upon the inference to be drawn by the court from the language used by the parties and the circumstances in which they use it.

Smith v Mottley (1993) 48 WIR 20 (BB)

Facts: The defendant, Cuthbert Mottley, a carpenter, agreed to build a house for the plaintiff, Velma Smith, on land belonging to the plaintiff and her spouse at lot 24, Durants, Christ Church. The plaintiff's case was that there was no written contract. There was also no stipulation in the agreement for the precise remuneration of the defendant, but the plaintiff sent goods to the defendant as a gesture of thanks, love and affection and told him that he should take his remuneration from the money which she sent from the United Kingdom. In pursuance of the agreement, she sent money from time to time from the United Kingdom

21 Incisive Media, Law.com Dictionary, 'Contract'.

to pay for labour and the purchasing of materials to complete the house. The parties corresponded with each other monthly during the period 1986 to 1987 when the construction of the house began and was taken to roof level. In July 1987 the plaintiff came to Barbados and observed that construction of the house had reached roof level and she agreed to send funds to the defendant to pay for the construction of the roof. In September 1987 she sent approximately BB$16,493.50. In July 1988 the plaintiff's husband and their daughters visited Barbados and discovered that the house had not been completed and that there were defects in the construction of the roof. They tried to contact the defendant to have him account for the state of affairs, but the defendant refused to make himself available and avoided them. Building contractors and a building inspector were then engaged to inspect the roof. They concluded that the roof had been badly constructed and needed to be replaced by a new roof. The walls of the house were raised and a new roof constructed costing BB$25,000. The claim was that the defendant was negligent, in that he supervised the construction of a roof which was built below the standard expected of a skilled builder and below the height recommended for buildings in Barbados which left the roof defective.

Held: Waterman, J

The evidence in this case shows that the plaintiff and the defendant are related. The plaintiff is the niece of the defendant. He agreed to construct the house for his niece. No contract, however, was recorded in writing. No sufficient thought appears to have been given as to the type of house to be built, as to the price of the house, as to the period over which the house was to be built and as to the defendant's remuneration for his services. By this rather loose arrangement it seems as if the uncle was trying to help his niece, who lived in England, build a house in Barbados for herself and her family and at the same time make some money for himself in supervising the building and assisting in doing some of the carpentry work on the house.

The first question to be decided is whether, on the evidence, the parties intended to create a legally binding contract or whether it is simply a family arrangement which has no legal effect . . . In *Jones v Padavatton* the mother invited her daughter to leave her lucrative job in Washington in the USA and go to England and read for the Bar, with a view to returning to Trinidad to practise law. The daughter accepted her mother's offer and went to England and entered on her studies at the Bar. Her fees and maintenance in England were provided by her mother. The mother later bought a house in England in which the daughter resided and from which she received the rents from the letting of some of the other rooms in the house. No terms of either of these arrangements were recorded in writing and there was no statement of the parties' respective obligations and, in particular, nothing as to the duration of these arrangements. The Court of Appeal held (*inter alia*) that the arrangement between the mother and the daughter was throughout a family arrangement depending on the good faith of the parties in keeping the promises made and not intended to be a rigid binding arrangement. Furthermore, that the agreement was far too vague and uncertain to be itself enforceable as a contract. Salmon LJ said (at page 621):

> Did the parties intend the arrangement to be legally binding? This question has to be solved by applying what is sometimes (although perhaps unfortunately) called an objective test. The court has to consider what the parties said and wrote in light of all the surrounding circumstances, and then decide whether the true inference is that the ordinary man and woman, speaking or writing thus in such circumstances, could have intended to create a legally binding agreement. Counsel for the mother has said, quite rightly, that as a rule when arrangements are made between close relations, for example between husband and wife, parent and child, or uncle and nephew, in relation to an allowance, there is a presumption against an intention of creating any legal relationship. This is not a presumption of law, but of fact. It

> derives from experience of life and human nature which shows that in such circumstances men and women usually do not intend to create legal rights and obligations, but intend to rely solely on family ties of mutual trust and affection.

In the present case, on the evidence, the true inference is that at the time when the arrangement was made to build the house neither the plaintiff nor the defendant intended to enter into a legally binding contract. I am satisfied that it was simply an informal family arrangement between an uncle and a niece whereby the uncle was helping his niece and her family build a house in Barbados. Furthermore, all the evidence shows that the terms of the arrangement for the building of the house were vague and uncertain. There is no written contract. There is, in particular, no agreement as to the defendant's remuneration for his work and services. In the circumstances therefore the agreement between the parties is unenforceable because of the absence of an intention to contract and because of the vagueness and uncertainty of the terms of the agreement.

CERTAINTY OF CONTRACT

For a contract to be binding, it must be certain and not suffer from vagueness or obvious incompleteness such that it cannot give rise to a binding contract. To determine certainty of contract, the court must be able to identify exactly what has been agreed,[22] although it does not expect commercial documents to be drafted with strict legal precision, as this poses the risk of the agreement being struck down.[23] If a contractual term is uncertain or unclear, it will not necessarily vitiate the contract if its meaning can be ascertained or the contract itself provides the method of supplying the meaning or deficiency. In deciding whether or not the agreement as a whole is sufficiently certain to amount to a contract, the court will try to determine what the reasonable man would have thought. Additionally, if the parties to the agreement have not agreed on some essential term of the contract or provided an effective machinery to ascertain certain requirements of a contract, a court will be reluctant to provide it. The court will not make contracts or supply to a contract a fundamental term for parties which have obviously not addressed it. It is the obligation of parties to make contracts with such certainty that is capable of being enforced.

Toojays Limited (Appellant) v Westhaven Limited (Respondent) Civil Appeal No. 14 of 2008 (BB)

Facts: The factual background to this appeal is not complicated. The Respondent is the owner of a restaurant property situate at Holetown, St. James. On May 1, 1998, the Respondent entered into a lease agreement to let that property to the Appellant for a period of five years commencing May 15, 1998. The Respondent and the Appellant operated under this agreement for a period of almost four years. In 2002, the Appellant informed the Respondent that in order to satisfy two potential investors, it, the Appellant, needed to offer these investors a 10 year lease minimum. The Respondent acceded to the Appellant's request and a second lease agreement was executed by the Respondent and the Appellant. In this second lease agreement, it was agreed that the Appellant 'shall rent the above-mentioned building for a period of 10 years commencing May I, 1998 to terminate on April 30, 2008 with an option of renewal for an additional five years to terminate on April 30, 2013'. This

22 Salzedo *et al, Briefcase on Contract Law*, p 33.
23 *Chitty on Contracts*, para 2–129, p 148.

agreement is undated. The Appellant sent to the Respondent a letter dated January 28, 2008 in which it sought to exercise the option to renew the lease contained in the second lease agreement. However, the Respondent claimed that the option to renew was not properly exercised and refused to renew the lease.

Held: Moore, CJ (Ag); Mason, Burgess, JJA
At the heart of this present case is the construction of an undated written lease agreement of premises at Holetown, St. James . . . As we have already noted, the core of the action here is the construction of a provision in the lease agreement purporting to grant an option to renew. First, the express language of clause 6 (C) of the agreement, namely, that 'the landlord shall not be bound to enter any negotiations regarding any new agreement' qualifies the preceding provisions in clauses 6 (A) and 6 (B). The unmistakable effect of the language in Clause 6 (C) is to negate any obligation on the part of the landlord to negotiate a renewal of the lease or to grant one. It is very doubtful, therefore, whether the agreement can reasonably be interpreted as conferring any option to renew. Second, it clear on the face of the agreement that the parties to the agreement have not agreed on an essential term of the 'option to renew', namely, the monthly rent for the period May 1st, 2008 to April 30th, 2011. There is a flood of case law supporting the argument of the Respondents that there is a general principle of contract law that, where, as is the case with the option to purchase in this matter, the parties do not agree on essential terms of an agreement, no binding contract can arise: see *May and Butcher v The King* [1934] 2 KB 17.

Adnan Mkhoul v Keith Henry and Etola Richards HC Civil Claim No. 121 of 2008 (SVG)

Facts: In July/August 2007, the Claimant Adnan Mkhoul held discussions with Defendant Keith Henry to purchase from him (Henry) 6335 sq ft of land on which there is a two storey building (the property), situate at Belvedere in the parish of Saint George in St. Vincent and the Grenadines. Money was paid by Mkhoul to Henry but the parties differ as to the quantum.

Held: Joseph, J

Is there a contract?
A valid contract comprises three components. One, agreement between parties; two, an identifiable subject matter; three, an ascertainable price. The subject matter is identifiable and there is no dispute about that. I shall consider the other two components, i.e., agreement between the parties and an ascertainable price. In his witness statement Henry states that he told Mkhoul that the purchase price of the property was $90,000.00. Mkhoul indicated that he would be unable to pay that sum and offered $45,000 which he (Henry) did not accept. Henry said that Mkhoul stated that if he (Henry) signed the deed Mkhoul would pay $90,000.00 in two installments . . . Mkhoul's witness statement:

> After a month or two Keith started to come by me and said to me I understand that you bought my sister's property[.] Keith then offered his property to me. I asked him how much he wanted for the property he said $60,000.00. I said No I give $40–45 thousand. He considered my offer and he came back and asked for $50,000.00 I agreed to pay the sum of $50,000.00 and he accepted the sum of $45,000.00.

Andy Mkhoul (Mkhoul's son) witness statement:

> I saw him (Henry) again at the Traffic Variety Store, on this occasion my father called me to listen to the conversation, Keith reduce the first offer from $60,000.00 to $50,000.00. My father said he was only paying $45,000.00 . . . . On third occasion when he came he accepted $50,000.00.

To constitute an agreement there must be an offer made by one party that is accepted by the other party. From the evidence, there was an offer of selling the property for $90,000.00 that was not accepted. Instead there was a counter offer of $50,000.00, and as will be seen later Mkhoul's claim is that he paid Henry $59,685.00. Hence there is no contract. The third component is that there must be certainty as to price. From the evidence there is no such certainty and there is therefore no contract between the parties. As there is no contract, any act that flows from that contract arrangement is of no effect and the parties cannot successfully claim any relief.

COUNTER-OFFERS

It is a principle that a counter-offer may, and indeed generally does, constitute a rejection of the offer and terminate it so that it is no longer open for acceptance. When a person makes an offer and the person to whom the offer is made responds by proposing changes to the terms of the offer, the law considers the response of that party not as an acceptance but rather as a counter-offer. Therefore an attempt to accept an offer on new terms (not contained in the offer) may be a rejection accompanied by a counter-offer.[24]

Singh v Chung 1995 CanLII 914 BCCA (CA)

Facts: The defendant listed for sale the subject property located at 9211 and 9215 Kilby Street, Richmond, British Columbia (the 'property') with HomeLife Richview Realty Limited on a standard exclusive listing agreement. This listing was taken by Greg Robertson representing HomeLife. On 1 June 1992 Paul Dhari prepared an offer by the plaintiffs to purchase the property for CAN$276,000 subject to the plaintiffs' arranging suitable financing by 5 June 1992. The offer was open for acceptance until 6:00 pm on 2 June 1992. Mr Dhari presented the counter-offer to the female plaintiff, Mrs Singh, later that night, namely 1 June 1992. Mrs Singh signed and initialled the counter-offer. Then, as a result of her concerns as to whether there were indeed two lots, Mr Dhari inserted a clause stating that: 'The vendor warrants that property has already been zoned and subdivided into two 33 × 122 lots, and will give copies of documents confirming this to purchaser by subject removal date' (the warranty clause). Upon Mr Dhari presenting to the plaintiffs the plan, they were satisfied that they were in fact purchasing two lots and Mr Dhari then proceeded to cancel out the clause that he had inserted and had the plaintiffs initial this cancellation, either personally or through the female person acting as authorised agent for and on behalf of her husband. On 3 June 1992 the agents advised the plaintiffs that the defendant declined to complete the sale because his offer had been rejected by the counter-offer in the warranty clause.

Held: Cumming, J
It is common ground that, as a general rule, a counter-offer may, and indeed generally does, constitute a rejection of the offer and terminate it so that it is no longer open for acceptance. See *Chitty on Contracts*, 27th edn para 2–063: 2–063, What amounts to rejection; counter-offers. A rejection terminates an offer, so that it can no longer be accepted. For this purpose, an attempt to accept an offer on new terms (not contained in the offer) may be a rejection accompanied by a counter-offer . . . A communication from the offeree

24 *Chitty on Contracts*, para 2–084, p 127.

may be construed as a counter-offer (and hence as a rejection) even though it takes the form of a question as to the offeror's willingness to vary the terms of the offer. But such a communication is not *necessarily* a counter-offer: it may be a mere inquiry or request for information made without any intention of rejecting the terms of the offer. Whether the communication is a counter-offer or a request for information depends on the intention, objectively ascertained, with which it was made . . .

I am satisfied, from the evidence of Mrs Singh which I have quoted, that she was genuinely concerned as to whether or not the proposed agreement did in fact relate to two lots rather than one, and that she raised the question with Mr Dhari in order to resolve her doubts . . . There was no counter-offer by the Singhs communicated to Mr Chung or his agent. And, Mr Chung's own counter-offer was accepted by Mr and Mrs Singh within the time limited for doing so. In the result, I would dismiss the appeal.

Battle of the forms

It is often the case that contracting parties rely on pre-printed forms (order, delivery, invoice) but this practice can prove problematic when parties are claiming that their respective separate forms are what dictate the terms and conditions of their contractual relationship. More often than not, the last form that is issued can be considered the operative form, especially when the party receiving the form accepted the contract by his conduct. If a party orders a product using his own order form but the product is delivered with a delivery note that governs the sale of the product, that can be considered a counter-offer. If the party making the order accepts delivery of the product, it may be considered that such party has accepted the delivery note as the binding contract and cannot rely on his order form as the operative contract. Nevertheless, if the difference in terms is so material that it would affect the price, the buyer ought not to be allowed to take advantage of the difference unless he draws it specifically to the attention of the seller. It must be noted that the delivery note must function and be intended to function as a contract and in some instances the court will merely hold the delivery note as proof of delivery and nothing more. Moreover, it must be ascertained whether or not persons in positions of authority have actually agreed to significant or onerous terms during the negotiation process. Once a deal is made by persons in authority, it cannot be unilaterally amended by clerical staff inserting pre-printed forms onto bills of lading, invoices or purchase orders as goods depart from or arrive at the loading dock. Such terms will not be held to be binding.

Brentwood Plastics Inc. v Topsyn Flexible Packaging Ltd. 2014 MBQB 97 (CA)

Facts: Brentwood is an American corporation based in the state of Missouri that manufactures, among other things, polyethylene film that is commonly used as commercial grade food wrap. Topsyn is a Winnipeg-based corporation that provides custom made packaging services, such as bread bags, to various clients in the food industry. In February of 2011, the parties entered into an oral agreement whereby Topsyn would purchase plastic film from Brentwood in accordance with quality specifications set out by Topsyn. The parties agree that during the discussions leading up to their oral agreement they never discussed an arbitration process that might come into effect should a dispute arise between them. Between February and September of 2011, Topsyn placed various purchase orders with Brentwood. Each purchase order contained written details as to a particular quality and quantity of plastic film. In particular, Topsyn printed the following clause on each purchase order:

> Film must have good clarity, gauge control, lay flat. No static or tackiness. Please send confirmation of order.

Upon receiving each purchase order Brentwood sent a written document entitled 'Terms and Conditions of Sale' to Topsyn, which included the following paragraph:

> Acceptance of your order by Brentwood Plastics Incorporated (Seller) is EXPRESSLY MADE CONDITIONAL TO THE TERMS AND CONDITIONS HEREIN SET FORTH and these constitute the only binding contact terms and conditions between the parties in the absence of a written agreement as provided in Paragraph 14.

The above document does not contain an arbitration clause and does not make any reference to an arbitration clause being contained in any other document, including the invoices issued after purchase orders were filled . . . In August of 2011, Topsyn took issue with the quality of the film provided by Brentwood and complained the film was not reasonably fit for its intended purposes. Topsyn provided Brentwood with details of the complaints and the damages it was claiming as a result of the defective film. Brentwood did not reply.

On September 2, 2011, Topsyn wrote to Brentwood and quantified its damages to be $83,803.94. Topsyn advised Brentwood that it would be available for further discussion and that it hoped for a speedy resolution. Topsyn did not receive a response to this letter from Brentwood but instead received a letter from the International Center for Dispute Resolution advising that a notice of arbitration had been received from Brentwood, and that an arbitration proceeding had started. Prior to receiving this letter, Topsyn was not aware that an arbitration process might be underway. Topsyn's response to the arbitration notice was to advise Brentwood in writing that the parties did not have an agreement that would entitle Brentwood to refer the matter to arbitration.

Held: Rempel, J

The Battle of the Forms

Proving what terms and conditions of an agreement were disclosed or reasonably ought to have been known and then subsequently agreed to by a commercial party can be a vexing task. The common law is replete with cases on the age old controversy surrounding instances of parties attempting to impose the wording from their standard form templates onto the opposing side of a commercial relationship. The common law appropriately labels these disputes as a 'battle of the forms'.

In the ***Stella-Jones*** case, the defendant inserted an arbitration clause on a bill of lading that was issued as cargo was being loaded onto a ship. The Court found the arbitration clause was an amendment to the standard form bill of lading and there was no evidence that the terms of that arbitration clause were ever agreed to by the plaintiff (paragraph 8). In upholding the decision on appeal, the Federal Court of Appeal stated at paragraph 20:

> It seems to me quite clear that the terms of contract proposed to Stella Jones by Hawknet were the terms contained in the 'Conline' booking note, which were to be superceded by the terms and conditions of the 'Conline' standard form of bill of lading, neither of which contained an arbitration clause. In my view, the fact that Mr. Kaddis of Stella Jones was not aware of these terms and conditions, or that he had never read them in the past, is irrelevant. Had he been aware of those terms or had he taken the time to read them, he would have noted that they did not include an arbitration clause. *If it was the appellant's intention to make the contract of carriage subject to an arbitration clause, it should have made its intention known to Stella Jones.* [*Mariana Maritime S.A. v Stella Jones Inc.*, [2002] FCA 215] [emphasis mine]

The result of that case makes abundant good sense as it cannot be fair for one party to add a term or condition of great significance to an agreement under circumstances where one cannot reasonably expect that this information would come to light and thus allow the other side to make an informed decision as to whether or not the deal should continue as originally contemplated. The notable concern arising from this case, and many other 'battle of the forms' cases, is whether or not persons in positions of authority are actually agreeing to significant or onerous terms during the negotiation process. Once a deal is made by persons in authority, it cannot be unilaterally amended by clerical staff inserting pre-printed forms onto bills of lading, invoices or purchase orders as goods depart from or arrive at the loading dock.

In order for the party arguing in favour of the existence of an arbitration clause to discharge its evidentiary burden, it must show that the 'battle of the forms' went beyond the stage where clerical staff, who were never part of the negotiation process, simply inserted pre-printed forms onto invoices or shipping records. Without evidence that a person in authority, with capacity to bind a party, knew or reasonably should have known about an agreement in writing during the negotiation process, it is difficult to persuade a trier of fact that the tipping point for a *consensus ad idem* has been reached. I hasten to add that the case law holds that parties can be deemed to be bound by terms common or standard to a particular industry and that such terms can be incorporated by reference, see *H & H Marine Engine Service Ltd. v Volvo Penta of the Americas Inc.* (2009) BCSC 1389, at paragraphs 56 & 57, but the burden of incorporation by reference is a high one.

This was confirmed by our Court of Appeal in *Western Processing & Cold Storage Ltd. et al. v Hamilton Construction Co. Ltd. et al. and Dow Chemical of Canada Ltd.* [1965] MJ No. 39 (MBCA) where the Court held at paragraph 19:

> . . . It would be grossly unjust to saddle Alsip with a responsibility which it never entered into or agreed to accept, unless it can be said that through the course of well-established prior business conduct Alsip knew that it was to be bound by an acknowledgment of order form to be mailed to it later and which would contain such a specially onerous term. . . .

I am satisfied that the evidence in this case clearly shows that persons in authority for the parties never discussed or communicated in writing about arbitration during the negotiation process. In point of fact, there was no way a person in authority at Topsyn could have even known arbitration was being contemplated until well after the deal was struck and the product arrived at Topsyn's premises. It is not at all surprising to me that the existence of the arbitration language inserted in the invoice did not come to the attention of a person in authority at Topsyn until the notice of arbitration arrived in the mail, which was well after the dispute about the quality of the film had erupted and the commercial relationship between the parties had collapsed.

CONSIDERATION

Meaning

A major development in contract law was the concept of consideration which had its origin in the desire to develop a legal basis for differentiating between promises which would be legally enforceable from those which would not. The law stipulated that promises supported by consideration would be legally enforceable. A moral obligation to pay is not regarded by the law as sufficient to make a promise legally enforceable. The purpose of the doctrine of consideration is to put some legal limits on the enforceability of agreements even where they are intended to be legally binding and are not vitiated by some factor such as mistake, misrepresentation, duress or illegality.[25]

The traditional definition of consideration concentrates on the requirement that something of value must be given and accordingly states that consideration is either some detriment to the promisee or some benefit to the promisor.[26] Consideration always moves from the promisee to the promisor.

National Insurance Board (Appellant) v [1] Ann Marie Duncan-Mason [2] Peter Mason (Respondents) HCVAP 2009/002 (GD)

Facts: By a mortgage made in the year 2003, the respondents charged certain land to the appellant. Monies advanced under the mortgage were used to construct a house on the said land. In the month of November 2004 heavy rains fell and the house collapsed as a consequence, it is suspected, of slippage/subsidence of the land. The appellant made certain concessions by way of assistance to the respondents and took a decision to waive interest on the loan. As a consequence the existing mortgage was released and a new mortgage was taken out on the same property. This mortgage was made by deed on 26th October 2004. Subsequently and upon the request of the respondents the Board of the appellant agreed to sell the property held pursuant to the mortgage deed for the price of $35,000.00 which said sum was to be paid towards the mortgage loan and informed the respondents of this decision by letter dated 6th May 2005. Subsequently, the appellant refused to sign a release of the property without payment of the mortgage debt in full or alternative collateral security which the respondents refused to give despite the appellant's requests. The respondents then took action against the appellant for loss of bargain and damages for breach of contract. The respondents relied solely on the said letter as a contract and alleged that the appellant was in breach thereof.

Held: George-Creque, Baptiste, Gordon (acting), JJA
I would be of the certain view that what the May 6th Letter meant was that in consideration of an early payment of $35,000.00 (which admittedly was not the whole debt) the appellant would release its security over the respondents' lands, thus permitting them to sell it if it were not for clause 4(c) of the Second Mortgage whilst at the same time retaining their right to be paid back the balance of the $100,000.00. The traditional definition of 'consideration' concentrates on the requirement that something of value must be given. It is sufficient that there either be a detriment to the promisee or a benefit to the promisor . . . I interpret the appellant's pleading as accepting that an agreement (offer and acceptance) was made between the parties. Unfortunately for the respondent, however that agreement lacked the essential ingredient, consideration to make the agreement a legally enforceable contract . . . In conclusion, I would[] reluctantly allow this appeal and reverse the whole of the order of the trial judge. I cannot help commenting, however, that the respondents have every right to feel hard done by the appellant who has acted in exercise of its legal rights without regard to the expectations of the respondent.

25 *Chitty on Contracts*, para 3–001, p 167. For more on these issues, see Chapter 3 below.
26 *Chitty on Contracts*, para 3–004, p 169.

The bargain

A significant aspect of the doctrine of consideration is what amounts to a good consideration and this translates into what can be sometimes viewed as the simplistic promise of consideration, namely a detriment to the promisee and a benefit to the promisor. The underlying basis of consideration is the notion of the 'bargain' that allows what may be a mere moral obligation to be transformed into a legal agreement capable of enforcement.

In unilateral contracts the consideration on the part of the offeree is completely executed by the doing of the very thing which constitutes acceptance of the offer. In cases of this class, it is necessary, in order that a contract may be established, that it should be made to appear that the statement or announcement which is relied on as a promise was really offered as consideration for the doing of the act (the bargain), and that the act was really done (the detriment) in consideration of a potential promise inherent in the statement or announcement.

Australian Woollen Mills Pty Ltd. v The Commonwealth (1954) 92 CLR 424 (AU)

Facts: The plaintiff company had for many years carried on a large business of manufacturing worsted cloth. In the course of its business it purchased, during the war years and up to the end of 1948, large quantities of raw wool, both greasy and scoured, for the purpose of manufacture into cloth. Its claim against the Commonwealth in the action was for a total sum of 176,153 pounds. This amount was split up in various ways in the statement of claim, and, as to some of the sums involved, various causes of action were alleged, and the amount alleged to be payable was calculated in various ways. In the last analysis, however, it would appear that the company's claim could only be framed as a claim for two distinct sums, which together made up the total of 176,153 pounds. The first was a sum of 108,871 pounds. The company alleged a contract, or rather a series of contracts, between itself and the Commonwealth, under which the Commonwealth bound itself to pay to it a sum, described as a subsidy, in respect of wool bought by it at auction for the purpose of manufacture. The sum of 108,871 pounds was, it said, payable to it under this contract or these contracts. The second sum claimed was a sum of 67,282 pounds. This was a sum which was in fact paid by the company itself to the Commonwealth in response to a demand made by the Commonwealth in circumstances which had to be considered. This sum was claimed as money and was received by the Commonwealth to the use of the company.

Held: Dixon, CJ; Williams, Webb, Fullagar, Kitto, JJ
The contract put forward by the plaintiff is thus seen to be of that type which is commonly said to be constituted by an offer of a promise for an act, the offer being accepted by the doing of the act. Such contracts are sometimes described as 'unilateral' contracts, but the term is open to criticism on the ground that it is unscientific and misleading. There must of necessity be two parties to a contractual obligation. The position in such cases is simply that the consideration on the part of the offeree is completely executed by the doing of the very thing which constitutes acceptance of the offer . . . In cases of this class it is necessary, in order that a contract may be established, that it should be made to appear that the statement or announcement which is relied on as a promise was really offered as consideration for the doing of the act, and that the act was really done in consideration of a potential promise inherent in the statement or announcement. Between the statement or announcement, which is put forward as an offer capable of acceptance by the doing of an act, and the act which is put forward as the executed consideration for the alleged promise, there must subsist, so to speak, the relation of a quid pro quo . . .

It is of the essence of contract, regarded as a class of obligations, that there is a voluntary assumption of a legally enforceable duty. In such cases as the present, therefore, in order that a contract may be created by offer and acceptance, it is necessary that what is alleged to be an offer should have been intended to give rise, on the doing of the act, to an obligation. The intention must, of course, be judged in the light of the principle laid down in *Freeman v Cooke* (1848) 2 Ex 654, at p 663 (154 ER 652, at p 656), but, in the absence of such an intention, actual or imputed, the alleged 'offer' cannot lead to a contract: there is, indeed, in such a case no true 'offer'. A test which has not seldom been applied in such cases in order to determine whether a contract has been made or not is to ask whether there has been a request by the alleged promisor that the promisee shall do the act on which the latter relies. Such a request may, of course, be expressed or implied . . .

It seems to have been thought at one time that it was necessary for a plaintiff, in any action at law in which he relied on an executed consideration, to allege in his declaration a request by the defendant that he should do the act which is relied on as providing the consideration. The presence or absence of an implied request that the act be done has been regarded as material in a number of cases . . .

Coming to the present case, it is impossible, in our opinion, to hold that any contract was constituted at any stage binding the Commonwealth to pay a subsidy to the plaintiff, or to any manufacturer, in consideration of a purchase of wool for local manufacture. It is impossible to suggest that the Government ever contracted with manufacturers to sell them appraisement wool at less than cost. The Government simply acquired wool and sold it to manufacturers at a price lower than it paid for it.

The problem has not changed in character since June 1946. The object to be attained is still to keep down the price of woollen goods to the consumer. And it is to be solved in the same way – that is to say, by a subvention. The only difference is that, because the Government will no longer be acquiring and selling wool, the old method is impracticable, and the subvention is to be paid direct to the manufacturer. No reason is suggested why the Government, which has not hitherto entered into any contract, should now propose to bind itself by contract . . .

If we ask (what we think is the real and ultimate question) whether there is a promise offered in consideration of the doing of an act, as a price which is to be paid for the doing of an act, we cannot find such a promise. No relation of quid pro quo between a promise and an act can be inferred. If we ask whether there is an implied request or invitation to purchase wool, we cannot say that there is. If we ask whether the announcement that a subsidy would be paid was made in order to induce purchases of wool, no such intention can be inferred.

Nature of the consideration

As noted, it is generally said that consideration is something, moving from the promisee, which is either a detriment to the promisee or a benefit to the promisor. It is often stated that while consideration must be sufficient, it need not be adequate. The courts will not attempt to measure the comparative value of the promise against the act done or promise made in exchange for it, nor will they denounce an agreement merely because it seems unfair.[27]

27 Furmston, M, *Cheshire, Fifoot & Furmston's Law of Contract*, 2001, London: Butterworths, p 90.

Even though it is expected that a party to a contract will be consciously aware of what consideration he provides for the promise he is accepting, it is not necessary that he be so aware of the consideration provided. This is such that although a party who has entered into an agreement for some benefit is unaware of the detriment to which he subjected himself, he is deemed to have provided good consideration.

Chappell & Co. Ltd. and Another v Nestle Co. Ltd. and Another [1960] AC 87 (HL) (UK)

Facts: The Hardy Record Manufacturing Co. Ltd, the second respondents, made gramophone records consisting of thin films of cellulose acetate. They entered into an agreement with the first respondents, the Nestle Co. Ltd, who were manufacturers of milk chocolate, to supply them with a number of records of a dance tune called 'Rockin' Shoes', the copyright of which was vested in the first appellants, Chappell & Co. Ltd, as sole licensees and in the second appellants, the Winneton Music Corporation, as owners. The price to Nestle of the records was fourpence; they were mounted on cardboard discs supplied by Nestle containing advertising matter. Nestle sold the records to the public at the price of 1s 6d, subject to a condition that the purchaser must also send three wrappers from their sixpenny milk chocolate bars. These wrappers were of no value in themselves and were thrown away when received. Nestle made a profit on each sale, but the purpose of the scheme was to advertise and promote the sale of their milk chocolate. The Hardy Record Manufacturing Co. gave notice of their intention to manufacture, in accordance with section 8(1) of the Copyright Act 1956, stating 1s 6d to be the ordinary retail selling price, and offered to pay royalties, which the appellants refused. In the action the appellants alleged that these transactions constituted a breach of copyright, as they did not involve a sale 'by retail' within the meaning of the section.

Held: Lord Reid
If a contract under which a person is bound to do something as well as to pay money is a sale, then either the price includes the obligation as well as the money, or the consideration is the price plus the obligation and I do not see why it should be different if he has to show that he has done something of value to the seller. It is to my mind illegitimate to argue – this is a sale, the consideration for a sale is the price, price can only include money or something which can be readily converted into an ascertainable sum of money, therefore anything like wrappers which have no money value when delivered cannot be part of the consideration. The respondents avoid this difficulty by submitting that acquiring and delivering the wrappers was merely a condition which gave a qualification to buy and was not part of the consideration for sale. Of course, a person may limit his offer to persons qualified in a particular way, for example, members of a club. But where the qualification is the doing of something of value to the seller, and where the qualification only suffices for one sale and must be re-acquired before another sale, I find it hard to regard the repeated acquisitions of the qualification as anything other than parts of the consideration for the sales. The purchaser of records had to send three wrappers for each record, so he had first to acquire them. The acquisition of wrappers by him was, at least in many cases, of direct benefit to the Nestle Co., and required expenditure by the acquirer which he might not otherwise have incurred. To my mind the acquiring and delivering of the wrappers was certainly part of the consideration in these cases, and I see no good reason for drawing a distinction between these and other cases. In my judgment this appeal should be allowed.

Forbearance and compromise

Forbearance and compromise pertain mainly to dispute settlement. With a trend to non-judicial settlement of disputes, parties tend to prefer executing settlement agreements. The settlement is a contract and often the consideration is the agreement by a party to forbear from engaging in legal proceedings. The courts have endorsed the notion of the settlement contract and the concept of forbearance and compromise as adequate consideration.

A creditor's forbearance from suing the principal may amount to good consideration to support a guarantee. There are two alternative circumstances in which forbearance to sue can constitute consideration:

(a) where the creditor promises to forbear in consideration for the guarantee; and
(b) the actual forbearance by the creditor given at the request of the guarantor and in return for something.

In the case of actual forbearance, the request of the guarantor may be express or implied. Although forbearance usually takes the form of the creditor refraining from instituting legal proceedings or proving in a bankruptcy or winding up, it may consist of the creditor refraining from asserting any legal right.

Stewart v Superior Canadian Livestock Auction Ltd 2014 SKQB 394 (CA)[28]

Facts: This case illustrates how the two year limitation period under *The Limitations Act*, SS 2004, c L-16.1 [*Act*] might surprise a farmer who grants credit to his neighbour to finance the purchase of livestock. The appellants, Andrew Drummond Stewart and Robert Murray Stewart [the Stewarts], the debtors under the credit arrangement, appeal the lower court's decision [2014 SKPC 72], awarding damages against them for breach of contract to pay the respondent, Superior Canadian Livestock Ltd. [Superior], for the purchase of five Simmental bulls. Layton Bezan, the principal of Superior, who has 20 years' experience buying and selling livestock, commenced an action in small claims court on September 25, 2013. The Stewarts maintained at trial that Superior's action was statute barred under the *Act*. The trial judge disagreed. The Stewarts now appeal the trial judge's decision.

Held: Layh, J
The Stewarts rest their appeal upon the simple assertion that the requirements of s. 11 of the *Act* pre-empt any other method to stay or modify the running of a limitation period (other than s. 21 which requires an *express extension of a limitation period* which no one suggests occurred in this instance). The Stewarts find error with the trial judge's disregard for s. 11. If Superior wanted to alter the limitation period, s. 11 provides the ready and only answer: seek the execution of a written acknowledgment or part payment of the debt. If neither is forthcoming, then Superior's option was to commence an action. The Stewarts maintain that permitting a 'verbal collateral contract' to be substituted for a statutorily prescribed written acknowledgment will create a 'floodgate' of plaintiffs mounting creative arguments that defendants have orally agreed to new terms of payment . . .

28 The statements made here are *obiter*.

However, resolving issue (1) is an alluring task, and I offer a brief assessment. One would expect that the essence of an agreement between a creditor and a debtor which effectively adjusts an expected payment date would accord with the common law's recognition of a forbearance agreement. The question, though, is whether a forbearance agreement is sufficient to add yet another method (in addition to those methods contemplated by s. 11 and s. 22 of the *Act*) to effectively push a limitation period forward in time. A good overview of the effect of a properly constituted forbearance agreement on a limitation period is offered in *Shook v Munro*, 1948 CanLII 8 (SCC), [1948] SCR 539 and *Hamilton (City) v Metcalfe & Mansfield Capital Corporation*, 2012 ONCA 156 (CanLII), 347 DLR (4th) 657 where Justice Laforme[] stated as follows:

> [73] At common law, a creditor and debtor can agree to forbear enforcement of a debt, and such an agreement would suspend the limitation period for the period of forbearance. In order to achieve this result, the creditor must promise not to enforce the debt, and the debtor must provide some consideration in exchange for this promise. In other words, a creditor's promise to forbear will not suspend the limitation period unless the debtor provides consideration for that promise: *Shook v Munro et al*, 1948 CanLII 8 (SCC), [1948] SCR 539.
>
> . . .
>
> [75] The cases relied on provide a means by which parties can agree to suspend the limitation period for an action to enforce payment on the debt. This makes sense because, if a creditor and debtor agree to change the repayment terms of the debt obligation, they have essentially renegotiated their debt agreement. So the limitation period for the creditor's action to collect on the debt would not run because – due to the agreement to change the repayment terms – the debtor is not effectively in default . . .

For the purposes of this appeal I will assume, but not determine, that the limitation period initially set by the terms of the original obligation to pay the purchase price of the five bulls could have been altered if Superior and the Stewarts had entered into a common law forbearance agreement.

Citibank NA v Blue Chateau Limited SC Civil Appeal No. 90/99, Suit No. 1998/E248 (JM)

Facts: The appellant, Citibank, NA, was a company duly incorporated in the state of New York, United States of America and was licensed under the Banking Act to carry on the business of banking in Jamaica. The respondent, Blue Chateau Limited, was a limited liability company duly incorporated under the Companies Act and was the registered proprietor of all that parcel of land part of Constant Spring Estates, comprised in Certificate of Title registered at Volume 1105, Folio 581 of the Register Book of Titles. The Company comprised 200 shares, 198 of which were held by Caldon Finance Group Limited (in liquidation), hereinafter referred to as Caldon, and one share by Henry Fullerton, the Executive Chairman of Caldon, and one share by Cynthia O'Sullivan, secretary of Caldon.

Dorothy Parkins, a vice president of the Jamaica branch of Citibank, swore to an affidavit on 7 May 1998 stating that from and since 29 March 1994, Caldon had opened a current account with Citibank. On 27 January 1998 Caldon's account became overdrawn in the sum of JM$7,718,568.50. By agreement made on 29 January 1998 between Citibank and Caldon further advances were made to Caldon by Citibank by way of overdraft on Caldon's account. On that date the total advances amounted to JM$13,911,189.24. It was agreed between Caldon and Citibank that interest would be charged on the overdraft on Caldon's account at the rate of 38 per cent per annum. By an agreement made orally and supported by memoranda in writing between 30 January 1998 and 3 February 1998, it was agreed between Citibank and Blue Chateau that in consideration for the former making the aforementioned advances by way of overdraft to Caldon, Blue Chateau would guarantee the payment of all sums of money up to a limit of JM$9,000,000 due by Caldon to Citibank by virtue of the overdraft on Caldon's account. The said agreement was arrived at in telephone conversations on 30 January and 2 February 1998 between Henry Fullerton, a director of Blue Chateau, on the one hand and Gerald Wight and Dorothy Parkins on behalf of Citibank. As security for the said guarantee, Blue Chateau by its servant or agent Henry Fullerton on 3 February 1998 deposited the duplicate Certificate of Title registered at Volume 1105, Folio 581 in respect of the mortgaged property with Citibank. A resolution of the Board of Directors of Blue Chateau dated 3 February 1998 was duly signed by Henry Fullerton and Cynthia O'Sullivan. A copy of the resolution is set out below.

> Resolution of Blue Chateau Limited resolved: that Blue Chateau Limited do guarantee the financial obligation to Citibank, N.A. of Caldon Finance Group Limited which financial obligation arises as a result of temporary facilities provided by Citibank, N.A. in the sum of nine million dollars ($9.0M). We, Henry A. Fullerton the Chairman and Cynthia O'Sullivan the Secretary of Blue Chateau Limited, hereby certify that the above is a true copy of a resolution duly passed by the Directors of the Company at a board meeting duly convened by the Directors and held on the Third day of February, 1998. Henry Fullerton, Chairman. Cynthia O'Sullivan, Secretary.

A valuation report dated 22 August 1996 prepared in respect of the mortgaged property by D.C. Tavores & Finson Co. Ltd Real Estate Appraisers was sent by Blue Chateau to Citibank in support of the security being provided by Blue Chateau for its guarantee. On 19 February 1998 Citibank registered the equitable mortgage as a charge against Blue Chateau Ltd at the office of the Registrar of Companies. Citibank also lodged at the office of the Registrar of Titles a caveat against any dealing with the mortgaged property without first advising the plaintiff. On 20 February 1998 Citibank's attorneys-at-law prepared and sent to Blue Chateau an instrument of mortgage in the form of a guarantor's mortgage for its due execution by Blue Chateau and return to sender but Blue Chateau failed or refused to return the instrument of mortgage duly executed.

On 12 March 1998, by a resolution passed by creditors of Caldon, Raphael Gordon of KPMG Peat Marwick was appointed Liquidator to wind up the affairs of Caldon. Citibank in a letter to the Liquidator dated 24 March 1998 made a formal demand for the sum of JM$5,959,592.63 which was currently due. On the following day Citibank wrote to Blue Chateau making a formal demand and referred to the equitable mortgage created by the deposit of the Title Deed. In addition, Citibank also gave formal notice pursuant to the Registration of Titles Act, indicating that if payment was not made within one month after service of the notice, the Bank would exercise its powers of sale.

Held: Forte, P; Walker, Langrin, JJA
The issue of forbearance to sue and past consideration: Reference was made to Section 2 of the *Mercantile Law Amendment Act* which provides that consideration for a guarantee need not appear by writing. Our attention was drawn to an extract from Law of Guarantees where it was stated that a creditor's forbearance from suing the principal may amount to good consideration to support a guarantee. There are two alternative circumstances in which forbearance to sue can constitute consideration:

(a) where the creditor promises to forbear in consideration for the guarantee, and
(b) the actual forbearance by the creditor given at the request of the guarantor and in return for something.

In the case of actual forbearance, the request of the guarantor may be express or implied. The author stated at p 22: 'Thus, if there is a pre-existing debt, the existence of which cannot in itself amount to consideration, the inference will often be drawn that the guarantee was given on the understanding that the creditor would forbear from taking action with respect to that debt.' It is instructive to observe that the authors also noted at p 22 that: 'Although the forbearance usually takes the form of the creditor refraining from instituting legal proceedings or proving in a bankruptcy or winding up, it may consist of the creditor refraining from asserting any legal right.' We were referred to a number of authorities on the issue of the forbearance to sue. In *Crears v Hunter* [1877] 19 QBD 341, the defendant's father owed the plaintiff a debt. For the purpose of inducing the plaintiff to give time to the defendant's father for payment of the debt, the defendant signed a promissory note whereby the defendant's father and the defendant jointly and severally promised to pay to the plaintiff the amount of the debt, with interest half-yearly at the rate of 5 per cent per annum until the amount was paid, the plaintiff having forborne to sue for several years. It was held that the plaintiff having forborne from suing the defendant's father at the defendant's request, there was good consideration for the defendant's liability on the note, although there was no contract by the plaintiff to forbear from suing. Lord Esher MR at page 344 had this to say:

> It may be true that there was no evidence of any request in express terms by the son that the plaintiff would forbear to sue the father, but what was the substance of the transactions contemplated in the minds of the parties? Was not the understanding obviously that if the plaintiff would forbear to sue the father, the defendant would become liable on the note?

Lindley LJ at page 345 said:

> Looking at the document and the history of the transaction, I cannot invent any rational theory by which to account for the defendant's giving the note except that it was for the purpose of benefiting his father by procuring for him time to pay the debt. To say otherwise appears to me inconsistent with human nature and the whole character of the transaction . . . But except on the theory that such was the understanding between the parties, the defendant's conduct is inexplicable.

Lopes LJ at page 347 said: 'Unless it were to procure forbearance, it is inconceivable why the defendant should have signed the note at all.'

In *Fullerton v Provisional Bank of Ireland* [1903] AC 309, a customer of a bank had overdrawn his account and being pressed by the bank undertook by letter to deposit a title deed of an Irish estate as security for his overdraft. The customer afterwards mortgaged the estate to the appellants, who registered their charge without notice of the prior charge. Lord Macnaghten stated at p 313:

> In such a case as this it is not necessary that there should be an arrangement for forbearance for any definite or particular time. It is quite enough if you can infer from the surrounding circumstances that there was an implied request for forbearance for a time, and that forbearance for a reasonable time was in fact extended to the person who asked for it.

Lord Davey quoted Lord Bowen in *Miles v New Zealand Alford Estate* Co. 32 CHD 206, 290 who said at p 316:

> So it will be sufficient here that the directors did forbear, if their forbearance was at the request expressed or implied of the guarantor and in consequence of his guarantee being given, and it seems to me there is no sort of necessity to discover language of any particular form, or writing of any particular character, embodying the resolution of the directors. We

> must treat the thing in a business way and draw an inference of fact as to what the real nature of the transaction was as between businessmen.

In *Glegg v Bromley* [1912] 3 KB 474 CA, Mrs G was largely indebted to her husband. He had requested her to give him further security and she executed in his favour a deed of assignment. Vaughan Williams LJ made reference to *Alliance Bank v Broom* [1864] 2DR & SM 289, where Kindersley VC said: 'if on the application for security being made, the defendant had refused to give security at all, the consequence certainly would have been that the creditor would have demanded payment of the debt and would have taken steps to enforce it.' He went on to say at p 486:

> the mere existence of an antecedent debt is not good consideration for an assignment even by way of further security. If there has been pressure and in response to that pressure the further assignment is made, that suffices. But the cases all show that even if there has not been pressure, but there has been a further assignment and it is known to the person who is the creditor and has power to put pressure upon the debtor that a further assignment has been made the law will if it possibly can give effect to the probability that the fact that the security has been increased will have influenced the creditor and made her more forbearing.

Mr Patrick Foster, counsel for the respondent, contended that the advances made before the giving of the guarantee could not have been good consideration for the giving of the said guarantee. The existence of a pre-existing debt could not validate a subsequent guarantee. This would amount to past consideration. Reliance was placed on *Wigan v English & Scottish Law Life Assurance Association* [1909] 1 Ch 291. The facts reveal that H was indebted to W who had pressed for payment or reduction of debt. H executed a deed of assignment and delivered it to his attorneys, telling them to use their discretion as to whether they should inform W of the assignment or not. In fact the solicitors obtained time from W for payment of the debt without producing the deed, and acting on the instructions destroyed it. It was held that there was no valuable consideration for the assignment. Parker J made the following observations at p 297:

> It appears to me to be reasonably clear that the mere existence of a debt from A. to B. is not sufficient valuable consideration for the giving of a security from A. to B. to secure that debt if such a security is given[. It] may of course be given upon some express agreement to give time for the payment of the debt, or to give consideration for the security in some other way, or if there be no express agreement, the law may very readily imply an agreement to give time. It may not be a definite time, but to forbear for some indefinite time in consideration of the security being given.

Based on the foregoing analysis of the relevant authorities, it is clear that neither the request for forbearance nor the consideration given need be in written form. The forbearance can in fact be implied from the circumstances. The court will also be willing to look at the nature of the transaction and the business sense that would undoubtedly be operating within the minds of the parties. It is clear from the foregoing analysis also, that forbearance does not only exist in the form of forbearance to sue, but can also be forbearance from exercising any other legal right. Citibank could be seen as withholding its power or its legal right to ask for immediate payment and such a right could in fact be exercised if the security were not given. In my view, forbearance includes refraining from asserting a legal right, which could have been asserted but for the security. Implicit in the giving and receiving of a guarantee must be some element of forbearance.

It cannot be gainsaid that Citibank, whether or not it had actually exercised it, had the power to make a demand for payment and the guarantee served the purpose of staying the

Bank's hand. That would be the element of forbearance which is that as long as the Bank had the security, it would not ask for immediate repayment. A reasonable inference may be drawn that Citibank must have requested some security. No person is going to volunteer to part with his title unless he is forced to do so. It is inconceivable that any financial institution would have increased a customer's indebtedness by such a substantial sum without any mention of a security. In my view, the agreement for the guarantee on 30 January was but the continuation of a process begun on 29 January which finally culminated in the lodging of the title on the 3 February 1998.

In light of the foregoing analysis on the issue of forbearance, it is abundantly clear that there was in fact good consideration for the giving of the guarantee and therefore the question of past consideration does not arise. In my judgment the learned judge fell into error when he said that the granting of overdraft facilities and the making of advances on 29 January 1998 could not be good consideration for the formation of a valid and binding contract of guarantee between Citibank and Blue Chateau.

Past consideration

A past consideration is, in effect, no consideration at all as it confers no benefit on the promisor, and involves no detriment to the promisee in return for his promise. It is merely an act or forbearance in time past by which someone has benefited without thereby incurring any legal liability. If afterwards, whether from good feeling or interested motives, he makes a promise to the person by whose act or forbearance he has benefited, and that promise is made upon no other consideration than the past benefit, it is gratuitous and cannot be enforced.

There is, however, one exception where past consideration will be held to be good consideration but it is dependent on three conditions being met:

(1) the act must be done at the promisor's request;

(2) the parties must have understood that the act was to be remunerated either by payment or conferment of some other benefit; and

(3) payment or the conferment of a benefit must have been legally enforceable had it been promised in advance.

Classic Maritime Inc v Lion Diversified Holdings & Anor [2009] EWHC 1142 (Comm) (21 May 2009) (GB)

Facts: The claimants (Classic) sought summary judgment against both defendants. The second defendant (Limbungan) sought a stay of the action so that the dispute between it and Classic could be decided in arbitration in accordance with an arbitration clause contained in a Contract of Affreightment (COA), and the first defendant (Lion) sought a stay on case management grounds. Classic brought the action against Lion under a written guarantee dated 28 August 2008 by which it guaranteed the obligations of its subsidiary, Limbungan, under the COA contained in or evidenced by an email Recap dated 13 August 2008 (the August COA), which in turn incorporated an earlier July COA. Lion raised two defences to the claim, one of which was that the guarantee was unenforceable because any consideration given was past consideration.

Held: Cooke, J

Past Consideration: Lion's argument that there was no valid consideration and only past consideration hangs upon the opening words of the guarantee itself, which reads as follows:

> In order to induce Classic Maritime Inc. to enter into a contract of affreightment dated 13 August 2008 (the 'Contract') with Limbungan Makmur Sdn Bhd of Kuala Lumpur, Malaysia, the undersigned (the 'Guarantor'): Represents that it owns, directly or indirectly, all of the equity interests in Limbungan Makmur Sdn Bhd and, accordingly, benefit from Classic Maritime Inc's entering into and performing its obligations under the Charterparty, and Guarantees and promises to pay to Classic Maritime Inc., on demand, any and all amounts (the 'Obligations') that Limbungan Makmur Sdn Bhd becomes obligated to pay to Classic Maritime Inc. as a result of Limbungan Makmur Sdn Bhd's failure to perform its obligations or otherwise under the Charterparty when each of the Obligations becomes due.

As already mentioned, the date of this guarantee is 28 August 2008 and the opening wording refers to the inducement of the contract of affreightment dated 13 August 2008, 15 days earlier. Lion submits that the guarantee, on its face, therefore refers to past consideration and it is therefore unenforceable. Moreover, Lion maintains that it is inadmissible to look at extrinsic evidence to show other consideration.

This argument is totally devoid of commercial sense and, I am glad to say, wrong as a matter of legal analysis. The Recap for the August COA stated that the COA was for the account of Limbungan but that its performance was to be fully guaranteed by Lion Industries. Limbungan was therefore under an obligation to procure such a guarantee from Lion Industries. The terms of the guarantee had not been negotiated at that stage but Limbungan had undertaken an obligation which was enforceable. There can be no doubt that if no guarantee from Lion Industries had been forthcoming (or from a suitable alternative as subsequently agreed) Classic would have been under no duty to fulfil the COA. Limbungan's capital apparently amounted to about 40p. Although it was argued by Lion that it was taken by surprise by an argument that the guarantee was a condition precedent to performance under the COA and that issues of factual evidence with regard to waiver, matrix, market conditions, knowledge of the parties and significance could arise, in my judgment, it is plain, as a matter of commercial construction of the COA, that the guarantee was an essential part of the bargain made with Limbungan. I cannot see the need for any prior notice to raise such a point, as a matter of law, nor how any facts which could be adduced in evidence could have any impact on this point which stares one in the face when looking at the terms of the COAs. Nor is there any realistic prospect of establishing any waiver for all time of such a condition precedent. The nomination of a vessel on 22 August by Classic, while at the time seeking to agree wording of the guarantee, cannot constitute a waiver of any kind. By the very nature of the July and August COAs, which each provided for four shipments a year for periods of five and a quarter and six years respectively, with a total value in excess of [US]$300 million, and the limited financial standing of Limbungan, a provision for a guarantee in such agreements must be considered so fundamental to them that the obligation to provide the guarantee amounts to a condition precedent to performance by Classic.

This is a similar situation to that set out in *Trans Trust v Danubian Trading* [1952] 2 QB 297 where Denning LJ found that the provision of a bankers' confirmed letter of credit was an essential term of the contract of sale and had to be seen as a condition precedent to the obligation of the seller to deliver the goods. There, if the buyer failed to provide the credit, the seller could treat himself as discharged from any further performance of the contract and could sue the buyer for damages for not providing the credit. When therefore, on its own case, it was subsequently discovered that Lion Industries could not give the guarantee, Limbungan would not have been able to enforce the COAs in the absence of an agreement by Classic to a substitute guarantee. When Classic accepted a substitute guarantee from Lion in place of the guarantee which Limbungan was obliged to procure from Lion Industries, Classic plainly gave up the right to sue Limbungan in respect of the failure to provide a guarantee from Lion Industries. This was plainly good consideration and no argument about illegality could avail Limbungan in respect of its failure to produce that guarantee from Lion Industries, particularly in view of the discussions in the course of negotiations which involved other Lion companies potentially giving the guarantees. Limbungan settled on Lion Industries and it was entirely its problem, if and when it was later discovered that Lion Industries was in no position to provide the guarantee as a matter of Malaysian law. Even if an argument was available to Limbungan in that respect, it cannot be doubted that there was good consideration in Classic giving up the potential right to sue Limbungan for the failure, when accepting the guarantee from Lion instead of that from Lion Industries. Consideration moved from Classic, the promisee, because it gave up its right against Limbungan in exchange for obtaining a right to sue Lion under the guarantee. Furthermore, even if the guarantee had been given by the entity named in the August COA, there would then have been good consideration since, when accepting the guarantee, Classic would be taken to have discharged Limbungan from its obligation to provide one. Once again consideration would move from the promisee in giving up that right.

The reality is that the guarantee was given as part and parcel of a single transaction, since it was specifically required by the August COA. There was no subsequent demand for a guarantee to be given, because it was already provided for in that COA. Consideration moved from Classic as the promisee in the context of the transaction as a whole. As originally set out in the August COA, the obligations undertaken by Classic were good consideration for the obligations undertaken by Limbungan, including the obligation to procure the guarantee. When the guarantee was given pursuant to Limbungan's obligations, (whether varied or not by the substitution of a different guarantor) the consideration it had in mind for the guarantee was the fulfilment by Classic of its obligations under the August COA. When Classic tendered performance for the first two voyages of the August COA by nominating the performing vessels and arranging for them to sail to the load ports, it was fulfilling its obligations under the August COA as part and parcel of the single transaction which included the guarantee. The performance of those obligations towards Limbungan in itself amounted to good consideration in relation to the third party guarantor, Lion. In paragraph 1 of the guarantee dated 28 August 2008, Lion represents that, by reason of its shareholdings in Limbungan, it benefits from Classic's performance of its obligations under the August COA. Presumably such benefit to a parent company is one of the reasons which could be put forward for the requirement suggested by Lion for a guarantee to be given only by a parent company. Regardless of that, there is no doubt that the clause specifically states that Lion benefits not only from Classic entering into the COA with Limbungan but also from performing its obligations under it and in those circumstances there can be no doubt that the future performance of the COA after 28 September, as actually occurred, does amount to good consideration moving from Classic. Furthermore, although the guarantee is dated 28 August and refers to the contract of affreightment already concluded on 13 August, there is an artificiality about Lion's argument, simply because the first few lines of the guarantee refer to the representations being made and the guarantee being given in order to induce Classic to enter into that COA. What is actually being stated is that the guarantee, whatever the date of its execution, operates to induce the conclusion of the COA. The reality of course is that it is part of a single transaction where the obligation to obtain the guarantee rested on the subsidiary Limbungan as at 13 August and the guarantee was executed pursuant to that obligation.

The promise of the future guarantee did induce Classic to enter the COA. It is merely that the guarantee itself, instead of being dated 13 August, is dated 28 August. Because of the closeness of parent and subsidiary, as referred to in the guarantee itself, there can be no doubt that the guarantee forms part and parcel of the single transaction and that, whatever the wording of the guarantee, it was provided by Lion, because without it, the transaction could not go ahead. In *Chitty on Contracts* (30th edition) paragraph 3–027 it is stated that, in determining whether consideration is past, the courts are not bound to apply a strictly chronological test. If the giving of the consideration and the making of the promise are substantially one transaction, the exact order in which these events occur is not decisive. It was accepted by Lion that the issue of a single transaction is always a question of degree but that what was envisaged by the authors was the case where the same parties were involved throughout. That does not however appear to me to be a sufficient answer to the point. It is the exchange of one obligation from one party for another from a different party which, in any event, changes the analysis, as set out earlier in this judgment.

There was argument about the decision of the Privy Council *Pao on v Lau Yiu Long* [1980] AC 614 and the statement in the judgment of the Board at page 631 that extrinsic evidence is admissible to prove the real consideration in three circumstances. The first is where no consideration or a nominal consideration is expressed in the instrument, which is not this case. The second is where the express consideration is in general terms or ambiguously stated. The third is where a substantial consideration is stated but an additional consideration exists which is not inconsistent with the terms of the written instrument. Lion submitted that, because the guarantee referred to the inducement of the COA by it, any reference to present or future consideration was inconsistent with that past consideration and could therefore not be admitted. I cannot accept this submission.

The inconsistency arises in the terms of the guarantee itself because an instrument dated 28 August 2008 is said to induce a contract of affreightment dated 13 August 2008. Given that, there is plainly room for reference to extrinsic evidence to clarify the anomaly. The guarantee, if executed on 28 August, without any prior commitment on the part of Lion could not induce the conclusion of the COA on 13 August. That in itself therefore could not be consideration at all, let alone past consideration. Since the guarantee refers to the benefit to Lion from Classic's performance of the obligations, there is reference to future consideration within the terms of the guarantee and the other matters to which I have already referred, insofar as they constitute additional consideration, are not inconsistent with that. As stated in *Halsburys Laws of Evidence* 4th edition Volume 12, as current in 1975, paragraph 1487: 'It is not in contradiction to the instrument to prove a larger consideration than that which is stated.' *Frith v Frith* [1906] AC 254 and the reference in it to *Clifford v Turrell* at pages 258–9 established that where there is one consideration stated, extrinsic evidence is allowed to prove any other consideration which existed and it is not in contradiction to the instrument to prove a larger consideration than that which is stated.

Performance of duty under existing contract

The traditional view is that there is no consideration if a party merely performs or promises to perform a duty already imposed on him under an existing contract.[29] Where parties are already in a contractual relationship, if one party promises to the other to do something above and beyond its contractual obligations while the other party simply performs as originally agreed,

29 See Furmston, *Cheshire, Fifoot & Furmston's Law of Contract*, pp 100–1.

the former will accrue no additional benefit as the promise to do more was not supported by good consideration. This rule is not always strictly applicable in light of developments in contract law. A benefit may exist if A promises to B to pay him more to fulfil his existing obligations where there is a risk of part or non-performance by B; it is, therefore, in A's, and even B's, interest to make such a promise, which may be considered to be based on good consideration. The courts are willing to expand their perspective on performing extra duties under existing contracts as good consideration, especially where fraud and economic duress are not involved.

Doucette v Marin 2008 CanLII 66625 (ON SC) (CA)

Facts: Victoria Doucette brought an action against Pauline Lisa Marin to enforce a warranty that there was no ureaformaldehyde foam insulation (UFFI) at the property Ms Doucette purchased at 742 9th Line, Innisfil, Ontario. The warranty was in a statutory declaration executed by Ms Marin on 27 January 2004 which stated at paragraph 9: 'The property above-described has not been insulated with Urea Formaldehyde Foam and this Warranty shall survive and not merge on closing.' Two weeks prior to executing the declaration containing the warranty, Ms Doucette and Ms Marin had executed an agreement of purchase and sale dated 8 January 2004. That agreement contained a UFFI warranty which stated at paragraph 22 that, 'to the best of Seller's knowledge no building on the property contains or has ever contained insulation that contains ureaformaldehyde'. The transaction closed on 30 January 2004. When Ms Doucette began to do renovations on the house, she discovered that the house was insulated with UFFI. Ms Marin's claim is that she executed the warranty concerning UFFI at the property with the advice of her lawyer Michael Telfer and such advice was negligent.

Ms Doucette's action was commenced against Ms Marin on 24 November 2006. She claimed a breach of the warranty and damages. Ms Marin issued the third party claim against Mr Telfer on 20 December 2006 alleging that she signed the declaration on Mr Telfer's advice and instruction. Mr Telfer delivered a defence to the third party claim and a statement of defence to the main action on 25 May 2007. Mr Telfer brought this motion to dismiss based on the fact that Ms Doucette was already contractually bound to close the transaction without an unconditional UFFI warranty and Ms Marin was contractually obligated to sell. Mr Telfer argued that since Ms Doucette was bound to complete the purchase under the contract, the closing of the purchase and sale was not consideration in law for the warranty. As there was no consideration, the unconditional warranty could not form the basis of Ms Doucette's claim against Ms Marin. Ms Doucette took the position that the court should not strike out the action as against Mr Telfer.

Held: Himel, J
In the case before me, at the time the unconditional UFFI warranty was given, the parties were already bound to complete the sale of the property on 30 January 2004 under the terms of the agreement of purchase and sale. In *Gilbert Steel Ltd. v University Construction Ltd.* [1973] 3 OR 268, the court wrote as follows at p 6: 'Long ago it was held that there is no consideration if all the plaintiff does is to perform, or promise the performance of an obligation already imposed upon him by a previous contract between himself and the defendant.' In *Yarlett v ReMax Realtron Realty Inc.* [1989] OJ No. 1379 (HC), in very similar facts to the case before me, the vendors signed a warranty in the agreement of purchase and sale that to the best of their knowledge the house they were selling contained no ureaformaldehyde. The vendors then signed a statutory declaration which stated that to the best of their knowledge and belief the property was not and never had been insulated with ureaformaldehyde and that the warranty would not merge on closing. They also signed a

written undertaking stating that in consideration of closing the transaction, they undertook that the property has not been insulated with ureaformaldehyde. The words 'To the best of our knowledge' were omitted. The plaintiff sued the vendors who added their lawyer for allowing them to execute the undertaking. Justice Granger dismissed the claim on the basis that there was no consideration for the signing of the declaration and undertaking . . . In the case before me, the statutory declaration which warrants the absolute truth of the statement and changes the warranty in the agreement of purchase and sale which states 'to the best of her knowledge and belief' was given without fresh consideration and was executed after the agreement of purchase and sale. Considering the jurisprudence under Rule 21.01, assuming that the facts as pleaded are true, and applying the decision of *Gilbert v Steel, supra*, I am of the view that it is 'plain and obvious' that the facts asserted disclose no reasonable cause of action against the third party.

Duty under law

Where a person or public officer is under a statutory obligation to perform a duty, his promise to discharge that duty is not good consideration, as he is legally bound to do so. A policeman is not expected to bargain with a member of the public over the price of protecting him,[30] as his legal duty is to 'protect and serve' the public. Where, however, that officer is asked to perform special duties or an act that is not within his usual scope of duties and so does, such as at a private event, depending on the nature of the request and the agreement concluded between the parties, this may be considered good consideration.[31]

Glasbrook v Glamorgan County Council [1925] AC 270 (GB)

Facts: The appellants were the owners of a valuable group of collieries about two miles from Swansea that was the subject of industrial action. Picketing which was not of a peaceful nature took place and as a result the safety men said they would no longer work because of insufficient police protection. The appellants requested that a police garrison be established at the mines but this request was refused. The police indicated that they already had a small presence at the colliery and were prepared to rapidly dispatch a large force at the sight of trouble but the appellants insisted on a garrison. The police agreed provided that a requisition be signed with a promise to pay as such a garrison would be a special duty. An agreement was signed and then the appellants refused to pay, claiming that the contract lacked consideration. It was argued that, when a subject has need of police protection and has done nothing to increase the risk, he is entitled to protection without payment and an agreement to pay is without consideration and contrary to public policy.

Held: Viscount Finley, LC; Shaw, Carson, Blanesburgh, LLJ
But it has always been recognised that, where individuals desire that services of a special kind which, though not within the obligations of a police authority, can most effectively be rendered by them, should be performed by members of the police force, the police authorities may . . . 'lend' the services of constables for that purpose on consideration of payment . . . I conclude therefore that the practice of lending constables for special duty in consideration of payment is not illegal or against public policy . . . I think that there

30 See Furmston, *Cheshire, Fifoot & Furmston's Law of Contract*, p 98.

31 See *Greater Manchester Police v Wigan Athletic AFC Ltd* [2008] EWCA Civ 1449 (19 December 2008) on this latter point.

was evidence to that effect, but it does not appear to me to follow that it was the duty of the police authority to provide the garrison. They were no doubt bound to protect the 'safety men' from violence, but it was not for the safety men to decide the form in which that protection should be given . . . I have come to the conclusion . . . that the appellants who deliberately entered into an agreement to pay for the services and maintenance of the police garrison and did not dispute their liability until they had had the benefit of those services for a period of nearly two months, cannot now repudiate their agreement.

Duty under contract in favour of third party

A question as to consideration based on the performance of duties arises when there is an examination of a situation where a promisor promises a benefit to a person to perform a contract which he is already obliged to perform for a third party. It has been held that an agreement to do an act which the promisor is under an existing obligation to a third party to do, may quite well amount to valid consideration since the promisee obtains the benefit of a direct obligation which he can enforce. While this may seem odd, as consideration is meant to move from the promisee as a detriment to him, in this particular case A's promise to C is said to be consideration for C's counter-promise to A; C was the promisor and the benefit that C got from A's promise satisfies the orthodox test of consideration for the counter-promise.[32]

New Zealand Shipping Co. Ltd. v A.M. Satterthwaite & Co. Ltd. [1975] AC 154 (PC) (GB)

Facts: On 5 June 1964 a bill of lading was issued by the agents for the Federal Steam Navigation Co. Ltd, the carrier, a wholly owned subsidiary company of the stevedore New Zealand Shipping Co. Ltd, to the Ajax Machine Tool Co. Ltd, the consignor, for the carriage of a drilling machine to Wellington in New Zealand. The respondent, A.M. Satterthwaite & Co. Ltd, was the consignee. The bill of lading bore on its face the following words: 'In accepting this bill of lading the shipper, consignee and the owners of the goods, and the holder of this bill of lading agree to be bound by all of its conditions, exceptions and provisions whether written, printed or stamped on the front or back hereof.' The consignee accepted the bill of lading and so the consignee agreed to its terms and conditions. In the course of its discharge from the ship at Wellington, the drilling machine was damaged by the negligence of the appellant, the stevedore, and the question for determination in this appeal was whether the appellant was exempted from liability for its negligence by the terms of the bill of lading which incorporated the Hague Rules in the Schedule to the Carriage of Goods by Sea Act 1924, and article III, rule 6, and discharged the carrier from all liability for loss or damage unless suit was brought within one year. This immunity was extended to the carrier's servants or agents, including independent contractors.

Held: Lord Wilberforce
The only question was, and is, the fourth question presented by Lord Reid, namely that of consideration . . . In their Lordships' opinion the present contract presents much less difficulty than others similar to it. It is one of carriage from Liverpool to Wellington. The carrier assumes an obligation to transport the goods and to discharge at the port of arrival.

32 *Chitty on Contracts*, fn 19, p 203.

The goods are to be carried and discharged, so the transaction is inherently contractual. It is contemplated that a part of this contract, viz discharge, may be performed by independent contractors – viz the appellant . . . There is possibly more than one way of analysing this business transaction into the necessary components; that which their Lordships would accept is to say that the bill of lading brought into existence a bargain initially unilateral but capable of becoming mutual, between the shipper and the appellant, made through the carrier as agent. This became a full contract when the appellant performed services by discharging the goods. The performance of these services for the benefit of the shipper was the consideration for the agreement by the shipper that the appellant should have the benefit of the exemptions and limitations contained in the bill of lading.

The conception of a 'unilateral' contract of this kind was recognised in *Great Northern Railway Co. v Witham* (1873) LR 9 CP 16 and is well established. This way of regarding the matter is very close to if not identical to that accepted by Beattie J in the Supreme Court: he analysed the transaction as one of an offer open to acceptance by action such as was found in *Carlill v Carbolic Smoke Ball Co.* [1893] 1 TB 256. But whether one describes the shipper's promise to exempt as an offer to be accepted by performance or as a promise in exchange for an act seems in the present context to be a matter of semantics. The words of Bowen LJ in *Carlill v Carbolic Smoke Ball Co.* [1893] 1 TB 256, 268 – 'why should not an offer be made to all the world which is to ripen into a contract with anybody who comes forward and performs the condition?' – seem to bridge both conceptions: he certainly seems to draw no distinction between an offer which matures into a contract when accepted and a promise which matures into a contract after performance, and, though in some special contexts (such as in connection with the right to withdraw) some further refinement may be needed, either analysis may be equally valid.

On the main point in the appeal, their Lordships are in substantial agreement with Beattie J. In their Lordships' opinion, consideration may quite well be provided by the appellant, as suggested, even though (or if) it was already under an obligation to discharge to the carrier. (There is no direct evidence of the existence or nature of this obligation, but their Lordships are prepared to assume it.) An agreement to do an act which the promisor is under an existing obligation to a third party to do, may quite well amount to valid consideration and does so in the present case: the promisee obtains the benefit of a direct obligation which he can enforce. This proposition is illustrated and supported by *Scotson v Pegg* (1861) 6 H & N 295 which their Lordships consider to be good law. The consignee is entitled to the benefit of, and is bound by, the stipulations in the bill of lading by his acceptance of it and request for delivery of the goods thereunder . . . Their Lordships will humbly advise Her Majesty that the appeal be allowed and the judgment of Beattie J restored.

TERMS

Contracts may be wholly in writing, partly in writing and partly oral, or wholly oral and the terms therein may be express or implied. Regardless of its form, for a contract to be valid and legally enforceable, it must contain all the essential terms necessary for the particular contract to be workable. It often happens, however, that an essential term may be inadvertently omitted as tacitly understood and will be supplied by the court to make the contract effective.[33] In other cases, the parties to the contract may have been unaware of legal obligations annexed by

33 See Furmston, *Cheshire, Fifoot & Furmston's Law of Contract*, pp 133–4.

statute to particular types of contracts which operate despite their ignorance or even contrary to what they intended.[34] One such statute, which deals with consumer protection, relates to the merchantability of goods and their fitness with respect to the purpose for which they were purchased where the buyer relies on the skill and specialist knowledge of the vendor in making the purchase (Sale of Goods Act).

Whether or not a statement becomes a term of the contract depends substantially on the intention of the parties. Some statements do not form part of the contract but may have been influential in closing the contract. While such statements are not part of the contract, if they are found to be false, this can give rise to an action on the basis of misrepresentation.

Sunset Crest Property Owners Inc v Peter Grannum Suit No. 1940 of 2007 (BB)

Facts: The issue which lay at the heart of the plaintiff's several claims against this defendant was whether the plaintiff and the defendant in his personal capacity were ever at any stage in a relationship of landlord and tenant. In other words, did the plaintiff and the defendant, Peter Grannum, ever enter into an agreement for a tenancy or lease?

Held: Crane-Scott, J
Even if the Court were in a position to accept the plaintiff's allegation that the defendant, Peter Grannum, was a sub-tenant of West Invest Inc and was in occupation of the premises when the head lease expired in August 2006, neither of the plaintiff's affidavits satisfactorily explains the nature of the relationship between the plaintiff and the defendant in the period immediately following the alleged termination of West Invest Inc's lease in August 2006. Given the unsatisfactory state of the evidence, many issues still remain unresolved and unexplained. For example, when West Invest Inc's lease with the plaintiff terminated in August 2006, the former sub-tenant (whoever this was) appears to have remained in occupation of the premises. Did the former sub-tenant become a tenant at sufferance of the plaintiff? Did the former sub-tenant continue to occupy the premises rent free? Did the plaintiff company overtly give the former sub-tenant permission to occupy the premises? If so, on what terms? Did the former sub-tenant at any time ever acknowledge the plaintiff as the owner of the premises and the person entitled to possession thereof? . . .

Whatever the relationship between the plaintiff and West Invest Inc's sub-tenant may have been prior to January 2007, the plaintiff's main point appears to be that an agreement for a periodic tenancy was concluded between the plaintiff company and the defendant following a conversation between Mr Armstrong and the defendant in January 2007. According to Mr Armstrong's affidavits, the agreed rent and other terms of the tenancy were subsequently set out in the plaintiff's letter of 16 February 2007 (AA1) confirming the arrangements . . .

The Court has had regard to Section 149 of the Barbados Property Act, Cap. 236 which, while providing that an instrument in writing is essential to create the relationship of lessor and lessee, also provides that an instrument in writing is not necessary for the creation of a periodic tenancy. Although an agreement for a periodic tenancy need not be in writing, it is incumbent on the plaintiff to prove the following essential terms of the contract:

(i) the parties to the contract;
(ii) the premises to be let or demised;

34 See Furmston, *Cheshire, Fifoot & Furmston's Law of Contract*, p 134.

(iii) the duration of the term; and

(iv) the amount of rent payable or the circumstances from which it can be ascertained . . .

In the absence of an instrument in writing signed by the defendant expressly recognising the existence of the terms of the agreement, the plaintiff may produce evidence that the agreement has been part performed. Such evidence must be certain and definite and the acts of part performance relied upon must also be unequivocally referable to the existence of a contract between the parties . . .

In the Court's view, the fact that a letter purporting to confirm an oral agreement which is said to have been reached between two parties is issued by one party to the other, does not by itself establish the existence of an agreement on the terms set out in the letter. In the absence of a written response or acknowledgment by the other party that he accepts what is stated in the letter as constituting the agreement there is no 'meeting of the minds' and one would necessarily have to deduce the existence of an agreement from the acts of the parties or from other circumstances. The plaintiff's letter of confirmation of 16 February 2007 (AA1) fails to support Mr Armstrong's evidence at paragraph 7 of his affidavit of 1 November 2007 that he had personally spoken to the defendant and reached an understanding in January 2007 about the terms on which he would be permitted to remain in occupation of the premises. While it is not clear whether this is a typographical error, the so-called letter of confirmation on which the plaintiff relies, refers instead to the conversation with the defendant having occurred on 31 January 2006. This adds additional confusion into an already uncertain state of affairs. Mr Weekes submitted that the defendant had part performed the alleged agreement and had paid rent pursuant to the agreement. However, Mr Armstrong's affidavits make no express mention of this, although there is some reference in the plaintiff's letter of confirmation (AA1) of West Side Scuba Centre having stopped paying the VAT Department garnished rent in October 2006. As the relationship between the defendant and West Side Scuba Centre has not satisfactorily been explained, and since the alleged agreement was concluded in January 2007 there is no evidence of part performance of the alleged agreement by the defendant after January 2007 . . .

In conclusion, the Court is of the view that the plaintiff has not satisfactorily established that it is entitled to summary judgment at this interlocutory stage. On the one hand, the plaintiff's two affidavits are unsatisfactory in that they fail to clearly establish how the defendant (in his personal capacity) came to be in occupation of the premises as alleged, initially as a sub-tenant of West Invest Inc and subsequently as a tenant of the plaintiff. No independent evidence was adduced in support of the facts asserted . . . In the circumstances, the plaintiff's application for summary judgment is refused and the defendant is permitted leave to defend.

Express terms

Express terms are those terms that are contained in a contract and are openly articulated by the parties to the contract, whether orally or in writing. Where an issue arises out of a written contract, there will not usually be any difficulty in discovering the problematic term and it will rest with the courts to interpret it. In the case of an oral contract, the courts will make a determination on the basis of the evidence presented.[35] In addition, the courts will have to objectively determine the original intention of the parties in interpreting the terms of the contract.

35 See Furmston, *Cheshire, Fifoot & Furmston's Law of Contract*, p 134.

Bariki International Limited et al v Jamaican Treat Limited Claim No. HCV-00545 of 2004 (JM)

Facts: Balteano Duffus, the second claimant, was a shareholder and director of Bariki International Limited and Jabico Investments Limited, the first and third claimants. Carlton Allen was the managing director of Jamaica Treat Limited, the defendant. These two gentlemen entered into contractual arrangements whereby Mr Duffus's company Bariki International Limited was retained to provide professional financial and management consulting services by Mr Allen's company Jamaican Treat Limited. Mr Allen in his witness statement/evidence-in-chief described Jamaica Treat Limited as an agro-processing company which primarily processed canned ackees and occasionally canned calaloo. The factory was located at Bushy Park in St Catherine and commenced production in about mid-August 2003. He alleged that he was introduced to Mr Duffus as someone able to provide expertise in getting the factory up and running. He was advised by Mr Duffus that he could 'obtain financing to obtain working capital for the defendant' through loans from either National Commercial Bank or the National Export-Import Bank of Jamaica also known as Ex-Im Bank. He authorised Mr Duffus to apply for and obtain these loans and as a result of the engagement of Mr Duffus the written agreements were signed on 2 January 2002. The first claimant contended that they provided the services pursuant to the contracts but were not paid fully as required by them. The defendant countered that he had paid what he ought to and further denied that Bariki International Limited provided any professional financial management consulting services as agreed or at all.

Held: Williams, J
The Law: The relationship between Bariki International Limited and Jamaican Treat Limited, it is agreed, is by virtue of two contracts dated 2 January 2002. It may therefore prove useful at this time to restate one of the basic principles of the law of contract as succinctly put by Justice PO Lawrence in *Jacobs v Batavia and General Trust* [1924] 1 Ch 287 at page 295:

> It is firmly established as a rule of law that parol evidence cannot be admitted to add to, vary or contradict a deed or other written instrument. Accordingly, it has been held that parol evidence will not be admitted to prove that some particular term, which had been verbally agreed upon, had been omitted (by design or otherwise) from a written instrument constituting a valid and operative contract between the parties.

As the law developed there have been cases in which extrinsic evidence has been held admissible. In one instance while the rule is said to prevent one party from relying on extrinsic evidence as to express terms of the contract, however, where the contract is silent on matters on which a term is usually implied, parol evidence may be given to support or rebut the usual implication. In this instant case, the defendant urges that to give efficacy to these contracts, terms need to be implied. The case of *The Moorcock* [1886–90] All ER at page 530 is relied on in support of this, and indeed the case is regarded as the leading authority on implied terms. A restatement of parts of the headnote proves useful:

> An implied warrant, as distinguished from an express contract or express warranty is founded on the presumed intention of the parties and upon reason. It is the implication which the law draws from what must obviously have been the intention of the parties, an implication which the law draws with the object of giving such efficacy to the transaction as both parties must have intended it should have and preventing such a failure of consideration as cannot have been within the contemplation of either of the parties. The reasonable implication which the law draws must differ according to the circumstances of the various transactions, and in business transactions what the law desires to effect by the implication is to give such business efficacy to the transaction as must have been intended by both parties, not to impose on one side all the perils of the transaction or to emancipate one side from all the burdens, but to

> make each party promise in law as much as it must have been in the contemplation of both parties he should be responsible for.

It is generally accepted that in a contract of employment the employee impliedly undertakes that he is reasonably skilled, that he will faithfully serve his employer and not act contrary to his employer's interest, and will use reasonable care and skill in the performance of his duties.

Application of the law to the facts found: There were two contracts – one dealt primarily with the issue of the sourcing of funds and the other the engaging of the services of the first claimant to perform consulting services. It is useful to note that only the latter spoke to a specific time the contract would last. The first claim by Bariki International arises out of the contract dealing with the sourcing of funds – referred to as the 'short form' contract. There is no dispute that funds were sourced in total a loan of [JM]$21.8 million from Ex-Im bank and a grant of US$50,000 from Cariforum Agribusiness Research and Trading Fund [CARTF]. The clause now in contention deals with the matter of payment for services rendered. The clause states:

> In consideration for services rendered, client agrees to pay consultant a service fee of 3% of the gross loan. Under the terms of such an agreement client will pay consultant 25% of the total fee in advance of the commencement of the consulting services. The remaining 75% of the fees shall be deemed earned and payable at the time and delivery and acceptance of the loan commitment.

The defendant's argument is that this clause is ambiguous and requires the implication of a term to provide the necessary business efficacy and reasonableness to the transaction. Further it is urged this clause should be construed *contra proferentem* such that it is to be construed against the party in whose favour it was made. The argument of the first claimant is of course that the terms are quite clear and unambiguous. The fee was 3 per cent of the gross loan – this fee was deemed to be earned and payable at the time and delivery and acceptance of the loan commitment. The defendant urged that the clause should be interpreted so that the fee would be 3 per cent of the loan amount actually received. The problem arose because only [JM]$7 million of the loan committed was actually disbursed. The defendant was unable to service the loan due to the fact that no production commenced at the defendant's factory. He defaulted on the loan and ultimately could not come up with requisite security requirement, and the commitment letter was withdrawn. Mr Allen for the defendant argues that Mr Duffus should have been in a position to recognise that the defendant would have been unable to meet the collateral requirements stipulated.

As to the Cariforum Agribusiness Research and Trading Fund [CARTF] agreement, the parties agree that the monies obtained [were] a grant and not a loan. Mr Duffus under cross-examination acknowledges the short-form contract related to loans and not grants. In his witness statement/evidence-in-chief he said it was agreed between the parties that the claimant would be paid 3 per cent of the funding secured including grants. In his evidence under cross-examination he said that rather than going and drafting up a separate contract for the grant, the spirit of the contract of 2002 [re loans] would be relied on for the grant. Mr Allen points to the fact that the involvement of Bariki with this project as service provider was completely separate from his earlier involvement meaning the payment structure as outlined in the short-form contract is not applicable. A separate agreement, he argued, covered the arrangements pursuant to the Cariforum Agribusiness Research and Trading Fund [CARTF] grant. Ultimately the parties are bound by the terms of the contract they signed and in this case where the terms, to my mind, are indeed clear, they will have to honour those terms.

Incorporation by express reference

Terms can be incorporated into a contract by express reference to another document. A reference to a popular term such as 'FOB' (Free on Board) or 'CIF' (Cost, Insurance and Freight), as defined by Incoterms,[36] in a contract is sufficient to incorporate the meaning ascribed in Incoterms as part of the express terms of a contract. Where, however, the incorporated terms conflict with the terms of the agreement, the clauses of the written agreement will prevail.

Barrack Construction Ltd v National Housing Corporation No. 1320 of 2001 (BB)

Facts: By a contract dated 13 August 1998 the plaintiff agreed to construct a five-storey office complex at Warrens, St Michael for the defendant. A dispute arose between the parties and the plaintiff wished to proceed to arbitration. He sought an order that the parties proceed to arbitration within 14 days. The defendant contended that the dispute, which related to a certificate of the architect as to the date that the works should reasonably have been completed, was not referrable to arbitration at that stage, but only after one of the events mentioned in clause 35(2) of the JCT Standard Form, which was incorporated into the agreement.

Held: Payne, J
The plaintiff's case is that clause 35(2) of the standard form is in conflict with clause 22 of the agreement and that the agreement should prevail. Counsel relies on the rule of interpretation expressed as follows at paragraph 8.12 in *The Interpretation of Contracts*, 2nd Edition by Kim Lewison, QC: 'Where a contract incorporates the terms of another document and the terms of that other document conflict with the terms of the contract, the terms of the contract will prevail.' Clause 22 of the agreement is as follows:

> In case any dispute or difference shall arise between the Employer and the Contractor either during the progress or after the completion or abandonment of the works as to the construction of the Contract or as to any matter or thing arising hereunder or in connection therewith either party may forthwith give to the other notice in writing of such dispute or difference and the same shall be and is hereby referred to arbitration in accordance with the Arbitration Act Cap. 110 of Barbados.

Clause 35 of the JCT Standard Form is as follows:

(1) Provided always that in case any dispute or difference shall arise between the Employer or the Architect on his behalf and the Contractor, either during the progress or after the completion or abandonment of the works, as to the construction of this contract or as to any matter or thing or whatsoever nature arising thereunder or in connection therewith (including any matter or thing left by this Contract to the discretion of the Architect or the withholding by the Architect of any certificate to which the Contractor may claim to be entitled or the measurement and valuation mentioned in clause 30(5)(a) of these Conditions or the rights and liabilities of the parties under clauses 25, 26, 32, or 33 of these Conditions), then such dispute or difference shall be and is hereby referred to the arbitration and final decision of a person to be agreed between the parties, or, failing agreement within 14 days after either party has given to the other a written request to concur in the appointment of an Arbitrator, a person

36 International Commercial Terms. These are standard trade definitions used in international sales contracts.

to be appointed on the request of either party by the President or a Vice-President for the time being of the Barbados Institute of Architects.

(2) Such reference, except on article 3 or article 4 of the Articles of Agreement, or on the questions whether or not the issue of an instruction is empowered by these Conditions, whether or not a certificate has been improperly withheld or is not in accordance with these Conditions, or on any dispute or difference under clauses 32 and 33 of these conditions, shall not be opened until after Practical Completion or alleged Practical Completion of the Works or termination or alleged termination of the Contractor's Employment under this Contract, or abandonment of the Works, unless with the written consent of the Employer or the Architect on his behalf and the Contractor.

Mr Shepherd submits that clause 35(2) above is merely a proviso to 35(1), which is in effect the same as clause 22 of the agreement. He contends that there is no conflict between clause 35(2) of the JCT Standard Form and clause 22 of the agreement. In *Pagnan SpA v Tradax* [1987] 3 All ER 565 it was a special condition of a contract of sale that the sellers would provide for an export certificate. The contract also incorporated the terms of GAFTA Form 119, clause 19 of which was a standard *force majeure* clause providing for cancellation of the contract where the sellers could not obtain the export certificate. The contract contained an 'inconsistency clause', which stated that the special conditions were to prevail over the standard terms. The sellers were unable to obtain the necessary export certificate.

The Court of Appeal (Dillon, Woolf and Bingham LJJ) held, quoting from the Headnote to the report, as follows:

> The special condition was to be construed fairly in the context of the contract as a whole and in its factual setting in order to ascertain the true intention of the parties. On its true construction, the special condition imposed an absolute obligation on the sellers to obtain an export certificate, and prima facie there had been a breach of that obligation. It followed that if there was inconsistency between the special condition and cl 19 of GAFTA Form 119 then, applying the inconsistency clause, the special condition would prevail and the sellers would be liable for their failure to obtain the export certificate. However, the mere fact that an apparently wide and absolute provision was subject to limitation, modification or qualification by other provisions did not necessarily make those other provisions inconsistent or repugnant, since for inconsistency to arise the clauses in question had to be incapable of being sensibly read together. In the circumstances, the special condition could be read in combination with cl 19 so that in the events specified in cl 19, but not otherwise, the sellers would be released from their contractual obligation to obtain a certificate and the contract or any unfulfilled part of it would be cancelled. Since the circumstances which prevented the sellers from obtaining the export certificate fell within the closely circumscribed ambit of cl 19, it followed that the sellers were excused from liability by cl 19. The appeal would accordingly be dismissed.

In *Forbes v Git* 1922 IAC 256, the appellant contracted with the respondents to carry out work in altering their restaurant. The contract by its first clause witnessed that in consideration of [BB]$3000 payable by three instalments, the appellant agreed to furnish the materials and perform the services stated in the contract. Details of the work followed, and there was a final clause to the effect that the respondents were to pay to the appellant the value of the materials provided and labour done, each at 12.5 per cent over cost, whether that value exceeded or was less than [BB]$3000. The materials and labour considerably exceeded that sum, and the appellant sued for a balance based upon the final clause. The Privy Council, reversing a decision of the Supreme Court of Canada, stated at page 259 per Lord Wrenbury:

> The principle of law to be applied may be stated in few words. If in a deed an earlier clause is followed by a later clause which destroys altogether the obligation created by the earlier clause, the later clause is to be rejected as repugnant and the earlier clause prevails. In this case the two clauses cannot be reconciled and the earlier provision in the deed prevails over the later. Thus if A covenants to pay 100 [pounds] and the deed subsequently provides that he shall not be liable under his covenant, that later provision is to be rejected as repugnant and void for it altogether destroys the covenant. But if the later clause does not destroy but only qualifies the earlier, then the two are to be read together and effect is to be given to the intention of the parties as disclosed by the deed as a whole. Thus if A covenants to pay 100 [pounds] and the deed subsequently provides that he shall be liable to pay only at a future named date or in a future defined event or if at the due date of payment he holds a defined office, then the absolute covenant to pay is controlled by the words qualifying the obligation in manner described. *Furnivall v Coombes* (1843) 5 Man & G 736) is an illustration of the former case; *Williams v Hathaway* (1877) 6 ChD 544 is an illustration of the latter. In the latter case there could be no question if the later provision of the deed were introduced by the word 'but' or the words 'provided always nevertheless', or the like. But there is no necessity to find any such words. If a later clause says in so many words or as matter of construction that an earlier clause is to be qualified in a certain way, effect can be given and must be given to both clauses.

I conclude therefore that a clause in the incorporated JCT Standard Form can be rejected as in conflict or inconsistent with a clause in the agreement only where the conflict or inconsistency is such that effect cannot fairly be given to both clauses. That plainly is not the case here. Clause 35(2) of the standard form merely limits, qualifies or controls, without destroying altogether, clause 22 of the agreement. Clause 35(2) is merely a proviso to clause 35(1), which is in effect the same as clause 22 of the agreement. The plaintiff's summons is therefore dismissed. Costs for the defendant to be agreed or taxed.

Implied terms

Where a contract is in writing and signed, the party signing it is usually regarded as bound by it whether or not he has read the document or understands its full legal effect. Although the primary obligations are contained in express terms, it is quite unusual for the parties to express all of the primary obligations, or to provide for every contingency. The court, in these circumstances, usually implies terms to fill in the gaps in the contract, based on the circumstances of the contractual relationship.

The court will only imply a term when the following conditions are satisfied:

(1) it must be reasonable and equitable;
(2) it must be necessary to give business efficacy to the contract, so that no term will be implied if the contract is effective without it;
(3) it must be so obvious that 'it goes without saying';
(4) it must be capable of clear expression;
(5) it must not contradict any express term of the contract.[37]

Apart from these specific requirements, terms may be implied in a contract: (1) based on custom or usage; (2) as the legal incidents of a particular class or kind of contract; (3) based

37 Zeller, B, 'Good Faith – Is it a Contractual Obligation?' (2003), *Bond Law Review* 15(2): 215–39, p 233. Available at: http://epublications.bond.edu.au/cgi/viewcontent.cgi?article=1268&context=blr.

on the presumed intention of the parties where the implied term must be necessary to give 'business efficacy' to a contract; (4) as meeting the 'officious bystander' test as a term which the parties would say, if questioned, that they had obviously assumed; (5) based on statutory obligations.

Ronicles Limited Claimant v 1. DCG Properties Ltd. 2. Stewart Title Eastern Caribbean Ltd. Defendants
Claim No. SLUHCV2011/0547 (LC)

Facts: The first defendant[] is a company undertaking the development of 'Le Paradis' a resort hotel and condominiums [in] Saint Lucia. The second defendant[] is registered in Saint Lucia as an external company, but is organized and exists under the Companies Act, Revised Statu[t]es of Anguilla, and is enjoined in these proceedings having assumed the responsibility of title guarantors and escrow agent under the Sale and Purchase Agreement between the claimant and first defendant and under the Service Agreement and Escrow Agreement.

On the 4th June 2007, the claimant and the first defendant entered a Sale and Purchase Agreement (SPA)[] for the sale to the claimant of a unit known as Unit No. 12–3-R, within the 'L[e] Paradis' development, the purchase price of which was US$945,000.00. The claimant at the time was interested in becoming an owner of one such condominium. The SPA contained various addenda including a financial addendum executed on the 4th June 2007. Scheduled to the SPA was a service agreement executed as between the two defendants an[] Escrow Agreement (EA) which appeared to be a set of escrow instructions and procedures. Both by reference were incorporated into and formed part of the SPA.

Under the SPA, the claimant was to have purchased the condominium unit by instalment payments, which payments were triggered by specific events. The SPA also detailed the recourse available to the claimant should the first defendant not meet its obligations under the agreement. The first defendant encountered difficulties and delays affecting its timely completion of 'Le Paradis', whereon the claimant sued the first defendant pursuant to article 1387 of the Civil Code of Saint Lucia for liquidated damages for breach of contract in the sum of US $94,500.00 or EC $256,747.05 and both defendants for the return and replenishment of the escrow account in the total sum of US $283,500.00 or EC $770,241.15. It transpired that the monies paid by the claimant to the second defendant as escrow agent had been disbursed to the first defendant by the second defendant. In particular the claimant has sued the second defendant for purportedly failing to honour its legal obligations as escrow agents. These proceedings are to determine the interpretation of the obligation of the second defendant as escrow agent.

Held: Taylor-Alexander, J
The vexing issues are the differing interpretation and import given to the clauses of the conjoined agreements by the various parties to it. The interpretation of their contractual obligation is to be derived from the objective common intention of the parties to the contract, which counsel for the claimant submits, on the authority of *Reardon Smith Line Ltd v Hansen-Tangen* [1976] 3 All ER 570 at 574[,] is to be taken as the intention which reasonable people would have had if placed in the situation of the parties. I agree with counsel for the claimant that the cardinal rule on the intention of parties to contractual agreements is first derived by reference to the clear and unambiguous words used in the contract. *Chitty on Contract[s]* provides thus:

> The cardinal presumption is that the parties have intended what they have in fact said so that their words must be construed as they stand, that is to say the meaning of a document or of a particular part of it is to be sought in the document itself. One must consider the words used,

> not what one may guess to be the intention of the parties. However this is not to say that the meaning of the words in a written document must be ascertained by reference to the words of the document alone. In principle the courts will look at all the circumstances surrounding the making of the contract which would assist in determining how the language of the document would have been understood by a reasonable man.

It is with caution that the court must imply any terms into a written agreement, as to do so would make the terms thereof binding on an unsuspecting party and change the nature of the contractual relationship. If the court were to imply any such term it would be on satisfaction of the requirements contained in *BP Refinery (Westernport) Pty Ltd v Shire of Hastings*, namely that:

a. It must be reasonable and equitable;
b. It must be necessary to give business efficacy to the contract so that no term will be implied if the contract is effective without it;
c. It must be so obvious that it goes without saying;
d. It must be capable of clear expression; and
e. It must not contradict any express term of the contract.

Clauses 2 and 4 of the SPA and clause 8 of the financial addendum are the provision over which much of the controversy between the parties rests. The relevant parts of the clauses read as follows:

Clause 2 SPA
Payment of the Purchase Price: Buyer agrees to make the following payments against the purchase price:

Payment	*Due Date*	*Amount*
Priority Reservation Deposit USD$2500	Paid/Refunded	
Initial Deposit USD$20,000	Upon execution of the Reservation Agreement or this Agreement by Buyer PAID	
30% of Purchase Price (less the Deposit previously paid by Buyer)	Within 7 days after execution of this agreement by Buyer	USD$263500
0	Upon completion of foundation pouring for the building within which the Unit will be located	$ 0
0	Upon commencement of the roofing for The building within which the Unit will be Located	$ 0
Balance of Purchase Price plus all remaining sums due by Buyer under this Agreement	At Closing (as defined in Section 10)	USD$661500

> All deposit payments are collectively referred to as the 'Deposit' or 'Deposits'. Deposits must be made by wire transfer to the escrow agent. The balance due at closing must be paid by wire transfer in United States. Unless otherwise agreed if the buyer fails to pay any deposit obligated to do, buyer will pay a late funding charge equal to interest on such deposit at a rate equal to 8% plus the prime lending rate per annum then applicable in St. Lucia . . .

Clause 4 SPA

> . . . buyer acknowledges and agrees that all the Deposits will be released from the escrow agent to the seller upon receipt upon a written request from the seller to the escrow agent together with written confirmation that the respective construction milestones set forth in section 2 have been satisfied, provided however that at all times at least 5%of the Purchase Price shall remain in escrow with the escrow agent. At closing any deposits not previously disbursed to the seller, will be released to the seller. Any interest earned on the deposits shall accrue solely to the benefit of the seller, and shall not be credited against the Purchase Price of the unit. No interest will assume to be earned.

Clause 8 Financial Addendum

> In the event Buyer waives with written notice to seller[] the financial contingency or obtains a financing commitment and does not terminate the purchase agreement, the buyer shall be under no obligation to pay any additional deposits, interest or fees until closing. Seller shall be obligated to fund the construction of the unit at its sole costs including any interest charges incurred during the construction period.

I am not persuaded that either of the defendants have overcome the requirements of *BP Refinery (Westernport) Pty Ltd v Shire of Hastings (ante)* to allow the court to imply into the agreements terms other than what is provided. I am satisfied that the words of the agreements read clearly and unambiguously, such that there is no need to read into it any clarifying words. To give the agreements the meaning that the defendants have ascribed to it will produce a commercially absurd result, removing any obligation or contractual responsibility of the second defendant/escrow agent to the claimant, which could not be the intention of the parties or the comfort and assurance the EA intended to give the claimant.

Jorge Raizman (Plaintiff) [As Principal Agent for a Business T/A Ride N' Style] v Aftabay Raja (Defendant) CV 1526 of 2006 (BB)

Facts: In August of 1999 Jorge Raizman ('the Plaintiff') and his business partner, Mr. Mark Harris, who is now deceased, went into business together under the business name 'Ride N' Style' which was duly registered with the Corporate Affairs and Intellectual Property Office. As its name implies, the 'Ride N' Style' business was intended by the partners to provide transportation services to the public by the operation of public service vehicles, namely, two route taxis or 'ZRs', as they are more commonly known. In furtherance of their 'Ride N' Style' business, the Plaintiff and Mark Harris purchased two route taxis, ZR-2774 and ZR-283, along with the relevant government permits through a loan of $167,000.00 which they obtained from Barclays Bank plc (as it then was). The loan to the partnership was secured by a charge against property owned by the Plaintiff at Chancery Lane in the parish of Christ Church. The Plaintiff and Mark Harris were joint principals on the loan and, as such, they were required to pay interest on all outstanding amounts due to the bank. With respect to the partnership arrangement, it appears not to be in dispute that Mark Harris was responsible for the daily operations of 'Ride N' Style', while the Plaintiff remained in the background as the silent partner who was consulted as necessary. By May, 2000, it became evident to both partners that their 'Ride N' Style' business not only required more time and effort than it was worth, but more importantly, was less profitable than expected. Mark Harris therefore advertised the route taxis for sale and entered into negotiations with the Defendant for the sale and purchase of both route taxis together with the relevant permits. The Defendant responded to Mark Harris' advertisement for the sale of the route taxis and entered into a written agreement dated June 1, 2000 with the Plaintiff and Mark Harris to purchase them for the sum of $150,000.00. The Plaintiff in his capacity as the principal agent and sole surviving partner of the 'Ride N' Style' business formerly operated by himself and his deceased partner, Mr. Mark Harris, instituted a claim in contract against the Defendant for the sum of $150,000.00 together with the interest of $9,419.44. In his Statement of Claim, the Plaintiff contended that it was an implied term of the Agreement that the amount of $150,000.00 to be paid by the Defendant for the purchase of the public service vehicles would be treated as a loan made by the Plaintiff and Mark Harris to the Defendant. The Plaintiff further alleged in his Statement of Claim that another implied term of the Agreement was that the Defendant would pay the customary interest charged by banks for any amount outstanding on the sum of $150,000.00. In his Defence, the Defendant further claimed that he had paid a sum of $90,000.00 into the account at Barclays Bank plc on diverse dates. He also alleged that his father had also paid on his behalf the sum of $80,000.000 to Mark Harris in full settlement of the claim and he was therefore discharged from the payment of any further sum due under the Agreement.

Held: Crane-Scott, J
The Court is required to interpret the Agreement to determine whether pursuant to the Agreement, the Defendant was obliged to pay not only the sum of $150,000.00 specified therein but any other sums due on the outstanding loan with Barclays Bank Plc, including interest and bank charges. The Court begins by observing that in interpreting a contractual agreement, the role of the Court is, according to Lord Hoffmann, to ascertain '. . . the meaning which the document would convey to a reasonable person having the background knowledge which would reasonably have been available to the parties in the situation in which they were at the time of the contract': *Investors Compensation Scheme v West Bromwich Building Society* [1998] 1 WLR 896 cited in Kim Lewison, *The Interpretation of Contracts* (Third Edition) at p 18. The Court is required to establish the mutual intentions of the parties as to the legal obligations assumed by each party under the contract, in so far as this can be determined from the language they have used, considered in light of the surrounding circumstances and the object of the contract: *Lewison (supra)* at para 2.02 and para 2.04. The Court is also required to construe the Agreement as a whole and to give the words used in the Agreement their ordinary and plain meaning, unless the context indicates otherwise: *Ibid* at para 2.01 and 5.01. Where there is any doubt as to the meaning of a contract or a term within it, the general principle is that the contract shall be construed against the party who was responsible for drafting the Agreement: *Ibid* at para 7.07. The Court accepts that terms may be implied into contracts where it appears from the language of the contract and the circumstances under which it was made that the parties had intended such a term to be inferred: *Chitty on Contracts* (Thirtieth Edition) Volume 1, para 13–004. However, in order for a term to be implied the term must be (1) reasonable and equitable; (2) necessary to achieve business efficacy; (3) obvious; (4) capable of clear expression; and (5) not contradict any express contractual term: *Lewison (supra)* at para 6.03 . . . Given the circumstances surrounding the Agreement and its provisions, including the Defendant's obligation to make payments directly to the loan account held by the Plaintiff and his partner, the Court is persuaded by the submissions of Counsel for the Plaintiff that it is reasonable and necessary, in order to give effect to the intention of the parties, for a term to be implied in to the Agreement that the Defendant was obliged to pay any interest and other bank charges associated with the loan.

Officious bystander

Whatever may be the precise legal criterion for implying terms into a contract upon which the parties have not expressly agreed, it would always be necessary for a court of the common law legal tradition to be very cautious about the imposition on the parties of a term that, for themselves, they had failed, omitted or refused to agree upon. Such caution is inherent in the economic freedom to which the law of contract gives effect. Absent some statutory or equitable basis for intervention, it is ordinarily left to the parties themselves to formulate any agreement to which they consent to be bound in law. As MacKinnon LJ, who is usually credited with inventing the fiction of the 'officious bystander', admitted: '[I]n most . . . cases the Court has . . . to find . . . the obvious common agreement, upon a matter as to which it must have the strongest suspicion that neither party ever thought of it at all, and that, if they had, they would very likely have been in hopeless disagreement what provision to make about it.'[38]

As far as implications in fact are concerned, it has been suggested that resorting to the officious bystander test for determining an implied contractual term may unduly restrain the importation of implied terms proper to a particular case. The officiousness of the bystander merely explains the intervention of that fictional person in the private business of the parties; it says nothing about the attitude or approach of the bystander concerned. There is no reason why officiousness and reasonableness should be incompatible. Nevertheless, the time may be coming when the fiction will be dispensed with completely and the courts acknowledge candidly that, in defined circumstances, the law to which they give effect permits, according to a desired policy, the imposition upon parties of terms and conditions for which they have omitted to provide expressly.

Carmel Smith v Statutory Authorities Service Commission (2007) HCA S-95 of 2004 (TT)

Facts: The respondent, Carmel Smith, was employed as the deputy director of the National Lotteries Control Board. She was charged with misconduct contrary to an implied term of her contract of employment that an officer must exercise his/her authority reasonably. The Particulars of Charge were as follows:

> That you Carmel Smith, deputy director, NLCB, did an act in breach of an implied term of your contract of employment namely not to exercise your authority unreasonably when during 2000 and 2002 you received a benefit above and beyond your entitlement as director, by accepting and using motor vehicle PBJ 3133 while enjoying an upkeep allowance on your personally owned motor vehicle.

It was alleged that the applicant breached this term by accepting a double benefit, namely, the upkeep allowance (of TT$1,000 per month) on her personal vehicle while enjoying the fully maintained NLCB vehicle. The contention was that the implied term, the breach of which she was accused, did not exist.

Held: Aboud, J (Ag)
It is well established that the courts have power to imply terms into contracts of every description, including contracts of employment. In these cases, a deficiency in the meaning or effect of the contract arises because a term is not expressed. The court implies the term to remedy the deficiency. The case law reveals various categories of terms that the courts have implied. In this case, the alleged term falls into the category of one that may be implied because it was so obviously a stipulation in the agreement that the parties must have intended it to form part of their contract . . .

38 Per Kirby, J in *Roxborough v Rothmans of Pall Mall Australia Pty Ltd* [2001] HCA 68 (6 December 2001) (AU), para 161.

Prima facie, that which is left to be implied and need not be expressed is something so obvious that it goes without saying; so that, if, while the parties were making their bargain, an officious bystander was to suggest some express provision for it in the agreement, they would immediately retort, 'oh, of course' . . .

A term will not, however, be implied unless the court is satisfied that both parties would, as reasonable men, have agreed to it had it been suggested to them. *Luxor (Eastbourne) Ltd v Cooper* [1941] AC 108. The term must, in all the circumstances, be equitable and reasonable. See *Young & Marten v Mc Manus Childs Ltd* [1969] 1 AC 454, 465. However, a term should not merely be implied because it would be reasonable to do so, or because it would improve the contract . . . The touchstone is always necessity and not merely reasonableness: *Liverpool City Council v Irwin* [1977] AC 239. The term to be implied must also be capable of being formulated with sufficient clarity and precision: *Shell UK Ltd v Lostock Garage Ltd* [1976] 1 WLR 1187.

The respondents submitted that the court should imply a term that the parties would not misconduct themselves in a manner that would undermine the trust and confidence necessary to maintain the relationship between employer and employee. In *Mahmud v BCCI* [1998] AC 20, such a term was implied into a contract made between an employer bank and its employee. The employer bank had conducted a dishonest or corrupt business, and the employee had suffered injury to his reputation when its misconduct was revealed and it went into liquidation. The employee sued for damages. In the course of the proceedings, the parties had agreed that such a term was implied. Lord Steyn, in the House of Lords, said this at p 45:

> The employer's primary case is based on a formulation of the implied term that has been applied at first instance and in the Court of Appeal. It imposes reciprocal duties on the employer and the employee. Given that this case is concerned with alleged obligations of an employer I will concentrate on its effect on the position of employers. For convenience, I will set out the term again. It is expressed to impose an obligation that the employer shall not: 'Without reasonable and proper cause, conduct itself in a manner calculated and likely to destroy or seriously damage the relationship of confidence and trust between an employer and employee.'

. . . In this passage, Lord Steyn describes the implied term as creating reciprocal obligations. It seems to me that a term must be implied in the contract of employment between the applicant and the respondent. I would define it exactly like Lord Steyn. I say so because the NLCB is a public authority and its officers are performing functions akin to public functions. An officer, especially one at the very highest level – such as the applicant – is put into a position of trust in a sphere of operations seemingly far removed from the ordinary commercial enterprise. She functions as the de facto 'chief executive officer' of a business that manages gambling and lotteries, but she does so on behalf of the taxpayer in whose name the respondent acts . . . In that context, the implied term of maintaining trust and confidence is crucial . . . If someone had asked either of these parties, at the time when the applicant was appointed, whether they would both maintain the trust and confidence of each other, both would have replied 'but of course, that goes without saying'. I therefore hold that this term is an implied term in their contract of employment.

Custom and usage

A term may be implied in a contract on the basis of industry custom and usage. There are four essential elements necessary to establish a valid custom:

(1) it must be immemorial;
(2) it must be reasonable;
(3) it must be certain in its terms, and in respect of both the locality where it is alleged to obtain and the persons whom it is alleged to affect; and
(4) it must have continued as of right and without interruption since its immemorial origin.

For the practice of the custom to amount to such a recognised usage, it must be certain, in the sense that the practice is clearly established; it must be notorious, in the sense that it is so well known in the market in which it is alleged to exist that those who conduct business in that market contract with the usage as an implied term; and it must be reasonable.

Dr P Samuels v Lakeland Farms Limited [2003] JMCA 8 (31 July 2003) (JM)

Facts: The respondent owned a stud farm which was in the business of breeding mares and providing for their daily needs. The appellant was the owner of two mares, 'Exotic Ruler' and 'Fiery Link'. He was also part owner of another mare, named 'Mekamara'. The issues on appeal arose out of an oral contract negotiated between the appellant and a Mr Murphy who was, at the relevant time, farm manager employed by the respondent. The contract concerned the 'keep and care' of the appellant's mares by the respondent. The appellant maintained at trial that he had entered into an oral contract with Mr Murphy, the farm manager of the respondent, who was his friend, to provide veterinary services to the farm at a reduced rate and in return Mr Murphy would keep and care for his mare 'Exotic Ruler' at the rate of JM$100.00 per day, which was an amount below that offered to other customers of the farm. The respondent contended that Mr Murphy had no authority to negotiate a reduction in the daily rates. In fact, the rates charged for these services were standard rates applicable to all mares on the farm including those owned by the owner of the respondent, Mr Richard Lake. One of the issues which arose in this appeal was: Was the respondent entitled to detain the mares pending payment of the outstanding fees according to industry custom?

Held: Forte, P; Bingham, Smith, JJA
I turn now to the question, whether custom and usages existing in the Industry, nevertheless entitled the respondent to exercise a lien over the mares of the appellant. The learned judge found that there was in fact:

> a custom or practice that when a customer falls into arrears his animals are not delivered to him unless he makes full payment or makes arrangements for payment and the plaintiff was entitled to detain the defendant's animals because there were sums outstanding and the defendant failed to pay or to make arrangements to pay . . . In the light of the finding above, the plaintiff had a lien on the horses and was entitled to detain them. In addition the costs incurred for their keep and care during the period of withholding must be borne by the defendant.

Mr Braham referred us to the four essential elements necessary to establish a valid custom. These are:

(1) it must be immemorial;
(2) it must be reasonable;
(3) it must be certain in its terms, and in respect of both the locality where it is alleged to obtain and the persons whom it is alleged to affect; and
(4) it must have continued as of right and without interruption since its immemorial origin. (See *Halsbury's Laws of England* paragraph 606)

(i) Immemorial. In theory for a custom to be immemorial, it must be in existence from the commencement of the reign of Richard I in 1189. Where, however, it is impossible to show a continued existence, the courts will support the custom if circumstances are proved which raise a presumption that the custom existed at that date. Evidence showing continuous use[] as of right as far back as living testimony can go is regarded as raising the presumption. [See paragraph 607 *Halsbury's* (*supra*)]. As a general rule proof of the existence of the custom as far back as living witnesses can remember is treated, in the absence of any sufficient rebutting evidence, as proving the existence of the custom from time immemorial. The periods during which living witnesses have been able to testify as to the existence of customs and which have been held sufficient to raise the presumption of existence of the customs from time immemorial, have varied greatly in different cases, but 20 years may be sufficient. [See *Halsbury's* (*supra*) paragraph 622, *R v Goffe* (1823) 2 B & C 54 and *Mercer v Denne* (1905) 2 Ch 538].

In the instant case, there was evidence[] establishing that over an average period of 27 years the witnesses recognise the detention of horses against contracts as a custom. Richard Lake, the owner of the respondent company who has been involved in the industry for 20 years, described the detention of the appellant's mares for non-payment as the 'norm in the industry'. Derrick White, owner and breeder of horses for 33 years and a Director of Caymanas Track for 10 years, testified that: 'Where customers who have horses for keep and care at a farm and do not pay fees, the custom is to hold the horses.' Mr White's testimony was based on his experience of keeping many horses at various stud farms. Elizabeth Miller testified that she has managed stud farms in Jamaica and England for the 'past 30 years'. She stated (page 76):

> I am aware of custom in industry in Jamaica when fees [are] not paid one gets in touch with client, sends invoice to client, if client does not pay I go and see them. If they have contract with them, if through verbal or written correspondence we get no reply, a letter is written by me with the permission of the owner of the farm to the Racing Commission and after a certain amount of time they give them to pay if they do not pay they are on the forfeit list. The horse will be retained (sic) and stay on the farm until the money is paid. That is the practice as far as I am aware. The cost of care and attention to horse would be the responsibility of owner of the horse. That is the custom or practice in the industry.

Mr Phillip Feanny, race-horse trainer and part owner of a stud farm, testified that he has been involved in the industry for 26 years. He stated at page 74:

> There is a custom if you don't pay, you don't get your horse or if you don't make arrangements to pay. That has been the case as far back as I can remember. The practice is that the individual who owns the horse would continue to pay while I detain horse. Bill continues to mount. This is the practice from [since] I have been involved.

Mr Braham contended, in the face of the above evidence, that the respondent had failed to prove that the custom existed, and that it had existed for the required period of time. He based this argument on two grounds, one that the testimony of Ms Miller which speaks to the horse going unto a forfeit list for non-payment meant that the owner of the farm would be entitled to sell or to take the ownership of the horse in lieu of fees. In the industry, however, it is not the name of the horse that is placed on the forfeit list but that of the owner. The placing of the owner's name on a forfeit list means merely that the horse could not be entered in a race, until the money is paid thereby removing the name of the owner from the forfeit list: (See Rules).

Second, Mr Braham relied on the fact that another witness, Mr David DeLisser and the appellant both testified that there was no such custom, and therefore the custom was not 'established to the required certainty'. In my view the evidence of those witnesses did no more than put the question of whether there was a custom in issue, and it was thereafter a question of fact for the learned judge. She rejected the evidence for the defence on this point and obviously by her finding accepted the evidence of the respondent's witnesses.

(ii) Reasonable. 'A custom must be reasonable. Reason for this purpose is not to be understood as meaning every unlearned person's reason, but artificial and legal reason warranted by authority of law. Consequently, a custom may be good even if no particular reason for it can be assigned; it is sufficient if there is no good legal reason against it. It is not for the party asserting a custom to prove its reasonableness, the rule is rather that a supposed custom may be rejected if it is unreasonable.' The above statement which is a correct statement of the law is taken from *Halsbury's* paragraph 609. The learned author of this noble work states also:

> Since customs are by definition inconsistent with the common law, they are not invalid merely because they are contrary to common law principles. *R v Abbot of Selby* [(1329) 97 Selden Soc 137]. They are only unreasonable if they are inconsistent with those general principles which, quite apart from particular rules or maxims, lie at the root of our legal system, or if they are contrary to the first principles of justice.

The contract in the instant case could not be held unreasonable merely because of the common law principle, which governs the question of the entitlement to detain the chattel under an agistment contract. In my view, the custom to detain horses by a party who undertakes its 'keep and care' cannot be held to be unreasonable as that party would have been put to expense and time in undertaking those responsibilities. Consequently, it must be reasonable to permit that party to detain the chattel (the horses) until payment for their care and upkeep is made.

(iii) Certainty. The custom must be one which is definite and certain, so that by the application of it, in each particular case it may be shown with certainty what are the rights which the custom gives in that case. There must be some definite limit to the right claimed to exist under an alleged custom (1) in respect of its nature generally, (2) in respect of the locality where the custom is alleged to exist, and (3) in respect of the persons alleged to be affected by it. (See *Halsbury's* paragraph 615). The authors of *Halsbury's* state that some definite limit must be assigned to the area in which the custom is said to obtain. However, in the instant case, no evidence was led as to the locality in which it is alleged that the custom obtained. Instead, it was contended that the custom existed within the Industry. However, the respondent also relied on the usage in the Industry. In dealing with the subject of usage, the authors of the text state at paragraph 445:

> Usage may be broadly defined as a particular course of dealing or line of conduct generally adopted by persons engaged in a particular department of business life, or more fully as a particular course of dealing or line of conduct which has acquired such notoriety, that where persons enter into contractual relationships in matters respecting the particular branch of business of life where the usage is alleged to exist, those persons must be taken to have intended to follow that course of dealing or line of conduct, unless they have expressly or impliedly stipulated to the contrary.

Also, in the case of *Cunliffe-Owen v Teather & Greenwood* [1976] 3 All ER 561, Ungoed-Thomas, J offers some assistance on the principles that govern 'usage', in the following words:

> 'Usage' is apt to be used confusingly in the authorities in two senses, (i) a practice, and (ii) a practice which the court will recognise. 'Usage' as a practice which the court will recognise

> is a mixed question of fact and law. For the practice to amount to such a recognised usage, it must be certain, in the sense that the practice is clearly established; it must be notorious, in the sense that it is so well known in the market in which it is alleged to exist that those who conduct business in that market contract with the usage as an implied term, and it must be reasonable. The burden lies on those alleging usage to establish it, in this case, the defendants. The practice that has to be established consists of a continuity of acts, and those acts have to be established by persons familiar with them, although, as is accepted before me, they may be sufficiently established by such persons without a detailed recital of instances. Practice is not a matter of opinion of even the most highly qualified expert as to what it is desirable that the practice should be. However, evidence of those versed in a market, so it seems to me, may be admissible and valuable in identifying those features of any transaction that attract usage and in discounting other features which for such purpose are merely incidental and if there is conflict of evidence about this, it is subject to being resolved like other conflicts of evidence.

The above dicta, with which I agree, show that the criteria to establish usage are almost in unison with the requirements to establish a custom. Both must be certain, reasonable and continuous in its [*sic*] application. A custom must be immemorial, while a usage must be notorious. The evidence in the instant case certainly establishes the elements of both custom and usage. Mr Braham, however, contended that a usage cannot operate to contradict the common law. For this proposition he relies on certain dicta in the case of *Myer v Dresser* [1864] 16 CB (NS) 646. The first is in the judgment of Erle, CJ at 660:

> It is a self-evident contradiction to my mind to say that the general law does not allow the deduction, and that there is a universally established usage to allow it. A universal usage which is not according to law cannot be set up to control the law . . . Such a general right as that claimed here would, I think, be very inconvenient; it would be giving opportunity for making unlimited claims for deduction, and lead to great confusion. No such difficulty arises in the case of particular usages confined to local districts. Many contracts are construed by the course of business in the particular trade or in the particular place where they are made. But that is not at all analogous to a universal usage pervading the whole world.

The other is in the judgment of Byles, J at 667 which reads:

> Then, can custom change the law? I need say no more than this, that, if this is to be considered as a general law for all mankind in all places, it is an attempt to prove the law by a usage, which cannot be done. If it is to be treated as a local custom it clearly is not a local custom. If it is a custom of a particular trade, it seems to be only a mode of settling accounts.

Though the learned Judges appear to use the term 'custom' and 'usage' interchangeably, as if they are the same, the words which fell from them speak to the inability of 'a universally established usage' to overrule the common law. Erle, CJ recognised, however, that no such difficulty would arise where the usage is confined to a local district, or to a particular trade.

In the instant case, it seems to me, and I so hold that all the elements of custom and usage were established by the appellants through the evidence of the witnesses which has been earlier recorded in this judgment. The evidence certainly supports a finding that in the thoroughbred industry it has always been recognised that a horse can be detained for the nonpayment of fees.

(iv) Continuity. There is no need for 'actual continuous use since 1189'. The evidence did not disclose any interruption in the custom, but instead demonstrated that it was practised in the Industry in excess of 20 years. In the event I would hold that the learned judge was correct when she found on the evidence that there is such a custom.

The legal incidents of a particular class or kind of contract

Terms can be implied as a legal incident to a particular class or kind of contract as 'necessary' for the very existence of the contract, such as those understood to bind banker and customer in their fiduciary relationship. This category of implied terms is distinguishable by its disregard for the actual or presumed intention of the parties. Terms implied are those that would necessarily be implied in all such contracts of a particular category or class.

Canadian Pacific Hotels Ltd v Bank of Montreal [1987] 1 SCR 71 (CA)

Facts: A number of forged cheques were drawn on the chequing account, at the respondent bank, of one of the appellant's operating units and were made payable to the defendant companies which were controlled by the defendant Sands. The cheques in issue were drawn during the period April 1976 to July 1977 inclusive on the chequing account, at the respondent Bank of Montreal (the Bank), of the operating unit or division of the appellant Canadian Pacific Hotels Limited (CP Hotels), at the Toronto International Airport, known as the Chateau Flight Kitchen (sometimes referred to as the Malton Flight Kitchen and hereinafter referred to as the Flight Kitchen). The banking operations of CP Hotels, including those of the Flight Kitchen, were part of the overall banking arrangements made with the Bank by Canadian Pacific Limited (CP) for itself and its subsidiary and associated companies. CP operated a centralised banking arrangement known as Treasury under which the Flight Kitchen maintained separate deposit and disbursement accounts with the Bank and a Treasury account with CP.

During the relevant period the defendant Sands forged the signature of Saunders on all 23, and the signature of Hird on 19, of the cheques for which the claim was made. He made the cheques payable to the defendant companies, Dundas Discounts Limited and Sig-Mor Sales Limited, which were controlled by him. The forgeries were not discovered until August 1977. CP Hotels gave the Bank notice of them on 25 August 1977.

In its defence, the Bank alleged that CP Hotels was 'estopped or otherwise denied' from recovering the amounts debited in respect of the forged cheques by the breach of a duty, arising out of the banker and customer relationship, to check its bank statements and vouchers on at least a monthly basis, with a bank reconciliation for such purpose, and to notify the Bank immediately of any errors. The Bank also set up in relation to this alleged duty the defence of a stated or settled account. The Bank further alleged the breach by CP Hotels of a duty to take reasonable precautions to prevent fraud by its employees in relation to dealings with the Bank by the maintenance of adequate supervision and internal accounting controls and also invoked the responsibility of a principal for the fraud of an agent acting within the scope of his actual or apparent authority.

Held: Le Dain, J
The duty to examine bank statements and vouchers with reasonable care and to report any discrepancies within a reasonable time, which was the duty principally contended for by the Bank, would, in my view, have to be a duty that applied to all customers . . . There is no doubt that the implication of terms in a contract on the basis of custom or usage is a well-recognised category of implication that has been particularly important with respect to commercial contracts . . . Implication on the basis of custom or usage was referred to by Lord Wilberforce in *Liverpool City Council*, where in his discussion of the various kinds of implication, he said at p 253:

> Where there is, on the face of it, a complete, bilateral contract, the courts are sometimes willing to add terms to it, as implied terms: this is very common in mercantile contracts where there is an established usage: in that case the courts are spelling out what both parties know and would, if asked, unhesitatingly agree to be part of the bargain.

. . . It is not too clear to me what the trial judge found in the present case to be the commercial custom on which he based the duties of care affirmed by him, but it would appear to have been the practice of a sophisticated commercial customer such as CP Hotels, which he found to be known and relied upon by the Bank, to operate a system of internal accounting controls which included a monthly bank reconciliation. With great respect, I would question whether this was sufficient to constitute a custom or usage on which a duty of care could be grounded as an implied term of the contract. It would seem to me that the evidence of the practice constituting such a custom or usage would have to be such as to support an inference of an understanding between the bank and the customer that the customer would examine his bank statements with reasonable care and report any discrepancies within a reasonable time, failing which he would be precluded from setting up the discrepancies against the bank. I question whether the evidence in the present case supports such an inference. In any event, there could be no such custom or usage with respect to the ordinary customer . . .

For similar reasons I am of the opinion that the duty contended for cannot be implied as a term of the banker and customer relationship in a particular case under the other category of implication based on presumed intention – the implication of a term as necessary to give business efficacy to a contract or as otherwise meeting the 'officious bystander' test as a term which the parties would say, if questioned, that they had obviously assumed. It is clear from the established law and practice, including the recognition and use of verification agreements, that the duty contended for is not necessary to the business efficacy of the banker and customer relationship and cannot otherwise be presumed to have been intended by the customer. Banks in this country have managed to get along without it for a very long time.

There remains the question whether the duty contended for can and should be implied under the third category of implication, which does not depend on presumed intention – the implication of terms as legal incidents of a particular class or kind of contract, the nature and content of which have to be largely determined by implication. Such is clearly the ordinary relationship of banker and customer with respect to the operation of an account. The issue here, as I see it, is whether the test for such implication is to be reasonableness or necessity. This is an important issue of judicial policy respecting the limits of judicial power to impose obligations or duties on the parties to a contract by implication. It is reflected in the differing opinions of the Court of Appeal in *Liverpool City Council*. Although what was said there was said with reference to implication on the basis of presumed intention under the business efficacy or 'officious bystander' tests, I think it applies equally to implication under what I have referred to as the third category. I am, therefore, with great respect, in agreement with the view expressed by the majority in the House of Lords in *Liverpool City Council* that the test in such a case of implication should also be one of necessity . . .

In my opinion, a duty, in the absence of a verification agreement, to examine bank statements with reasonable care and report discrepancies within a reasonable time is not necessary or required by the contractual relationship in this sense. It should not, therefore, be imposed by judicial decision . . . In conclusion, then, I am of the opinion that a customer of a bank does not, in the absence of a verification agreement, owe a duty to the bank to examine his bank statements and vouchers with reasonable care and to report any discrepancies within a reasonable time, nor does a customer, 'sophisticated' or otherwise, owe a duty to its bank to maintain an adequate system of internal accounting controls for the prevention and minimisation of loss through forgery.

Business efficacy

A term will be implied in a contract if it is necessary to give efficacy to the contract. In business transactions, what the law desires to effect by the implication of a term is to give such business efficacy to the transaction as must have been intended at all events by both parties who are businessmen.[39] As with the officious bystander test, this is not to say that consideration of what is reasonable plays no part in determining whether or not a term should be implied. The court has no right to imply in a written contract any such stipulation, unless, on considering the terms of the contract in a reasonable and business manner, an implication necessarily arises that the parties must have intended that the suggested stipulation should exist.

RBTT Bank Jamaica Limited v YP Seaton, Earthcrane Haulage Limited and YP Seaton and Associates Claim No. [2014] JMSC Civ 34 (JM)

Facts: It was the year 1990. Jamaica was in the throes of an extreme shortage of foreign exchange. The Bank of Jamaica ('BoJ') had little or no foreign exchange. Those who needed foreign exchange in large quantities had to find those who had it and work out an exchange rate. Not even government companies could rely on the BoJ to provide them with needed foreign exchange to pay for goods and services from overseas. The Jamaica Commodity Trading Company ('JCTC') was one such company. So short was foreign exchange that JCTC entered into agreements to purchase milk powder with an overseas company which accepted Jamaican dollars thus relieving JCTC of the obligation to find foreign exchange to pay under the sale contract. Throughout, this case[] no one has remotely suggested that BoJ had any foreign exchange to sell to anyone or to make available to government companies. Therefore even in this opening paragraph it can be stated with absolute certainty that the contracts that have precipitated this dispute did not require JCTC or BoJ to provide foreign exchange to the seller. Any sentient reader would immediately ask, how then was the seller to be paid? This case is a story about paying the seller; the arrangements that were made to do so; the payment mechanism established for payment; how it was effected and the consequences of giving effect to the payment mechanism.

JCTC was responsible for importing a number of goods. It had a recurring problem: lack of foreign exchange. The company now wanted to purchase milk powder but had no foreign exchange. It invited tenders from suppliers. Prolacto SA ('Prolacto'), a Belgian company responded and placed bids with JCTC. One of the attractive features of this company was that it was prepared to accept payment in Jamaican dollars. JCTC was delighted.

Two contracts were concluded – the first in August/September 1990 and the second in December 1990. Under the first contract, Prolacto offered a cash price. This was available if JCTC paid, in full, the Jamaican dollar equivalent of the full purchase price. Prolacto offered an alternative: 180 days payment by an irrevocable letter of credit and the price went up by US$55.00 per metric tonne. It appears that even on these exceptionally favourable terms for an international sale JCTC was unable to take advantage of the offer. JCTC

39 *The Moorcock* (1889) 14 PD 68, quoted in Furmston, *Cheshire, Fifoot & Furmston's Law of Contract*, p 157.

simply did not or could not pay the full cash price in Jamaican dollars. The second contract also offered a cash price per metric tonne provided that the full purchase price was paid in Jamaican dollars.

Prolacto appointed EarthCrane Haulage Limited ('EarthCrane') as its agent. Mr Seaton is the major shareholder of EarthCrane. He is also the major shareholder in YP Seaton and Associates Company Limited ('YPSACL'). He is the major human persona in this case who was the alter ego of both companies. The relationship between JCTC and Prolacto deteriorated and both contracts were terminated. JCTC then made claim against RBTT (formerly 'ECB'), Mr Seaton, EarthCrane and YPSACL to recover the money it claims was overpaid, that is to say improperly withdrawn by EarthCrane, from the deposit in respect of the first contract . . . In summary the bank's claim in CL 1993/E083 is about (a) recovering the overpayments; (b) recovering interest it claims to be entitled to and (c) a declaration that the taking of the JA$15,254,583.69 from Mr. Seaton was lawful . . .

Held: Sykes, J

Background against which to interpret the contracts and understand the conduct of the parties

The court will say that not all the documents are before the court and to that extent the court is hampered but not prevented from deciding what were the basic terms of the contract between the JCTC and Prolacto. It is important to come to some conclusion about the contract between Prolacto and JCTC because it is this contract that precipitated the agreement between ECB, Prolacto and JCTC. ECB's claim rests substantially on establishing what the terms of the sale contracts were between JCTC and Prolacto on the one hand and then the terms of the payment agreement between JCTC, ECB and Prolacto. RBTT's case theory cannot succeed unless it can show what the payments which it seeks to recover in action E-083 ought to have been . . .

The first important factor which is part of the background to this case is the severe shortage of foreign exchange in Jamaica at the time. As RBTT's own witness, Mr Keith Senior, a senior officer at ECB, testified that even though there was something known as the BoJ rate, in practice no one used it in the purchase and sale of foreign exchange because the BoJ rate was such that one could not purchase any significant amounts of the scarce commodity at that rate. He put forward the view that it was perhaps only government bodies such as customs which would use it for their purposes but certainly for commercial transactions between private citizens it was virtually ignored. From what he said, it was pure market forces that determined the exchange rate. He went as far as saying that if a person had significant amounts of foreign exchange commercial banks were willing to entertain discussions on the rate of exchange. The sense of his testimony was that these were well-known facts or as Lord Hoffmann would say, facts which were reasonably available to the parties.

The second important dimension to this case is that the purchase of the milk powder was an international sale. It is now accepted that the legal context and legal principles are part of the matrix of fact which a court can use to interpret a contract. JCTC, as a government company entering into the international arena for the purchase of goods, must be taken to have known and was willing to abide by what was then and now considered to be the standard basic understanding of insisting on certainty of payment in an international sale. A fundamental principle in an international sale contract is that there must not be any uncertainty regarding payment. This court will be very inclined to favour the honouring of any payment mechanism agreement between JCTC and Prolacto and interpreting the payment arrangements in a manner that would make the contract efficacious . . .

The third important factor in this case is that Jamaican currency was not legal tender outside of Jamaica and therefore would have had little or no intrinsic value for Prolacto.

Prolacto had no rational reason to wish to have large amounts of Jamaican currency unless it could be converted to foreign exchange . . .

The court wishes to say that there is another basis on which it would be prepared to say that the agreement between Prolacto and JCTC must have included Prolacto's direct access to the deposit. If the court were to find that there was no express agreement that Prolacto would have access to the deposit, the court would be prepared to hold that it was a necessary term of the contract in *Attorney General of Belize v Belize Telecom* (2009) 74 WIR 203. Lord Hoffmann in *Belize Telecom* held at paragraphs 17–22:

> The question of implication arises when the instrument does not expressly provide for what is to happen when some event occurs. The most usual inference in such a case is that nothing is to happen. If the parties had intended something to happen, the instrument would have said so. Otherwise, the express provisions of the instrument are to continue to operate undisturbed. If the event has caused loss to one or other of the parties, the loss lies where it falls.
>
> **[18]** In some cases, however, the reasonable addressee would understand the instrument to mean something else. He would consider that the only meaning consistent with the other provisions of the instrument, read against the relevant background, is that something is to happen. The event in question is to affect the rights of the parties. The instrument may not have expressly said so, but this is what it must mean. In such a case, it is said that the court implies a term as to what will happen if the event in question occurs. But the implication of the term is not an addition to the instrument. It only spells out what the instrument means.
>
> **[19]** The proposition that the implication of a term is an exercise in the construction of the instrument as a whole is not only a matter of logic (since a court has no power to alter what the instrument means) but also well supported by authority. In *Trollope & Colls Ltd v North West Metropolitan Regional Hospital Board* [1973] 2 All ER 260 at 267–268, [1973] 1 WLR 601 at 609 Lord Pearson, with whom Lord Guest and Lord Diplock agreed, said:
>
>> [T]he court does not make a contract for the parties. The court will not even improve the contract which the parties have made for themselves, however desirable the improvement might be. The court's function is to interpret and apply the contract which the parties have made for themselves. If the express terms are perfectly clear and free from ambiguity, there is no choice to be made between different possible meanings: the clear terms must be applied even if the court thinks some other terms would have been more suitable. An unexpressed term can be implied if and only if the court finds that the parties must have intended that term to form part of their contract: it is not enough for the court to find that such a term would have been adopted by the parties as reasonable men if it had been suggested to them: it must have been a term that went without saying, a term necessary to give business efficacy to the contract, a term which, though tacit, formed part of the contract which the parties made for themselves . . .
>
> **[20]** More recently, in *Equitable Life Assurance Society v Hyman* [2000] 3 All ER 961 at 970, [2002] 1 AC 408 at 459, Lord Steyn said: 'If a term is to be implied, it could only be a term implied from the language of [the instrument] read in its commercial setting.'
>
> **[21]** It follows that in every case in which it is said that some provision ought to be implied in an instrument, the question for the court is whether such a provision would spell out in express words what the instrument, read against the relevant background, would reasonably be understood to mean. It will be noticed from Lord Pearson's speech that this question can be reformulated in various ways which a court may find helpful in providing an answer—the implied term must 'go without saying', it must be 'necessary to give business efficacy to the contract' and so on—but these are not in the Board's opinion to be treated as different or additional tests. There is only one question: is that what the instrument, read as a whole against the relevant background, would reasonably be understood to mean?
>
> **[22]** There are dangers in treating these alternative formulations of the question as if they had a life of their own. Take, for example, the question of whether the implied term is

> 'necessary to give business efficacy' to the contract. That formulation serves to underline two important points. The first, conveyed by the use of the word 'business', is that in considering what the instrument would have meant to a reasonable person who had knowledge of the relevant background, one assumes the notional reader will take into account the practical consequences of deciding that it means one thing or the other. In the case of an instrument such as a commercial contract, he will consider whether a different construction would frustrate the apparent business purpose of the parties. That was the basis upon which *Equitable Life Assurance Society v Hyman* [2000] 3 All ER 961, [2002] 1 AC 408 was decided. The second, conveyed by the use of the word 'necessary', is that it is not enough for a court to consider that the implied term expresses what it would have been reasonable for the parties to agree to. It must be satisfied that it is what the contract actually means . . .

The court has set out this rather long passage to reinforce the point that when considering a contract it is not what the parties meant but what a reasonable person who had the relevant information and was in the position of the parties [would consider]. The reasonable person would consider whether one interpretation would give effect to the contract or frustrate the business purpose. The court has already set out what it concludes were the terms of the agreement between JCTC and Prolacto and has indicated how the terms were arrived [at] and the effect of them in terms of the price per metric tonne. The other part of the background is that this was an international sale and as stated already, having regard to that fact the court must insist on the payment mechanism being honoured and it is not open to the seller to change the terms without agreement from the buyer. Other background is the shortage of foreign exchange. The seller was to have his payment in foreign exchange. The seller agreed to accept Jamaican dollars. The commercial context meant that JCTC was under an obligation to provide Jamaican dollars so that the seller could buy foreign exchange which would be sent to him as payment for the goods shipped. The price was never quoted in Jamaican dollars and no one has suggested that the seller was to get Jamaican dollars with no possibility of getting foreign exchange. There is no evidence that Prolacto had any other business in Jamaica that would make Jamaican dollars of value to the company and so it cannot be said that they would have simply taken the Jamaican dollars without trying to convert it to foreign currency. A necessary term of the contract had to be that the foreign exchange was going to be purchased from the Jamaican dollars deposited. It may be said that no document actually says this. This court would hold that this must be a necessary term of the contract if it was going to work. Parties do not make contracts with a view to them not working. There cannot be many persons who engage with each other by contract with the clear unstated intention not to perform. On the facts of this case and relying on *Belize Telecom* this court would hold that a reasonable person armed with the background knowledge reasonably available would have concluded that Prolacto would have had to have access to the Jamaican dollar to get paid.

The court also concludes that the reasonable person would say that for the contract to work Prolacto would necessarily have to pay for the foreign exchange at market rates since part of the matrix of fact is that the BoJ had little or no foreign exchange to give to JCTC to make the payment for the milk powder.

The conclusion then is that Prolacto had every right to use the Jamaican dollars to get the foreign exchange needed for it to be paid in foreign currency. This means that Prolacto had every right to permit its agent to use the money in accordance with Prolacto's instructions or within the boundaries permitted by Prolacto. RBTT has not established what these market rates were and indeed could not because it was never a party to the transactions between Prolacto's agents and the sellers of the foreign exchange. From the evidence Prolacto's agent was free to negotiate the exchange rate with whomever had foreign currency. In light of this it is difficult to see how RBTT can succeed in its overpayment claim.

Combined business efficacy/officious bystander test

There are situations in which the court will be prepared to imply a term if there arises from the language of the contract itself, and the circumstances under which it was entered into, an inference that the parties must have intended the stipulation in question. An implication of this nature may be made in two situations: first, where it is necessary to give business efficacy to the contract, and, second, where the term implied represents the obvious, but unexpressed, intention of the parties. The two criteria often overlap, and, in many cases, have been applied cumulatively, although they are alternative grounds.

Starry Benjamin Claimant v Caribbean Commercial Bank (Anguilla) Limited Defendant Claim No. AXAHCV2013/0079 (AI)

Facts: On the 12th August 2013, the Eastern Caribbean Central Bank (ECCB) assumed control of the affairs of the Defendant Bank (CCB) acting pursuant to section 5B of the Eastern Caribbean Central Bank Agreement Act (the Act). The Act states that when ECCB is of the view that the interests of depositors or creditors of a financial institution are being threatened or that the financial institution is likely to become unable to meet its obligations or it is not maintaining high standards of financial probity or sound business practice, it may exercise such powers. Further in order to assume control of the affairs of the financial institution, ECCB must be of the opinion that the financial system is in danger of disruption, substantial damage, injury or impairment as a result of the circumstances giving rise to the exercise of such powers. Where ECCB proposes to exercise these powers, a notification stating the property and undertaking that ECCB proposes to take over and the powers of control that ECCB proposes to exercise must be published in the Official Gazette. The said notification with respect to CCB was published in the Official Gazette of Anguilla on the 12th August 2013.

Section 5 D of the Act states that[:]

> Where the Bank (ECCB) has under Article 5B assumed control of a financial institution, it may terminate or retain the services of any or all of the directors, officers and employees of the institution and the directors so retained shall manage the affairs of the institution subject however to any directions of the Bank.

On the 19th November 2013, the Claimant (Ms. Benjamin) filed a claim against CCB for a declaration that she was summarily dismissed without cause or notice and for a declaration that Article 5D of the Act did not supersede her Contract of Employment (*the Contract*). Ms. Benjamin states that on the 12th August 2013, she was summoned to meet with representatives of the ECCB and was presented with a letter from the Governor of ECCB which indicated that CCB was under conservatorship and all Directors were immediately terminated.

Ms. Benjamin states that she was terminated from her position as Managing Director of CCB without notice and without cause on the 12th August 2013, which, she states is in breach of her Contract with CCB. The Contract was for a period of 3 years with the commencement date being the 1st May 2012. CCB admits in its defence that Ms. Benjamin's employment was terminated on the 12th August 2013. Counsel for the claimant submits that the relevant section of the Contract with reference to termination is Clause 16 which states as follows[:]

> **Termination without Cause**
>
> 16. The Bank may terminate this Agreement without cause by giving the Managing Director three (3) months['] written notice. Upon termination, the Managing Director shall be entitled to all compensation and gratuity calculated for the term of the Agreement.

Pursuant to clause 16, Ms. Benjamin claims 3 months['] pay for failure of CCB to give her notice of termination, compensation for the unexpired balance of the employment contract and gratuity for the term of the Contract. She also claims outstanding vacation pay and relocation expenses as well as costs and interest. In response, CCB contends that the power to terminate under Article 5D of the Act supersedes the Contract, that clause 16 referred to above is a penalty clause and that the Contract was frustrated by the intervention of the ECCB.

Held: Mathurin, J
The Effect of Article 5D

CCB submits that there was implied into the Contract a term that the Contract could also be terminated by the ECCB without notice. In support of this submission, CCB relies on the business efficacy and officious bystander tests which determine whether or not a term can be implied into a contract based on the intention of the parties.

CCB submits that the business efficacy test was explained by Bowen L.J. in *The Moorcock* (1886–90) All ER 53 where he stated as follows[:]

> In business transactions such as this, what the law desires to effect by the implication is to give such business efficacy to the transaction as must have been intended at all events by both parties who are business men; not to impose on one side all the perils of the transaction, or to emancipate one side from all the chances of failure, but to make each party promise in law as much, at all events as it must have been in the contemplation of both parties that he should be responsible for in respect to those perils or chances[.]

Counsel also relies on the summarization by McKinnon LJ in *Shirlaw v Southern Foundries* (1939) 2 KB 206 at 277 of the officious bystander test where he stated[:]

> Prima facie that which in any contract is left to be implied and need not be expressed is something so obvious that it goes without saying; so that, if, while the parties were making their bargain, an officious bystander were to suggest some express provision for it in their agreement, they would testily suppress him with a common 'Oh, of course!'.

Counsel for CCB has asked that the court should imply into the Contract, a term that termination under Article 5D would end obligations by CCB to Ms. Benjamin under section 16 of the Contract for the following reasons[:]

(a) That the power to terminate conferred on ECCB cannot be taken away by contract
(b) That the intervention by ECCB would occur only when the institution is distressed and requires rehabilitation or restructuring
(c) All parties must be taken to be aware of the provisions of the Act
(d) If the parties were asked whether the contractual provisions were subject to the right of ECCB to terminate they would have said 'Of course!'

A term can only be implied if it is necessary in the business sense to give efficacy to the contract; that is if it is such a term that it can be confidently be said that if at the time the contract was being negotiated someone had said to the parties, 'What will happen in such a case?', they would both have replied, 'Of course, so and so will happen; we did not trouble to say that; it is too clear'.

Whether a term will be implied is a question of law for the court. A term will not be implied so as to contradict any express term; and, in fact, a term ought not to be implied unless on considering the whole matter in a reasonable manner it is clear that the parties must have intended that there should be the suggested stipulation. Where a contract contains an express obligation by a party to the contract, it is for that party to show that there is some implied term which qualifies the obligation.

The assumption of control of CCB and the termination of employees are both statutory powers of the ECCB so it may very well be that termination by ECCB can reasonably be implied into the Contract. I am not however persuaded that the premises on which CCB is asking the court to consider implying a term that a person can be dismissed *without notice or in breach of the terms of a fixed term contract* between the parties can assist CCB. Can the Court conclude that if Ms. Benjamin had discussed the possibility of ECCB control when negotiating the Contract, that she would have agreed to termination without notice and in breach of the Contract? . . .

Having heard the evidence and considered the submissions and authorities of Counsel, I am not satisfied that CCB has shown that there was an implied term that qualified the obligations to Ms. Benjamin upon termination by ECCB and as such the claim that termination under Article 5D operates to extinguish all rights accruing to Ms Benjamin pursuant to her Contract. In the absence of a definition of termination under the ECCB Agreement Act, the Court will not readily imply such a qualification where the parties have entered into a carefully drafted written agreement containing detailed terms.

Terms implied by law

In many classes of contract, statutory terms annexed to a contract will often not be expressly included in the contract. Certain terms will be implied in contracts related, for example, to the sale of goods, unless the implication of such a term would be contrary to the express words of the agreement.[40] Again, the implication of such terms does not depend on the intention of the parties but on more general considerations.

Sale of Goods Act, Ch. 82:30 (Revised Laws of Trinidad and Tobago, 2013)

Section 14(1) In a contract of sale . . . there is an implied condition on the part of the seller that in the case of a sale he has the right to sell the goods . . . (2) In a contract of sale, . . . there is an implied warranty that – (a) the goods are free, and will remain free until the time when the property is to pass . . . and (b) the buyer will enjoy quiet possession . . . Section 16(2) Where the seller sells goods in the course of business, there is an implied condition that the goods supplied under the contract are of merchantable quality, except that no such condition – (a) as regards defects specifically drawn to the buyer's attention before the contract is made; or (b) if the buyer examines the goods before the contract is made, as regards defects which that examination ought to reveal. (3) Where the seller sells goods in the course of a business and the buyer, expressly or by implication, makes known – (a) to the seller, or (b) where the purchase price or part of it is payable by instalments and the goods were previously sold by a credit broker to the seller, to that credit broker, any particular purpose for which the goods are being bought, there is an implied condition that the goods supplied under the contract are reasonably fit (and where appropriate reasonably durable) for that purpose whether or not that is a purpose for which such goods are commonly supplied, except where the circumstances show that the buyer does not rely, or that it is unreasonable for him to rely, on the skill or judgment of the seller or credit broker.

40 *Chitty on Contracts*, para 13–003, p 643.

Ian Hoyte v Toyota Trinidad and Tobago Limited (2013) CV2012–02049 (TT)

Facts: The Defendant, Toyota Trinidad and Tobago Limited, ('Toyota') is a motor vehicle dealer engaged in the business of selling new and pre-owned motor vehicles. On the 12th of May 2008 the Claimant, Ian Hoyte ('Hoyte') purchased a pre-owned motor vehicle ("the Vehicle") from Toyota for $160,000.00. At the time of the sale the Vehicle was nine years old and had a mileage of 120,000 km. Prior to the purchase Hoyte inspected the Vehicle and identified certain repairs that he wanted done. Toyota agreed to perform these repairs on the Vehicle prior to its delivery. The vehicle was delivered on 23rd May at 4:15 p.m. After inspecting the vehicle Hoyte took delivery of it. The next day at around 8.15 a.m. while driving along the Beetham Highway Hoyte heard a rumbling sound followed by an explosion from the underneath and to the rear of the vehicle. The vehicle then violently pulled towards the median of the Highway and overturned several times. The airbags failed to activate. As a result of the accident Hoyte suffered injury and the Vehicle was damaged. By this action Hoyte alleges that Toyota has breached the terms of the contract between them and its duty under the Sale of Goods Act and seeks declarations in that regard and damages. In particular Hoyte contends that Toyota orally represented to him that it would rectify any and all defects in the Vehicle to a satisfactory quality and to a standard that was acceptable to be roadworthy and safe before delivery of the said Vehicle. He contends that, among other things, Toyota failed to ensure that the Vehicle was of merchantable or satisfactory quality; failed to carry out proper repairs to the Vehicle; failed to check the quality of the tyres to ensure that they were in a standard and quality reasonable and acceptable for road use and failed to ensure that the airbags, the Vehicle's primary safety mechanism, was functional and operating.

Held: Jones, J

What were the terms or conditions of sale?
The Sale of Goods Act Chap 82:30 ('the Act') sets out the conditions to be implied with respect to the sale of goods. With respect to the quality or fitness for any particular purpose of goods supplied under a contract for sale the Act provides that there is no implied condition or warranty with respect to those goods except where the seller sells goods in the course of a business. Where, as in this case, the seller sells goods in the course of business, there is an implied condition that the goods supplied under the contract are of merchantable quality. This condition does not however apply with respect to (a) defects specifically drawn to the buyer's attention before the contract is made; or (b) if the buyer examines the goods before the contract is made with respect to defects which that examination ought to reveal. In this regard it is not in dispute that Hoyte examined the Vehicle prior to its purchase. As a result there is no implied condition as to merchantable quality with respect to the defects which ought to have been revealed by his examination.

In addition to the conditions implied by the Act Hoyte relies on certain representations which he says were made by Toyota's employees at the time of sale. At the end of the day therefore I have to determine what were these representations and their effect. According to Hoyte these representations were with respect to certain repairs agreed to be done by Toyota prior to the delivery of the Vehicle and to the condition of the Vehicle . . .

With respect to the repairs agreed to be done by Toyota I accept Hoyte's evidence that Toyota agreed to repair the light to the Vehicle, repair the power windows and cover four bolt holes. I am also satisfied that Toyota warranted that the repairs would be performed before delivery and to a satisfactory standard . . . I am satisfied that Hoyte was given the express assurance by Toyota's representatives that the Vehicle was roadworthy and in good working condition. With respect to the roadworthiness and working condition of the

Vehicle this was against the background of it being a second-hand or pre-owned vehicle as described. I am satisfied that in these circumstances it matters not whether Hoyte was told that the vehicle was being sold 'as is' or not. The vehicle was sold in the condition that it was at the time subject to the agreement by Toyota to do the specific repairs to a satisfactory standard. It is in respect of this condition that the assurances were made by Toyota.

With respect to the conditions implied by the Sale of Goods Act, on the evidence, it is clear that there was an examination of the Vehicle by Hoyte prior to the purchase. In these circumstances section 16 (2) (b) applies with respect to those to defects which Hoyte's actual examination ought to have revealed. With respect to defects not ascertainable on the examination there is an implied condition of merchantable quality. To this end, the Act provides that goods are of merchantable quality within the meaning of the section if they are fit for the purpose for which goods of that kind are commonly bought as is reasonable to expect having regard to any description applied to them, the price if relevant and all the other relevant circumstances. The repairs agreed to be done apart I am satisfied that the guarantee made by Toyota that the Vehicle be roadworthy is no more stringent than the conditions of sale implied by section 16 of the Act. In this regard I agree with the dicta of Lord Denning when in dealing with the question of whether a second-hand car is reasonably fit for the purpose in *Bartlett v Sidney Marcus Ltd* he says: 'A second-hand car is reasonably fit for the purpose if it is in a roadworthy condition fit to be driven along the road in safety, even though not as perfect as a new car.'

In my opinion therefore with respect to the defects which were apparent on Hoyte's examination and agreed to be addressed by Toyota there was a guarantee that those repairs would be done prior to delivery and be to a satisfactory standard. In the context of the specific repairs I am satisfied that this required the lights and the power windows to be working and the bolt holes closed. With respect to defects which Hoyte's examination ought to have revealed there was no implied condition as to merchantable quality. With respect to any other defects which would not have been apparent upon Hoyte's examination there was an implied condition that the Vehicle would have been of merchantable quality. Further I am satisfied that the express guarantees made by Toyota as to the condition of the Vehicle were no more than the requirement of merchantable quality provided by the Act. In this regard however I am satisfied that the express guarantees made by Toyota were not limited to those defects not revealed or revealable on Hoyte's examination . . .

The question of whether the Vehicle was of merchantable quality is a question of fact for my determination. In the particular circumstances of this case of relevance here is the close proximity in time of the accident to the delivery of the Vehicle and Hoyte's evidence as to the cause of the accident. The case as presented by Hoyte it is that the accident occurred as a result of a defective tyre and that the injury to him was made more severe because the airbags failed to deploy . . .

At the end of the day therefore I am asked to assess whether the Vehicle was of merchantable quality on the basis of the evidence of Hoyte as to how the accident occurred; the proximity of the accident to the date of delivery and the fact of a damaged tyre. With respect to the tyre, given my rejection of the evidence of *Boodoosingh*, I have no way of knowing whether the damage to the tyre was the cause of or as a result of the accident. Accordingly I have no information as to the cause of the accident. On the other hand it is not in dispute that this was a 9 year pre-owned Vehicle with a mileage of 120,000 km which was subject to certain conditions as to merchantable quality. In this regard I am cognisant of the dicta of Lord Denning in *Bartlett v Sidney Marcus Ltd* when he says:

> A buyer should realise that when he buys a second-hand car effects may appear sooner or later; and, in the absence of an express warranty, he has no redress. Even when he buys from

> a dealer the most ran that he can require is that it should be reasonably fit for the purpose when driven along the road.

In that case the purchaser drove the car for more than four weeks before putting it into the garage to have its clutch repaired. The clutch required more work than the purchaser had anticipated. It was determined, however, but that did not mean that at the time of sale it was not fit for use as a car. In the instant case Hoyte had the benefit of the Vehicle for less than 24 hours after delivery. During which period he drove the vehicle twice, one of those journeys being to his home from Toyota's compound. It was on the second journey that the accident occurred.

I am satisfied that with respect to the conditions implied under the Sale of Goods Act there was a requirement that insofar as there were defects in the Vehicle which could not have been revealed by the examination conducted by Hoyte, Toyota was required to provide a vehicle which was of merchantable quality. In this regard therefore there was no examination of the engine by Hoyte nor did he test drive the Vehicle. On the evidence it is clear that at the time of his examination of the Vehicle there was no visual indication of any damage to the tyres. The evidence of Sheppard confirms this. It is clear therefore that in accordance with the Act Toyota was required to provide a Vehicle which was of merchantable quality with respect to both the engine and defects to the tyres not obvious on a visual examination.

I satisfied that with respect to the express representations made by Toyota it was required to provide a vehicle that was roadworthy, regardless of Hoyte's examination. I am satisfied that in both cases the requirement of merchantable quality required that the Vehicle be fit for the purpose for which Vehicles are commonly bought, that is to be driven along the road, as is reasonable to expect, having regard to the fact that the Vehicle was nine years old, pre-owned with a mileage of 120,000 km and purchased for $160,000.

There has been no challenge to Hoyte's evidence as to how the accident occurred. He says that he was driving at approximately 60 kilometers per hour when without warning he heard rumbling sound followed by an explosion from beneath and to the rear of the Vehicle. The Vehicle immediately malfunctioned and pulled violently in an uncontrollable manner to the right, slammed into the median of the Highway and overturned several times. It would seem to me therefore that, given all the pre-delivery checks made by Toyota with respect to this Vehicle and given the fact that the Vehicle was driven for less than 24 hours before it literally self-destructed the inescapable inference to be drawn is that the Vehicle was not of merchantable quality. It was not reasonably fit for the purpose of being driven along the road.

Conditions

Conditions are terms that are considered to be critical to a contract, the breach of which may entitle a party to terminate the contract and claim damages for loss sustained on account of the breach.

Gerard Kraakman DBA 'The Woodshop' v Donna Sterling (2011) HCVAP 2010/12 (VG)

Facts: The appellant, Mr. Gerard Kraakman, is the owner of a well[-]established wood shop, known as 'The Woodshop' at Baughers Bay, Tortola, in the Territory of the Virgin Islands. The respondent, Mrs. Donna Sterling, along with her husband Mr. Wayne Sterling, were at the relevant time building a luxury home in Long Bay, Tortola. The couple contracted with Mr. Kraakman to manufacture the doors and windows for their new home, after Mrs. Sterling had had many meetings with him. It was an implied term of the contract that the fixtures and fittings required would be of a high standard. From her negotiations with Mr. Kraakman, as well as after having observed work that he had done for other clients, Mrs. Sterling was confident that he would be capable of carrying out the work to the required standard. After the doors and windows had been manufactured, Mrs. Sterling completed payment for the items but later discovered that the quality of the work was rather poor and the goods had not been manufactured to the required standard. She ultimately demanded that Mr. Kraakman repay her in full and brought a claim against him in the court below when he refused to do so.

Held: Mitchell (Ag), Edwards, Baptiste, JJA
Whether the goods conformed with the contract description

This was the first question for the judge. Questions arose concerning the measurements, conformity to a template or templates, poor workmanship, and whether the goods were fit for purpose. These issues arise under the Sale of Goods Act ('the Act'). Contracts for sale of goods are not to be found only in the express written and oral and implied terms and conditions agreed to by the parties. Some of the terms and conditions of such a contract are implied by the Act. The relevant sections are:

> 15. Where there is a contract for the sale of goods by description, there is an implied condition that the goods shall correspond with the description; and if the sale be by sample, as well as by description, it is not sufficient that the bulk of the good[s] corresponds with the sample if the goods do not also correspond with the description.

And, section 16 provides:

> 16. Subject to the provisions of this Act and of any statute in that behalf, there is no implied warranty or condition as to the quality or fitness for any particular purpose of goods supplied under a contract of sale, except as follows-
>
> (a) where the buyer, expressly or by implication, makes known to the seller the particular purpose for which the goods are required, so as to show that the buyer relies on the seller's skill or judgment, and the goods are of a description which it is in the course of the seller's business to supply (whether he be the manufacturer or not), there is an implied condition that the goods shall be reasonably fit for such purpose, provided that in the case of a contract for the sale of a specified article under its patent or other trade name, there is no implied condition as to its fitness for any particular purpose;
>
> (b) where goods are bought by description from a seller who deals in goods of that description (whether he be the manufacturer or not), there is an implied condition that the goods shall be of merchantable quality; provided that if the buyer has examined the goods, there shall be no implied condition as regards defects which such examination ought to have revealed;
>
> (c) . . .
>
> (d) an express warranty or condition does not negative a warranty or condition implied by this Act unless inconsistent therewith.

. . . The judge found as a matter of fact that Mrs. Sterling was building a costly home and that Mr. Kraakman knew that. He also knew that Mrs. Sterling was relying on his expertise to fabricate exterior doors and windows reasonably fit for installation in that particular house. As he testified, Mrs. Sterling had visited his workshop on many occasions and had an opportunity to see the doors and windows that were being made for other clients. She had asked for a quote for the doors and windows because she had been so impressed with the quality of his workmanship. The judge found that Mr. Kraakman, as a result of the many flaws in the fabrication of the doors and windows, had failed in his obligation to supply goods reasonably fit for the purpose as required by section 16(a). This finding was supported by the evidence that she accepted . . .

Was Mrs. Sterling entitled to reject the goods as a whole?

The judge found that Mrs. Sterling was not obliged to incur the cost of taking delivery of every item and measuring and inspecting each minutely but was entitled to reject the lot without incurring further expense as she could reasonably infer from her inspection of some of the items that they were not reasonably fit for the particular purpose and did not meet the contract description. Mr. Farara QC takes issue with that finding. He suggests that the judge was applying section 15 of the Act which deals with sale of goods by sample. However, this, he submits, was a sale by description and Mrs. Sterling was obliged to inspect each and every one of the items and find whether it did or did not conform to the description before she could lawfully reject it.

Section 13 of the Act deals with when a condition of a contract of sale may be treated as a warranty. It provides:

> 13. (1) Where a contract of sale is subject to any condition to be fulfilled by the seller, the buyer may waive the condition, or may elect to treat the breach of such condition as a breach of warranty, and not as a ground for treating the contract as repudiated.
>
> (2) Whether a stipulation in a contract of sale is a condition, the breach of which may give rise to a right to treat the contract as repudiated, or a warranty, the breach of which may give rise to a claim for damages but not to a right to reject the goods and treat the contract as repudiated, depends in each case on the construction of the contract. A stipulation may be a condition, though called a warranty in the contract.
>
> (3) Where a contract of sale is not severable, and the buyer has accepted the goods, or part thereof, or where the contract is for specific goods, the property in which has passed to the buyer, the breach of any condition to be fulfilled by the seller can only be treated as a breach of warranty, and not as a ground for rejecting the goods and treating the contract as repudiated, unless there be a term of the contract, express or implied, to that effect.

The claimant in her pleadings did not directly state what express or implied term of the contract was the condition that was breached, which entitled her to reject all of the items and repudiate the contract. However, she pleaded at paragraph 3 in her Defence to Counterclaim that 'she was legally entitled to reject the items and did so as a result of a breach of the Agreement', having already pleaded at paragraph 5 of her statement of claim that: 'It was an implied condition of the agreement and an understanding between the parties . . . that the work would be performed in a professional manner and that the items would be fit for the purpose for which they were fabricated' . . .

In my view it is the implied condition in section 16(a), i.e., that the goods shall be reasonably fit for the purpose, that is operative. The question whether the contract is severable or not is decided on the facts of the case in question. The terms of the contract and the evidence accepted by the judge[] admit the conclusion that the contract was indivisible, and so I am of the view that the parties intended the contract not to be severable. If the contract is severable, the buyer loses his right to reject that part of the goods which he has accepted; but he may still reject the remainder: *Jackson v Rotax Motor and Cycle Co.* The respondent by her conduct clearly did not elect to waive this implied condition, or to treat the breach of this implied condition as a breach of warranty; and having regard to our prior findings, the respondent did not accept any of the goods or any portion of the goods thereby causing property to pass to the respondent. Consequently, she would not lose her right to reject all of the goods according to the law.

Having regard to the construction of the contract, and the conduct of the parties, the respondent's right to repudiate would not be negatived by the express warranty in the contract either in my view. In light of the respondent's pleadings previously referred to, the law, evidence, and the extent of the unfitness of the items which led the respondent to refuse to accept them, I am of the view that the respondent was entitled to repudiate.

Warranties

Warranties, like conditions, are also important terms in a contract. However, the breach of a warranty does not entitle the innocent party to rescind the contract; he may only claim damages. If, however, the warranty was used to induce the innocent party to enter into contractual relations, he may be entitled to have the contract rescinded on the ground of misrepresentation.

Aaron Krohn (Claimant) v Jose Tun (First Defendant), Ali Safa (Second Defendant) and Walid Jundi (Third Defendant); The Attorney General and The Comptroller of Customs (Interested Parties) Claim No. 78 of 2011 (BZ)

Facts: The Claimant, Aaron Krohn claims the sum of $14,074.89 from the first Defendant, being monies expended by him which he paid to the Belize Customs Department to release a blue in color 2004 Isuzu D-Max motor vehicle (hereinafter referred as 'motor vehicle') that was confiscated by the said Department because it was alleged that the motor vehicle was stolen goods and was uncustomed. He also claims damages for breach of contract. Mr. Krohn paid the first Defendant, Mr. Jose Tun $25,000 for the vehicle but, Mr. Tun denies that he is the seller. He claims that Mr. Krohn was aware that he held the vehicle as collateral for a loan given to the third Defendant, Walid Jundi. He claims that he had also given a loan to the second Defendant, Ali Safi and held the vehicle as collateral. The Certificate of title for the motor vehicle was[,] however, in the name of Mr. Tun. He claims that he was doing business with an Open Transfer which was acceptable at the time at the Belize Traffic Department, hence the reason the vehicle was not transferred back to the true owner. The issue arose as to whether Mr. Tun breached the implied warranty that Mr. Krohn should enjoy quiet possession of the motor vehicle when it was seized by the Customs Department.

Held: Hafiz-Bertram, J
Learned Counsel, Mr. Musa submitted that Mr. Tun sold a stolen, uncustomed motor vehicle to Mr. Krohn and as such, the recourse available to him is governed by the *Sale of Goods Act, Chapter 261 of the Laws of Belize, Revised Edition, 2000*. Learned Counsel submitted that pursuant to *section 14* there is an implied condition on the part of Mr. Tun who is the seller that he had a right to sell the motor vehicle and an implied warranty that the buyer shall have and enjoy quiet possession of the goods. However, it had been proven that he did not have such right as the motor vehicle turned out to be stolen from Guatemala and was not declared to the Belize Customs Department upon entry into Belize. Learned Counsel, Mr. Musa further submitted that since Mr. Tun breached the implied condition that he had the right to sell vehicle, Mr. Krohn had the right to treat the contract as repudiated and recover the purchase price of $25,000.00. Mr. Krohn in the claim before the amendment had claimed $25,000. He later amended the claim to recover damages since he entered into negotiations with the Belize Customs Department and he paid the

duties for the uncustomed vehicle so that it could be released to him. The breach therefore, was converted to a breach of warranty. Learned Counsel, Mr. Musa submitted that since Mr. Krohn waived his right to treat the breach as a breach of a condition, the breach is then converted to and treated as a breach of a warranty which gives rise to a claim for damages. He relied on *Halsbury's Laws of England*, Fourth Edition, and Volume 41 at para. 64 where the distinction was shown between warranties and conditions of sale. '*64.* ***Warranties, conditions and innominate or intermediate terms distinguished.*** Where a stipulation in a contract of sale is a warranty, its breach may give rise to a claim for damages but not to a right to reject the goods and treat the contract as repudiated; but, where a stipulation in a contract of sale is a condition, its breach may give rise not only to a claim for damages but also generally to a right to treat the contract as repudiated. *Where, however a seller is in breach of any one of three of the terms implied in a contract of sale by the Sale of Goods Act 1979 or of any one of the three conditions implied in a contract for the transfer of property in goods, or, as the case may be, in a contract for the hire of goods by the Supply of Goods and Services Act 1982 and where the breach is so slight that it would be unreasonable for the buyer to reject the goods, then, if the buyer does not deal as consumer, the breach is not to be treated as a breach of condition but as breach of warranty . . .*' (emphasis added). Learned Counsel further relied on *Halsbury's Laws of England*, Fourth Edition, Volume 41 at paragraphs 65 and 66 which state that the buyer can waive the condition and treat the breach as a warranty: '*65.* ***Parties' voluntary election as regards conditions.*** *Where a contract of sale is subject to a condition to be fulfilled by the seller, the buyer may, where the breach of condition would entitled him to reject the goods*, waive the condition *or may elect to treat the breach of the condition as a breach of warranty and not as a ground for treating the contract as repudiated. The position of the seller is the same in relation to a condition to be fulfilled by the buyer. A party will be treated as having waived a stipulation if his conduct is reasonably interpreted by the other party and relied on by him as amounting to a waiver, provided that it clearly and unambiguously bears that interpretation, even if the first party did not intend to waive the stipulation. 66.* ***Buyer's compulsory election****. Subject to the buyer's right of partial rejection, where a contract of sale is not severable and the buyer has accepted the goods or part of them, the breach of a condition to be fulfilled by the seller* can only be treated as a breach of warranty *and not as a ground for rejecting the goods and treating the contract as repudiated, unless there is an express or implied term of the contract to that effect.*' The court is in agreement with the legal submissions as stated by Learned Counsel, Mr. Musa . . . I find that the vehicle which was transferred to Mr. Krohn by Mr. Tun was the same vehicle that was seized by the Customs Department. As a consequence, the court finds that Mr. Tun breached the implied warranty that Mr. Krohn should enjoy quiet possession of the motor vehicle when it was seized by the Customs Department. *Section 14* of the *Sale of Goods Act applied.* It has been proven above that Mr. Tun breached the implied warranty that Mr. Krohn should enjoy quiet possession of the motor vehicle when it was seized by the Customs Department. This breach of warranty may give rise to a claim for damages as shown in paragraph 47 above. Learned Counsel, Mr. Musa further relied on *Halsbury's Laws of England*, Fourth Edition, Volume 41 at para. 312 which states: '*Buyer exposed to penalty or damages. Where, as a result of the breach of warranty, the buyer, is through using the goods in the normal manner contemplated by the seller*, exposed to proceedings for a penalty or other penal proceedings or to an action for damages, he may, for so long as he is entitled as against the seller to rely on the warranty, recover the penalty or the damages, his costs and his other losses from the seller. *At least where no criminal offence is committed, this will be the case, even if the buyer is liable in negligence to a third person*' (emphasis added) . . . It has been proven that Mr. Krohn had to pay to the Customs Department the duties for the stolen vehicle so that it could be released to him. This is a loss suffered as a result of the breach of the implied warranty for quiet possession and of the implied condition, treated as a warranty, that Mr. Tun had the right to sell the car. Mr. Krohn also claims other losses which he said resulted as a consequence of the breach. I agree with Learned Counsel Mr. Musa's submission that that Mr. Krohn is entitled to recover the penalty or damages or other loss against the Seller, Mr. Tun. This however, must result as a consequence of the breach of the implied warranty that Mr. Krohn should enjoy quiet possession of the motor vehicle when it was seized by the Customs Department.

Exemption clauses

Contracts commonly include exemption clauses designed with the hope of excluding or restricting the liability of one party which would otherwise accrue to him. A party relying on an exemption clause must demonstrate that the clause is incorporated into the contract (by signature, notice or course of dealing) governing his performance of the contract and that it provides protection against the consequences of the breach of contract for which he is accused. Nonetheless, if these considerations are established in favour of the person in breach, there are still several other hurdles that must be overcome in order to establish the operability of the exemption clause.

The law of exemption clauses has been revolutionised by the Unfair Contract Terms Act, which seeks to level the playing field between consumers and vendors. The Act precludes exemption clauses purporting to exempt liability for death or personal injuries caused by someone acting negligently. Moreover, where damage has been caused to property, reliance by the negligent party on an exemption clause may only obtain where notice of the exemption clause has been reasonable.

Unfair Contract Terms Act, Ch. 82:37 (Revised Laws of Trinidad and Tobago, 2013), section 5:

(1) A person cannot by reference to any contract term or to a notice given to persons generally or to particular persons exclude or restrict his liability for death or personal injury resulting from negligence.
(2) In the case of other loss or damage, a person cannot so exclude or restrict his liability for negligence except in so far as the term or notice satisfies the requirement of reasonableness.
(3) Where a contract term or notice purports to exclude or restrict liability for negligence a person's agreement to or awareness of it is not of itself to be taken as indicating his voluntary acceptance of any risk.

Coles v Clarenville Drydock Ltd. 1998 CanLII 13306 (NL SCTD) (CA)

Facts: As a preliminary point of law and fact, the parties sought a determination of whether a marine service centre operator, whose crane dropped a fishing vessel while lifting it back into the water, was exempted from all liability by exclusion of liability and assumption of risk clauses in an agreement with the vessel owner. This raised the difficult question of when a court should refuse to enforce an exclusion clause after a fundamental breach of the contract containing it. The question to be determined was whether CDL should be excused from any liability to the plaintiffs because Coles signed the Statement of Acceptance of Responsibility on 19 June 1995. Subsidiary issues included whether the exclusion of liability and assumption of risk clauses were unenforceable because (a) on a strict construction they did not exclude liability for CDL's own negligence or (b) to enforce the clauses would have resulted in a fundamental breach of the contract between Coles and CDL or (c) the clauses were unconscionable and would have imposed an unreasonable bargain upon an unequal party.

Held: Barry, J

The Law and Analysis. Exempting clauses generally. In Fridman, *The Law of Contract in Canada* (3rd edn 1994), at pp 561–600, one finds a good analysis of the approach taken by Canadian courts to the enforcement of clauses exempting risk. To summarise the relevant points:

(a) An exempting clause will not be enforced if an innocent misrepresentation by one party has misled the other to enter into the contract with such a clause (p 571).

(b) An exempting clause will not be enforced if the party seeking protection did not bring its existence and inclusion in the contract sufficiently to the notice of the other party at the time of, or prior to the making of the contract (p 573). Normally notice will be inferred where the clause is in a written agreement, the party signing can read, and that party has not been rushed into signing (pp 573–8).

(c) Once the courts accept that an exempting clause is included in a contract, the courts still regard it with a critical or jaundiced eye, approaching the interpretation of such a clause strictly, applying the ordinary rules of construction, including the *contra proferentem* rule, which says the clause, particularly in a standard form contract, is to be strictly construed against the party who drafted it (p 578). A clause will not exclude liability for the drafter's own negligence, unless it does so expressly or by necessary implication. The latter case arises only where the words could not reasonably apply to some ground other than the drafter's negligence (p 580).

(d) Where the exempting clause purports to exempt from a fundamental breach of the contract, that is, where 'the performance of the contract becomes something totally different from that which the contract contemplates', or the breach 'goes to the root of the contract', or 'undermines the whole contract', or involves 'a totally different performance of the contract from that intended by the parties' (pp 565–6), the law is somewhat confusing . . .

Whichever approach one takes, the following circumstances of the present case warrant non-enforcement of the exemption clauses:

(a) Coles did not enjoy equality of bargaining power with CDL. He was in a 'take it or leave it' position. If he did not sign the standard form, he would have had a 35 to 40-hour steam to the next available marine service centre.

(b) Whether or not the circumstances would permit a plea of *non est factum* by Coles, the way in which CDL modified the government form required in fairness that the changes be brought directly to the attention of vessel owners. On the evidence, CDL did expressly point out the changes to certain owners. But CDL could not say it did so for Coles. He denies receiving any notice of the changes. Also, leaving displayed the signs previously erected by government, after the form had been modified, would have the effect of lulling Coles into the belief that the form he was signing in 1995 was the same as that signed in 1994. The sign erected by CDL over the customer service wicket was not sufficiently explicit to alert vessel owners that the rules of the Centre had changed.

(c) As a matter of public policy, there will be greater incentive to properly maintain and operate equipment at marine service centres if the operator of the centre incurs liability in these circumstances. The centre has the better opportunity to spread the risk by obtaining appropriate insurance and charging vessel owners any increased costs from so doing. I doubt if vessel owners would be able to obtain insurance on a cost-effective basis to cover damages caused by negligent crane operators who are untrammelled in their conduct.

Summary and Disposition. 1. The exemption clauses on a strict construction do not apply to CDL's own negligence in the maintenance or operation of its crane. 2. Even if the clauses, on a proper construction, do purport to exclude CDL's own negligence, they are unenforceable because to do so would not be fair and reasonable but, on the contrary, would be unconscionable, considering (a) the unequal bargaining power of the parties, (b) the potentially confusing manner in which the forms were changed but signs were not, and (c) the better position of the Centre operator to spread the risk in these sorts of cases.

Roger Rahamut and National Insurance Property Development Company Limited v Airport Authority of Trinidad and Tobago HCA No. S-732 of 1995 (TT)

Facts: On 9 February 1995 the plaintiff parked the car in Car Park B. He had asked the attendant whether it could be left for three days and the cost of doing so. He was then given a car park ticket which sets out certain 'conditions of parking' on the reverse side. On 12 February 1995 the plaintiff returned to the car park where he discovered his car was missing. On 13 February 1995 the plaintiff reported the matter and sought to negotiate a settlement for damages to his vehicle. This was futile. He claimed damages for negligence. The plaintiff claimed that he was not aware of a sign/notice on the eastern wall of the car park showing the rates. There was no warning sign on the guard booth or a disclaimer sign. He did not see a disclaimer in block letters. He got the ticket after he parked the car. He did not look at the words on the ticket 'PTO for conditions of parking'.

Held: Lucky, J
The conditions on the reverse side of the ticket must be strictly construed. There is no condition for disclaimer with respect to theft of a car. The test of reasonableness is set out in the Unfair Contracts Act 28/85 (the Act) and guidelines for the application of reasonableness are specified in the Second Schedule to the Act . . .

In this case, the disclaimer provision reads: 'While every effort will be made to ensure the safety of cars while in the car park, The Airports Authority disclaims all liability for loss or damage to any car or any property therein. Personal property left in a car will be at the owner's sole risk.' The plaintiff says he did not read the clause on the reverse of the ticket, neither did he observe the notice of disclaimer on the booth. There is no evidence that anyone drew it to his attention. But, if he did see the condition on the reverse, the question must be considered: What is the contractual representation set out in the first sentence? It must mean that efforts will be made to ensure safety of the plaintiff's car . . . This seems to be negligent on the part of the owners of the car park . . .

The witness said there is a notice on the booth which reads: 'The Company hereby disclaims all liability to any loss or damage to any vehicle left therein or any person using the car park.' I think the Court must take a practical and commonsensical approach in these matters. Will a person, driving a Sedan, (not open-top car), who comes to a standstill at a booth to a car park see a notice on the lower part of the booth? I do not think so. Further, there is no evidence that the attendant directs a driver's attention to the notice or points it out to drivers who intend to use the car park . . .

In the instant case, the ticket must be kept at all times by the owner of the car; charges are fixed by calculating the time of parking and leaving. The ticket must be presented and the prescribed amount paid before the exit barrier is lifted and the car driven out. Second, a person cannot drive out a car that had been parked unless the calculated sum is paid to the official at the gate. This is also the position at Car Parks A and B at Piarco . . . The first question is whether the disclaimer has been incorporated into the contract? The second is how must the disclaimer be construed? The third is whether the customer was notified or his attention drawn to the disclaimer or exempting condition.

The general rule is that if a person pays for a service and receives a ticket which contains a disclaimer on the reverse he is not bound by the conditions therein, because the ticket is a receipt for the money paid . . . I do not pause to enquire whether the exempting condition is void for unreasonableness. All I say is that it is so wide and so destructive of rights that the court should not hold any man bound by it unless it is drawn to his attention in the most explicit way . . .

In my opinion, the notice was not put in a prominent place; neither was it drawn to his attention by the attendant in any explicit way. The general rule regarding disclaimer notices (exemption clauses) is that they are to be construed strictly against the party who introduced them and seeks to rely on them – the *contra proferentem* rule. Therefore, an ambiguous disclaimer should be construed so that the meaning is not extended in favour of the party seeking to rely on it . . . I think there is an ambiguity. The Airports Authority who issued the ticket/card are thereby making a representation that efforts will be made to ensure the safety of cars and in the very next sentence it disclaims liability for loss. The disclaimer is dependent upon the first statement which requires a degree of care. In any event, there is no evidence of any effort to ensure the safety of cars in accordance with this representation. The car park is private, it is fenced and there is an entrance and exit with barriers, one of which had been moved.

I do not think that is enough to satisfy the representation. The Unfair Contracts Act (28/85). This Act is obviously important . . . Section 4(2) reads: '(2) In the case of other loss or damage, a person cannot so exclude or restrict his liability for negligence except in so far as the term or notice satisfies the requirement . . . of reasonableness.' . . . Applying the 'reasonableness' test, set out in the above Schedule, to the evidence, it seems to me that the bargaining position of the parties was unequal. The plaintiff had to park his car in one of the car parks; the card/ticket is ambiguous (a representation and a disclaimer), the plaintiff was not informed nor was the disclaimer or notice drawn to his attention. The contract was unfair to the plaintiff. He could not bargain. For the above reasons I find in favour of the plaintiff.

CHAPTER 3

LAW OF OBLIGATIONS: ATTACKING THE CONTRACT

Can you do another draft of this? There's still a couple of sentences people might actually understand...

Reproduced with the permission of CartoonStock

CAPACITY

Legal ability

For a contract to be binding, it must be made by parties with the requisite capacity, that is, the legal ability to make the contract. There are several factors that may adversely affect a person's ability to contract. A mentally ill person or a drunk may argue that they are not bound by a contract made during a period of illness or drunkenness. This argument would be based on the reasoning that, at the time of making the contract, they lacked the capacity to understand the implications of the contract and, therefore, should not be bound by the contract. In the case of minors, there may be no issue of the minor's intelligence but the courts have expressed a desire to protect those that have not yet attained the age of majority.

Minors

Where a minor enters into a contract with another person for the purchase or supply of necessaries, the contract will bind the minor. The courts have considered it in the minor's interest (as well as that of the other party) that he should be able to enter into binding contracts for necessaries. What constitutes necessaries will depend largely on the individual circumstances and requirements of the minor. Generally, necessaries include food, drink, clothing, medical aid, board and lodging. There are, however, some interesting extensions to the concept of necessaries.

First Charter Financial Corp. Ltd. v Musclow 49 DLR (3d) 138 1974 (BCSC) (CA)

Facts: On 3 October 1967 McLennan Motors Ltd sold a motor vehicle to the defendant Musclow (who was not represented at the trial and whose whereabouts, apparently, were unknown) under a conditional sales contract for a total price of CAN$4,274.06. To secure payment of this amount, Musclow executed a promissory note payable in monthly instalments of CAN$115. McLennan Motors Ltd then assigned the agreement in the promissory note to the plaintiff. Following a payment which he made on 16 May 1968, Musclow's indebtedness to the plaintiff was CAN$3,474.06.

Around this time, William H Butler, the manager of the plaintiff company, became aware of the fact that Musclow had transferred, or was contemplating transferring his interest in the motor vehicle to the defendant Alan MacDonald, who was then 20 years of age. Apparently Mr Butler informed Musclow that the plaintiff would not consent to the transfer unless it approved the purchaser. Alan MacDonald then submitted a loan application to the plaintiff, indicating that his net monthly income was CAN$440. On the evening of 29 May 1968 a meeting took place in the offices of the plaintiff in New Westminster. Mr Butler said, so far as he recalled, he simply told Mrs MacDonald that she would have to guarantee her son's financial commitment because her son could not be held financially liable because he had not yet attained his majority (the age of majority then being 21 years of age in British Colombia).

On 19 October 1968 Alan MacDonald telephoned the plaintiff company and advised that the car had been stolen in September, that it had been subsequently found, but that the car had been stripped of all parts. By letter dated 23 October 1968 the plaintiff wrote to the defendant Dorothy MacDonald stating her son's position and demanding payment of the balance owing, namely CAN$2,048.41 plus incidental costs.

Held: Craig, J
Whether goods are 'necessaries' is a question of mixed law and fact. The first consideration is whether a good is capable of being a necessary. If it is so held to be, the next question is whether in the particular circumstance, which is a question of fact, the goods are necessaries. Obviously, the determination of what is 'necessary' must change with the times. What was not a necessary 10 years ago may very well be a necessary today. It seems to me in present-day circumstances, many goods, which at one time clearly would be unnecessary, now must clearly be a 'necessary'. The ownership of a motor vehicle is a clear illustration of this proposition. At one time the ownership of a motor vehicle was a luxury even for a small group of people. Today in this country, ownership of a motor vehicle is a commonplace thing and many young people from 26 years and up not only drive motor vehicles regularly, but own a motor vehicle.

In this case, the defendant Alan MacDonald did not give evidence, but his mother testified that she had said on examination for discovery that her son was using the motor vehicle to commute from his home to his employer's place of business and that this answer was true. I do not think this evidence is sufficient to bring the motor vehicle within the category of a 'necessary' . . . I do not agree with the decision of Oliver J in *Coutts & Co. v Browne-Lecky et al.* I think it is wrong. In principle, to allow a person who has guaranteed an infant's financial obligation to contend successfully that he is not liable because the infant's contract which he guaranteed is void when he has made that guarantee knowing that the infant could not be liable for the debt and knowing, too, that the other party would not have entered into the contract unless the adult had guaranteed the debt. Even if there is a distinction between the legal effect of a guarantee and an indemnity relating to a void contract, as Oliver, J suggests in the *Coutts & Co.* case, I am satisfied that on the facts of this case, Mrs MacDonald was giving an indemnity . . Accordingly, Mrs MacDonald's defence on this aspect of the case fails.

Education will also be deemed a necessary where it is likely to lead to the future profit of the infant.

Norman Aviation Flight Training Academy Inc. Claimant/Respondent v Leroy Smith, Dulani Smith Defendants/Applicants (2014) Claim No. ANUHCV 2013/0523 (AG)

Facts: The respondent operates a flight training institution for profit. By way of an agreement dated September 5, 2009 (hereinafter the agreement), the second applicant enrolled to obtain 'flight and academic/ground school training'. The agreement states the cost of the training at USD$68,500.00. The first applicant signed the said agreement as guarantor. The applicants also signed two promissory notes (hereinafter the notes); the first note predates the agreement being signed on August 31, 2009. The second note is dated September 5, 2009, the date of the agreement. While the obligations are the same in both notes, they list different dates for payment of the sums due for the tutelage offered to the second applicant. As is the case with the agreement, the first applicant signs as guarantor on the notes[.]

On August 8, 2013 the respondent filed a claim form and statement alleging breaches of both the agreement and the notes by the applicants. The respondent claims that the applicants only paid the sum of (E.C) $10,000.00 and a balance of (E.C) $174,950.00 remains outstanding[.]

The applicants filed a defence on October 16, 2013 in which they denied that the first applicant contracted with the respondent to provide flight training to the second applicant. The first applicant contended that he only signed the notes and he did so in the capacity of a guarantor. The applicants also plead that the notes were conditional on the respondent providing flight training to the second applicant to the value of $174,950. This was not done and as such the respondent was only entitled to the sum of $9500.00 which had already been paid. Additionally, there was no presentment or demand made to either of the applicants and as such the notes cannot be enforced against the applicants. The second applicant also makes the point that at the time of contracting, he was a minor and the agreement, not being one for necessaries, could not be enforced against him. In any event, having attained the age of majority, he specifically repudiated the agreement in the defence.

Held: Glasgow, M (Ag)

The agreement
The applicants strenuously maintain in both their pleadings and their submissions that the first applicant was not a party to the agreement. The evidence contradicts that assertion. The agreement is attached to the statement of claim as 'exhibit GN 1'. This document is signed by both applicants; the first applicant signed as guarantor[.]

The evidence is also pellucid that at the time of signing the agreement, the second applicant was a minor. The respondent specifically denied the second applicant's minority in the reply but this position was, appropriately, not maintained in the affidavit in response to the application and the submissions filed in support of the respondent's submissions opposing the grant of the summary judgment. As it relates therefore to the second applicant, the only remaining contention is whether the agreement is enforceable regard being had to his minority at the time of signing[.]

The law is on this issue could not be more well settled. An agreement entered into by a minor is generally voidable at his instance. The only agreement which may be absolutely enforced against a minor is an agreement for what are termed 'necessaries'. *Coke upon Littleton*, page 172(A) recites the position that 'an infant can bind himself to pay for his necessary meat, drink, apparel, necessary physicke and such other necessaries and likewise for his good teaching or instruction whereby he may profit himself afterwards.' *Chitty on Contracts*, recited above, restates the law as to what are considered as [necessaries] to be 'confined to necessary goods and services supplied to the minor . . . it extends to contracts for the minor's benefit and in particular to contracts of apprenticeship, education and service.'

It has therefore been held that a minor could be sued on a covenant in a deed of apprenticeship since the instructions he received were to profit his endeavors to become a tradesman. A minor was also held bound by the terms of a contract of service which were, as a whole, for his benefit. *Roberts v Gray* was another claim involving instructions to a minor whereby he entered on a tour as a professional billiards player. The court there observed that looking at the agreement as a whole, it was one for the instruction of the minor and in such a form for his future benefit. The contract was therefore binding on the minor as a contract for his necessaries and could not be repudiated by him[.]

Lord Esher expounded on the law in this way in *Walter v Everard* where he explained at page 374 that:

> Food and clothing always are necessaries, if the infant cannot obtain them in any other way. Is education a necessary for an infant? Looking at it independently of authority, I should say that education in a trade with a view to making an infant a useful citizen must always in this working country have been thought of the greatest importance, and must always have been considered a necessary for an infant. But on this point we have the authority of the passage in *Coke upon Littleton*, p. 172 (A), in which Lord Coke lays it down in effect that education in a trade is a necessary for an infant, or rather I should say one of that class of things which may be a necessary. What will make it a necessary? If the infant can obtain the education which he requires in another way, it may not be a necessary. You must have regard to the condition of the infant in life – whether, for instance, he is a young man who will have to earn his living by his own exertions . . . The person who sues the infant on his covenant must shew that he did in fact supply him with the necessary education, and that the premium which he charged was reasonable in amount. If he does this he brings himself within all the conditions which would entitle him to recover from the infant . . .

In terms of a minor's education, Fry LJ makes the point a bit more succinctly –

> I think that education, which, whether it is or is not in strictness a necessary, is likely to lead to the future profit of the infant, falls within the same rule. In my opinion, it is really a necessary for an infant . . . I have no doubt that the proper education of an infant stands in the same position under English law as food and clothing supplied to him . . .

Whether or not the contract was one for necessaries is a question of fact based on all the facts available to the court . . .

In these proceedings it is clear that the agreement was not one for the supply of goods and services or for apprenticeship or service but rather one for the second applicant's education and instruction. The crucial question it would seem to me would be whether the instructions in this case were of such that, as Lord Coke put it, the second applicant 'may profit himself afterwards' or as *Halsbury's Laws* puts it 'clearly for his benefit.' This is also a question of fact to be resolved on the material before this court. However, this issue is hotly controverted. For the applicants it is contended that the contract could not be one for necessaries. They also go on to point out that at the material time the second applicant was undergoing mandatory state educational pursuits. The flight training program was therefore not a necessity in view of his age and station in life. I would consider this an attempt to distinguish the second applicant's circumstances from that of, for example, the minor in the *Roberts v Gray* decision who embarked on his instruction with a view to becoming a professional billiards player. Evidently the respondent has a different disposition to the entire affair. In the respondent's estimation the program offered was one which would secure a commercial pilot's licence to the second applicant. They contend that the second applicant's career ambition of becoming a commercial pilot would be thereby realized[.]

The applicant's success on the applications would rest on my determination that it is clear from the evidence that the agreement was one which the second applicant could avoid and thus avoided because the agreement was not for his necessaries. In that regard it must be apparent on the facts before me that the flight training given to the second applicant were not instructions from which he stood to benefit in the future. I cannot say that this is the case here. Without even venturing a forensic analysis of the evidence, I am sure that it would not be idle supposition to state that, as a general proposition, the second applicant would benefit from any vocational training he receives, in particular, training at a flight school offering professional courses. But I do not need to venture into the realm of speculation. It is my view that there is material on which the respondent can establish the claim that the course was for the benefit of the second applicant, chief among which is the fact that the course itself is one which will confer the second applicant with a commercial pilot's licence, whether or not he chose to utilize it in the future for profit . . .

In addressing contracts with minors, the courts have attempted to articulate certain key principles. If the entire contract or a particular term of a contract is so disadvantageous to the minor as to render the entire contract unfair, the court will not enforce the contract. It is clear that the true question is whether the particular stipulation complained of is so unfair as to make the entire contract disadvantageous to the infant. One may find in any contract a clause which by itself is not to the advantage of the infant; but that is not enough: the contract as a whole must be disadvantageous.

Bromley v Smith [1909] 2 KB 235 KBD (GB)

Facts: The plaintiff carried on the business of a baker at Great Clacton, in the county of Essex. Part of Great Clacton had become known as Clacton-on-Sea and was a watering place consisting of a sea front along which were a number of lodging and boarding houses and shops. The plaintiff's practice was to send men with carts containing bread, which was in part sold to regular customers on whom his men called habitually and in part hawked about and sold to any persons who were disposed to buy it. The plaintiff did not himself go on these rounds, but attended to the business in the shop at Great Clacton.

In November 1895 the plaintiff was in want of an assistant to go daily with a horse and cart on a round, which he described as the town round. By means of an advertisement he got into communication with the defendant, a young man of the age of 18 years, who lived at Great Baddow in the county of Essex, and had been from the age of 12 years engaged in the bakery trade or business. On 18 November 1895 an agreement was entered into between the plaintiff and the defendant with a restrictive covenant if the defendant left the employ of the plaintiff on a time and area basis. On 30 October 1908 the plaintiff brought an action against the defendant in the county court of Essex, held at Colchester and Clacton-on-Sea, claiming in his particulars of summons an injunction restraining the defendant for three years from 9 October 1908 from being engaged either as principal, servant or agent or otherwise in the business of a baker or manufacturer of flour, meal, bread or confectionery, wholesale or retail, at Little Clacton or elsewhere within 10 miles from Great Clacton.

Held: Channell, J
The question which I have to decide is whether the agreement of 18 November 1895 is binding upon the defendant. The law on this subject has been laid down in general terms in a number of cases. A man cannot restrict himself in the future exercise of his work and labour unless there is good reason for so doing. One principle which has been recognised as a good reason for a man restricting himself in this way is that the restriction is necessary for the protection of the person for whose benefit it is imposed . . . But then the restriction must coincide with what is necessary for the protection of the master's business . . . In my opinion, therefore, this agreement, in so far as it seeks to restrain the defendant from engaging in the business of a restaurant-keeper, goes beyond what was necessary for the protection of the business carried on by the plaintiff in supplying bread on a round.

Then comes the question whether this unenforceable restriction vitiates the whole agreement. It is well settled that, if the void portion is severable from the valid portion, the agreement is binding as to the valid portion . . . in the present case I think the agreement can be severed . . .

Then the question arises, would this contract, if so limited, be binding on an infant? There is abundant authority that contracts for service may be binding on infants although they contain restrictive terms. A contract which contains the only terms on which an infant can reasonably expect to get employment must, I think, be for his benefit. The defendant could not get employment in the plaintiff's or any other similar business on any better terms than those I have suggested, and I think it was for his benefit to get employment on those terms; by entering into the plaintiff's service on those terms he was only giving up the chance of setting up in business in a place where he was not known, and it is quite right that when leaving that service he should forgo the right of soliciting customers whom he would never have known but for that service. Common honesty demands that forbearance . . . Omitting the invalid restrictions to which I have referred, I think the contract with this restriction was on the whole for the benefit of the defendant and was therefore binding upon him.

At the same time, the policy of the law is to mitigate some of the hardships that might be imposed on persons dealing with a minor, so as to encourage them to enter into contracts that are for the minor's benefit.

Chaplin v Leslie Frewin (Publishers) Ltd. and Others [1966] Ch 71 (GB)

Facts: The infant plaintiff, Michael Chaplin, was the son of a rich and famous father, Charles Chaplin, who had been an actor in films and a producer. Michael was born in

California on 6 March 1946, and at the material time was 19, his father being 76. At the age of 18, while on a visit to Spain, he wished to get married to Patrice Johns, a girl who was a few years older than himself. But he could not marry without his father's consent. His father refused because he had no job. The couple came back and went to Scotland and got married there. They had no money and had a child to support. At the end of March 1965, when he was just 19, he got National Assistance for his wife, the child and himself. That received wide publicity.

Michael Chaplin received an offer to write a book about his life and on 17 April 1965 two contracts were signed. Michael Chaplin was to tell his life story to the two journalists, who were to write it up in the form of a book, and the publisher's company, the first defendants, Leslie Frewin (Publishers) Ltd, were to publish it. The publishers were to pay Mr and Mrs Chaplin a royalty on all sales. In just over a fortnight the book was in typescript. There were only two copies. The publishers sent one copy to the printers, and the other to their solicitors so that they could read the book for libel. On 10 May 1965 the solicitors wrote to the publishers drawing attention to several passages which might be defamatory of various people, including Charles Chaplin senior, adding that other passages might be hurtful, if not very harmful, to him.

By the middle of June 1965 the galley proofs were ready, and Frewin showed them to Mr and Mrs Chaplin, together with the solicitor's letter. He told them that any alterations they wished would be incorporated in the page proofs. He also told them that the alterations suggested by the solicitors would be incorporated. In the middle of July 1965 Mr and Mrs Chaplin showed the galley proofs to one or two friends, who expressed their disapproval of the book. That roused Mr and Mrs Chaplin to action. They told the publishers that they took serious objection to several passages in the book, to its style and other matters. In consequence the publishers arranged a meeting at which amendments could be made. Over two days there were long meetings with the publisher's representatives at which a number of small amendments were made, and at the end, on 21 July, Mr and Mrs Chaplin signed a certificate approving the print.

A few days later, on 28 July, Michael Chaplin was short of money again. He telephoned to Frewin, who gave him a further cheque for £100 against his royalties. Three or four weeks later Michael Chaplin went to solicitors for the first time, and showed them the page proofs. They wrote on 26 August 1965 to the publishers and claimed to avoid the agreement of 17 April 1965. Early in September 1965, a writ was issued in the name of Michael John Chaplin (an infant) by his wife and next friend, Patrice Frances Chaplin, claiming against the publishers and the printers.

Held: Danckwerts, LJ
I now turn to the first question – whether the contract is revocable or is binding on the infant. On this question we were referred to *Doyle v White City Stadium*, in which Doyle (an infant) had agreed to be bound by the rules regulating professional boxing because otherwise he could not pursue the career of a professional boxer. The contract and the rules were held binding upon him. It is plain that it was a case treated as within or analogous to the exceptions to the general rule in respect of infants' contracts and the contract was held binding on the infant because it enabled him to earn his living and so was for his benefit.

I think the principle of that case applies to the present case. The advantage of the contract to the plaintiff in the present case was that it would enable the plaintiff to make a start as an author and thus earn money to keep himself and his wife. The time to judge the question of whether the contract is beneficial must, I think, be the date when the contract is made: see *Halsbury's Laws of England*, 3rd edn (1957), Vol. 21, p 145. It cannot be right to enable a contract made in good faith to be avoided because it turns out at a later date that the benefits are not as great as the parties anticipated.

It was contended by Mr Roche that this contract could not be beneficial to the plaintiff because (1) the book exposed him to the risk of actions for defamation, and (2) the book presented the plaintiff himself as being a bad character. As regards the first, the defendants allege that they can justify, and on this ground the judge declined, according to practice, to grant an injunction. As regards the second ground, the contract did confer substantial benefits. I find it difficult to sympathise with a person who, for the purpose of gain, has approved of a book which is calculated to denigrate his character and afterwards wishes to change his mind. How far the book will affect readers I do not know, but it may be that the publicity which the book has now received will increase the sales of the book and thus increase the benefits to the plaintiff which were the object of the contract. The mud may cling but the profits will be secured. Taste is a matter of opinion. The plaintiff has failed to make out a case.

Drunkards

Cases involving the issue of intoxication as it affects capacity are approached with great caution. It has been asserted that mere drunkenness affords no ground for resisting a suit to enforce a contract. Where, however, there is real ground for thinking that the judgment of one party was, to the knowledge of the other, seriously affected by drink, the courts will be more willing to invoke the capacity defence and generally refuse specific performance at the suit of that other.

Blomley v Ryan (1956) 99 CLR 362 (AU)

Facts: The appellant was the plaintiff in the action. He brought it to enforce a contract made on 21 April 1953 by which the respondent, who was the defendant, sold a grazing property to the appellant for the price of 25,000 pounds. This property was a settlement lease of 3,696 acres at Boggabilla, a town in New South Wales. The respondent was about 78 years of age and his mental and physical powers were much impaired by old age and addiction to rum. He left school at the age of 14 years; he was uneducated and of humble social station. His mental weakness did not amount to continuous contractual incapacity. He owned and managed this valuable grazing property named 'Worrah' at Boggabilla. He had held it since 1926. The area of the property was 3,696 acres: it was carrying, in April 1953, about 3,000 sheep and 50 head of cattle owned by the respondent. He lived in an unpretentious house on the property.

Rather late in life, Ryan contracted a habit of indulging in extended bouts of drinking. He usually went on one of these sprees at shearing time. He was so intoxicated at times that he could not manage himself or his affairs. When he was drunk at shearing time, he took no interest in what was going on and moped about the place. Drinking was then his preoccupation.

The shearers arrived on 19 April and began shearing on the next day. A few days before they arrived the respondent obtained a supply of rum from stock and station agents at Goondiwindi. When the shearers came, he was drunk and dirty and his house was in a filthy condition. On 13 April 1953 EF Blomley, his son (the appellant) and Stemm drove to the respondent's house on the property. Stemm brought a bottle of rum. Before bargaining began, and when it ended for the day, Stemm poured drinks for the respondent, his companion, 'Scotty' Turner, EF Blomley and himself and all had several drinks. The bottle was left behind with a small residue in it. The bargaining took place between EF Blomley and Stemm on one side and the respondent, Ryan, on the other. According to their evidence, EF Blomley offered 25,000 pounds, the respondent firmly refused to take less than 30,000 pounds, saying he would sell at that price on terms, and Blomley told the respondent that as he would give terms, his son, the appellant, would be the buyer.

On 20 April 1953 EF Blomley and Stemm drove again to the respondent's house. This time the appellant did not come but his brother-in-law, B Doran, a son of the witness WJ Doran, came with them. Again Stemm brought a bottle of rum. He knew that the respondent had a few days previously obtained a supply of rum from his principal's store at Goondiwindi in the ordinary course of business. Stemm said he brought a bottle of rum with him as 'a friendly gesture'. Disclaiming that it was an artifice, Stemm said that he would have brought more if he were minded to use it to get a bargain. It is certain, upon the weight of the evidence, that the respondent was very drunk when these three persons arrived, and that nobody who saw him could have any doubt that he was. A bargain was made for the sale of the farm.

Held: Taylor, McTiernan, Fullagar, Kitto, JJ
The authorities which I have cited show, I think, that, when a court of equity is asked to refuse specific performance of, or to set aside, a contract at the instance of a party who says that he was drunk at the time of making it, the principles applied do not differ in substance from those applied in such cases as *Clark v Malpas* (1862) 31 Beav 80 (54 ER 1067), 4 De G F & J 401 (45 ER 1238); *Fry v Lane* (1888) 40 Ch D 312, and the other cases cited by Taylor J. But they show also that cases in which an allegation of intoxication is a main feature are approached with great caution by courts of equity. This is, I think, not so much because intoxication is a self-induced state and a reprehensible thing, but rather because it would be dangerous to lend any countenance to the view that a man could escape the obligation of a contract by simply proving that he was 'in liquor' when it was made. So we find it said again and again that mere drunkenness affords no ground for resisting a suit to enforce a contract. Where, however, there is real ground for thinking that the judgment of one party was, to the knowledge of the other, seriously affected by drink, equity will generally refuse specific performance at the suit of that other, leaving him to pursue a remedy at law if he so desires. And, where the court is satisfied that a contract disadvantageous to the party affected has been obtained by 'drawing him in to drink', or that there has been real unfairness in taking advantage of his condition, the contract may be set aside . . .

The defendant did not repudiate the contract until 22 July. In the meantime he had bought another property, in which he proposed to reside, and he had allowed certain stock to be placed on 'Worrah' by the plaintiff or his father. But Rogers had not supplied him with a copy of the contract, and I do not think, on the evidence, that he had any real understanding of the position until early in July, when he obtained a copy of the document, and, after a conversation with the witness Barden, consulted a firm of solicitors at Moree. After obtaining their advice he acted promptly enough. His drinking bout continued for some days after 21 April, and Taylor J thought that at its conclusion he had, at the best, only a hazy recollection of what had actually happened. When – to use his own expressive phrase – the 'booze got out of his system', he seems to have begun to think seriously about the position, but there is nothing to suggest that he was aware that the transaction might be successfully challenged, or even alive to what he had really done in April. In all the circumstances it would be wrong, in my opinion, to hold that there was any affirmation of the contract or any failure to repudiate in due time a transaction which, even when he became sober, he did not fully understand and appreciate until the document was in his hands.

The contract of a man too drunk to know what he is about is voidable only, and not void, and therefore capable of ratification by him when he becomes sober.

Matthews v Baxter (1872–73) LR 8 Ex. 132 Ex Ct (GB)

Facts: The contract of a man too drunk to know what he is about is voidable only, and not void, and therefore capable of ratification by him when he becomes sober. The plaintiff alleged a breach of contract by the defendant in not completing the purchase of houses and land bought of the plaintiff at a sale by auction. The plea was that, at the time of making the alleged contract, the defendant was so drunk as to be incapable of transacting business or knowing what he was about, as the plaintiff well knew. The replication was that, after the defendant became sober and able to transact business, he ratified and confirmed the contract.

Held: Kelly, CB
I am of opinion that our judgment must be for the plaintiff. The contract cannot be voidable only as regards one party, but void as regards the other; and if the drunken man, upon coming to his senses, ratifies the contract, I think he is bound by it.

Held: Martin, B
I am of the same opinion. The judges in *Gore v Gibson* use the word 'void', it is true, but I cannot think they meant absolutely void. They simply meant to say that a drunken man's contract could not be enforced against his will. But it by no means follows that it is incapable of ratification . . . I think that a drunken man, when he recovers his senses, might insist on the fulfilment of his bargain, and therefore that he can ratify it, so as to bind himself to a performance of it.

Held: Pigott, B
I agree with the rest of the Court, although with some hesitation. The language of the judges in *Gore v Gibson* must be taken with regard to the subject then under consideration; and the word 'void' must be taken to mean no more than that the contract could not be enforced *in invitum* against the defendant. Upon the whole, I think the contract was voidable only, and therefore capable of ratification.

Mentally ill

A contract made by a person of unsound mind is not voidable at that person's option if the other party to the contract believed at the time he made the contract that the person with whom he was dealing was of sound mind. In order to avoid a fair contract on the ground of insanity, the mental incapacity of the one must be known to the other contracting parties. A defendant who seeks to avoid a contract on the ground of his insanity must plead, and prove not merely his incapacity, but also the plaintiff's knowledge of that fact, and unless he proves these two things he cannot succeed.

The Imperial Loan Company, Limited v Stone [1892] 1 QB 599 CA (GB)

Facts: The action was brought on a promissory note which the defendant, who had since the making of the note been found by inquisition to be a lunatic, signed as surety. The statement of defence alleged that the defendant when he signed the note was so insane as to be incapable of understanding what he was doing, and this allegation was repeated with the further allegation added that the insanity of the defendant was known to the plaintiffs.

Held: Lord Esher, MR
When a person enters into a contract, and afterwards alleges that he was so insane at the time that he did not know what he was doing, and proves the allegation, the contract is as

binding on him in every respect, whether it is executory or executed, as if he had been sane when he made it, unless he can prove further that the person with whom he contracted knew him to be so insane as not to be capable of understanding what he was about. It can hardly be doubted that for a long series of years, if insanity was set up in answer to an action for breach of contract, it must have been pleaded, and the plea was not good unless it went on to allege knowledge on the part of the plaintiff. The fact of such a plea being required, and having to go to that extent, shews that the law as I have stated it was generally accepted. The burden of proof, in such a case, must lie on the defendant; the jury have disagreed on a material question in the cause, and as there is no finding on that question, the case must go back for a new trial.

Held: Lopes, LJ
It seems to me that the principle to be deduced from the cases may be summarised thus: A contract made by a person of unsound mind is not voidable at that person's option if the other party to the contract believed at the time he made the contract that the person with whom he was dealing was of sound mind. In order to avoid a fair contract on the ground of insanity, the mental incapacity of the one must be known to the other of the contracting parties. A defendant who seeks to avoid a contract on the ground of his insanity must plead, and prove, not merely his incapacity, but also the plaintiff's knowledge of that fact, and unless he proves these two things he cannot succeed. Applying that in the present case, it is apparent that the verdict entered for the defendant cannot stand, but that there must be a new trial.

Hilda Elisabeth Stoutt (By Her Guardians and Next Friends Peggy Stoutt-Harewood and Preston Stoutt), Peggy Stoutt-Harewood, Preston Stoutt Appellants v Firstbank Puerto Rico Respondent (2011) HCVAP 2010/016 (VG)

Facts: An elderly and mentally challenged housewifely mother put up her only real estate, her home, to secure the business debts of a company owned by her two sons. The bank described the loan as a 'residential loan' on its documentation. The bank would have been aware that the mother did not play any part in the business of the company; that she did not obtain any benefit from the loan; that as an elderly, housewifely mother she may have been susceptible to undue pressure. The bank did not insist that she obtain independent legal advice prior to accepting her mortgage charge. The business loan went into default and the bank attempted to enforce its security over the mother's house by selling it. Two of her children, having been appointed her legal guardians, applied to the court to set aside their mother's securities. The trial judge found that the bank had no knowledge of their mother's mental disorder at the time she executed the charges and that the charges could not be set aside.

Held: Mitchell, Edwards, Baptiste, JJA
The medical evidence was that Mrs. Stoutt had been treated by Dr. Leonard C. Vander Linde of Michigan in the USA from the year 1991 to 1999 for a Schizoaffective Disorder. In 1999, Dr. Vander Linde came to the Territory at her family's request because she was unable to travel. He found her at that time to be 'clearly psychotic, paranoid, disorganised and hostile. She was unable to adequately care for herself and could only manage with the help of her family.' In his opinion, from 1999 to 2005 she was 'chronically psychotic and mentally ill and she was not competent to enter into any legal contract.' From September 2005, Mrs Stoutt was treated for her mental condition by Dr. June Samuel of the Community Mental Health Services in the Territory. At that time Mrs. Stoutt was admitted to a facility for mental treatment. Dr. Samuel recorded that Mrs. Stoutt had a long

history of psychiatric illness and had become non-compliant. She explained Schizoaffective Disorder as being:

> a mental disorder characterised by symptoms including delusions, hallucinations, thought disturbances and inappropriate interactions. However, unlike schizophrenia, in Schizoaffective Disorder there is a significant mood component and affected individuals may become depressed or manic or agitated. This disorder is ongoing and permanent and is controlled by medication. It also affects various aspects of brain functioning so individuals may have ongoing difficulties with social functioning.

These two psychiatric reports were not disputed by the bank, and the judge had no difficulty in finding that Mrs. Stoutt was suffering from a mental disorder such that her capacity to contract was impaired when she executed all three of the charges . . .

The princip[al] ground of appeal was that the judge, having found as a fact that Mrs. Stoutt was suffering from a mental disorder and that her capacity to contract was impaired at the time she executed all three of the charges, fell into error in concluding that Mrs. Stoutt was nevertheless bound by the charges. Yet, that is the law. A person who is not mentally capable of entering into a legal contract will nevertheless be bound by its terms unless she can prove that at the time the contract was made the other party to the contract had either actual or constructive notice of her incapacity. The law has been so at least since the case of *The Loan Company Limited v Stone*. The principle was there laid down that:

> A contract made by a person of unsound mind is not voidable at that person's option if the other party to the contract believed at the time he made the contract that the person with whom he was dealing was of sound mind. In order to avoid a fair contract on the ground of insanity, the mental incapacity of the one must be known to the other of the contracting parties. A defendant who seeks to avoid a contract on the ground of his insanity, must plead and prove, not merely his incapacity, but also the plaintiff's knowledge of that fact, and unless he proves these two things he cannot succeed.

The learned trial judge had the benefit of seeing and hearing the witnesses and it is now difficult to fault her conclusion from the evidence before her that the bank had neither actual nor constructive knowledge through Mr. Melvin Stoutt of Mrs. Stoutt's mental disorder. I find no merit in this ground of appeal.

Taking advantage

A person may, strictly speaking, possess a legal capacity to contract; yet, the courts may be inclined to set aside a contract on the basis that such capacity may be suffering from a defect that would move the court to offer relief from contractual obligations incurred while under the claimed defect.

Undue influence

Although the courts of equity have never set aside contracts on the ground of folly, imprudence or want of foresight, the doctrine of undue influence is founded on the principle that the courts of equity have always sought to protect people from being forced, tricked or misled in any way by others into entering into contracts. The equitable relief of undue influence has two categories: actual or expressed undue influence and presumed undue influence. Actual undue influence comprises overt acts of improper pressure or coercion, such as unlawful threats; it is an equitable wrong committed by the dominant party against the other which makes it unconscionable for the dominant party to enforce its legal rights against the other. It is typically some express conduct overbearing the other party's will. Presumed undue influence arises out of a relationship between two persons where one has acquired a measure of influence or ascendancy over another, of which the ascendant person then takes unfair advantage.

Tanya Susanne Phillips Applicant v RBC Royal Bank (Jamaica) Limited Respondent [2014] JMCC Comm. 2 (JM)

Facts: Mrs. Tanya Phillips (claimant) seeks an interlocutory injunction to restrain the defendant Royal Bank Jamaica Ltd[] (defendant) from exercising its powers of sale over her matrimonial home. Mr. Phillips, her husband[,] is the owner of National Meats which is heavily indebted to RBC. In 2007 the claimant and her husband guaranteed a loan to National Meats and in 2009 she signed a Loan Agreement, guarantee and mortgage with her husband to finance National Meats. In seeking to restrain the defendant, Mrs. Phillips is asserting undue influence. In support of that assertion, she avers that she is entirely dependent on her husband and she is dyslexic. She contends that the bank failed in its responsibility to ensure that she understood the contents of the document she was signing. The bank, however maintains that it discharged its duty to her.

Held: Sinclair-Haynes, J
The law (as distilled from Lord Nicholls' speech in *Etridge*[)], provides protection for certain persons who are vulnerable to undue influence because of their special relationship with others who are liable to abuse the influence they wield. The important consideration is the degree of trust and confidence which the vulnerable party reposes in the other. The relationship a wife shares with her husband falls into this category. The court recognizes that persons within this category can be subject to undue influence without any manifest act of inducement.

The court is mindful that it is also unremarkable for a wife to accede to her husband's requests purely out of love and affection although the result might be wholly disadvantageous to her. The court is however cognizant that a husband can misuse the trust and confidence she reposes in him. Whether he has, is a question of fact . . . (see Lord Nicholls' speech in *Royal Bank of Scotland plc v Etridge (No 2)*).

In *Etridge*, at pages 799 and 798 of the case, he said:

> 27 The problem has arisen in the context of wives guaranteeing payment of their husband's business debts In recent years judge after judge has grappled with [the] baffling question whether a wife's guarantee of her husband's bank overdraft, together with a charge on her share of the matrimonial home, was a transaction manifestly to her disadvantage.
>
> 28 in a narrow sense, such a transaction plainly (['']manifestly') is disadvantageous to the wife. She undertakes a serious financial obligation, and in return she personally receives nothing. But that would be to take an unrealistically blinkered view of such a transaction. Unlike the relationship of solicitor and client or medical adviser and patient, in the case of husband and wife there are inherent reasons why such a transaction may well be for her benefit. Ordinarily, the fortunes of husband and wife are bound up together. If the husband's business is the source of the family income, the wife has a lively interest in doing what she can to support the business. A wife's affection and self-interest run hand-in-hand in inclining her to join with her husband in charging the matrimonial home, usually a jointly[-]owned asset, to obtain the financial facilities needed by the business. The finance may be needed to start a new business, or expand a promising business, or rescue an ailing business.
>
> 29 Which, then, is the correct approach to adopt in deciding whether a transaction is disadvantageous to the wife: the narrow approach, or the wider approach? The answer is

> neither. The answer lies in discarding a label which gives rise to this sort of ambiguity. The better approach is to adhere more directly to the test outlined by Lindley LJ in *Allcard v Skinner* 36 Ch D 145, and adopted by Lord Scarman in *National Westminster Bank plc v Morgan* [1985] AC 686, in the passages I have cited.
>
> 30 I return[] to husband and wife cases. I do not think that, in the ordinary course[], a guarantee of the character I have mentioned is to be regarded as a transaction which, failing proof to the contrary, is explicable only on the basis that it has been procured by the exercise of undue influence by the husband. Wives frequently enter into such transactions. There are good and sufficient reasons why they are willing to do so, despite the risks involved for them and their families. They may be anxious, perhaps exceedingly so. But this is a far cry from saying that such transactions as a class are to be regarded as prima facie evidence of the exercise of undue influence by husbands.
>
> 31 I have emphasised the phrase 'in the ordinary course'. There will be cases where a wife's signature of a guarantee or a charge of her share in the matrimonial home does call for explanation. Nothing I have said above is directed at such a case.

The guarantee which Mrs. Phillips signed in September 2007 was manifestly to her disadvantage. That fact, in isolation, is not sufficient to place her claim within the realm of undue influence in the absence of evidence that her husband misused the influence he had over her. Lord Nichols cautioned that:

> Undue influence has a connotation of impropriety. In the eye of the law, undue influence means that the influence has been misused. Statements or conduct by a husband which do not pass beyond the bounds of what may be expected of a reasonable husband in the circumstance should not, without more, be castigated as undue influence. [Similarly], when a husband is forecasting the future of his business, and expressing his hopes or fears, a degree of hyperbole may be only natural. Courts should not too readily treat such exaggeration as misstatements.
>
> Inaccurate [explanations] of a proposed transaction are a different matter. So are cases where a husband, in whom a wife has reposed trust and confidence for the management of their financial affairs, prefers his interests to hers and makes a choice for both of them on that footing. Such a husband abuses the influence he has. He fails to discharge the obligation of candour and fairness he owes a wife who is looking to him to make the major financial decisions . . .

Lord Nicholls outlined the bank's responsibility to the wife in a most lucid manner. It is necessary to quote him extensively. He said:

> 64 In the type of case now under consideration . . .
>
> 65 Typically, the advice a solicitor can be expected to give should cover the following matters as the core minimum. (1) He will need to explain the nature of the documents and the practical consequences these will have for the wife if she signs them. She should lose her home if her husband's business does not prosper. Her home may be her only substantial asset, as well as the family's home. She could be made bankrupt. (2) He will need to point out the seriousness of the risks involved. The wife should be told the purpose of the proposed new facility, the amount and principal terms of the new facility, and that the bank might increase the amount of the facility, or change its terms, or grant a new facility under her guarantee. The solicitor should discuss the wife's financial means, including her understanding of the value of the property being charged. The solicitor should discuss whether the wife or her husband has any other assets out of which repayment could be made if the husband's business should fail. These matters are relevant to the seriousness of the risks involved. (3) The solicitor will need to state clearly that the wife has a choice. The decision is hers and hers alone. Explanation of the choice facing the wife will call for some discussion of the present financial position including the amount of the husband's present indebtedness, and the amount of his current overdraft facility. (4) The solicitor should check whether the wife wishes to proceed.

> She should be asked whether she is content that the solicitor should write to the bank confirming he has explained to her the nature of the documents and the practical implications they may have for her, or whether, for instance, she would prefer him to negotiate with the bank on the terms of the transaction. Matters for negotiation could include the sequence in which the various securities will be called upon a specific or lower limit to her liabilities. The solicitor should not give any confirmation to the bank without the wife's authority.
>
> 66 The solicitor's discussion with the wife should take place at a face-to-face meeting, in the absence of the husband. It goes without saying that the solicitor's explanations should be couched in suitable non-technical language. It also goes without saying that the solicitor's task in an important one. It is not a formality.
>
> 67 As already noted, the advice which solicitor can [be] expected to give must depend on the particular facts of the case. But I have set out this 'core minimum' in some detail, because the quality of the legal advice is the most disturbing feature of some of the present appeals. The perfunctory nature of the advice may well be largely due to failure by some solicitors to understand what is required in these cases.

Mrs. Phillips signed a document entitled 'Waiver of Independent Legal Advice' which reads:

> The bank has advised me of my right to obtain Independent Legal Advice from an attorney-at-law with regards to my right to my guarantee for loans amounting to the total of the sum of the following amounts:
>
> US $13,510,346.96 and (b) J50,000,000.00 to National Meats and Foods Distrtibutors Limited. I further certify that the bank has explained the nature of the Guarantee document to me and I fully understand that by giving it I will be become liable for the debt.

She affixed her signature at the bottom of another form entitled 'Certificate of Independent Legal Advice.' The document was a declaration by the attorney. The said declaration was in standard form which required the erasure of the pronouns which did not relate to the applicant. The form stated that the attorney explained the nature of the document and advised her fully of the liability she was incurring by executing the document. It also stated that she was advised by the attorney as to the manner in which such liability could be enforced by the bank against her and she informed the attorney that she was satisfied.

It is useful to quote that portion of the form verbatim. The document reads:

> That she fully understands the nature and effect of having executed such documents. I am satisfied that she fully understand (a) the nature and effect of having executed such documents. I am also satisfied that she noted freely and voluntarily and was not under any undue influence by David George Phillips (borrower) or any other person.

On Mrs. Phillip's evidence, what transpired at the lawyer's office fell woefully short of the requirements outlined by Lord Nichols. On her evidence, the seriousness of the risk involved was not adequately driven home to her. [T]he attorney failed to:

(a) explain the purpose for his involvement and the fact that he could be called upon to counteract any allegation that she might make of undue influence;

(b) determine whether she wished him to act for her;

(c) explain fully the nature of the document ;

(d) inform her that she could become a bankrupt;

(e) inform her what was the amount of the principal and interest and the fact that it could be increased without her knowledge;

(f) discuss her means with her;

(g) a[s]certain whether she understood the value of the property charged; and
(h) inquire whether there were other assets from which payment could be made in the event the husband's business failed.

The attorney also failed to:

(a) inform her that that it was entirely her decision;
(b) discuss with her the state of her husband's finances, for example his [indebtedness] and overdraft facility;
(c) ascertain whether she wished to proceed;
(d) enquire whether she desired to confirm with the bank the nature of the documents and what the practical implications were;
(e) determine whether she wished to nego[t]iate with the bank; or
(f) obtain her permission before confi[r]ming with the bank.

Further, the meeting took place in the presence of her husband and his employee . . .

Importantly, the bank failed to inform the attorney of the dire financial situation of National Meats of which they had knowledge. The precarious position of National Meats caused the bank to seek the advice of the Special Loans Group. It had determined, by virtue of Mr. Glen Smith's report, that National Meats did not have the cash flow to meet its obligations. This critical fact was not conveyed to the attorney to enable her to properly advise Mrs. Phillips. If Mrs. Phillips was informed that National Meats could not meet the existing obligations and the implications that not only were they likely to lose their source of income but also the matrimonial home, she may very well not have signed.

The 2009 document which Mrs. Phillips signed was a complex document which captured the 2007 guarantee which she signed without . . . proper legal advi[c]e. The bank sought to combine guarantees, that is the 2007 and 2009, loans with a mortgage . . . Further, she was 'borrowing' from the bank to finance her husband's business in which she had no interest. The 'loan' was not to finance the matrimonial home or to a[c]quire property in which she would have an interest. Although the general rule is that a bank is under no obligation to the wife where she is a borrower with her husband, the facts of this case are exceptional . . .

The bank was well aware that she was not an owner nor had she any shares in National Meats. They were put on enquiry and was therefore obliged to 'take reasonable steps to satisfy itself that she understood and freely' signed the 2007 guarantee and the 2009 Loan Agre[e]ment. They failed to properly do so.

Mr. Panton is of the opinion that the facts of the instant case are [distinguishable] from *Etridge* as the loan was granted [in] both the Phillip's names to revive a business which provided her and her family to live comfortably. The matrimonial home and other properties were purchased in their joint names with monies from National Meats. With that submission, this Court disagrees. A reading of the cases does not reveal that a wife who benefits from her husband's business is disentitled to raise undue influence. In any event there is no evidence that at the time, the matrimonial home was purchased from the proceeds of a 'cash-rich' National Meats; the defendant provided National Meats with a loan.

Unconscionability

The courts of equity will set aside a contract on the basis of it being unfair and unconscionable in circumstances where one of the parties has imposed objectionable terms in a morally reprehensible manner. Unconscionability can be pleaded as a defence against having to perform contractual obligations where one party has been at a serious disadvantage to the other, whether through poverty, ignorance, lack of advice or otherwise. Where circumstances exist under which unfair advantage could be taken and this weakness is exploited by the other in some morally culpable manner with the result that the ensuing transaction is not merely hard or improvident, but overreaching and oppressive, a plea of unconscionability may hold.

Rasheed Mohammed Claimant v Dheerajie Benny Defendant (2010) Claim No. CV 2007–00205 (TT)

Facts: By his Statement of Case, the Claimant further alleged that by Memorandum of Transfer dated the 22nd February, 2006 ('the Memorandum of Transfer') the Defendant in consideration of the sum of $800,000.00 transferred unto the Claimant her one half share and interest in the said lands. The Claimant alleged at paragraph 3 of the Statement of Case that the Defendant agreed to sell her half interest in the said lands to the Claimant at the price of $800,000.00. It is further alleged at paragraph 3 that on the 25th January, 2006, the said lands were valued by Mr. Cecil Alcantara at $500,000.00, but the Claimant agreed to pay the Defendant the sum of $800,000.00 for her half share.

The Court will set out in full what was further alleged at paragraph 3 of the Statement of Case:

> The Memorandum of Assent was prepared by Mr. Mervyn Campbell Attorney at Law who advised the Defendant to obtain independent legal advice. Mr. Eric Noel Etienne Jr., Attorney at Law, independently advised the Defendant and fully explained to her the nature of the transaction and Mr. Etienne also read over the Memorandum of Transfer to the Defendant. The Defendant having agreed to the transaction placed her thumb print on the Memorandum of Transfer as her act and deed in the presence of her said Attorney at Law Mr Etienne and also in the presence of her grand daughter Ms Shamalar Selal. Both Mr Etienne and Ms Selal signed the Memorandum of Transfer as having witnessed the placing of her thumb print thereon by the Defendant. The Memorandum of Transfer was duly registered, the Stamp Duty Section of the Board of Inland Revenue having accepted the figure of $800,000.00 as being a bona fide purchase price for the half share and interest in the said parcel of land.

At paragraph 4 of the Statement of Case, the Claimant contended that the allegation that the transfer of the Defendant's interest in the said lands was obtained by deceit, undue influence and coercion on the part of the Claimant against the Defendant was untrue. The Claimant contended that the Defendant agreed to the transaction having had the benefit of independent legal advice from an attorney at law who read over the Memorandum of Transfer to her and explained to her the nature of the transaction . . .

The Defendant . . . contended that the sale was at a gross undervalue. Further, she contended that she trusted the Claimant and had developed a confidential relationship with him by reason of their several conversations and her confiding in him about her family dispute. Accordingly, the Defendant contended that the Claimant became and was at all material times under a duty of trust and confidence towards her in relation to any transaction relating to the said lands.

Held: Rajnauth-Lee, J
As to the law of unconscionable bargain, it is succinctly set out at paragraph 38–27 *Snell's Equity* (supra) as follows: A contract may be set aside in equity if one party lacks sufficient mental capacity, if that lack of capacity is unknown to the other party, and there is in the conduct of the latter unfairness amounting to equitable fraud which would have entitled

the former to rescind the contract even if he had been sane. But, while a transaction will not be set aside merely because it is improvident, the intervention of equity does not stop short at want of mental capacity. Under a well-established jurisdiction, equity will set aside a purchase from a poor and ignorant vendor at a considerable undervalue, where the vendor acts without independent advice, unless the purchaser satisfies the court that the transaction was fair, just and reasonable. It has been said that 'poor and ignorant' may nowadays be understood as 'member of the lower income group' and 'less highly educated', the latter requirement being applied in particular to the person's understanding of property transactions. The jurisdiction will not be exercised unless the purchaser was guilty of unconscionable conduct; it is not sufficient that the parties had unequal bargaining power or that the terms of the bargain were more favourable to one party than to another.

The well-known case of *Inche Noriah v Shaik Allie Bin Omar* [1929] A 127 was cited by both parties. In that case, a Malay woman, who was of great age and wholly illiterate, executed a deed of gift of landed property in Singapore in favour of her nephew, who had the management of all her affairs. Before executing the deed the donor had independent advice from a lawyer who acted in good faith. He was unaware, however, that the gift constituted practically the whole of the donor's property, and did not bring home to her mind that she could more prudently, and equally effectively, benefit the donee by bestowing the property upon him by will. It was held by their Lordships of the Judicial Committee of the Privy Council that the gift should be set aside. It was held that where the relations between a donor and donee raise a presumption that the donee had influence over the donor, the Court will set aside the gift unless (as laid down in *Allcard v Skinner* (1887) 30 Ch D 145, 171) the donee establishes that it was the spontaneous act of the donor, acting in circumstances which enabled him to exercise an independent will, and which justified the Court in holding that it was the result of a free exercise of the donor's will. If the evidence establishes the fact above stated it should not be disregarded merely because the donor did not receive independent legal advice. On the other hand the receipt of independent legal advice may rebut the presumption although it is not acted upon. But to have that effect it must be given with a knowledge of all the relevant circumstances, and be such as a competent and honest adviser would give if acting solely in the interest of the donor . . .

In the judgment of the Court, Mrs. Maharaj has correctly submitted that an examination of the evidence in the case shows that the Defendant was a sickly, aged, illiterate person, without education and knowledge of business transactions. She was being badly treated by her own son, Preetam, and turned to the Claimant, whom she perceived would take the place of a good and caring son to assist her to get back into her property. According to Mrs. Maharaj, not only did she repose trust and confidence in the Claimant but she also placed trust in Mr. Campbell.

Mrs. Maharaj has also correctly submitted that the granting of the Power of Attorney by the Defendant in the circumstances set out in the evidence of the Claimant and of Mr. Campbell demonstrated the absolute trust and confidence that the Defendant reposed in the Claimant. The Defendant gave her rights over to the Claimant by virtue of a general Power of Attorney although Mr. Campbell admitted that he had not explained the effect of the document to her. By the Claimant's own admission, the Defendant had become attached to him. In fact, he said the Defendant's whole family had become attached to him. According to the Claimant, from the Defendant's conversations and dealings with him, the Defendant regarded him more as a son than Preetam. According to him, from the Defendant's dealings with him, she relied on him and trusted him. She had given him all her information and all her documents.

In addition, the Court agrees with Mrs. Maharaj's submission that, based on Mr. Etienne's evidence, the extent of his independent legal advice was his reading the document to the Defendant (who was illiterate and hard of hearing) and his asking both parties if they understood. According to Mr. Etienne, he then handed the document to the relative with the child (presumably Vashti) to read for herself. It is not in dispute that the Claimant was also in the room when Mr. Etienne was allegedly giving the Defendant 'independent legal advice.'

The Court also agrees with Mrs. Maharaj's submissions that the Defendant did not have the benefit of any, let alone, independent legal advice and that when she affixed her thumb print to the Memorandum of Transfer she had no understanding that what she was doing was parting with her property, her home, her inheritance for a sum of $800,000.00; no understanding that in doing so she would no longer have her home that she and her husband had built and on which they had given their children permission to build their homes; no understanding that when a property was being sold that the purchase price that is, the consideration, should be paid before or at the time when the transaction was being completed and certainly before it was registered. Mrs. Maharaj has correctly submitted that nobody told the Defendant and nobody advised her . . .

Further, the Court finds that a case of unconscionable bargain has been made out. The Claimant, the purchaser, has taken advantage of the Defendant, a poor and ignorant vendor, in circumstances where the sale was at a considerable undervalue and the vendor acted without independent legal advice . . . A declaration is hereby granted that the Memorandum of Transfer dated the 22nd February, 2006 and registered as No. T200603080001 95963 on the 8th March, 2006 was executed and obtained by the Claimant from the Defendant by undue influence and at an undervalue and as an unconscionable bargain.

Unequal bargaining power

Unequal bargaining power is often perceived as another manifestation of the broader doctrine of unconscionability. A person is not in a position of relevant disadvantage simply because of inequality of bargaining power. Most contracts are made between parties of unequal bargaining power, and good conscience does not require parties to contractual negotiations to forfeit their advantages, or neglect their own interests. However, courts of equity may intervene whenever one party to a transaction is at a special disadvantage in dealing with the other party because illness, ignorance, inexperience, impaired faculties, financial need or other circumstances affect his ability to conserve his own interests, and the other party unconscientiously takes advantage of the opportunity placed in his hands.

Schroeder Music Publishing Co. v Macaulay (formerly Instone) [1974] 1 WLR 1308 (GB)

Facts: The appellants were publishers of music. The respondent was a writer of songs. In 1966 the respondent was aged about 21. He and a Mr McLeod had collaborated in writing a few songs, but it appears that none of them had been published. He obtained an interview with Mr Schroeder who, with Mrs Schroeder, controlled an American music publishing corporation with worldwide connections. The appellant company was a subsidiary of the corporation. The respondent wished to get a different kind of contract but agreed to sign the agreement which was in the appellants' standard form with a few alterations. On 12 July 1966 they entered into a somewhat elaborate agreement under which the appellants engaged the exclusive services of the respondent for a term of five years which in a certain event was to be extended to 10 years. In 1970 the respondent raised this action claiming a declaration that the agreement was contrary to public policy and void.

Held: Lord Reid

In the present case the respondent assigned to the appellants 'the full copyright for the whole world' in every musical composition 'composed created or conceived' by him alone or in collaboration with any other person during a period of five or it might be 10 years. He received no payment (apart from an initial £50) unless his work was published and the appellants need not publish unless they chose to do so. And if they did not publish he had no right to terminate the agreement or to have copyrights reassigned to him. I need not consider whether in any circumstances it would be possible to justify such a one-sided agreement. It is sufficient to say that such evidence as there is falls far short of justification. It must therefore follow that the agreement so far as unperformed is unenforceable.

Held: Lord Diplock

My Lords, the provisions of the contract have already been sufficiently stated by my noble and learned friend, Lord Reid. I agree with his analysis of them and with his conclusion that the contract is unenforceable. It does not satisfy the test of fairness as I have endeavoured to state it. I will accordingly content myself with adding some observations directed to the argument that because the contract was in a 'standard form' in common use between music publishers and songwriters the restraints that it imposes upon the songwriter's liberty to exploit his talents must be presumed to be fair and reasonable.

Standard forms of contracts are of two kinds. The first, of very ancient origin, are those which set out the terms upon which mercantile transactions of common occurrence are to be carried out. Examples are bills of lading, charterparties, policies of insurance, contracts of sale in the commodity markets. The standard clauses in these contracts have been settled over the years by negotiation by representatives of the commercial interests involved and have been widely adopted because experience has shown that they facilitate the conduct of trade. Contracts of these kinds affect not only the actual parties to them but also others who may have a commercial interest in the transactions to which they relate, as buyers or sellers, charterers or shipowners, insurers or bankers. If fairness or reasonableness were relevant to their enforceability the fact that they are widely used by parties whose bargaining power is fairly matched would raise a strong presumption that their terms are fair and reasonable.

The same presumption, however, does not apply to the other kind of standard form of contract. This is of comparatively modern origin. It is the result of the concentration of particular kinds of business in relatively few hands. The ticket cases in the nineteenth century provide what are probably the first examples. The terms of this kind of standard form of contract have not been the subject of negotiation between the parties to it, or approved by any organisation representing the interests of the weaker party. They have been dictated by that party whose bargaining power, either exercised alone or in conjunction with others providing similar goods or services, enables him to say: 'If you want these goods or services at all, these are the only terms on which they are obtainable. Take it or leave it.' To be in a position to adopt this attitude towards a party desirous of entering into a contract to obtain goods or services provides a classic instance of superior bargaining power.

It is not without significance that on the evidence in the present case music publishers in negotiating with songwriters whose success has been already established do not insist upon adhering to a contract in the standard form they offered to the respondent. The fact that the appellants' bargaining power vis à vis the respondent was strong enough to enable them to adopt this take-it-or-leave-it attitude raises no presumption that they used it to drive an unconscionable bargain with him, but in the field of restraint of trade it calls for vigilance on the part of the court to see that they did not.

Duress

A contract may be set aside in the presence of economic duress. A finding of economic duress is dependent on the extraction of a promise as a result of the exercise of 'pressure', whether characterised as a 'demand' or a 'threat' and the exercise of that pressure must have been such that the coerced party had no practical alternative but to agree to the coercer's demand.

Yassim Ali, substituted on behalf of the Estate Of Dean Mohammed Ali (pursuant to the order of the Honourable Justice Jones dated 8th July, 2009) v Salesh Ramnarine [CV 2008–01471] Salesh Ramnarine; St. Augustine Gas Station Limited v Yassim Ali, substituted on behalf of the Estate of Dean Mohammed Ali [2010] Claim No. CV 2009–00958 (TT)

Facts: This case is all about the purchase of a gas station for the sum of $4,700,000.00. Unfortunately, as simple as this may seem, the means adopted by the parties to achieve this result was far from straightforward and has resulted in Yassim Ali seeking in these actions the sum of $1,720,608.10 which he claims is due to him . . . Briefly and by way of overview, negotiations for the sale of the gas station began in or around November 2003. In January 2004 an agreement for its sale for the price of $4,700,000.00 was signed. On the 18th December 2004 the gas station was transferred to SAGSL for the sum of $3,000,000.00. On the 12th June 2007 SAGSL sold the gas station to the United Independent Petroleum Marketing Company ('UNIPET') for $4,665,350.00. Along the way there were executed by or on behalf of the parties five agreements:

(i) the principal agreement dated the 28th January 2004 by which it was agreed that the property be sold for $4,700,000.00;

(ii) a variation agreement and an agreement for the sale of the equipment and goodwill of the gas station both dated the 16th August 2004 the effect of which was to divide the agreed purchase price for the gas station into the sum of $3,000,000.00 for the leasehold property and the building and the sum of $1,700,000 for the goodwill and equipment;

(iii) a first shareholders' agreement dated the 8th September 2004 whereby the parties agreed to the issue to Ali of 1,700,000 shares in SAGSL valued at $1.00 and the transfer of those shares to Salesh Ramnarine at a minimum of 14,000 and a maximum of 42,000 shares a month at a price of $1.10 per share;

(iv) a second shareholders['] agreement dated the 20th May 2005 whereby the shares were transferred to Ramnarine and Ramnarine agreed to pay for the said 1,700,000 shares within 30 months at the price of $1,880,000.00 together with interest at a rate of 11% per annum

All the agreements, except the last, were prepared by Ramnarine's attorneys.

As told by these documents therefore the transaction for the sale of the gas station for a consideration of $4,700,000.00 was transformed to a sale of the leasehold premises and building thereon for $3,000,000.00 and the goodwill and equipment of the gas station for $1,700,000.00. The consideration for the sale of the goodwill and equipment was then converted to shares in SAGSL and provision made for the purchase of those shares by Ramnarine at an increased price of 10 cents a share. Thereafter the leasehold property was transferred to SAGSL. Some 5 months after the transfer of the property the parties then entered into a new agreement for the payment [] by Ramnarine within 30 months of the purchase price of the shares at a price over and above the $1.10 a share originally agreed together with interest. The initial dispute between the parties began as a disagreement, some 25 months after the execution of last agreement, as to the application of interest to the cost of the purchase of the shares by Ramnarine and thereafter escalated to challenges to first one and then to all the agreements made by the parties by way of allegations by Ramnarine of economic duress, misrepresentation, deceit and fraud.

Held: Jones, J

Were the agreements executed on the 16th August, 8th September and the 20th May entered into by Ramnarine as a result of duress, economic or otherwise, by Ali?

The case as presented by Ramnarine is one of economic duress. Economic duress has now been firmly established in the common law as one of the means by which a party may avoid an unfair agreement. It renders the agreement voidable at the option of the offended party. According to Ramnarine[,] Ali coerced, threatened and pressured him first with respect to continuing with the transaction despite the fact of the encumbrances on the property and then into entering the two shareholders['] agreements.

The basis of the defence of economic duress is that where pressure, which the law recognises as illegitimate, is put on the other contracting party the consent is treated in law as revocable unless approbated either expressly or by implication after the illegitimate pressure has ceased: per Lord Diplock in *Universe Tankships v International Transport Workers Federation and Others* [1983] AC 366 at page 384B. The defence allows a party to avoid a contract on the ground of duress even though the threats are in the nature of commercial pressure and not associated with threats to the person or to the seizure or withholding of goods.

The elements of the defence were succinctly stated by Peter Millett QC sitting as a deputy High Court judge in the case of *Alec Lobb (Garages) Ltd v Total Oil Great Britain Ltd.* [1982] 1 WLR 87 at page 93 paragraph G: '. . . commercial pressure may constitute duress and render a transaction voidable, provided the pressure amounts to a coercion of the will which vitiates consent: see *Pao On v Lau Yin Long* [1980] AC 614. Economic duress, however, is still a form of duress. A plaintiff who seeks to set aside a transaction on the grounds of economic duress must . . . establish that he entered into it unwillingly (not necessarily under protest, though the absence of protest will be highly relevant); that he had no realistic alternative but to submit to the defendant's demands; that his apparent consent was exacted from him by improper pressure exerted by or on behalf of the defendant; and that he repudiated the transaction as soon as the pressure relaxed.'

In his evidence in chief Ramnarine claims that he first sought to rescind the contract sometime after the signing of the agreements of the 16th of August. He says this was as a result of Ali telling him that there was a further debt of $1,600,000.00 on the property and that the property was in danger of being foreclosed. According to him he had discussions with Ali about this debt and tried to rescind the contract. He says that Ali told him that he could not refund the money as it had all been used to repay his creditors. Thereafter between the 16th August 2004 and the 8th September 2004 he says that Ali pressured and coerced him so that he had no choice but to enter into the first shareholders agreement . . . It is hardly likely that Ali would claim to have a greater encumbrance on the property than he really had. I do not accept Ramnarine's evidence that Ali told him that there was an additional encumbrance of $1,600,000.00 on the property.

The reality is that [at] this stage there was nothing that would have allowed Ramnarine to avoid the agreement without losing his money. Both the principal agreement and the variation drafted by his attorneys provided for the retention of all sums paid under the agreement if Ramnarine failed to complete. The fact that the monies already paid under the agreement had been used to meet the debts of Ali was of no consequence. The truth was that if Ramnarine did not complete the transaction he would have been unable to recover the monies paid by him. In the circumstances I do not accept Ramnarine's assertion that he was pressured by Ali into continuing with the transaction and entering into the first shareholder agreement.

With respect to the second shareholders['] agreement Ramnarine says that he was forced to enter into an agreement on terms which were financially onerous to him. The question here is not whether the terms of the second shareholders['] agreement were more onerous to Ramnarine but rather whether undue pressure, amounting to coercion of his will, was put on Ramnarine to enter into that contract. While the terms of the contract may have some relevance to whether it was entered into voluntarily or not the fact that a contract contains onerous terms is not conclusive of duress. The contract may be the result of the usual commercial pressure that exists whenever one party is in a stronger bargaining position than the other. A stronger bargaining position does not necessarily equate with coercion. If that were the case most commercial contracts would be open to challenge.

Indeed this was recognised in the *Pao On v Lau Yiu Long* case. In dealing with whether in case[s] where duress is not established public policy may intervene to invalidate the consideration if there has been a threat to repudiate a pre-existing contractual obligation or an unfair use of a dominating bargaining position, at page 634C-E Lord Scarman said: 'Their Lordships' conclusion is that where businessmen are negotiating at arm's length it is unnecessary for the achievement of justice, and unhelpful in the development of the law, to invoke such a rule of public policy. It would require an unacceptable anomaly. It is unnecessary because justice requires that men who have negotiated at arm's length be held to their bargains unless it can be shown that their consent was vitiated by fraud, mistake or duress. If a promise is induced by coercion of a man's will, the doctrine of duress suffices to do justice. The party coerced, if he chooses and acts in time, can avoid the contract. If there is no coercion there can be no reason for avoiding the contract where there is shown to be real consideration which is otherwise legal.' To take the transaction out of the realm of normal commercial activity there must be some element of illegitimacy or undue pressure being put on the party seeking to avoid the transaction.

The first question to be answered therefore is whether any pressure was put to bear on Ramnarine to enter into the second shareholders['] agreement and if so was that pressure undue or illegitimate or was it normal commercial pressure imposed by a person in a stronger bargaining position and permissible in the circumstances? Despite Ramnarine's claim in his pleadings and the letter from his Attorneys dated the 6th November 2007 there is no evidence of any indication by Ali to either the Ministry or UNIPET with respect to the withdrawal of the use of the licence.

In his evidence in chief however Ramnarine claims that he was pressured into signing the second shareholders['] agreement by (a) Ali's refusal to accept payments pursuant to the first shareholders['] agreement and (b) Ali's threats to revoke the licence. He says he explained to Ali that his financial position made any increased payments impossible and as a result Ali refused to accept any further payments under the agreement. Ali denies this claim. According to Ali it was Ramnarine who refused to make any further payments after March 2005.

By January 2005 Ali had already executed the deed transferring the gas station to Ramnarine. The only security that Ali had for the $1,700,000 owed to him therefore was the first shareholders['] agreement. It seems to me very unlikely that Ali would have refused to accept any payments made by Ramnarine pursuant to the agreement. I accept Ali's evidence that it was Ramnarine who stopped payment of the first shareholders['] agreement and that the last payment made by Ramnarine was in March 2005.

In any event Ramnarine's evidence as to the reason for Ali's refusal to accept the payments is contradictory. On one hand he says that Ali's refusal was as a result of a disagreement between them as to the true price of the shares. According to Ramnarine the agreement erroneously calculated the price for the purchase of the shares to be $1.10 instead of $1.00 and Ali refused to accept payments for shares calculated at less than $1.10 a share and threatened to withdraw the licence. However later in his evidence he says that Ali's refusal was based on a demand that he purchase more than the minimum share purchase obligation [and] Ali threatened to withdraw the licence and declined to accept any payment. These demands he says were made in the month of April. Despite this he claims that Ali accepted payment for the month of April.

I do not accept Ramnarine's claim that the first shareholders['] agreement erroneously fixed the price of the shares at $1.10 a share. The agreement was prepared by Ramnarine's attorneys. The agreement converted Ramnarine's responsibility to pay the $1,700,000.00 by way of a lump sum payment to payment by monthly instalments which if made in accordance with the terms of the agreement provided at best for the debt to be liquidated in excess of three years. The agreement did not provide for the payment of interest. Ali was being credited with shares which did not give him any rights in SAGSL. It is reasonable to assume that in these circumstances the price of $1.10 per share was to compensate Ali for being out of his money for so long a period.

With respect to the threats to withdraw the use of the licence Ali denies making any threats to withdraw the licence prior to the execution of the second shareholders['] agreement[;] he says he did threaten to withdraw the licence but that this was after the second shareholders['] agreement had been signed. He says that he made this threat when he received the letter from UNIPET in June 2006 threatening to sue for monies owed with respect to gas supplied to Ramnarine. I find that Ali's evidence is the more credible on these issues. In the circumstances I reject Ramnarine's evidence that Ali threatened to withdraw the use of the licence if Ramnarine did not enter into the second shareholders['] agreement.

Even if I were to accept Ramnarine's evidence that there was a threat by Ali to withdraw the use of the licence prior to the execution of the second shareholders['] agreement the question to be answered would be whether this threat amounted to undue or illegitimate pressure on Ramnarine or was reasonable exercise of commercial pressure by Ali. Assuming the facts as claimed by Ramnarine the threat would have been made against the following background: the original agreement had provided for the purchase of the gas station by Ramnarine for the sum of $4,700,000.00 by June 2004; by virtue of agreements made at Ramnarine's request and for his benefit the gas station had been transferred to Ramnarine for $3,000,000.00; Ali no longer had the gas station and 9 months after the original date for completion had only received some $3,042,600.00 of the agreed $4,700,000.00; the only security for the outstanding sums was 1,700,000 shares in a company which did not allow him any say in the company; in the meanwhile Ramnarine was making only the minimum monthly share purchases while operating the gas station pursuant to a licence in the name of Ali's father.

It seems to me that in all the circumstances of the case it cannot be said that the threat to withdraw the use of the licence was anything more than a reasonable exercise of the commercial pressure available to businessmen. It did not in my opinion constitute a breach of contract by Ali. Indeed the agreement between the parties provided that by the date of completion Ali take all necessary steps and execute all documents to transfer to Ramnarine or to ensure Ramnarine's rights to purchase gas from the relevant dealers. It is not in dispute that [by] December 2004 Ali had done all that he was required to do to ensure that Ramnarine was authorised to purchase gas.

There was no requirement by the contract that after the transfer of the gas station to Ramnarine that Ali continue to facilitate the supply of gas to the gas station by the continued use of the licence in his father's name. The fact that Ali continued to facilitate the supply of gas to Ramnarine was [as] much for his benefit as for Ramnarine's. It seems to me clear on the evidence that there was no hope of Ramnarine being able to pay the outstanding sums unless there was a supply of gas for sale. It would seem to me that it was in those circumstances that Ali was prepared to continue to facilitate such a supply but there was no contractual requirement in this regard.

In these circumstances in my opinion, if there was a threat by Ali which encouraged Ramnarine to enter into the second shareholders['] agreement there was nothing in these circumstances that would amount to undue or illegitimate pressure. This in my opinion would have been nothing more tha[n] ordinary commercial pressure exerted by a party in a stronger bargaining position.

Even if the threat was undue or illegitimate there must also be some factor which in law could be regarded as a coercion of his will so as to vitiate his consent: 'in determining whether there was a coercion of will such that there was no true consent it is material to enquire whether the person alleged to have been coerced did or did not protest; whether at the time he was allegedly coerced into making the contract he did or did not have an alternative course open to him such as a[n] adequate legal remedy whether he was independently advised and whether after entering the contract he took steps to avoid it.' : per Lord Scarman in *Pao On v Lau Yui Long* at page 635C-D.

While it has not been submitted that there was a viable alternative open to Ramnarine, nor is there any evidence that he was independently advised, although according to Ali[,] Ramnarine said he was taking the agreement to his lawyers[,] of relevance is Ramnarine's conduct after the signing of the agreement. The first objection by Ramnarine to the agreement was made in June 2007. That objection was not to the agreement but rather to what Ramnarine considered to be a breach of that agreement. It would seem to me that rather than protesting the agreement Ramnarine was in fact affirming its validity.

This position continued even after Ramnarine's Attorneys became involved. Indeed it is only after a series of correspondence between attorneys with respect to the application of the payments under the agreement[,] the assertion by Ali's Attorneys that all the monies payable under the agreement were now due and a threat to commence proceedings on Ali's behalf that in October 2007 Ramnarine alleges economic duress. His claim of economic duress however is only with respect to that provision in the agreement that provides for the payment of interest. By the letter rather than repudiate the agreement he seeks time to pay what he claims is due under the said agreement.

It would seem to me therefore that it cannot be said that Ramnarine repudiated the agreement as soon as the pressure relaxed. On Ramnarine's case the pressure would have relaxed when he sold the gas station with UNIPET[;] by that time he would have had no need for the use of the licence in Dean Mohammed Ali's name. But at that stage Ramnarine was still affirming the agreement.

In my opinion the position taken by Ramnarine goes to answer the question of whether in fact the alleged pressure was the reason for entering the contract, the 'but for' question.

It clearly was not. If it was then once the pressure was removed one would expect an immediate attempt to avoid the contract. Instead what we have is a clear affirmation by Ramnarine of the agreement which affirmation continues until Ali's letter threatening court action.

In my opinion therefore the agreements of the 16th August 2004, 8th September 2004 and the 20th May 2005 were not entered into by Ramnarine in circumstances which amounted to duress, economic or otherwise, placed on him by Ali.

Jimmy Robinson (Claimant) v Prinselsio Rivero (Defendant) Claim No. 311 of 2012 (BZ)

Facts: On the 16 June, 2011 at about 7:30 p.m., the claimant was driving his motor vehicle bearing licence plate No. D-6526 on Princess Margaret Drive, Belize City when another vehicle, Nissan Altima No. D-6903 driven by Jose Barrera collided to the claimant's vehicle from behind causing physical injuries to the claimant. The Nissan Altima was owned by the defendant and one Jose Mendez and insured by RF & G Insurance Company of Coney Drive, Belize City. Jose Barrera was at all material times authorized by the defendant to drive the Nissan Altima. In relation to the injuries suffered by the claimant as a result of the accident, the insurance company paid to the claimant $21,882.64 for medication, therapy, doctor visits, hospital services and loss of earnings. On 27 October, 2011, the claimant signed a document, entitled 'Deed of Release And Discharge' in which the insurance company, the owners of the Nissan Altima, the driver Barrera, and the claimant are named as parties, all of whom signed the Deed which was witnessed by others. The claimant says that the Deed is not enforceable because it was signed under duress. Mr. Hubert Elrington SC in his written submissions, submitted as follows: 'The behaviour of the defendant's insurance company was offensive and bordered on extortion. There is ample evidence that the claimant was in serious pain, needing medical attention abroad urgently and needed his money to look after his health and to get some relief from his pain.'

Held: Legall, J
The claimant filed a witness statement and also gave evidence and not once did he mention anything about extortion. I do not find evidence that he signed the Deed because he was in serious pain, or needed medical attention abroad urgently. And, as we saw above, the claimant said no one forced him to sign the document. Considering the evidence, I am not satisfied on a balance of probabilities that the claimant has proven that he signed the Deed or receipt under duress or undue influence.

MISTAKE

If one, or both, of the parties to a contract enter into it under some misunderstanding or misapprehension, in certain circumstances the courts are prepared to permit the parties to rely on the defectiveness of the contract on the basis that if the parties had known of the correct fact, they would not have entered any contractual arrangement.

> The effect of a mistake may be to prevent the formation of a contract, because for example, the parties are at cross purposes. But the fact that a mistake has been made is not sufficient, of itself, to set aside the contract. The reason for this is that the law adopts an objective rather than a subjective approach to agreement.[1]

1 McKendrick, E, *Contract Law: Text, Cases and Materials*, 2008, Oxford: Oxford University Press, p 525.

Mistakes can be unilateral or mutual but in both instances relief against a contract can be granted by the courts.

Great Peace Shipping Limited v Tsavliris (International) Limited 'Great Peace'/'Cape Providence' [2002] EWCA Civ 1407 (GB)

Facts: The story concerned two vessels, the *Cape Providence* and the *Great Peace*. In September 1999 the *Cape Providence* was on her way from Brazil to China with a cargo of iron ore when she suffered serious structural damage in the South Indian Ocean. The defendants learned that the vessel was in difficulties and offered their salvage services, which were accepted on the terms of Lloyd's Open Form of salvage agreement. To find a tug, they approached a firm of London brokers, Marint. The individuals involved at Marint were Mr Graeme Little and Mr Andrew Holder. A tug was found, but it was going to take five or six days for the tug to reach the *Cape Providence* from Singapore. There was serious concern that in the meantime the vessel might go down with the loss of her crew.

Mr Little contacted Ocean Routes and this company gave Mr Little the names of four vessels reported to be in the area. He was told that the *Great Peace*, a vessel owned by the respondents, was the nearest to the *Cape Providence* and should be close to a rendezvous position within about 12 hours. Shortly after midnight Mr Lee, an agent for the *Great Peace*, phoned Mr Holder (who had taken over from Mr Little) and put forward an offer for the chartering of the *Great Peace*. They went through and confirmed the terms of the fixture. As requested, Mr Lee faxed instructions to the master of the *Great Peace* to alter course towards the *Cape Providence*. He sent a copy of the fax to Mr Holder. At 08.17 am Mr Lee gave Mr Holder contact details of the *Great Peace*, which Mr Holder passed on to Captain Lambrides. A few minutes later, at 08.29, the master of the *Great Peace* sent a message to Worlder Shipping Ltd that he had contacted the *Cape Providence* to find her latest position and was altering course 'right now'. Meanwhile, at 08.25 am Captain Lambrides called Mr Holder to say that the vessels were 410 miles away from each other. This was not something known to Mr Holder or Mr Lee.

About the same time as that message was being sent, the *Cape Providence* was passed by a vessel called the *Nordfarer*. By chance the charterers of the *Nordfarer* were also the charterers of the *Cape Providence* and so had an interest in assisting her. At 10.10 am the appellants told Mr Holder that they had contracted with the owners of the *Nordfarer* directly and instructed him to cancel the *Great Peace*. At 10.25 am Mr Holder told Mr Lee that the *Great Peace* was no longer required, that is she was cancelled. They discussed possible financial terms. At 11.00 am Mr Lee sent a fax to Mr Holder, confirming the cancellation and saying that he would do his best to persuade the owners of the *Great Peace* to accept two days' daily hire in place of the minimum five days due under the contract. After speaking to the appellants, Mr Holder told Mr Lee that the appellants were not prepared to pay any sum. So the respondents issued proceedings.

Held: Lord Phillips, MR; May, Law, LLJ
A mistake can be simply defined as an erroneous belief. Mistakes have relevance in the law of contract in a number of different circumstances. They may prevent the mutuality of agreement that is necessary for the formation of a contract. In order for two parties to conclude a contract binding in law each must agree with the other the terms of the contract. Whether two parties have entered into a contract in this way must be judged objectively, having regard to all the material facts. It may be that each party mistakenly believes that he has entered into such a contract in circumstances where an objective appraisal of the facts reveals that no agreement has been reached as to the terms of the contract . . .

Another type of mistake is that where the parties erroneously spell out their contract in terms which do not give effect to an antecedent agreement that they have reached. Such a mistake can result in rectification of the contract. Again, this case is not concerned with that type of mistake.

In the present case the parties were agreed as to the express terms of the contract. The defendants agreed that the *Great Peace* would deviate towards the *Cape Providence* and, on reaching her, escort her so as to be on hand to save the lives of her crew, should she founder. The contractual services would terminate when the salvage tug came up with the casualty. The mistake relied upon by the defendants is as to an assumption that they claim underlay the terms expressly agreed. This was that the *Cape Providence* was within a few hours sailing of the *Great Peace*. They contend that this mistake was fundamental in that it would take the *Great Peace* about 39 hours to reach a position where she could render the services which were the object of the contractual adventure. Thus what we are here concerned with is an allegation of a common mistaken assumption of fact which renders the service that will be provided if the contract is performed in accordance with its terms something different from the performance that the parties contemplated . . . We shall describe it as 'common mistake', although it is often alternatively described as 'mutual mistake' . . . If one applies the passage from the judgment of Lord Alverstone CJ in *Hobson v Pattenden* . . . it suggests that the following elements must be present if common mistake is to avoid a contract:

(i) there must be a common assumption as to the existence of a state of affairs;

(ii) there must be no warranty by either party that that state of affairs exists;

(iii) the non-existence of the state of affairs must not be attributable to the fault of either party;

(iv) the non-existence of the state of affairs must render performance of the contract impossible;

(v) the state of affairs may be the existence, or a vital attribute, of the consideration to be provided or circumstances which must subsist if performance of the contractual adventure is to be possible . . .

It was unquestionably a common assumption of both parties when the contract was concluded that the two vessels were in sufficiently close proximity to enable the *Great Peace* to carry out the service that she was engaged to perform. Was the distance between the two vessels so great as to confound that assumption and to render the contractual adventure impossible of performance? If so, the appellants would have an arguable case that the contract was void under the principle in *Bell v Lever Brothers Ltd* . . . The fact that the vessels were further apart than both parties had appreciated did not mean that it was impossible to perform the contractual adventure. The parties entered into a binding contract for the hire of the *Great Peace*. That contract gave the appellants an express right to cancel the contract subject to the obligation to pay the 'cancellation fee' of five days' hire. When they engaged the *Nordfarer* they cancelled the *Great Peace*. They became liable in consequence to pay the cancellation fee. There is no injustice in this result. For the reasons that we have given, we would dismiss this appeal.

Mutual mistakes

One of the more frequent manifestations of the mistake doctrine is that of common mistake. This occurs when there is a common mistaken assumption of fact which renders the service that will be provided, if the contract is performed in accordance with its terms, something different from the performance that the parties contemplated. Common mistakes are also sometimes called 'mutual mistakes'. The law appropriate to mutual or common mistakes is based on the establishment of certain propositions. The starting principle is that the law ought to uphold rather than destroy apparent contracts. Rules as to a mistake regarding the quality of the subject matter, such as the common law rules regarding commercial frustration, are designed to cope with the impact of unexpected and wholly exceptional circumstances on apparent contracts. In order to attract legal consequences, mutual mistakes must be substantially shared by both parties and must relate to facts as they existed at the time the contract was made. Moreover, the mistake must render the subject matter of the contract essentially and radically different from the subject matter which the parties believed to exist. It must also be emphasised that there is growing recognition of the principle that a party cannot be allowed to rely on a common mistake where the mistake consists of a belief which is entertained by him without any reasonable grounds for such belief.

Typically, there are four main types of operative mutual mistake:

(1) mistake as to the existence of the subject matter of the contract;
(2) mistake as to title;
(3) mistake as to the substance of the thing contracted for;
(4) a false and fundamental assumption going to the root of the contract.

Eastern Canada Coal Gas Venture Ltd. (Venture) v Cape Breton Development Corp. (Devco) 2001 (NSCC) 196 (CA)

Facts: This was an action by Eastern Canadian Coal Gas Venture Limited (Venture) against the Cape Breton Development Corporation (Devco). On the application of Venture, the Attorney General of Canada was substituted as the named defendant. In June 1992 Devco and Venture signed a Coal Gas Agreement (CGA) and a Memorandum of Understanding (MOU) to use coalbed methane to produce electricity. The only gas available on 1 April 1993 was from Devco's Lingan Colliery. Venture knew that Phalen gas would not be available until early in 1994. Despite the terms of its contract with Devco for Phalen gas, Venture decided to start electrical generation on 1 April 1993 using Lingan gas. Unfortunately, Lingan Colliery flooded in November 1992. Lingan gas was suddenly and permanently not available. Venture then took the position that Devco was obliged to provide Phalen gas as of 1 April 1993. Venture denied that it had ever been its intention to start electrical generation using Lingan gas. Both Venture and Devco had proceeded in the mistaken belief that Phalen gas alone could support the project.

Held: Edwards, J
'Mutual mistake' fundamental to the parties' agreement results in rescission of the agreement. Devco was justified in terminating its involvement with the project . . . If one, or both, of the parties to a contract enter into it under some misunderstanding or misapprehension, in what circumstances will they be permitted to allege that the contract is defective, on the ground that, if they had known the true facts, they would never have entered into the agreement? . . .

At the present time, however, the courts are very reluctant to intervene in this manner. The reasons for this change are twofold. In the first place, at common law, if a contract is entered into under a legally operative mistake, it is void *ab initio*; it has no legal effect whatsoever . . . Second, there is a feeling that, once the parties are ostensibly in agreement in the same terms and upon the same subject matter, they ought to be held to their bargain; they must rely on the stipulations of the contract for protection from the effect of facts unknown to them. Nevertheless, cases will undoubtedly arise in which it would be unjust to hold the parties strictly to their agreement . . .

This case raises the fundamental issue of there never having been sufficient gas for the project. Again, as succinctly set out in *Anson's Law of Contract* at p 256, under the heading 'Mistake as to the Existence of the Fact at the Root of the Contract', the authors summarise the situation as follows: 'In this type of mistake, the parties, though genuinely *ad idem*, contract on the basis of an assumption which subsequently proves to be false.' The text describes cases of operative mistake and divides them into two categories – mutual mistake and a second, unilateral mistake. The description on p 256 of *Anson's Law of Contract* is as follows:

> The cases with which we have to deal fall into two main classes:
>
> (i) cases in which the parties, though genuinely agreed, have both contracted in the mistaken belief that some fact which lies at the root of the contract is true. This type of mistake is generally known as a mutual mistake, as it is shared by both parties.
>
> (ii) cases where, although to all outward appearances the parties are agreed, there is in fact no genuine consensus between them, and the law therefore does not regard a contract as having come into existence. This type of mistake is sometimes known as a unilateral mistake, as the mistake is on one side only.

The text discusses the leading case on mutual mistake, which is *Bell v Lever Brothers Ltd.* [1932] AC 161, and suggests at pp 258 and 259 as follows:

> It is suggested that some guidance may be obtained by an examination, in the light of decided cases, of the examples of mistake put forward in the speeches [in *Bell v Lever Brothers Ltd.*]; these envisage four main types of operative mutual mistake: mistake as to the existence of the subject matter of the contract; mistake as to title; mistake as to the substance of the thing contracted for; a false and fundamental assumption going to the root of the contract.

Mistake as to the existence of the subject matter of the contract does not seem particularly relevant. It applies if the subject matter either ceased to exist or perhaps had never been in existence, and that fact was always unknown to the parties. An example might be with respect to a contract for the carriage of specific goods, which goods did not exist on the date of the contract, or a contract for an annuity bought on the life of a person who, unknown to both parties, was already dead. The second example also does not seem particularly relevant, as to mistake as to title. If, for example, the buyer is already the owner of the goods which the seller purports to sell, and if the parties intended to transfer ownership in the goods, then the transfer is impossible. Likewise, the third example as to mistake as to the substance of the thing contracted for does not seem particularly relevant. In addition, it is very difficult to distinguish between mistake which is as to the substance of the contract, as compared to a mistake as to the quality of the goods.

The cases consider facts as to a sound horse versus an unsound horse, old oats versus new oats, horse beans versus feveroles. However, the final category as to a false and fundamental assumption is more analogous to the facts before the Court. On p 266, the authors of *Anson's Law of Contract* state as follows:

> Where the parties contract under a false and fundamental assumption, going to the root of the contract, and which both of them must be taken to have had in mind at the time they entered into it as the basis of their agreement, the contract is void. This should not be regarded as a category separate and distinct from those categories of mistake already mentioned, but rather as a more compendious statement of the type of error required.

> It received the approval of both Lord Atkin and Lord Thankerton in *Bell v Lever Bros.*, although some doubts were expressed as to its value owing to the necessary vagueness of its formation . . .

Treitel, *The Law of Contract* 8th edition states at p 249 as follows: 'Consent may be nullified if both parties make a fundamental mistake of fact.' In such cases, the extreme injustice of holding one of the parties to the contract outweighs the general principle that apparent contracts should be enforced. The authors then go on to classify what mistakes might be considered as 'fundamental' for purposes of the analysis, and include a discussion of mistake as to the existence of the subject matter, mistake as to the identity of the subject matter, mistake as to quality, mistake as to quantity, and, the most significant in light of the fact situation in issue, 'mistake as to the possibility of performing the contract'. The authors state that consent may be nullified if both parties believe that the contract is capable of being performed when this is not the case. They give as examples physical impossibility, citing the *Sheikh Bros. Ltd. v Ochsner* case referred to above . . .

The authors also talk about legal impossibility and finally, commercial impossibility. Under the latter heading they discussed the 'Coronation Cases' including *Griffith v Brymer* (1903) 19 TLR 434 which was a contract made for the hire of a room for the purpose of viewing Edward VII's coronation procession. The contract was held void because when the contract was entered into, the procession had already been cancelled. That fact was unknown to the parties. While performance of the contract may have been both physically and legally possible, its commercial object had been defeated . . .

I will now turn to the facts in this case in relation to 'mutual mistake'. Mutual mistake is a difficult concept, the subject of numerous commentaries and controversies . . . Mistake at common law means that the contract is void. If mistake is established in equity, the contract is voidable . . . It might be useful if I now summarised what appears to me to be a satisfactory way of approaching this subject. Logically, before one can turn to the rules as to mistake, whether at common law or in equity, one must first determine whether the contract itself, by express or implied condition precedent or otherwise, provides who bears the risk of the relevant mistake. It is at this hurdle that many pleas of mistake will either fail or prove to have been unnecessary. Only if the contract is silent on the point is there scope for invoking mistake.

That brings me to the relationship between common law mistake and mistake in equity. Where common law mistake has been pleaded, the court must first consider this plea. If the contract is held to be void, no question of mistake in equity arises. But, if the contract is held to be valid, a plea of mistake in equity may still have to be considered: see *Grist v Bailey* [1966] 2 All ER 875, [1967] Ch 532 and the analysis in *Anson's Law of Contract* (26th edn 1984) pp 290–91.

Turning now to the approach to common law mistake, it seems to me that the following propositions are valid although not necessarily all entitled to be dignified as propositions of law. The first imperative must be that the law ought to uphold rather than destroy apparent contracts. Second, the common law rules as to a mistake regarding the quality of the subject matter, like the common law rules regarding commercial frustration, are designed to cope with the impact of unexpected and wholly exceptional circumstances on apparent contracts. Third, such a mistake in order to attract legal consequences must substantially be shared by both parties, and must relate to facts as they existed at the time the contract was made. Fourth, and this is the point established by *Bell v Lever Bros. Ltd.*, the mistake must render the subject matter of the contract essentially and radically different from the subject matter which the parties believed to exist. While the civilian distinction between the substance and attributes of the subject matter of a contract has played a role in the development of our law (and was cited in the speeches in *Bell v Lever Bros. Ltd.*), the principle enunciated in *Bell v Lever Bros. Ltd.* is markedly narrower in scope than the civilian doctrine. It is therefore no longer useful to invoke the civilian distinction. The principles enunciated by Lord Atkin and Lord Thankerton represent the *ratio decidendi* of *Bell v Lever Bros. Ltd.*

Fifth, there is a requirement which was not specifically discussed in *Bell v Lever Bros. Ltd.* What happens if the party who is seeking to rely on the mistake had no reasonable grounds for his belief? An extreme example is that of the man who makes a contract with minimal knowledge of the facts to which the mistake relates but is content that it is a good speculative risk. In my judgment a party cannot be allowed to rely on a common mistake where the mistake consists of a belief which is entertained by him without any reasonable grounds for such belief: cf. *McRae v Commonwealth Disposals Commission* (1951) 84 CLR 377 at 408. That is not because principles such as estoppel or negligence require it, but simply because policy and good sense dictate that the positive rules regarding common mistake should be so qualified. Curiously enough this qualification is similar to the civilian concept where the doctrine of error *in substantia* is tempered by the principles governing *culpa in contrahendo*. More importantly, a recognition of this qualification is consistent with the approach in equity where fault on the part of the party adversely affected by the mistake will generally preclude the granting of equitable relief . . . 'Where the parties contract under a false and fundamental assumption, going to the root of the contract, and which both of them must be taken to have had in mind at the time they entered into it as the basis of their agreement, the contract is void.'

. . . on the face of the written agreements there was a 'mutual mistake' going to the foundation of the agreements entitling Devco management to terminate Devco's involvement without any liability to Venture. Devco relied reasonably on Venture, and Venture induced Devco's understanding that the project was viable on the available gas using Venture's generating plant as specified by Venture. Venture knew that Devco had no independent source of information on gas volumes from Phalen Colliery for the project, and Devco certainly was not in a position to and did not examine Venture's proposed generating plant with an eye to independently determining its saleable output. Devco's mistaken belief was induced by Venture, and in the circumstances of Venture's promotion of the generating project, Devco's belief was reasonable . . .

In the circumstances of this case, there would be no damages payable by Devco to Venture, as the mutual mistake was entirely due to Venture's work in relation to determining the volume and quality of coal gas from Phalen Colliery for its project in relation to the technical requirements including efficiency of the project which it designed. Devco relied reasonably on the information and assurances provided by Venture . . . In all of the circumstances of this case, there was no reason for Devco to have investigated the issue of gas availability and the issue of what saleable electricity generation could be expected from the gas available to the project. In conclusion, there was a fundamental mutual mistake of fact. Devco was therefore justified in terminating its involvement in the project. Accordingly, the Agreements are rescinded and there is no liability on the part of Devco to Venture.

In addition, the courts are now prepared to extend the ability to bring an action based on a mistake of fact to include a mistake of law such that the latter is no longer addressed as a separate cause of action under English law.

Kleinwort Benson Ltd v Lincoln City Council [1999] 2 AC 349 (GB)

Facts: The appellant in each of the four consolidated appeals was Kleinwort Benson Ltd, a bank which was an early participant in the market for interest rate swaps. Each of the respondents was a local authority. They may be described in brief as Birmingham City Council, Southwark London Borough Council, Kensington and Chelsea London Borough Council and Lincoln City Council. Kleinwort Benson entered into interest rate swap transactions with each of the respondents. Following the decision in *Hazell*, Kleinwort Benson commenced proceedings against each of the respondents claiming restitution of the sums it had paid to them under these transactions. The total of the net payments made under them by Kleinwort Benson was £811,208.90.

There were two features of these transactions which were of particular relevance to these appeals, no doubt flowing from the fact that Kleinwort Benson participated in interest rate swaps at an early stage. The first is that, at the time when proceedings were commenced by Kleinwort Benson, each of the transactions was fully performed by both parties according to its terms across the whole of the agreed period. The second is that not all of the sums paid by Kleinwort Benson to the respondents were paid within the six-year limitation period expiring with the date of the issue of the writ. Of the net sum of £811,208.90 paid by Kleinwort Benson, £388,114.72 was paid within the six-year period, and £423,094.18 represented earlier payments. The former sum had been paid by the relevant local authorities to Kleinwort Benson. The latter sum was in issue, and was the subject of the cases under appeal.

The claim of Kleinwort Benson in each of these cases was that the money in question was paid by it under a mistake, viz a mistaken belief that it was paid pursuant to a binding contract between it and the relevant local authority.

Held: Lord Goff
It is plain, however, that here the mistake relied upon is a mistake of law; and under the law as it stands at present restitution will in general not be granted in respect of money paid under a mistake of that kind . . . I am satisfied that your Lordships should, if you decide to consider the point yourselves rather than leave it to the Law Commission, hold that the mistake of law rule no longer forms part of English law . . . I would therefore conclude . . . that the mistake of law rule should no longer be maintained as part of English law, and that English law should now recognise that there is a general right to recover money paid under a mistake, whether of fact or law, subject to the defences available in the law of restitution.

In certain cases, equity will relieve against the consequences of mutual mistake, even though the mistake would not vitiate the contract at law. The remedy of rescission may be given to set aside a contract where the parties were under a common misapprehension as to their relative or respective rights, provided that the misapprehension was fundamental and that the party seeking to set it aside was not at fault.

Dammer v Wallace and Others (1993) 45 WIR 161 (AI)

Facts: Thomas Alexander Webster (the deceased) died in Anguilla on 23 September 1931 intestate. He was survived by his wife Zellie Augusta Webster (the testatrix) and 10 children, two of whom were the appellant and John Augustus Webster. The deceased owned large acreages of lands in Anguilla, of which an area measuring a size of 135.75 acres recorded on the Land Register of Anguilla formed part. At the time of the death of the deceased the Real Representative Act was in force in Anguilla and by its terms the real property of the deceased would have devolved on his personal representatives. Letters of administration of the estate of the deceased were granted on 10 February 1932 to the testatrix.

The Intestates Estates Act 1945 came into force in Anguilla on 11 December 1945. It followed the provisions of the Administration of Estates Act 1925 (United Kingdom) by abolishing the concepts of heirship and dower. Under the provisions of the law which were in force at the date of death of the deceased, therefore, his real property after administration would have belonged to his heir subject to his widow's right to dower (which was a life interest in one-third of the deceased's real property). So that when the testatrix obtained letters of administration to the estate of the deceased in 1932, she held the estate in her capacity as personal representative of the deceased to give effect to those interests.

It would appear that the testatrix (who died in 1966) took no steps to administer the estate during her lifetime. But, by the provisions of her will dated 24 September 1956, she purported to make several devises of the property in respect of which her husband had died intestate, to her children and others. She died on 21 September 1966, and probate of her will was granted on 15 July 1975 to Peter Adams, who had been named sole executor thereunder.

Meanwhile, on 6 June 1972 the appellant had entered into an agreement with her brother John Augustus Webster for the sale to him of her 'interest and share' in the will of her mother. The first respondents were granted letters of administration *de bonis non* to the estate of the deceased on 18 May 1983. They sold that area of land forming part of the estate of the deceased consisting of 135.75 acres to Rosano Spadaro and Coral Cove Ltd, who by 1988 had duly paid for those lands and the sum of US$1,561,125 became available to the first respondents, who technically should have held this sum on behalf of the persons entitled in accordance with the rules of intestacy which prevailed at the time of the death of the deceased. The appellant alleged, and this was admitted by the second respondent, that the purchase money was divided into 10 equal shares among the children of the deceased and that all the children (except the appellant) received from the first respondents a one-tenth share of the proceeds of sale. The appellant therefore instituted these proceedings against the first respondents as administrators of the estate of the deceased in order to recover the sum of US$156,112.50 which (she claimed) represented her one-tenth share which has been withheld from her.

Held: Liverpool, JA
What falls to be decided in this case is the interpretation of the contract of 6 June 1972 pure and simple. I start off therefore by rejecting the submission of the appellant that she could have had nothing to sell. In construing a written contract the intention of the parties must be gathered from the instrument itself, and the function of the court is to ascertain what the parties meant by the words which they have used. While it is true that the appellant's contract referred to 'my interest and share', these words are not to be taken in a technical sense. One has only to examine the language used by the law lords of the Privy Council in *Lord Sudeley v Attorney-General* [1897] AC 11 to appreciate the difficulty which can be encountered if a proper choice of words is not used. I accept the statement of law contained in the authorities cited by counsel for the appellant to the effect that a devisee, legatee or person interested under an intestacy does not have a defined or specific legal or equitable interest to which a claim may be laid before the estate has been administered. The cases, *Barnardo's Homes v Income Tax Special Commissioners* [1921] 2 AC 1 and *Commissioner of Stamp Duties (Queensland) v Livingston* [1965] AC 694, cited by counsel for the appellant, support this legal principle as it pertains to a will, and *Eastbourne Mutual Building Society v Hastings Corporation* [1965] 1 All ER 779 illustrates the case of an intestacy. But I am unable to agree to the proposition that such a legatee, devisee or other person interested under a

will or an intestacy may not enter into a perfectly valid contract to sell that entitlement if any, whatever it may be.

In my view what the appellant purported to sell was whatever she may have been entitled to under the will of her mother; and that this 'share' or 'interest' or 'entitlement' by whatever name it may be called could only have meant what was due to her after the estate was administered . . . The purchaser, in my view, bought and obtained a right to an expectancy, or as it is often more elegantly put a *spes successionis*. Since it has turned out that there was no property real or personal which lawfully reached the appellant under the testatrix's will, the second respondent is entitled to nothing under the agreement. The findings of the trial judge were therefore based on a false legal premise and his decision cannot be upheld.

The authorities reveal that where performance of a contract is impossible at the time of contracting, the case is one of initial impossibility or mistake, and such a contract is generally void *ab initio*, the reason being that a binding contract cannot arise from a promise which is manifestly incapable of performance either in fact or in law at the time when it is made (see 9 *Halsbury's Laws of England* (4th edn) paragraphs 441, 442 and 447). Further, where the initial impossibility is not known to either party (and this will be so in a case where the property has never existed, even though the parties believed otherwise) the contract will, as a general rule be void (*Galloway v Galloway* (1914) 30 TLR 531 and *Law v Harrigan* (1917) 33 TLR 381). The parties to the contract intended to effectuate a transfer of the appellant's entitlement under the will of her mother, but such a transfer was impossible for the reasons already stated. The question which arises as a consequence is, will this court assist a purchaser in a position such as this where the consideration has wholly failed?

In certain cases equity will relieve against the consequences of mistake, even though the mistake would not vitiate the contract at law; and the remedy of rescission may be given to set aside a contract where the parties were under a common misapprehension as to their relative or respective rights, provided that the misapprehension was fundamental and that the party seeking to set it aside was not at fault (see 9 *Halsbury's Laws of England* (4th edn) paragraph 449). This is clearly a case where both parties were under a common and fundamental misapprehension as to the rights of the appellant both under the intestacy of the deceased and also under the will of the testatrix. I would therefore order that the contract be rescinded and the purchase price returned to the second respondent.

Unilateral mistakes

The law is now clear that a unilateral mistake will only invalidate a contract if equity will set it aside. A party who has entered into a written contract under a serious mistake about its contents in relation to a fundamental term will be entitled in equity to an order rescinding the contract. This applies where the other party is aware that the first party is entering the contract under some serious mistake or misapprehension about either the content or subject matter of that term and deliberately sets out to ensure that the first party does not become aware of the existence of his mistake or misapprehension.

RBTT (Claimant) v Almon Nisbett (Respondent) and Almon Nisbett (Claimant) v RBTT (Respondent) (2012) Consolidated Claims Nos. NEVHCVI996/0 177 & NEVHCV200110113 (KN)

Facts: On 29th March 1993, Almon Nisbett mortgaged the property registered at Book 6 Folio 78 ['the First Property'] of the Register of Titles to the Bank in consideration of the sum of $900,000.00. The terms of that mortgage ['the First Mortgage'] included *inter alia* that interest was at the rate of 13% per annum on the reducing balance repayable on demand and until demand by monthly instalments of $2,780.00, with the first payment commencing on 4th September 1992 and thereafter on the 4th day of each and every succeeding month.

On 4th June 1993, the First Mortgage was filed in the Registry of Deeds and noted as a Mortgage on the Certificate of Title of the First Property. On 6th September 1993, a Notice to Pay Off was filed requiring Almon Nisbett to pay off the sum of $958,102.94 with interest at the rate of 13% per annum in accordance with the First Mortgage. On 30 May 1994, upon a lump sum payment of $700,000.00 towards the First Mortgage, and in consideration of the discharge of the First Property, another mortgage was executed to cover the remaining balance on the First Mortgage. A Discharge of the First Mortgage was filed on 30 May 1994. Also on 30 May 1994, a Memorandum of Mortgage – Demand ['the Second Mortgage'] in the sum of $387,088.81 was registered. Almon Nisbett's property registered at Book 31 Folio 349 on the Register of Titles ['the Second Property'] was used to secure the Second Mortgage. Under the terms of the Second Mortgage, interest was calculated at the rated of 13% per annum calculated on the reducing balance payable by instalments of $2,780.00 [rate] per week commencing on 30 April 1994 and ending on 31 January 2003 or until demand. In October 1996, the Bank instructed its solicitor to commence legal proceedings against Almon Nisbett to recover all sums due and owing. On 4th November 1996, the Bank filed a Summons in Misc. Suit No. 177 of 1996 to settle the Articles of Sale of the Second Property. The Summons was issued under Section 75 of the Title by Registration Act Cap. 279 ['Cap. 279'] of the Laws of the Federation of Saint Christopher and Nevis. An affidavit in support, Notice to Pay Off, Instructions to Seize Property and Act of Seizure were also filed on the same date. On 18 January 2001, the Bank filed a Writ of Summons Indorsed with Statement of Claim in the same Suit claiming monies due and owing to the Bank from Almon Nisbett in respect of a loan extended to him at his request on 30th March 1994. The amount due to the Bank was stated to be $839,502.83. Interest on the debt until payment was also claimed. On 6 March 2001, Almon Nisbett filed a Defence and Counterclaim. He admitted that he had failed to pay the Bank the sum of $387,088.81 or the sum of $534,220.07 as referred to in the Notice to Pay Off or any such sum. He denied that he was liable to the Bank for the sums claimed or any sums at all . . .

The pleadings raise several issues requiring determination but in my view, they are all related to the following: 1) Was the Second Mortgage void because there was a mistake in the material particular of its terms? . . .

Held: Leigertwood-Octave, J

Mistake

The first issue that I will deal with relates to mistake. The contention by Almon Nisbett is that the Second Mortgage is void because there was a substantial mistake in the material particulars of its terms. Phillips MR in the case of *Great Peace Shipping Limited v Tsavliris Salvage (International) Limited* defined mistake simply as an erroneous belief. At common law, a contract may be vitiated on the ground of mistake of one party or both depending on the circumstances of the case. Three types of mistakes have been identified in contract: unilateral mistakes; mutual mistakes; and common mistakes. The two sides do not agree which type or types of mistake apply in this case. Miss Harper submitted that there was a mistake in communication between the Bank and Almon Nisbett and that he had operated under a mistake or understanding about the terms of the Second Mortgage . . .

The leading cases on unilateral mistake are *Smith v Hughes* and *Hartog v Colin and Shields*. Miss Harper has relied on the latter. These authorities indicate that a unilateral mistake is where only one party to a contract is mistaken as to the terms or subject-matter contained in a contract . . .

In her written submissions, Ms. Walwyn referred to the case of *Great Peace Shipping Ltd. v Tsavliris Salvage (International) Ltd*; the Great Peace, which considered common mistake. Common mistake arises where the parties to a contract share the same mistake. It exists in three main sets of circumstances:

1) a common mistake as to the existence of the subject matter of the contract;
2) a common mistake as to the ownership of the subject matter of the contract; and
3) a common mistake as to the qualities or attributes of the subject matter of the contract.

Lord Atkin held in *Bell v Lever Brothers*, where a contract expressly or impliedly contains a condition of a contract, it is voidable if the assumption is not true. In that case, common mistake arose because both parties believed that they were bargaining about a service contract, which could only be terminated with compensation. In fact, the contract could have been terminated without compensation.

I have considered the authorities and [] no circumstances in this case gave that rise to common mistake. The Bank has never agreed that there was any erroneous belief on its part in relation to the Second Mortgage, therefore mutual mistake must be discounted. I have therefore concluded that Almon Nisbett is relying on unilateral mistake.

Where a party asserts that the validity of a contract is affected by a unilateral mistake, he must prove that:

1) The mistake was fundamental to the terms of the contract or 'an essential and integral element of the subject matter;
2) The other party to the contract was aware of the mistake, or
3) In the circumstances, the mistake would have been apparent to any reasonable man'.

Miss Harper has submitted that Almon Nisbett operated under a mistake or understanding about the terms of the Second Mortgage and that the Second Mortgage was of a different class and character from what Almon Nisbett believed. The mistake was not just as to content of the document but was fundamental and Almon Nisbett did not intend to accept its terms. The mistake was fundamental because the effect was to ask Almon Nisbett to pay more than what he was entitled to pay. The Bank knew or should have known of the mistake regarding the terms of the contract and they acted recklessly by not rectifying it.

I turn to the evidence presented in support of those submissions and I come [] one matter that impacts . . . the evidence in this case, the death of Almon Nisbett. It is accepted that this matter has continued after Almon Nisbett's death by the substitution of Masefield Nisbett, as the Administrator of his Estate. However, there are certain evidential matters that neither Masefield Nisbett nor any other witness can speak to, in the place of Almon Nisbett. I have no evidence before me as to what was Almon Nisbett's mistake in relation to the terms of the Second Mortgage or what mistake he was operating under. That evidence would have to come [from] Almon Nisbett. I have heard submissions and conclusions drawn on the part of the Bank but I have no evidence [] adduced in this trial in support of the allegations . . . It is my judgment therefore that the Second Mortgage is not void on the ground of mistake.

The court will not grant an equitable remedy, such as specific performance, where the person seeking to enforce a contract knew of a mistake but was seeking to benefit from it.

Yambou Development Co Ltd v Kauser (2000) 59 WIR 141 (VC)

Facts: On 9 August 1989 the appellant Yambou Development Co Ltd issued a writ against Helen Hadley for specific performance of a contract for the sale by Mrs Hadley of a property at Villa in St Vincent (the property). Mrs Hadley died in the course of the proceedings and the respondent was her executrix. The action was dismissed by Mitchell J and an appeal from his judgment was unanimously dismissed by the Court of Appeal (Satrohan Singh, Redhead and Matthew JJA) on 20 April 1998. The appellant then appealed to the Board.

The original contract for sale was made on 13 November 1981 between Mrs Hadley (acting through an estate agent) as vendor and Norton and Lesline Bess as purchasers. The purchase price was EC$400,000. Mr and Mrs Bess paid an agreed deposit of EC$23,000. The balance of the purchase price, amounting to EC$377,000, was to be paid on completion. This was fixed for 13 December 1981, and time was expressly made of the essence of this date. Mr and Mrs Bess were unable to raise the balance of the purchase price by 13 December 1981 and were granted successive extensions of time, first to 15 January 1982 and finally to 15 March 1982. The terms of the second extension of time were recorded in a document dated 15 November 1981 and signed by both parties. Again time was made of the essence of the date for completion. Mr and Mrs Bess were, however, still unable to raise the finance to enable them to complete, and Mrs Hadley offered to assist them. On or about 29 January 1982 it was orally agreed that, provided Mr and Mrs Bess made an immediate further payment of EC$107,000, the balance of the purchase price, amounting to EC$270,000, would be left outstanding on mortgage. The terms of the mortgage were agreed. Repayment was to be made by fixed but increasing yearly instalments of [the] principal over a period of five years together with interest at the rate of 1 per cent per month on the balance of the purchase price for the time being outstanding.

These terms were confirmed by Mrs Hadley's solicitor, Mr Commissiong, in a letter addressed to Mr and Mrs Bess and dated 30 January 1982. The letter contained a repayment schedule which showed the amount of principal to be repaid in each of the five years and correctly recorded the rate of interest as 1 per cent per month. The schedule also purported to show the combined amount of principal and interest which were 'thus' to be repaid in each of the five years, but unfortunately the interest element of each payment was incorrectly calculated at the rate of 1 per cent per annum. On 9 March 1982 Mr Commissiong wrote to Mr Sylvester, the Bess's solicitor, pointing out the error which he had made in his previous letter. On 24 March 1982 Mr Commissiong wrote again to Mr Sylvester, noting that Mr and Mrs Bess had not indicated their intention to complete the purchase. He explained that, now that the completion date of 15 March 1982 had passed, his client had instructed him to return the full downpayment, and he enclosed a cheque for EC$130,000 made payable to Mr and Mrs Bess. Mr and Mrs Bess had by then issued a writ against Mrs Hadley claiming specific performance of the contract on the terms of the letter of 30 January 1982.

Held: Lord Millett
The judge found that Mr and Mrs Bess were aware of the mistake and dishonestly tried to take advantage of it. But even if they had not noticed the mistake and were wholly innocent, they could not have resisted Mrs Hadley's claim to have the mortgage deed rectified to accord with the terms which the parties had agreed. Mrs Hadley was not obliged

to accept the terms of a mortgage which differed from those which she had agreed with Mr and Mrs Bess merely because her solicitor had made a mistake in recording them. Fortunately, the mistake was noticed in time. Once it came to light, Mrs Hadley was entitled to have the transaction completed on the agreed terms. She was not obliged to buy a lawsuit by completing on the terms which her solicitor had incorrectly recorded and bringing proceedings for rectification . . . Thereafter Mrs Hadley was discharged from all further obligation to convey the property to Mr and Mrs Bess. They had no right to have the contract specifically performed.

MISREPRESENTATION

The classical position is that if a party enters into a contract on the basis of certain statements of fact which turn out to be untrue, the court may be prepared to hold that the presence of such untrue statements of fact can form the basis of relief for an aggrieved party. The courts are not impressed by statements that are mere puffs, opinions, beliefs, representations as to the future or representations with regard to the law.

Asha Charan v Omar Mohammed (2011) CV2008–00683 (TT)

Facts: The claimant purchased a used vehicle from the defendant at a price of $90,000.00. She claims that in the course of oral negotiations taking place between November and December 2007, the Defendant represented to her that: a. Everything was working well with the vehicle; and b. That the claimant was buying a very good vehicle . . . The claimant claims she relied on the said representations and therefore did not take a mechanic to inspect the said vehicle . . . On the same day of the claimant taking possession of the said vehicle, it was discovered that the *air conditioning* in the said vehicle was malfunctioning. . . . Two days after her taking possession the vehicle broke down and it was discovered that the *power steering line had burst* . . . She claims that the defendant made representations that were untrue, either well knowing that they were false and untrue, or recklessly, not caring whether they were true or false . . . 'it was discovered that the *entire braking system* as well as *power steering line* required overhauling; *the tyres required cambering* and the *wheels aligning* . . .' . . . '. . . it was also discovered that the *entire air condition system* required overhauling . . .'

Held: Rajkumar, J
Chitty on Contracts, Volume 1, 30th Edition

(a) A false statement of fact
A misrepresentation must be a false statement of fact, past or present, *as distinct from a statement of opinion*, or of intention or mere commendatory statements. *Mere 'puffs' do not amount to representations: Dimmock v Hallet* (1866) LR 7 Ch App 21 at 27. A mere statement of opinion which proves to have been unfounded, will not be treated as a misrepresentation, Hummingbird *Motors Limited v Hobbs* [1986] RTR 276 . . . as a general rule these cannot be regarded as representations of fact, except insofar as they show that the opinion or intention is held by the person expressing it. Moreover statements must be construed as they would reasonably be understood by the recipient in the context in which the statement was made. Thus a statement as to the nature of a policy made to an experienced loss adjuster, who had a copy of the policy schedule that described it correctly, and was thought to have a copy of the policy itself, was regarded as 'a contention, not as a representation' – in other words, it was merely an expression of opinion . . .

Statement of opinion may amount to statement of fact

However, in certain circumstances *a statement of opinion or of intention may be regarded as a statement of fact, and therefore as a ground for avoiding a contract if the statement is false*. Thus, *if it can be proved that the person who expressed the opinion did not hold it, or could not, as a reasonable man having his knowledge of the facts, honestly have held it, the statement may be regarded as a statement of fact. Connolly Limited v Bellway Homes Limited* [2007] EWCH 895.

Opinion not honestly held

If a person states as his opinion something which he does not in fact believe, or which given the facts known to him, he could not honestly hold, he makes a false statement of fact. So where at a sale of property, the vendor described the occupier as 'a most desirable tenant', while in fact he knew that the rent was considerably in arrear[s], this was held to entitle the purchaser to rescind the contract. *Smith v Land and House Property Corp* (1884) 28 Ch D 7. . .

Reasonable reliance on statements of opinion or statements as to the future

. . . It is suggested that the fundamental principle which underlies all the cases of misrepresentation, . . . is not so much that statements as to the future, or statements of opinion, cannot be misrepresentations[,] but rather that *statements are not to be treated as representations where, having regard to all the circumstances*, it is unreasonable of the representee *to rely on the representor's statements rather than on his own judgment. In general this seems to be the reason why statements as to the future and statements of opinion have been held not to ground relief; in dealing with statements of this nature it has usually been felt that the representee ought not to have relied on the representor.* It has been recognized that sometimes a statement which on its face a statement of fact was really only one of opinion because it was apparent that the maker had no real knowledge or was simply passing on information for what it was worth . . . On the other hand there are circumstances in which it is perfectly reasonable for the representee to rely on the representor's statements even where those statements are matters of opinion, or statements as to the future, and where this is the case, it is thought that the statement should be treated as a representation in the relevant sense.

For example if the statement were made that everything was in its original condition then knowing that the vehicle was a foreign used vehicle, had an odometer reading of 100,000 km, as clearly stated in Motor Critic report, and had been in use as a taxi, such a statement if made at all, must have been recognized by a reasonable person as being mere puff or exaggeration, and treated with healthy sceptism. It would be unreasonable to ascribe such weight to a statement of that nature and it would not be reasonable for the claimant to rely on such a statement, as she claims she did, to enter into the contract of sale without performing basic inspection of the vehicle either herself or with an adviser . . .

I do have reason to doubt whether they constituted representations, and whether they could constitute terms of the contract for sale. I find that even if they were made they would not amount in law to representations such that the claimant; (a) could credibly state that she was induced by them to purchase the vehicle (b) ought to have relied on these rather than on her own judgment.

I find that any such statements made were mere puff[s] and / or statements of opinion (such as *the vehicle does work top of the line*) and could not, by their nature, constitute representations. In any event even if they could I find that they were not made negligently or fraudulently, because the defendant had no knowledge of any unremedied defects in the said vehicle, (save for the gas tank float valve), which fundamentally affected the operation, performance or safety of the said vehicle. There is no evidence that he deliberately concealed from the claimant knowledge which he had of any such defect . . .

I find that the statements allegedly made by the defendant, even if made, did not amount to representations or terms of the contract of sale.

However, further inroads have been made into the limited definition of misrepresentation and statements as to the law can now successfully give rise to an action based on misrepresentation.

Vraj Pankhania, Joshna Pankhania v The London Borough of Hackney, The Receiver for the Metropolitan Police District (2002) WL 1876382 (GB)

Facts: On Wednesday 8 November 1999, at an auction of commercial properties held in the Ballroom at the Langham Hilton Hotel, Mr James Cannon of Nelson Bakewell, a firm of chartered surveyors, brought down his gavel to signify that bidding for the 'star lot' (which combined two neighbouring properties in Shoreditch) was at an end. The properties were in separate ownership. After a vigorous contest, the successful bid, of £3,925,000, was made by the first claimant (often called Mr Victor) bidding in person. He was acting on behalf of himself and his wife, who together conducted business under the name 'Westcombe Homes'. The first claimant paid 10 per cent of the purchase price, and signed a Memorandum of Sale, the same day. The purchase was completed on 9 February 2000. As Mrs Pankhania featured very little in the evidence, for convenience, references to 'the claimant' are to Mr Pankhania. The purchasers alleged that they purchased in reliance on two representations which were false, namely:

(a) that National Car Parks Ltd (NCP), who occupied a car park which formed part of the property, was represented to be a contractual licensee, whose occupation was terminable upon three months' notice, whereas NCP was in fact a tenant, protected in its occupation by the Landlord and Tenant Act 1954;
(b) that the likelihood that the purchasers would be granted planning consent for residential or live/work development on the car park, and the attitude of the first defendant, London Borough of Hackney (Hackney) to such an application, was misrepresented. Hackney was not only a co-vendor, but also the local authority within whose area both sites lay, and thus the local planning authority. The vendors were alleged to have represented that Hackney had no objection to residential or live/work development, whereas the true position was said to be that Hackney intended to adhere strictly to the terms of a Unitary Development Plan, and Guidance Notes, which militated against residential development in favour of employment-based use, the property being within a defined employment area.

Held: Tedd, J
The defendants argue that the misrepresentation was as to law, not fact, and that there is a long-established rule that no action lies for a misrepresentation of law. The leading academic authors regard that as a debatable proposition, awaiting reconsideration in the light of the decision of the House of Lords in *Kleinwort Benson Ltd. v Lincoln City Council* [1999] 2 AC 349 . . . In *Kleinwort Benson*, the House of Lords held that 'the rule precluding recovery of money paid under a mistake of law could no longer be maintained' . . . Does the 'misrepresentation of law' rule survive that decision? . . .

The rules of the common law should, so far as possible, be congruent with one another, and based on coherent principle. The survival of the 'misrepresentation of law' rule following the demise of the 'mistake of law' rule would be no more than a quixotic anachronism. Its demise rids this area of the law of a series of distinctions, such as the 'private rights' exception, whose principal function has been to distinguish the 'mistake of law' rule, and confine it to a very narrow compass, albeit not to extinguish it completely . . . The consequence is that the claimant has established that the defendants are liable to him in damages in respect of the first limb of his claim, namely the car park representations, and damages must be assessed. I invite the parties to consider what directions may be appropriate to progress the remainder of the case. However, the claimant has failed on the second limb of his claim, namely the planning representations, and that limb must be dismissed.

A simple formulation of the principle of misrepresentation is that a person can rescind a contract (representee) where it is proved that the other party to the contract (representor) made a material statement that was unambiguous and likely to induce the representee to enter into a contract. The representee must have relied on the said statement and entered into the contract, resulting in the incurrence of damages.

Sylvan Lashley (First Plaintiff) and Gloria Lashley (Second Plaintiff) v Azul Dacosta Lashley (Defendant) (2011) No CV 1996 of 2006 (BB)

Facts: The parties to the proceedings are family members, the First and Second Plaintiffs being the Defendant's younger brother and sister-in-law respectively. The Plaintiffs both reside in the United Kingdom, while the Defendant resides and conducts business in Barbados as an electrical contractor trading as 'Lashley's Electrical'. At the heart of the proceedings is the Plaintiffs' claim that they are entitled to rescind the Conveyance which they executed in favour of the Defendant on August 25th, 1993 because they allege that they had been induced by and had acted to their detriment in reliance upon certain false and fraudulent misrepresentations made to them by the Defendant at various times during the year 1992. The Plaintiffs claimed as follows: That by a deed of charge by way of legal mortgage dated the 4th day of July, 1991 the Plaintiffs, by the Defendant as their agent and duly constituted attorney on record by Power of Attorney aforesaid 'as surety', obtained a loan from the Canadian Imperial Bank of Commerce 'stamped to cover $235,000.00' 'by way of overdraft and otherwise' for the purpose of completing the said building construction which consisted of four (4) two (2) bedroom apartments. The Plaintiffs proceeded to make prompt monthly payments at the said bank [CIBC] from the month of July 1991 right up to December, 1998. In or about the month of April 1992, the Defendant telephoned the Plaintiffs and in order to induce the Plaintiffs to transfer an interest or share of the Plaintiffs' said property to the Defendant, the Defendant represented to the Plaintiffs that the Plaintiffs were not sending any money to Barbados to pay the mortgage and that he the Defendant, 'as surety', was making all of the repayments on the said mortgage. The Defendant then demanded a one-half share of the Plaintiffs' said property. The Plaintiffs denied the allegation, but nevertheless increased the amount of the mortgage money they were repaying to the bank on the property from £500 per month to £600 per month. Induced however, by and in reliance upon the Defendant's representation, by letter dated the 23rd September, 1992, the Plaintiffs wrote to the Defendant thanking him for all that he had done for the Plaintiffs, including making good the 'shortfall' which the Defendant claimed he was making on the Plaintiffs' behalf, the Plaintiffs therein offered the Defendant a one-third (1/3rd) share of the property. On receipt of the Plaintiffs' said letter, the Defendant again telephoned the Plaintiffs in an angry mood, shouting loudly and demanded a one-half (1/2) share. The Defendant insisted that he did not want a one-third (1/3rd) share. He further represented that with all the work he has done on the apartments and the amount of money in making good the 'shortfalls' one third (1/3rd) was not enough. Induced by and acting in reliance upon each of the representations, and in fear of losing the entire property, the Plaintiffs trusted the Defendant, who is a family member and who at the time was their agent in Barbados, with the sole control and management of the Plaintiffs' business in Barbados, they having no knowledge of what was actually taking place except as advised by the Defendant, the Plaintiffs transferred the one-half (1/2) share in the property to the Defendant as he demanded by a conveyance dated the 25th day of August, 1993 prepared by the Defendant's Attorney-at-law and sent to the Plaintiffs in England for their signature, the said transfer purporting to be for the sum of $85,000.00, which sum was never paid by the Defendant to the Plaintiffs. The Defendant filed a Defence and Counterclaim on May 8th, 2008 in which he expressly denied making the alleged representations to the Plaintiff as alleged or at all.

Held: Crane-Scott, J
The law governing proceedings for rescission based on misrepresentation is that where one person ('the representor') makes a misrepresentation [i.e. a false statement of fact] to another ('the representee') which has the object and result of inducing the 'representee' to enter into a binding transaction with him, the 'representee' may generally elect to regard the transaction as rescinded. Furthermore, a transaction which is induced by a misrepresentation may be rescinded or set aside irrespective of whether the misrepresentation was made fraudulently, negligently or wholly innocently. [*See Halsbury's Laws of England*, 4th Edition, Volume 31, paras 701–814; *Chitty on Contracts, General Principles*, 30th Edition, at paragraph 6–103.] The proper parties to proceedings for rescission are the parties to the alleged representation, that is to say, the 'representee' as the person claiming relief on the one hand, and the 'representor' being the person who allegedly made the representation and against whom relief is sought on the other. [*Halsbury's Laws*, 4th Edition, Volume 31, paras 725 & 819.] The law may also deem a person to be a 'representee' and a proper party to the proceedings in special situations. Accordingly, where the representation is made to one person through another, but with the intention that the person through whom the representation is conveyed will also be influenced and act on it (as where the 'representor' knows or believes that the two persons are partners or business associates) in such a case either or each of the persons in question, if either or each acts on the faith of the representation, is deemed a 'representee'. [*Halsbury's Laws*, 4th Edition, Volume 31, para 736.] Where a misrepresentation is alleged, the burden lies on the 'representee', as the party alleging that misrepresentations were made, to prove 'that degree of falsity which is required to establish that the representation is a misrepresentation'. It is also imperative that the precise representation relied upon be distinctly stated in the pleadings. [*Halsbury's Laws of England*, 4th Edition, Volume 31, para 744; *Hallows v Fernie* (1868) 3 Ch App 467 at 477.] A representation is deemed to have been false, and therefore a misrepresentation in law, if it was *at the material date* false in substance and in fact. Accordingly, it will be for the 'representee' to establish that the representation relied on was false *at the date when the 'representee' altered his position because of it.* [*Halsbury's Laws of England*, 4th Edition, Volume 31, para 742 and 753; *Briess v Woolley* [1954] AC 333 at 354.] . . . In law, no misrepresentation, however gross or fraudulent, will attract any civil consequences, unless the 'representee' is able to establish that: (i) it was material in the sense that its tendency or its 'natural and probable result' was to induce the 'representee' to act on the faith of it in the way in which he was shown to have acted; and (ii) that the misrepresentation was intended to and did influence the mind of the 'representee' so as to affect his conduct. [*Halsbury's Laws of England*, 4th Edition, Volume 31, paras 765–780.] As the party alleging that misrepresentations were made, the legal burden of proving the falsity of the second representation rested on the Plaintiffs. However following its review of the Plaintiffs' case, the Court found that the

Plaintiffs had also failed to adduce cogent evidence from which the Court could find that the Defendant's statement that he had been making good shortages had, in fact, been false . . . In the circumstances, that Court finds as a matter of law that it would have been no misrepresentation for the Defendant to represent to the Plaintiffs that he had been making good shortfalls on the loan repayments due to the bank and I so hold.

Materiality

The statement being relied upon by a party seeking to rescind a contract on the basis of misrepresentation must be significant or important.

Andrene Brown (Claimant) v Insurance Company of the West Indies (Defendant) (2011) Claim No. HCV 04439 of 2007 (JM)

Facts: The Claimant is, and was at all material times, a civil servant employed in the Ministry of Labour as a Labour Administrator. She is a graduate of the University of the West Indies with a Bachelor's Degree and also holds a [Master's] Degree in Human Resource Development. It is not disputed that in or around January 2005 the Claimant entered into a contract of insurance with the Defendant to provide comprehensive insurance coverage of a 2005 Mitsubishi Pajero motor vehicle, licence # 2847 EL, which the Claimant had purchased with the benefit of a Twenty Per Cent (20%) duty concession, awarded to the Claimant by virtue of her position as a travelling officer and civil servant. To assist in the financing of the purchase of the said motor vehicle, she acquired a loan from RBTT Bank which loan was secured with the assistance of Mr. Jamelah Skeene, her then fiancé, and her main witness in this case. The policy of insurance was renewed up to 2007. On or around the night of December 31, 2006, the vehicle, the subject of the insurance contract, was allegedly taken from Mr. Skeene when he was purportedly held up at gun point in the vicinity of the Old Harbour Main Road, in the Parish of St. Catherine. In consequence of this loss, the Claimant claimed against the Defendant on the policy of insurance. Subsequently, the Defendant purported to accept the claim and offered to indemnify the Claimant for her loss. However, after investigating the circumstances in which the claim had been made, the Defendant sought to deny the Claimant's claim and to assert that it was entitled to reject it based on the terms of the policy. The Claimant in her claim insists that she is entitled to compensation from the Defendant insurer as she had a valid comprehensive policy of insurance over the vehicle and pursuant to her loss, her policy must be honoured. The Defendant, on the other hand, says it is entitled to deny the Claimant's claim on the basis of material non-disclosure and on the further basis that by virtue of a breach of a provision of the contract which was a warranty, it is entitled to avoid the policy. The Defendant has sought to deny the Claimant's claim on the basis that the Claimant has breached her duty of utmost good faith, a fundamental premise of contracts of insurance, by non disclosure of material facts or deliberate misstatements of facts in the completion of the proposal form. The Defendant also avers that by virtue of the declaration made by the Claimant in the proposal form, her answers to questions in the proposal were made warranties, the breach of which allowed the Defendant to avoid the policy.

Held: Anderson, J

Has there been Misrepresentation and/or Non-Disclosure.
The evidence accepted by the Court is that the Claimant made the certain representations on the proposal form which were not true. She had stated that the motor vehicle would

be garaged overnight in a carport and that the Claimant would normally be the one who would have had custody and control of the vehicle. This was shown to have been untrue. When asked for 'details of persons who would drive the car', the only name inserted was that of the Claimant but, as the Claimant herself said in cross examination, it was always intended that Mr. Skeene would also be a driver. In fact in her statement to the private investigator she had said that from the time of its acquisition, Mr. Skeene was the 'regular driver of the vehicle'. When asked why she had not put Mr. Skeene's name on the proposal form, she said it was not asked for and the insurance was comprehensive.

On the evidence I have accepted, there was non-disclosure in that she had not revealed [] the person who would be the main person who would have control of the vehicle. She did not, in that context, reveal that she would continue to drive her Toyota Camry motor car while Mr. Skeene would mostly drive the Pajero. She did not reveal that the other likely driver of the vehicle was Mr. Skeene who was a self employed businessman and who carried on the business as a wholesaler and entertainment co-ordinator. It is not in dispute, and the Court so finds, that the insurance profile of Mr. Skeene was significantly different from that of the Claimant.

Was the misrepresentation or non-disclosure 'material'?
The definition of what is material has already been set out above in the submissions of the Defendant. A circumstance is material if it would have had an effect on the mind of a prudent insurer in weighing up the risk. (*Pan Atlantic Insurance Co. Ltd.*) It was the submission of the Claimant that if there were non-disclosure or misrepresentation, they were not material, that materiality had to be proven and shown to have induced the insurer to enter into the particular contract. Thus the citations above, of the *Pan Atlantic Insurance Co.* case and *MacGillvary on Insurance Law* were made by the Claimant's attorney. In *Drake Insurance v Provident Insurance* [2003] EWCA Civ. 1834, (also referred to below in the judgment of Karl Harrison JA in *ICWI v Elkhalili*) the English Court of Appeal reaffirmed that inducement had to be proved by the insurer.

It is the law that there are instances in which the non-disclosure or the misrepresentation is so clearly material that the Defendant would not have to prove materiality. I would find as proven that in the instant circumstances the misrepresentation as to where the motor vehicle would be kept was material. I would also be prepared to hold that the non-disclosure of the fact that the person who would be more often the driver of the vehicle and in whose custody and control it would more often be, is also material as likely to affect a reasonable underwriter's mind in considering whether to accept the risk at all or at the premium decided upon. The evidence of Mrs. Washington-Hoilett for the Defendant, was that the nature of the information which had not been provided by the insured in the proposal form was such as could have affected the insurer's consideration as to whether the risk should be accepted and at the premium at which it was . . .

I adopt without reservation the reasoning of his lordship set out above. In particular, I adopt his reference to *Condogianis* which he says supports the proposition that 'where the truth of the statements is made the basis of the contract, it is unnecessary to consider whether the fact inaccurately stated is material or not, or whether the applicant knew or did not know the truth'. In the circumstances, I give judgment for the Defendant and I award costs to the Defendant, to be taxed if not agreed.

Ambiguity

The statement that is being relied upon must not be ambiguous, that is, a statement capable of more than one meaning.

Clotelle Holder-Delves (First Plaintiff), Patrick Delves (Second Plaintiff) and Renaldo Springer (Third Plaintiff) [suing by his mother and next friend Rhonda Holder] v BS&T Motors (Defendant) No. 1724 of 2002 (BB)

Facts: It is alleged that on 24 August 2000 the first plaintiff, on her own behalf and as agent for the second plaintiff, purchased from the defendant a white BMW motor vehicle which was subsequently licensed as O-580 for the sum of $76,373.00. The purchase was made in reliance on false representations by the defendant's servants or agents that the vehicle was a 2000 model, new and had not been previously used. The vehicle was delivered to the plaintiffs on 15 September 2000. The first plaintiff alleged that the vehicle had significant mechanical defects which resulted in the vehicle being returned to the defendant on several occasions. On each occasion the first plaintiff indicated her intention to reject the said vehicle and requested a replacement. It is alleged that while the second plaintiff was driving the vehicle on 11 February 2002, an accident occurred when, in negotiating a right turn, the steering became unstable, causing the vehicle to veer out of control. It collided with an embankment, causing personal injuries to the plaintiffs.

Held: Goodridge, J
The first plaintiff claimed that, during the course of the negotiations for the purchase of the vehicle, the defendant falsely represented that the vehicle was a 2000 model, new and unused. She alleged that the vehicle was in fact a 1999 model having been manufactured between June 1998 and March 1999. It was not new and unused as there was substantial wear and tear on the front suspension; severely damaged right front bottom ball joint; worn front and rear brake pads and worn brake discs. Fraudulent misrepresentation occurs when one person (the representor) makes a false representation to another (the representee) which induces that person to enter into a contract. In the case of *Derry v Peek* (1889) AC 337 Lord Hers[c]hell stated at p. 374: 'Fraud is proved when it is shown that a false representation has been made (1) knowingly, or (2) without belief in its truth, or (3) recklessly, careless whether it be true or false.' The first plaintiff's evidence is that Mr. Tudor said that the car in the showroom was a 2000 model and the one on the outside (O-580) was a 1999 model . . . On the first plaintiff's own admission, the defendant's agents did not state that the car was a 2000 model. The evidence does not disclose that the defendant made the representation as to the year model of the vehicle as alleged in the claim. It is the finding of the court that the first plaintiff has failed to prove that the defendant made any misrepresentation in respect of the year of manufacture of the vehicle. The first plaintiff's evidence is that Mr. Tudor told her that while the vehicle was on display on the front lawn someone had jumped on the roof and they had to do some fixing and repainting of the roof and that the car was never used . . . In the case of *Morris Motors Ltd v Lilley* [1959] 1 WLR 1185 it was stated that a vehicle remains new 'even when it leaves the manufacturer's hands, until it is made the subject of a retail sale by a distributor or dealer, it is registered with the local county council, number plates are put upon it and it is driven away by the purchaser.' In *R v Ford Motor Company Limited* (1974) 59 Cr App R 281 it was held that: 'If the damage which the new car after leaving the factory has sustained is, although perhaps extensive, either superficial in character or limited to certain defined parts of the car which can be replaced by new parts, then provided such damage is in practical terms perfectly repaired so that in truth it can be said after repairs have been effected that the car is as good as new, then it would not be a false representation to describe such a car as new.' It is the opinion of the court that the work done to the roof did not prevent the vehicle from being described as a new vehicle. In any event, the first plaintiff admitted she was told of the repair to the damaged roof prior to purchase and yet she purchased the vehicle.

She would have waived her right to reject the vehicle. However, there is the fact that the defendant represented to the first plaintiff that the vehicle was not used when it had in fact been used as a test drive vehicle. This statement amounted to a representation but I am not satisfied on the evidence that the first plaintiff has established on a balance of probabilities that the representation was fraudulent or that she was induced into entering into the contract for the sale of the vehicle on the basis of that representation.

The Court however found for the Plaintiffs on the basis that 'while some of the defects could be classified as resulting from normal wear and tear, others were mechanical defects of a serious nature which lead the court to hold that the vehicle was not of merchantable quality and was not fit for the purpose for which it was bought'.

Inducement

It is essential for a representee to prove that he was induced by his belief as to the truth of the representation to enter into the contract and consequently suffered damage as recognised by law. A warranty as to the truth of a statement will suffice for a cause of inducement.

Andrene Brown (Claimant) v Insurance Company of the West Indies (Defendant) (2011) Claim No. HCV 04439 of 2007 (JM)[2]

Held: Anderson, J
But the authorities seem clear that in addition to materiality, inducement must be demonstrated if the contract is to be avoided. In *Ansari v New India Insurance Co. Ltd.* [2009] EWCA Civ 93, Moore-Bick LJ, referring to *Pan Atlantic v Pine Top* said:

> *Pan Atlantic v Pine Top* was concerned with the *concept of materiality* (My emphasis) in the context of misrepresentation and non-disclosure in the course of negotiations leading to the formation of a contract of insurance. It is trite law that the insured is obliged to disclose to the insurer before the contract is made all material circumstances known to him, a material circumstance being defined as one which would influence the judgment of a prudent insurer in fixing the premium, or determining whether he will take the risk. That principle, which is contained in section 18 of the Marine Insurance Act 1906, applies to contracts of insurance of all kinds. The question for determination in *Pan Atlantic v Pine Top* was whether, in order to influence the judgment of a prudent insurer, a circumstance must be of such importance as to have a decisive effect on his decision whether to accept the risk at all and if so on the terms to be applied, or whether it is sufficient that it is something he would take into account when making his decision, without it[] necessarily having a decisive effect on his mind. *The House of Lords held that the latter was the case, recognising that an insurer who seeks to avoid the contract on the grounds of misrepresentation or non disclosure must also establish that it induced him to accept the risk on terms to which he would not otherwise have agreed.* (my emphasis) . . .

Despite the evidence of Mrs. Washington Hoilett, it is not at all clear to me that the Defendant has established that it was *induced* by the misrepresentation or non-disclosure, to enter into the particular contract with the Claimant.

Notwithstanding this finding, I do accept the alternative submission of the Defendant that the signing of the declaration at the foot of the proposal form amounted to a warranty

2 See case brief above.

to the Defendant, the breach of which allows the Defendant to avoid the policy. A recent decision which makes me satisfied that this is the correct view in the instant matter is that of the Jamaican Court of Appeal in the case of *ICWI v Abdulhadi Elkhalili* SCCA # 90 of 2006. In that case, Karl Harrison JA, in delivering the main judgment of the Court stated: 'This appeal raises issues of some general importance: what constitutes material facts which ought to be disclosed in a proposal form for motor vehicle insurance and what is the legal effect of the warranty clause in this form?'

These were, in my view, the same issues which the Court faces here. In *Elkhalili*, the Court of Appeal reversed the earlier decision of Lawrence-Beswick J at first instance. That decision was strongly relied upon by the Claimant in its submissions on materiality. The learned judge, Karl Harrison JA provided a comprehensive analysis of the law both in relation to materiality as well as to the effect of signing of the declaration. The declaration in the case before the Court of Appeal was in the following terms: 'I/WE HEREBY DECLARE that all the above statements and Particulars are true' and . . . 'I agree that this Proposal and declaration shall be the basis of and be considered as incorporated in the policy issued hereunder which is in the ordinary form used by the INSURANCE COMPANY OF THE WEST INDIES LIMITED for this class of Insurance and which I/WE agree to accept'.

This was the same declaration as is contained in the instant case. There, as in this case, the Claimant claimed not to have read the proposal form. He also said that he did not fully understand it owing to his limited grasp of English. I hope I may be forgiven if I quote extensively from the extremely well-reasoned judgment of his lordship. His lordship said:

12. Before examining the several grounds of appeal, I think it convenient at this stage to set out the legal principles which apply to proposal forms and to the conditions of an insurance policy vitiated by fraud or misrepresentation.
13. A contract of insurance is one of utmost good faith (*uberrimae fidei*) and, as such, the requirement of good faith must be observed by both the insured and the insurer throughout the existence of the contract. In practice, the requirement of *uberrima fides* means simply that an applicant for insurance has a duty to disclose to the insurer all material facts within the applicant's knowledge which the insurer does not know. There is a duty of disclosure and a duty not to misrepresent facts.
14. The test of materiality has been settled by the House of Lords in *Pan Atlantic Insurance Co. Ltd. v Pine Top Insurance Co. Ltd.* [1994] 3 All ER 581, [1995] 1 AC 501 on a 3:2 majority. The majority held that, for the purposes of marine and nonmarine insurance, a circumstance is material if it would have had an effect on the mind of a prudent insurer in weighing up the risk. The House also held that, for an insurer to be entitled to avoid a policy for misrepresentation or non-disclosure, the alleged misrepresentation or non-disclosure must be material and must have induced the making of the policy. Recently, the English Court of Appeal held in *Drake Insurance v Provident Insurance* [2003] EWCA Civ 1834 that inducement must be proved by the insurer.
15. The proposal form which precedes the issuance of the policy of insurance is the document which helps the insurer to make an informed decision as to whether he will indeed insure the proposer's risk. In order therefore, to ensure the utmost good faith on the part of the insured, it is commonplace among insurers to require that the proposal form be filled up accurately and to have the proposer for insurance warrant the accuracy of the answers and statements made on the form. Thus, as in this appeal, the proposer (Mr. Elkhalili) was required to sign and did sign the declaration (reproduced at (9), above). The critical element in the declaration is the phrase which states that 'this proposal and declaration shall be the basis of and be considered as incorporated in the policy . . .' This declaration, in my view, forms

the basis of the contract, so that, the declaration at the foot of the proposal form that the statements are true, and that the declaration shall be considered as part of the policy of insurance, makes the truth of the statements a condition precedent to the liability of the insurer. A proposer, by signing it, signifies his agreement to it.

...

20. Of similar effect is the case of *Dawsons Ltd v Bonnin* [1922] 2 AC 413. Viscount Haldane, approving an earlier passage of Lord Blackburn in *Thomson v Weems* (1884) 9 App Cas 671, held that the basis clause made the truth of the statements contained in the proposal a condition precedent to the liability of the insurers quite apart from the question of materiality.
21. The law does not require that the word 'warranty' be used in the declaration. Viscount Finlay explained in *Dawsons* (supra) at 428–429 that- 'any form of words expressing the existence of a particular state of facts as a condition of the contract is enough to constitute a warranty. If there is such a warranty the materiality of the facts in themselves is irrelevant; by contract their existence is made a condition of the contract'.
22. Breach of warranty then entitles the insurer to terminate the contract of insurance and avoid the policy.

... I am of the view that the 'form of words expressing the existence' of the particular state of fact as a condition of the insurance contract herein, is 'enough to constitute a warranty'. That warranty has been breached and the Defendant is therefore entitled to avoid the policy ... In the circumstances, I give judgment for the Defendant and I award costs to the Defendant, to be taxed if not agreed.

Reliance

An important issue is whether the representee relied on the statement that is being characterised as untrue. If the statement was never made to the representee, could there have been reliance?

Dave Lopez and Versatile Investment Trust Limited v The Bank of Nova Scotia Trust Company of Trinidad and Tobago Limited and Constantine Mendez (2001) HCA No. 3418 of 1986 (TT)

Facts: The action arose out of an agreement for sale of lands by the defendant to the first plaintiff in his own right, dated 16 August 1982. The lands referred to in the agreement were 15 lots situate at St Joseph Village, San Fernando (hereinafter called the said lands). The date fixed for completion in the agreement was 14 November 1982. The agreement was a simple one. The purchase price of the said lands was TT$1,648,104.00 of which the first plaintiff paid 10 per cent upon the execution of the agreement. The agreement fixed the completion date. It provided that the sale was subject to a good marketable title. It provided for the payment of interest at the rate of 13 per cent per annum if the balance was not paid at the completion date. It provided for the vendor to give the purchaser 14 days' notice to complete and that time was of the essence. Should the purchaser not then complete there were provisions for forfeiture of the deposit and the ability of the vendor to sell and recover any deficit from the purchaser. The agreement was signed by one Clyde A Jones on behalf of the defendant and by the first plaintiff. There was a survey plan of 1977 of one Stoute attached to the agreement.

On 24 May 1993 the said lands were conveyed to the second plaintiff at the direction of the first plaintiff. It was pleaded that the first plaintiff was the majority shareholder (70 per cent) of the second plaintiff. This was not put in issue by the defendant in its pleading. The plaintiffs claimed that the said lands were not developed as per the agreement for sale.

Held: Kangaloo, J
The second plaintiff has proved damage to the extent of TT$17,000 it paid to Mr Greene for the installation of storm water drains. This is the only damage that it has proved. The question remains even if there was a representation made by either of the third party or Mr Jones on behalf of the defendant, whether the representation was made to the second plaintiff at all. On the evidence there is nothing to suggest that the defendant even knew of the existence of the second plaintiff until the letters passing between attorneys for the plaintiffs and the defendant towards the end of March 1983. All the representations are pleaded before this date and the evidence led by the plaintiffs similarly do not contradict this. No representation was made by anyone to the second plaintiff specifically. However it is not necessary that the statement be made directly to the plaintiff; communication to an intermediary is sufficient. But it is necessary that the defendant knows that his statement will be communicated to the plaintiff either specifically or as a member of an ascertainable class and that the statement is likely to be acted upon by the plaintiff for the purpose for which the statement was made and that such was objectively the intention of the defendant (See *Halsbury's Law of England* 4th edn Vol. 33 paragraph 614).

Damage

It is essential for a representee to prove not only that he acted upon or suffered in consequence of his belief in the truth of the representation, but that such action or suffering resulted in damage recognised by law.

Dave Lopez and Versatile Investment Trust Limited v The Bank of Nova Scotia Trust Company of Trinidad and Tobago Limited and Constantine Mendez HCA No. 3418 of 1986 (TT)

Held: Kangaloo, J
In *The Law of Actionable Misrepresentation* (1974) Spencer Bower at paragraph 141 it is stated that in an action for misrepresentation it is essential for a representee to prove not only that he acted upon or suffered in consequence of his belief in the truth of the representation, but that such action or suffering resulted in damage recognised by law. Thus there must be a representation to a representee who, acting on the representation, suffered damage. In the case of the first plaintiff there is no plea that he was induced by any representation to enter into the agreement for sale. There was consequently no evidence led that he was so induced. Additionally, as has already been pointed out even if there was such a plea substantiated by evidence, the first plaintiff on the evidence suffered no damage. This plaintiff's case therefore is bound to fail.

Knowledge of representee

In ascertaining whether any unfounded representation is open to redress, the court may at times look to the knowledge of the parties involved. There would appear to be some attempt to incorporate some form of the principle of *caveat emptor* into the law pertaining to misrepresentation.

If it is on a subject peculiarly within the knowledge of the party making the representation and is relied on by the other party, it may well be held to be legally cognisable; however, where the facts are available to the other party and such party applies or might apply unrestricted means of inquiry, and is not induced to withhold inquiry, the alleged representation which turns out to be untrue may not lead to an opportunity to rescind a contract as the court may be inclined to treat such representations as mere puffs.

Miller v Edelweiss International Franchise Corp. 1996 BCSC C914895 (CA)

Facts: The plaintiffs entered into a series of agreements with the defendant corporations under which the plaintiffs became franchisees. The plaintiffs claimed that they were induced to enter into these contracts by oral representations made by the defendant corporations. The plaintiffs sued for damages claiming that the oral representations inducing them to enter into the contracts were innocent misrepresentations and/or negligently made. The defendants misrepresented to the plaintiffs that they would be purchasing a store with ever-increasing income and without any real or pending competition, which with hands-on management could readily gross CAN$400,000 or so per year. The defendants made that representation knowing that it was false in its essential particulars, namely, that the store's revenue was increasing when it was, if anything, declining and that there would be in the immediate future no significant competition from Overwaitea when the defendants knew full well that this was imminent.

Held: Owen-Flood, J
I accept the evidence of Mr and Mrs Miller that at that meeting, representations were made by Mr Dallas. Those representations, I find, were untrue and the defendants knew them to be untrue . . . if the misrepresentation was *in substantialibus*, that is, if it concerned a point of substance, such that if it had been known the representation was false at the time it was made, then it might reasonably be supposed that the party to whom the representation was made would not have entered into the contract, then the exclusion clause is no defence for the person making the misrepresentation. I find that to be the case at bar. The misrepresentations here were indeed substantial. In the result I hold that the misrepresentations constitute not only breach of contract but also negligence on the part of the defendants who held themselves out as knowledgeable and who knew that the plaintiffs were relying upon their knowledge . . .

This gives rise to the second issue of whether it was reasonable for the plaintiffs to rely upon the misrepresentations, or whether this is simply a case of *caveat emptor*, that is to say buyer beware, in which it was unreasonable for the plaintiffs to rely upon what was held out to them. The defendants point to the principle that a statement of opinion or what is sometimes called puffery does not generally give rise to liability. That is true but it has no application at bar. I hold that the statements were not mere expressions of opinion but purported to be fact and mixed fact and opinion. They certainly were not statements of pure opinion. The misrepresentation was made that the deli's revenue was steadily increasing. In fact, the reverse was true . . .

The defendants also argue that at law there is no liability for misrepresentation where the facts at issue are not solely within the knowledge of the representor, but are also subject to discovery upon investigation and inquiry by the representee. The defendants say that in such circumstances it is not reasonable for the representee to rely without undertaking further investigation . . . I follow the law set out by Robson, JA speaking for the Court in *Rasch v Horne* (1930) 1 WWR 816 (Man CA) at 820 where he wrote:

> An element to be considered in ascertaining whether any unfounded representation is open to redress in any form is the means of knowledge of the parties involved. If it is on a subject

> peculiarly within the knowledge of the party making the representation and to be relied on by the other party, it may well be held to be legally cognisable, but where the facts are available to the other party and not only so but he applies or might apply unrestricted means of inquiry, and is not induced to withhold inquiry, the alleged representation is probably no more than the dealer's talk in which each party from his own standpoint of buyer or seller usually indulges.

At bar the subject matter of the representations, namely past financial performance and future prospects, the status of the head lease, and the pending expansion of the Overwaitea delicatessen, were all matters peculiarly within the knowledge of the defendants, the parties making the representations . . . The fact of the matter is that because of the misrepresentations they [the plaintiffs] did not get what they had bargained for.

Verona Robinson (Claimant) v Marcia Robinson (Defendant) [2014] JMSC Civ 19 (JM)

Facts: In this matter, the claimant claims against the defendant for recovery of the sum of $586,410.00. This sum is allegedly the balance owing to the claimant arising from her sale to the defendant of her stock in her female-clothing store located in the Bank House Mall in Mandeville, Manchester. She contends that the original full sale price was $1,086,410.00 and that the balance was left after the defendant paid the sum of $500,000.00 on or about November 14, 2006, the day on which she took possession and delivery of the claimant's stock and began operating a business from the claimant's former store. On the other hand, the thrust of the defendant's case is that there was no concluded agreement. She contends that although the sum of $500,000.00 was paid, the exact amount of the balance had not been agreed. The agreement between the parties was for some items in the stock that were old and/or otherwise unusable[] to have been taken out by the claimant before the final price could have been agreed on. A written agreement was sent to her by the claimant, but she refused to sign it for that reason.

Held: Williams, J

. . . there are some aspects of the defendant's case with which the court had serious issues. For example, where she admits in cross-examination that she instructed her lawyer more or less in the terms in which he wrote to the claimant, that would suggest, not that there was not a completed agreement, as the defendant contends, but that the real reason for failing to complete was her disappointment with the sales that she had envisaged – perhaps based on representations that the claimant had made to her. This suggests a lack of due diligence on her part and undermines her contention that there was not a completed agreement. It suggests, further, that she did not pay because she could not afford to; not that there was no final agreement on the balance. In this regard, if it was that the real reason for non-completion was her disappointment with the sales, the maxim *caveat emptor* (let the buyer beware) – to the extent that it still exists today, would be applicable. In the case of *Miller v Jamieson* 2007 BCSC 1064 (Supreme Court of British Columbia), Meiklem, J (at paragraph 120) made the following observation on the maxim *caveat emptor* in a case relating to housing:

> [120] Caveat emptor has been described as operating passively because the vendor need not do anything to inform himself about the state of the property being sold or the existence of any defects: that burden falls to the purchaser. A vendor therefore has no obligation to review the condition of the home in order to be able to describe to prospective purchasers which areas are worn out, in need of repair, were constructed in a shoddy fashion or to the highest standard. Partly for historical reasons and in part because the buyer is in the best position to

> determine the quality of the home he wishes to purchase, the law has put the onus on the purchaser to determine the state and quality of the property being sold.

... There is no evidence of fraud or misrepresentation on the part of the claimant in this case; nor any evidence of any latent defect in the goods that the defendant inspected during the stock-taking exercise.

FRUSTRATION

Early developments

The early common law courts took the view that a contract, after its formation, must be performed even where events beyond the control of a party occurred and prevented the party obligated to perform the contract from so performing.

Redmond v Dainton [1920] 2 KB 256 (GB)

Facts: The plaintiff claimed:

(1) possession of a dwelling house and premises, No. 175, Belsize Road, Hampstead, upon a forfeiture for breach of a covenant to repair;
(2) damages for breach of covenant; and
(3) mesne profits.

By an indenture of lease dated 1 May 1867, the premises were demised by the plaintiff's predecessor in title to one Dale for a term of 99 years from Christmas 1855, at the yearly rent of £8 8s. The defendant was the assignee of the term and was in possession of the premises. The lease contained the following covenants by the lessee, his executors administrators or assigns:

> To keep the dwelling-house insured against fire during the term, and to expend upon the demised premises all money received from the insurance in rebuilding restoring or reinstating the premises; at all times during the term sufficiently and substantially to repair, uphold, support, sustain, and maintain the dwelling-house, walls and premises, and every part thereof; and at the end or other sooner determination of the term to surrender and yield up the premises being well and sufficiently repaired etc. as aforesaid.

On 28 January 1918 the house was struck by a bomb discharged from a German aeroplane, and was very seriously damaged. With the exception of some repairs to the party wall between the house and an adjoining one, no repairs were done to the house by the defendant after 28 January 1918 and on 27 January 1919, the plaintiff served the defendant with a notice under s14 of the Conveyancing Act 1881, specifying breaches of the covenant to repair and requiring the defendant to remedy them. The defendant did not comply with the notice and on 29 May 1919 the plaintiff issued the writ in this action.

Held: Darling, J
Then it was argued that the defendant is not bound to make good damage which has resulted, not from a fire, but from an act of the King's enemies, and *Paradine v Jane* was cited in support of that contention. It appears to me that, so far from *Paradine v Jane* helping the defendant, it is a distinct authority against him, for in that case:

> . . . it was resolved that the matter of the plea was insufficient; for though the whole army had been alien enemies, yet he ought to pay his rent. And this difference was taken, that where the law creates a duty or charge, and the party is disabled to perform it without any default in him, and hath no remedy over, there the law will excuse him. As in the case of waste, if a house be destroyed by tempest, or by enemies, the lessee is excused . . . But when the party by his own contract creates a duty or charge upon himself, he is bound to make it good, if he may, notwithstanding any accident by inevitable necessity, because he might have provided against it by his contract so that it is no excuse if that which happens might have been provided against by the contract.

The report goes on: 'And therefore if the lessee covenant to repair a house, though it be burnt by lightning, or thrown down by enemies, yet he ought to repair it.'

As I have said, *Paradine v Jane* appears to me to be a distinct authority against the defendant. No case has been cited to show that where a lease contains a covenant to keep a building in repair, the lessee is not liable under the covenant if the building is damaged by lightning or the King's enemies . . . 'Rent is a duty created by the parties upon the reservation, and had there been a covenant to pay it, there had been no question but the lessee must have made it good, notwithstanding the interruption by enemies, for the law would not protect him beyond his own agreement, no more than in the case of reparations.' Hold, therefore, that there has been a breach of the covenant to repair.

Contemporary formulation

The law has changed from the days of strict enforcement even when performance of a contract has been prevented by acts beyond the control of a party. However, it should be noted that the courts are not yet ready to release a party from its contractual obligations except in limited circumstances and where there is no reasonable opportunity for the contract to be substantially performed. There is generally reluctance by the courts to give a generous interpretation to factual circumstances that would lead to a finding of frustration. This narrow approach is based on the principle that a bargain must be upheld unless exceptional circumstances prevail.

National Carriers Ltd. v Panalpina (Northern) Ltd. [1981] AC 675 HL (GB)

Facts: Kingston Street, Hull, was a continuation of English Street (of which originally it may have been part) and terminated by running perpendicularly into a T-junction with Railway Street. Before it reached this end, it crossed more or less at right angles an intersection with Commercial Road and Manor House Street. At one side of it, at the point nearest the intersection, was a derelict and ruinous Victorian warehouse which at some time has become, under the laws for the conservation of national heritage, a 'listed building', which meant that it could not be demolished without the consent of the Secretary of State for the Environment. Even assuming a result favourable to demolition, the total process would be likely to last a year.

In the events which happened, the process was not yet complete, but, on the material before us, was likely to be concluded by the end of December 1980 or the beginning of January 1981. By that time, it would have lasted about 20 months. Since, in course of time, the Victorian warehouse became dangerous as well as derelict, it evidently presented problems of safety to the Kingston-upon-Hull City Council. In 1978 they placed a restriction order on Kingston Street, and on 16 May 1979 they closed it altogether to vehicular traffic. Access to Kingston Street was not merely prohibited to vehicles, but rendered physically impossible, by the erection across it by the local authority of a fenced barrier.

Opposite the ruinous listed building there was another warehouse, more or less triangular in shape, the only access to which (except perhaps on foot) was via a loading bay in Kingston Street. The consequence of the application for demolition, and the subsequent proceedings, was that, from 16 May 1979 until the time when the barriers were finally removed and the prohibition order lifted, this triangular warehouse was rendered totally useless for the one purpose, that of a commercial warehouse, for which alone it was fitted, and for which alone, by the terms of the contract between the parties, it may have been lawfully used. In 1974 the triangular warehouse had become the subject of a demise between the plaintiffs/respondents to these proceedings, the lessors, and the defendants/appellants. This demise was contained in a lease dated 12 July 1974, and was expressed to run for 10 years from 1 January 1974. The sole defence raised by the defendants/appellants to their obligation to pay rent was that, by reason of the events described above, the lease had become frustrated and was therefore wholly at an end.

Held: Lord Hailsham, LC
This question is the applicability of the law of frustration to leases and agreements for a lease . . . The doctrine of frustration is of comparatively recent development. The general rule of common law laid down as early as 1647 in *Paradine v Jane*, Aleyn, is that the performance of absolute promises is not excused by supervening impossibility of performance . . .

This . . . brings me to the central point at issue in this case which, in my view, is whether or not there is anything in the nature of an executed lease which prevents the doctrine of frustration, however formulated, applying to the subsisting relationship between the parties . . . I conclude that the matter is not decided by authority and that the question is open to your Lordships to decide on principle. In my view your Lordships ought now so to decide it. Is there anything in principle which ought to prevent a lease from ever being frustrated? I think there is not . . .

In the result, I come down on the side of the 'hardly ever' school of thought. No doubt the circumstances in which the doctrine can apply to leases are, to quote Viscount Simon LC in the *Cricklewood* case, at p 231, 'exceedingly rare'. Lord Wright appears to have thought the same, while adhering to the view that there are cases in which frustration can apply, at p 241. But, as he said in the same passage: 'the doctrine of frustration is modern and flexible and is not subject to being constricted by an arbitrary formula.' To this school of thought I respectfully adhere. Like Lord Wright, I am struck by the fact that there appears to be no reported English case where a lease has ever been held to have been frustrated. I hope this fact will act as a suitable deterrent to the litigious, eager to make legal history by being first in this field.

Held: Lord Ratcliffe
Frustration occurs whenever the law recognises that, without default of either party, a contractual obligation has become incapable of being performed because the circumstances in which performance is called for would render it a thing radically different from that which was undertaken by the contract. It is not the hardship or inconvenience or material loss itself which calls the principle of frustration into play. There must be as well such a change in the significance of the obligation that the thing undertaken would, if performed, be a different thing from that contracted for.

Nelson Pierre, Claimant v Millenium Holdings Ltd (MHL) and Frederick Sahadeo, Defendants (2013) Claim No. MNIHCV2009/0025 (MS)

Facts: Nelson Pierre, a resident and national of Dominica, was employed by the Government of Montserrat as an engineer. His employment came to an end on 31 March 2009.

During his employment, he met the second defendant where he was staying and enquired into any vacancies with MHL. There arose a temporary vacancy as Project Manager. Pierre assured the defendant that getting a work permit would not be an issue. They agreed that Pierre would submit to an interview with the government representative on the project and seek approval to work as the Project Manager at MHL. Nevertheless, his request for the work permit was denied and he claims for breach of contract.

Held: Redhead, J
If frustration involves a question of law, then there is no requirement that it should have been pleaded . . . 'the doctrine of frustration is modern and flexible and is not subject to being constricted by any arbitrary formula' . . . [In] *Chitty on Contracts*, the learned authors tell us 'a contract may be discharged on the ground of frustration when something occurs after the formation of the contact which renders it physically or commercially impossible to fulfil the contract or transforms the obligation from that undertaken at the moment of the entry into the contract.' The case at bar . . . falls squarely within the first limb of that definition. After the contract agreement was signed by the parties, the authorities refused to permit the Claimant to work on the Millenium project or to grant the Claimant a work permit which made it impossible for the Claimant to carry out his duties in Montserrat. The granting of the work permit or refusal to do so was beyond the control of the parties. In *National Carriers* . . . Lord Radcliffe said: 'Frustration occurs whenever the law recognizes that without default of either party a contractual obligation has become incapable . . . [of] being performed because the circumstances in which performance is called for would render it a thing radically different from that which was undertaken by the contract . . . It was not this I promised to do.' . . . In light of the foregoing . . . the refusal of the Government to allow the Claimant to work on its project at Little Bay or to grant a work permit to the Claimant frustrated the contract.

Foreseeability of a frustrating event will generally exclude the operation of the doctrine.

Devcon Ltd Claimant v Cap Juluca Properties Ltd (Doing Business As Cap Juluca Resort) Defendant (2012) Claim No. AXAHCV 0041/2009 (AI)

Facts: Cap Juluca, acting through its agent DCK, contacted Devcon and invited a proposal for beach replenishment at Cap Juluca. Devcon submitted a proposal which was ultimately accepted by Cap Juluca and formed the basis of the agreement between the parties. The proposal indicated that Devcon was to have undertaken the work for thirty (30) days utilizing the fixed daily rate . . . On the previous occasion when the parties had dealt with each other the circumstances were different. On that occasion, there was a total meeting of minds in relation to Devcon's importation of the equipment with which it had to work. As a result, all of the requisite permissions and approvals had been obtained from the relevant officials. Importantly, the equipment was not seized on the basis that they had entered Anguilla through an unlawful port. On the prior occasion, Devcon's equipment had arrived at Maunday's Bay beach where it cleared customs at that very site . . . In order to fulfill the terms of the Agreement, Devcon arranged for its equipment and barge to leave from Turks and Caicos en route to Anguilla in order to commence the replenishment of Maundays Bay beach. During discussions between DCK's representatives and Devcon's officials, Devcon was advised that the equipment and barge, upon entering Anguilla, should go straight to the Cap Juluca site; this is not an official port of entry in Anguilla. There was no discussion between the parties about the prior clearance of the barge and equipment. Devcon's barge entered Anguilla and went straight to Maundays Bay beach without stopping at the official port of entry. A few hours after its illegal entry into Anguilla, the

Customs authorities went to Cap Juluca and immediately seized the barge and equipment. The Customs authorities took away a truck and other equipment from the site but ordered Devcon's officials to leave its barge and other equipment exactly where they were. The barge remained in the rough seas for three (3) days . . . After the seizure by the Customs authorities and in spite of pleas from Devcon's officials and in the face of the inclement weather, the barge was forced to remain in the rough seas for approximately three (3) days while negotiations ensued with the Customs authorities. Meanwhile and unbeknownst to Devcon's officials, its equipment was damaged as a result of being kept in the rough seas and choppy waters. Having had the barge released, Devcon commenced working and after a period of three (3) days its barge got damaged. It nevertheless persisted and its barge became so severely damaged that Devcon had to discontinue the work altogether. One of the issues that arises is whether the contract has been frustrated.

Held: Blenman, J
Mr. Browne's evidence was that Devcon commenced work on 22nd November 2008 when they were given the approval to do so, but by 28th November 2008 the work had to stop because the spuds had completely broken. Learned counsel Mrs. Richardson Hodge submitted that this frustrated Devcon's ability to continue to render beach replenishment services to Cap Juluca in the manner originally contracted for between the parties. The continued existence or availability of the barge to conduct the beach replenishment was essential to the performance of the Agreement.

Mrs. Richardson Hodge referred the Court to paragraph 23–001 of *Chitty on Contracts* which states that:

> [A] contract may be discharged on the ground of frustration when something occurs after the formation of the contract which renders it physically or commercially impossible to fulfill the contract or transforms the obligation to perform into a radically different obligation from that undertaken at the moment of entry into the contract.

The type of frustration which applies to the case at bar is frustration of the adventure which occurs where the commercial venture envisaged by the parties is no longer capable of performance. The essential conduit to determining whether the contract is frustrated is to ascertain whether the contract made is, on its true construction, wide enough to apply to the new situation created by the supervening event. If it is not, then the original commercial adventure envisaged by the parties is considered frustrated and thereby incapable of performance.

Mrs. Richardson Hodge reminded the Court that the barge along with other equipment were seized when it entered into Anguilla waters due to Cap Juluca's failure to clear the barge's arrival with Customs. The barge was seized and restricted to the rough seas for three days. The damage to the barge resulting from compliance with this Customs order led to the barge being incapable of use. The only thing Devcon could do then to assist with beach replenishment was to lease the truck it had in its possession to Cap Juluca. Mrs. Richardson Hodge submitted that without the use of the barge, the contract had undergone a fundamental change, one which struck at the root of the contract, as the barge was the primary instrument by which the sand replenishment was to be completed. The commercial venture (beach replenishment through use of the barge) envisaged by the parties was no longer possible and the original contractual terms could no longer apply to this new set of circumstances.

Mrs. Richardson Hodge admitted that any claim of frustration, however, is subject to several limitations which may serve as a bar to a party's reliance on the doctrine. These are inclusive of, but not limited to whether the frustration was self-induced or whether the supervening/frustrating event was foreseeable.

Mrs. Richardson Hodge urged the Court to accept Devcon's evidence that the barge was seized by Customs and the spuds on the barge had to be placed in the seabed in rough waters at the Cap Juluca site. The spuds broke and the barge became inoperable. The Agreement entered into between Devcon and Cap Juluca was based on the use of the spud barge. It was unforeseeable that the spuds would break and the barge become inoperable. In the circumstances, Mrs. Richardson Hodge submitted that foreseeability does not operate as a bar to Devcon's reliance on the doctrine of frustration. Mrs. Richardson Hodge said that it is essential to note that as per paragraph 23–069 of *Chitty*, frustration does not rescind the contract *ab initio*, but it brings it to an end forthwith, without more and automatically. It releases both parties from any further performance of the contract and may even allow recovery of monies which were paid on a basis which had wholly failed (total failure of consideration), but it does not affect obligations undertaken by the parties before the contract was frustrated in some instances . . .

According to G. H. Treitel in *Frustration and Force Majeure* at pages 147–148, a contract may be discharged where a thing is destroyed which is not the subject-matter of the contract but the continued existence or availability of which is essential for the performance of the contract. Thus, if one took the view that the subject matter of a voyage charter under which a specific cargo were to be carried was the ship (and the ship alone), the contract would nevertheless be frustrated by the unavailability of the specific cargo on the ground that the availability of that cargo was essential for the performance of the contract. The same point can be made in relation to a situation where a seaman's contract of service could be discharged by loss or capture of the ship: here again it seems that the subject matter of the contract is the service to be rendered and the ship is a thing essential for its performance.

Mrs. Richardson Hodge opined that where the ground on which frustration is claimed is the destruction or unavailability of a thing which is not itself the subject matter of the contract, the question arises whether that thing is indeed essential for performance. In *Appleby v Myers*, a contract to install machinery in a factory and to maintain the machinery for two years was held to be discharged when the factory was destroyed before the work of installing the machinery had been completed. In that case, the services under the contract were to be rendered by the supplier in the factory which was destroyed; thus, the availability of the factory to install and maintain the machinery therein was essential to the performance of the contract . . .

It bears stating that even though the barge and equipment were inadvertently brought into Anguilla at an illegal port, perhaps the better course was for Customs not to have ordered that the detained barge remain in the rough seas. The Court reiterates that it was the detention of the barge in the rough seas for three (3) days that caused its initial damage. The contract was clearly frustrated. The occurrence of the frustrating event brings the contract to an end forthwith, without more and automatically.

The courts are also vigilant to prevent self-induced frustration as a mechanism to escape contractual obligations.

Maclean-Beaudet v Belanger 2012 CanLII 97365 (ON SCSM) (CA)

Facts: This is a replevin action by the plaintiff against the defendants for the return of a female Chihuahua called Princess and her three puppies. The dog is presently in the *de facto* possession of the defendants, Jamie Belanger and Ashley Dicks ('the defendants'). The defendants testified that they had a contract with the plaintiff for the purchase of Princess which they made with the plaintiff a few days after they took possession of Princess in May of 2010. The contract was for renovations to the plaintiff's home which included framing and drywall work in the home, as well as exterior siding work. They maintained that the terms of the contract are set out in a handwritten document which they stated was partly in the plaintiff's handwriting and initialled by the plaintiff. They stated that they intended to prepare a more formal contract for signing but misplaced the handwritten document for a period of time. The plaintiff denied that there was such a contract or that her handwriting appears on the document. She particularly denied that she agreed to siding work. I have some difficulty in accepting the plaintiff's evidence about the contract. When looking at the document, it clearly identifies the names of the defendants and has the initials 'LB.' It itemizes the renovation work to be done. It refers to 'Princess and papers,' the term 'papers' being the Purebred Dog Certificate. More importantly, there is the uncontradicted evidence of the defendant, Jamie Belanger, that he performed part of the work under the contract. He purchased material for the framing, did the framing and wiring in the plaintiff's bathroom, and reset windows and doors as itemized in the handwritten document. This, in my view, corroborates that a contract was in existence for the purchase of Princess no matter what the precise terms of the contract were. No other reason has been given why Mr. Belanger did the work for the plaintiff. Mr. Belanger was precise in his testimony about what work was to be done under the contract and I accept his evidence over that of the plaintiff's. She admitted in her examination-in-chief that she has a medical condition that affects her memory and her denial of the contract is insufficient to explain away the existence of the document which sets out the terms of the contract.

Held: Lange, Deputy Judge
The plaintiff argued in the alternative that, if there is a contract, the defendants only partly performed the contract and ownership of Princess cannot be conveyed to the defendants on this basis. The defendant, Jamie Belanger, testified that he did not do the drywall and siding work because the plaintiff never provided the materials to do the work although he was prepared to do the work. It is reasonable to assume that the plaintiff was to supply the drywall and siding materials. Construction materials are expensive and these materials would far exceed the plaintiff's suggested purchase price for Princess of $1,000 to $1,200. I am supported in this conclusion by the handwritten document itself which states '[indecipherable word] sup[p]ly Material of Siding . . . (Drywall 4 × 8.)' The reference to the amount of drywall to be supplied is also indecipherable. In my view, the plaintiff failed to perform her end of the bargain and the doctrine of self-induced frustration applies. The plaintiff has rendered performance of this part of the contract impossible by her own fault. As stated by the Supreme Court of Canada in *Wells v Newfoundland*, 1999 CanLII 657 (SCC), [1999] SCJ No. 50 at par. 51: 'Self-induced frustration does not excuse non-performance' of a contract. As stated in *Church of Scientology of British Columbia v Ahmed*, [1982] BCJ No. 2399 (SC) at par. 47 '. . . it was the appellants' own default which frustrated the adventure: the appellants cannot rely on their own default to excuse them from liability under the contract.' As stated in *Pan Pacific Specialities Ltd. v Shandong Machinery and Equipment I/E Corp.*, [2001] BCJ No. 48 (SC) par. 87: 'Self-induced frustration does not terminate a contract . . .' I conclude that the defendants performed what they could under the contract and are entitled to ownership of Princess. It follows that ownership of Princess includes ownership of her three puppies.

ILLEGAL CONTRACTS

It stands to reason that a contract that is contrary to law or public policy will not be enforced. Contracts that are tainted by the element of illegality will be rejected by the courts. No court ought to enforce an illegal contract or allow itself to be made the instrument of enforcing obligations alleged to arise out of a contract or transaction which is illegal.

If a contract is illegal as formed, or the parties intend that the contract should be performed in an illegal manner, the courts will neither enforce the contract nor provide any other remedies arising out of the contract. However, in respect of the latter category, the performance of a contract which is in contravention of a statute means that the contract is *prima facie* legal. The governing principle would appear to be that the court will not give sanction to persons benefitting from performance of an illegal contract and then seeking to rely on the said illegality as the basis for not upholding their part of the contract.

Kings Beach Hotels Limited and JGL Hotels Limited (Appellants) v Johanna Kesmin Marks (Respondent) (2011) Civil Appeal No. 23 of 2006 (BB)

Facts: By virtue of two loan agreements between the parties to this action, funds totalling over GBP 1,600,000 were lent and advanced to Kings Beach Hotels Limited and JGL Hotels Limited by Johanna Kesmin Marks. Johanna Kesmin Marks was at all times a resident of the United Kingdom and, as such, the permission of the Exchange Control Authority (the Authority) pursuant to section 33 of the Exchange Control Act, Cap. 71 (the Act) was required for the granting of the loans and the issuing of Debenture/Mortgages to secure the sums advanced under the said loans.

Held: Waterman, JA
In essence the issue raised by the grounds of appeal can be stated succinctly thus: whether failure to obtain permission from the Authority pursuant to *section 33* of *the Act* rendered the Debenture/Mortgage null and void . . . *Chitty on Contracts* (29th edition) states at paragraph 17–007 that illegal contracts are traditionally placed in two categories. The first is illegality as to formation, while the second is illegality as to performance. With regard to the former, if a contract is illegal as formed, or the parties intend that the contract should be performed in an illegal manner, the courts will neither enforce the contract nor provide any other remedies arising out of the contract. However, in respect of the latter category, the performance of a contract which is in contravention of a statute means that the contract is prima facie legal. Additionally, the test for illegality laid down by the House of Lords in *Tinsley v Milligan* [1994] 1 AC 340 was whether the claimant needed to rely on the illegality to found the claim. In *Grant v Williams* JM 1987 CA 103, the Jamaican Court of Appeal discussed the validity of a contract for the sale of property, where the vendor was a resident of the United States and had not acquired the requisite permission from the Jamaican Exchange Control Authority under the Jamaican Exchange Control Act. The Court of Appeal upheld the judgment of *Downer J* that the contract was valid and enforceable as the prohibitory provisions of *the Act* were concerned with performance and not with the formation of the contract . . . The Court finds that Kings Beach Hotels Limited and JGL Hotels Limited benefitted significantly from the proceeds of Johanna Kesmin Marks's funds in the furtherance of its business objectives, and cannot now use *the Act* to perpetrate a fraud on Johanna Kesmin Marks, nor ask the Court to uphold its immoral conduct in this regard. In the result, the appeal is dismissed.

Restraint of trade

A restrictive covenant in a contract of employment will be void *ab initio* unless the restraints that it imposes are reasonable having regard to the interests of the parties and of the public.

In practice, this test of what is reasonable tends to be resolved by considering whether or not the restrictive covenant is reasonably necessary to protect legitimate interests of the employer in preserving goodwill and confidential information. It is well settled that the reasonableness of a restraint clause is to be tested by reference to the position as at the date of the contract of which it forms part.

Esso Petroleum Co. Ltd. v Harper's Garage (Stourport) Ltd. [1968] AC 279 (GB)

Facts: The appellants were a large company whose most important product was Esso petrol, most of which was sold by them to garages and filling stations for resale to the public. The respondent company owned two garages: they contracted with the appellants under what are known as solus agreements and bound themselves for the periods of those agreements, *inter alia*, to sell at their garages Esso petrol and no other. When cheaper 'cut price' petrol came on the market, they began to sell it and ceased to sell Esso petrol. The appellants then raised two actions, which were consolidated, to prevent this: they sought injunctions to restrain the respondents from buying otherwise than from them any motor fuel for resale at these garages. The tie-in period was for four years and five months for the Mustow Green Garage and a period of 21 years in respect of the Corner Garage.

Held: Lord Reid
So I can now turn to the first question in this appeal – whether this agreement is to be regarded in law as an agreement in restraint of trade . . . The most general statement with regard to restraint of trade is that of Lord Parker in *Attorney-General of the Commonwealth of Australia v Adelaide Steamship Co Ltd.* He said: 'Monopolies and contracts in restraint of trade have this in common, that they both, if enforced, involve a derogation from the common law right in virtue of which any member of the community may exercise any trade or business he pleases and in such manner as he thinks best in his own interests.' ([1913] AC 781, 794; 29 TLR 743, PC).

But that cannot have been intended to be a definition: all contracts in restraint of trade involve such a derogation but not all contracts involving such a derogation are contracts in restraint of trade. Whenever a man agrees to do something over a period he thereby puts it wholly or partly out of his power to 'exercise any trade or business he pleases' during that period. He may enter into a contract of service or may agree to give his exclusive services to another: then during the period of the contract he is not entitled to engage in other business activities. But no one has ever suggested that such contracts are in restraint of trade except in very unusual circumstances . . .

The leading case of *Nordenfelt v Maxim Nordenfelt Guns & Ammunition Co. Ltd.* fell within the old categories, and it may be misleading to take the well-known passages out of context and try to apply them to cases of quite different nature. Lord Macnaghten said: 'The public have an interest in every person's carrying on his trade freely: so has the individual. All interference with individual liberty of action in trading, and all restraints of trade of themselves, if there is nothing more, are contrary to public policy, and therefore void.' . . . In general unless a contract is vitiated by duress, fraud or mistake its terms will be enforced though unreasonable or even harsh and unconscionable, but here a term in restraint of trade will not be enforced unless it is reasonable and in the ordinary case the court will not remake a contract: unless in the special case where the contract is severable, it will not strike out one provision as unenforceable and enforce the rest . . . Restraint of trade appears to me to imply that a man contracts to give up some freedom which otherwise he would have had . . .

In the present case the respondents before they made this agreement were entitled to use this land in any lawful way they chose, and by making this agreement they agreed to restrict their right by giving up their right to sell there petrol not supplied by the appellants. In my view this agreement is within the scope of the doctrine of restraint of trade as it had been developed in English law. Not only have the respondents agreed negatively not to sell other petrol but they have agreed positively to keep this garage open for the sale of the appellants' petrol at all reasonable hours throughout the period of the tie . . .

It is now generally accepted that a provision in a contract which is to be regarded as in restraint of trade must be justified if it is to be enforceable, and that the law on this matter was correctly stated by Lord Macnaghten in the *Nordenfelt* case. He said:

> restraints of trade and interference with individual liberty of action may be justified by the special circumstances of a particular case. It is a sufficient justification, and indeed it is the only justification, if the restriction is reasonable – reasonable, that is, in reference to the interests of the parties concerned and reasonable in reference to the interests of the public, so framed and so guarded as to afford adequate protection to the party in whose favour it is imposed, while at the same time it is in no way injurious to the public.

So in every case it is necessary to consider first whether the restraint went farther than to afford adequate protection to the party in whose favour it was granted, second whether it can be justified as being in the interests of the party restrained, and, third, whether it must be held contrary to the public interest . . . we can assume that both the garage owners and the companies thought that such ties were to their advantage and it is not said in this case that all ties are either against the public interest or against the interests of the parties. The respondents' case is that the ties with which we are concerned are for too long periods . . . A tie for 21 years stretches far beyond any period for which developments are reasonably foreseeable . . . I would therefore dismiss the appeal as regards the Corner Garage agreement.

Dranez Anstalt and Others v Zamir Hayek and Others [2002] EWCA Civ 1729 (GB)

Facts: The claimants in the proceedings included Breasy; its holding company, Charenton Limited, to which Dr Hayek had transferred the rights conferred by the patents in 1986; Dranez Anstalt, to which the patent rights had been transferred by Charenton in 1988, and Flexco, to which the rights to manufacture and distribute the Oscillator had been granted by Dranez Anstalt, also in 1988. Breasy was incorporated in the United Kingdom. Charenton, Dranez Anstalt and Flexco were incorporated or constituted in Liechtenstein. Breasy carried on business under licences granted by Dranez Anstalt and Flexco.

On 8 March 1994 Dr Hayek and two brothers involved in the development of the Oscillator signed a side letter which included the following paragraphs:

> not to act, other than in Dranez [Anstalt], DH and the Other Corporate Bodies, directly or indirectly in Dranez's, DH's and the Other Corporate Bodies' range of activities in connection with present and future generations and applications of the Oscillator and/or emanating therefrom and to undertake not to compete directly or indirectly with the above entities.

In March 1995 matters came to a head. Dr Hayek left his employment with Breasy and was removed as a director. Later that year he incorporated Medivent. He turned his powers of invention to the development of a new ventilator. He sought to describe that as 'the Hayek Respirator'; but in response to complaints from the claimants, changed that name to 'the RTX Respirator'.

Held: Chadwick, LJ
The question which the judge had to address, therefore, was whether, in the circumstances of this case, a covenant which sought to prevent Dr Hayek, as the inventor of the Oscillator, from competing in the business of manufacturing and selling ventilators, worldwide, for so long as the companies were conducting that business was reasonable having regard (i) to the respective interests of Dr Hayek and the persons to whom the side letter was addressed and (ii) to the interest of the public at large that Dr Hayek should not be restricted from applying his inventive skills in a field of medical science in which he was expert and in the development of which there was an obvious public benefit . . .

[T]o my mind, the more powerful criticisms of the judge's approach are, first, that (in addressing the question whether the restriction was reasonable as between the parties) he failed to relate the protection from competition which the investors sought to obtain under the side letter to the nature of the investment which they were making; and, second, that (in so far as he did address the question whether the restriction was reasonable in the public interest) he failed to give any (or any sufficient) weight to the interest of the public at large that Dr Hayek should not be restricted from applying his inventive skills in a field of medical science in the development of which there was an obvious public benefit . . . In particular, it must be a wholly exceptional case in which the imposition of such restraints on a pioneer in a field of medical science – in the development of which there is, at least prima facie, such an obvious public benefit – can be justified. There is nothing in his judgment to indicate whether, and if so why, the judge thought that this was such a case. In my view he ought to have concluded that it was not.

Exceeding product area of business

The restraining clause should apply to an area where the person being restrained had meaningful exposure and could affect a legitimate interest of the person seeking to enforce the restraining clause.

BFi Optilas v Blyth & Others [2002] EWHC 2693 QBD (GB)

Facts: The claimant company was the UK trading company of an international group, which distributed and marketed specialised optical and electronic equipment. The company comprised a merged business of Optilas Limited and BFI. The first defendant was formerly employed as the general manager of the Optilas part of the business, which dealt in lasers, fibre optics and other associated products. BFI was concerned primarily in the selling of RF products, magnetic products and sensing products. The second defendant was the former sales manager within the Optilas part of the claimant's business, and from February 2001 until September 2002 was the business development director. These two defendants were then in business together as partners in the third defendant, a limited liability partnership. The claimant sought an interim injunction against all three defendants to enforce the terms of express restrictive covenants contained in contracts of the first and second defendants.

Held: Hawkesworth, J
Turning to the claim against the second defendant . . . It is common ground that the second defendant's previous conditions of employment did not include any restrictive covenant. However, it is not disputed that the second defendant did subsequently sign the 'terms of employment' containing the restrictive covenant, neither was the point, initially at least, taken in correspondence . . .

The second point taken against the restrictive covenant relied upon by the second defendant is that it is too wide in its terms, going far beyond what would be necessary to protect the legitimate business interests of the claimant. Mr Campbell points to a number of features in the covenant, which he submits make it wider than was reasonably necessary. At the relevant date, that is the date of the contract, the second defendant was the business development director. He had previously been a sales manager within the Optilas part of the company. However, in his role as business development director he had what he describes as a general marketing role, and although he had contact with suppliers he did not have such a close relationship as existed when he was a sales manager. It is therefore submitted that it is unreasonable to require the covenant at all since no significant interest needed protection, and that furthermore, since no type of product or area of business was identified, it was far too wide, including, as it purports to do, products sold by both the Optilas part of the business and the BFI side. Those latter objections do, it seems to me, have validity . . .

In these circumstances it seems to me that it was unreasonable on the part of the claimant to seek to protect its whole customer base without geographical limitation and without limitation to the product area of the company for which the second defendant had responsibility. Further objection is taken to the absence of any requirement within the covenant to limit the customers or suppliers to those with whom the second defendant had personal dealings . . . Thus I hold that in respect of the covenant relied upon against the second defendant, its wording is wider than is reasonably necessary to protect the legitimate and commercial interests of the claimant, applying, as it purports to do, to the whole product range of the claimant and to areas outside the responsibility of the second defendant. Accordingly, I refuse the application for an interim injunction against the second defendant.

Restraining use of specialist skills

It is always challenging for a person to justify a restrictive covenant that purports to restrain someone from using a skill or profession where the first party did not contribute to its development.

Idameneo (No 123) Pty Ltd v Dr Teresa Angel-Honnibal [2002] NSWSC 1214 (AU)

Facts: In these proceedings the plaintiff sought an injunction restraining the defendant, a medical practitioner in general practice, from continuing to conduct her practice in breach of covenants in agreements whereby the defendant sold the goodwill of her practice to the plaintiff, agreed to work exclusively in the plaintiff's premises for a period of five years, and agreed not to conduct a medical practice within a certain area for a further period after ceasing to carry on her practice in the plaintiff's premises. In addition, the plaintiff sought liquidated damages for breach of contract. Further, or in the alternative, the plaintiff claimed return of the consideration which it had paid for the purchase of the defendant's medical practice as money had and received to the use of the plaintiff on the ground of unjust enrichment. The defendant said that: 'the covenants not to practice are void as an unreasonable restraint of trade and contrary to the public interest'.

Held: Palmer, J
The difference in wording is important. Do the restrictive trade covenants prohibit the defendant only from establishing her surgery within the proscribed area, or do they

also prohibit her from providing any sort of medical service, such as making house calls or attending patients in hospitals or nursing homes, anywhere within the proscribed area? . . .

I regard the restraint of trade covenants in the Sale of Practice Contract and the Practitioner Contract as prohibiting only the rendering of medical services by the defendant within the premises in which she has established her practice . . . [T]he common law has developed the principle that in determining whether a restraint of trade is void as a matter of public policy, the Court has to consider two questions: first, is the restraint reasonable as between the parties and, second, is the restraint contrary to the public interest? . . . In the present case, therefore, I hold that the plaintiff bears the onus of establishing that the restraint imposed in Clause 10.1 and 10.2 of the Sale of Practice Contract and in Clause 5.5(a) of the Practitioner Contract is reasonable as between the parties, and that the defendant bears the onus of establishing that the restraint is contrary to the public interest . . .

[T]he ultimate consideration for the Court is whether public policy has been served in striking down restraints of trade which go further than is reasonably necessary to protect the legitimate interests of those seeking to benefit from them or which are otherwise contrary to the public interest. Accordingly, while the Court gives weight to the fact that the parties have agreed upon the terms of a restraint, the party seeking to enforce the restraint still bears the onus of showing, by sufficiently persuasive evidence, that the protection of the covenant is no greater than is reasonably necessary between the parties. In discharging that onus, that party must do more than merely point to the existence of a bargain; it must justify the restraint by reference to the circumstances of the particular case. For example, where a restraint of trade covenant is obtained to protect the goodwill of a medical practice it will be relevant to know what is the type of practice conducted and what are the characteristics of the locality in which it is conducted. If the practice having the benefit of the covenant is a general practice, a restraint wide enough in terms to prohibit the covenantor from establishing [a] practice nearby as a neurosurgeon or as an anaesthetist may well be wider than is reasonably necessary because a specialist of that type does not see patients directly, as does a doctor, but only upon a referral from a general practitioner so that, in truth, there is no real likelihood of competition between the specialist and the general practitioner for the same patients . . .

Again, a restraint protecting the goodwill of a general practice from competition within a radius of twenty kilometres of the surgery may be no greater than is necessary if the practice is the only practice in a small country town, so that established patients of a retiring partner may be quite willing to drive twenty kilometres to the nearest town if the retiring partner sets up practice there. However, such a covenant might well be completely unreasonable if the practice happens to be conducted in the demographic centre of Sydney. In the present case, I have come to the conclusion that the restraints imposed in Clause 10.1(a) and (b) of the Sale of Practice Contract are greater than are reasonably necessary for the protection of the goodwill purchased by the plaintiff.

Protecting an excessively wide range of products or services

A restrictive covenant must be reasonable to the extent of not seeking to prevent someone from working in an entire industry rather than some specific area where there is a legitimate basis for protecting a particular interest.

Mont (J.A.) UK Limited v Mills [1993] FSR 577 (GB)

Facts: This was the defendant's appeal from an interlocutory injunction granted by Laws J on 16 September 1992, restraining him until 28 February 1993, or further order, from working for a number of named companies in the paper tissue industry, and from supplying paper tissue products for retail by any of a further number of named companies. The intended and immediate effect of that injunction was to prevent the defendant from continuing his employment as joint managing director of FH Lee Ltd (Lee), which he had commenced on 22 June 1992, Lee being trade competitors of the plaintiffs in the retail sector of the paper tissue industry.

The defendant was aged 43. He had spent 20 years in the paper tissue industry. It was, indeed, the only work he knew. For some five years from 1986 he worked as sales and marketing director for Invercon Paper Mills Ltd, until, in January 1991, that company was amalgamated with the plaintiffs, and the defendant's job disappeared. Although the plaintiffs attempted to find him a suitable alternative position, that proved impossible. In the event, having been involved throughout 1991 in a variety of projects, the defendant finally, in February 1992, entered into a written severance agreement with the plaintiffs terminating his employment with effect from 29 February 1992. The defendant had been entitled to one year's notice. Under the severance agreement he was paid compensation and a bonus . . . in respect of 1991. He was permitted to retain his company motor car until 31 March 1992. His BUPA membership was continued until April 1993, or such earlier date as he commenced alternative employment. In broad terms he was being paid the equivalent of a year's emoluments without discount for accelerated receipt, and he was being released from any obligation to work for the plaintiffs during the year in question. He was, however, crucially to these proceedings, required to submit to a restrictive condition in these terms: 'This total payment is made on condition that you do not join another company in the tissue industry within one year of leaving our employment.'

Having left the plaintiffs' employment, the defendant initially received 'out-placement counselling' and then sought work outside the tissue industry. Before finding it, however, in early June 1992 he received an unsolicited offer from Lee and, as stated, he took it up and on 22 June 1992 became their joint managing director. The plaintiffs first learned of this in early July. On 14 July they wrote to the defendant seeking wide undertakings, including his agreement not to work for Lee before February 1993. On 15 July the defendant's then solicitors replied; they offered contractual undertakings as to confidentiality, but nothing more.

Held: Brown, LJ
It would always be said that the covenants were basically 'just and honest', and designed solely to protect the employer's legitimate interests in the confidentiality of their trade secrets rather than to prevent competition as such. And it would be no easier to refute that assertion in other cases than it is here. Thus would be perpetuated the long-recognised vice of ex-employees being left subject to apparently excessive restraints and yet quite unable, short of expensive litigation and at peril of substantial damages claims, to determine precisely what their rights may be. *Mason v Provident Clothing and Supply Company Ltd* [1913] AC 724 provides, indeed, House of Lords authority to this effect. As Lord Moulton stated at page 745:

> It would in my opinion be *pessimi exempli* if, when an employer had exacted a covenant deliberately framed in unreasonably wide terms, the courts were to come to his assistance and, by applying their ingenuity and knowledge of the law, carve out of this void covenant the maximum of what he might validly have required. It must be remembered that the real sanction at the back of these covenants is the terror and expense of litigation, in which the

> servant is usually at a great disadvantage, in view of the longer purse of his master. It is sad to think that in this present case this appellant, whose employment is a comparatively humble one, should have had to go through four courts before he could free himself from such unreasonable restraints as this covenant imposes, and the hardship imposed by the exaction of unreasonable covenants by employers would be greatly increased if they could continue the practice with the expectation that, having exposed the servant to the anxiety and expense of litigation, the court would in the end enable them to obtain everything which they could have obtained by acting reasonably.

. . . [A]s a matter of policy, it seems to me similarly that the court should not too urgently strive to find within restrictive covenants *ex facie* too wide, implicit limitations such as alone could justify their imposition . . . In short, the covenant clearly means that the defendant shall not, during that year, be joined to another company in the tissue industry . . . It is, in short, only because the covenant they drew was altogether too wide that it fails. Its width cannot be justified and thus it is void as being in unlawful restraint of trade. It is upon that sole but central ground that I would allow this appeal.

Excessive geographical width

With respect to restraints based on space, the courts pose two questions: first, is it against the public interest? And second, does that which has been stipulated exceed what is necessary for the protection of both parties?

Fitch v Dewes [1921] 2 AC 158 (GB)

Facts: The respondent was a solicitor practising for more than 20 years in the county of Warwick. In 1899 the appellant who was then a youth of some 15 years of age, entered into employment with the respondent in the capacity of junior clerk and continued in that employment until June 1914. In 1912 the appellant undertook to serve the respondent as managing clerk for a term of three years and that he, upon determination of the contract of employment, would not work as a solicitor within a seven-mile radius of the town hall of Tamworth in Warwick.

Held: Lord Birkenhead
The clause only restricts him from being directly or indirectly engaged in the office, profession or business of a solicitor within a radius of seven miles of the town hall of Tamworth. We need not, therefore, trouble ourselves with any question as to restriction in respect of space, but may confine ourselves to the complaint which is made that the agreement cannot stand because the restriction in respect of time is unlimited and is against the public interest. But it is to be noticed here . . . that guidance may be derived in dealing with a restriction relating to time from an examination of the restriction which is made in respect of space . . . Therefore, I say plainly, and I hope, simply, that it has for long now been accepted that such an agreement as this, if it is impeached, is to be measured by reference to two considerations. First: Is it against the public interest? And second: Does that which has been stipulated far exceed what is required for the protection of the covenantee? It might perhaps be more properly stated, does it exceed what is necessary for the protection of both the parties? . . .

I am of the opinion that it is in the public interest that a proper restrictive covenant of this kind between an established solicitor, possibly an elderly man, and a younger man should be allowed. It is in the public interest because, otherwise, solicitors, perhaps carrying on their business without a partner, would be extremely chary of admitting competent young men to their offices . . . There is, therefore, nothing in the clause which I have read which conflicts with the public interest . . . the appeal [should] be dismissed.

Unreasonable period of restraint

In the case of covenants designed to protect a legitimate business interest, the question that often arises is what is the minimum time required to protect the legitimate business interest. The answer may vary between different types of business interests and must satisfy the requirement of protecting a legitimate business interest and not going beyond that which is reasonable.

Allied Protection Limited (Claimant) v John Barnes and John Barnes v Donald Williams [2013] JMCC Comm. 12 (JA)

Facts: Allied Protection Limited ('Allied') is a limited liability company incorporated under the laws of Jamaica. The company is in the business of providing security service[s] to individuals and companies throughout the island. Mr. John Barnes is a former shareholder and former Managing Director of Allied. Mr. Donald Williams is the Chairman and the majority shareholder of Allied. Mr. Williams and Mr. Barnes entered into an agreement to purchase the shares of Mr. Barnes. This was a private contract between the two men. Mr. Williams and Mr. Barnes orally agreed that Mr. Barnes would not solicit any of Allied's clients. Mr. Williams did secure Mr. Barnes' oral agreement or assurance that he would not solicit or attempt to obtain any of Allied's contracts for the period of 12 months from April 1 2011 to May 1 2012.

Held: Mangatal, J

(c) Restraint of trade – is the convenant/agreement not to solicit enforceable?

Covenants in restraint of trade are generally considered contrary to public policy. However, the cases also establish that if the restraint is reasonable in reference to the legitimate interests of the party concerned, and is not injurious to the public, it may be held enforceable. For a restraint to be reasonable in the interests of the parties, it must afford no more than adequate protection to the party in whose favour it is imposed: *Morris v Saxelby* [1916] AC 688. Non-solicitation clauses are often used in employment agreements to prevent a key employee from competing with the employer's business after leaving the company. These clauses are also commonly found in share purchase / sale agreements. In those situations, the purpose of the clause is to protect and ensure that the departing shareholder does nothing that would undermine the value of the goodwill of the company, for which the person purchasing the shares would be paying [] The distinction is important because restraint of trade [covenants] entered into between vendors and purchasers are treated with less disfavour than those entered into between master and servant . . .

Even in the business context, however, of a sale of shares, if a covenant goes further than reasonably necessary to protect a legitimate interest, it will be held void and not enforced – *Nordenfelt*. The questions therefore regarding the covenant not to solicit are (1) what are the interests that it is legitimate to protect? And (2) Is the protection taken no more than is reasonably necessary to protect those interests? I do not find that there was any ordinary relationship of Master and Servant between Mr. Barnes and Allied. Mr. Barnes in his evidence stated that he considered himself at all times a part owner of Allied. In his witness statement, Mr. Williams indicated that when Allied was formed after the merger, a decision was taken by the Board of Directors, including Mr. Barnes, to keep directors' salaries at a minimum and at the end of each quarter depending on the profit realized, a director's fee would be paid out accordingly, thereby allowing for a more liquid cash flow.

The interests that it seems legitimate to protect in this case appear to me to be that of a vendor-purchaser covenant between Mr. Barnes and Mr. Williams, with Mr. Barnes as Managing Director, rather than a Master-Servant restraint of trade covenant between Allied and Mr. Barnes. It is also to be noted that there is no claim by Allied against Mr. Barnes as a director or for any breach of fiduciary duties in that regard. Mr. Barnes was Managing Director for 9 years for Allied Protection Systems & Sales Limited, before it was merged with United Protection and Allied Protection Systems and Sales Limited to form Allied. At Allied, Mr. Barnes worked for another 9 years as Managing Director before he resigned in January 2011. In that capacity, he would have been exposed to Allied's customers and trade connections. He would have had confidential and sensitive information about Allied, for example, its customers, rates and charge strategies. More significantly, Mr. Barnes was a vendor of shares in Allied and in respect of the business of which he considered himself part-owner. These contracts that Allied had were very important in determining the value of the Company and were used by Mr. Barnes as a bench mark to arrive a sale price for []his shares. Mr. Williams would therefore have a legitimate interest in wanting to protect and retain the clients of Allied and the non-solicitation term would no doubt be a reasonable way to achieve that protection.

Indeed, Mr. Barnes was asked by Counsel, Mrs. Mayhew about the factors that were taken into consideration when the parties were trying to agree to a purchase price for his shares. Mr. Barnes indicated that he had a very good idea of what the value of the company was and consequently what the value of his shareholding would be. He further went on to say that in arriving at the purchase price, he would have taken the quantity and quality of Allied's contracts into account, because ultimately the value of the company would be based on the number and quality of its contracts. Mrs. Mayhew's submitted in her closing submission[] that[,] on Mr. Barnes own evidence, there seems to be a nexus between the price paid for the shares and the contracts which the Company had. She submitted that it would be reasonable to conclude that the issue of the non-solicitation of Allied's clients by Mr. Barnes would have been discussed between the two men and an agreement reached.

In *Alec Lobb Limited v Total Oil (Great Britain) Ltd* [1985] 1 WLR 173 (CA), the court pointed out that when the question of reasonableness is being looked at, the quantum of the consideration may be part of the overall assessment. The parties had agreed that the price to be paid for the shares is $10,000,000.00. Mr. Williams in investing time and money in getting these shares would therefore want to capitalise on his investment, particularly in ensuring that nothing is done by the seller that would affect adversely the status quo of the company in which the shares are being sought. Lord McNaughten in *Trego v Hunt* [1895–1899] All ER Rep 804, which was cited by Mrs. Mayhew in her closing submissions, at page 814 reasoned that

> *A man may not derogate from his own grant; the vendor is not at liberty to destroy or depreciate the thing which he has sold;* there is an implied covenant on the sale of goodwill that the vendor does not solicit the customer he has parted with; it would be a fraud on the contract to do so. *These, as it seems to me, are the different turns and glimpses of a proposition that I take to be elementary. It is not right to profess and to purport to sell that which you do not mean the purchaser to have; it is not an honest thing to pocket the price and then recapture the subject of sale, to decoy it away or call it back before the purchaser had time to attach it to himself and make it his very own.* (my emphasis)

(d) Was it an implied term of the agreement relating to the sale of shares that Mr. Barnes would not solicit the clients of Allied?
The decision in *Trego v Hunt* has been applied many times, and was referred to in the recent English Court of Appeal's decision in *Baldwins (Ashby) Ltd. v Maidstone* [2011] EWHC B12, cited by Mrs. Mayhew. The case establishes that whether there was or was not an express agreement by Mr. Barnes not to solicit Allied's clients, it would be an implied term of the agreement for the sale of his shares to Mr. Williams that he would not solicit Allied's clients within a reasonable period after the sale. It would seem that the principles apply whether it is the sale of shares in the whole business that is the subject of the agreement or whether it is a portion of the shares of the business, such as is the situation in the present case where Mr. Barnes as Managing Director was selling his not insignificant[] 9% portion of the shares in Allied. See *Halsbury's Laws of England*, 4th edition, Vol. 47 paragraph 24, footnote 1, *Nordenfelt* and *Connors Bros. v Connors* [1940] 4 All ER 179. The particular non-solicitation term agreed to is not in my view unnecessarily wide. As Mrs. Mayhew points out in her written submissions, and as I have found, it did not limit Mr. Barnes ability to work in the security industry on leaving Allied. It also did not preclude him from setting up a rival company or seeking clients for himself. It was suitably limited in scope and time, in so far as it simply sought to restrict Mr. Barnes from soliciting the clients of Allied for a period of 12 months. It is therefore in my view enforceable. Even if there was no express agreement about the non-solicitation or the period of 12 months, as stated above, there would be an implied term not to solicit for a reasonable time and I think in the circumstances 12 months would appear to be a reasonable time. I should add, that even if I am wrong and that it is in fact a covenant in restraint of trade between Allied and Mr. Barnes as employer-employee, as well as, or instead of an agreement having to do with the sale of the shares, the term is reasonable in the interests of the parties and enforceable.

Contracts contrary to public policy

The public policy which a court is entitled to apply as a test of validity to a contract is in relation to some definite or governing principle which the community as a whole has already adopted, either formally by law or tacitly in its general course of community life. The court is not a legislator: it cannot initiate the principle; it can only state or formulate one if it already exists. The courts refuse to give effect to such a bargain, not for the sake of the defendant – indeed they do not fail to notice that his failure to abide by the agreement sometimes adds dishonesty to illegality – but for the sake of the community, which will be prejudiced if such a bargain were countenanced.

Niedermeyer v Charlton 2014 BCCA 165 (CanLII) (CA)

Facts: The appellant was injured returning to Whistler Village after participating in a zip line experience operated by the respondent, Ziptrek Ecotours Incorporated ('Ziptrek'), when a bus operated by the respondent, left the road returning from the area where the zip line activities were conducted. On a summary trial, a Supreme Court judge held that the document entitled 'Release of Liability, Waiver of Claims Assumption of Risk and Indemnity Agreement' signed by the appellant, was a complete defence to the appellant's claim, and dismissed her action.

Held: Garson, Bennett, JJ
I begin my analysis by turning to Mr. Justice Binnie's discussion of the public policy branch of the test laid out in *Tercon Contractors Ltd. v British Columbia (Transportation and Highways)*,

2010 SCC 4 (CanLII), for determining the enforceability of an exclusion clause, also known as a release of liability. Though Binnie J was dissenting in the result, the Court was unanimous on the correct approach to exclusion clauses, including on the question of public policy. First, I note that Binnie J made clear why public policy interests are not closed to judicial consideration when courts are asked to determine the enforceability of a contract. He wrote:

> [115] I agree with Professor Waddams when he writes:
>
>> [I]t is surely inevitable that a court must reserve the ultimate power to decide when the values favouring enforceability are outweighed by values that society holds to be more important. [para. 557]
>
> [116] While memorably described as an unruly horse, *public policy is nevertheless fundamental to contract law, both to contractual formation and enforcement and (occasionally) to the court's relief against enforcement.* As Duff CJ observed:
>
>> It is the duty of the courts to give effect to contracts and testamentary dispositions according to the settled rules and principles of law, since we are under a reign of law; *but there are cases in which rules of law cannot have their normal operation because the law itself recognizes some paramount consideration of public policy which over-rides the interest and what otherwise would be the rights and powers of the individual.* (*Re Millar Estate*, 1937 CanLII 10 (SCC), [1938] SCR 1, at p. 4)
>
> . . .

Thus, the Court rejected the notion that the heads of public policy were closed to all but those well recognized in the jurisprudence: contracts in restraint of trade, injurious to the justice system, injurious to the state, affecting marriage or immoral contacts: Brandon Kain and Douglas T. Yoshida, 'The Doctrine of Public Policy in Canadian Contract Law' in Todd L. Archibald and Randall Scott Echlin, eds., *Annual Review of Civil Litigation* (Toronto: Thomson Carswell, 2007) 1 at 18–28. That said, Binnie J continued to endorse significant judicial restraint when invoking public policy as justification for interfering with a contract freely entered into by competent adults. He cautioned courts to remember that, 'Freedom of contract will often, but not always, trump other societal values': para. 117.

Citing with approval the comments of Duff CJ in *Re Millar Estate*, 1937 CanLII 10 (SCC), [1938] SCR 1, Binnie J recognized that given the importance of the 'certainty and stability of contractual relations' only where harm to the public is 'substantially incontestable' will the court use its residual power to decline to enforce a contract: para. 117. The examples given in *Tercon* illuminate the high threshold a party must meet in order to defeat an otherwise valid exclusion clause. A court should not allow the party responsible to escape civil liability simply because the relevant contracts included waiver clauses if, for example, a milk supplier uses a toxic compound in baby formula to increase profitability at the cost of sick or dead babies or if toxic cooking oil is recklessly sold creating a public health crisis: para. 118. Despite what could be considered the clear moral blameworthiness enshrined in these examples, Binnie J made clear that the conduct resulting in a breach of contract 'need not rise to the level of criminality or fraud to justify a finding of abuse': para. 118.

As is perhaps evident from the preceding paragraphs, the discussion of public policy in *Tercon* tends to focus on the *conduct* of the party who seeks to rely on the exclusion clause. This Court has similarly focused on the public policy interest in disavowing the knowing or reckless misconduct of a party who endangers the public and then points to a limitation of liability clause in answer: *Lam v University of British Columbia*, 2010 BCCA 325 (CanLII) at para. 71; *Loychuk v Cougar Mountain Adventures Ltd.*, 2012 BCCA 122 (CanLII) at para. 46 leave to appeal ref'd [2012] SCCA No. 225. However, it is important to note that there is nothing in *Tercon* that limits the consideration of public policy to the conduct of the party relying on the exclusion clause. Indeed, the Court recognizes in *Tercon* that the nature of the breach *or* the contract itself could give rise to a public policy interest capable of overriding freedom of contract: para. 117. What *Tercon* requires is that a plaintiff seeking to avoid the effect of an exclusion clause identifies the public interest that he or she says outweighs enforcement of the contract freely entered into. In my view, Ms. Niedermeyer has done so.

Contract to commit a crime

The court will not countenance a contract to commit a crime and will refuse to uphold or attach legal sanction to such a bargain.

Spyglass v McCabe 2010 SKPC 164 (CanLII) (CA)

Facts: The plaintiff sues the defendant for the value of a dog and one of its pups. The plaintiff gave the male dog to the defendant on the understanding that the plaintiff would be given first pick of the first litter sired by the dog and, further, that if the defendant ever decided not to keep the dog, she would offer it back to the plaintiff. The dog belonged to a third party who had no knowledge of the transaction. The issue is whether this is an illegal contract which is not enforceable.

Held: Meekma, J
There is a longstanding basic principle in common law that an illegal contract is unenforceable. Courts have been vigilant in preventing abuse of their process and may refuse to give effect to illegal contracts . . .

Bastarache J also discussed the Doctrine of Illegality with respect to acts contrary to public policy:

> 86 . . . The development of the law in this area can be traced to *Holman v Johnson* (1775), 1 Cowp 341, 98 ER 1120, where Lord Mansfield stated, at p. 1121:
>
> > The principle of public policy is this; *ex dolo malo non oritur actio*. No Court will lend its aid to a man who founds his cause of action upon an immoral or an illegal act. If, from the plaintiff's own stating or otherwise, the cause of action appears to arise *ex turpi causâ*, or the transgression of a positive law of this country, there the Court says he has no right to be assisted. It is upon that ground the Court goes; not for the sake of the defendant, but because they will not lend their aid to such a plaintiff.
>
> 87 Since *Holman*, the courts have examined many transactions which involve what the courts considered to be immoral or illegal acts. The public policy in the present case is similar to the public policy recognized in the case law where the courts have refused to uphold a contract to commit a crime. To enforce a contract of this type is to recognize that it is valid to agree to circumvent the law for economic gain. As *Cheshire, Fifoot and Furmston's Law of Contract* (13th ed. 1996), explains, at p. 375: 'An allied rule of public policy is that no person shall be allowed to benefit from his own crime.'

The statutory basis for the illegality of the contract which the plaintiff seeks to enforce can be found in s. 322(1)(a) of the *Criminal Code of Canada* which describes the offence of theft as follows:

> 322(1) Every one commits theft who fraudulently and without colour of right takes, or fraudulently and without colour of right converts to his use or to the use of another person, anything, whether animate or inanimate, with intent,

(a) to deprive, temporarily or absolutely, the owner of it, or a person who has a special property or interest in it, of the thing or of his property or interest in it;

'Conversion' includes the disposal of goods by selling or delivering them to a third party. The plaintiff's delivery of the dog to the defendant without the knowledge and consent of the true owner was a theft by conversion. The secrecy supports intent to deprive the rightful owner of the dog. As such, the contract is illegal as it is in breach of a statute, i.e., the *Criminal Code of Canada*, the purpose of the section being to protect and preserve property to its rightful owner and prevent his being deprived of it without his consent.

The remedy sought by the plaintiff would not benefit the true owner, Clayton McCarthy, but the plaintiff, who had no claim to the dog at the point in time where she disposed of it. There is no unjust enrichment to the defendant in finding the contract unenforceable, as she offered to return the dog to the true owner and he agreed that she could keep it. Clayton McCarthy is the only party who could pursue any claim against the defendant and he has opted not to do so . . .

Applying the modern approach to the Doctrine of Illegality, I find that the contract between the plaintiff and the defendant was illegal and is unenforceable.

PRIVITY

Although not a mechanism to attack the validity of contract, the privity of contract doctrine is designed to limit access to the benefits accruing under a contract. It was once the case that only a person who was party to a contract could commence legal proceedings with respect to the contract. This is based on the rule of privity of contract and largely on the notion of consideration, as a third party to a contract would not have provided the requisite consideration to turn an obligation, moral or otherwise, into a contract. The situation has changed tremendously, especially as concerns contracts for insurance for the benefit of a third party, and there have been so many exceptions to the rule of privity of contract that it is now considered more of a fossil from the days of classical contractual dogma.

Claudette Edwards v Quest Security Services Ltd (2005) Claim No. 2005 HCV 01124 (JM)

Facts: In April 2000, Quest entered into a contract of insurance with Guardian. By that contract, Guardian agreed to provide insurance coverage for the employees of Quest which would become payable on the occurrence of certain events such as death or injury to the employee. Clause 8 of the contract clearly states that the proposer (Quest) should not have any beneficial interest in the policy. Quest employed Miss Lettera Thompson. She worked as an office helper. Unfortunately, she was diagnosed with leukaemia in 2003. In February 2005, her health significantly declined to the extent that she was hospitalised on February 5, 2005. At some point on February 5, Miss Lettera Thompson executed a change of beneficiary from naming Quest as the beneficiary. Before this change was effected, Miss Thompson had named Claudette Edwards, the claimant, as the beneficiary. The document is alleged to have been executed at the home of Mr and Mrs Joseph Dibbs, directors of Quest. Miss Thompson died on April 9, 2005. Miss Edwards then brought this claim.

Held: Sykes, J
Mr. Dabdoub suggested that the cases he cited on the privity issue (*Beswick* and *Cleaver*) have conclusively settled the matter once and for all that non-parties to a contract have

no standing to bring any claim concerning it. However, is this really so? I am of the view that unless there is a decision from the Judicial Committee of the Privy Council on appeal from Jamaica or from the Court of Appeal of Jamaica that has precluded, irrevocably, a re-examination of the doctrine of privity in the context of insurance contracts generally and life and/or accident insurance contracts in particular then it is appropriate to see whether the[re] are developments in other common law jurisdictions that may be of assistance . . . what the research reveals is growing judicial impatience with the rule and the tardiness of legislative intervention and but for the apparent timidity of counsel the judges would have acted long ago.

Twenty seven years after *Beswick*, it was the turn of Steyn LJ to express his despair in *Darlington BC v Wiltshier Northern Ltd* [1995] 1 WLR 68. His Lordship described the inability of third parties to sue on contracts for their benefit as rule having 'no doctrinal, logical or policy reason' . . . The learned Lord Justice said at pages 76G–78C:

> The genesis of the privity rule is suspect. It is attributed to *Tweddle v Atkinson* (1961) B.& S. 393. It is more realistic to say that the rule originated in the misunder standing of *Tweddle v Atkinson.* See Atiyah, The Rise and Fall of Freedom of Contract, 1979, 414; Simpson, A History of the Law of Contract: the Rise of the Action of Assumpsit, 1975, 475. While the privity rule was barely tolerable in Victorian England, it has been recognized for half a century that it has no place in our more complex commercial world. Indeed as early as 1915 in *Dunlop v Selfridge* 1915 AC 847, at 855, when the House of Lords restated the privity rule, Lord Dunedin observed in a dissenting speech that the rule made:
>
> > it possible for a person to snap his fingers at a bargain deliberately made, a bargain not in itself unfair, and which the person seeking to enforce it has a legitimate interest to enforce.
>
> Among the majority Viscount Haldane, the Lord Chancellor asserted as a self-evident truth that 'only a person who is a party to a contract can sue on it': at 853. Today the doctrinal objection to the recognition of a *stipulatio alteri* continues to hold sway. While the rigidity of the doctrine of consideration has been greatly reduced in modern times, the doctrine of privity of contract persists in all its artificial technicality.
>
> In 1937 the Law Revision Committee in its Sixth Report proposed the recognition of a right of a third party to enforce the contract which by its express terms purports to confer a benefit directly on him: Cmd. 5449, para 41 8. In 1967 in *Beswick v Beswick* [1968] AC 58, 72, Lord Reid observed that if there was a long period of delay in passing legislation on the point the House of Lords might have to deal with the matter. Twelve years later Lord Scarman, who as a former Chairman of the Law Commission usually favoured legislative rather than judicial reform where radical change was involved, reminded the House that it might be necessary to review all the cases which 'stand guard over the unjust rule': *Woodar Investment Development Ltd v Wimpey Construction UK Ltd.* [1980] 1 WLR 277, at 300G . . .
>
> But as important as judicial condemnations of the privity rule is the fact that distinguished academic lawyers have found no redeeming virtues in it. See, for example, Markesinis (1987) 103 LQR 354; Reynolds (1989) 105 LQR 1; Beatson (1992) 44 CLP 1; and Adams and Brownsword (1993) 56 MLR 722. And we do well to remember that the civil law legal systems of other members of the European Union recognize such contracts. That our legal system lacks such flexibility is a disadvantage in the single market. Indeed it is a historical curiosity that the legal system of a mercantile country such as England, which in other areas of the law of contract (such as, for example, the objective theory of the interpretation of contracts) takes great account of the interests of third parties, has not been able to rid itself of this unjust rule deriving from a technical conception of a contract as a purely bilateral *vinculum juris.*
>
> In 1991 the Law Commission revisited this corner of the law. In cautious language appropriate to a consultation paper the Law Commission has expressed the provisional recommendation that 'there should be a (statutory) reform of the law to allow third parties to

> enforce contractual provisions made in their favour': Privity of Contract: Conflicts for the Benefit of Third Parties, Consultation Paper No. 121, at 131. The principal value of the Consultation Paper lies in its clear analysis of the practical need for the recognition of a contract for the benefit of third parties, and the explanation of the unedifying spectacle of judges trying to invent exceptions to the rule to prevent demonstrable unfairness. No doubt there will be a report by the Law Commission in the not too distant future recommending the abolition of the privity of contract rule by statute. What will then happen in regard to the proposal for legislation? The answer is really quite simple: probably nothing will happen.
>
> But on this occasion I can understand the inaction of Parliament. There is a respectable argument that it is the type of reform which is best achieved by the courts working out sensible solutions on a case by case basis, e.g. in regard to the exact point of time when the third party is vested with enforceable contractual rights: See Consultation Paper, No. 121, at par. 5.8. But that requires the door to be opened by the House of Lords reviewing the major cases which are thought to have entrenched the rule of privity of contract. Unfortunately, there will be few opportunities for the House of Lords to do so. After all, by and large, courts of law in our system are the hostages of the arguments deployed by counsel. And counsel for Darlington, the third party, made it clear to us that he will not directly challenge the privity rule if this matter should go to the House of Lords. He said that he is content to try to bring his case within exceptions to the privity rule or what Lord Diplock in *Swain v The Law Society*, supra, at 611D, described as 'judicial subterfuges . . . to mitigate the effect of the *lacuna* resulting from the non recognition of a *jus quaesitum tertio*'.
>
> . . .

The passage by Lord Justice Steyn demonstrates what while the condemnation of the doctrine was virtually universal in England the issue was not whether the rule should be reformed by the means by which it would be reformed and the extent of the modification. Some favoured legislation while others favoured judicial intervention. One gets the impression that but for counsel's disinclination to challenge the rule Steyn LJ was prepared to begin judicial reform of the rule itself rather than trying to look for dubious 'exceptions' to the rule. The disappointment of the Lord Justice is palpable. In Australia, the High Court suffered no such disappointment. Counsel on behalf of the respondent [in] *Trident General Insurance Company Limited v McNiece Bros Proprietary Limited* (1998) 165 CLR 107 boldly argued that there should be an exception to the privity rule in the case of public risk policies where the parties to the contract intend to confer a benefit on an identified third party. Led by Chief Justice Mason the High Court of Australia, by a majority of 5:2, on varying grounds, upheld the decision of the Court of Appeal of New South Wales, which decided that McNiece Bros could recover under an insurance policy to which they were not parties and did not contribute any of the premiums because in the opinion of the court, the contract was clearly made for the benefit of McNiece. The insurance company resisted the claim by squarely the issue of privity of contract . . . To recognise an obligation on the part of a promisor who has accepted agreed consideration for a promise to benefit a third party[] is not to abrogate the doctrine of privity of contract. It is merely to confine it to the only area in which it can properly operate, viz the area of rights and obligations having their source in contract.

In the case before me, Miss Thompson was the intended beneficiary of the contract. That is indisputable. The clear intention of the parties was to confer a benefit on Miss Thompson or a beneficiary identified by her. In other words, Miss Thompson was given the option of disposing her benefit to whomever she pleased. She chose Miss Edwards. But for the alleged change of beneficiary, Miss Edwards would have stepped into the shoes of Miss Thompson once she (Miss Thompson) died. The injustice of saying Miss Edwards in the event of Miss Thompson's death cannot bring action is patent. Following on from the logic of Gaudron J, why should the initially named beneficiary be prevented from attempting to establish that the second named beneficiary secured the benefit by inequitable conduct, which if established can have the effect of setting aside the purported change of beneficiary? . . . To permit Miss Edwards to maintain this claim does not require wholesale destruction of the privity rule. It would simply be a demonstration of what the common law has always done – updating the law to do justice while maintaining the stability of the law.

The claimant has reasonable grounds to bring the claim because the developments in the law of contract, particularly in the area of insurance . . . suggest that a person who is not a party to a contract may bring an action . . . It would be wrong to ignore the high authority that has condemned the privity rule in its current form and inexcusable to ignore a decision from a well-respected final appellate court that has opened the door to judicial re-examination of the doctrine of privity.

REMEDIES FOR BREACH OF CONTRACT

Damages

Underlying principle

The underlying principle of damages as a remedy for breach of contract is to put the plaintiff in the position he would have been in if the contract which had been breached had been performed as agreed.

Mohamed Ali v Guyana Teachers' Union (1991) 50 WIR 203 (GY)

Facts: On 14 July 1983 the appellant (Mr Mohamed Ali), then the acting head teacher of the Bush Lot Secondary School, West Coast, in the county of Berbice, received a letter from the Teaching Service Commission terminating his services; but it disclosed no reason for the precipitate course. Quite naturally, the appellant, who had been a teacher for some 19 years, was distraught and, two days later, went to the headquarters of his union, the respondents. He protested his innocence and demanded to be reinstated. One year after the union promised to represent him, the appellant again met its officials and, on that occasion, a minister of the government, a Mr Salahuddin, was present. The appellant's disappointment led to this litigation in which he claimed (*inter alia*) damages for breach of contract that on several occasions up to two and a half years later, he was never reinstated and he felt the respondents never represented him.

Held: Bishop, JA
I am prepared to hold, and do hold, even at this stage, that the appeal should be allowed, the union not having put forward favourable aspects of the claim of the appellant in an effort to protect his interests . . . *Damages for breach of contract are given by way of compensation for loss suffered, and not to inflict punishment on those responsible for the breach: per* Lord Atkinson in *Addis v Gramophone Co Ltd* [1908–10] All ER 1 at page 4. Here, the union officials, on behalf of the union, displayed *gross dereliction of a contractual duty that was owed to the appellant* . . . The principle to be borne constantly in mind is that the claim for damages must be based upon loss occurring as the natural consequence of the breach or on what was in the contemplation of both parties at the time they made their contract, that is when the appellant joined the union and received his copy of the rule book. The vital question, therefore, is not what

damages should have been foreseen by the union, or what the effluxion of time has shown the appellant to have lost or will lose, but whether the probability of the loss should reasonably have been within the contemplation of both parties, when they entered into their contractual relationship . . .

I have shown that the appellant lost the opportunity of representation, to which, on the facts of this case, he was entitled. Therefore, in the light of my review, an award of damages would be in order . . . Counsel admitted that it was very difficult to formulate his proposition, but he ultimately said that where the volition of another comes between the contractor and what he hopes to get under the contract, no damages can, as a matter of law, be given. I can find no authority for that proposition . . . But there is no other universal principle as to the amount of damages than that '*it is the aim of the law to ensure that a person whose contract has been broken shall be placed as near as possible in the same position as if it had not*' [*emphasis supplied*].

Remoteness of damages

Damages should be awarded when arising naturally or as may reasonably be supposed to have been within the contemplation or knowledge of both the parties at the time they made the contract. Knowledge can be based on awareness (or what the party in breach ought to be aware of) in the ordinary course of things or special circumstances outside the ordinary course of things which the party in breach was made aware of at the time of the making of the contract.

Winston Walters v Jose Cartellone Construcciones Civiles S.A. (2009) HCV No. 05597 of 2008 (JM)

Facts: Mr Winston Walters was a trucker and marl pit operator. He was what could be called a self-made man. In his capacity as a marl pit operator, he entered into a written contract, dated 13 February 2004, with Cartellone to provide Cartellone with marl for use on what is known as the North Coast Highway. This highway was an ambitious project undertaken by the Government of Jamaica. It runs along the entire north coast of Jamaica from Negril in the west (the haven for spring breakers from the United States of America) to Port Antonio in the east (the home of the famous Boston Jerk Pork). Clause 4 governed restoration of the marl pit after the execution of the marl and this restoration was said to be the responsibility of Cartellone. Clause 4 reads: 'After the Contractor (*sic*) finish (*sic*) the extraction of marl, the Quarry will be left in a suitable condition. There will be no pits.'

It was alleged that the defendant completed the extraction of the marl in early 2005 but he failed to restore the marl pit. The precise date was not stated in the pleaded case. On the face of it, there was a breach of contract. The marl pit to which this contract related was located at Cranbrook in the parish of St Ann. Mr Walters's case was that Cartellone was to reclaim the mined-out areas of the marl pit and the failure to do this was a breach of clause 4. Mr Walters claimed that this failure to reclaim the marl pit by Cartellone prevented him from being awarded another licence to operate another marl pit at Bengal in Trelawny.

Mr Walters further alleged that he applied for another quarry licence on 13 July 2005. This application was after the breach of contract alleged against Cartellone. Mr Walters pleaded that by letter dated 4 November 2008 from the Mines and Geology Division of the Ministry of Mining and Telecommunication, over the signature of Mr Paul Henry, Inspector of Mines, he was told that there needed to be a 'complete restoration' of the

Cranbrook marl pit before he would be considered for the grant of a marl pit licence at the proposed site at Bengal, Trelawny. This inability to secure a marl pit licence, the argument went, prevented him from earning from specific lucrative contracts which came his way.

Held: Sykes, J
The current state of the law makes it clear that losses under contracts of the type under consideration, in the instant case, are not recoverable unless they were brought to the attention of the defendant specifically, at the time the contract was made. It is true that from one point of view, it can be said that a claimant may lose specific contracts with third parties if the defendant is in breach of his contract with the claimant, but the law has never held that these losses are recoverable unless they were brought to the attention of the defendant at the time of the contract . . .

I should point, that even though I have said that the party undertaking the risk should be told specifically of any additional risk, this only applies if the risk is beyond what is ordinarily expected in the circumstances of the contract. What is ordinarily expected is taken to be within the contemplation of the parties and so need not be spelt out with specificity. What this means is that when the parties contract, there is a factual matrix against which the agreement is concluded, and that factual matrix may be such that, in the event of a breach, then certain losses "would arise generally" because they would occur 'in the great multitude of cases', and those losses would be recoverable even if the parties had not expressly spoken about it. The reason for this is that the losses that resulted were so very obvious or so virtually certain, that it can be taken that the parties must have had these losses in mind at the time they contracted. Thus losses that arise from a general loss of business because of a breach of contract are virtually certain. There is no need to know of any specific contract whereas loss under a particularly lucrative contract cannot be known to the contract breaker unless he was told about the contract at the time he contracted with innocent party.

This is the real basis of the decision in the *Heron 11*. The House emphasised that the ship owner, while not knowing what the charterers had in mind, nonetheless knew enough to know that a delay in arriving may result in losses generally. He knew that the charterers were sugar sellers. He knew that there was a market for sugar in Basrah. He knew that the charterers wanted to get there by a specific date. He knew that the price of sugar fluctuated in the Basrah market. Therefore he must have appreciated that delay may result in some loss . . .

If in cases where the special contract has already been entered into between the claimant and the third party, such losses are not recoverable unless the contract [was] brought to the attention of the contract breaker at the time of the contract between the claimant and the contract breaker, then it must follow as a matter of logic[] that[,] contracts that were not in existence at the time of the contract between the claimant and the contract breaker, could not conceivably be within the contemplation of third parties, and thus are even more remote than third party contracts that existed at the time of the contract between the parties . . . The claimant does not have a good arguable case in relation to these special contracts.

Mitigating losses

Once the defendant has breached his obligations or stated his intention to breach his obligations, the plaintiff has a duty to mitigate his loss, unless the plaintiff had 'substantial and legitimate interest' in actual performance.

Saffron Limited (Claimant) v Angel Estates Limited (Defendant) (2012) Claim No. ANUHCV2008/0641 (AG)

Facts: By a contract dated 2nd October 2006, the Defendant granted a 21 year lease to the Claimant whereby the Claimant leased a portion of the Defendant's building; that building also housed the Defendant's casino and sports bar and restaurant, which were on the ground floor of the building. Included in the terms of the lease was the provision of utility services to the Claimant to include electricity and water, which services were to be paid for by the Claimant to the Defendant for onward payment to the relevant statutory bodies. It was therefore understood that the leased premises would be supplied with electricity and that it would be the duty of the Defendant as the landlord so to do, and not that of the tenant, whose duty was to pay for the electricity supplied. In late 2007, the Defendant's company was in dire financial straits and unable to pay for its electricity; as a result, APUA suppressed electricity to the Defendant's premises. As a result of the suppression, the Defendant ran its generators for approximately one (1) year into 2008. Throughout that period, the Claimant continued its operations, using electricity provided by the Defendant. According to the evidence of Mr. Velardi, the Managing Director of the Defendant Company, in the beginning of May 2008, the Defendant was unable to purchase diesel to run its generators due to its finances. He informed Mr. Martel, the Managing Director of the Claimant company, that the Defendant company would be obliged to discontinue providing electricity from its generators. The Claimant company rented a generator and continued the running of the Saffron restaurant until the 2nd October 2008. During that period of time and until the end of August 2008, the Claimant paid rent to the Defendant. Mr. Velardi further states that, at the end of August 2008, Mr. Martel informed him that he would be sending their chefs on vacation, in anticipation of the upcoming season. Mr. Martel did not tell him that he would be closing down the restaurant; he was of the opinion that Mr. Martel was preparing to re-open as normal during the peak season. As a result of the Defendant becoming bankrupt, it ceased its operations of the casino, sports bar and restaurant, on the ground floor of the building. Mr. Martel closed the restaurant sometime in mid-September 2008 for holidays for three weeks. According to the Claimant's Reply to Defence, the Claimant did in fact re-open its restaurant after the 2008 annual vacation, but on opening night, 'the lights went out'. The Defendant however alleges that, after the holiday closure, the Claimant never re-opened the restaurant. It is Mr. Martell's contention that the closure of his company's restaurant was due to the Defendant's failure to provide electricity for which they have been found liable. He states that the Defendant acted in breach of its obligation with respect to the supply of electricity and because of this, the Claimant's restaurant was forced to close.

Held: Remy, J
The law is settled that damages for breach of contract are intended to put the injured party (the claimant) in the position, as far as money can do it, as he would have been if there had been no breach. The claimant must, however, take all reasonable steps to mitigate the loss consequent on the breach. As stated by the learned writers of *McGregor on Damages*:

> 'The first and most important rule is that the claimant must take all reasonable steps to mitigate the loss to him consequent upon the defendant's wrong and cannot recover damages for any such loss which he could thus have avoided but has failed, through unreasonable action or inaction, to avoid. Put shortly, the claimant cannot recover for avoidable loss.' The learned writers go on to state that 'it is the loss that has to be avoided and not the wrong itself.' (see the first supplement to the 18th edition.)

. . .

The case of *Payzu Limited v Saunders* tells us that 'the question what steps a plaintiff in an action for breach of contract should take towards mitigating the damage is a question of fact and not of law.'

In assessing reasonableness, while it has been said that the claimant is 'not bound to nurse the interests' of the defendant, it has also, and for long, been said that the claimant must act with the defendant's as well as his own interest in mind[,] per Channell J in *Smailes v Hans Dessen*. The claimant is not under any obligation to do anything other than in the ordinary course of business. He need not risk his money too far; he need not do anything to damage his commercial reputation. He is however obliged to take some action; inaction is not an option.

Turning to the instant case. What would a reasonable businessman[] in the shoes of the Claimant do? The Claimant had a 21-year lease. Only 18 months of this lease had elapsed. The Claimant closed the restaurant ostensibly for vacation for three weeks, and did not re-open. It is the Claimant's contention that it was forced to cease the operation of its restaurant on account of the Defendant's non-provision of electricity. If, as stated by the Claimant, connecting to CDAL power was not an option, was the Claimant absolved from taking any other steps towards mitigating its loss? Based on the authorities, the answer cannot be in the affirmative. It is the view of the Court that, notwithstanding the Defendant's breach, the Claimant was compelled, in the circumstances, to take one or other of the following steps:

a) Renting or purchasing a generator to provide electricity. The evidence before the Court is that when the Defendant stopped supplying electricity from their generators to the Claimant in late May 2008, the Claimant rented a generator at a cost of $100 U.S. per day. Mr. Martel's evidence is that this generator powered the restaurant and 'other areas that they needed to function.' He stated that this generator was a 125 KVA which was 'the minimum that was needed.' He stated that he attempted to find the cost of a generator like the one he rented, but when asked under cross-examination what was the cost, he responded, 'I did not investigate that.'
b) Re-locating to alternative premises.

Would a reasonable businessman in the shoes of Mr. Martel seek alternative premises to re-locate the restaurant as submitted by the Defendant? The Court is of the view that the answer to this question has to be in the affirmative. Mr. Martel and/or the other Directors or Managers of the Claimant company ought to have, as reasonable businessmen, sought an alternative venue to operate their restaurant. There is no evidence before the Court that they even attempted to obtain alternative premises. There is no evidence that the premises occupied by the Claimant had a distinctive feature which no other premises could provide, or that the ambience could not be duplicated elsewhere.

Mr. Martel also gave evidence that he made enquiries of APUA and offered a deposit of $20,000.00 as a gesture to encourage them to supply electricity to his company's restaurant. He adds that this offer was not acceptable 'given the millions owed by the Defendant Company to APUA.' The Court notes that Mr. Martel offers not a shred of evidence of this. There is no evidence of any correspondence between Mr. Martel and APUA either by letter, fax, email or otherwise. The Claimant chose the option of closing the restaurant at the Defendant's premises. Having done so, it did not re-locate the restaurant to alternative premises. At the time of the closure of the restaurant, the Claimant had another 19 years on the lease remaining; it chose to sue for the unexpired portion of the lease, i.e., the remaining 19 years.

It is the Claimant's contention that it did all that it reasonably could do to stay in business. I disagree. The facts do not support the Claimant's contention. What the facts do disclose is that the Claimant sat back and did nothing; there was no attempt to find alternative premises; there was also no attempt made to obtain an alternative power source by way of purchase or lease of a generator so as to keep the Saffron Restaurant open. Mr. Martel did not even attempt to find out what a generator would cost. He cannot therefore even suggest that the purchase of a generator would have exposed the Claimant Company to unreasonable financial risk.

The rule of law in relation to mitigation of damages was stated by Cockburn CJ in *Frost v Knight* as follows:

> In assessing the damages for breach of performance, a jury will of course take into account whatever the plaintiff has done, or has had the means of doing, and, as a prudent man, ought in reason to have done, whereby his loss has been, or would have been, diminished.

In similar vein, Saunders JA in *International Motors Limited and Ronnie Thomas* stated:

> The law is that a person bringing a claim for damages should act reasonably in seeking to mitigate the damages. Even though you have a good, solid claim against a defendant, the law expects you to behave in a reasonable and responsible manner to ensure that the damages suffered or incurred are not greater than they reasonably ought to be. The law will not allow you to recover loss that could and should have been avoided.

The Court is of the view that the response of the Claimant to the Defendant's breach was not reasonable in the circumstance. The Claimant was required to take all reasonable steps to lessen the damage resulting from the Defendant's breach. It was not entitled to sit back and suffer loss which was avoidable by taking steps which a reasonable and prudent businessman would take. It took no steps to mitigate its loss.

Principle of quantum meruit

Quantum meruit literally translates as 'as much as he deserves'. It is trite law that when a contract is terminated under a termination clause or at common law, both parties are discharged from the further performance of the contract; however, rights which have already been unconditionally acquired are not divested or discharged unless the contract provides to the contrary. *Quantum meruit* is an equitable doctrine based on the principle that one who benefits from the labour and materials supplied by another should not be unjustly enriched thereby. Under circumstances where contracts are not enforceable because of uncertainty or where there has been no contract (for example, the voluntary provision of goods and services under certain circumstances), the law implies a promise to pay a reasonable amount for the materials and labour which have been furnished. A claim for damages on a *quantum meruit* basis can be sustained in the absence of a concluded contract or even where the work performed is not used at all by the person against whom a claim is being made.

Joseph Henry v Tobago Plantations Limited (2009) Claim No. CV2007–03427 (TT)

Facts: Mr. Joseph Henry, the Claimant was employed by Tobago Plantations Limited, the Defendant, as its Manager-Development by letter dated 3rd August 1995. He was so employed with the Defendant until 28th February 2001 when he was made redundant due to 'internal restructuring.' The Defendant was in that period engaged in the construction of infrastructure and building projects for the Defendant at Lowlands, Tobago. This included the Hilton Tobago with 74 condominiums, 20 villas, a golf course and a maintenance facility ('the Project'). It is the work performed by the Claimant in the construction of the Project which forms the backdrop to this action.

As Manager-Development, the Claimant was responsible for the co-ordination and supervision of the construction of the Defendant's infrastructure and building projects. The Claimant was accountable to the Defendant's Board through the *Director-in-charge*, Mr. Keith Ian McLachlan. One aspect of the infrastructure at the Project which fell under the Claimant's supervision was the design and construction of an underground electrical distribution system ('the UED System'). The Defendant had engaged Exeqtech Limited to design the civil and electrical infrastructure for the Project, in particular the UED System. However in mid-1996, the Claimant advised Mr Mc Lachlan of the difficulties being encountered by Exeqtech Limited in designing the UED System for it to meet with the approval of the Trinidad and Tobago Electricity Commission ('T&TEC'). In that conversation Mr. Mc Lachlan asked the Claimant whether he '*could get through doing it.*' This, the Claimant understood to mean, whether he could himself get through with obtaining the approvals in designing the UED System. He told Mr. Mc Lachlan '*I could do it*' who then told him '*to go ahead.*'

This UED System was a novel idea at that time. It was a system in which all the wires for the electrical infrastructure are placed underground so that the landscape is not aesthetically disrupted by above ground wires and poles. The Claimant eagerly set about researching, planning and executing the design of the system and effectively became the Design Engineer for the electrical work to advise Alpha Engineering and Design Limited ('Alpha'), which firm was eventually selected by the Defendant to replace Exeqtech Limited in 1996. Alpha was responsible for the infrastructural design at the Project such as roads, water, sewage and drainage.

No agreement however was made between the parties for the Claimant's remuneration for his execution of this task. However the Claimant continued working on the UED System and liaising with Alpha, suppliers of equipment, and representatives of T&TEC to implement the UED System until it was successfully implemented at the Project on or about July 2000. During that time the Claimant continued to perform his regular duties as Manager-Development in co-ordinating and supervising the civil infrastructural work executed by the Defendant's contractors.

After the Claimant's employment was terminated on the grounds of redundancy, the Defendant, having had the benefit of the UED System installed by the Claimant's intervention, paid the Claimant severance benefits pursuant to the Retrenchment and Severance Benefits Act as well as other benefits pursuant to his contract as Manager-Development. However these sums which were paid to the Claimant by March 2001 did not include any compensation for the work done on the UED System despite the Claimant having raised the issue of remuneration for this work during the course his employment.

The Claimant now makes his claim in these proceedings against the Defendant for the payment of the sum of $437,500.00 as the sum due and owing to him for the performance of the task of designing the UED System. The Claimant contends that the design and establishment of the UED System was additional to his duties as Manager-Development and that he undertook this task at the request of Mr. Mc Lachlan. The Defendant having paid the [Claimant] his regular salary under his contract as Manager-Development denies that it is liable to pay to the [Claimant] any additional remuneration.

The short point to be decided in this case therefore is whether the Defendant requested the Claimant to perform works which were additional to or outside the scope of his duties as Manager-Development.

Held: Kokaram, J
The Claimant having been asked to perform the works of designing the UED system, whether the Claimant is entitled to be paid extra remuneration beyond his monthly pay depends upon a construction of the terms of his contract of employment. In the analysis of extra remuneration in the context of an employment relationship paragraph 553 of *Halsbury Laws of England* Vol. 6 states as follows:

> A promise to pay extra remuneration is however founded on good consideration, and will be enforced[] when the employee is no longer bound by the original contract by reason of the risk having become greater than that within the contemplation of that contract, or because of the nature of the service has been entirely changed, or in a case where the employee undertakes increased responsibility, or more work.

The Claimant submits in this case that he undertook increased responsibility or 'more work' in the design and preparation of the System. The Defendant however submits that in the context of an employment contract services which are-

- directly related to an employee's ordinary duties;
- might reasonably have been anticipated as being likely to arise in the course of the employee's ordinary duties; and/or
- cannot be differentiated in kind from the scope of the employee's ordinary duties;

do not amount to 'additional' duties and do not entitle an employee to receive additional remuneration. In support of this contention the Defendant relies upon *Mackison's Trustees v The Magistrates of Dundee*. Lord Guthrie at page 822 noted:

> In the case of a servant hired for certain work, who, in addition, does other and unrelated work, it may be possible, by that circumstance alone, or by that circumstance taken along with others, to raise up an implication for separate and additional remuneration, which, I suppose, would be calculated on the basis, not as here, of ordinary professional charges, but of quantum meruit, for which, as I have said, there is no material. But in this case I am unable to discover any work, in the office or on the ground, Parliamentary or local, done by Mr. Mackison as an engineer, an architect, or a surveyor, which had not a direct relation to his admittedly official work, and which, on his appointment, might not reasonably have been anticipated as likely to arise, although, it may be, not to the extent actually developed.

Even if the Claimant cannot prove in fact that there was an agreement between the parties to pay to him extra remuneration, the Claimant's demonstration that the design of the UED System bore no direct relation to his official work or which does not form part of his original contract is the quintessential of a quantum mer[u]it claim. Such claims are an obligation arising *quasi ex contract*. In such claims, the obligation to pay reasonable remuneration for work done is imposed by a rule of law when there is no binding contract between the parties. The law will imply a promise to pay on the part of a person who requests another to perform services. The existence of a contract between the parties in respect of the services rendered is not a requirement for the implication of a promise to pay. See *Craven Ellis v Cannons Limited*[.] Green LJ observed in that case that the fact that there was no valid contract between the Defendant company and the Plaintiff presented no obstacle to the implied promise to pay on a quantum mer[u]it basis which arises from the performance of the services and such implied acceptable of the same by the company. Indeed Green LJ commented[] that:

> The company having had the full benefit of these services declined to pay either under the agreement or on the basis of a quantum mer[u]it. Their defence to the action is a purely technical defence and if it succeeds . . . the company would be in the position of having received and accepted valuable services and refusing for purely technical reasons to pay for them . . .

Quantum mer[u]it claims are appropriate where there is no concluded contract between the parties on material terms such as the price for which services will be performed by one party and who has provided the services that were requested and accepted by the client. In those cases the law implies a promise to pay a reasonable fee. Therefore where parties have a defined contract between them for remuneration for services rendered, it stands to reason that quantum mer[u]it claims cannot be based on an entitlement derived from that contract. It must be for work outside of that contract and for which there is no contract to pay an agreed sum.

In *S&W Process Engineering Limited v Cauldron Foods Limited* P Gouldson J stated:

> It is trite law that a claim on a quantum mer[u]it cannot arise if there is an existing contract between the parties to pay an agreed sum . . . However where there is contract for specified work but the contractor does work outside the contract at the employer's request the contractor may be entitled to be paid a reasonable sum of the work outside the contract on the basis of an implied contract. However this will always turn on what is meant in a particular instance by 'outside the contract'.

In the context of this case therefore for the Claimant to be entitled to reasonable remuneration for the design of the system, it must be demonstrated that the request made was not referable to the contract of employment as Manager-Development. If the performance of the work is not referable to any contract, the law will impose an obligation on the Defendant sounding in quasi contract to pay the Claimant a reasonable remuneration. There will still be liability even if the system had not been put into operation so long as the Claimant performed services at the Defendant's request to execute works which was not part of his original bargain . . .

The Court holds that the design of the system was a task that was assigned to the Claimant by his supervisor. That this duty was not within the contemplation of the parties at the date of the Claimant's appointment and was not within the scope of the Claimant's duties as a Manager-Developer. The Claimant is entitled to reasonable remuneration for the performance of the said services which is assessed in the sum of $434,851.76.

Liquidated damages and penalty clauses

The parties to a contract may anticipate the possibility of a breach and include in the contract a term that a certain sum shall be paid to the injured party by the party in default if a specified breach occurs. If this sum is a genuine pre-estimate of the damage, the term is known as liquidated damages; if it is in excess of a genuine pre-estimate, it may be deemed a penalty and not enforceable.

Dunlop Pneumatic Tyre Co. Ltd v New Garage and Motor Co. Ltd [1915] AC 79 (GB)

Facts: The appellants through an agent entered into a contract with the respondents under which they supplied them with their goods, which consisted mainly of motor tyres, covers and tubes. By this contract, the respondents agreed to pay £5 for each tube, cover or tyre sold in breach of the terms of the contract for supply. The appellants having discovered that the respondents had breached the contract by selling below the agreed cover price, brought an action for breach. The court in its assessment of damages used the £5 as liquidated damages and awarded £250 to the appellants. The decision was reversed in the Court of Appeal and was then appealed.

Held: Lord Dunedin

(i) Though the parties to a contract who use the words penalty or liquidated damages may prima facie be supposed to mean what they say, yet the expression used is not conclusive. The court must find out whether the payment stipulated is in truth a penalty or liquidated damages . . .

(ii) The essence of a penalty is a payment of money stipulated as *in terrorem* of the offending party; the essence of liquidated damages is a genuine pre-estimate of damage . . .

(iii) The question whether a sum stipulated is a penalty or liquidated damages is a question of construction to be decided upon the terms and inherent circumstances of each particular contract; judged of as at the time of the making of the contract, not as at the time of the breach . . .

(iv) To assist this task of construction various tests have been suggested, which, even if applicable to the case under consideration, may prove helpful or even conclusive. Such are:

(a) It will be held to be a penalty if the sum stipulated for is extravagant and unconscionable in amount in comparison with the greatest loss that could conceivably be proved to have followed from the breach . . .

(b) It will be held to be a penalty if the breach consists only in not paying a sum of money, and the sum stipulated is a sum greater than the sum which ought to have been paid . . .

(c) There is a presumption (but no more than a presumption) that a clause is penal when 'a single lump sum is made payable by way of compensation on the occurrence of one or more or all of several events, some of which may occasion serious and others but trifling damage' (Lord Watson in *Lord Elphinstone v Monkland Iron and Coal Co*) . . .

(d) It is no obstacle to the sum stipulated being a genuine pre-estimate of damage that the consequences of breach are such as to make precise pre-estimation an impossibility. On the contrary, that is just the situation when pre-estimated damage was the true bargain between the parties . . .

Turning now to the facts of the case; it is evident that the damage apprehended by the appellants owing to the breaking of the agreement was an indirect and not a direct damage . . . To arrive at the indirect damage in this case, supposing no sum had been stipulated, that is just what a judge would, in my opinion, have had to do. On the whole . . . the appeal [should] be allowed.

Brown's Bay Resort Limited (Appellant) v Luca Possoni (Respondent) (2014) ANUHCVAP2010/0033 (AG)

Facts: The respondent leased commercial premises from the appellant for a period of two years, beginning 1st November 2006, for the purpose of operating a restaurant and beach bar business ('the Lease'). The respondent also operated a day charter and fishing tours business from the premises. Clause 19 of the Lease made provision for a penalty fee of

US$4000.00 in the event of an interruption of the contract. In or about September 2007, the appellant's representative told the respondent that the appellant was selling the property and that the Lease would not be continued. In December 2007, the locks to the property were changed and the premises were padlocked. The respondent accepted the appellant's repudiation of the Lease and cancelled the contract he had with a new chef and hostess/manager that he had engaged for the second year of the term. He also had to pay the chef and hostess/manager compensation. The respondent brought a claim against the appellant for loss of profits, losses caused by the forced termination of the contract with the chef and hostess/manager and for damages for unlawful termination of the Lease. The learned trial judge granted judgment for the respondent and ordered the appellant to pay to the respondent general damages of $123,347.02 which represented *inter alia* loss of revenue from the appellant's breach of the Lease and costs of the aborted contract of service with the chef and manager. The appellant appealed on the grounds that the learned trial judge erred in (1) failing to construe clause 19 of the Lease as a liquidated damages clause; (2) accepting the damages claimed by the respondent in the absence of sufficient or adequate proof; (3) awarding damages for loss from a fishing and charter business; and (4) failing to apply the principle that damages are to compensate a claimant only in respect of what he has lost.

Held: Webster, QC, JA (Ag), Thom, (Ag), Baptiste, JJA
. . . Clause 19 applies where one party has conducted himself or itself in such a way as to interrupt the contract, not to a case where the conduct results in a repudiation and termination of the contract. This finding by the learned judge is, in my view, sufficient to dispose of the issues relating to clause 19 and ground 1 of the notice of appeal. However, the learned judge went on in his judgment to deal with the alternative position of what would happen if clause 19 applied to the facts of the case and whether it limited the respondent's claim for damages to the stipulated sum of $4,000.00. In other words, is clause 19 a true liquidated damages clause or a penalty. The learned judge analysed the relevant principles and authorities and concluded at paragraph 40 of the judgment –

> In any event, the principles to be extracted from the case of *Dunlop Pneumatic Tyre Company Limited v New Garage and Motor Company Limited*, which both sides accepted as the pre-eminent authority on the determination of whether an amount stipulated in a contract is a penalty or liquidated damages, lead in the Court's view to a conclusion that the sum of US$4,000 stipulated in clause 19 of the lease agreement is not a genuine pre-estimate of the damages likely to accrue from a breach of the agreement so as to be characterised as liquidated damages – the amount is stated in the agreement to be 'a penalty fee' and not liquidated damages; it is single lump sum made payable by way of compensation on the occurrence of one or more or all of several events, some of which may occasion serious and others but trifling damage; and the damages caused by a breach of the agreement (as in the present case) are quite capable of being ascertained by the normal measure of damages.

I agree with and would adopt the learned judge's conclusion that clause 19 is not a liquidated damages clause, and his reasons for so concluding. I do so with deference to the very careful and detailed submissions on the point by Dr. David Dorsett, counsel for the appellant. The respondent's claim for damages is not limited to the stipulated amount of $4,000.00. Damages are at large. I would dismiss ground 1 of this appeal.

Specific performance

Specific performance is exceptional and ordered only when an award of damages would be 'inadequate'. Specific performance is often the preferred remedy with respect to land contracts.

More often than not, the court would order the party in breach to perform his contract primarily due to the irreplaceable character of the goods or services covered. Specific performance is a 'coercive' remedy and is a creation of equity, thus making those seeking specific performance subject to the rules of equity.

Powercor Australia Ltd v Pacific Power [1999] VSC 110 (AU)

Facts: In or about August 1996 representatives of the parties commenced exploratory discussions in respect to futures trading. The initial discussions culminated in an agreement known as the ISDA Master Agreement (the Master Agreement) being entered into between the parties dated 21 November 1996 but exchanged on or about 16 December 1996. Pursuant to that agreement the parties agreed to enter into futures transactions in the New South Wales and Victoria electricity market on the terms and conditions contained therein. The terms of the Master Agreement formed part of each transaction by reason of the fact that the parties provided that each futures transaction was to be an amendment to the Master Agreement. The Master Agreement was varied on or about 8 October 1997.

During the period from 4 November 1996 to 27 May 1998 the parties entered into 35 separate undisputed commodity transaction agreements in respect of the provision of notional electricity. The periods of the contracts varied from one month to 10 years. These contracts were not in dispute. They had been or were being performed. PCA alleged that between 13 November 1997 to 15 June 1998 the parties entered into 11 additional contracts in respect of the notional supply of electricity for periods ranging from 2.5 years up to 10 years. These alleged contracts were in dispute. PCA originally asserted there were 12 but in final address PCA's counsel abandoned the claim in respect of disputed contract number 12. In respect of each contract, PP denied that any final binding contract was concluded because the parties were still negotiating. In the alternative it alleged it was agreed that no contract was concluded until a confirmation agreement was signed and exchanged. Further it alleged the person acting on behalf of PP was not authorised to enter into the particular contract on behalf of PP. PP further asserted that the employee of PCA who negotiated each agreement was not authorised to conclude the particular contract on behalf of PCA. PP raised issues of mistake and conventional estoppel and PCA delivered a reply raising, *inter alia*, estoppel.

PP also counter-claimed relying upon Sections 52 and 53 of the Trade Practices Act. PP at all times had in place a trading policy to the effect that it would not hedge in excess of 85 per cent of its generated electricity. At the end of May 1998 the senior trader at PP, Mr Murphy, realised that PP had or was about to exceed 85 per cent of its capacity. On 29 May 1998 he wrote a letter to PCA which, contrary to the hitherto harmonious trading relationship, raised doubts about a number of transactions. It appears that Mr Murphy took it upon himself to break off relations but his conduct over the following 12 days was bizarre. The letter of 29 May 1998 contained errors of fact and was confusing. Thereafter he had further discussions of a relatively friendly nature with PCA, blamed the confrontation on others, continued negotiations and then wrote a letter on 10 June 1998 disputing there was agreement and raising questions of authority. On 19 June 1998 PP wrote a letter in which it stated it was not bound and thereafter refused to honour the alleged agreements. On 21 August 1998 PCA issued a writ against PP seeking specific performance of the disputed agreements, sought equitable damages and in the alternative sought damages in lieu of specific performance.

Held: Gillard, J

The other option was to seek an order that PP perform its side of the bargain. PCA was entitled to sue for specific performance. The remedy of specific performance is a creature of equity and it evolved to overcome deficiencies in the remedies available at common law. Writing in his first edition in 1858 Edward Fry in his treatise on *The Specific Performance of Contracts* wrote at p 1:

> The specific performance of contracts is an ancient branch of the equitable jurisdiction of the Court of Chancery, arising out of the incapacity of the courts of common law to enforce the actual performance of the contract: for these courts, they recognising the obligation of the parties to a contract to perform their respective parts, enforce its obligation, not specifically, but only by way of damages.

As a general rule specific performance is not available if damages that can be awarded give the victim full compensation, but it is an essential condition of that rule that the award will put the victim in a position as good as he would have been in if the agreement had been performed. It follows that in cases involving payment of money specific performance is not usually granted. But again that is only a general rule and if money is to be paid pursuant to a contract periodically, common sense and justice demands that the contract be specifically performed to avoid numerous proceedings being brought to recover payment. See *Beswick v Beswick* (1967) Ch 538 at 560–1. The reasoning of Danckwerts LJ was expressly approved in the House of Lords – see [1968] AC at 97. The principle was stated by Lord Upjohn in the *Beswick* case when he said – 'Equity is to do true justice to enforce the true contract that the parties have made and to prevent the trouble and expense of a multiplicity of actions. This has been well settled for over a century.'

No doubt Mr Downes QC had these principles in mind when he accepts that specific performance is appropriate in respect of future obligations. What Mr Downes QC is seeking to do is to divide up the remedies available to PCA between common law damages for the past and the equitable remedy of specific performance for the future. PCA has elected to claim specific performance. It is entitled to do so. It has the carriage of the proceeding and is entitled to pursue any remedy that the law permits it. Whether or not it is open to divide remedies in the way submitted by PP is a moot point. I suspect the issue is not one of jurisdiction because this court has unlimited jurisdiction but a question of whether the court should divide up the remedy in the circumstances. If this is correct, in the end it is a question of doing practical justice between the parties.

The fact is that PCA has the legal right to have its contracts fully performed. That right it seeks in the present proceeding. This means the contracts in their entirety and not a portion thereof. PCA referred to *Turner v Bladin* (1951) 82 CLR 463. This is an example of specific performance being decreed in respect of past and future obligations. The case does not address the issue whether a court should divide up the remedy in the way sought by PP. See also the observations of Lord Pearce in *Beswick v Beswick, supra*, at p 92 (B–C).

CHAPTER 4

LAW OF OBLIGATIONS: TORTS

Reproduced with the permission of CartoonStock

THE LAW OF TORTS

Tortious liability arises from the breach of a duty primarily fixed by law; such duty is towards persons generally and its breach is redressible by an action for unliquidated damages.[1] This much-venerated definition by *Winfield* has not managed to quell the difficulties experienced by many writers in defining 'tort'. *Street* offers a definition that states:

> Tort is that branch of the civil law relating to obligations imposed by operation of law on all natural and artificial persons. These obligations, owed by one person to another, embody norms of conduct that arise outside contract and unjust enrichment. Tort enables the person to whom

1 Rogers, WVH, *Winfield and Jolowicz on Tort*, 2002, London: Sweet & Maxwell, p 4.

> the obligation is owed to pursue a remedy on his own behalf where breach of a relevant norm of conduct infringes his interests to a degree recognized by the law as such an infringement.[2]

Steele acknowledges the difficulties inherent in attempting to define the law of torts and the absence of a widely accepted definition of tort but offers her own definition.[3] According to Steele, 'Torts are 'wrongs'. To be slightly more precise, torts are civil wrongs for which law will provide a remedy. This remedy will be enforceable against one party, to the benefit of the other, and it will reflect (and perhaps correct) the wrong committed.'[4] As succinctly put by *Street*, what the law of torts does is to define the obligations imposed on one member of society by his or her fellows and to provide for compensation for harms caused by breach of such obligations.[5]

Just as members of the business community must honour their legal undertakings whether written or oral, so too must they honour social undertakings that are underpinned by the principles of tortious liability. What is being upheld is the social contract that creates obligations to each other and to the wider community. The law of torts defines the obligations imposed on one member of society to his or her fellows and provides for compensation for harms caused by breach of such obligations.

NEGLIGENCE-GENERATED TORTS

The tort of negligence is one of the main platforms of liability within the business community in terms of its interaction with the wider society and its own employees, servants and/or agents. There are four basic components that must be present for the successful presentation of an action founded on negligence.

General principles of negligence

The concept of duty

The notion of duty examines whether the law acknowledges the possibility of tortious liability in a given situation. Duty helps to:

> demarcate the range of people, relationships and interests that receive the protection of the law from the effects of negligently inflicted harm. Thus, even where the defendant's carelessness can be shown to have caused damage to the claimant, the law may nevertheless not acknowledge the existence of a 'duty situation', thereby refusing to impose liability.[6]

The emerging law had its genesis in the 1932 decision of *Donoghue v Stevenson*, where Lord Atkin, in the House of Lords, made the now famous pronouncements on the duty concept. Lord Atkin cast the duty concept within the framework of the 'neighbour principle' and mandated that one should take reasonable care to avoid acts or omissions which can be reasonably foreseen as likely to injure one's neighbour. This then led to his response to the consequential question, who, in law, is one's neighbour? Lord Atkin firmly answered this question by asserting that one's neighbour includes persons who are so closely and directly affected by one's act that

2 Murphy, J, *Street on Torts*, 2012, Oxford: Oxford University Press, p 4.
3 Steele, J, *Tort Law: Text, Cases and Materials*, 2007, Oxford: Oxford University Press, p 3.
4 Steele, *Tort Law*, p 3.
5 Murphy, *Street on Torts*, p 4.
6 Deakin, S, Johnston, A and Markesinis, B, *Markesinis and Deakin's Tort Law*, 2007, Oxford: Oxford University Press, p 116.

one ought to reasonably have them in contemplation as being so affected when directing one's mind to the acts or omissions which are called in question and under examination by the law.

Donoghue v Stevenson [1932] AC 562 (GB)

Facts: On August 26 1928, the Appellant drank a bottle of ginger beer, manufactured by the Respondent, which a friend had bought from a retailer and given to her. The bottle contained the decomposed remains of a snail which were not, and could not be, detected until the greater part of the contents of the bottle had been consumed. As a result she alleged, and at that stage her allegations were accepted as true, that she suffered from shock and severe gastroenteritis. She accordingly instituted the proceedings against the manufacturer which gave rise to this appeal. The foundation of her case was that the Respondent, as the manufacturer of an article intended for consumption and contained in a receptacle which prevented inspection, owed a duty to her as consumer of the article to take care that there was no noxious element in the goods, that he neglected such duty and was consequently liable for any damage caused by such neglect.

Held: Lord Atkin
At present I content myself with pointing out that in English law there must be, and is, some general conception of relations giving rise to a duty of care, of which the particular cases found in the books are but instances. The liability for negligence, whether you style it such or treat it as in other systems as a species of '*culpa*', is no doubt based upon a general public sentiment of moral wrongdoing for which the offender must pay. But acts or omissions which any moral code would censure cannot in a practical world be treated so as to give a right to every person injured by them to demand relief. In this way rules of law arise which limit the range of complainants and the extent of their remedy. The rule that you are to love your neighbour becomes in law, you must not injure your neighbour; and the lawyer's question, Who is my neighbour?, receives a restricted reply. You must take reasonable care to avoid acts or omissions which you can reasonably foresee would be likely to injure your neighbour. Who, then, in law is my neighbour? The answer seems to be persons who are so closely and directly affected by my act that I ought reasonably to have them in contemplation as being so affected when I am directing my mind to the acts or omissions which are called in question . . . There will no doubt arise cases where it will be difficult to determine whether the contemplated relationship is so close that the duty arises.

The law has now evolved somewhat and the test to determine the presence of a duty of care is somewhat more complicated. In assessing liability for a harm sustained by a plaintiff, it is necessary to consider the matter not only by inquiring about foreseeability but also by considering the nature of the relationship between the parties (proximity) and to be satisfied that in all the circumstances it is fair, just and reasonable to impose a duty of care. These elements are not to be looked at as mutually exclusive but must be analysed within the context of their interrelationship.

Marc Rich & Co. AG v Bishop Rock Marine Co. Limited [1996] AC 211 (GB)

Facts: A ship was on a loaded voyage from South America to Italy when a crack appeared in her hull. Further cracks developed when she was anchored off Puerto Rico. A surveyor, called in by the master, recommended permanent repairs, at which the owners baulked. Temporary repairs were made and the ship sailed. The temporary repairs broke down and the ship sank. The question for the court was whether the surveyor's employers, a Japanese classification society, were liable for his negligence in finally agreeing that temporary repairs were sufficient and whether the surveyor owed a duty of care to the cargo owners.

Held: Lord Steyn
In this case the question is whether a classification society owed a duty of care to a third party, the owners of cargo laden on a vessel, arising from the careless performance of a survey of a damaged vessel by the surveyor of the classification society which resulted in the vessel being allowed to sail and subsequently sinking. It is a novel question.

In England no classification society, engaged by owners to perform a survey, has ever been held liable to cargo owners on the ground of a careless conduct of any survey . . . [S]ince the decision in *Dorset Yacht Co. Ltd. v Home Office* it has been settled law that the elements of foreseeability and proximity as well as considerations of fairness, justice and reasonableness are relevant to all cases whatever the nature of the harm sustained by the plaintiff. Saville LJ explained: 'whatever the nature of the harm sustained by the plaintiff, it is necessary to consider the matter not only by inquiring about foreseeability but also by considering the nature of the relationship between the parties; and to be satisfied that in all the circumstances it is fair, just and reasonable to impose a duty of care. Of course . . . these three matters overlap with each other and are really facets of the same thing. For example, the relationship between the parties may be such that it is obvious that a lack of care will create a risk of harm and that as a matter of common sense and justice a duty should be imposed . . . Again in most cases of the direct infliction of physical loss or injury through carelessness, it is self-evident that a civilised system of law should hold that a duty of care has been broken, whereas the infliction of financial harm may well pose a more difficult problem. Thus the three so-called requirements for a duty of care are not to be treated as wholly separate and distinct requirements but rather as convenient and helpful approaches to the pragmatic question whether a duty should be imposed in any given case. In the end whether the law does impose a duty in any particular circumstances depends upon those circumstances . . .' That seems to me a correct summary of the law as it now stands . . .

I am willing to assume (without deciding) that there was a sufficient degree of proximity in this case to fulfil that requirement for the existence of a duty of care. The critical question is therefore whether it would be fair, just and reasonable to impose such a duty . . . By way of summary, I look at the matter from the point of view of the three parties concerned. I conclude that the recognition of a duty would be unfair, unjust and unreasonable as against the shipowners who would ultimately have to bear the cost of holding classification societies liable, such consequence being at variance with the bargain between shipowners and cargo owners based on an internationally agreed contractual structure. It would also be unfair, unjust and unreasonable towards classification societies, notably because they act for the collective welfare and unlike shipowners they would not have the benefit of any limitation provisions . . . In my judgment the lesser injustice is done by not recognising a duty of care.

The standard of care

The standard of care lies at the heart of the law of torts. The standard of care defines the conduct that must be present to establish negligence in law.

The question, as a whole, of whether the defendant has broken a duty of care is a mixed one of law and fact; but the standard of care required of the defendant is an exclusively legal construct and based on the standard of a hypothetical reasonable person. If the defendant causes loss or injury to the claimant, but is able to show that he acted in a way that a reasonable person would have acted, no liability would attach.[7]

This second element in the establishment of a claim in tort must ascertain the appropriate standard of care and whether such standard of care was breached by the defendant.

Javier Arthurton BNF, Sandra Arthurton, Claimant v Winston Skeete, First Defendant and Wesk Limited, Second Defendant (2012) Claim No. NEVHCV2007/0024 (KN)

Facts: Javier Arthurton [Javier], by his next friend and mother Sandra Arthurton [Mrs. Arthurton] has brought this Claim against Winston Skeete [Mr. Skeete] and Wesk Limited for damages as a result of injuries he suffered in accident which occurred on 24th January 2004 on the *MV Sea Hustler*, a vessel, operated by Wesk Limited and captained by Mr. Skeete. At about 7:30 p.m. on 24th January 2004, Javier, who was 12 years old at the time, was at the Nevis Pier with other persons, including his mother. The group was intending to travel to St. Kitts on the MV Sea Hustler, which is a passenger and cargo vessel. Javier's left foot was severely damaged when he stepped on to the ramp to board the boat. In his Claim, Javier alleged that the accident was caused by the Defendants' negligence. Both Mr. Skeete and Wesk Limited deny any liability and they allege that the accident was caused by the negligence of Javier or his mother. The pleadings raise one question for determination and that is was the accident caused or contributed to by the negligence of Mr. Skeete or Wesk Limited?

Held: Leigertwood-Octave, J
To succeed in a negligence claim, a claimant must prove that: the defendant owed him a duty of care; that defendant breached that duty; the breach of that duty caused damage and the damage was not too remote. Carriers of passengers are liable when negligence is proved and in their written submissions, the Claimant referred the court to authorities where the duty of care in relation to carriers of passengers and/or their servants was considered. In *Readhead v Midland Railway Co*, the court held that the duty of a railway company and its servants, in relation to their passengers, was to take all due and reasonable care, including the use of skill and foresight, to carry them safely. 'Due care' means that having reference to the nature of the contract to carry, a high degree of care, and casts on carriers the duty of exercising all vigilance to see whatever is required for the safe conveyance of their passengers is in fit and proper order.

Although[] the House of Lords in *Barkway v South Wales Transport Company* placed the standard of care at 'a very high degree', the obligation does not appear to be greater tha[n] the general duty at common law to take reasonable care in the circumstances to avoid acts or omissions which can reasonably be foreseen as likely to injure the person or property of another. The authorities that the Defendants have relied on are consistent with the finding in *Barkway's case*. The Defendants' standard of care is that which might be expected from a person of ordinary prudence or a person of ordinary care and skill, engaged in the type of activity in which they were engaged. A professional is required to meet the standard of the ordinary skilled man exercising and professing to have the special skill[] in question. It is sufficient that he exercises the ordinary skill of an ordinary competent man exercising that particular art. A carrier's duty to exercise reasonable care must depend on the circumstances of each case, as particular circumstances are likely to require particular precautions

7 Murphy, *Street on Torts*, p 111.

> . . . Having considered, the authorities and reviewed the evidence and the submissions from both sides, it is my judgment that neither the Defendants nor their servants were negligent, in that they had exercised the duty of care at the standard of care required in relation to the Claimant.

It is beyond dispute that the test for determining the required standard of care is an objective one; however, the courts will do so in a manner which considers the attributes of a defendant that are idiosyncratic to a class or category of persons to which the defendant belongs.

> *Orchard v Lee* [2009] EWCA Civ 295 (GB)
>
> **Facts:** At about 1.40 pm on 27th January 2004 the respondent (SL) a thirteen and three-quarters year old boy was playing tag with another thirteen and a half year old boy (LR), originally the second defendant to the proceedings. They were playing in the courtyard and part of a walkway which was the social area for their age group when, running backwards and taunting LR, SL ran into the appellant who was working as a lunchtime assistant supervisor at the school. The back of his head came into contact with the appellant's cheek and although at first any injury seemed slight it has developed and her injuries are quite serious. The appellant brought proceedings naming SL, LR and the School as defendants. We were told that no proceedings were ever in fact commenced against the school and the matter proceeded to trial before His Honour Judge Iain Hughes QC with the only defendants, the two boys. The judge dismissed the claim against the boys, the essence of his conclusion being that, despite his sympathy for the appellant, he was satisfied that it was a simple accident caused by 'horseplay between two 13 year old boys in and around an outside courtyard . . . boys doing what boys do'. The appeal is against his finding relating to SL alone.
>
> **Held:** Waller, LJ
> No real criticism is made of that direction but I am not sure it is a complete statement of the law as the judge actually, and in my view rightly, applied. First, to test negligence simply by reference to a realisation that actions may cause injury makes for too broad a test. In one sense obviously running around on playgrounds may well lead to boys bumping into each other so that one or other may fall over and receive the odd scratch or bruise, and it would be difficult to say that 13 year olds do not appreciate the risk of that sort of injury. A 13 year old boy will not however be liable simply because in playing around on the playground he foresees that in the way the games are played there is risk of injury of some kind . . .
>
> In *Mullin v Richards* [1998] 1 WLR 1304 Hutchison LJ who gave the lead judgment approached the issue as to whether a 16 year old girl should be held liable by addressing primarily the question of foreseeability of injury. It is for that reason the judge in this case directed himself in the way he did. That question is very much interlinked with the question whether conduct should be held culpable, as his reasoning at page 1310 D to H would show. But I respectfully suggest that the primary question should be whether the conduct of the child is culpable, i.e. whether it has fallen below the standard that should objectively be expected of a child of that age. That will be assisted by what injury the child could foresee as likely to be caused by that conduct, but is still a separate question. It is to culpability that the High Court of Australia addressed their observations. It seems to me that *McHale* was approved in *Mullins* and that it establishes the correct approach.

I should mention one further authority put before us in which the issue was whether one 15 year old participant in 'horse play', in which pieces of bark were thrown one at another, was liable for the injury to the eye of another 15 year old. In the Court of Appeal Dyson LJ, with whose judgment Clarke LJ and the Vice Chancellor agreed, held that a breach of duty of care owed by one participant to another in such horseplay would only be established where the conduct amounted 'to recklessness or a very high degree of carelessness.' See *Blake v Galloway* [2004] EWCA Civ 814. It does not seem that *McHale* or *Mullins* were considered by the Court of Appeal in *Blake.* That may be because the case in the court below had been argued by reference to the question whether the injured child was consenting (encapsulated in the maxim *volenti non fit injuria*) and it was only in the Court of Appeal with new counsel that it was suggested that the claim in negligence should have been dismissed.

In the instant case, although we are not concerned with participants and the duty of care owed by participants one to the other, but are concerned with two 13 year old boys playing tag and the duty of care owed to persons supervising them, I am doubtful whether when considering the culpability of their conduct there will be any significant difference. The truth is that *McHale* and *Mullins* demonstrate consistently with *Blake* that for a child to be held culpable the conduct must be careless to a very high degree and where a child of 13 is partaking in a game within a play area, not breaking any rules, and is not acting to any significant degree beyond the norms of that game, he or she will not be held culpable.

I would summarise the position in this way. It is not in issue that SL owed a duty of care. But if there is to be found a breach of that duty of care it would have to be established that SL, a 13 year old, was running about and playing tag in a way which was to a significant degree outside the norm for 13 year olds. The answer to that question can be assisted by considering whether SL was conducting himself in the way he played tag in a manner in which a 13 year old boy would reasonably foresee there was likely to be injury beyond that normally occurring while a game of tag was in progress . . .

The accident was of course most unfortunate but the conduct of SL described seems to me to be simply the conduct to be expected of a 13 year old playing tag. No part of the conduct seems to me to be outside the norm where a game of tag is being played, let alone a significant degree outside the norm . . .

I, of course, feel sympathy for the appellant. But it seems to me that the judge's assessment of this case was clearly right. 13 year old boys will be 13 year old boys who will play tag. They will run backwards and they will taunt each other. If that is what they are doing and they are not breaking any rules they should not be held liable in negligence. Parents and schools are there to control children and it would be a retrograde step to visit liability on a 13 year old for simply playing a game in the area where he was allowed to do so. I would dismiss the appeal.

Causation

In establishing legal liability in tort, the defendant must be shown to have caused the loss or damage in question. English law generally applies a two-test approach to the making of a finding on causation. The first test is generally referred to as factual causation, which consists of the application of the 'but for' test. This test 'consists of posing the question: would the loss have been sustained but for the relevant act or omission of the defendant?'[8]

8 Deakin *et al, Markesinis and Deakin's Tort Law*, p 244.

Barnett v Chelsea and Kensington Hospital Management Committee [1969] 1 QB 428 (GB)

Facts: William Patrick Barnett, the deceased, died from arsenical poisoning at about 1.30 pm on 1 January 1966. At the time of his death he was employed as a nightwatchman at the Chelsea College of Science and Technology. At about 9.30 pm on 31 December 1965 he reported for duty in company with two other nightwatchmen, Frederick Whittall and Herbert Weighall, the senior watchman. At about 5 am on 1 January 1966, all three watchmen shared some tea. Immediately after drinking the tea, the deceased complained of the heat in the room and, within 20 minutes, all three men started to vomit. The three watchmen then made their way in the deceased's car, which he drove quite normally, to the casualty department of St Stephen's Hospital. After a delay of several minutes Weighall became angry and demanded to see a doctor. The nurse then spoke on the telephone to the doctor who advised that the men go home to their bed and call their own doctors. The nurse passed that message to the three men and they all left the hospital. The deceased drove them back to the college. As soon as they reached the college the deceased went into the telephone room where he lay down with a cushion under his head. Later in the morning he was seen by a member of the college staff sitting on a packing case close to a radiator in the hall. At approximately 1 pm a doctor retained by the college was called to see the deceased, but by the time the doctor arrived it was too late to do anything for him. He was taken back by ambulance to St Stephen's Hospital and found to be dead on arrival.

Held: Nield, J
In my judgment, there was here such a close and direct relationship between the hospital and the watchmen that there was imposed upon the hospital a duty of care which they owed to the watchmen. Thus I have no doubt that Nurse Corbett and the medical casualty officer were under a duty to the deceased to exercise that skill and care which is to be expected of persons in such positions acting reasonably . . . Let me say at this stage that there is no complaint against Nurse Corbett that she failed in her duty.

There are two main questions here: Has the plaintiff established, on the balance of probabilities, (1) that the medical casualty officer was negligent, and, if so, (2) that such negligence caused the death of the deceased? . . . It remains to consider whether it is shown that the deceased's death was caused by that negligence or whether, as the defendants have said, the deceased must have died in any event . . .

There has been put before me a timetable which I think is of much importance. The deceased attended at the casualty department at five or ten minutes past eight in the morning. If the casualty officer had got up and dressed and come to see the three men and examined them and decided to admit them, the deceased (and Dr Lockett agreed with this) could not have been in bed in a ward before 11 am. I accept Dr Goulding's evidence that an intravenous drip would not have been set up before 12 noon, and if potassium loss was suspected, it could not have been discovered until 12.30 pm. Dr Lockett, dealing with this, said: 'If this man had not been treated until after 12 noon the chances of survival were not good.' . . . I regard that evidence as very moderate, and it might be a true assessment of the situation to say that there was no chance of BAL being administered before the death of the deceased. For those reasons, I find that the plaintiff has failed to establish, on the balance of probabilities, that the defendants' negligence caused the death of the deceased.

A claimant pleading a negligence claim does not have to prove that the defendant's breach of duty was the sole or even the main cause of damage, provided he can demonstrate that it made a material contribution to the damage.

Dr James Boyce (Appellant) v Corine Lorde and Stephen Lorde (Respondents) (2011) Civil Appeal No. 20 of 2008 (BB)

Facts: The respondents, Stephen and Corine Lorde, are husband and wife. Mrs. Lorde who was pregnant with twins was a patient of the appellant, a consultant obstetrician/gynaecologist. Her estimated date of delivery was 25 January 1999 but on 3 January, her membranes ruptured prematurely as a result of which she was admitted to the Bayview Hospital where she underwent an emergency caesarian section performed by the appellant. Mrs. Lorde was delivered of healthy twin girls. Mrs. Lorde remained in the hospital for five days during which time her temperature fluctuated. On 4 January, Mrs. Lorde was reported to have a temperature of 37.5°C and had now become tachycardic (rapid pulse) with a pulse rate of 100 per minute. On 5 January, her temperature remained elevated with a mild tachycardia. She was medicated with an oral antibiotic. On 6 January, she complained of feeling tired and dizzy and her pulse rate was still slightly elevated and her temperature again rose after having reduced a little earlier on that day. On 7 January, her temperature became even more elevated and she complained of feeling unwell. On 8 January, a high temperature and elevated pulse were again recorded. Later in that day, Mrs. Lorde suffered a panic attack and complained of feeling unwell. She was 'seen' by the appellant and in spite of her misgivings she was discharged. A review of the graphic sheet during the period of hospitalization shows that Mrs. Lorde was febrile from the time of admission with spiking temperatures and her temperature never reverted to normal up to the time of her discharge. The next day, 9 January, after complaining of feeling unwell, she was visited at her home by the appellant who examined her and readmitted her to the Bayview Hospital. The appellant's diagnosis was postoperative pyrexia secondary to infection. On readmission Mrs. Lorde was treated intravenously with antibiotics for 3 days. On 10 January her temperature remained elevated. On that day blood cultures, a complete blood count and sputum were taken. On 11 and 12 January, Mrs. Lorde's temperature and pulse rate remained elevated and she complained of pain. On 13 January her temperature was recorded as normal and she was discharged. Following that discharge and until 21 January, Mrs. Lorde's health deteriorated to the point where she fell unconscious and suffered a stroke. She had again to be hospitalized, this time in the Medical Intensive Care Unit at the Queen Elizabeth Hospital. Mr and Mrs. Lorde claimed damages against the appellant and the Bayview Hospital on the grounds that they negligently managed Mrs. Lorde's case.

Held: Mason, JA
One question for consideration before the trial judge was whether on a balance of probabilities it had been established that the appellant had failed to exercise the care required of a doctor professing the relevant special skill in circumstances which require the exercise of that special skill . . . However the onus of proving breach of that duty lay with Mrs. Lorde. It was incumbent upon her to establish on a balance of probabilities that the appellant was negligent and that that negligence caused or materially contributed to the damage complained of. But the standard of civil proof is a balance of probabilities . . . In our view therefore there was a failure to exercise reasonable skill and care in carrying out the relevant examination of Mrs. Lorde in order to ascertain her condition. This therefore resulted in a failure to properly assess the risks and to take the appropriate steps. This lack of reasonable

> skill and care culminated in the decision to prematurely discharge Mrs. Lorde on two occasions before her condition had been properly ascertained and stabilized. This negligence on the part of the appellant thus led to the inappropriate treatment of the infection which Mrs. Lorde had contracted. We accept the opinions expressed by the majority of the experts that if Mrs. Lorde had been given appropriate peri-operative antibiotic proplylaxis, the pelvic infection would have been prevented. Further, if appropriate investigations and treatment for possible septicaemia had been initiated during Mrs. Lorde's second admission to Bayview Hospital, the septicaemia would have been controlled. We are satisfied that based on the evidence reviewed here, the judge was correct in her findings that Mrs. Lorde contracted an infection as a result of poor management and that there was a general failure to properly manage the situation to determine and treat the source or cause of the infection . . . The main thrust of the appellant's appeal relates to the issue of causation, namely that the evidence does not support the judge's determination that the stroke suffered by Mrs. Lorde was as a result of infection or any negligent treatment by the appellant . . . The judge determined that she could conclude that there was negligence in so far as the doctor was concerned if she found *as a fact* that there was a chain of causation establishing liability. She clearly identified that there was a need for her to find that there was a direct causal link between the caesarian section, the infection and the stroke . . . The legal authorities on medical negligence affirm the principle that the onus of proving causation lies on the claimant. There must be inferred from the facts that the defendant's negligence had caused or materially contributed to the claimant's injury. Thus causation is an issue of fact to be determined according to evidence but the criteria for its determination raise issues of law in which the burden of proof is on the claimant and the standard of proof is the balance of probabilities. However the determination of the issue of causation is independent of the determination of negligent conduct . . . The House of Lords held in *Bonnington Castings Ltd v Wardlaw* [1956] AC 613 that the claimant does not have to prove that the defendant's breach of duty was the sole or even the main cause of damage, provided he can demonstrate that it made a material contribution to the damage, that anything which did not fall within the principle *de minimis non curat lex* would constitute a material contribution. However, before an inference can be drawn that the defendant's breach of duty made a material contribution, there must be some evidence to link the defendant's breach of duty to the claimant's harm other than the simple assertion that it increased the general risk of harm . . . It is therefore not enough to show that the appellant's negligent treatment of Mrs. Lorde increased the likelihood of the resulting stroke and *may* have caused it. It must be proved on a balance of probabilities that the appellant's negligent treatment *did* cause the stroke in the sense that it would not otherwise have happened . . . Mrs. Lorde's case was based upon whether there was the exercise of proper care and if that proper care had been exercised in all respects and had continued to be exercised whether Mrs. Lorde would have suffered the stroke. There was in our opinion abundant evidence entitling the judge to determine that the appellant's neglect in providing the proper care required caused or materially contributed to the stroke which Mrs. Lorde suffered.

Where a third party voluntarily breaks the chain of causation, liability will not attach to the defendant.

Topp v London Country Bus (South West) Ltd. [1993] 1 WLR 976 (GB)

Facts: On 25 April 1988 Mr Green, a bus driver employed by the defendants, ended a shift driving an Austin Freight Rover minibus on route E1 at about 2.35 pm. He left the bus at the bus stop unlocked with its ignition keys in it to begin a 40-minute rest period before resuming his duties driving a different bus. Such rest periods are required by statute. The next driver, Mr McFadyen, was supposed to pick up the bus at about 2.43 pm, but he did not do so. He had been scheduled to work non-compulsory overtime from 2.43 pm until about 4.50 pm, but he had been involved in a minor accident on a preceding shift during the morning and had been shaken up. And so he did not report for his overtime.

Mr Green was working the same route during the afternoon with a different bus. He saw the bus where he had left it outside the pub. He was concerned because its absence meant that he was picking up a double load of doubtless angry passengers. So he telephoned the controller and told him that the vehicle was there. This, he said, was between 4 pm and 5 pm when he was busy with school children. By that time, therefore, at the latest, those at the depot knew that the bus was abandoned at the bus stop. Mr Green said that, when he telephoned, he got the impression from what was said that those at the depot already knew. The defendants took no steps to recover the bus before it was stolen.

At about 11.10 pm Mrs Lydia Fay, who lived in a house opposite the bus stop, heard the sound of an engine revving up. She saw the bus in the bus stop moving forwards and backwards. She heard the sound of crashing gears and then saw the bus move erratically into the middle of the road. Its headlights were not then on. It then drove west along Dorking Road. By the time it had travelled some 350 metres its headlights were on. It drove about 50 metres past Woodcote Side and then suddenly the near side wheel mounted the pavement before it careered out towards the middle of the road and then pulled in again. In the course of this manoeuvre the bus struck Mrs Topp's bicycle, causing her to be dragged along before her body fell at the side of the road. The criminal driver of the bus has never been identified. Despite first aid Mrs Topp was certified dead soon after she arrived at Epsom District Hospital. The plaintiff's claim was dismissed and an appeal was filed.

Held: Dillon, LJ
Mr Hetherington submitted that there was a particular danger because the lay-by was outside or near to a public house. I do not think he suggested that its proximity to the hospital added any particular danger. He put his case in three ways: first, that the bus was in a special category of risk as a source of danger on the highway; second, that even if it was not in a special category as a source of danger, there was a sufficiently high risk to attract a duty of care; third, that the judge, in seeking to apply the tests laid down in *Caparo Industries Plc. v Dickman* [1990] 2 AC 605, drew too rigid a line, instead of dealing with the case simply on its own facts, and his reasons were flawed. But Mr Hetherington has to accept the general proposition which is to be found in the speech of Lord Goff of Chieveley in *Smith v Littlewoods Organisation Ltd.* [1987] AC 241, 272:

> even though A is in fault, he is not responsible for injury to C which B, a stranger to him, deliberately chooses to do . . . [that] may be read as expressing the general idea that the voluntary act of another, independent of the defender's fault, is regarded as a *novus actus interveniens* which, to use the old metaphor, 'breaks the chain of causation'.

In so far as the case is put on the basis that to leave the bus unlocked, and with the key in the ignition, on the highway near a public house is to create a special risk in a special category, it is pertinent to refer to a passage in the judgment of Robert Goff LJ in *P. Perl (Exporters) Ltd. v Camden London Borough Council* [1984] QB 342, 359: 'In particular, I have in mind certain cases where the defendant presents the wrongdoer with the means to commit the wrong, in circumstances where it is obvious or very likely that he will do so – as, for example, where he hands over a car to be driven by a person who is drunk, or plainly incompetent, who then runs over the plaintiff . . .' But the sort of cases to which Robert

Goff LJ was there referring are far different from the present case. It may be added that there is no evidence that the malefactor had been frequenting the public house; we do not know who he was, nor is there any evidence or presumption that persons who do frequent that particular public house are particularly likely to steal vehicles and engage in joy-riding . . .

I see no basis for interfering with the determination by May J with which I agree, and I would dismiss this appeal.

Damages

The main issue arising in tort law after establishment of the critical factors of a duty of care, breach of the standard of care, and causation is whether the breach has caused damage and what can be recovered.

REMOTENESS

Having established a duty of care, the appropriate standard of care, breach of that standard of care and that such breach caused the damage suffered, a plaintiff cannot recover damages for tortious acts where the damage is of such a kind that the reasonable man could not have foreseen. In other words, liability is imposed where the damage is such that it should have been reasonably foreseen.

Overseas Tankship (U.K.) Ltd. v Morts Dock & Engineering Co. Ltd. [1961] UKPC 1 (18 January 1961) (AU)

Facts: In the action the respondents sought to recover from the appellants compensation for the damage which its property known as the Sheerlegs Wharf, in Sydney Harbour, and the equipment thereon had suffered by reason of fire which broke out on 1 November 1951. The respondents at the relevant time carried on the business of shipbuilding, ship-repairing and general engineering at Morts Bay, Balmain, in the Port of Sydney. In October and November 1951 a vessel known as the *Corrimel* was moored alongside the wharf and was being refitted by the respondents. A number of the respondents' employees were working upon the vessel itself, using for that purpose electric and oxyacetylene welding equipment. At the same time the appellants were charterers by demise of the *SS Wagon Mound*, an oil-burning vessel, which was moored at the Caltex Wharf on the northern shore of the harbour at a distance of about 600 feet from the Sheerlegs Wharf.

During the early hours of 30 October 1951 a large quantity of bunkering oil was, through the carelessness of the appellants' servants, allowed to spill into the bay, and by 10.30 on the morning of that day it had spread over a considerable part of the bay, being thickly concentrated in some places and particularly along the foreshore near the respondents' property. The appellants made no attempt to disperse the oil. The *Wagon Mound* unberthed and set sail very shortly after. The respondents' works manager inquired of the manager of the Caltex Oil Company, at whose wharf the *Wagon Mound* was then still berthed, whether they could safely continue their operations on the wharf or upon the *Corrimal*. The results of the inquiry coupled with his own belief as to the inflammability of furnace oil in the open led him to think that the respondents could safely carry on their operations. He gave instructions accordingly, but directed that all safety precautions should be taken to prevent inflammable material falling off the wharf into the oil. At some time the oil under or near the wharf was ignited and a fire, fed initially by the oil, spread rapidly and burned with great intensity. The wharf and the *Corrimal* caught fire and considerable damage was done to the wharf and the equipment upon it.

Held: Viscount Simonds
It is inevitable that first consideration should be given to the case of *In re Polemis and Furness Withy & Co. Ltd.* . . . What, then, did *Polemis* decide? . . . There can be no doubt that the decision of the Court of Appeal in *Polemis* plainly asserts that, if the defendant is guilty of negligence, he is responsible for all the consequences whether reasonably foreseeable or not . . . Enough has been said to show that the authority of *Polemis* has been severely shaken though lip-service has from time to time been paid to it. In their Lordships' opinion it should no longer be regarded as good law . . .

It is, no doubt, proper when considering tortious liability for negligence to analyse its elements and to say that the plaintiff must prove a duty owed to him by the defendant, a breach of that duty by the defendant, and consequent damage. But there can be no liability until the damage has been done. It is not the act but the consequences on which tortious liability is founded. Just as (as it has been said) there is no such thing as negligence in the air, so there is no such thing as liability in the air . . .

Their Lordships conclude this part of the case with some general observations. They have been concerned primarily to displace the proposition that unforeseeability is irrelevant if damage is 'direct'. In doing so they have inevitably insisted that the essential factor in determining liability is whether the damage is of such a kind as the reasonable man should have foreseen . . It is a departure from this sovereign principle if liability is made to depend solely on the damage being the 'direct' or 'natural' consequence of the precedent act. Who knows or can be assumed to know all the processes of nature? But if it would be wrong that a man should be held liable for damage unpredictable by a reasonable man because it was 'direct' or 'natural,' equally it would be wrong that he should escape liability, however 'indirect' the damage, if he foresaw or could reasonably foresee the intervening events which led to its being done: cf. *Woods v Duncun*. Thus foreseeability becomes the effective test . . .

Their Lordships will humbly advise Her Majesty that this appeal should be allowed, and the respondents' action so far as it related to damage caused by the negligence of the appellants be dismissed with costs.

Liability may be imposed, however, even where the loss is not reasonably foreseeable, if there is a 'possibility' or 'real risk' of damage which the defendant by his conduct made no attempt to avoid.

Wright v Davidson (1992–02–07) BCCA CA011480 (CA)

Facts: Mrs Wright was injured in a motor vehicle collision on 10 October 1986 when a vehicle driven by the appellant, Bradley Davidson, collided with the rear of the vehicle driven by Mrs Wright. As a result of the collision, Mrs Wright struck the left side of her head and suffered a minor laceration to her left temple but did not lose consciousness. After the collision she was taken to the emergency department of the Langley Memorial Hospital where she complained of a sore neck, right shoulder and chest. X-rays of her shoulder and neck showed no injury. In the month following the collision, she complained of soreness in the neck radiating into her shoulder, jaw pain, headaches, low-back pain,

pain in the head, dizzy spells and noise in her left ear. A neurologist, Dr Knazan, who examined her on 16 December, described the pain in her neck area as 'whiplash'. He found on examination that she was oriented but appeared quite tense and anxious, and somewhat depressed. He considered that her symptoms were related to soft-tissue injury and post-traumatic syndrome associated with the motor vehicle accident. Before the accident, Mrs Wright had had no known history of emotional or mental problems. On 8 July 1987 Mrs Wright was admitted to hospital after ingesting an overdose of an insignificant amount of Ativan in an apparent suicide attempt. On the morning of 24 July she told her husband that she did not wish to attend her daughter's band concert because the noise would bother her and she stayed home by herself. Later on 24 July she committed suicide by hanging.

Held: Legg, J
Mr Justice Gould adopted the reasoning of Mr Justice Hudson (dissenting) in *Haber v Walker* [1963] VR 339 (SC Victoria, Full Ct) that 'the death must be shown to have been the natural and probable consequence of the negligence or, to use the more common expression of modern times, a consequence of the negligence which is reasonably foreseeable'. Gould, J then stated (at p 24): 'The test which must be satisfied is that which emerges from the well-known series of cases, beginning with *Overseas Tankship (UK) Ltd. v Morts Dock & Enrg. Co. (The Wagon Mound (No. 1))*, [1961] 1 AC 388, [1961] 1 All ER 404 (PC); the foresight of a reasonable man determines responsibility.' The test was altered somewhat by the case of *Hughes v Lord Advocate*, [1963] AC 837, [1963] 1 All ER 705 (HL), where it was held that one need not foresee the exact way in which an accident occurs, as long as one anticipates the general type of consequences which occur. Further qualifications were made on *The Wagon Mound (No. 1)* case by the case of *Overseas Tankship (U.K.) Ltd. v Miller SS. Co. Pty. (The Wagon Mound (No. 2))*, [1967] 1 AC 617, [1966] 2 All ER 709 (PC); liability may be imposed, even where the loss is not reasonably foreseeable, if there is a 'possibility' or 'real risk' of damage which the defendant by his conduct made no attempt to avoid . . .

What is determinative of liability in the case under appeal is that when Mrs Wright took her life she made a conscious decision, there being no evidence of disabling mental illness to lead to the conclusion that she had an incapacity in her faculty of volition. Accordingly, her suicide must be taken as a *novus actus interveniens* such that it cannot be said that her death was a reasonably foreseeable consequence of the wrongdoing.

One need not foresee the exact way in which an accident occurs, as long as one anticipates the general type of consequences which might occur.

Hughes v Lord Advocate [1963] AC 837 (GB)

Facts: Shortly after 5 pm on Saturday, 8 November 1958 the appellant (then aged 8) and his companion (then aged 10) were in Russell Road, Edinburgh; they could not resist the opportunity of exploring the unattended canvas shelter. In and around it they found aids to exploration readily at hand. Within the canvas shelter or tent was the uncovered manhole. Nearby was a section of a ladder. Nearby also there were lighted lamps. Pursuing their boyish whims, they must have thought that as a place for play it was bounteously equipped. Furthermore, somewhere outside the tent they found a rope and a tin can (which apparently were no part of the Post Office material). The ladder and the rope and a lamp proved helpful in exploring the hole and the chamber below the road. In all this, however, as anyone might have surmised, was the risk that in some way one of the boys might fall down the hole or might suffer some burn from a lamp. The lamps were doubtless good and safe lamps when ordinarily handled, but in the hands of playful, inquisitive or mischievous boys there could be no assumption that they would be used in a normal way. Exercising an ordinary and certainly not an over-exacting degree of prevision the workmen should have decided, when the tea-break came, that someone had better be left in charge who could repel the intrusion of inquisitive children. If, of, course, there was no likelihood that children might appear, different considerations would apply. A risk that he might in some way burn himself by playing with a lamp was translated into reality. In fact he was very severely burned. Though his severe burns came about in a way that seems surprising, this only serves to illustrate that boys can bring about a consequence which could be expected, but yet can bring it about in a most unusual manner and with unexpectedly severe results. After the pursuer tripped against the lamp and so caused it to fall into the manhole, and after he contrived to be drawn into or to be blown into or to fall into the manhole, he was burned. His burns were, however, none the less burns although there was such an immediate combustion of paraffin vapour that there was an explosion.

Held: Lord Reid
It was argued that the appellant cannot recover because the damage which he suffered was of a kind which was not foreseeable. That was not the ground of judgment of the First Division or of the Lord Ordinary and the facts proved do not, in my judgment, support that argument. The appellant's injuries were mainly caused by burns, and it cannot be said that injuries from burns were unforeseeable. As a warning to traffic the workmen had set lighted red lamps round the tent which covered the manhole, and if boys did enter the dark tent it was very likely that they would take one of these lamps with them. If the lamp fell and broke it was not at all unlikely that the boy would be burned and the burns might well be serious. No doubt it was not to be expected that the injuries would be as serious as those which the appellant in fact sustained. But a defender is liable, although the damage may be a good deal greater in extent than was foreseeable. He can only escape liability if the damage can be regarded as differing in kind from what was foreseeable.

So we have (first) a duty owed by the workmen, (second) the fact that if they had done as they ought to have done there would have been no accident, and (third) the fact that the injuries suffered by the appellant, though perhaps different in degree, did not differ in kind from injuries which might have resulted from an accident of a foreseeable nature. The ground on which this case has been decided against the appellant is that the accident was of an unforeseeable type. Of course, the pursuer has to prove that the defender's fault caused the accident, and there could be a case where the intrusion of a new and unexpected factor could be regarded as the cause of the accident rather than the fault of the defender. But that is not this case. The cause of this accident was a known source of danger, the lamp, but it behaved in an unpredictable way.

RECOVERY OF PURE ECONOMIC LOSSES

Most Commonwealth jurisdictions recognise the possibility of recovery of pure economic losses as a result of the tortious act of another. It is easier to recover such pure economic losses where they are a result of a physical loss or damage to property. In the area of negligent misstatements (dealt with later on in this chapter), it is generally acknowledged that pure economic losses are recoverable based on the special relationship that must be established between the person making the statement and the recipient. The English jurists have been reluctant to widen the scope of recovery for pure economic losses.

McFarlane and Another v Tayside Health Board [2002] 2 AC 59 (GB)

Facts: Mr McFarlane underwent a vasectomy operation on 16 October 1989; by letter of 23 March 1990 he was told that his sperm counts were negative. In September 1991 (following the resumption of intercourse without contraceptive measures), Mrs McFarlane became pregnant and their fifth child, Catherine, was born on 6 May 1992. They claimed that Mrs McFarlane suffered pain and distress from the pregnancy and birth and that they both have incurred and will incur costs in rearing Catherine, all due to the negligence of the defenders.

Held: Lord Slynn
The doctor undertakes a duty of care in regard to the prevention of pregnancy: it does not follow that the duty includes also avoiding the costs of rearing the child if born and accepted into the family. Whereas I have no doubt that there should be compensation for the physical effects of the pregnancy and birth, including of course solatium for consequential suffering by the mother immediately following the birth, I consider that it is not fair, just or reasonable to impose on the doctor or his employer liability for the consequential responsibilities, imposed on or accepted by the parents to bring up a child. The doctor does not assume responsibility for those economic losses. If a client wants to be able to recover such costs he or she must do so by an appropriate contract.

This conclusion is not the result, as it is in some of the American cases of the application, of 'public policy' to a rule which would otherwise produce a different conclusion; it comes from the inherent limitation of the liability relied on. A line is to be drawn before such losses are recoverable. I would accordingly dismiss the board's appeal in respect of the claim for solatium by Mrs McFarlane and her claim for expenses caused directly and immediately by the pregnancy and birth, including medical expenses (if any) and the costs of the layette, but I would allow the Board's appeal in respect of the claim for damages for the rearing of the child.

Held: Lord Hope
This is a claim for economic loss . . . As to the law, it has not been suggested that the costs of rearing the child are too remote, in the sense that they were not a reasonably foreseeable consequence of the defender's negligence. For my part, I would regard these costs as reasonably foreseeable by the wrongdoer. But in the field of economic loss foreseeability is not the only criterion that must be satisfied. There must be a relationship of proximity between the negligence and the loss which is said to have been caused by it and the attachment of liability for the harm must be fair, just and reasonable. The mere fact that it was reasonably foreseeable that the pursuers would have to pay for the costs of rearing their child does not mean that they have incurred a loss of the kind which is recoverable . . .

These observations were taken a step further in *Murphy v Brentwood District Council* [1991] 1 AC 398. In the course of his discussion of the relevant principles Lord Oliver said this at pp 486H–487C:

> In the straightforward case of the direct infliction of physical injury by the act of the plaintiff there is, indeed, no need to look beyond the foreseeability by the defendant of the result in order to establish that he is in a 'proximate' relationship with the plaintiff . . . The infliction of physical injury to the person or property of another universally requires to be justified. The causing of economic loss does not. If it is to be categorised as wrongful it is necessary to find some factor beyond the mere occurrence of the loss and the fact that its occurrence could be foreseen.

There must be a relationship of proximity, and the attachment of liability for the harm must be just, fair and reasonable.

I do not wish to place undue emphasis on the fact that the pursuers chose to keep the child. The fact is, as Mrs Smith so ably demonstrated, they had no other choice. The law is not so harsh as to drive parents, in the very difficult situation in which the pursuers found themselves, to the alternatives of abortion or placing for adoption, which, for obvious reasons, they would have found quite unacceptable. Nevertheless they are now bringing the child up within the family. There are benefits in this arrangement as well as costs. In the short term there is the pleasure which a child gives in return for the love and care which she receives during infancy. In the longer term there is the mutual relationship of support and affection which will continue well beyond the ending of the period of her childhood. In my opinion it would not be fair, just or reasonable, in any assessment of the loss caused by the birth of the child, to leave these benefits out of account. Otherwise the pursuers would be paid far too much. They would be relieved of the cost of rearing the child. They would not be giving anything back to the wrongdoer for the benefits. But the value which is to be attached to these benefits is incalculable. The costs can be calculated but the benefits, which in fairness must be set against them, cannot.

The logical conclusion, as a matter of law, is that the costs to the pursuers of meeting their obligations to the child during her childhood are not recoverable as damages. It cannot be established that, overall and in the long run, these costs will exceed the value of the benefits. This is economic loss of a kind which must be held to fall outside the ambit of the duty of care which was owed to the pursuers by the persons who carried out the procedures in the hospital and the laboratory.

Mid Island Poultry Ltd (Claimant) v Electrical Rewind Services Ltd (1st Defendant) and John Salter (2nd Defendant) [2012] JMSC Civ 175 (JM)

Facts: This is an action for a breach of contract and negligence for the service and repair of a blast freeze refrigerator unit which has been detained for lack of payment.

Held: Anderson, J

The Claimant has also claimed damages for the Defendants' negligence and/or breach of contract, in essence, arising from that which he has alleged as being the Defendants' failure to repair or properly repair the Claimant's blast freeze unit . . . The Court of Appeal of Jamaica has made it clear . . . that a Claim founded on negligence seeking to recover damages for that which constitutes pure economic loss and which thus, does not arise from damage to property or injury to a person, cannot lawfully be pursued and must, of necessity, fail.

Other Commonwealth countries have not been as hesitant as the English to expand the areas for recovery of pure economic losses. In Canada it is possible in some cases to recover damages for pure economic losses caused by a defendant's negligence depending on: (1) whether sufficient proximity or 'closeness' can be established, and (2) whether extension of recovery to this type of loss is desirable from a practical point of view.

Canadian National Railway Co. v Norsk Pacific Steamship Co. [1992] 1 SCR 1021 (CA)

Facts: The New Westminster Railway Bridge, which spans the Fraser River between Surrey and New Westminster, was built in 1904. It carries a single railway track. Its sole purpose is to service railway traffic, both passenger and freight, but it incorporates a swing span to permit marine traffic to navigate the waterway. On 28 November 1987 the barge *Crown Forest No. 4*, while being towed downstream by the tug *Jervis Crown* in heavy fog, collided with the bridge. The *Jervis Crown* was owned and operated by the Norsk Pacific Steamship Co. and the Norsk Pacific Marine Services Ltd, both hereafter referred to as Norsk. The accident caused extensive damage to the bridge and it was closed for several weeks while repairs were made. The appellants admitted liability for negligence as to the collision itself.

While the bridge was closed, the four railway companies that used the bridge had to reroute traffic over another bridge further upstream. Freight was either delayed or not transported at all. The use of the waterway was also interfered with, and cargo was delayed or transported by land. This accident gave rise to a number of legal actions which were consolidated in the judgment of Addy J. The Department of Public Works (PWC), representing The Queen in right of Canada, claimed damages as owner of the bridge against both Norsk and the owners of the barge *Crown Forest No. 4* and the tug *Westminster Chinook* (another tug which was helping the *Jervis Crown* at the time of the accident). Only the action against Norsk succeeded. Norsk was held liable to PWC for all damages resulting to PWC from the collision. This decision was not appealed.

In addition to the action by the owner, three of the four railway companies claimed for economic loss against Norsk and the other defendants. The smallest railway user, Canadian Pacific Ltd (CP), did not participate in the litigation. Before trial there was an agreement that the entitlement of the other two railways, the Burlington Northern Railway and the B.C. Hydro and Power Authority Railway, to recover for pure economic loss would stand or fall on the result of the *Canadian National Railway Co* (CN) claim. It was therefore only the CN claim that was directly in issue. The trial judge allowed CN's claim against Norsk and dismissed its claim against the other defendants. Norsk's appeal was denied in the Court of Appeal. Leave to appeal to this Court was granted to Norsk on 15 November 1990.

Held: The judgment of L'Heureux-Dubé, Cory and McLachlin, JJ was delivered by McLachlin, J

A fundamental proposition underlies the law of tort: that a person who by his or her fault causes damage to another may be held responsible . . . While the criterion of physical damage successfully avoided the spectre of unlimited damages, it suffered from the defect that it arbitrarily, and in some cases, arguably unjustly, deprived deserving plaintiffs of recovery. Why, it was asked, should the right to recover economic loss be dependent on whether physical damage, however minuscule, had been inflicted on the plaintiff's property? Why should a plaintiff who waits for a defective machine to break and cause physical injury or damage be able to recover, while one who prudently repairs the machine before the physical damage or injury occurs be left without remedy? Is there really a generic distinction between the loss resulting from repair of physical damage and loss resulting from loss of use in a commercial situation where the only real loss is one of profit? While it may be argued that physical injury is inherently more deserving than economic loss, particularly where the economic loss is not associated with physical damage (see Feldthusen, *Economic Negligence* (2nd edn 1989), at pp 8–14), that does not explain why the law should not permit recovery for economic loss where justice so requires nor how damage to property and economic losses can be distinguished in many situations . . .

A summary of how different courts in different jurisdictions have dealt with this problem affords us perspective both on the nature of the problem and the possible solutions.

United Kingdom. The traditional exclusionary rule of *Cattle v Stockton Waterworks Co.* restricted recovery of economic loss to cases where the plaintiff had suffered physical damage. This rule was lifted to allow recovery for pure economic loss in an action for negligent misstatement in *Hedley Byrne & Co. v Heller & Partners Ltd.* [1964] AC 465 (HL). The exception was pinned on the concept of reliance. Where the defendant negligently made a misstatement which the defendant should have foreseen others would rely on, and where the plaintiff relied on it and suffered financial loss, the plaintiff was entitled to recover that loss, notwithstanding the absence of any physical harm to the plaintiff. This exception is now firmly fixed in the law of tort. Various courts in the following two decades attempted to widen the exceptions to the exclusionary rule. For example, it was extended to products liability cases in *Junior Books Ltd. v Veitchi Co.* [1983] 1 AC 520 (HL). And it was allowed in maritime law where the plaintiff could be said by reason of its contract to be in a 'joint venture' with the owner of damaged property: *Morrison Steamship Co. v Greystoke Castle (Cargo Owners) (The Greystoke Castle)* [1947] AC 265. These cases culminated in the dictum of Lord Wilberforce in *Anns v Merton London Borough Council* [1978] AC 728 (HL), which suggested that recovery should not depend on the category of case, but should lie wherever two general conditions were found:

(1) foreseeability and sufficient proximity between the negligent act and the loss; and
(2) the absence of considerations which call for a limitation on liability.

The House of Lords recently resiled from *Anns* and returned to the old proposition that economic loss could be recovered in negligence only where the plaintiff had suffered physical damage or in the reliance situation of *Hedley Byrne: Murphy v Brentwood District Council* [1991] 1 AC 398 . . . In subsequent years this Court repeatedly held that economic loss can be recovered in tort in the absence of injury to the plaintiff's person or property in appropriate cases . . .

It is my view that the incremental approach of *Kamloops* is to be preferred to the insistence on logical precision of *Murphy*. It is more consistent with the incremental character of the common law. It permits relief to be granted in new situations where it is merited . . . If this approach is followed, as it has been to date in Canada, new categories of cases will from time to time arise. It will not be certain whether economic loss can be recovered in these categories until the courts have pronounced on them. During this period, the law in a small area of negligence may be uncertain. Such uncertainty however is inherent in the common law generally. It is the price the common law pays for flexibility, for the ability to adapt to a changing world. If past experience serves, it is a price we should willingly pay, provided the limits of uncertainty are kept within reasonable bounds.

The foregoing suggests that the incremental approach to the problem of determining the limits for the recovery of pure economic loss which was adopted by this Court in *Kamloops* should be confirmed. Where new categories of claim arise, the court should consider the matter first from the doctrinal point of view of duty and proximity, as well as the pragmatic perspective of the purposes served and the dangers associated with the extension sought . . . As more cases are decided, we can expect further definition on what factors give rise to liability for pure economic loss in particular categories of cases. In determining whether liability should be extended to a new situation, courts will have regard to the factors traditionally relevant to proximity such as the relationship between the parties, physical propinquity, assumed or imposed obligations and close causal connection. And they will insist on sufficient special factors to avoid the imposition of indeterminate and unreasonable liability. The result will be a principled, yet flexible, approach to tort liability for pure economic loss. It will allow recovery where recovery is justified, while excluding indeterminate and inappropriate liability, and it will permit the coherent development of the law . . .

Where there is physical injury or damage, one posits proximity on the ground that if one is close enough to someone or something to do physical damage to it, one is close enough to be held legally responsible for the consequences. Physical injury has the advantage of being a clear and simple indicator of proximity. The problem arises when it is taken as the only indicator of proximity. As the cases amply demonstrate, the necessary proximity to found legal liability fairly in tort may well arise in circumstances where there is no physical damage . . .

The plaintiff CN suffered economic loss as a result of being deprived of its contractual right to use the bridge damaged by the defendants' negligence. Applying the *Kamloops* approach, its right to recover depends on: (1) whether it can establish sufficient proximity or 'closeness', and (2) whether extension of recovery to this type of loss is desirable from a practical point of view . . . I conclude that here, as in *Kamloops*, the necessary duty and proximity are established, that valid purposes are served by permitting recovery, and that recovery will not open the floodgates to unlimited liability. In such circumstances, recovery should be permitted.

INJURED FEELINGS

Damages for a tortious act may include compensation for injury to feelings. The assessment of compensation for an injury or loss, which is neither physical nor financial, presents special problems for the judicial process, which aims to produce results objectively justified by evidence, reason and precedent. Subjective feelings of upset, frustration, worry, anxiety, mental distress, fear, grief, anguish, humiliation, unhappiness, stress, depression and so on, and the degree of their intensity, are incapable of objective proof or of measurement in monetary terms.

Essa v Laing Ltd. [2004] EWCA Civ 2 (GB)

Facts: Mr Essa, the applicant, was a Welshman who lived all his life in Cardiff. He was black. He earned his living as a labourer and construction worker and represented Wales many times as an amateur boxer. In the spring and summer of 1999 he was employed by a Mr Rogers on the construction of the Millennium Stadium at Cardiff Arms Park. The applicant was a member of a gang of about 15 subject to the instructions and supervision of Mr Pritchard, who was employed by the company, the main contractors, as a foreman. They were working under pressure because of the need to complete the stadium in time for the Rugby World Cup and, as the tribunal found, Mr Pritchard's quite abrasive style of foremanship achieved highly effective results.

On 28 July Mr Pritchard was giving instructions on the allocation of work to a Mr Grayson Williams who was employed by Mr Rogers but who supervised Mr Pritchard's gang. There were about 15 men present on this occasion. According to Mr Essa, Mr Pritchard said to Mr Williams 'get the boys organised'. He then turned and, pointing at Mr Essa who was sitting down reading his payslip, he said 'and make sure that black cunt doesn't wander off'. Mr Essa was extremely hurt and in tears. Mr Essa expressed his hurt in highly emotional terms, he wept and said: 'He called 20 men "boys" and he called me a black cunt.'

He said: 'He looked at me like an animal. It took my humanity from me.' He stressed over and over that he was born in Cardiff only around the corner from the stadium.

The Employment Appeal Tribunal held that the statutory tort created by section 54 was designed to protect persons from all kinds of discrimination on the grounds of race and any subsequent injury, including personal injury such as psychiatric damage, and that compensation was recoverable in respect of all harm caused directly by the act of discrimination, whether or not it was reasonably foreseeable.

Held: Pill, LJ
Psychiatric illness is regarded as a species of personal injury (*Page v Smith*). A claimant can, in present circumstances, recover in respect of a recognisable psychiatric illness. The claimant can also, by virtue of section 57(4), claim in tort for 'injury to feelings'. I do not find the presence of subsection (4) in section 57 decisive upon the present issue. It was inserted at a time when there may well have been doubt as to whether 'injury to feelings' was a proper head of damage in personal injury cases. For the avoidance of doubt, it was declared that damages for the present tort may include damages for such injury. Injury to feelings will most frequently occur, of course, without there being a psychiatric illness but both may result from the conduct complained of. They are different, as stated by Stuart-Smith LJ in the *Sheriff* case, but they are not, in my judgment, different kinds of damage in the sense contemplated in cases such as *Hughes v Lord Advocate*. I agree with the analysis of section 57(4) by Stuart-Smith LJ in the *Sheriff* case, with the proviso that, while there is a difference between 'injury to health or personal injury' and 'injury to feelings', the two are not inconsistent, may overlap and injury to feelings may contribute to injury to health. In *Vento v Chief Constable of the West Yorkshire Police* [2003] ICR 318 an award including sums for both psychiatric damage (clinical depression and adjustment disorder) and injury to feelings was upheld in this court, though that for injury to feelings substantially reduced. Giving the judgment of the court Mummery LJ commented, at p 335, para 63, that during the period of psychiatric disorder there must have been a substantial degree of overlap with the injury to the applicant's feelings. This approach does not support a conclusion that the damages are of a different kind.

In present circumstances a requirement that psychiatric illness must reasonably have been foreseen by the wrongdoer does not in my view arise. If I am wrong about that, I would hold that on the facts of this case foreseeability of significant injury to feelings is obvious and, for the reasons given, the foreseeability test is thereby satisfied with respect to psychiatric illness. Causation needs to be established and issues including intervening act and mitigation considered. I would dismiss this appeal. I agree with the conclusion of the Employment Appeal Tribunal that the case should be remitted to the employment tribunal.

NERVOUS SHOCK

The recovery of damages for nervous shock is a constantly evolving area of tort law. It would seem, under the present law, the general position is that a person who suffers a reasonably foreseeable recognisable psychiatric illness, as a result of another person's death, injury or imperilment, cannot recover damages for negligence unless he can satisfy three main requirements:

(i) that he had a close tie of love and affection with the person killed, injured or imperilled;
(ii) that he was close to the 'accident' in time and space;
(iii) that he directly perceived the 'accident' rather than, for example, hearing about it from a third person.

Page v Smith [1996] AC 310 (GB)

Facts: On 24 July 1987 the plaintiff, Mr Page, was involved in a motor accident. He was driving his Volvo car along a road in Bury St Edmunds when the defendant, Mr Smith, driving his Datsun car in the opposite direction, cut across to enter a side road. A collision occurred. The plaintiff sustained no bodily injury. Neither did the defendant or his wife and child who were with him in his car. However, the plaintiff had for a very long time been suffering from a condition variously described as myalgic encephalomyelitis (ME), or chronic fatigue syndrome (CFS) or post-viral fatigue syndrome (PVFS), which had manifested itself from time to time with different degrees of severity. The plaintiff had suffered a particularly severe attack in March 1987, apparently as a result of a viral infection, but his evidence was that he was recovering from it and hoped to be able to return to his work as a teacher in September 1987. The plaintiff took proceedings against the defendant claiming damages for personal injuries caused by the defendant's negligence. His case was that his condition CFS had as a result of the accident become chronic and permanent so that he would never be able to work again.

Held: Lord Lloyd
In the present case . . . the plaintiff was a participant. He was himself directly involved in the accident, and well within the range of foreseeable physical injury. He was the primary victim. This is thus the first occasion on which your Lordships have had to decide whether, in such a case, the foreseeability of physical injury is enough to enable the plaintiff to recover damages for nervous shock.

The factual distinction between primary and secondary victims of an accident is obvious and of long-standing . . . Though the distinction between primary and secondary victims is a factual one, it has, as will be seen, important legal consequences. So the classification of all nervous shock cases under the same head may be misleading. In *Alcock's* case Lord Oliver said, at p 407:

> It is customary to classify cases in which damages are claimed for injury occasioned in this way under a single generic label as cases of 'liability for nervous shock'. This may be convenient but in fact the label is misleading if and to the extent that it is assumed to lead to a conclusion that they have more in common than the fact of similarity of the medium through which the injury is sustained – that of an assault upon the nervous system of the plaintiff through witnessing or taking part in an event – and that they will, on account of this factor, provide a single common test for the circumstances which give rise to a duty of care.

It is of cardinal importance in the present case to bear that warning in mind. Although the plaintiff was, as I have said, the primary victim, the peculiarity of the present case is that, by good fortune, he suffered no broken bones and no bruising; indeed he had no external physical injury of any kind. But as a direct result of the accident he suffered a recrudescence of an illness or condition known variously as ME, CFS or PVFS, from which he had previously suffered in a mild form on sporadic occasions, but which, since the accident, has become an illness of 'chronic intensity and permanency' . . . Since physical injury to the plaintiff was clearly foreseeable, although it did not in the event occur, the judge did not consider, as a separate question, whether the defendant should have foreseen injury by nervous shock . . . The court will, as ever, have to be vigilant to discern genuine shock resulting in recognised psychiatric illness . . . In the case of a secondary victim, the question will usually turn on whether the foreseeable injury is psychiatric, for the reasons already explained. In the case of a primary victim the question will almost always turn on whether the foreseeable injury is physical. But it is the same test in both cases, with different applications. There is no justification for regarding physical and psychiatric injury as different 'kinds' of injury. Once it is established that the defendant is under a duty of care to avoid causing personal injury to the plaintiff, it matters not whether the injury in fact sustained is physical, psychiatric or both . . .

Applying that test in the present case, it was enough to ask whether the defendant should have reasonably foreseen that the plaintiff might suffer physical injury as a result of the defendant's negligence, so as to bring him within the range of the defendant's duty of care. It was unnecessary to ask, as a separate question, whether the defendant should reasonably have foreseen injury by shock; and it is irrelevant that the plaintiff did not, in fact, suffer any external physical injury . . . In the result, I would restore the judgment of Otton J but subject to one last caveat. One of the grounds of appeal from Otton J's judgment was that his finding on causation was against the weight of the evidence. Ralph Gibson LJ upheld this ground of appeal, but it was left open by Farquharson LJ and Hoffmann LJ. Unless, therefore, the claim can now be settled, the case will have to go back to the Court of Appeal for a finding on this issue.

In judging whether the personal injury was foreseeable, the court looks at a person of 'ordinary fortitude' or at a particular plaintiff with his particular vulnerabilities. The law has consistently held that the question is what a person of ordinary fortitude would suffer.

Mustapha v Culligan of Canada Ltd. 2008 SCC 27 (CA)

Facts: The plaintiff, Mr Mustapha, sued for psychiatric injury sustained as a result of seeing the dead flies in a bottle of water supplied by the defendant, Culligan. In the course of replacing an empty bottle of drinking water with a full one, Mr Mustapha saw a dead fly and part of another dead fly in the unopened replacement bottle. He became obsessed with the event and its 'revolting implications' for the health of his family, which had been consuming water supplied by Culligan for the previous 15 years. The plaintiff developed a major depressive disorder with associated phobia and anxiety. He sued Culligan for damages. The trial judge found that seeing the flies in the water resulted in psychiatric injuries to Mr Mustapha, and awarded him CAN$80,000 in general damages, CAN$24,174.58 in special damages, and CAN$237,600 in damages for loss of business . . . The Ontario Court of Appeal overturned the judgment, on appeal.

Held: McLachlin, CJC
The fourth and final question to address in a negligence claim is whether the defendant's breach caused the plaintiff's harm in fact and in law. The evidence before the trial judge establishes that the defendant's breach of its duty of care in fact caused Mr Mustapha's psychiatric injury We are not asked to revisit this conclusion. The remaining question is whether that breach also caused the plaintiff's damage in law or whether it is too remote to warrant recovery. The remoteness inquiry asks whether 'the harm [is] too unrelated to the wrongful conduct to hold the defendant fairly liable' (Linden and Feldthusen, at p 360). Since *The Wagon Mound (No. 1)*, the principle has been that 'it is the foresight of the reasonable man which alone can determine responsibility' (*Overseas Tankship (UK) Ltd. v Morts Dock & Engineering Co.*, [1961] AC 388 (New South Wales PC), at p 424).

Much has been written on how probable or likely a harm needs to be in order to be considered reasonably foreseeable. The parties raise the question of whether a reasonably foreseeable harm is one whose occurrence is *probable* or merely *possible*. In my view, these terms are misleading. Any harm which has actually occurred is 'possible'; it is therefore clear that possibility alone does not provide a meaningful standard for the application of reasonable foreseeability. The degree of probability that would satisfy the reasonable foreseeability requirement was described in *The Wagon Mound (No. 2)* as a 'real risk', that is 'one which would occur to the mind of a reasonable man in the position of the defendant . . . and which he would not brush aside as far-fetched' (*Overseas Tankship (UK) Ltd. v Miller Steamship Propriety Ltd.* (1966), [1967] 1 AC 617 (New South Wales PC), at p 643).

The remoteness inquiry depends not only upon the degree of probability required to meet the reasonable foreseeability requirement, but also upon whether or not the plaintiff is considered objectively or subjectively. One of the questions that arose in this case was whether, in judging whether the personal injury was foreseeable, one looks at a person of 'ordinary fortitude' or at a particular plaintiff with his or her particular vulnerabilities. This question may be acute in claims for mental injury, since there is a wide variation in how particular people respond to particular stressors. The law has consistently held – albeit within the duty of care analysis – that the question is what a person of ordinary fortitude would suffer: see *White v Chief Constable of South Yorkshire Police* [1998] 3 WLR 1509 (UK HL); *Devji v Burnaby (District)* (1999) 180 DLR (4th) 205, 1999 BCCA 599 (BC CA); *Vanek*. As stated in *White*, at p 1512: 'The law expects reasonable fortitude and robustness of its citizens and will not impose liability for the exceptional frailty of certain individuals.' As the Court of Appeal found, at para 49, the requirement that a mental injury would occur in a person of ordinary fortitude, set out in *Vanek*, at paras 59–61, is inherent in the notion of foreseeability. This is true whether one considers foreseeability at the remoteness or at the duty of care stage. As stated in *Tame v New South Wales* (2002) 211 CLR 317, [2002] HCA 35 (Australia HC), *per* Gleeson CJ, this 'is a way of expressing the idea that there are some people with such a degree of susceptibility to psychiatric injury that it is ordinarily unreasonable to require strangers to have in contemplation the possibility of harm to them, or to expect strangers to take care to avoid such harm' (para 16). To put it another way, unusual or extreme reactions to events caused by negligence are imaginable but not reasonably foreseeable. To say this is not to marginalise or penalise those particularly vulnerable to mental injury. It is merely to confirm that the law of tort imposes an obligation to compensate for any harm done on the basis of *reasonable* foresight, not as insurance.

The law of negligence seeks to impose a result that is fair to both plaintiffs and defendants, and that is socially useful. In this quest, it draws the line for compensability of damage, not at perfection, but at reasonable foreseeability. Once a plaintiff establishes the foreseeability that a mental injury would occur in a person of ordinary fortitude, by contrast, the defendant must take the plaintiff as it finds him for purposes of damages. As stated in *White*, at p 1512, focusing on the person of ordinary fortitude for the purposes of determining foreseeability 'is not to be confused with the "eggshell skull" situation, where as a result of a breach of duty the damage inflicted proves to be more serious than expected'. Rather, it is a threshold test for establishing compensability of damage at law. I add this. In those cases where it is proved that the defendant had actual knowledge of the plaintiff's particular sensibilities, the ordinary fortitude requirement need not be applied strictly. If the evidence demonstrates that the defendant knew that the plaintiff was of less than ordinary fortitude, the plaintiff's injury may have been reasonably foreseeable to the defendant. In this case, however, there was no evidence to support a finding that Culligan knew of Mr Mustapha's particular sensibilities.

It follows that in order to show that the damage suffered is not too remote to be viewed as legally caused by Culligan's negligence, Mr Mustapha must show that it was foreseeable that a person of ordinary fortitude would suffer serious injury from seeing the flies in the bottle of water he was about to install. This he failed to do. The only evidence was about his own reactions, which were described by the medical experts as 'highly unusual' and 'very individual' (CA judgment, at para 52). There is no evidence that a person of ordinary fortitude would have suffered injury from seeing the flies in the bottle; indeed the expert witnesses were not asked this question. Instead of asking whether it was foreseeable that the defendant's conduct would have injured a person of ordinary fortitude, the trial judge applied a subjective standard, taking into account Mr Mustapha's 'previous history' and 'particular circumstances' (para 227), including a number of 'cultural factors' such as his unusual concern over cleanliness, and the health and well-being of his family. This was an error. Mr Mustapha, having failed to establish that it was reasonably foreseeable that a person of ordinary fortitude would have suffered personal injury, it follows that his claim must fail.

An important issue in the debate on the recovery of damages for nervous shock pertains to the position of secondary victims, that is, persons not being in proximity to the accident but suffering nervous shock. Existing case law suggests that it is not enough for a plaintiff to show that his mental suffering as a secondary victim is a reasonably foreseeable consequence of the defendant's negligence towards the primary victim. As stated above, to establish the necessary proximity a secondary victim must show:

(1) a close tie of love and affection to the immediate victim;
(2) closeness in time and space to the incident or its aftermath; and
(3) perception by sight or hearing, or its equivalent, of the event or its aftermath.

Taylor (Respondent/Claimant) v A Novo (Appellant/Defendant) (UK) Ltd [2013] EWCA Civ 194 (GB)

Facts: On 27 February 2008, Cindy Taylor (Mrs Taylor) was injured in an accident at work as a result of which she sustained injuries to her head and left foot. She was injured when a fellow employee caused a stack of racking boards to tip over on top of her. The accident was caused by the admitted negligence of the appellant her employer (Novo). She was apparently making a good recovery when on 19 March 2008 she suddenly and unexpectedly collapsed and died at home. Her sudden collapse and death were due to deep vein thrombosis and consequent pulmonary emboli, which themselves were due to the injuries that she had sustained in the accident. Her daughter, Crystal Taylor (Ms Taylor) did not witness the accident, but she did witness her mother's death. It is not in dispute that, as a result of witnessing her mother's death, she suffered significant post traumatic stress disorder (a well known psychiatric injury). The only issue at the trial before HHJ Halbert was whether Ms Taylor was entitled as a matter of law to claim damages from Novo as a 'secondary victim' of the accident to her late mother (Mrs Taylor being the 'primary victim'). The judge held that she was. The issue before this court is whether he was right to do so.

Held: Master of the Rolls
The law on secondary victims
The classification of primary and secondary victims appears to have derived originally from the speech of Lord Oliver in *Alcock v Chief Constable of South Yorkshire Police* [1992] 1 AC 310. The plaintiffs in that case alleged that the impact of what they saw and heard at

the Hillsborough stadium disaster had caused them nervous shock resulting in psychiatric illness. At p 407D-E, Lord Oliver said:

> Broadly [the cases] divide into two categories, that is to say, those cases in which the injured plaintiff was involved, either mediately or immediately, as a participant, and those in which the plaintiff was no more than the passive and unwilling witness of injury caused to others.

He proceeded to refer to these two categories of plaintiff respectively as 'primary' and 'secondary' victims. In the case of secondary victims, the starting point is whether psychiatric injury caused to the claimant was a reasonably foreseeable consequence of the defendant's negligence; and in addition to the requirement of reasonable foreseeability of psychiatric illness, there must be a relationship of proximity between the claimant and the alleged tortfeasor.

He explained at p 410D that the reasonable foreseeability test had been described by Lord Atkin in *Donoghue v Stevenson* [1932] AC 562 at 580 as 'demonstrably too wide' and was refined by him into the more restricted 'neighbour' test which introduced the 'essential but illusive (sic)' concept of proximity. Lord Oliver then said this at p 410E:

> The failure of the law in general to compensate for injuries sustained by persons unconnected with the event precipitated by a defendant's negligence must necessarily import the lack of any legal duty owed by the defendant to such persons. That cannot, I think, be attributable to some arbitrary but unenunciated rule of 'policy' which draws a line as the outer boundary of the area of duty. Nor can it rationally be made to rest upon such injury being without the area of reasonable foreseeability. It must, as it seems to me, be attributable simply to the fact that such persons are not, in contemplation of law, in a relationship of sufficient proximity to or directness with the tortfeasor as to give rise to a duty of care, though no doubt 'policy,' if that is the right word, or perhaps more properly, the impracticability or unreasonableness of entertaining claims to the ultimate limits of the consequences of human activity, necessarily plays a part in the court's perception of what is sufficiently proximate.
>
> What is more difficult to account for is why, when the law in general declines to extend the area of compensation to those whose injury arises only from the circumstances of their relationship to the primary victim, an exception has arisen in those cases in which the event of injury to the primary victim has been actually witnessed by the plaintiff and the injury claimed is established as stemming from that fact. That such an exception exists is now too well established to be called in question. What is less clear, however, is the ambit of the duty in such cases or, to put it another way, what is the essential characteristic of such cases that marks them off from those cases of injury to uninvolved persons in which the law denies any remedy for injury of precisely the same sort. Although it is convenient to describe the plaintiff in such a case as a 'secondary' victim, that description must not be permitted to obscure the absolute essentiality of establishing a duty owed by the defendant directly to him – a duty which depends not only upon the reasonable foreseeability of damage of the type which has in fact occurred to the particular plaintiff but also upon the proximity or directness of the relationship between the plaintiff and the defendant. The difficulty lies in identifying the features which, as between two persons who may suffer effectively identical psychiatric symptoms as a result of the impression left upon them by an accident, establish in the case of one who was present at or near the scene of the accident a duty in the defendant which does not exist in the case of one who was not. The answer cannot, I think, lie in the greater foreseeability of the sort of damage which the plaintiff has suffered. The traumatic effect on, for instance, a mother on the death of her child is as readily foreseeable in a case where the circumstances are described to her by an eye witness at the inquest as it is in a case where she learns of it at a hospital immediately after the event. Nor can it be the mere suddenness or unexpectedness of the event, for the news brought by a policeman hours after the event may be as sudden and unexpected to the recipient as the occurrence of the event is to the spectator present at the scene. The answer has, as it seems to me, to be found in the existence of a

> combination of circumstances from which the necessary degree of 'proximity' between the plaintiff and the defendant can be deduced. And, in the end, it has to be accepted that the concept of 'proximity' is an artificial one which depends more upon the court's perception of what is the reasonable area for the imposition of liability than upon any logical process of analogical deduction . . . in each case there was not only an element of physical proximity to the event but a close temporal connection between the event and the plaintiff's perception of it combined with a close relationship of affection between the plaintiff and the primary victim. It must, I think, be from these elements that the essential requirement of proximity is to be deduced, to which has to be added the reasonable foreseeability on the part of the defendant that in that combination of circumstances there was a real risk of injury of the type sustained by the particular plaintiff as a result of his or her concern for the primary victim.

The five common features identified by Lord Oliver have since been referred to as the 'control mechanisms' for limiting the class of persons who can recover damages for psychiatric illness as secondary victims: see per Lord Lloyd in *Page v Smith* [1996] 1 AC 155, 197E-H. There follows a detailed consideration by Lord Oliver of some of the cases culminating in his conclusion at p 415G that there is no 'logic and no virtue in seeking to lay down as a matter of "policy" categories of relationship within which claims may succeed and without which they are doomed to failure in limine'. At p 416D, he summarised the position in these words:

> . . . To use Lord Wilberforce's words in *McLoughlin's* case [1983] 1 AC 410, 422–423:
>
> > As regards proximity to the accident, it is obvious that this must be close in both time and space. . . . The shock must come through sight or hearing of the event or of its immediate aftermath.
>
> Grief, sorrow, deprivation and the necessity for caring for loved ones who have suffered injury or misfortune must, I think, be considered as ordinary and inevitable incidents of life which, regardless of individual susceptibilities, must be sustained without compensation. It would be inaccurate and hurtful to suggest that grief is made any the less real or deprivation more tolerable by a more gradual realisation, but to extend liability to cover injury in such cases would be to extend the law in a direction for which there is no pressing policy need and in which there is no logical stopping point. In my opinion, the necessary proximity cannot be said to exist where the elements of immediacy, closeness of time and space, and direct visual or aural perception are absent.

. . .

This case does not raise questions of the kind which typically arise in secondary victim cases such as whether the claimant (i) had a close tie of love and affection with the primary victim; or (ii) was close in time and space to the incident for which the defendant was negligently responsible; or (iii) directly perceived the incident rather than, for example, hearing about it from a third person. The issue raised in this case is whether the death of Mrs Taylor was a relevant incident for the purposes of Ms Taylor's claim as a secondary victim. If it was, then her claim would succeed because, on this hypothesis, it would not founder on the rock of any of the control mechanisms.

I accept the submission of Mr Cory-Wright that, in order to succeed, Ms Taylor must show that there was a relationship of proximity between Novo and herself. The word 'proximity' has been used in two distinct senses in the cases. The first is a legal term of great importance in the law of negligence generally. It is used as shorthand for Lord Atkin's famous neighbour principle. Used in this sense, it is a legal concept which is distinct from and narrower than reasonable foreseeability. It describes the relationship between parties which is necessary in order to found a duty of care owed by one to the other. In his speech in *Alcock* Lord Oliver refers to proximity in this sense more than once in the passages which

I have cited above. Lord Atkin's neighbour principle itself is concerned with the relationship between parties. You must take reasonable care to avoid acts or omissions which you can reasonably foresee would be likely to injure 'persons who are so closely and directly affected by my act that I ought reasonably to have them in contemplation as being so affected when I am directing my mind to the acts or omissions which are called in question.' Lord Bridge made the same point in *Caparo v Dickman* [1990] 2 AC 605 at 617H:

> What emerges is that, in addition to the foreseeability of damage, necessary ingredients in any situation giving rise to a duty of care are that there should exist between the party owing the duty and the party to whom it is owed a relationship characterised by the law as one of 'proximity' or 'neighbourhood'. . .

But in secondary victim cases, the word 'proximity' is also used in a different sense to mean physical proximity in time and space to an event. Used in this sense, it serves the purpose of being one of the control mechanisms which, as a matter of policy, the law has introduced in order to limit the number of persons who can claim damages for psychiatric injury as secondary victims or to put it in legal terms, to denote whether there is a relationship of proximity between the parties. In a secondary victim case, physical proximity to the event is a necessary, but not sufficient, condition of legal proximity.

I accept the submission of Mr Cory-Wright that the correct question is whether Ms Taylor and Novo were in a relationship of proximity in the legal sense. The difficulty in answering this question is that, as Lord Oliver said, the concept of proximity depends more on the court's perception of what is the reasonable area for the imposition of liability than any process of logic. In the context of claims by secondary victims, the control mechanisms are the judicial response to how this area should be defined. This has involved the drawing of boundaries which have been criticised as arbitrary and unfair. But this is what the courts have done in an area where they have had to fix the ambit of liability without any guiding principle except Lord Atkin's famous, but elusive, test.

In the present case, Novo's negligence had two consequences which were separated by three weeks in time. The judge described them as two distinct events. The use of the word 'event' has the tendency to distract. In reality there was a single accident or event (the falling of the stack of racking boards) which had two consequences. The first was the injuries to Mrs Taylor's head and arm; and the second (three weeks later) was her death. There was clearly a relationship of legal proximity between Novo and Mrs Taylor. Moreover, if Ms Taylor had been in physical proximity to her mother at the time of the accident and had suffered shock and psychiatric illness as a result of seeing the accident and the injuries sustained by her mother, she would have qualified as a secondary victim on established principles[.] But in my view, to allow Ms Taylor to recover as a secondary victim on the facts of the present case would be to go too far . . .

Ms Taylor would have been able to recover damages as a secondary victim if she had suffered shock and psychiatric illness as a result of seeing her mother's accident. She cannot recover damages for the shock and illness that she suffered as a result of seeing her mother's death three weeks after the accident.

Contributory negligence

When contributory negligence is set up as a defence, its existence does not depend on any duty owed by the injured party to the party sued. All that is necessary to establish such a defence is to prove that the injured party did not, in his own interest, take reasonable care of himself and contributed by this want of care to his own injury. Contributory negligence is based on the principle that where a man is part author of his own injury, he cannot call on the other party to compensate him in full. Where the defence of contributory negligence is raised, the court will objectively assess the reasonableness and forseeability of the plaintiff's action taken to protect himself while simultaneously determining the appropriate standard of care required of the defendant.

Clive Morris (Plaintiff) v Francis Furniture Limited (Defendant) (2010) No. 735 of 2006 (BB)

Facts: The Plaintiff alleges that on 11 January 2006 whilst in the course of his employment, he was operating a router machine which has dangerous parts when his fingers came into contact with the dangerous parts and he was injured. The Defendant denies that any injury, loss or damage was caused as a result of any breach of statutory duty or negligence on its part. The Defendant states that the specified risks were reduced by the installation of guards on the router machine and the implementation of a system requiring users of the machine to use safety apparatus. The Defendant further stated that the Plaintiff caused and contributed to the accident in that he failed and/or refused and/or neglected to: (a) make proper use of the safety apparatus provided to him; (b) heed and to obey the several written and posted signs on the defendant's premises; (c) heed and to obey the defendant's oral instructions and warning as to the dangers of him operating the router machine without the use of safety apparatus; and, (d) [] take appropriate care for his own safety. Further, the Defendant claimed that the Plaintiff had full knowledge of the risk of injury, loss and damage to himself by his own actions or conduct and voluntarily and impliedly consented to run such risk. It relies on the defence *volenti non fit injuria*.

Held: Goodridge, J
Counsel for the Plaintiff submitted that if the Court is of the view that this case warrants a finding of contributory negligence it should bear in mind the following factors. Firstly, according to the Defendant's own evidence it was aware that the Plaintiff had in the past not used the safety jigs when routing panels and had warned him of the same on occasions prior to the accident. Secondly, given the non-enforcement of the safety rules and the fact that there were others who used their bare hands as well, it would seem as though the Defendant condoned such conduct. The Defendant contended that the Plaintiff failed to have regard for his own safety in that he failed to use the safety equipment provided by the Defendant and the Court should find that the Plaintiff's injury was in part due to his negligence. The Defendant cited the case of *General Contractors v Christmas* [1958] 2 All ER 1110 but submitted that it should be distinguished from the facts in the present case. The Defendant submitted that the Court should find that the Plaintiff was 90% liable for the injury which he suffered . . . As *Lord Denning LJ* said in *Jones v Livox Quarries Ltd.* [1952] 2 O.B. 608 at 615: 'Just as actionable negligence requires the foreseeability of harm to others so contributory negligence requires foreseeability of harm to oneself. A person is guilty of contributory negligence if he ought to have reasonably foreseen that, if he did not act as a reasonabl[y] prudent man, he might hurt himself, and in his reckonings he must take into account the possibility of others being careless'. The Court is satisfied that the Plaintiff contributed to his injuries in that, although he was provided with the necessary safety equipment and copies of the safety rules, the Plaintiff failed to comply with those rules or to use the safety jig but instead chose to use his bare hands. The Plaintiff was an experienced

joiner having had some 14 years' experience prior to joining the Defendant. He should have exercised greater care for his own safety . . . I assess his responsibility at 40%.

Andy Bhagwandeen (Claimant) v The Attorney General of Trinidad and Tobago (First Defendant), Deonarine Mahadeo and Sasenarine Deonarine (T/A Deonarine Mahadeo and Son) (Second Defendant), and The Chairman, Alderman, Councillors and Electors of the Region of Princes Town (Third Defendant) (2012) Claim No. CV2010–03421 (TT)

Facts: There is a tendency to use our nation's roads as storage bays while construction works are being carried out for the maintenance of highways and public roads. In those cases dangers are created for road users and there is an obligation to ensure that the construction works are executed taking into account the safety of road users. This case highlights the corresponding obligations of both the authorities executing such construction[] works and road users when such works are being carried out. I have found in this case that the Ministry of Works (the 1st Defendant) and its contractors, Deonarine Mahadeo and Son (the 2nd Defendant)[,] caused a load of gravel to be deposited on [] Garth Road in Princes[] Town without any signage or warning and which blocked the entirety of the left side of the roadway causing motorists, in this case the Claimant, travelling on the left side of the roadway to adopt a maneuver inherent with risk. The Claimant was forced to 'overtake' or cross over to the opposite lane without any assurance that that lane was clear as his view of oncoming traffic was obscured by the obstruction caused by the load of gravel. He collided with an oncoming vehicle. I also find that the Claimant, the driver of the vehicle however was not entirely without blame and that he contributed to the accident by failing to slow down to execute the maneuver. I have assessed his liability at 20% and the liability of the Defendants shared equally at 40% each.

Held: Kokaram, J
On the issue of contributory negligence I accept that driving at 50km was not too fast in the circumstances. However, I equally accept that at that time of the day on seeing the load of gravel and obvious danger, the prudent step to take by the motorist would be at least to slow down before executing the maneuver. It appears to me that the Claimant simply drove unto the opposite lane oblivious of the dangerous maneuver and it was almost a matter of course as though he had the right of way or was entitled to be on that side of the road. Clearly he failed to drive with due care and caution having noticed the impending danger. It does not appear that Attorney for the Claimant has with any vigor advanced a case that the Claimant is not without blame. Hamel Smith J.A in *Eugene v T&TEC* CA191/97 observed that a party is contributor[il]y negligent where he did not act as a reasonably prudent man would, by failing to take into account the carelessness of others:

> The burden is always on the party alleging contributory negligence but this can be inferred from the evidence adduced on the plaintiff's behalf (see *Sharpe v S. Ry* [1925] 2 KB 311) or from the primary facts so found by the trial judge. While the standard of care in contributory negligence is the same as that in negligence, contributory negligence does not depend on a duty of care but rather on foreseeability of harm to oneself. The injured person would be guilty of contributory [negligence] if, for example, he ought reasonabl[y] to have foreseen that if he did not act as a reasonably prudent man, he might injure himself; and in his reckonings he must take into account the possibility of others being careless. (See *Jones v Livox Quarries Ltd.* [1952] 2 QB 608 at 615).

For whatever reason the Claimant did not in his own interest take reasonable care of himself and contributed by his want of care to his own injury. In terms of his contribution I would attribute his blame at 20%.

SPECIFIC ASPECTS OF NEGLIGENCE: TORT-BASED LIABILITY AS PART OF BUSINESS ACTIVITIES

Product liability

The classic statement on product liability emerged in the case of *Donoghue v Stevenson*. Lord Atkin asserted that a manufacturer of products, which he sells in such form as to show that he intends them to reach the ultimate consumer in the form in which they left him with no reasonable possibility of intermediate examination, and with the knowledge that the absence of reasonable care in the preparation or putting up of the products will result in an injury to the consumer's life or property, owes a duty to the consumer to take that reasonable care.

Donoghue v Stevenson [1932] AC 562 (GB)[9]

Held: Lord Atkin

A manufacturer puts up an article of food in a container which he knows will be opened by the actual consumer. There can be no inspection by any purchaser and no reasonable preliminary inspection by the consumer. Negligently, in the course of preparation, he allows the contents to be mixed with poison. It is said that the law of England and Scotland is that the poisoned consumer has no remedy against the negligent manufacturer. If this were the result of the authorities, I should consider the result a grave defect in the law, and so contrary to principle that I should hesitate long before following any decision to that effect which had not the authority of this House. I would point out that, in the assumed state of the authorities, not only would the consumer have no remedy against the manufacturer, he would have none against any one else, for in the circumstances alleged there would be no evidence of negligence against any one other than the manufacturer; and, except in the case of a consumer who was also a purchaser, no contract and no warranty of fitness, and in the case of the purchase of a specific article under its patent or trade name, which might well be the case in the purchase of some articles of food or drink, no warranty protecting even the purchaser-consumer . . .

My Lords, if your Lordships accept the view that this pleading discloses a relevant cause of action you will be affirming the proposition that by Scots and English law alike a manufacturer of products, which he sells in such a form as to show that he intends them to reach the ultimate consumer in the form in which they left him with no reasonable possibility of intermediate examination, and with the knowledge that the absence of reasonable care in the preparation or putting up of the products will result in an injury to the consumer's life or property, owes a duty to the consumer to take that reasonable care. It is a proposition which I venture to say no one in Scotland or England who was not a lawyer would for one moment doubt. It will be an advantage to make it clear that the law in this matter, as in most others, is in accordance with sound common sense. I think that this appeal should be allowed.

9 See case brief above.

Range of defendants

While Lord Atkin's classical definition of product liability was limited to manufacturers, current legal trends extend such liability to a wider range of persons including assemblers, repairers and suppliers.

Haseldine v Daw and Son Limited (1941) 2 KB 343 (GB)

Facts: The access to upper floor flats in a block which was let out in a number of tenancies was by a hydraulic lift which remained in the occupation of the landlord of the flats. The landlord made a contract with a firm of engineers to adjust, clean and lubricate the machinery of the lift once every month, to repack the glands when needed, and to report to him if any repairs to the lift were necessary. The engineers told the landlord that the rams of the lift were badly worn and scored and ought to be replaced by new rams, but they did not consider, and, therefore, did not tell the owner, that the lift was dangerous to use. They doubted whether they could obtain the necessary bars and tubes for the replacement owing to the war, and so they suggested that they should make an extra visit each month to grease the rams. An employee of the engineers repacked one of the glands and he negligently failed to replace it properly, thereby causing the gland to fracture when the lift was worked. The next day the plaintiff, who wished to visit one of the tenants, used the lift to reach the tenant's flat, when, owing to the fracture of the gland, the lift fell to the bottom of the well and the plaintiff was injured.

Held: Scott, LJ
I content myself with saying that I find myself in general agreement with that closely reasoned judgment, and I merely add that, if ever there was a case where a repairer, when sending out for immediate use a machine in a condition made dangerous by his professional want of skill or care, could not and would not 'reasonably anticipate any intermediate examination before use', it is the case of a repair to a lift which is intended to be used by a non-expert porter as soon as the repair is finished for taking people up to a higher floor. The facts of this case, therefore, in my opinion, clearly show that the engineers did owe a duty of care to any person using the lift in the ordinary way up to the time of their next examination of it, for they realised, or ought to have realised, that no effective examination was in the least likely before then. The order of the court will be that the appeal of the landlord be allowed and judgment entered for him with costs here and below, that the appeal of the engineers be dismissed with costs, the costs of the landlord in the court below to be paid direct to him by the engineers.

Defective products

Any products generally in use are fit subjects for claims based on product liability; however, it must be established that the product causing the harm was in some way defective. The meaning of 'defective' must be determined with some flexibility but must be generally assessed in the context of what was reasonable to expect of the product in all the circumstances. Even if the fault did not lie in the product, liability can be established in law where the labelling of the product was defective. Labels must generally be explicit as to the dangers associated with a product; however, where products are not generally manufactured for use by the wider public, but by experts, the courts have, at times, recognised that the instructions as to the use of such products need not be as explicit as if the product would be used by a member of the general public.

Holt v P.P.G. Industries Canada Ltd. (1983) 25 CCLT 253 (CA)

Facts: On 17 June 1978, while the plaintiff Walter Holt was using a cleaning solvent known as 'Mix & Match Blanket Wash 200' at the business premises rented and occupied by the plaintiff Presto Print and Copy Centre Ltd (Presto), a flash explosion and fire occurred causing injury to himself and his two infant sons. In addition damage was caused to the business premises and Presto's printing press. Walter Holt was the major shareholder and principal officer of Presto. The plaintiff was an experienced printer, and had used this brand of solvent without mishap on at least a thousand previous occasions. The label on each can of the solvent contained the following warning: 'Caution: Inflammable mixture. Do not use near fire or flame'.

Held: Stratton, J
From the circumstances of the flash explosion and fire including the situation immediately preceding it as described by Walter Holt, I have formed the inference that the flash occurred as a result of a spark emanating from the motor ignition switch or from the motor itself igniting the vapours formed by the evaporation of Blanket Wash 200 during its use in the cleaning process and from discarded cleaning rags and cleanup mats . . .

Thus it seems increasingly clear that the trend in Canadian/English Courts is to allow an inference of negligence to be more readily drawn particularly as against a manufacturer. This inference, however, comes into prominence only in the event that the product in question is found to be defective and thus we come to what I consider to be the prime issue here, namely, whether Blanket Wash 200 is a defective product. The question simply put is whether the plaintiffs have satisfied me, by a preponderance of evidence, that Blanket Wash 200 was defective in either its formulation or its labelling and that either or both of these defects caused the explosion and fire and resulting damage and injury. The test to be applied to determine whether any defect exists was dealt with at p 13 of the Ontario Law Reform Commission Report on Products Liability (*op. cit.*). After referring to Lord Atkin's test in *M'Alister (Donoghue) v Stevenson, supra*, the report continued as follows:

> For there to be liability under Lord Atkin's statement, it is clear that a product must fall short in some way of what it ought to be; a product, in other words, must be defective. Some test of the concept of 'defect', therefore, is required. This must be a general and flexible test; and, it would seem that the concept cannot be defined except in terms of what it was reasonable to expect of the product in all the circumstances. (The underlining is mine.) . . .

It was also established that Blanket Wash 200, or for that matter all blanket washes, had to be quite volatile (readily vaporising) and flammable to be effective to dissolve the printing ink and thus properly clean printing press rollers. The whole of the evidence has not satisfied me that, under the present state of the art, the product could have been made significantly safer in its formulation and still perform the function for which it was designed. Thus I do not find from the evidence that Blanket Wash 200 was defective in its formulation . . .

I must next review the circumstances relating to the label design and content and, in the light of these circumstances, determine whether the defendants acted with reasonable care. The plaintiffs rely heavily on the *Lambert* case, *supra*, wherein Chief Justice Laskin in dealing with the label on the can of lacquer sealer at issue in that case stated as follows:

> In my opinion, the cautions on the labels affixed to the container cans of Supremo W-200 lacked the explicitness which the degree of danger in its use in a gas-serviced residence demanded. A home owner preparing to use that lacquer sealer could not reasonably be expected to realize by reading the three cautions that the product when applied as directed gives off vapours to such a degree as likely to create a risk of fire from a spark or from a pilot light in another part of the basement area.

Although the plaintiff in the *Lambert* case was a professional engineer and knew that the sealer he was using gave off vapours and was inflammable, he was clearly not an experienced commercial user of the product and must therefore be contrasted to Mr Holt in our present facts. Mr Holt had used the same or comparable product in the very same process on the same press and in the same building on 1,000 to 1,800 prior occasions.

In the English case of *Holmes v Ashford* [1950] 2 All ER 76 (CA), in holding that the manufacturer of a hair dye gave adequate warning to inform a professional hairdresser of the potential danger of the dye, Tucker LJ said at p 80: 'In my view, if they [meaning the manufacturer] give a warning which, if read by a hairdresser, is sufficient to intimate to him the potential danger of the substance with which he is going to deal, that is all that can be expected of them.' The decision in *Murphy v St. Catharines Gen. Hosp.* [1964] 1 OR 239, 41 DLR (2d) 697 at 712 (HC), recognises that certain products are designed for use only by experts and that therefore it would follow that the instructions as to the use of such products need not be as explicit as if the product would be used by a member of the general public. At p 712 of his decision Gale J said: 'it has always to be borne in mind that this instrument [in this case an intravenous unit] was never intended or expected to be handled by a member of the public but only by doctors or under their close supervision or instruction.' In *Schulz v Leeside Dev. Ltd.* [1978] 5 WWR 620, 6 CCLT 248, 90 DLR (3d) 98 [leave to appeal to the Supreme Court of Canada dismissed 25 NR 609n], the British Columbia Court of Appeal overturned a judgment of the trial court which held that there was a duty on the lessor of a motor boat to inquire of the lessee as to his boating experience and to warn him of the dangers of not being properly seated. In that case the plaintiff sat on the bow of the boat rather than the seat. In delivering the judgment of the British Columbia Court of Appeal, Seaton JA at p 630 [WWR] highlighted the basic distinction from the facts before the British Columbia Court and two other decisions, including the *Lambert* decision, in the following words: 'Neither [decision] supports the proposition that the supplier must warn a competent person against obvious dangers or applies to the use of an instrument other than the use for which it was designed.' Earlier in his decision Seaton JA at p 629 deals at length with the duty to warn a user of dangers which are either obvious or known to him:

> The specific limitation that in my view is applicable here is set out most clearly in *Prosser's Law of Torts*, 4th edn, p 649: Obvious Dangers. One limitation commonly placed upon the duty to warn, or for that matter the seller's entire liability, is that he is not liable for dangers that are known to the user, or are obvious to him, or are so commonly known that it can reasonably be assumed that the user will be familiar with them. Thus there is certainly no usual duty to warn the purchaser that a knife or an axe will cut, a match will take fire, dynamite will explode, or a hammer may mash a finger. There is a close analogy here to the rule that the possessor of land is not liable to an invitee for similar dangers.

In *Austin v 3M Can. Ltd.* (1975) 7 OR (2d) 200, 54 DLR (3d) 656 (HC), McCart J distinguished the situation before his court from the facts of the *Lambert* decision. In the *Austin* case the use of the grinder involved high-speed operation which in turn meant that the grinder was difficult and dangerous to handle. The court found that those facts were common knowledge among persons in the auto body business and it was therefore held that the user of the disc, being a reasonably competent auto body repairman, was not a member of the general public in the sense contemplated by Chief Justice Laskin.

In the present case the evidence is that Blanket Wash 200 was intended for the use of industrial printers and was not offered for sale to the general public. As I found earlier Walter Holt was an experienced printer and had lengthy experience in the use of both the product itself and the printing press being cleaned. In addition, the evidence indicated that Blanket Wash 200, under one or other of its generic names of lactol spirits of V M & P naptha, had been used as a blanket wash in the printing industry on presses similar to the AB Dick 360 for approximately 50 years. Of the witnesses who were questioned on the point, both expert and otherwise, no one had any real knowledge of a fire being caused in the process of using blanket wash in the cleaning of a printing press. It is my view that the warning presented by Canada Printing's label, in its general content and tone, is reasonably comparable with labels of competing products and in particular AB Dick's Blanket Wash and a blanket wash known as Pronto manufactured by Varn Chemicals; this latter company apparently has the largest sales volume of any blanket wash in at least the immediate area. As observed earlier, Mr Holt learned the cleaning procedure from instructions given by AB Dick in the use of both AB Dick's Blanket Wash and the AB Dick 360 printing press and Mr Holt knew that AB Dick's Blanket Wash had the same or closely comparable properties to Blanket Wash 200 . . .

Thus I have concluded that under all the circumstances the label was adequate and not defective. Even if I had found the label to be inadequate and therefore that Canada Printing was negligent, to succeed the plaintiff would have to also establish that the defect in the label caused the loss and injury. It would be difficult for the accused to establish this causation having in mind that his evidence was that he did not take note of any label on the Blanket Wash 200 and never asked Canada Printing for instructions in connection with it but instead relied on the verbal and written instructions he had earlier received relating to the AB Dick 360 press and that company's blanket wash.

Lack of foreseeability of damage due to a defect in a product at the time of its manufacture may be a successful defence in an action based on product liability.

Iman Abouzaid v Mothercare (UK) Ltd [2000] EWCA Civ 348 (GB)

Facts: The respondent sustained an accident on 16 November 1990 when he was 12 years old. He was helping his mother to attach a product known as a Cosytoes to a pushchair. The product had been purchased from one of the appellant's stores. It was a fleece-lined sleeping bag for use by a young child and had been purchased for use by the respondent's younger brother. The product was intended to be attached to the pushchair by elasticated straps passed around the back of the pushchair from each side of it and joined by a metal buckle attached to one of the straps. The buckle was intended to pass through a loop on the other strap. The straps were respectively seven and eight inches long and just under an inch wide. The buckle was of light construction. The respondent was attempting to join the straps by attaching the buckle when one of the elastic straps slipped from his grasp and the buckle hit him in the left eye and he suffered injury.

Held: Wright, J

The existence of a duty upon a manufacturer to take reasonable care to avoid injury to the consumer of his product is beyond question. The issue that falls for decision in this appeal is whether the care that this defendant took to avoid such injury fell below the standard of what is reasonably required in the particular circumstances. A primary question in this context is the likelihood of harm resulting from the manufacturer's decision to equip his product with this particular kind of securing device; and that likelihood is to be gauged with reference to the state of knowledge which could be attributed to the defendant at the time of the occurrence . . .

There was no dispute between the parties as to the circumstances in which this accident occurred, and the claimant's description of the event went unchallenged. In such circumstances we in this Court are in as good a position to decide what the outcome in law of such circumstances should be. The evidence of the expert witness plainly establishes that in 1990 the occurrence of such an accident as this would not have been within the reasonable contemplation of the defendant in the light of his then state of knowledge. On that evidence, in my judgment, the claimant fails to establish a claim based on common law negligence.

Ultimate customer

While Lord Atkin referred to the ultimate customer in his enunciation on product liability, courts are prepared to expand the range of negligence liability to include persons that are not ultimate customers but who may have been injured by a defective product.

Stennett v Hancock and Peters [1939] 2 All ER 578 (GB)

Facts: The plaintiff was walking along the pavement when the first defendant lorry driven by his servant approached from the opposite direction in which the plaintiff was walking. Suddenly the flange which kept the tyre on one of the wheels of the first defendant lorry became detached and bowling along the road, it mounted the pavement and injured the plaintiff. The first defendant claimed that he entrusted his vehicle to have the particular wheel repaired by the second defendant and he was not liable as the second defendant, who was a competent repairer, repaired the wheel negligently.

Held: Branson, J

Therefore it seems to me that every element which was considered . . . in *M'Alister (Donoghue v Stevenson)* to be necessary to render the maker of the article in that case responsible to the ultimate user of it who was damaged thereby is present here . . . What is said is that he is liable by reason of his negligently repairing the vehicle which he knew would, if so used, be liable to inflict injury upon a passer-by . . . That, as I have said, seems to come within the principle of the decision in *M'Alister (Donoghue v Stevenson)* . . . I think that the cause of the trouble was the inefficient and careless re-assembly of the wheel by Bryant, and for the reasons I have given, I think the plaintiffs are entitled to recover against Bryant.

Sale

It would seem trite law that the word 'sale', as echoed by Lord Atkin, must be given a more expansive meaning, considered more in the context of supply rather than a transfer of ownership for valuable consideration. This means that a manufacturer may be held liable for distributing defective products as samples in the post or the supermarket if they cause damage. Free services rendered negligently may also incur liability. This position was explained as *obiter dictum* by Lord Denning in the following case.

Hawkins v Coulsdon and Purley UDC [1954] 1 QB 319 (GB)

Obiter dictum: Denning, LJ

It is as well to pause at this point and consider this analogy of a gift; for you will find that just as the law of master and servant has changed in the last hundred years so has the law of gifts. The decision of the House of Lords in *Donoghue v Stevenson* makes the earlier cases on gifts quite out of date. There can be little doubt that the cases of *Blakemore v Bristol and Exeter Railway Co.* and *MacCarthy v Young*, on which Willes J relied, would be decided differently today. Let me give some modern instances.

Suppose that the manufacturer of a special soap sends out samples by way of gift to members of the public, and owing to negligence in manufacture a user of the soap suffers from dermatitis. Surely there is a cause of action, even though the manufacturers did not actually know of its evil character at the time. Again, suppose that hospital authorities treat a patient negligently, they are liable, even though they give their services gratuitously. If they give him food which through their carelessness has been mixed with some injurious ingredient, are they not also liable even though they did not know of its injurious character? There is no difference in principle between such a case and the case where the driver of a car gives a friend a lift.

Intermediate examination

> The effect of intermediate examination seems . . . to be this: If someone in the place of the manufacturer would reasonably contemplate that the defect in the goods would remain there at the time of their use by the claimant despite their passing through the hands of intermediaries, he is still liable.[10]

The existence of a mere opportunity to examine will not allow a manufacturer to escape liability. Rather, there must be a reasonable probability or possibility that an examination would reveal any defects or concealed dangers in the product before use. The intended examination must be one that is practicable or contemplated by the parties.

Howmet Ltd v Economy Devices Ltd & Ors [2014] EWHC 3933 (TCC) (GB)

Facts: On 12 February 2007 there was a disastrous fire at the Claimant's factory in Exeter. The Claimant ('Howmet') says that it was caused by the failure of a probe that was supposed to detect a loss of liquid in a hot water tank. As a result of the combination of some rather unusual events the heater to the tank was switched on at a time when the tank was virtually empty. The probe, being out of the water, should have isolated

10 Murphy, *Street on Torts*, p 404.

the heating units in the tank. It failed to do so and so the heaters overheated and set fire to the tank, and the fire quickly spread to the factory. It caused losses in excess of £20 million. The First Defendant, Economy Devices Ltd ('EDL'), was the manufacturer of the probe. The Second Defendant, Electrochemical Supplies Ltd ('ECS'), was engaged to design, supply and install a new grain etch line ('GEL'), which included the tank that caught fire. The Third Defendant, MJD Technologies Ltd ('MJD'), purchased the probe from EDL and installed it as part of a subcontract with ECS for the electrical system for the new GEL. MJD is now dormant and has neither assets nor insurance. It has not served a Defence and has effectively played no part in the litigation. Howmet has now settled its claim against ECS and so the trial was confined to the issues between Howmet and EDL. Howmet claims that the probe, known as a Therm O Level ('thermolevel'), was negligently designed with the result that it was unreliable in service and, in any event, was not a failsafe device. It complains also about the brochure produced by EDL which, it says, contained misleading information as to the qualities of the product. EDL denies liability. It contends that the losses sustained by Howmet were not within the scope of any duty owed by EDL, that the fire was caused by acts of Howmet which broke the chain of causation and that there was nothing wrong with what it says was a simple and relatively low grade product. In the alternative, it relies on the defence of contributory negligence.

Held: Edwards-Stuart, J
The expert evidence suggests very strongly that the design and manufacture of the thermolevels was deficient: it is not easy to see how a properly and carefully designed and manufactured device could have so many defects. Boyle's tests showed that an unsophisticated and simple test regime revealed serious deficiencies in the operation of the thermolevels. Such tests would have been relatively easy for a manufacturer to carry out and, if carried out on a reasonable sample of EDL's output, would surely have revealed the flaws discovered by Mr. Boyle. In the absence of any evidence from EDL, I can only conclude that EDL did not implement any form of satisfactory test regime. As a manufacturer of a piece of equipment that it described as a 'safety low level cut out' that 'prevents heater burn-outs [and] fires', I consider that EDL should have had in place a proper system of testing a reasonable proportion of the thermolevels that it manufactured. Its failure to do so amounted in my judgment to a want of proper care.

The scope of the duty of care and the possibility of intermediate examination
Howmet relies on the fundamental principle formulated by Lord Atkin in *Donoghue v Stevenson* [1932] AC 562, at 599:

> A manufacturer of products, which he sells in such a form as to show that he intends them to reach the ultimate consumer in the form in which they left him with no reasonable possibility of intermediate examination, and with the knowledge that the absence of reasonable care in the preparation or putting up of the products will result in an injury to the consumer's life or property, owes a duty to the consumer to take that reasonable care.

EDL submitted that the principle in *Donoghue v Stevenson* applied only when the product caused a direct injury to the claimant's property, and not when the product simply failed to prevent another device from causing that injury. I can find no such restriction or limitation in the passage quoted above. Take the example of a negligently manufactured brake cable in a car. Driving too fast, the driver loses control on the approach to a bend. The brakes fail to work. The car leaves the road and crashes into a tree. The driver is severely injured. Had the brake cable not been defective, the speed on impact would have been greatly reduced and the driver's injuries either minor or avoided altogether. I can see no reason why the driver should not have a claim in negligence against the manufacturer of the defective brake cable.

EDL suggests that there was an expectation that the thermolevel would be subject to an intermediate examination. However, insofar as any physical examination or testing is concerned, I am unclear as to precisely what type of examination (if any) might have been anticipated or, if carried out, what it would have revealed. EDL's case on this aspect, as developed in cross-examination, was that a careful reading of EDL's literature would have revealed to a competent engineer that the device might not be suitable for use in a safety critical function. For example, it was suggested that because the literature included no statement that the thermolevel would operate reliably in circumstances such as those in which Howmet proposed to use it, the reader should infer that it was not reliable. When cross-examined about this Mr. Braund appeared to be as puzzled as I was. His view was that somebody looking at the literature would infer that the thermolevel would work reliably when called upon to do so . . . I agree: in my view there was nothing whatever in this point, particularly since I have already found that the use to which Howmet put the thermolevel was a use typical of those which could be expected.

. . . In the context of his evidence as a whole, what I understood Mr. Braund to mean by this answer was that whilst EDL's literature may have raised a question about the adequacy of the device, it was reasonable for a designer to assume that it had been properly designed with appropriate safety features so as to make it fit for its purpose. That seems to me to be a reasonable view and I accept it.

I do not accept EDL's submission that a designer in the position of ECS should have appreciated, on the basis of EDL's literature, that the thermolevel was or might be inadequate for its purpose. In my view, there was no other form of examination that could have been anticipated that would have revealed that the thermolevel was or might be defective, and EDL has not suggested any. As Mr. Braund observed, the operation of the probe would be a mystery to anyone who had not looked into it in detail . . .

Accordingly, if Howmet reasonably relied on the thermolevel as a protection against fire at the relevant time, then a failure by the thermolevel to operate properly was in my view within the scope of the duty of care owed by EDL to Howmet . . . Nevertheless, the claim of negligence against EDL failed due to want of proof of causation.

Negligence

The elements of negligence must be established to ensure successful product liability litigation. There must be a breach of a standard of care to someone who is owed a duty of care.

Graham Barclay Oysters Pty Ltd v Ryan 211 CLR 540 (2003) (AU)

Facts: In December 1996 and early January 1997, Mr Ryan and his family consumed oysters purchased from Barclay Distributors Pty Ltd. The oysters were grown in the Wallis Lake in New South Wales. In late January 1997 Mr Ryan began to feel unwell. Blood tests revealed that he was suffering from the hepatitis A virus (HAV). The Department of Health reported that notifications of HAV began to increase in the week commencing 20 January 1997, peaking on 3 February 1997. By 10 February 1997 the Department had established a link between those infected with HAV and the consumption of oysters grown in the Wallis Lake. A New South Wales government taskforce ultimately attributed 444 cases of HAV to the consumption of oysters grown in the Lake.

HAV is spread by the 'faecal-oral route' – it is contracted when humans ingest material contaminated with human faeces which contains the virus. It can only be transmitted through human faeces. HAV has an incubation period of between 15 and 50 days; most cases of infection occur within 30 days of contact. It is a resilient virus that can survive in the environment for periods of three months or longer. Oysters are filter feeders, processing 10 to 20 litres of water per hour by sucking water in and excreting particles through the oyster's normal digestive processes. Some particles, including those that contain HAV, are retained while others are excreted. HAV does not attack oysters; ordinarily the virus is retained in the oyster's flesh. Viral contamination of the oyster is likely to be at a level of concentration that far exceeds the concentration of the virus in the water.

Following heavy rain – known as a 'fresh' – the practice of the industry was to suspend harvesting until the water had cleared. In accordance with this practice, Graham Barclay Oysters Pty Ltd did not harvest oysters between 23 and 27 November 1996. On 11 February 1997, when the Barclay companies became aware of the HAV outbreak, they ceased harvesting and recalled oysters they had sent to distributors and retailers. On 14 February 1997 all Wallis Lake oyster growers voluntarily ceased harvesting. The Barclay companies did not resume harvesting until the 1997–98 season.

Held: McHugh, J
The Barclay companies accepted that they owed oyster consumers a duty of care to ensure that the oysters were safe for human consumption. The issues in relation to the Barclay companies related to the scope of the duty of care that they owed to oyster consumers and whether there was a breach of that duty. At all material times, Mr Barclay knew that potential sources of viral pollution existed in Wallis Lake, that depuration was not adequate to remove viruses completely and that E-coli oyster meat testing would not necessarily reveal the existence of viruses. On this evidence, the learned trial judge held that a prudent oyster grower needed to do more than depurate and rely on E-coli flesh tests because those steps provided insufficient protection against a known danger. His Honour said that the only real protection to consumers was to prevent viral contamination from occurring and the Barclay companies were obliged to take the steps reasonably open to it to obtain a virus-free growing environment. Failing this, the companies had to refrain from selling oysters unless they contained a warning about the risks of consumption. His Honour saw the carrying-out of a survey of sanitary sources as one way of reducing the risk of a contaminated environment. His Honour recognised that any sanitary survey would require state or local government involvement. But he said that, given that the Barclay companies produced a product that put consumers at risk, they could not say that the making of a sanitary survey was someone else's responsibility. The trial judge said that neither the Barclay companies nor any of the committees with which they were associated had attempted to procure any governmental involvement in making a survey. His Honour concluded that in selling oysters, grown in waters known to be open to possibly undetectable viral contamination, and without any warning as to this danger, the Barclay companies had breached the duty of care they owed to oyster consumers.

In the Full Court, Lee and Kiefel JJ formulated the duty differently from the trial judge but they dismissed the Barclay companies' appeal. Lee J said the content of the duty required the Barclay companies to refrain from harvesting and selling oysters from the lake when conditions had arisen which they knew had increased the risk of oyster contamination. Until the Barclay companies had taken the necessary steps to show that the resumption of oyster harvesting was safe, sales of oysters should have been halted. His Honour said that, if the trial judge had intended to limit the scope of the duty to the provision of notice to consumers of the nature of the risk at the time of sale, his statement of the duty was inadequate. Kiefel J found that the duty required the Barclay companies to refrain from selling oysters for human consumption until a 'sufficient period' had elapsed for the risk of contamination to be regarded as acceptable or testing indicated this to be so. Lindgren J would have allowed the Barclay companies' appeal. His Honour referred to the fact that no previous outbreak of health problems from the consumption of Wallis Lake oysters had occurred. And Mr Barclay did not know 'of the existence of an actual problem as distinct from potential sources of faecal contamination of the Lake'. Accordingly, the Barclay companies' duty of care did not reasonably require them to take steps to ensure that the lake was free from contamination or to cease their operations until they could be 'completely assured' that they were providing an uncontaminated product.

The duty of care owed by a manufacturer or producer to a consumer is a duty to take reasonable care to avoid injury to the consumer. To formulate the duty in more specific terms invites error because it is likely to mix a question of law (whether a duty existed) with a question of fact (whether a breach occurred). If the duty is formulated in specific terms, the issue on breach is whether the duty has been performed in accordance with the terms of the duty as formulated. But, as *Wyong Shire Council v Shirt* shows, the question of breach is far more complex than an affirmative or negative answer to the question whether the defendant carried out the duty as formulated. It involves evaluating and weighing a number of competing considerations. Both the trial judge and the majority judges in the Full Court did not attempt to evaluate and weigh the competing considerations. In failing to do so, they erred in law.

Because the facts are not in dispute, it is appropriate for this Court to determine the question of breach. As I have pointed out, the risk of injury from contaminated oysters was reasonably foreseeable to the State and the Council. The risk was also reasonably foreseeable by the Barclay companies. That they knew of the risk and consequences of faecal contamination appears from the facts that Mr Barclay was aware of potential sources of faecal contamination around the Lake, that he knew of Professor Brown's reports about the potential pollution of the Lake as at August 1994, that they ceased harvesting immediately after the heavy rainfall in November 1996 and they used salinity tests after the rainfall in addition to the usual practice of depuration. So the critical question is what would be the reasonable producer's response to this risk?

As Mason J pointed out in *Shirt*, the reasonable producer would consider the magnitude of the risk of contamination, the degree of probability that such contamination might occur and cause harm to individuals and the expense, difficulty and inconvenience to the Barclay companies of taking the suggested alleviating action. The Barclay companies conceded that it was not far-fetched or fanciful to think that oyster consumers could contract a viral disease such as HAV as the result of a 'fresh'. However, the evidence indicated that the rainfall and resultant fresh in November 1996 was no different to hundreds of others that had occurred for nearly a century. None of them had resulted in an outbreak of viral disease. Accordingly, although the magnitude of the risk was great, the probability of it eventuating was very low. The response of the Barclay companies was to cease harvesting during and immediately after the rainfall in November 1996. They resumed harvesting when they observed the water was clear, salinity tests showed that the fresh was spent and oyster-flesh tests for the E-coli bacteria were within normal limits. In addition, harvested oysters were subjected to depuration for 36 hours. While depuration does not fully protect oyster consumers, in the then state of technology it was the most effective method for doing so.

As I earlier indicated, in November 1996 PCR testing was still in the research stage, was expensive and destroyed the oyster tested. Counsel for Mr Ryan contended that harvesting should not have resumed until a 'sufficient period' had elapsed after the fresh to make the risk of contamination minimal. However, he accepted that the sufficient period would not elapse until the carrying-out of a sanitary survey and the identification of the sources of pollution. The notion that the Barclay companies should have gone to the expense of doing these things and closing down its business in the meantime sounds like a counsel of perfection rather than a reasonable response to a risk of injury that had a low degree of probability of occurring. Be that as it may, the Barclay companies did not have the statutory powers of entry and inspection necessary to render a sanitary survey effective or the legal power to compel others to remedy the defects in sanitary systems that caused the lake to become faecally contaminated.

Given the Barclay companies' lack of power to do these things, it had only two realistic alternatives to what it did. It could have closed down indefinitely until the 'sufficient period' elapsed or it could give a warning notice. Given the very low degree of probability of the risk occurring, it was not unreasonable for the Barclay companies to resume harvesting when they did. No doubt the magnitude of the risk, if it eventuated, was high. But so are the magnitudes of many risks that reasonable people run because the alternative is too costly or too inconvenient. The magnitude of the risk of being involved in a motor car accident is very high, and the risk could be minimised, if not eliminated, by no car ever travelling at more than 10 km per hour. But few would contend that travelling at 10 km per hour was the only reasonable response to the risk of a motor car accident. The question of reasonableness has to be looked at from the point of view of a reasonable producer considering the matter at the end of 1996 before the outbreak was notified. With great respect to the learned judges in the Federal Court, I do not think that any such producer would have contemplated shutting down his or her business for the 'sufficient period'. And I certainly do not think that any such producer would have thought it a reasonable response to sell the oysters accompanied by a warning of the danger of eating them. An oyster distributor would have little hope of selling oysters that carried a label stating that the oysters could be subject to viral contamination, for it would be a brave oyster consumer who purchased oysters with such a warning. More importantly, the risk was so low, that it was not unreasonable for the Barclay companies to sell their oysters without such a warning, a warning that would substantially harm, if it did not destroy, their sales.

In my opinion, the steps that the Barclay companies took were a reasonable response to a very low risk of viral contamination. Reasonable care did not require them to go to the expense of conducting sanitary surveys – even if they could have done so effectively – or shutting down their business indefinitely or labelling their oysters with a warning concerning the risk of viral contamination. In nearly a century, no previous outbreak had occurred. What they did was in accordance with industry practice and at the time was a reasonable response to the slight possibility that consumers would suffer harm because of viral contamination caused by the heavy rain that occurred in November 1996. It follows that the appeal by Graham Barclay Distributors Pty Ltd must be allowed.

However, Graham Barclay Oysters Pty Ltd did not appeal against the finding that it had breached ss 74B and 74D of the Trade Practices Act. Accordingly, the appeal by Graham Barclay Oysters Pty Ltd should be allowed only to the extent that it concerns the issue of negligence. Otherwise, the judgment in favour of Mr Ryan against that company should stand.

Negligent misstatement/misrepresentation

The tort of negligent misstatement/misrepresentation arises when a false statement is made by a person owing a duty of care to the recipient. This is particularly the case where a fiduciary relationship exists. In *Caparo Industries Plc v Dickman and Others* [1990] 2 AC 605, the well-known four-element test for negligent misstatement/misrepresentation was articulated. The necessary relationship between the maker of a statement or giver of advice (the adviser) and the recipient who acts in reliance upon it (the advisee) may typically be held to exist where:

(1) the advice is required for a purpose, whether particularly specified or generally described, which is made known, either actually or inferentially, to the adviser at the time when the advice is given;
(2) the adviser knows, either actually or inferentially, that his advice will be communicated to the advisee, either specifically or as a member of an ascertainable class, in order that it should be used by the advisee for that purpose;
(3) it is known, either actually or inferentially, that the advice so communicated is likely to be acted upon by the advisee for that purpose without independent inquiry; and
(4) it is so acted upon by the advisee to his detriment.

Caparo Industries Plc. v Dickman and Others [1990] 2 AC 605 (GB)

Facts: The appellants were the auditors of a public limited company, Fidelity Plc. (Fidelity), which carried on business as manufacturers and vendors of electrical equipment of various kinds and whose shares were quoted on the London Stock Exchange. On 22 May 1984 the directors of Fidelity announced the results for the year ended 31 March 1984. These revealed that profits for the year fell well short of the figure which had been predicted, and this resulted in a dramatic drop in the quoted price of the shares which had stood at 143p per share on 1 March 1984 and which, by the beginning of June 1984, had fallen to 63p. Fidelity's accounts for the year to 31 March 1984 had been audited by the appellants and had been approved by the directors on the day before the results were announced.

On 12 June 1984 they were issued to the shareholders, with notice of the annual general meeting, which took place on 4 July 1984 and at which the auditor's report was read and the accounts were adopted. Following the announcement of the result, the respondents Caparo Industries Plc. (Caparo) began to purchase shares of Fidelity in the market. On 8 June 1984 they purchased 100,000 shares but they were not registered as members of Fidelity until after 12 June 1984 when the accounts were sent to shareholders, although they had been registered in respect of at least some of the shares which they purchased by the date of the annual general meeting, which they did not attend. On 12 June 1984 they purchased a further 50,000 shares, and by 6 July 1984 they had increased their holding in Fidelity to 29.9 per cent of the issued capital. On 4 September 1984 they made a bid for the remainder at 120p per share, that offer being increased to 125p per share on 24 September 1984. The offer was declared unconditional on 23 October 1984, and two days later Caparo announced that it had acquired 91.8 per cent of the issued shares and proposed to acquire the balance compulsorily, which it subsequently did.

The action in which this appeal arose is one in which Caparo alleges that the purchases of shares which took place after 12 June 1984 and the subsequent bid were all made in reliance upon the accounts and that those accounts were inaccurate and misleading in a number of respects and in particular in overvaluing stock and underproviding for after-sales credits, with the result that an apparent pre-tax profit of some £1.3m should in fact have been shown as a loss of over £400,000.

Held: Lord Oliver
Words are more volatile than deeds. They travel fast and far afield. They are used without being expended and take effect in combination with innumerable facts and other words.

Yet they are dangerous and can cause vast financial damage. How far they are relied on unchecked . . . must in many cases be a matter of doubt and difficulty. If the mere hearing or reading of words were held to create proximity, there might be no limit to the persons to whom the speaker or writer could be liable . . . In my judgment, accordingly, the purpose for which the auditors' certificate is made and published is that of providing those entitled to receive the report with information to enable them to exercise in conjunction those powers which their respective proprietary interests confer upon them and not for the purposes of individual speculation with a view to profit . . . To widen the scope of the duty to include loss caused to an individual by reliance upon the accounts for a purpose for which they were not supplied and were not intended would be to extend it beyond the limits which are so far deducible from the decisions of this House.

Sylvia Steens (Claimant) v National Commercial Bank of Jamaica Limited (Defendant) [2013] JMSC CIV 104 (JM)

Facts: The Claimant Miss Sylvia Steens was a customer of the Defendant. Miss Sandra Cunningham a long-time friend of the Claimant was employed to the defendant and was personal banker to Miss Steens. Miss Cunningham resigned from the bank in November 2007. Miss Steens had savings of over Euro 100,000.00 at National Commercial Bank (NCB) Capital Markets Limited. She claims that in May and June 2007 Sandra Cunningham gave her unsolicited advice that she should invest funds in an investment programme which would earn her more money than would be earned on the Euro account. In reliance on this advice the Claimant signed certain documents presented to her by Miss Cunningham and endorsed a cheque payable by the defendant NCB to her and gave this cheque to Miss Cunningham. Miss Cunningham, she claims, used part of the proceeds of the cheque to invest in Higgins Warner, an unregistered investment scheme. Miss Steens claimed that she suffered loss of $2,004,475.28 plus interest. The Defendant contends that any advice that Miss Cunningham may have given was not given in her capacity as an employee of NCB. In any event the advice could not have been relied on by Miss Sylvia Steens to place deposits with Higgins Warner because the first of the deposit was placed with Higgins Warner long before the proceeds of the loan was secured. If the first deposit was placed before the advice given, the second could not have been as a result of the advice given. The express purpose of the loan was to purchase real estate and for personal expenses. This does not encompass depositing money in an unregistered scheme. Miss Steens did accept the proceeds of the loan and therefore must be obliged to repay it on the terms set out in the commitment letter.

Held: Thompson-James, J
I have found that Miss Cunningham was placed in a fiduciary position in relation to Miss Steens, holds a position of trust in relation to her and must therefore act for her benefit. I have also found that in her dealings with Miss Steens['] accounts and giving her advice in relation to Higgins Warner Miss Cunningham did not act for Miss Steens benefit. I have also found that the advice given was given at the bank and in the capacity of a personal banker. Further Miss Cunningham's dealings are wholly inconsistent with proper dealings on the part of a personal banker. I also agree with Lord Giffords submission that the bank has adduced no evidence to show that Miss Steens knew that Miss Cunningham was only authorized to convey information about the bank's services and not authorized to give investment advice.

In *Hedley Byrne & Co. Ltd. v Heller & Partners Ltd* it was pointed out that[:]

If in the ordinary course of business or professional affairs, a person seeks information or advice from another who is not under contractual or fiduciary obligation to give the

> information or advice in circumstances in which a reasonable man so asked would know that he was being trusted or that his skill or judgment was being relied on, and the person asked chooses to give the information or advice without qualifying his answer as to show that he does not accept responsibility, then the person replying accepts a legal duty to exercise such care as the circumstances require in making his reply; and for failure to exercise care on action for negligence will lie if damages result.

In this case [I] have found no evidence on a balance to indicate that M[i]ss Cunningham clearly or otherwise qualified her advice or her information as to show that she was not accepting responsibility. Therefore she has a legal duty to exercise such care as the circumstances require in giving the advice or information.

Salmon and Heuston on the Law of Tort 19th Edition p 233:

> Hedley Bryne affirms and extends the principle that a duty to be careful (as distinct from a duty to be honest) may exist where there is a fiduciary relationship. It extends that principle by suggesting that the duty extends to all relationship[s] where the inquirer was trusting the other to exercise a reasonable degree of care, and when the other know[s] or ought to have known that the inquirer was relying on him.

Further in *Banbury v Bank of Montreal* Lord Findlay LC propounds[:]

> [] while it is not part of the ordinary business of a banker to give advice to a customer as to investments generally, it appears to be clear that there may be occasions when advice may be given by a banker as such and in the course of his business – a banker may as such give advice on investments to a customer who consults him, or indeed, to anyone who comes to him for advice, and when he chooses to advi[s]e. If he undertakes to advi[s]e, he must exercise reasonable care and skill in giving the advice. He is under no obligation to advise but if he takes upon himself to do so, he will incur liability if he does so negligently.

I have no hesitation in holding that Miss Cunningham in the context of a client and personal banker relationship owed a duty to exercise reasonable care and skill in giving the advice to Miss Steens but she omitted to do so and was indeed negligent in giving the advice. It even goes beyond that. I find on a balance of probability that not only did Miss Cunningham use her position at NCB in an unreasonable manner but also in a manipulative and perhaps dishonest manner. In *Banbury v Bank of Montreal* Lord Findlay LC further propounds[:]

> Negligence in a case of this kind involves a breach of duty. There can be no negligence in law unless it is the failure or omission to perform or disclose some duty which is imposed upon you.
>
> Further in *National Commercial Bank (Jamaica) Ltd. v Hew* at p 188 it is stated[:]
>
> A banker cannot be liable for failing to advise a customer if he owes the customer no duty to do so.

This I find is not Miss Cunningham's position.

Further in *Woods v Martins Bank Ltd.* Salmon LJ states at page[s] 173[–4]:

> I find that it was and is within the scope of the defendant's bank business to advise on all financial matters and that they owed a duty to the plaintiff to advise him with reasonable care and skill in each of the transactions . . . as he chose to advise him, the law in those circumstances impose[s] on him to advise with reasonable care and skill.
>
> . . .

The proximity between Miss Steens and Miss Cunningham was sufficiently close for Miss Cunningham to owe a duty of care to Miss Steens. In giving her the advice and in her dealings with Miss Steens, Miss Cunningham was negligent resulting in a breach of this duty. The loss to Miss Steens was a direct[ly] foreseeable result of Miss Cunningham's negligence. Further it is just and reasonable to impose the duty.

The Canadian courts articulate the *Hedley Byrne* principle a little differently. They hold that, in order to establish liability for negligent misrepresentation, the plaintiff must prove five elements: (1) the defendant owed a duty of care to the plaintiff based upon a special relationship; (2) there was a false representation made by the defendant to the plaintiff; (3) the defendant was negligent in making the false representation; (4) the plaintiff reasonably relied upon the false representation; and (5) the plaintiff suffered a detriment.

Yeomans v Wilkins 2011 NBQB 85 (CanLII) (CA)

Facts: The plaintiffs seek damages from the defendants for water problems they say they experienced with respect to a residential property they purchased from the defendants. The plaintiffs claim that the defendants knew or ought to have known that there were water problems and failed to disclose this information when specifically asked about the issue and made fraudulent and/or negligent misrepresentations in this regard prior to the purchase of the property by the plaintiffs.

Held: Glennie, J

Liability for Negligent Misrepresentation
In *Gauthier v Canada (Attorney General)* 2000 CanLII 20261 (NB CA), 2000 CanLII 20261 (NBCA), (2000) 225 NBR (2d) 211 Drapeau JA, as he then was, discussed the tort of negligent misrepresentation at pp. 221–3:

> 14. The tort of negligent misrepresentation is a relatively recent feature of the common law. Its origins can be traced to the case of *Hedley Byrne & Co. Ltd. v Heller & Partners Ltd.*, where the five Law Lords expressed the then novel view that, in appropriate circumstances, liability in tort could result from negligent misrepresentation. Previously, it was generally accepted that liability in tort could not be founded on negligent misstatements in the absence of some contractual or fiduciary obligation or unless fraud was proven. Since *Hedley Byrne & Co.*, the scope of liability in tort for negligent misrepresentation has mushroomed. It is now accepted that the *prima facie* duty of care that accompanies the making of a representation is one that is owed not only by professional advisors but, as well, by all those who find themselves in a 'special relationship' with the person relying on the representation. See *Queen v Cognos Inc.*, 1993 CanLII 146 (SCC), 1993 CanLII 146 (SCC), [1993] 1 SCR 87, at p. 110, per Iacobucci J. Such a 'special relationship' will be found to exist where the representor should reasonably foresee that his statements will be relied upon by the plaintiff and the latter's reliance would be reasonable in the circumstances. Absent policy considerations negating that *prima facie* duty of care, its breach will attract liability in tort.

In *Queen v Cognos Inc.* 1993 CanLII 146 (SCC), 1993 CanLII 146 (SCC), [1993] 1 SCR 87 the Supreme Court of Canada reviewed the law relating [to] negligent misrepresentation and outlined five general requirements for imposing liability for negligent misrepresentations. Justice Iacobucci lists the requirements at p. 110:

(1) there must be a duty of care based on a 'special relationship' between the representor and the representee;
(2) the representation in question must be untrue, inaccurate or misleading;
(3) the representor must have acted negligently in making said representation;

(4) the representee must have relied, in a reasonable manner, on said negligent misrepresentation; and

(5) the reliance must have been detrimental to the representee in the sense that damages resulted.

Applying those requirements to the circumstances of this case, I find as follows:

1. Special Relationship.
A special relationship existed between the plaintiffs and the defendants in this case. They were parties to the Agreement of Purchase and Sale relating to the sale of the property. There is a clear contractual setting. Justice Allen M. Linden, in his text *Canadian Tort Law*, Sixth Edition (Butterworths, 1997), writes at p. 439:

> Difficulties have arisen in the past when negligent statements have been made in contractual settings, mainly because the courts were reluctant to enlarge contractual liability through the back door of liability for negligent statements.
>
> . . . In *Central Trust Co. v Rafuse* (1986), 1986 CanLII 29 (SCC), 37 CCLT 117 (SCC); rehearing [1988] 1 S.C.R. 1026, the concurrent liability theory 'conclusively triumphed['] . . . Mr. Justice LeDain, in a learned and comprehensive opinion, explained that the existence of a contract 'should not preclude reliance on a concurrent or alternate liability in tort' and that the plaintiff has the right 'to assert the cause of action that appears to be most advantageous to him'. Mr. Justice LeDain warned, however, that 'concurrent liability in tort will not be admitted if its effect would be to permit the plaintiff to circumvent or escape a contractual exclusion or limitation of liability.[']
>
> In *B.C. Hydro & Power Authority v B.G. Checo Int'l. Ltd.* 1993 CanLII 145 (SCC), [1993] 1 SCR 12, at p. 27, the Supreme Court reinforced and clarified this point. Madame Justice McLachlin and Mr. Justice La Forest explained:
>
> > [A] plaintiff may sue either in contract or in tort, subject to the limit the parties themselves have placed on that right by their contract . . . The rule is that one cannot sue concurrently in contract and tort where the contract limits or contradicts the tort duty. It is rather that the tort duty, a general duty imputed by the law in all relevant circumstances, must yield to the parties' superior right to arrange their duties in a different way. In so far as the tort duty is contradicted by the contract, it remains intact and may be sued upon . . .
>
> Following the *B.C. Hydro* case, the contract will affect the tort duty only if the parties restrict or wa[i]ve the duty respecting representations. This attitude demonstrates that negligence law protects negotiating parties in the same way as it assists others in the community in other situations, which is as it should be. Negligent statements are no more defensible in a pre-contractual context than elsewhere. The courts should combat it in that situation in the same way as they do in other contexts.

In my view there was foreseeability and proximity in the circumstances of this case. Mr. Wilkins could easily foresee that Mr. Yeomans would rely on his representations with respect to water flooding on the property. The plaintiffs' reliance is reasonable in the circumstances. There was no contractual waiver or restriction on the representations made by Mr. Wilkins.

2. Untrue, Inaccurate or Misleading Representation.
The representation by Mr. Wilkins with respect to the extent of water flooding the property was untrue, inaccurate or misleading. Justice Linden, in his text *Canadian Tort Law*, supra, states at p. 44:

> Beyond instances where a plaintiff is misled through implication or omission are cases, replete in number, where straight untruth has formed the basis for a negligence action.

I am satisfied on the evidence that Mr. Wilkins knew he had serious water problems resulting from the flooding of his property when he owned it. He failed to disclose this fact to Mr. Yeomans and Mr. McLean when he was specifically asked the question. As well, he did not disclose the extent of the property's flooding problems in the past. Mr. Wilkins says that Mr. Yeomans did not ask him any other questions regarding any water on the property other than whether the water had ever come onto the property to which he says he told Mr. Yeomans that 'the ditch running east to west along Waterford Road did fill with water approximately three days each year when the snow melted.' Mr. Yeomans says he asked Mr. Wilkins if he had 'any flooding problems on the grounds of the property' and that Mr. Wilkins 'responded that he did not'. I accept Mr. Yeomans testimony in this regard. It is corroborated by John McLean, the real estate agent, who says that while showing the property Mr. Yeomans asked Mr. Wilkins if he had ever had any water problems with the property and that Mr. Wilkins replied that 'he had not'.

3. Negligent Action.
I find on the evidence that Mr. Wilkins acted negligently in making the misrepresentation. Justice Linden in *Canadian Tort Law*, supra writes at pages 443 and 444:

> Stated otherwise, the defendant must have breached the standard of care. The standard of care applicable to negligent misrepresentation cases was discussed by Iacobucci J. in *Cognos* where he stated:
>
> > The applicable standard of care should be the one used in every negligence case, namely the universally accepted, albeit hypothetical 'reasonable person'. The standard of care required by persons making representations is an objective one[.]
>
> The objective nature of the test was stated by the court as follows:
>
> > Although the representor's subjective belief in the accuracy of the representations and his moral blameworthiness, or lack thereof, are highly relevant when considering whether or not a misrepresentation was fraudulently made, they serve little, if any, purpose into an inquiry into negligence. As noted above, the applicable standard of care is that of the objective reasonable person, The representor's belief in the truth of his or her representations is irrelevant to that standard of care. See *Queen v Cognos*, supra, at p. 121.

4. Reasonable Reliance
I find on the evidence that the plaintiffs reasonably relied upon the representation made in this case concerning the lack of water problems or flooding on the property after Mr. Yeomans put the question directly to Mr. Wilkins. Although there was no reliance on a property condition statement in this case, there was a clear verbal representation made by Mr. Wilkins to Mr. Yeomans when he inspected the property with Mr. McLean.

Mr. Yeomans says Mr. Wilkins told him he had not had any flooding problems on the grounds of the property. I find the testimony of Mr. Yeomans to be clear and reliable, as well as being corroborated by Mr. McLean, and accordingly I have no hesitation in accepting it. In my opinion, Mr. Yeoman's reliance on Mr. Wilkin's representation in this regard is reasonable in the circumstances.

5. Resulting Damage
The final requirement is that damage must have ensued. I am satisfied that the plaintiffs have incurred losses, damages and expenses as the result of Mr. Wilkin's negligent misrepresentation.

Liability for Negligent Misrepresentation
I conclude from the evidence that the five general requirements set forth by the Supreme Court of Canada in *Queen v Cognos, supra*, for imposing liability negligent misrepresentation

have been met in this case. I find on a balance of probabilities that Mr. Wilkins made a negligent misrepresentation to the plaintiffs. Accordingly, the defendants are legally liable to the plaintiffs for negligently misrepresenting to them the nature and extent of the water and flooding problems on the property.

The courts are reluctant to widen the scope of the relationship that is required to establish an action based on negligent advice.

George Burchell v Desmond Tomlinson HCV 03126/2006 (JM)

Facts: JCAL was allotted 44 parks at the Sangster International Airport. These parks were allocated to JCAL members who have a bus in that area at the airport. The defendant was the president of JCAL. The members of JCAL had to pay a monthly fee for the parks which was remitted by JCAL to the Airport Authorities. In 1998 the claimant, who lived in the USA, had no bus. He returned to Jamaica after a telephone conversation with the defendant and contracted with one Richard Lawson for the purchase of an Isuzu bus. He deposited JM$675,000.00 in a bank account in relation to the agreement. He did not receive the bus. He did not recover his money. Mr Richard Lawson was later arrested and charged for fraud in relation to the transaction. He was subsequently sentenced to a term of imprisonment. Mr Burchell brought this action against Mr Tomlinson to recover damages. He asserted that Mr Tomlinson induced him to enter into the contract with Richard Lawson falsely and negligently misrepresented to the claimant that Richard Lawson was an honest, reputable and trustworthy businessman with whom he could entrust his money for the delivery of the motor bus.

Held: Straw, J
The issue for determination is whether the claimant has proved that a special relationship existed between Mr Tomlinson as president and Mr Burchell as a member that would create a duty of care on the part of Mr Tomlinson to all the members at the time he made the recommendation . . . It is clear that there appears to be no simple formula to which recourse can be had in order to provide in every case a ready answer to the question whether, given certain facts, the law will or will not impose liability for negligence . . . In the circumstances of the particular case, the court has made a finding that Mr Tomlinson made a recommendation to Mr Burchell and that the offices of JCAL were used to facilitate the payment of money by Mr Burchell to one Richard Lawson. That recommendation, essentially, consisted of information given by Mr Tomlinson to the effect that Mr Lawson was someone who could import a vehicle into the island on Mr Burchell's behalf. There is no evidence of any fiduciary relationship between any of the parties involved. There is no evidence that Mr Lawson was a person of previous delinquent conduct and that Mr Tomlinson ought to have known this. There is no evidence to suggest that the defendant held himself out as being in a position to advise Mr Burchell on the reputation of Mr Lawson. The court cannot infer that Mr Tomlinson held himself out as a professional or other advisor to give an opinion on the reputation of Mr Lawson and that he ought to have known that his recommendation was one on which a reasonable person would rely. In fact, Mr Burchell gave no evidence that Mr Tomlinson stated that Mr Lawson was honest and trustworthy. Neither did Mr Burchell request or solicit his opinion on the reputation of Mr Lawson. There is no justification to induce the court to enlarge the category of cases in which people are held liable for negligent misstatements by imposing a duty of care on Mr Tomlinson.

Occupiers' liability

There is a common law duty to take such care as in all the circumstances of the case is reasonable to see that a visitor is reasonably safe in using the premises for the purposes for which he is invited or permitted by the occupier to be there.[11] In most common law jurisdictions, this area of law, referred to as 'occupiers' liability', has been dominated by statutory intervention.[12]

Occupiers' liability generally arises from occupancy or control, not on ownership. Responsibility for the condition of premises resides with the person in actual occupation or possession, whether or not such person enjoys legal or beneficial ownership.

> *Anthony Walrond (Appellant) v National Assistance Board (Respondent)* (2010) Civil Appeal No. 16 of 2008 (BB)
>
> **Facts:** On 25 April 1995, Mr. Walrond as was his custom took lunch for his brother's mother-in-law, Ms. Millicent Alleyne, at Gall Hill, Christ Church. However, on exiting the house on the said day, as he stepped on the front step it broke and he fell between the suspended slabs. He struck his hip and 'got pains right after that'. He gave no details as to the circumstances of the accident nor was evidence given in support of the allegation of negligence against the NAB. On 7 January 2000, over four years after the accident, Mr. Walrond as plaintiff filed a writ and statement of claim against the defendant, NAB. The statement of claim pleaded that the NAB was a corporate body established by the *National Assistance Act, Cap. 48* and that in pursuance of its statutory function it provided a house for Ms. Alleyne. The statement of claim also pleaded that the NAB retained control of the said house to which the only mode of access was by a staircase of about eight flights suspended on concrete columns. Further, unknown to the plaintiff, the condition of the staircase was such that it was a danger of which the defendant gave no warning. It was alleged that 'the concrete, although apparently intact, was old, defective and dangerous'. The loss and damage were alleged to have been occasioned by the breach of statutory duty under the *Occupiers Liability Act, Cap. 208* (the *Act*) and/or by the negligence of the NAB, its servants and/or agents. The NAB in its defence denied that it retained control of the house occupied by Ms. Alleyne. The NAB further denied breach of statutory duty under the *Act* and negligence of its servant or agents.
>
> **Held:** Williams, Moore, Mason, JJA
> The most helpful case in determining whether the NAB was an occupier of the premises is the House of Lords case of *Wheat* referred to by the judge and relied upon by Mr. Gollop. *Wheat* was a case on the (English) Occupiers' Liability Act, 1957 which in all material respects is identical to our *Act*. Occupier is not defined in either statute but *Lord Denning* in *Wheat* at *pages 577* and *578* provided the following insight as to who was an occupier:
>
> > [T]he word 'occupier' is used in the same sense as it is used in the common law cases on occupiers' liability for dangerous premises. It is simply a convenient word to denote a person who had a sufficient degree of control over premises to put him under a duty of care towards those who came lawfully on the premises . . . wherever a person has a sufficient degree of control over premises that he ought to realise that any failure on his part to use care may result in injury to a person coming lawfully there, then he is an 'occupier' . . . In order to be an 'occupier' it is not necessary for a person to have entire control over the premises. He need not have exclusive occupation. Suffice it that he has some degree of control. He may share the control with others. Two or more may be 'occupiers'.

11 Murphy, *Street on Torts*, p 224.
12 The majority of common law jurisdictions have legislation entitled *Occupiers' Liability Act.*

The *Act* refers to: 'an occupier of premises', 'capacity as an occupier', 'a person's occupation or control of premises', 'any invitation or permission [the occupier] gives to another to enter or use the premises, 'the visitor will be reasonably safe in using the premises for the purposes for which he is invited or permitted by the occupier to be there' and 'a person occupying or having control of the premises'. 'Premises' is given a broad interpretation. The essence of occupation for the purpose of the *Act* is control for the duty of care is imposed on a person actually in charge of the state of the premises. *Lord Pearson* at *page 589* in interpreting the legislation stated: '*The foundation of occupier's liability is occupational control, i.e., control associated with and arising from presence in and use of or activity in the premises.*' The *Act* envisages that the duty should be on the person who is himself physically in occupation; or someone who is vicariously in occupation through his servants or agents; or the person who is in control in relation to the relevant danger. The occupier is the person who is in command of the state of the premises (in this case the staircase and the steps) that brought about the injury and should in law bear the responsibility for the damage. Both *Viscount Dilhorne* and *Lord Denning* quoted the statement in *Salmond on Torts* as to who is generally an occupier. The current edition of *Salmond and Heuston on the Law of Torts*, Twenty-First Edition (1996) at *page 259* defines and describes the person who is generally the occupier as follows: 'Who is responsible? In dealing with dangerous premises it is necessary to distinguish between the responsibilities of the owner, those of the occupier or possessor, and those of third parties on the premises. Generally speaking, liability in such cases is based on occupancy or control, not on ownership. The person responsible for the condition of the premises is he who is in actual occupation or possession of them for the time being, whether he is the owner of them or not. For it is he who has the immediate supervision and control and the power of permitting or prohibiting the entry of other persons.'

The evidence did not provide proof of ownership by the NAB . . . Even if the NAB was the owner of the house, the appellant still had to prove that the NAB was an occupier of the premises for the purpose of the *Act*. The NAB was obviously not in physical occupation of the premises, which could only be through a servant or agent, and there was no evidence that it exercised any control by, for example, carrying out inspections of and repairs to the property. In the circumstances it is difficult to appreciate how the NAB had a sufficient degree of control over the premises to place it under a duty of care towards the appellant. Ms. Alleyne had lived in the house for 19 years prior to the date of the accident; she was the obvious person in physical occupation and control of the premises but she was not a party to the proceedings. It is therefore unnecessary to make any finding as to her responsibility in the matter. Two persons may be occupiers of the same premises at the same time and both under different duties of care towards lawful visitors as explained in *Wheat*. However, the evidence in this case does not support any finding of occupation on the part of the NAB. It follows that there was no corresponding duty to take care to see that the premises were reasonably safe for persons coming on to them.

Audrey Baratt (Claimant) v Hawksbill Limited (Defendant) (2012) Claim No. ANUHCV 2009/0343 (AG)

Facts: During the period 16 May 2008 to 23 May 2008, the Claimant Audrey Barratt and her husband Roger Barratt were vacationing at the Hawksbill Hotel (the Hotel) operated by the Defendant company. The Claimant alleges that on the third day of her vacation at the Hotel, namely the 19 May 2008, at approximately 7 p.m., after leaving her room for dinner at the restaurant of the Hotel, and while walking on the pathway outside her room, she slipped and fell and suffered injury to her left foot and ankle. She further alleges that 'the said accident was caused by the negligence and/or breach of contract of the Defendant, its servants or agents.'

Held: Remy, J
According to *Clerk and Lindsell on Torts* at page 415, paragraph 8–04, there are four requirements of the tort of negligence, namely:

1. the existence in law of a duty of care situation, i.e., one in which the law attaches liability to carelessness,
2. breach of the duty of care by the defendant, i.e, that he failed to measure up to the standard set by law,
3. a causal connection between the defendant's careless conduct and the damage,
4. that the particular kind of damage to the particular claimant is not so unforeseeable as to be too remote.

Gilbert Kodilinye in *Commonwealth Caribbean Tort Law*, at page 64 states that 'There are a number of common situations in which it is well established that a duty of care exists, for example: . . . (b) the occupier of premises owes a duty of care to lawful visitors to ensure that the premises are reasonably safe.'. . .

Once the determination is made that a duty of care is owed to the Claimant, the Court's next task is to determine whether the Defendant was in breach of that duty. The applicable test is as enunciated by Alderson B in *Blyth v Birmingham Waterworks Co.*:

> Negligence is the omission to do something which a reasonable man, guided upon those considerations which ordinarily regulate the conduct of human affairs, would do, or doing something which a prudent and reasonable man would not do.

The Claimant needs to satisfy the Court that the ingredients of duty, breach and resulting damage are made out in order for the Defendant to be held liable in negligence.

Occupier's Liability
There are no statutory provisions in Antigua and Barbuda with respect to occupier's liability; the liability of occupiers is governed by common law principles. According to Gilbert Kodilinye in *Commonwealth Caribbean Tort Law*, 'At common law, the occupier of premises owes an invitee a duty to exercise reasonable care to prevent damage to the invitee from an unusual danger known to the occupier or of which the occupier ought to have known.' It is undisputed that the Claimant, as a paying guest of the Hotel, clearly falls within the definition of an 'invitee' based on the leading case of *Indermaur v Dames*. In that case, an 'invitee' was defined as a person who enters premises upon business which concerns the occupier, and upon his invitation, express or implied.

What constitutes an UNUSUAL DANGER was defined in *London Graving Dock Co. v Horton* as follows:

> I am not conscious that it has been stated in plain terms, but it is noticeable that what is declared to be the duty is not to prevent unusual danger but to prevent damage from unusual danger . . . I think 'unusual' is used in an objective sense and means such danger as is not usually found in carrying out the task of fulfilling the function which the invitee has in hand, though what is unusual will, of course, vary with the reasons for which the invitee enters the premises . . .

To ground an action for breach of duty owed by the Defendant as operators of the Hotel, the Claimant must prove that the Defendant/occupier failed to take reasonable care that the Hotel is in such a state of repair that would not expose the Claimant to any hazards that the Defendant ought to be aware of. The Defendant must take reasonable care to ensure that the Claimant was not injured by an UNUSUAL DANGER on the premises of which the occupier knows or ought to have known, and of which the Claimant did not know or of which she could not have been aware.

In the Bahamian case of *Cox v Chan*, Sawyer J. pointed out that the occupier's duty is 'not an absolute duty to prevent any damage to the plaintiff, but is a lesser one of using reasonable care to prevent damage to the plaintiff from an unusual danger of which the defendant knew or ought to have known, and of which the plaintiff did not know or which he could not have been aware.'

. . .

The undisputed evidence before the Court is that there were only two (2) steps leading to and from the Unit. There is no evidence before the Court that these steps were built in non-compliance with any building code in Antigua and Barbuda. Further, no evidence is adduced that the steps were broken or slippery, or that they were in a state of disrepair. There is also no evidence that anyone had fallen down the stairs on that night or indeed on any other occasion.

. . .

I am therefore of the view that, on the evidence, the Defendant did not breach its duty to take such care as was reasonable in the circumstances to see that the Claimant was reasonably safe.

This liability on the part of occupiers can extend also to protecting visitors from the acts of independent contractors.

Airline Freight Services Ltd. v Rosalind Morris and Exhibition & Building Contractors Ltd. (2005) CA No. 25 of 1997 (BB)

Facts: According to the evidence of the plaintiff/respondent (Rosalind Morris), she reported for duty on 9 January 1990 at 8.00 am; at that time the entrance to her office in the Customs Department was free from any obstruction. Sometime between 11.30 am and 12 noon that day, she left her office to go to lunch, and as she exited the door of the Customs Department and turned left, making two to three steps to walk along the ramp, she tripped and fell on an unrolled BRC wire which extended from that portion of the ramp in front of the offices of the first defendant/appellant (Airline Freight Services Ltd) to about two to three steps away from the door to the Customs Department. The BRC wire was part of the materials which the second defendant/respondent (Exhibition & Building Contractors Ltd) was using to carry out renovations to the first defendant/appellant's offices at Terminal 2.

In its defence, the first defendant/appellant admitted that the plaintiff/respondent had tripped on the BRC wire, but denied negligence or that it was in control of the area where the incident occurred. It further contended that the second defendant/respondent was an independent contractor whom it had engaged to carry out renovations to its office at Terminal 2, and accordingly, it claimed an indemnity against the second defendant/respondent in respect of any damages recovered by the plaintiff/respondent.

Held: Williams, JA
The circumstances in which an employer can be made liable for the acts of an independent contractor are succinctly set out in *Clerk & Lindsell on Torts*, 17th edition, at 5–46 . . . :

> Of course even though the damage complained of may have been caused by the wrongful act or omission of an independent contractor or his employee, it may also be attributable to

> the negligence or other personal fault of the employer. If, for example, he has negligently selected an incompetent contractor, or has employed an insufficient number of men, or has himself so interfered with the manner of carrying out the work that damage results, he will himself have committed a tort for which he can, of course, be held liable. Again if the employer has authorised or ratified the independent contractor's tort then, on normal principles, he will be jointly liable for such tort.

Winfield & Jolowicz on Tort, 17th edition, at 20–21, expressed it in similar terms . . .

> In principle an employer is not responsible for the torts of his independent contractor. It is no exception to say that he is liable:
>
> (1) for torts authorised or ratified by him or where the contractor is employed to do an illegal act, for here they are both liable as joint tortfeasors; or
>
> (2) for his own negligence, for example in failing to take care to select a competent contractor or procure adequate resources;
>
> (3) cases of strict liability are sometimes treated as exceptions, but it is doubtful if they are so in theory;
>
> (4) nor is it an exception that he is liable if he personally interferes with the contractor or his servants and in fact directs the manner in which the work is to be done, for he is then again liable as a joint tortfeasor: *M'Laughlin v Pryor* (1842) 4 Man & G 48; *Hardaker v Idle DC* (1896) 1 QB 335.

The action of Freight in directing Exhibition to place the BRC partition flat on the ramp also brought into focus the 'neighbour' principle as pronounced by Lord Atkin in *Donoghue v Stevenson* [1933] AC 562, 580: 'You must take reasonable care to avoid acts or omissions which you can reasonably foresee would be likely to injure your neighbours. Who then, in law, is my neighbour? The answer seems to be – persons who are so closely and directly affected by my act that I ought reasonably to have them in contemplation as being so affected when I am directing my mind to the acts or omissions which are called in question.'

If one applies this principle to the facts of the present case, it becomes clear that both Freight and Exhibition had a duty of care to all persons who were likely to use the ramp – including, of course, Morris. It is plain that Mr Ward (employee of Freight) was aware of the potential danger involved in placing the BRC partition flat on the ramp. When he gave instructions to Exhibition's workmen to move the BRC partition from where it was leaning on the wall and place it flat on the ramp, he told Exhibition's workmen to place markers on the BRC (paragraph [42] above). Even without this clear evidence that Mr Ward was aware that danger could result to persons using the ramp if proper precautions were not taken, it must have been obvious to Mr Ward that danger could result from laying the BRC flat on the ramp, to which the general public had access, yet he did not ensure that markers were in fact placed on the BRC (as he had instructed) to draw the presence of the BRC partition to the attention of any person using the ramp . . .

In *McLaughlin v Pryor* (*supra*), Pryor had rented a carriage with a driver to take him and some friends to races at Epsom, so that, as between him and the owner and driver of the carriage, he was the employer and the owner and the driver were independent contractors. On the way to Epsom, they met a build-up of traffic at a toll gate. Pryor's driver tried to get ahead of another carriage, and in attempting to do so the driver collided with the other carriage and caused damage and injuries. Pryor was held liable for the damage caused to the second carriage and its occupant because the evidence showed that he had assented to and assumed control over the driver of his carriage and later acknowledged responsibility for the accident. It was his interference with the work and his approval of the work of the independent contractor and the result thereof that attracted liability to the employer of the independent contractor and not the nature of the work or activity which the agent of the independent contractor undertook. The same principle is well illustrated by a hypothetical example in *Commonwealth Caribbean Tort Law* by Professor Kodilinye, 2nd edition, at page 445: 'An example commonly given of liability for authorizing an independent contractor's tort is that of the passenger in a taxi who orders the driver to drive fast or to take other risks. In such a case, both the taxi driver and the passenger will be liable for any damage caused by the former's reckless driving.'

In addition, I think that the principle applicable to extra-hazardous and inherently dangerous work can be applied, by analogy, to a case in which the employer directs that a specific part of the work should be executed in a manner that is likely to present a danger to the general public. Although the refurbishing work that Freight originally entrusted to Exhibition did not appear to be inherently dangerous or hazardous, the same could not be said of that part of the work which Freight specifically instructed Exhibition to do, that is, placing the BRC partition flat on the ramp to which access was had by all members of the general public who had business in any of the offices abutting the ramp. The Trial Judge found that Freight ordered the removal of the BRC 'from an apparent place of little danger to one of clear danger' (page 94). Freight was aware of the danger involved in its instructions (paragraph [42] *supra*), so it was incumbent upon Freight itself not only to give instructions to take care but also to ensure that the necessary precautions were put in place to avoid danger to third parties.

In sum, Freight engaged the services of Exhibition to do some alterations to Freight's office; the work involved the removal of a BRC partition, which Exhibition moved and propped against Freight's wall in a safe position; Freight interfered with Exhibition's work by giving instructions to place the partition flat on a ramp which provided access to and between all the offices in Terminal 2; Freight realised the possible danger of the partition in its new position to the general public using the ramp, but did not see to it that its warning instructions were followed. As a result, both Exhibition and Freight are to blame for the injuries sustained by Morris when she tripped and fell on the BRC partition.

While the duty of care on the part of occupiers is generally towards visitors, the courts have developed some sensitivity towards trespassers.

Arthur Belisle (Appellant) v Anna Crawford (Respondent) Civil Appeal No. 30 of 2009 (BZ)

Facts: In October 1999, the respondent entered into a contract of tenancy with the appellant in respect of premises at 202 East Collet Canal, Belize City. The Tenancy was in respect of the upper flat of the two storey wooden structure on the premises, at a monthly rental of $250.00. She was at that time employed as an office assistant at the Ministry of Housing earning $150.00 per week. On 30 August 2001, while the respondent was on the wooden verandah of the upper flat, the floor collapsed, causing her to fall some distance to the ground and to suffer serious physical injuries. Those injuries, which included a severely broken leg, required surgical intervention and extensive rehabilitative treatment here in Belize and subsequently, on two separate occasions, in Havana, Cuba. The appellant admitted in his defence that the respondent had brought the need for repairs to the verandah to his attention. However, he averred, the respondent was warned not to use the verandah until the repairs were completed and, in particular, 'not to do laundry on the said verandah as this was the cause of the rotting'. Despite the respondent being in arrears of rent, the repairs were in fact commenced in June 2002, 'but could not continue as the [respondent] kept throwing water on the workmen[']. The respondent ignored the warning not to do laundry on the verandah and continued to do so clandestinely and it was while she was so engaged that the accident, which was admitted, occurred. The appellant also pleaded that at the time of the accident the respondent was a trespasser at the time of the accident, having been served on 30 June 2002 with notice to quit the premises on 31 July 2002, for failure to pay rent when due.

Held: Morrison, JA
As regards ground 1, *British Railways Board v Herrington*, upon which Mr Staine relied, established that although, as a general rule, a person who trespassed on the land of another did so at his own risk, and the occupier of the land did not owe him the common duty of care owed to persons lawfully on the land, it did not follow that an occupier was never, in any circumstances, under a duty to take steps to protect the trespasser from potential danger. Where an occupier knew that there were trespassers on his land and also knew of facts giving rise to potential dangers to persons on the land who were unaware of those facts, he was under a duty to take reasonable steps to enable the trespasser to avoid the danger. In other words, it is not the law that no duty of care is owed by an occupier of land to trespassers. In the contrary as Lord Denning MR put it in *Pannett v P McGuinness & Co Ltd*, the other case cited by Mr Staine on this point (at page 141), '[t]he long and short of it is that you have to take into account all the circumstances of the case and see then whether the occupier ought to have done more than he did'. In the instant case, on the evidence which the judge accepted, the respondent remained on the premises after June 30, 2002, believing that the verandah had been properly repaired, which it had not been. This, in my view, created a clear potential of danger to the respondent, which it was the appellant's duty to take reasonable care to protect her against and which he failed to do, as the judge found. So that, it seems to me, even on the appellant's case, he would still be liable.

Jane Craig (Claimant) v LJ Williams (Defendant) (2012) Claim No. CV2009–01023 (TT)

Facts: This claim was filed on 20 March 2009 for an injury sustained by the claimant on 21 March 2005. The claimant says she visited the defendant's place of business at Shaw Park when an object fell on her head and caused her injury. She had set out in her statement of case it was a steel iron frame. In her evidence she could not say exactly what the object was. She said it could have been an iron chair or table. She glanced at it. It was made of iron. The claimant says she had gone to the defendant's place to buy items for a small grocery business she had. She said she regularly went there to make purchases.

Held: Boodoosingh, J
That the defendant owes a duty of care to persons in the premises is not in doubt. What the defendant contends is that the claimant went to an area which is restricted and where there were signs marked 'Employees Only'. There was also a sign painted on the ground saying 'STOP'. The area where the claimant went, according to the defendant, was a restricted area. By going into that area, she became a trespasser, and the defendant owed a duty of 'common humanity' only in those circumstances: *British Railways Board v Herrington* [1972] 1 All ER 749. In this case it was held that, whereas an occupier does not owe a duty of care to trespassers, he does owe a duty of 'common humanity' or a duty to act 'in accordance with common standards of civilised behaviour'.

Given the evidence presented by both sides, I accepted the claimant's evidence on a balance of probabilities on the location of the incident and how it occurred. I did not find any reason to disbelieve her based on the cross-examination.

What is also clear is that notwithstanding the denials by the defendant, the claimant was able to gain very easy access to the area. If there was a barrier, it was meant for vehicles. Also, any 'STOP' sign on the ground could only be for vehicles. The defendant ought to have had someone stationed there to restrict access or have a gate or some other protective barrier to prevent access in those circumstances. I accepted the claimant's evidence that after making her purchases, she customarily would go to the area she went to on 21 March 2005 to await the delivery of her goods. Given this evidence, it is expected that more would have been done by the defendant to keep persons out of an area like this to which the claimant frequently had access without apparent hindrance. Also, the object fell from above. The claimant denied she had leaned on any objects such as wooden pallets to cause something to fall. The defendant produced no evidence on this. I accepted the claimant's evidence that an iron object fell from above and she had not leaned to cause this to happen. This suggests that it was not properly secured. This would be an unusual danger such as would ordinarily make an owner liable. In those circumstances, I find there was a breach of the duty of care owed by the defendant to the claimant.

Employers' liability

It is hardly surprising that Lord Atkin's neighbour principle extends to the imposition of responsibility upon one person for the failure of another with whom the person has a special relationship, such as that of employer and employee, to exercise such care as a reasonably prudent person would use under similar circumstances. The duty of care of the employer to the employee extends to the provision of competent staff, a safe place of work, safe equipment and a safe system of work. It would appear that the provision of a safe system of work includes ensuring its proper operation[13] through reasonable supervision where required and adherence to it by employees.

Clive Morris (Plaintiff) v Francis Furniture Limited (Defendant) (2010) No. 735 of 2006 (BB)[14]

Held: Goodridge, J
Counsel for the Plaintiff submitted that at common law there is implied into every contract of employment terms that seek to protect the health and safety of all employees. He referred to the case of *Wilson & Clyde Coal Co. Ltd. v English* [1938] AC 57 where *Lord Wright* described the employer's obligation as three-fold: the provision of competent staff, adequate material and a proper system of work and effective supervision. It was counsel's further submission that an employer must organize a safe system of working for his employees and must ensure that the system is adhered to. Counsel pointed out that the duty to provide a safe system of work is by no means limited to the mere provision of safety apparatus and or the issuing of safety instructions . . . While the evidence shows

13 Deakin *et al*, *Markesinis and Deakin's Tort Law*, p 697.

14 See case brief above.

that the Defendant did provide a safe system of work, did the Defendant ensure that there was strict compliance by the Plaintiff with those rules? . . . The Plaintiff did not recall ever being warned by any officer of the Defendant about using his bare hands when routing panels. However, the Defendant's officers gave evidence to the contrary. When questioned about the failure to take strong action against the Plaintiff for his continued disobedience of the rules, Mr. Francis said that the Plaintiff was a first[-]class worker and they could not dismiss him because there was a shortage of skilled joiners. The net effect of this testimony is that the Defendant chose to ignore the Plaintiff's failure to comply with its safety rules. . . . The Defendant did not ensure compliance with its own rules. This failure to ensure that the Plaintiff used the safety devices is a breach of the Defendant's duty of care to its employees. The duty is not only to provide devices but to ensure their use. It is clear that the Defendant was well aware of the Plaintiff's negligence but chose to ignore it because he was a good worker. I therefore find the Defendant to have been negligent because of this breach and accordingly liable in damages for the Plaintiff's injuries occasioned by the breach.

Anthony Francois (Claimant) v Maritime Preservation Limited (Defendant) (2011) CV2008–00055 (TT)

Facts: The Claimant was Foreman of the Defendant Company for two (2) years with responsibility of overseeing approximately twenty (20) workers. At about 7:45 a.m. on 26th January 2005, the Claimant instructed workers to remove certain equipment from the hull of a ship on the Defendant's property at Slipway Guide Jetty in Port-of-Spain. However, one of the workers employed with the Defendant, Elton Johnson, refused to take instructions from the Claimant. A scuffle ensued between the parties. The said Elton Johnson later struck the Claimant on his head with a piece of pipe. He continued to beat the Claimant who had fallen, whilst he was on the ground, thereby causing him severe injuries, loss and damage. The Claimant contends that throughout the two years that he worked with the Defendant, Elton Johnson had displayed violent and aggressive tendencies towards several other employees besides himself. As a result, the Claimant made numerous complaints to his supervisors but no steps were taken to provide security on the premises or to relocate Elton Johnson; the latter was dismissed once but re-hired shortly thereafter. The Claimant alleges that it is as a result of the Defendant's negligence and/or breach of Employer's Duty that he suffered various injuries.

Held: Charles, J
The employer's duty to his employee to employ fellow competent workers has long been recognised and the employer is answerable for his own default in failing to employ a competent employee. In *Hudson v Ridge Manufacturing Co. Ltd.*, the Defendant Company was held liable on this ground for continuing to employ a man who was known to be addicted to acts of horseplay and who by such acts injured the claimant. Slade J. opined that:

> . . . where it existed, as it were in the system of work, a source of danger, through the conduct of one of the defendant's employees, of which they knew, repeated conduct which went on over a long period of time, and which they did nothing whatever to remove, except to reprimand and go on reprimanding with no effect . . . the injury was sustained as a result of the defendant's failure to take proper steps to put an end to that conduct, to see that it would not happen again, and if it did happen again to remove the source of it.

This aspect of the duty may extend to failing to control staff who are harassing an employee. In *Waters v Commissioner of Police of Metropolis*, the House of Lords held that there was a breach of duty where an employer knew that acts done by employees during their employment might cause physical or mental harm to a particular fellow employee and did nothing to supervise or prevent such acts when he had the power to do so.

The question now arises of whether the Defendant Company knew of Elton Johnson's disposition towards the Claimant. The Claimant contended that he made more than one complaint to the Defendant of the harassment he suffered at the hands of Elton John[son]. The Defendant denies any such complaints were made. Whilst the Defendant's sole witness admitted that the Company kept records of complaints and reports made by employees of indiscipline and/or misconduct these records were not produced to the Court to verify whether or not the Claimant made any reports. Having heard the Claimant and the Defendant's witness, D. Williams, testify on this issue, I accepted the evidence of the Claimant. I found him to be a more credible, forthright witness than Mr. Williams on the whole. The Claimant having asserted and established prima facie that he did report to the Defendant prior incidents of threats and acts of aggravation by Mr. Johnson against him, the onus of displacing this prima facie case fell to the Defendant. It was open to the Defendant Company to adduce evidence to displace the Claimant's testimony on this point; they have not done so. Accordingly, I drew an adverse inference against the Defendant Company that prior reports about Mr. Johnson's hostility and aggression toward the Claimant had been reported to them and they had done nothing about it.

I therefore hold that the acts of violence by Mr. Johnson were reasonably foreseeable by the Defendant Company who had taken no steps to remove this employee from the workplace. I also hold that the Claimant's injuries were caused by the Defendant's failure to take steps to end the conduct complained of by the Claimant. Therefore, the Defendant failed to provide a safe system of work for the Claimant and is responsible for the injuries he sustained as a result of their failure.

Premnath Jaikaran (Plaintiff) v Saiscon Limited (Defendant) (2011) CV2007–2813 (TT)

Facts: The Plaintiff's claim is for damages for personal injuries, including the loss of his right eye and consequential loss suffered as a result of the Defendant's negligence in failing to provide a safe system of work in the course of his employment with the Defendant. The Plaintiff pleaded that the explosion was a direct result of the negligence of the Defendant, its employees or agents acting in the course of their employment in that the Defendant:

a) Failed to take all reasonable and effective measures whether by inspection, examination, supervision or otherwise to ensure a safe system of work;
b) Failed to devise, institute or operate or ensure the institution or operation of a safe system of work;
c) Failed to ensure that the Plaintiff was provided with suitable personal protection equipment;
d) Failed to provide plant and equipment namely eye protection that was suitable for the task at hand;
e) Failed to warn the Plaintiff of the dangers of working as above in the circumstances or otherwise to prevent him from so doing or to supervise him to see that he did not do so;
f) Exposed the Plaintiff to a danger or a trap or foreseeable risks of injury;
g) Caused or permitted the Plaintiff to do the work aforesaid when they knew or ought to have known that there was an attendant risk of the barrel exploding and the lid hitting the Plaintiff.
h) Failed to provide any or any adequate supervision, control, guidance and direction to the Plaintiff;

i) Failed to take reasonable care for the safety of the Plaintiff and/or to provide the Plaintiff with a safe place of work or to keep it safe, and/or a safe system of work thereby exposing the Plaintiff to unnecessary risks.

Held: Tiwary-Reddy, J

> Negligence is the omission to do something which a reasonable man, guided upon those considerations which ordinarily regulate the conduct of human affairs, would do, or doing something which a prudent and reasonable man would not do. Per Alderson B in *Blyth v Birmingham Waterworks Co.* [1843–60] All ER AER Rep 478 at 479.

At common law, employers have a duty to take reasonable care for the safety of their employees in all the circumstances of the employment. This general duty has been elaborated upon by the courts over the years, to involve the following four categories of specific responsibilities:

a. The duty to provide competent staff;
b. The duty to provide proper plant and work appliances and apparatus;
c. The duty to provide a safe work place; and
d. The duty to provide a safe work system.

This Plaintiff contended that the Defendant breached its duty to provide a safe work system, that is, the employer had a duty to ensure that the actual mode of conducting the work was safe and that the Defendant failed to do so. For its part the Defendant maintained that the Plaintiff was expressly forbidden from using the welding torch. Therefore the Defendant did not breach its duty to provide a safe system of work.

As noted before an employer has a duty to take reasonable care to provide a system of work, which does not subject his employees to unnecessary risk.

> I do not believe it to be part of the common law of England that an employer is bound through his foreman, to stand over workmen of age and experience every moment they are working and every time that they cease work, in order to see that they do what they are supposed to do. That is not the measure at common law. The duty is to take reasonable care in their operations as not to subject those employed to unnecessary risk . . .
>
> If there are young people or trainees in a factory obviously the need for watching them is greater than in the case of the skilled and experienced men. Per Singleton L J in *Woods v Durable Suites Limited* [1953] 1 WLR 857 at 862–863.
>
> ***Supervision*** *When there is a duty to provide a safe system of work, the employer does not discharge the whole duty merely by providing it, but must take reasonable steps to see that it is carried out. This involves instruction of the workman in the system as well as some measure of supervision. It does not mean 'that an employer is bound, through his foreman, to stand over workmen of age and experience every moment they are working and every time that they cease work, in order to see that they do what they are supposed to do.' The employer must take reasonable care to see that the system is followed, and it is a question of degree and of fact whether this has been done in every individual case.* In *Nolan v Dental Manufacturing Co. Ltd.* [1958] 1 WLR 936 at 942 per *Paull J a workman was blinded while sharpening a tool on a grinder when a chip flew off and entered his eye. It was held that the common law duty of the defendants was not only to provide him with goggles but also to issue 'strict orders that they were to be used, and to supervise their workmen, at any rate to a reasonable extent, in order to ensure that their orders were obeyed.'* Per *Clerk and Lindsell on Torts* 19th Edn. at paragraph 13–14.

From the foregoing it becomes obvious that in actions based on an unsafe system of work the Plaintiff must establish four separate issues of facts, viz:

(i) That the Defendant's operations involved a risk of injury which was reasonably foreseeable;
(ii) That there was a reasonably practicable means of obviating such risk;
(iii) That the Plaintiff's injuries were caused by the risk in question; and
(iv) That the failure of the Defendant to eliminate the risk showed a want of reasonable care for the Plaintiff's safety.

The Defendant knew or ought reasonably to have known that the containers were used for the storage of hydraulic oils and other oils. Yet the Defendant took no reasonable care to ensure that the containers were properly cleaned or to ensure that the residue of whatever was stored in the container was properly discarded. Guerra admitted that such containers, if left in the sun, could become hazardous.

This Court holds that the Defendant owed a duty to the Plaintiff to provide a safe system of work. It matters not whether the Plaintiff was hired as a welder or not. Any one of the employees could have been required to pour the oil into the drum. Any of the employees could have been unscrewing the cap of the drum and suffered a similar fate as the Plaintiff. In *CV A 27/03 Tajo Beharry v BWIA International Airlines* the Appeal Court per Mendonca JA stated:

> . . . to argue that the Respondent is not liable because the Appellant was not required to be where he was at the time he was injured is, in the circumstances, not factually correct. It is also a technical argument and one that is not sound in law. It conjures up notions that an employer will not be liable to an employee if he is engaged in a frolic of his own. This concept has no relevance to the liability of the employer to his employee in negligence (*Allen v Aeroplane and Motor Aluminium Castings Limited* [1965] 3 All ER 377). An employer may be liable even when the employee was injured when engaged in an activity for the employee's use and not directly connected with his work (*Davison v Handley Page Limited* [1945] 1 All ER 235). Whether the Appellant is performing a duty or not does not exclude him from the class of persons to whom a duty of care is owed by the Respondent. The fact of the matter is that the Respondent should have had in its contemplation that flight engineers including those from a crew going off duty might go under the aircraft in execution of their duties. The Respondent ought therefore to have such persons in their contemplation and ought to have reasonably foreseen that its conduct could expose such persons to personal injury . . .

The Defendant's instructions to the Plaintiff to cut open the sealed barrel which had residual oils and gases by welding involved a risk of injury which was reasonably foreseeable and there was a reasonably practicable means of avoiding such a risk by cleaning the barrel of any residue or by releasing the build-up of gases before lighting the torch. There is no dispute that the Plaintiff's injuries were caused by the said risk. Accordingly the Defendant's failure to eliminate the risk showed a want of reasonable care for the Plaintiff's safety.

This Court has concluded that the Defendant owed the Plaintiff a duty to provide him with a safe system of work which did not subject the Plaintiff to un-necessary risk. The Defendant breached this duty as a result of which the Plaintiff suffered serious personal injuries. This Court therefore holds that the Plaintiff has discharged the burden placed on him to establish a breach of the duty to provide a safe system of work.

An employer may be liable even when the employee is injured when engaged in an activity for the employee's use and not directly connected with his work. Whether the employee is performing a duty or not does not exclude him from the class of persons to whom a duty of care is owed by the employer.

Tajo Beharry v BWIA International Airways Limited (2006) Civ. App. No. 27 of 2003 (TT)

Facts: On 7 March 1994 the appellant was the flight engineer or third pilot on the respondent's Tri Star L1011 aircraft on flight 981 from Frankfurt, Germany to St Lucia. On the way to St Lucia the appellant discovered what he described as a 'snag'. He observed that the hydraulic fluid reservoir gauge showed depletion in the hydraulic fluid in the 'C' hydraulic system of the aircraft. The C hydraulic system is one of four hydraulic systems in the aircraft and is considered the most important. It was policy that in the event of such an occurrence, if the aircraft is in range of its destination, that ground engineers at its destination should be informed of the problem. The appellant in accordance with this policy notified the ground engineers in St Lucia of the snag and recorded it in the aircraft's technical log. When a mechanical default is recorded in the aircraft's technical log, that entry has to be cleared by ground engineers before the aircraft becomes airborne again.

The aircraft landed safely in St Lucia and parked at its ramp. According to the appellant the normal procedure was for the ground engineers to board the aircraft to be briefed. This they did not do and so the appellant, accompanied by co-pilot Mr Emmy Nathaniel, came off the aircraft. The appellant said that he came off the aircraft to look for the engineers in order to brief them about the snag. The appellant also testified that he was concerned as to where the leak was because of certain notices to pilots that the respondent had sent out. According to the appellant the notices warned that hydraulic fluid leaking on a 'hot component' such as a pump could cause a fire. His major concern, he said, was to find out where the leak was and if there were any 'burns' or damage to the aircraft and to see the engineers. The appellant agreed that while in transit he had briefed the engineers and that there was nothing further for him to tell them and that he had gone under the aircraft out of curiosity.

When the appellant came off the aircraft he went under it in the vicinity of the hydraulic bay. There are two access panels or doors to the hydraulic bay and the appellant observed both doors opened and a ladder was under one of them. The appellant went under one of the doors to see what he could see. As soon as he got there he heard a 'hum' and a 'jet stream' of hydraulic fluid went straight into his right eye. The appellant then re-entered the aircraft and washed his eye in accordance with the respondent's standard procedure for dealing with such an occurrence. After he washed his eye, the appellant stated that it was burning a lot and he had blurred vision. The next day, however, the burning subsided but the eye was still a little sore. The appellant as a consequence saw a doctor and he was advised that his eye would be okay. However, the condition of the eye did not improve but on the contrary it deteriorated. It turned out that as a consequence of the incident, the appellant suffered a detachment of the retina of the right eye leading to permanent diminished vision in that eye.

Held: Mendonça, JA

To argue that the respondent is not liable because the appellant was not required to be where he was at the time he was injured is, in the circumstances, not factually correct. It is also a technical argument and one that is not sound in law. It conjures up notions that an employer will not be liable to an employee if he is engaged in a frolic of his own. This concept has no relevance to the liability of the employer to his employee in negligence (*Allen v Aeroplane and Motor Aluminium Castings Limited* [1965] 3 All ER 377). An employer may be liable even when the employee was injured when engaged in an activity for the employee's use and not directly connected with his work (see *Davison v Handley Page Limited* [1945] 1 All ER 235). Whether the appellant is performing a duty or not does not exclude him from the class of persons to whom a duty of care is owed by the respondent.

The fact of the matter is that the respondent should have had in its contemplation that flight engineers, including those from a crew going off duty, might go under the aircraft in execution of their duties. The respondent ought therefore to have such persons in their contemplation and ought to have reasonably foreseen that its conduct could expose such persons to personal injury. It is not relevant in those circumstances that the appellant may have had nothing further to tell the ground engineers when he came off the aircraft or (which is not the case) that he may have even gone under the aircraft out of simple curiosity.

In my judgment, therefore, the answer to the question whether the respondent ought reasonably to have foreseen that its conduct could expose the appellant to the risk of personal injury so as to come under a duty of care to him, must be answered in the affirmative. The respondent was therefore under a duty of care to the appellant not to expose him to the risk of personal injury.

As I mentioned, counsel for the respondent submitted that in the event that the appellant is owed a duty of care by the respondent, the duty is only one to warn the appellant of risks of which he did not know. The respondent contends that the appellant knew of the risk of coming into contact with hydraulic fluid. In this case, therefore, the occasion to exercise the duty of care did not arise . . . I have already mentioned that the real danger here was not the simple fact of hydraulic fluid coming into contact with the appellant but the pressurisation of the C hydraulic system. Here the appellant did not know that the system was about to be pressurised or would be pressurised. It therefore cannot be said that he knew or appreciated the risk involved.

So far as the use of smoke goggles is concerned, the appellant did accept a suggestion put to him by counsel in cross-examination that he could have used the smoke goggles to protect his eyes. The respondent not surprisingly seized on this answer and has drawn attention to it in advancing its submission. But this answer by the appellant was given, no doubt, with the benefit of hindsight. I do not doubt that the appellant 'could have' worn the goggles as no doubt he could have, in hindsight, taken a number of other protective measures. There is, however, no evidence that smoke goggles were provided by the respondent for the use by flight engineers when leaving the aircraft to carry out inspections. The description 'smoke goggles' carries a certain connotation and suggests that they are to be used in circumstances of a smoke-filled cabin. The name of the goggles does not suggest that they are to be used in external inspections of the aircraft. It seems that flight engineers were required to check for leaks on a routine basis and to do so without eye wear. What evidence there is does not indicate that the goggles were used in external inspections of the aircraft. In those circumstances I do not think that any criticism can be directed at the appellant for not wearing the goggles even where he acknowledges that he could have worn them. I would think that if having left the cockpit to see if there was a fire threat as a consequence of the leak, it would not have been apparent to him that he should have protected his eyes from injury. This is particularly so in this case where the appellant said that on approaching the hydraulic bay at the material time he saw no evidence of a leak. The position . . . may very well have been different had the appellant been told that the system was to be pressurised. It would have brought home to him that fluid might come shooting at him under a 'jet stream' from the possible leak in the system and hence the need to protect his eyes. This was not done.

In the circumstances I see no basis on which to hold the appellant contributorily negligent.

An employer should take into account any peculiarity, weakness or special susceptibility of an employee, which is known or ought to be known.

Ann Marie Redman (Claimant) v Hillary Samuel (Defendant) (2009) Claim No. CV2007–02664 (TT)

Facts: The Claimant was employed in October 2005 by the Defendant as a legal secretary. The Defendant is an Attorney-at-law and practices at No. 1 2nd Panchoo Lane, San Juan. The office in which the Claimant worked was about 24 feet x 12 feet and housed a waiting area for clients, filing cabinets, desks and chairs. The Claimant is 43 years old, is 5 feet 4 inches tall, weighs 269 pounds and has a hip measurement of 44 inches. The Claimant used a desk about 2 feet wide and 4 feet long and says that she also used a plastic chair with a fabric cover on a pedestal with 5 wheels. These wheels had no wheel locks. The seat of the chair was approximately 16 inches x 15 inches with no arm rests. It weighed about 20 pounds. The desk and the chair stand within a tiled area and there is no mat on the tiles. The Defendant says that the chair assigned for her use, as well as the chairs for use by her fellow employee, Shamilla Ali, and clients was made of steel with four legs and no wheels. The Claimant says that on the day in question she went to the filing cabinet, retrieved a file and returned to her desk. She put the file on her desk, held the ends of the desk and lowered herself to sit on the chair. In doing so, the chair moved backwards as soon as her buttocks touched the seat. She fell to the ground.

Held: Stollmeyer, J (as he then was)
Charlesworth & Percy On Negligence 11th Ed. at paragraph 10–12 summarises the employer's duty as follows:

> The duty is owed to each employee as an individual. This means that an employer should take into account any peculiarity, weakness or special susceptibility of an employee, which is known or ought to be known. The employer's 'liability in tort arises from his failure to take reasonable care in regard to the particular employee and it is clear that, if so, all the circumstances relevant to that employee must be taken into consideration.'

It is clearly an employer's duty to provide a safe place and system of work.

Providing a chair for a secretary that is too small in seat – or cushion – size is not the proper or appropriate chair to provide for any member of staff. A chair without wheels is not a proper or appropriate chair to provide for a secretary. I do not agree with the Claimant's contention that providing a non-skid surface is necessarily a part of the employer's duty, and it is debatable whether providing a chair with wheel locks is. Nor is it, in my view, necessarily the case that the chair must have arm or side rests. It will all depend upon the particular circumstances. If, therefore, it is necessary to provide wheel locks and/or armrests given the particular characteristics of work place and/or the employee, then this should be done. The chair provided for the Claimant's use should in my view have been larger, of sturdier construction, and fitted with wheels. It should also have had arm rests which would have allowed her to more easily ensure that the chair was held steady and stationary while she was attempting to sit. In the present claim, the chair provided, whether it was the chair actually used or not, did not meet those requirements. Consequently, the Defendant did not provide the Claimant with a chair proper or appropriate for her personal use.

Where the employee knows or appreciates the risk involved and still assumes the risk, the employee may be held to have contributed to the injury which he may have sustained.

Nevertheless, the courts recognise that economic pressures make it unjust to allow an employer, where a servant has been injured, to say in defence that the servant ran the risk with his eyes open, being fully aware of the danger that occurred.

Benton Brooks (Appellant/Plaintiff) v Syne Contractors Limited (Respondent/Defendant) (2012) Cv App No. 195 of 2003 (TT)

Facts: On 22nd May 2003, Brenton Brooks (the appellant) was working on the compound of Syne Contractors Limited (the respondent) when he was instructed by Mr. Ramsingh (the respondent's foreman) to start a forklift and bring it down a hill. As a labourer, the appellant was not authorized to drive the forklift but proceeded to do so as he was instructed by the foreman. While the appellant was driving the forklift down the hill, it went into a pothole and tilted over to the left side. The appellant's foot became trapped under the forklift and remained there for some time until the forklift was lifted off his foot. He sustained a broken instep as a result . . . On the facts as found by the trial judge the issue to be determined on appeal is whether the respondent should be liable for injury to the appellant in circumstances where the injury occurred when he was carrying out an act that he knew he was unauthorized to do, but upon the instructions of a foreman who knew that the act was not authorized by the employer.

Held: Narine, Stollmeyer, Smith, JJA

In *Imperial Chemical Industries Ltd. v Shatwell* (1965) AC 656, the respondent suffered injury when together with a co-worker he deliberately tested an electrical circuit in a manner which was expressly forbidden by his employers and in plain breach of statutory safety regulations. At first instance the trial judge gave judgment for the respondent, but reduced his damages by one half due to the respondent's contributory negligence. The Court of Appeal dismissed the appeal. On appeal to the House of Lords it was held that where two fellow servants combine to disobey an order deliberately, although they knew the risk involved, '*volenti non fit injuria*' was a complete defence if the employer was not himself at fault, and was only liable vicariously for the acts of the fellow servant within the scope of his employment.

. . .

In this case, the appellant was employed as a labourer. His duties had nothing whatsoever to do with driving a forklift. In fact he knew that he was not authorized to do so. Accordingly, there is no issue in this case as to whether the accident was caused by the workman carrying out his duties in an improper manner.

. . .

In *I.C.I. v Shatwell* (*supra*) (at page 685 D) Lord Pearce provided a particularly lucid explanation of the rationale underlying the principle of vicarious liability:

> The doctrine of vicarious liability has not grown from any very clear, logical or legal principle but from social convenience and rough justice. The master having (presumably for his own benefit) employed the servant, and being (presumably) better able to make good any damage which may occasionally result from the arrangement, is answerable to the world at large for all the torts committed by his servant within the scope of it. The doctrine maintains that liability even in respect of acts which the employers had expressly prohibited (see *Canadian Pacific Railway v Lockhart*) and even when the employers are guilty of no fault themselves (*Staveley Iron & Chemical Co. Ltd. v Jones*, and see *per* Fullagar J. in *Darling Island Stevedoring & Lighterage Co. Ltd. v Long*). It follows that they are liable for the torts of one servant against another.

In this case, on the facts found by the trial judge, the foreman instructed the appellant to drive the forklift, although they both knew that the appellant was not authorized to do so. The appellant was employed as a labourer. His duties did not include driving the forklift. In doing so he was clearly carrying out an act which did not fall within the scope of his employment. Following the reasoning in the cases of *Kay* (supra) and *Canadian Pacific Railway* (supra), it cannot be said that the wrongful act of driving the forklift was so connected with his duties as to be an authorized mode of carrying them out.

. . .

In *Joseph Smith v Charles Baker and Sons* (HL) (1891) AC 325, at 355 the House of Lords discussed the maxim of '*volenti non fit injuria*' in the context of an employer/employee relationship as follows[:]

> In its application to questions between the employer and the employed, the maxim as now used generally imports that the workman had either expressly or by implication agreed to take upon himself the risks attendant upon the particular work which he was engaged to perform, and from which he has suffered injury. The question which has most frequently to be considered is not whether he voluntarily and rashly exposed himself to injury, but whether he agreed that, if injury should befall him, the risk was to be his and not his masters. When, as is commonly the case, his acceptance or non-acceptance of the risk is left to implication, the workman cannot reasonably be held to have undertaken it unless he knew of its existence, and appreciated or had the means of appreciating its danger.

In *Bowater v Rowley Regis Corporation* [1944] KB 476 the plaintiff a carter was ordered by his foreman to take out a horse, which to the knowledge of both of them had run away on two previous occasion. The plaintiff was thrown from the cart and sustained injuries. In rejecting the defence of *volenti*, Lord Goddard LJ stated at pages 480–481:

> The maxim '*volenti non fit injuria*' is one which in the case of master and servant is to be applied with extreme caution. Indeed, I would say that it can hardly ever be applicable where the act to which the servant is said to be *volens* arises out of his ordinary duty, unless the work for which he is engaged is one in which danger is necessarily involved. Thus, a man in an explosives factory must take the risk of an explosion occurring in spite of the observance and provision of all statutory regulations and safeguards . . . A man, however, whose occupation is not one of a nature inherently dangerous but who is asked or required to undertake a risky operation is in a different position. To rely on this doctrine the master must show that the servant undertook that the risk should be on him. It is not enough that, whether under protest or not, he obeyed an order or complied with a request which he might have declined as one which he was not bound either to obey or to comply with. It must be shown that he agreed that what risk there was should lie on him.

. . .

In *I.C.I. v Shatwell* (supra) at p. 680 E Lord Hudson commented that since the decision of the House in *Joseph Smith* (supra), the defence of *volenti* as between employer and employee almost disappeared. He referred with approval to the judgment of Goddard LJ In *Bowater v Rowley Regis Corporation* (supra) and remarked at p. 681B:

> Economic pressures are usually present which make it unjust to allow an employer where a servant has been injured to say in defence that the servant ran the risk with his eyes open, being fully aware of the danger that occurred.

The mere fact that the appellant obeyed the instruction of the foreman without protest knowing that the brakes of the forklift were not functioning properly and he was familiar with the terrain does not mean that he voluntarily undertook the risk of injury. He was obeying the instruction of someone who exercised authority over him, and would have apprehended possible adverse consequences to him, had he failed or refused to comply with the instruction. In the circumstances, I am of the view that the maxim '*volenti non fit injuria*' does not apply in this case.

Vicarious liability

"Under the principle of vicarious liability, an employer will be liable for the tort of his employee, provided that the tort is sufficiently connected with the individual's employment."[15] It is clear that the test is whether the wrongful conduct of the employee is so closely connected with acts the employee was authorised to do that, for the purpose of the liability of the employer to third parties, the wrongful conduct may fairly and reasonably be regarded as done by the employee while acting in the ordinary course of the employee's employment.

Sylvia Steens (Claimant) v National Commercial Bank of Jamaica Limited (Defendant) [2013] JMSC CIV 104 (JM)[16]

Held: Thompson-James, J

The Applicable Law

Bernard (Clinton) v Attorney General [2004] WIR 245

> In the case of intentional wrongs, the correct approach to determine whether the employer is liable . . . ? is to concentrate on the relative closeness of the connection between the nature of the employment and the particular tort, and to ask whether it is just and reasonable to hold the employer vicariously liable.

Dubai Aluminium Co. Ltd. vs Salaama & Others [2003] 2 AC 366

> A was acting in his capacity as a partner, his assistance in the fraudulent scheme by drafting the necessary agreements was so closely connected with the acts which he was authorized to do that for the purpose of the firms' liability he could fairly and properly be regarded as having acted in the ordinary course of the firms' business; that the assistance coupled with the dishonesty was sufficient to give rise to equitable liability on A's part and that accordingly the defendant's firm was vicariously liable for A's conduct.

Bazley vs Curry (1999) 174 DLR (4th); 45 per Mclachin J at p 62

> The policy purposes underlining the imposition of vicarious liability on employees are served only when the wrong is so connected with the employment that it can be said that the employer has introduced the risk of the wrong and is thereby fairly and usefully charged with its management and minimization.

. . .

Can NCB be held vicariously liable for the advice? I have found that Miss Cunningham gave advice in her capacity as Miss Steens' personal banker and that a wrong was committed by Miss Cunningham in her employment. I have also found that in the circumstances

15 Steele, *Tort Law*, p 564.
16 See case brief above.

NCB introduced the risk of the wrong. I therefore cannot agree with Learned Counsel Mrs. Minott-Phillips that if such a negligence existed [i]t would not be just and reasonable to hold NCB liable for Miss Cunningham's negligence.

. . .

Further in *Bernard (Clinton) v Attorney General* it is stated that[:]

> In the case of intentional wrongs, the correct approach to determine whether the employer is liable – is to concentrate on the relative closeness of the connection between the nature of the employment and the particular tort, and to ask whether it is just and reasonable to hold the employer vicariously liable.

I have no hesitation in holding that for the purpose of liability, Miss Cunningham's act may fairly and properly be regarded as done by her while acting in the course of the banks' ordinary business and that NCB is liable because of Miss Cunningham's fault. Further as pointed out at page 388 of the Judgment in *Dubai Aluminium Co. Ltd v Salaama & Others*: The vicariously liable employer has in law the same responsibility as his employee.

Jasmat Ramanand and Shyam Ramanand (Plaintiffs) v Ramcharran Singh and Shiva Woodworking Establishment Limited (Defendants) (2010) No 213-W (GY)

Facts: The action arose out of an accident which occurred on the Melanie Public Road, East Coast Demerara, and in which Lackram Ramanan [d] who was then in the employ of Shiva Woodworking Establishment Limited fell off the tray of motor lorry GHH 4243, suffered personal injuries and died therefrom. The canter was in the process of transporting furniture and a mattress for the second-named defendant and was being driven by the first-named defendant . . . Both defendants, while denying any negligence on their part, claimed the accident and the resultant injuries and death of the deceased were caused or contributed to by the negligence on the part of the deceased. Alternatively, they claimed that the accident was an Act of God which they could not reasonably have foreseen.

The only evidence as to how the accident occurred came from the witness, Loxley Watson . . . [H]e observed a long-based Canter pass . . . going West with furniture and a mattress in its tray. Two boys were sitting on the mattress. At that time, a high breeze was blowing and was lifting the mattress. The boys got up and made efforts to hold down the mattress with their hands. However, the high winds caused the mattress to fly off the tray throwing the boys onto the centre of the road. The Canter . . . continued its journey without stopping . . . Persons who had gathered at the scene stopped a vehicle and one of the boys was taken to the hospital. The other boy, who was bleeding from the mouth and ears, remained at the scene for about twenty minutes when a man claiming to be the owner of the Canter and the employer of the boys took him into his vehicle and they left for the hospital.

Held: Chang, CJ (Ag)
It is the view of the court that the mattress was forcibly blown by the wind off the tray of the canter despite the best efforts of the deceased and his co-worker to keep it down on the tray not merely because the wind was high but also because of the speed of the canter on the road in the prevailing conditions. The defendant company could have easily made provision against the reasonable possibility of the mattress being blown off the tray of the canter by high winds by properly securing the mattress by having it firmly strapped to the tray of the canter rather than seeking [to] rely on the efforts of the deceased and his co-worker to keep the mattress from blowing off the canter by the use of the body weight.

> . . .
>
> The overall operations of the defendant company extend beyond the premises of manufacture and embraces transporting of the company's products by way of canter on the public road. As an employer, the defendant company was under a duty to take reasonable efforts and precautions to ensure a minimum of danger to the employees including danger arising from their own carelessness and also to ensuring that the system of safe working was complied with . . .
>
> This court has no doubt that the deceased himself in the performance of his duties as worker and porter was guilty of carelessness along with his co-workers and that such carelessness contributed to the accident in which he suffered death. But, the carelessness of the co-workers is attributable to the company as employer and the company must be held [] liable for damage or injury resulting for such carelessness.

An act is deemed to be in the course of employment if it is either authorised by the employer or can be considered a mode, albeit an improper mode, of doing an authorised act.

Curtis Arthurs (Claimant) v James Jackson (Trading as Negril Tree House Resort) (Defendant) (2010) Claim No. CL 1999/A0–42 (JM)

Facts: The last year of one's teenage years is always a special time for those standing on the brink of a new decade. Although they have passed the legal age of being able to exercise their franchise, for them the portals of life are just beginning to open. And so it must have been for Curtis Arthurs, who at nineteen (19) years of age in 1993, had been employed in the water sports department as a spotter at the Negril Tree House Resort in the tourist mecca of Negril, on the north coast of the island. Two (2) years had passed since the commencement of his employment with the resort[] and[,] as a spotter, his were the eyes of the driver of the boat, ensuring that the vessel's projected path was clear of swimmers, other sea craft and any form of floating debris. His primary function was to alert the operator of the boat of any likely danger in the water, so that timely measures could be taken to avoid injury or damage. His duties as a spotter provided Curtis Arthurs with what must have been exhilarating exposure to sun, sea breeze and the thrill of an accelerating power speedboat, propelling adventurous tourists skyward in their enjoyment of parasailing activities. While perhaps his involvement with the visitors' experience could only be enjoyed vicariously, it was nevertheless a good life for a young man of his age. Alas, it was not to last.

On the 25th May, 1993, at about 4:30 pm, after water sports activities had ended, Curtis Arthurs and Gladstone Bailey, the driver of the marine vessel 'Seacraft' set out to dock the boat at Bloody Bay for safe keeping, which was approximately three (3) to four (4) miles away from the Resort. Suddenly and without any warning, Gladstone Bailey caused the speedboat to surge forward and swing out to splash a passing boat. That manoeuvre resulted in Curtis Arthurs being thrown from the boat into the water, where he came in contact with the boat's propeller and suffered severe traumatic injuries, in particular, the amputation of his right leg above the knee. He instituted legal proceedings against the owner of Negril Tree House Resort, James Jackson, his servants and/or agents claiming damages for negligence, breach of duty and/or breach of the contract of employment, as consequence of which he suffered loss and damage and incurred expense.

Coram: Rattray, J

The next issue to determine is whether James Jackson is liable for the actions of Gladstone Bailey in the circumstances of this case. As a general principle, 'an employer is liable for the negligence of the employee, if committed in the course of his employment, but is not liable for negligence, which is committed outside the scope of his employment.' See *Charlesworth and Percy on Negligence* 9th Edition, paragraph 2–246, page 153. The case of *Canadian Pacific Railway Company v Lockhart* [1942] AC 591, a Privy Council decision on Appeal from the Supreme Court of Canada is also instructive. The head note reads:

> Where a servant of the appellant company in disregard of written notices prohibiting employees from using privately owned motor cars for the purpose of the company's business unless adequately protected by insurance, used his uninsured motor-car on a journey for the purpose of, and as a means of execution of work which he was ordinarily employed to do, and by negligent driving injured the respondent:
>
> Held, that the means of transport was incidental to the execution of that which he was employed to do, and that the prohibition of the use of an uninsured motor-car merely limited the way in which, or by means of which he was to execute the work, and that breach of the prohibition did not exclude the liability of the company to the respondent.

Lord Thankerton who delivered the Judgment of the Court stated at page 599:

> The general principles ruling a case of this type are well known, but, ultimately, each case will depend for decision on its own facts. As regards the principles, their Lordships agree with the statement in Salmond on Torts, 9th ed. p. 96, namely: 'It is clear that the master is responsible for acts actually authorised by him: for liability would exist in this case, even if the relation was merely one of agency, and not one of service at all. But a master, as opposed to the employer of an independent contractor, is liable even for acts which he has not authorised, provided they are so connected with acts which he has authorised that they may rightly be regarded as modes – although improper modes – of doing them. In other words, a master is responsible not merely for what he authorises his servant to do, but also for the way in which he does it . . .'

There is no dispute that at the material time, Gladstone Bailey was employed as the driver of the 'Seacraft', which entailed his maintaining control over and the selection of the direction in which the vessel travelled. On that particular afternoon, he was instructed to take the boat to Bloody Bay for safe keeping, which is what he was doing when he embarked upon the 'splashing' of another vessel. I am of the view that the prohibition issued by the employer merely limited the way [i]n which the boat operator was to carry out the work for which he was employed. The breach of that prohibition then does not exclude the liability of the employer to an injured third party. In the circumstances, I find that by his actions, Gladstone Bailey was performing, in an unauthorised and improper manner, an act that he was employed to perform. As such, I find his employer James Jackson liable for the consequences of the actions of his employee, Gladstone Bailey.

The applicable test is whether the wrongful act of the employee is so closely connected with the acts he was authorised to do that, for the purposes of liability, it is assumed to be the act of the employer. Where, however, the wrongful act of the employee is not so connected, it can fall within the classic phrase of 'being a frolic of his own' and the employer may not be held liable for the wrongful act of the employee. Nevertheless, the language now used is that of 'closeness of the alleged tortious act with the employee's job'.

Curlon Orlando Lawrence Claimant v Channus Block And Marl Defendant/Ancillary Claimant Quarry Limited And Owen Bailey Ancillary Defendant [2013] JMSC Civ 6 (JM)

Facts: Mr Anthony Charley, managing director of Channus Block[,] and Marl Quarry Limited ('the company'), seem agitated by the possibility that the company may be held liable for injuries suffered by Mr Curlon Lawrence on September 23, 2006 while working as a labourer at the company's plant at Brown's Town, St Ann. Mr Lawrence suffered severe injury to both legs, which resulted in both legs being amputated above the knee, when Mr Owen Bailey, another employee of the company, switched on the paddle of a mixer on a block making machine. Mr Lawrence was inside the mixer cleaning it. He has framed his claim in both the torts of negligence and breach of the employer's duty to provide a safe system of work. In respect of the tort of negligence, Mr Lawrence is relying heavily on the principle of vicarious liability, that is, the company is to be held liable for the negligence of Mr Owen Bailey even though the company may not be at fault.

Held: Sykes, J

Whether the company is vicariously liable for the acts of Mr Owen Bailey

It has been said that vicarious liability is based on social and economic policy. That policy has decided that the employer should bear the damage arising from any negligent acts by his employee if the negligent conduct is sufficiently connected to the employee's job so that it can be said that he was acting on the employer's behalf at the crucial time. Vicarious liability does not depend on the employer being at fault. Indeed, the employer need not be at fault and no such conclusion is necessary. In fact, the employer may have done all that he could possibly have done to avert or prevent the injury which has occurred but the law, based on social and economic policy, will still hold him liable because he has engaged in an activity that carries with it certain risks. The employer, like the injured party, may be innocent of any blameworthy behaviour. The serious social question that arises in vicarious liability is this: of the two innocent parties which of them should bear the actual loss that arises from the negligent conduct of the employee? It has been said that justice and fairness dictate that the employer be responsible for those torts which are reasonably incidental to the business he operates. Why should this be so? The very general proposition is that anyone who employs another (excluding independent contractors) for his own purposes inevitably creates the risk that the person so employed may act negligently and therefore once the employer creates that risk (by employing another) then social and economic policy concludes that he should bear the risk of loss or damage which may arise (*Lister v Hall* [2001] 2 AC 215, [64] Lord Millett). The negligent conduct of one employee to another employee or to a third party is one of those risks which are reasonably incidental to any kind of business or activity. In practical terms, vicarious liability is [a] loss-distribution device (*Lister* [64] Lord Millett).

The difficulty many have in accepting this principle of vicarious liability is compounded when one is dealing with intentional torts (that is torts where the employee embarks upon a deliberate course of conduct such as killing, maiming or drafting documents that facilitate fraud), or where the tort is not presented by the claimant as an intentional one but the employer's defence resists the claim on the basis that the conduct of the employee was motivated by malice, spite or ill will. The problem also arises even if the tort is not presented in the forms just indicated by either the claimant or the defendant but the defendant asserts that the employee acted beyond 'the scope of his employment.'

. . .

Any of the responses by the defendant just indicated always necessitates a close examination of the facts to see whether vicarious liability arises. In this regard the language now used is that of closeness of the alleged tortious act with the employee's job. This new found language is said to be more appropriate than the hitherto now-frowned-upon phrases such as 'within the scope of employment', 'on [a] frolic of his own', 'unauthorised mode of doing the job', 'unauthorised act' and such like. The new language, it is said, has not introduced a new concept but simply sharpened the focus of the analytical lens. This analytical model was triggered by the Canadian Supreme Court's decisions in *Bazley v Curry* (1999) 174 DLR (4th) 45 and *Jacobi v Griffiths* (1999) 174 DLR (4th) 71. These decisions greatly influenced the House of Lords in *Lister* and *Dubai Aluminium Ltd v Salaam* [2003] 2 AC 366. These influences were eventually felt in Jamaica through the Judicial Committee of the Privy Council's decisions in *Bernard v The Attorney General of Jamaica* (2004) 65 WIR 245 and *Brown v Robinson* (2004) 65 WIR 258 – both decisions from Jamaica. The Board also considered the matter in *Attorney General v Hartwell* (2004) 64 WIR 103, an appeal from the Court of Appeal of the Eastern Caribbean (British Virgin Islands). The Court of Appeal of Jamaica in *Wright v Morrison* [2011] JMCA Civ 14 held that the new language found in the advice of Privy Council and the judgments of the House of Lords applies to torts generally and is not restricted to intentional torts.

This sharpened analysis necessitated the reinforcement of some basic ideas. First, in order to make the defendant liable, the claimant must do more than show that the job created the opportunity to commit the tortious act. Second, he must show that the conduct complained of was so closely connected with the job functions of the employee at the material time that it is fair and just to hold the employer vicariously liable.

The Court of Appeal of England and Wales have held that where it can be said that the tortious act is closely connected to the job function of the employee then it will normally be fair and just to impose liability on the employer [] (*Gravil v Redruth Rugby Football Club Ltd* [2008] IRLR 289; [2008] EWCA Civ 689).

The focus is on the nature of the employment, the duties of the employee and the act complained of. If, looking at the matter broadly, the act is closely connected with the employment and duties required then the employer will be held liable. The analysis by Lord Steyn of *Lloyd v Grace, Smith & Co* [1912] AC 716 in *Lister* provides a classic example of what is intended by the new language. In the *Grace, Smith* case, had the managing clerk rummaged through the bag of the client while she was sitting in the waiting room to see an attorney and stole the document to commit his tortious act then that would be a case of the job providing the opportunity to commit the tort. However, the firm held out the managing clerk as someone to whom the claimant could legitimately hand the documents which she did. Likewise in *Morris v C W Martin & Sons Ltd* [1966] 1 QB 716, the claimant handed the fur to a furrier who in turn handed over to the defendant for cleaning. The defendant's employee stole the fur. The defendant was has held liable because their employee got the fur in his capacity as an employee to clean the fur. He took it and stole it. The result would have been different if the employee had broken into the claimant's house and stole the fur.

. . .

Where the law stands the position is as follows: a defendant cannot escape liability by arguing that what was done by the employee was deliberate, intentional or even criminal. He has to show that what was done was not closely connected to the employee's job. On the other hand, the claimant cannot simply say, 'He is your employee. He injured me, so compensate me.' He must show that the tortious act was so closely connected to the job of the employee that it is fair and just to hold the employer liable.

Turning now [to] the facts of this case. In the view of this court there is a far more reasonable explanation than malice for what Mr Owen Bailey did. This is the absence of proper training of Mr Owen Bailey and Mr Lawrence for the task of cleaning the mixer as well as lack of implementation of proper safety procedures, on the day in question, that the company said that it had.

The evidence from Mr Charley was that two of the safety procedures for cleaning the mixer were (a) the isolator switches should be padlocked and (b) the key for the padlock should be in the pocket of the person cleaning the mixer. This meant that on the day in question the isolator switches should have been padlocked[;] Mr Lawrence should have the key in his pocket if the mixer was to be cleaned. None of this happened. In this context, Mr Owen Bailey was fiddling with the switch not because he was malicious but because he was negligent.

. . .

The isolator switch enables power to go [to] the on/off switches that turn on the mixer. Mr Charley said that [the] two isolator switches would both have to be turned on and then the on/off switch for the paddle of the mixer would have to be pressed in order for the paddle to move. The company, through Mr Charley and Mr Donovan Bailey, is endeavouring to say that Mr Owen Bailey must have turned on the two isolator switches and then pressed the on/off switch thereby activating the paddle and injuring Mr Lawrence. Mr Owen Bailey accepts that he pressed only one switch which was the on/off switch. This switch turned out to be the one that activated the paddles. This is why the company defended the claim on the basis that the act(s) causing injury to Mr Lawrence must have been deliberately done with malevolent intent and therefore it is not liable.

Mr Owen Bailey said that he pressed only one button and it was after he did this that the mixer was activated. When he heard Mr Lawrence exclaim he realised something had happened. On inquiring, he found Mr Lawrence severely injured. On Mr Owen Bailey's account, he did not turn on the isolator switch. It does not matter whether he did or did not switch on the isolator switch. What is clear is that he pressed the switch that actually activated the mixer.

Even accepting Mr Donovan Bailey's evidence that he turned off one or both isolator switches, Mr Owen Bailey's action of turning on one or both switches and then turning on the mixer was so closely connected with what he was assigned to do (assist Mr Lawrence to clean the mixer) that the deliberate nature of his conduct does not exonerate the company from liability.

When the company asked Mr Lawrence to clean the mixer and accepted the suggestion from Mr Owen Bailey that he would assist Mr Lawrence the risk of injury to Mr Lawrence was created if a negligent employee switched on the machine while Mr Lawrence was actually in the mixer. It was therefore incumbent on the company to put in place measures to eliminate or reduce that risk. The evidence is that the company had the measure but regrettably it was not fully implemented on that fateful day. The negligent conduct of Mr Owen Bailey was the switching on of the paddle while Mr Lawrence was cleaning the mixer.

From all that has been said the court concludes that the company is vicariously liable for the injuries to Mr Lawrence.

TORTS OF INTERFERENCE WITH USE AND ENJOYMENT OF PROPERTY

Nuisance

'A private nuisance may be defined as any activity or state of affairs causing a substantial and unreasonable interference with a claimant's land or his use or enjoyment of that land.'[17] There are three kinds of interest 'which nuisance law affords protection: the protection of land *per se*; the protection of the use of land; the protection of the enjoyment of the land. In each case, the damage must always be referable to the land, and not merely chattels which happen to be on the land'.[18]

Wilton Innis (Plaintiff) v Guyana Telephone & Telegraph Company Limited (Defendant) (2012) 1998 No. 392/W (GY)

Facts: The plaintiff who resides at 49 Melanie Damishana, East Coast Demerara claim damages in nuisance as a result of damage he says he suffered as a result of the operation of a generator which was operated by the defendant and which was located a few feet from his home. The defendant denied the plaintiff's claim and put him to strict proof of the damage claimed and stated that its generator was placed there to facilitate the provision of telephone service to the area. The defendant pleaded that it provided a telephone service to the community including the plaintiff in the Melanie Damishana area and that it had permission from the Local Democratic Council to locate its facility, an International Outside Plant Access Cabinet, on the Council's Property.

Held: George, J
Despite my finding that the major claims of the plaintiff have not been proven, I, however, do accept the plaintiff's evidence that he owns the premises where he lives and that in the period leading to the filing of this action the defendant's generator did emit noise (though there is no evidence of the level or degree of noise in the period leading up to and at the filing of this action) that there was smoke from the exhaust of the generator and that his curtains were dirtied often by the smoke. The plaintiff did not testify how, if at all, the noise affected him personally and I have given my findings that the plaintiff has not proven that the smoke affected him personally. The issue therefore is whether what the plaintiff has actually proven can amount to nuisance so as to make the defendant liable in damages.

. . .

This may be a case of private nuisance however, for as Prof Kodilinye has stated (p 193–194) 'the law of private nuisance has been designed to protect the individual or occupier of land from substantial interference with his enjoyment thereof.' . . .

> The main problem in the law of private nuisance is in striking [a] balance between the right of the defendant to use his land as he wishes as the right of the plaintiff to be protected from interference with his enjoyment of his land. In order to strike this balance, two main requirements have been developed: the injury of interference complained of will not be actionable unless it is (a) sensible (in the case of material damage to land); or (b) substantial (in the case

17 Murphy, *Street on Torts*, p 438.
18 Murphy, *Street on Torts*, p 438.

of interference with enjoyment of land); the defendant will not be held liable unless his conduct was unreasonable in the circumstances.

Sensible material damage

'Sensible material damage' means damage (a) which is not merely trifling or minimal; and (b) which causes a reduction in the value of the plaintiff's property.

. . .

Substantial interference with enjoyment of land

Where an action in nuisance is founded on interference with enjoyment of land, such as where a plaintiff complains of inconvenience, annoyance or discomfort caused by the defendant's conduct, the interference must be shown to be substantial. (Emphasis mine.)

. . .

In *Winfield & Jolowicz on Tort* by WVH Rogers . . . the learned author has this to say on the issue of damage:

> In the case of a private nuisance, however, although it is said that damage must be proved, the law will often presume it . . . This inference appears to apply to any nuisance where the damage is so likely to occur as to be superfluous to demand evidence that is has occurred. *The inference cannot be made if the discomfort is purely personal, for personal sensitivity to smells, smoke and the like varies considerably and it is only fair that evidence of substantial annoyance should be required.* (Emphasis mine.)

. . .

Another issue that is relevant in this case is the reasonableness of the defendant's conduct. Professor Kodilinye has this to say at pp 196–197 on this and the related issue of utility of the defendant's conduct.

> Reasonableness of the defendant's conduct: Whether the plaintiff claims in respect of injury to property or in respect of interference with enjoyment of land, the primary question in any action in private nuisance is: 'Was the defendant's activity reasonable according to the ordinary usages of mankind living . . . in a particular society?['] There are no precise criteria for determining this question; all depends upon the circumstances of the individual case. However, a number of factors have been taken into account in determining this issue . . .

The factors to which reference has just been made are identified by Professor Kodilinye as follows:

> (1) locality, (2) utility of the defendant's conduct, (3) the plaintiff's abnormal sensitivity, (4) the defendant's malice, and [(6)] the duration of the harm.

. . .

Mr. Trotman cited the Canadian case of *Suzuki v Munroe* 2009 BCSC 1403 (CanLII) where at para 36 Verhoeven J cited the Supreme Court of Canada decision of *St Lawrence Cement Inc v Barrette* 2008 SCC 64 (CanLII) at para 77 where it was stated as follows:

> At common law, nuisance is a field of liability that focuses on the harm suffered rather than on prohibited conduct. Nuisance is defined as unreasonable interference with the use of land. Whether the interference results from intentional, negligent or non-faulty conduct is of no consequence provided that the harm can be characterized as a nuisance. The interference must be intolerable to an ordinary person. This is assessed by considering factors such as the nature, severity and duration of the interference, the character of the neighbourhood, the sensitivity of the plaintiff's use and the utility of the activity. The interference must be substantial, which means that compensation will not be awarded for trivial annoyances.

In this case, the plaintiff lived in the community of Melanie Damishana. No description of the community was given e.g. whether it was residential, farming, industrial or mixed, though I gathered from the evidence that there were residences nearby . . . there is no evidence that the facility was unlawfully placed where it was located. Be that as it may, even it if had been proven that permission was sought from and granted by the local government authority, this would not mean as I said that the defendant would not be liable in nuisance once proven. Given my finding that based on the plaintiff's evidence he has proven that the generator did emit noise and that there was smoke from the exhaust of the generator which dirtied his curtains, the questions is – has the plaintiff proven that he suffered 'sensible material damage' or 'substantial annoyance'?

. . .

And in *Greenidge* (supra) while it was agreed that it was not a defence for the defendant to say that it had obtained permission to erect and operate its power generation facility, it was found by the court that permission to operate a facility did not exempt the company from proceedings in nuisance and that 'the law has always insisted that an owner of property cannot use his property unreasonably and it is an unreasonable use of property to cause substantial damage to another.' . . . Further . . .

> The law of nuisance does not allow as a defence that the place is a convenient or suitable one for committing the nuisance or that the business or operations causing the nuisance is useful to persons generally in spite of the annoyance to the plaintiff. It is likewise no defence to say that the best known means have been taken to reduce or prevent the nuisance complained of or that the cause of the nuisance is the exercise of a business or trade in a reasonable and proper manner. Moreover, the fact that an area is an industrial one does not rule out the possibility of an actionable nuisance on the ground of excessive noise.

In this case, the facility was used to provide telephone service to Melanie Damishana and the surrounding community. In the context of reasonableness of the defendant's conduct, there is no evidence to support a conclusion that by placing the facility in that particular location and by having an automatic generator to power it when there were power outages the defendant was acting unreasonably. This is not a case where the defendant was acting out of malice or spite, in which case nuisance would be actionable. And 'some consideration [can] be given to the fact that the offensive enterprise is essential and unavoidable in the particular locality, like a coal mine, quarry or some public utility or service['] . . . While this latter sentence would be relevant to this case as the telephone service provided by the defendant to the community may be considered essential, in appropriate cases, despite the necessity of the conduct, the fact that conduct associated with a defendant's enterprise is so offensive as to cause proven substantial damage then the nuisance would be actionable and liability would follow.

In this case, however, at the end of the day what the plaintiff has actually proven is very limited; no serious material or substantial damage or substantial annoyance has been proven and I am constrained to hold that the plaintiff's case has to be dismissed.

Rule in *Rylands v Fletcher*

The Rule in *Rylands v Fletcher* is an important example of a strict liability tort. Blackburn J famously stated:

> We think that the true rule of law is that the person who for his own purposes brings on his lands and collects and keeps there anything likely to do mischief if it escapes, must keep it in at his peril,

and if he does not do so, is *prima facie* answerable for all the damage which is the natural consequence of its escape.[19]

The House of Lords, in the same decision of *Rylands v Fletcher*, made it clear that the rule was confined to cases involving a non-natural use of land.[20] Things which have been held to be capable of giving rise to *Rylands v Fletcher* liability include electricity, explosives, fire and things likely to cause fire, water and sewage.[21] However, because of the strict liability nature of *Rylands v Fletcher*, there is growing reluctance by courts to apply it. Indeed, in the Australian case of *Burnie Port Authority v General Jones Pty Limited* (1994) 120 ALR 42, the High Court held that the principle of *Rylands v Fletcher* should be regarded as overtaken and replaced by the principles of liability in negligence.

In the case of *Transco Plc v Stockport Metropolitan Borough Council* [2004] 2 AC 1, the House of Lords confirmed that the rule in *Rylands v Fletcher* was a subset of nuisance and that it should be confined to circumstances where the occupier has brought some dangerous thing onto his land which poses an exceptionally high risk to neighbouring property should it escape, and which amounts to an extraordinary and unusual use of land.

Transco Plc v Stockport Metropolitan Borough Council [2004] 2 AC 1 (GB)

Facts: Brinnington Housing Estate forms part of the metropolitan borough of Stockport. The estate was built by the predecessor of the respondent, the Stockport Metropolitan Borough Council (the council) between 40 and 50 years ago and is the mixture of semi-detached houses and tower blocks characteristic of the urban planning of that time. The estate stands on a low escarpment from which the land slopes down westward to the Reddish Vale Country Park and eventually the River Tame. The estate and the country park are separated by the bed of a disused branch railway which used to run from Stockport town centre in the south to Denton in the north.

In 1966 the North Western Gas Board, pursuant to an agreement with the British Railways Board, laid a 16-inch high-pressure steel gas main beneath the surface of the old railway. The pipe now belongs to the appellant, which used to be called British Gas plc, then BG plc and is now Transco. At some time in the summer of 1992 a leak developed in a high-pressure pipe belonging to the council which supplied water to Hollow End Towers, an 11-storey tower block on the Brinnington Estate. Although the pipe was not part of the North West Water Authority's mains system, it was a good deal bigger than the kind of pipe which would normally lead from the mains to a single dwelling. This was because it had to supply the large tanks in the basement of Hollow End Towers from which the water was pumped to tanks on the roof which supplied all 66 flats in the block. The pipe was made of asbestos cement and had an internal diameter of three inches, giving it a capacity 16 times greater than the 3.25-inch pipe in common domestic use. It is not clear why the pipe fractured but the judge found that it was probably the result of the subsidence of tipped material in a landfill site under part of the tower, which was itself supported on piles.

The leak was first discovered on 24 September 1992, when the well of the lift shaft at Hollow End Towers was found to be flooded. The fracture was found and quickly repaired. But later events showed that water must have been escaping from some time in considerable

19 (1866) LR 1 Exch 265, at 279–80.
20 (1866) LR 1 Exch 265, at 338–40.
21 Murphy, *Street on Torts*, p 489.

quantities, because two days after the leak had been found, water was seen bubbling up near the old railway below the tower. The old landfill site below the tower, which had been soaking up water like a sponge, was now saturated. The water ran along the tightly packed surface of the footpath along the railway bed and then, where the path was carried upon an embankment, spilled down the sides. On 28 September 1992 a section of embankment, sodden with water, gave way and spilled over the golf course sited on the edge of the country park. A 27-metre section of Transco's gas pipe line was left unsupported and exposed. The possibility of a fracture in the unsupported gas pipe was obviously hazardous and Transco quickly took steps to repair the damage. The cost of the works required to restore support and cover the pipe was £93,681. Transco sued the council to recover the cost of repair. Transco's main claim was that the council was liable without proof of negligence under the rule in *Rylands v Fletcher* (1868) LR 3 HL 330.

Held: Lord Bingham
The rule in *Rylands v Fletcher* is a sub-species of nuisance, which is itself a tort based on the interference by one occupier of land with the right in or enjoyment of land by another occupier of land as such.

Held: Lord Hobhouse
I consider that the rule in *Rylands v Fletcher* should not be abrogated. The rationale for it was and remains valid. The content of the rule has been clearly spelled out by Blackburn J and the relevant constituent elements can be easily stated as I have done in para 54 above. The academic and judicial criticisms of the rule are largely the result of later confusions. The rule itself and the laws of private nuisance already in existence in the mid-nineteenth century and still in existence today provide appropriate defences or, to adopt the current jargon, sufficient control mechanisms. In the decision of disputes there are always bound to be cases which fall just on one side of the line or the other.

The present case is no exception. The source of the leakage was a water pipe large enough to supply the defendants' flats. The accumulation of ground water arose because of unforeseen and undetected leakage over a period of time; the leakage was fortuitous. The case cannot be brought within the principle of shared benefit or implied consent nor was any act of God or *vis major* involved. But the necessity remains that the plaintiffs must show that the defendants brought onto their land something dangerous which involved a risk of damaging the plaintiffs' property. Stored water might constitute such a danger as could a high-pressure water main laid under a city street: *Charing Cross Electricity Supply Co v Hydraulic Power Co* [1914] 3 KB 772. But the present is not such a case. The water pipe which the defendants laid to supply the flats was not such a danger; it falls on the wrong side of the line. The plaintiffs' claim rightly failed.

Williams v Murraine (1987) 40 WIR 160 (MS)

Facts: The appellant, Leslie Williams, was a commercial bee-keeper who had in a state of reclamation or captivity 20 hives of bees on his land at Harris in Montserrat, which land was comprised of one and a half acres. The respondent, Gabriel Murraine, farmed a small portion of land adjacent to that where the appellant had his bees hived some 50 yards away on the hillside. Up to 31 May 1986 the respondent had farmed his piece of land on a regular basis for a period of two years, and there was no complaint about his being stung by the appellant's bees. Indeed when the respondent commenced working his land, the appellant already had his bees on his one and a half acres of land.

On 31 May 1986, while the respondent was working on his piece of land, he was stung in four places by bees. There was no contest that the bees belonged to the appellant. The contention put forward by the appellant was that the respondent swatted the bees while they were foraging, despite being warned by the appellant not to do so and being told that the bees would not sting him unless they were molested. It was while he was nonetheless so engaged in swatting the bees from the flowers, that he was stung. The appellant also stated in his evidence that he had imported from the USA a queen bee, and because of the presence of the queen bee on the land, wild bees were also attracted thereto.

Held: Robotham, CJ
Can he succeed under the rule in *Rylands v Fletcher* as the magistrate found? I think not. The rule in *Rylands v Fletcher* can only be invoked if the defendant is making a non-natural use of the land, as Lord Moulton said in *Rickards v Lothian* [1913] AC 263 at page 280: 'It is not every use to which land is put that brings into play that principle in *Rylands v Fletcher*. It must be some special use bringing with it increased danger to others and must not merely be the ordinary use of land or such a use as is proper for the general benefit of the community.' I do not consider (as I have already indicated) that the appellant here was making a non-natural use of the land. A further application of the rule shows that there must be some escape of the dangerous thing from the place in which it was confined. The magistrate found that bees were not dangerous creatures. This finding alone would take this case out of the application of the rule. In any event bees by their nature forage for miles so it cannot be said they 'escaped' on to the respondent's land. I am of the view that the magistrate erred in coming to the conclusion which he did. I would allow the appeal and enter judgment for the appellant defendant with no order as to costs.

Andre Alexander (Claimant) v St Lucia Golf Resort & Country Club Limited (Defendant) (2011) SLUHCV2007/0715 (LC)

Facts: This is a claim for damages in nuisance and negligence as well as personal injury brought by the claimant against the defendant alleging that the defendant by itself its servants and/or agents wrongfully caused or permitted 'grey water' used to sprinkle its golf course to enter the defendant's land/premises situate adjacent to the defendant's property thereby interfering with and considerably diminishing his enjoyment of his property on which he had built his home by the droplets of water entering upon his property and the odour emerging from the sprinkler system when it is turned on.

Held: Georges, J
Regarding the alleged liability in nuisance the burden of proving loss rests on the claimant to prove that the defendant's use of 'grey water' to irrigate its golf course was unreasonable and interfered with his use and enjoyment of his land. This is a question of fact and critical to the issue of private nuisance is the question whether the damage done was foreseeable. It is now well established beyond any doubt that there cannot be liability in nuisance unless the harm was reasonably foreseeable.

As stated in the headnote of the Privy Council decision in *Overseas Tankship (UK) Ltd. v Miller Steamship Co. Pty.*:

> Foreseeability of the injury is a necessary element in the measure of damages recoverable in cases of nuisance and it is not sufficient that the injury suffered was the direct result of the nuisance if that injury was in the relevant sense unforeseeable.

With regard to liability under the rule in *Rylands v Fletcher* in order to succeed the claimant must show that the defendant's activities constituted a 'non-natural' use[] of land and the claimant's burden would clearly be less if the defendant's use of his land is inherently unreasonable. Fault in *Rylands v Fletcher* is assessed therefore having regard to reasonable use[] and remoteness considerations. Thus in *Cambridge Water v Eastern Counties Leather* it was held that the concept of 'non-natural use[]' was a valid one and whilst what the defendants were engaged in constituted a non-natural use nevertheless the same test for remoteness as applied in negligence also applied to the rule and as a result the loss suffered by the claimant was not of a type foreseeable by the defendants and the damage was therefore too remote.

As regards the law in respect of the recovery of damages under the rule in *Rylands v Fletcher* this has been clarified and settled by the dictum of Lord Goff in *Cambridge Waters v Eastern Counties Leather* supra 'that knowledge or foreseeabilty of damage of the relevant type is a prerequisite for the recovery of damages'.

As stated at the foot of paragraph 38 a defendant is not liable in negligence nuisance or under the rule in *Rylands v Fletcher* for a particular kind of loss, damage or injury suffered by a claimant as a result of the defendant's act or omission if a reasonable man who possessed the defendant's knowledge would not have foreseen a substantial degree of probability – as distinct from a bare or remote possibility – that the particular loss damage or injury or risk thereof would be a consequence of his act or omission.

On the basis of the legal principles enunciated and the case authorities referred to I hold on the facts found that on a balance of probability the defendant is not liable to the claimant for loss or damage or personal injury in negligence nuisance or under the rule in *Rylands v Fletcher.*

Escape of the thing likely to cause mischief will not attract liability when such escape is caused by the act of a stranger.

Mandraj and Mandraj v Texaco Trinidad Inc (1969) 15 WIR 251 (TT)

Facts: The appellants were the registered proprietors and tenants respectively of certain contiguous parcels of land comprising approximately 31.5 acres situated near Rajoo Trace, Penal, of which 30 acres were planted in pasture grass and about 1.5 acres cultivated in rice. The respondent company owned and operated, *inter alia*, a trunk oil pipeline passing through the Penal area and which at about a quarter of a mile from the appellants' land traversed a small watercourse called the Sakal Channel, which subsequently becomes known as the Guanapo Channel, situated in close proximity to the said parcels of land.

On 23 September 1963 an oil leak occurred in the said trunk pipeline at the point at which it crosses the Sakal Channel, with the result that a considerable quantity of oil was carried along by the watercourse (which was at that time apparently in flood) and deposited over much of the appellants' pasture and rice cultivation, causing damage not only to the growing crops but also to cattle grazing in the pasture. It was found by the Board that this escape of oil was promptly and effectively stopped by the respondent company's engineers, who affixed a substantial metal screw clamp (a model of which was produced to the court) over a hole in the pipeline which caused the leakage. Expert witnesses called by the respondent company maintained at the hearing that the nature of this hole was such as to show that it had been made by a deliberate act of drilling and was not due to any defect in the metal of which the pipe was manufactured. This opinion was accepted by the Board.

Held: De La Bastide, JA

It was conceded by counsel that the legal liability of the respondent company was *prima facie* governed by the rule in *Rylands v Fletcher* ((1868), LR 3 HL 330, 37 LJEx 161, 19 LT 220, 33 JP 70, affirming *Fletcher v Rylands* (1866), LR 1 Exch 265, 2 Digest (Repl) 313, 164), in which the House of Lords affirmed the decision of the Court of Exchequer Chamber, speaking for whom Blackburn J, formulated the rule as follows ((1866), LR 1 Exch at p 279):

> The question of law therefore arises, What is the obligation which the law casts on a person who, like the defendants, lawfully brings on his land something which, though harmless while it remains there, will naturally do mischief if it escapes out of his land? It is agreed on all hands that he must take care to keep in that which he has brought on the land and keeps there, in order that it may not escape and damage his neighbours: but the question arises whether the duty which the law casts upon him under such circumstances is an absolute duty to keep it at his peril or is, as the majority of the Court of Exchequer have thought, merely a duty to take all reasonable and prudent precautions in order to keep it in, but no more . . . We think that the true rule of law is that the person who for his own purposes brings on his lands and collects and keeps there anything likely to do mischief if it escapes, must keep it in at his peril, and if he does not do so is prima facie answerable for all the damage which is the natural consequence of its escape. He can excuse himself by showing that the escape was owing to the plaintiff's default; or, perhaps, that the escape was the consequence of *vis major* or the act of God; but as nothing of the sort exists here, it is unnecessary to inquire what excuse would be sufficient.

It has long been recognised that the deliberate act of a stranger ousts the application of the rule in *Rylands v Fletcher* . . . In my judgment, the Board's findings were such as to justify their conclusion that the present case fell within this exception to the rule in *Rylands v Fletcher.*

ENGAGING IN UNFAIR TORTIOUS BUSINESS PRACTICES

Passing off

Lord Diplock, in the landmark decision of *Erven Warnink BV v J Townend & Sons (Hull) Ltd.* [1979] 2 All ER 927 (GB), identified five elements that must be present to create a valid cause of action for passing off, namely, (1) a misrepresentation (2) made by a trader in the course of trade, (3) to prospective customers of his or ultimate customers of goods or services supplied by him, (4) which is calculated to injure the business or goodwill of another trader (in a sense that this is a reasonably foreseeable consequence) and (5) which causes actual damage to a business or goodwill of the trader by whom the action is brought or (in a *quia timet* action) will probably do so. Simply put, the tort of passing off protects commercial undertakings against misrepresentations aimed at their customers which are calculated to damage their business or goodwill.

Similar products/business

There are two main forms of passing off. The first type deals with competitors engaged in a common field of activity and the plaintiff has alleged that the defendant has named, packaged or described its product or business in a manner likely to lead the public to believe the defendant's product or business is that of the plaintiff.

Kay Mart Ltd., Steve Khemlani and Raju Khemlani v K-Mart Corporation (Plaintiff/Respondent) CA No. 85 of 1997 (JM)

Facts: The allegations were that the appellants operated a general merchandising business at a five-storey retail store styled as 'KMART' located within the Manor Centre Shopping Centre at 195 Constant Spring Road in the parish of St Andrew. That commencing on or about November 1994 the appellants passed off and attempted to pass off the appellants' business as being the business of the respondent and infringed the respondent's trademark.

Held: Forte, JA
One of the questions which call[s] for decision in this appeal is whether a corporation which carries on no business in Jamaica, but has developed a reputation and goodwill in Jamaica, can successfully bring an action for passing off against another party who has invaded its right of property in that reputation and goodwill, by misrepresentations made in passing off the goods or business of that party as that of the corporation . . .

The practicality of the heavy traffic of persons moving between the United States of America and Jamaica and the consequent familiarity and knowledge of the respondent's business will be as relevant to this case as it appears to have been in the *McDonald* case (*supra*). There is an abundance of evidence in the affidavits of both parties which speak to the factual issues such as those described in the judgment of Rattray J (*supra*). In the event that on an analysis of the law and the facts, the trial judge determines that in Jamaica the softer approach, apparently preferred by the more recent cases, is correct, then there will of course be a requirement to determine also, based on the evidence, whether in spite of the fact that the respondent has no business in Jamaica, it nevertheless enjoys goodwill and reputation in Jamaica to which the appellants' actions have caused damage. For those reasons we would conclude that in respect of the claim of passing off, there is a serious question to be tried and that the respondent has a real chance of success in his claim for a permanent injunction . . .

In so far as the balance of convenience is concerned, the fact that the respondent is the proprietor of the trade mark must also be a matter to be considered in determining the balance of convenience (see the *McDonald* case (*supra*) at pg 9) and were the issues in this appeal only related to the infringement of the trademark, we would nevertheless find that the learned judge was correct in ordering the interlocutory injunction.

Passing off with respect to similar products may occur even where names are distinctly different in circumstances where the packaging is the mechanism used to generate the misrepresentation.

Colgate-Palmolive Limited and Another v K.F. Pattron [1978] RPC 635 PC (TT)

Facts: The plaintiffs sold and distributed 'Colgate' toothpaste in Trinidad and Tobago. 'Colgate' toothpaste had been sold in Trinidad for some 35 years and prior to the commencement of these proceedings, had commanded three-quarters of the local toothpaste market. It was sold in two forms, 'ordinary' and 'with fluoride' in packaging . . . the predominant colours of which were red, white and dark blue. The plaintiffs were the proprietors of two trademarks, one consisting of the word COLGATE and the other consisting of a label containing the word COLGATE printed in a distinctive white script on a bright red background. The defendant, a manufacturer of various toilet products in Trinidad, began to sell toothpaste under the name TRINGATE in packaging coloured red, white and blue . . . The plaintiff commenced proceedings for infringement of the trademarks and for passing off.

Held: Lord Edmund-Davies
That the Court of Appeal paid due regard to the reasons given by D Malone, J for dismissing the plaintiffs' claim is beyond doubt – indeed, the learned Chief Justice, in particular, subjected it to a close analysis. Nevertheless, all three members concluded that the appeal must be allowed. It is not, their Lordships think, necessary to consider in detail the reasons which led to this unanimous conclusion, and it should suffice to select some typical passages from the judgments: Hyatali, CJ, after considering defence submissions regarding differences between the 'get-up' of the plaintiffs' and the defendant's goods, continued:

> I am not however impressed with the significance of, or the conclusion drawn from these differences, and for two reasons. Firstly, because it is clear to me from the evidence and my examination of all the packages that what the [defendant] really did was to borrow features from the packages, tubes and label of the [plaintiffs], and to knit them together, as it were, into the name and label which he used as a trade mark; and secondly, because the ordinary purchaser of ordinary memory purchasing with ordinary caution could not be expected to make the close and careful side by side examination of the two products which the learned judge obviously made to identify and highlight the differences which he enumerated . . . The court must in the end trust to its own perception into the mind of the reasonable man. This is in accordance with the dictum of Lord Parker of Waddington in *Spalding v Gamage* (1915) 32 RPC 273 at 286.

Approaching the matter in this way, on the body of undisputed evidence – oral, documentary, and 'real' (in the shape of the toothpaste cartons and tubes) – which had to be evaluated, it is in their Lordships' judgment impossible to hold that the Court of Appeal were disentitled to arrive at the conclusions they did. On the contrary, these were, in the words of Viscount Simonds in *Benmax v Austin* (*ante*, at p 373), 'inferences from facts specifically found', and the process of 'perception and evaluation' of which he spoke was conducted by the Court of Appeal in relation to a body of evidence which abundantly supported those conclusions. Indeed, had this appeal come direct to this Board from the learned trial judge, their Lordships would have formed exactly the same view. They will accordingly dismiss the appeal.

Different products

The second type of passing off is where it is alleged that a person has promoted his product or business in such a way as to create the false impression that his product or business is in some way approved, authorised or endorsed by another or that there is some business connection between the person promoting the product and the person with whom a business connection is being made. By these means a person may hope to 'cash in' on the goodwill of another. This type of passing off may occur by using a similar name or design for a distinctly different product.

Walt Disney Productions v Fantasyland Hotel Inc. [1996] 6 WWR 403 (CA)

Facts: The company operated a number of theme parks worldwide, each containing an attraction known as 'Fantasyland'. The company sued a company related to the mall owners to enjoin them from using the name 'Fantasyland' for a hotel on the same property as the amusement park.

Held: Belzil, Bracco and Picard, JJA
The court in *Greystone* accepted a statement from the *National Hockey League* case, at p 401:

> Passing-off cases fall into two broad categories. In the first are those where competitors are engaged in a common field of activity and the plaintiff has alleged that the defendant has named, packaged or described its product or business in a manner likely to lead the public to believe the defendant's product or business is that of the plaintiff . . . The second, and nowadays perhaps more common type of passing-off, is where it is alleged that a defendant has promoted his product or business in such a way as to create the false impression that his product or business is in some way approved, authorized or endorsed by the plaintiff or that there is some business connection between the defendant and the plaintiff. By these means a defendant may hope to 'cash in' on the goodwill of the plaintiff.

The appellant says this case is of the second type because the respondent in using the name Fantasyland for its hotel, is creating the false impression that it is authorised or connected with the appellant, in other words, the respondent is 'cashing in' on the appellant's goodwill. The appellant's theory of the law of passing off contains a fatal weakness. Even the 'more common type of passing off' referred to requires proof of the essentials of goodwill; misrepresentation or confusion, which the trial judge found, as a fact, did not exist in this case. In other words, the allegation or even the belief that the respondent is benefiting from the use of the name Fantasyland is not enough to found the tort of passing off.

The British Columbia cases cited do not support a modification in the requirements for the tort of passing off. Furthermore, the appellant's claim for the protection of its right breaks down when it depends merely on the common location and ownership of two business enterprises in which it has no goodwill. It has no goodwill in an amusement park not named Fantasyland and it has not challenged the finding of fact that it does not have goodwill in the name Fantasyland used for a hotel or at large . . . The appellant has not proven that it is entitled to an injunction restraining the respondent from naming a hotel attached to West Edmonton Mall, the Fantasyland Hotel.

Robyn Rihanna Fenty, Roraj Trade LLC, Combermere Entertainment Properties, LLC Claimants/Respondents v Arcadia Group Brands Limited Topshop/Topman Limited Defendants/Appellants [2015] EWCA Civ 3 (GB)

Facts: These proceedings concern a complaint by Rihanna, the world famous pop star, about the sale of fashion garments bearing her image. The appellants (collectively 'Topshop') own and operate the well known Topshop retail fashion stores. In 2012 Topshop began to sell in its stores and through its website a fashion t-shirt displaying a clearly recognisable image of Rihanna. The image was derived from a photograph of Rihanna which was taken when she was on a video shoot for a single from her 'Talk That Talk' album. Rihanna is looking directly at the camera with her hair tied above her head with a headscarf. It is, as the judge thought, a striking image and similar images had been used by Rihanna in connection with the Talk That Talk album. This particular photograph was, however, taken by an independent third party photographer. He, as owner of the copyright in the photograph, licensed the use of the image to Topshop.

Rihanna (and two of her corporate licensing vehicles) thereupon issued these proceedings and alleged that, whatever may have been the position in relation to the copyright in the photograph, the use of her image in relation to fashion clothing was not licensed and that a substantial number of people buying the t-shirt would think that she had endorsed it when, in fact, it was not connected with her at all. Rihanna contended that Topshop's activities therefore amounted to passing off. Topshop responded that Rihanna had not asserted that this particular image or any features of it had become distinctive of her or her clothing and that she was, by these proceedings, claiming an image right, that is to say a right to control the licensing of her name and likeness, and that no such right is recognised in English law.

The judge accepted that the mere sale by a trader of a t-shirt bearing an image of a famous person does not, in and of itself, amount to passing off. But he found the sale by Topshop of this t-shirt was, in the particular circumstances of this case, likely to lead people to buy it in the belief that it was a t-shirt which Rihanna had approved or authorised, and that this had caused her damage. He found that Topshop's activities therefore amounted to passing off and he granted an injunction prohibiting Topshop from dealing in it any further without clearly informing prospective purchasers that it had not been so approved or authorised. It is against that decision and order that Topshop now appeals.

Held: Kitchin, LJ
A celebrity seeking to control the use of his or her image must therefore rely upon some other cause of action such as breach of contract, breach of confidence, infringement of copyright or, as in this case, passing off. However, as Mr Hobbs has properly reminded us, the law of passing off is not designed to protect a person against fair competition. Nor does it protect a person against the sale by others of the same goods or even copied goods. What it protects is goodwill and it prevents one person passing off his goods or services as those of another. As Lord Oliver of Aylmerton explained in *Reckitt & Colman Products Ltd v Borden Inc & Ors* [1990] RPC 341 at page 406, a claimant must establish three elements in order to succeed in such a claim. First, he must establish a goodwill or reputation attached to the goods or services which he supplies in the mind of the purchasing public by association with the particular name or get up under which the goods or services are offered to the public, such that the name or get up is recognised by the public as distinctive of the claimant's goods or services. Second, he must demonstrate a misrepresentation by the defendant to the public leading or likely to lead the public to believe that the goods or services offered by him are the goods or services of the claimant. Third, he must demonstrate that he suffers or, in a *quia timet* action that he is likely to suffer, damage by reason of the erroneous belief engendered by the defendant's misrepresentation that the source of the defendant's goods or services is the same as the source of those offered by the claimant.

It is of course inherent in these propositions that, registered trade marks aside, no-one can claim monopoly rights in a word or a name. Conversely, however, no-one may, by the use of any word or name, or in any other way, represent his goods or services as being the goods or services of another person and so cause that other person injury to his goodwill and so damage him in his business. Further, it is enough that the goods or services are represented as being in some way connected or associated with that other person provided that the connection is a material one in the sense that it has caused or is likely to cause him such damage in his business.

It is not necessary for the purposes of these proceedings to attempt to define all of the circumstances in which the law of passing off law may be invoked to prevent the unauthorised use of a name or likeness of a famous real or fictitious person, for here Rihanna contended that she had a reputation and goodwill in connection with her business activities and further, that the use of her image on the t-shirt amounted to a misrepresentation and was likely to deceive members of the public into believing it was approved of and authorised by her and so, in short, that she was happy to be associated with it and had endorsed it. Put another way, it was her case that the misrepresentation that she was associated with the t-shirt made it more attractive and so played a material part in the decision of the public to buy it.

In my judgment this allegation did disclose a sustainable case in passing off. In substance Rihanna alleged that she had suffered damage to the goodwill in her business as a result of the misrepresentation, implied in all the circumstances, that she had endorsed the t-shirt. In the *Irvine* case Laddie J proceeded to consider the development of this area of the law before summarising the position in these terms:

> 38. In my view these cases illustrate that the law of passing off now is of greater width than as applied by Wynn-Parry J in *McCulloch v Lewis A May (Produce Distributors) Ltd* [1947] 2 All ER 845. If someone acquires a valuable reputation or goodwill, the law of passing off will protect it from unlicensed use by other parties. Such use will frequently be damaging in the direct sense that it will involve selling inferior goods or services under the guise that they are from the claimant. But the action is not restricted to protecting against that sort of damage. The law will vindicate the claimant's exclusive right to the reputation or goodwill. It will not allow others to so use goodwill as to reduce, blur or diminish its exclusivity. It follows that it is not necessary to show that the claimant and the defendant share a common field of activity or that sales of products or services will be diminished either substantially or directly, at least in the short term. Of course there is still a need to demonstrate a misrepresentation because it is that misrepresentation which enables the defendant to make use or take advantage of the claimant's reputation. 39. Not only has the law of passing off expanded over the years, but the commercial environment in which it operates is in a constant state of flux. Even without the evidence given at the trial in this action, the court can take judicial notice of the fact that it is common for famous people to exploit their names and images by way of endorsement. They do it not only in their own field of expertise but, depending on the extent of their fame or notoriety, wider afield also. It is common knowledge that for many sportsmen, for example, income received from endorsing a variety of products and services represents a very substantial part of their total income. The reason large sums are paid for endorsement is because, no matter how irrational it may seem to a lawyer, those in business have reason to believe that the lustre of a famous personality, if attached to their goods or services, will enhance the attractiveness of those goods or services to their target market. In this respect, the endorsee is taking the benefit of the attractive force which is the reputation or goodwill of the famous person.

After emphasising that character merchandising cases which do not involve any endorsement may raise rather different issues, Laddie J continued:

> 46. It follows from the views expressed above that there is nothing which prevents an action for passing off succeeding in a false endorsement case. However, to succeed, the burden on the claimant includes a need to prove at least two, interrelated facts. First, that at the time of the acts complained of he had a significant reputation or goodwill. Second, that the actions of the defendant gave rise to a false message which would be understood by a not insignificant section of his market that his goods have been endorsed, recommended or approved of by the claimant. I shall turn to those two issues.

In the present case I am entirely satisfied that the judge did have proper regard to the distinction between endorsement and general character merchandising. He began his analysis of the law by reminding himself that to make good any claim in passing off it must be established that the claimant has a goodwill, that the defendant has committed a misrepresentation and that the claimant has, as a result, suffered damage. He then referred to the decision of Laddie J in *Irvine* and acknowledged that it is not a necessary feature of merchandising that members of the public will think that the products in issue are in any sense endorsed by the celebrity or creator of the character in issue. He continued that it must be shown that the claimant has a relevant goodwill and that the impugned activity involves a false representation that there is a connection between the claimant and the goods in issue of a relevant kind, that is to say that the claimant is materially responsible for their quality.

Finally, of course, the belief which this false representation engenders in the minds of the purchasers must play a part in their decision to buy.

The judge found on the evidence, as I believe he was entitled to, that the image itself is striking because it is oversized and shows Rihanna's face and shoulders; that Rihanna is looking straight at the camera with her hair tied above her head in a head scarf, in other words that she is in a pose; and that similar images had been used for the recent Talk That Talk album and associated video. It seems to me that, having come this far, the judge was also entitled to go on and make the finding that he did at paragraph [69], namely that the relationship between this image and the images for the album and video would be noticed by her fans. Indeed the nature of the image may be thought to have made it very likely indeed that it would be taken to be an authorised publicity shot for what was then her recent musical release.

It follows that the judge was entitled to find that the sale by Topshop of the t-shirt amounted to passing off.

Locality-based action

It is not necessary that a plaintiff, in order to maintain a passing off action, has a place of business or a business presence in the country where the action is being brought; nor is it necessary that his goods be sold there. It is sufficient if his goods have a reputation in the country among persons there, whether residents or otherwise, of a sufficient degree to establish that there is a likelihood of deception among consumers and potential consumers and of damage to his reputation.

McDonald's Corporation v McDonald's Corporation Ltd and Another (1996) 55 WIR 226 (JM)

Facts: On 7 July 1996 Chester Orr J refused an application by the appellant (McDonald's Corporation) for an interlocutory injunction restraining the respondents (McDonald's Corporation Ltd and Vincent Chang) from 'using upon any sign, banner, advertisement or other article the name "McDonald's" or "McDonald's Corporation" or "McD" or any imitation thereof whether at the respondents' store at 1 Cargill Avenue, Kingston 10, in the parish of St Andrew or in connection with any other business, or from passing off or attempting to pass off any business carried on by the respondents or any of them as the business of the appellant or doing any act to infringe the appellant's trade mark', pending the hearing of the action filed by the appellant in this matter. In the same judgment the trial judge ordered on an application for an interlocutory injunction by the respondents that the appellant be restrained from opening a restaurant in the Corporate Area (as defined in the Kingston and St Andrew Corporation Act) trading under the name 'McDonald's' pending the hearing of the action filed.

The application for the interlocutory injunction arose out of a suit filed by the appellant against the respondents in which the appellant claimed that the respondents had since January 1995 passed off or attempted to pass off the respondents' business and restaurant at 1 Cargill Avenue, Kingston 10, as being the business of the appellant. Furthermore, it was claimed that the respondents had infringed the registered trade marks of the appellant by using a colourable imitation of the appellant's arched 'M' corporate logo on the respondents' sign displayed at 1 Cargill Avenue, Kingston 10. Consequently, the appellant asked the court for an injunction to restrain the respondents from:

(1) the doing of acts infringing the appellant's trade mark registered in Jamaica;
(2) passing off the business as that of the appellant;

(3) using the names 'McDonald's Corporation', 'McDonald's' or 'McD' in a false or misleading respect contrary to the provisions of the Fair Competition Act; and
(4) carrying on business at 1 Cargill Avenue or in any other restaurant under the names of 'McDonald's', 'McD' or 'McDonald's Corporation'.

Held: Rattray, P
There are in my view two issues of law which can be conveniently determined in these proceedings, and indeed it would be a negation of our appellate function if we did not determine them now. These issues are: (a) must the appellant have maintained a place of business in the jurisdiction before it can sustain a passing-off action? . . .

In respect of issue (a), in my view the law has moved in more recent times from a concept of goodwill and reputation being annexed to the carrying-on of the business in a specific location to an appreciation of the fact that in an age of satellite communication, television imagery, and easy communication and movement of persons between countries, goodwill and reputation can attach to a business, not only in its locality, but likewise in other countries if the relevant factors are established. Particularly, is this so in the Jamaican locality and specifically in relation to the USA a few hundred miles to our north where large numbers of Jamaicans reside who travel home to Jamaica from time to time. Furthermore, we are a country which is the beneficiary of a continuously expanding tourism industry fuelled with increasing frequency by large numbers of US residents. In practical terms, the many airline flights daily between Kingston and Miami, the constant traffic of Jamaicans on holiday and business to that US city (and vice versa) can almost be said to make each an extension of the other.

I prefer in our jurisdiction to move away from the decision of Pennycuick J in *Alain Bernardin & Cie v Pavilion Properties Ltd* [1967] RPC 581 (the *Crazy Horse* case) which wedded goodwill and reputation to the location of the business, to subsequent cases like *Baskin-Robbins Ice-Cream Co v Gutman* [1976] FSR 545, *Maxim's Ltd v Dye* [1978] 2 All ER 55 and *Pete Waterman Ltd v CBS (UK) Ltd* [1993] EMLR 107, which switched the focus away from location and concentrated on the question of the existence of goodwill and reputation which in every case is a question of fact . . . The law with respect to passing off essentially relates to the right possessed by a business which has established reputation and goodwill in a jurisdiction not to be exposed to the risk of injury by another business which adopts features so closely resembling that of the first business as to create the misrepresentation made by passing off one person's goods as the goods of another . . .

Bearing in mind my view of the trade marks of the appellant and the other factors in relation to the Montego Bay business which I have already enunciated, as well as, in relation to the Kingston business, the restaurant which was on the brink of opening when these proceedings came before the court, the trial judge was in error in granting the interlocutory injunction against the appellant's opening of the Kingston restaurant on the basis of a balance of convenience and a status quo which relied on the fact the business had not already opened but which failed to take into account the other relevant factors. In the circumstances, I would dismiss the appeal as it relates to the refusal by the trial judge of the appellant's application for an interlocutory injunction to restrain the respondents from continuing their business at 1 Cargill Avenue. I would, however, allow the appeal in respect of the grant by the trial judge of an injunction to the respondents to restrain the appellant from opening and carrying on its restaurant business in the Corporate Area.

The discerning consumer

There is now a growing attempt in certain circumstances to credit the modern consumer with a sense of discernment that would negate the impact of a person attempting to misrepresent his product as that of another. Passing off hinges on the likelihood of confusion on the part of an unwary consumer. The courts have indicated that the test is that of a casual consumer and not a careless consumer.

Dairy Distributors Ltd. v Nestle Trinidad and Tobago Limited [2005] HCA 528 of 2003 (TT)

Facts: It was not disputed that the plaintiff was incorporated in 1991 and introduced this pour and splash design in 1997. The plaintiff's only product was Dairy Dairy powdered milk of three types, full cream, low fat and skimmed. All these products were packaged in pillow packs. The defendant's parent company had been in business since 1868 and the defendant had been incorporated locally since 1914. The defendant dealt in liquid milk of various types, liquid milk products and powdered milk. All its liquid milk and liquid milk products were packaged in tetra paks. Its powdered milk brands were Svelty Calcium Plus, Klim 1–2–3 and Klim Full Cream. Svelty Calcium Plus was sold in cans alone. The label on Klim 1–2–3 had no splash of white liquid. Klim Full Cream was the only powdered milk product of the defendant which was sold in pillow packs as well as in cans. While this label had a pour of white liquid into a glass and ended in a splash, the rest of the label was deep yellow or mustard in colour. Further the word KLIM was in white and deep yellow against a rich brown background. On the plaintiff's pillow packs were the words 'Dairy Dairy' in large bold letters while the defendant's products carried its brand 'NESTLE' in white against a royal blue background. Further the defendant's brand name appeared in much smaller letters than the plaintiff's. An examination of the designs on the packaging of both parties revealed that the plaintiff's design was of a vertical pour of white liquid falling on to a flat surface resulting in a splash, while the defendant's design was of a slanted pour of white liquid into a tilted glass ending in a splash inside the glass, which is more than half filled. Further, the colour scheme of the plaintiff's packaging was in shades of blue and green while the defendant's Klim Full Cream package was in bright yellow.

Held: Tiwary-Reddy, J

In order to prove passing off the plaintiff must first establish that the particular get-up which he has been using has become associated exclusively with his business. Next the plaintiff must prove the likelihood of confusion by an unwary purchaser . . . In assessing the strength of each party's case I think it is highly unlikely that an unwary purchaser will confuse liquid milk with powdered milk especially where the liquid milk is in tetra paks and the powdered milk is in pillow packs. Further, there are major differences in the design and colour schemes of the packaging of the powdered milk products of both parties. It is to be noted that the test is of the casual shopper not of the careless shopper. In the circumstances, it appears that the plaintiff has an uphill task to prove the likelihood of confusion.

Conspiracy

This tort takes two forms. The first form is conspiracy to injure which occurs when several persons combine together with the aim of injuring the plaintiff, with resulting damage.[22]

22 Murphy, *Street on Torts*, p 402.

Lonrho Plc. v Fayed and Others [1991] 3 WLR 188 (GB)

Facts: The plaintiff in this action, Lonrho Plc., had been anxious to acquire control of House of Fraser since early 1981. Following a reference by the Secretary of State for Trade and Industry to the Monopolies and Mergers Commission (the MMC) under section 64 of the Fair Trading Act 1973 of the 'merger situation' arising from the proposed acquisition and a report of the MMC dated 9 December 1981, Lonrho gave an undertaking to the Secretary of State not to acquire more than 30 per cent of the equity share capital in House of Fraser. A further reference relating to the proposed acquisition by Lonrho was made to the MMC on 31 May 1984. The MMC's report on this reference was expected to be made not later than 28 February 1985. If this report were favourable to Lonrho, it was to be expected that the Secretary of State would release it from the undertaking and that Lonrho would be free to proceed to bid for control of House of Fraser.

The first three defendants in the action were brothers named Fayed. The Fayeds owned and controlled a company called House of Fraser Holdings Plc. (Holdings). In November 1984 Holdings acquired most of Lonrho's shares in House of Fraser and were intending to acquire a controlling interest. This gave rise to a new merger situation under section 64 of the Act of 1973. If the Secretary of State had referred this merger situation to the MMC, the Fayeds and Holdings would have been prevented from acquiring control of House of Fraser unless and until the MMC had made a favourable report on the reference. In the event no such reference was made.

On 3 March 1985 Holdings made a cash offer of 400p per share for the whole of the issued ordinary share capital of House of Fraser which was recommended to the shareholders by the board of directors of House of Fraser and was publicly announced on 4 March. By 11 March Holdings had acquired more than 50 per cent of the shares. Following a favourable report by the MMC on the May 1984 reference relating to Lonrho's proposed acquisition of House of Fraser, the Secretary of State, on 14 March 1985, released Lonrho from the undertaking given in December 1981.

Lonrho's pleaded case, in very short summary, was as follows. Lonrho at all material times intended to acquire control of House of Fraser. The Fayeds and Holdings induced the Secretary of State to abstain from referring their proposed acquisition of House of Fraser to the MMC by false and fraudulent representations about themselves, their commercial background and the source of the finance available to them for the acquisition of House of Fraser. If the Secretary of State had known the truth, he would have made a reference either before or after Holdings had acquired control. If the reference had been made before Holdings had acquired control, this would have left Lonrho, when released from its undertaking, in a position to bid for control of House of Fraser without competition from the Fayeds or Holdings. If the reference had been made after Holdings acquired control, this would probably have led to an order under the Act of 1973 requiring Holdings to divest itself of its controlling interest, which again Lonrho would have had the opportunity to acquire.

The fifth and sixth defendants to the action were Mr MacArthur, a director of Kleinwort Benson Ltd, and Kleinwort Benson Ltd, the merchant bankers who were advising the Fayeds and Holdings in connection with the take-over. Lonrho pleaded that some of the relevant false statements which induced the Secretary of State not to refer Holdings' proposed acquisition to the MMC were made by these defendants fraudulently, not in the sense that they knew of the falsity, but in the sense that they acted recklessly not caring whether the statements were true or false. As against all the defendants, Lonrho's statement of claim pleaded that their intention was both to benefit the Fayeds and Holdings by furthering their interest in the acquisition of House of Fraser and to injure Lonrho by preventing them from acquiring House of Fraser. Lonrho claimed to have lost the opportunity to acquire House of Fraser by bidding for the shares without competition from the Fayeds or Holdings and thereby to have suffered damage. Lonrho asserted that these facts were sufficient to establish a cause of action for the common law tort of interfering with business by unlawful means. But the statement of claim also relied additionally or alternatively on the same allegations of fact as establishing the tort of conspiracy to injure.

Held: Lord Bridge
In *Rookes v Barnard* [1964] AC 1129, 1204, Lord Devlin said: 'There are, as is well known, two sorts of conspiracies, the *Quinn v Leathem* [1901] AC 495 type which employs only lawful means but aims at an unlawful end, and the type which employs unlawful means.' . . . The civil tort of conspiracy to injure the plaintiff's commercial interests where that is the predominant purpose of the agreement between the defendants and of the acts done in execution of it which caused damage to the plaintiff, must I think be accepted by this House as too well established to be discarded however anomalous it may seem today . . . But in the many cases where plaintiffs have asserted a conspiracy to injure, but have been unable to prove that any unlawful means were used, judgments in the Court of Appeal and speeches in your Lordships' House emphasising the requirement of a predominant purpose to injure have repeatedly included *dicta* indicating that this requirement does not apply where the means used to effect the conspirator's purpose are unlawful . . . Where conspirators act with the predominant purpose of injuring the plaintiff and in fact inflict damage on him, but do nothing which would have been actionable if done by an individual acting alone, it is in the fact of their concerted action for that illegitimate purpose that the law, however anomalous it may now seem, finds a sufficient ground to condemn their action as illegal and tortious. But when conspirators intentionally injure the plaintiff and use unlawful means to do so, it is no defence for them to show that their primary purpose was to further or protect their own interests; it is sufficient to make their action tortious that the means used were unlawful . . .

It follows from this conclusion that Lonrho's acceptance that the pleaded intention on the part of the appellants to cause injury to Lonrho was not the predominant purpose of their alleged unlawful action is not necessarily fatal to the pleaded cause of action in conspiracy and therefore affords no separate ground for striking out that part of the pleading . . . I have reached the conclusion that it would be inappropriate to strike out the statement of claim and that the case must accordingly proceed to trial.

The second form of conspiracy is where the persons come together intending to use unlawful means as a mechanism for inflicting harm.

David Wong Ken and Others (Claimants) v National Investment Bank Jamaica Limited and Others (Defendants) [2012] JMSC Civ 32 (JM)

Facts: The allegations against each of the defendants claim will be better understood if the claimant's theory is explained. Messieurs David Wong Ken, Jack Koonce, Shirley Shakespeare and Robert Cartade came together to establish WCC [Western Cement Company Limited] which had as its objective the production of quicklime and ultimately, the manufacturing of cement. Quicklime is used in many industries including the bauxite/alumina and sugar industries.

There were three bauxite companies operating in Jamaica at the material time. These were: (a) Jamalco which operated at Halse Hall, Clarendon; (b) Alpart which operated at Naine in St. Elizabeth and (c) Alcan which operated at Ewarton, St. Catherine, and Kirkvine in Manchester. Of these three companies, Jamalco was the single largest user of quicklime. All three companies had their own quicklime producing capability but generally they never produced enough to meet their own demand. The quicklime producing factories at these plants were old and tended to breakdown frequently. The companies tended to be chronically short of quicklime and therefore imported the balance of their needs.

WCC's goal, as stated earlier, was to produce quicklime and cement. To this end, it bought land in Maggotty, St. Elizabeth. This land was the site of Revere Alumina Company which had long ceased operating at that location. After purchase, WCC invested heavily in equipment and other material to begin the production of quicklime. WCC obtained loans from a consortium of local banks to finance the project. In 1996, WCC decided that it needed to secure additional funding to complete the plant for production. It sought and obtained a loan from NIBJ. This was the first time WCC was borrowing from NIBJ. WCC made the application in September 1996 and by February 1997 the loan was approved and disbursement in the form of payments to third parties began. At the time WCC began its investment in this sector, the only other quicklime producer in Jamaica, other than the bauxite/alumina companies[,] was another company known as Chippenham Park. WCC took the view that Chippenham Park was not a serious rival.

When NIBJ made the loan to WCC, it did so by becoming an equity partner (preference shares) in WCC, that is to say, it became a shareholder. Under the terms of the first loan, NIBJ was entitled to appoint a director to the board of NIBJ. This option was not exercised until November 27, 1997, when WCC made a second loan application to NIBJ.

WCC is saying that the first application to NIBJ made two things possible. First, NIBJ was able to acquire critical confidential information about WCC because NIBJ as lender required WCC to submit information which contained its production and marketing strategy (see para. 27 of supplemental witness statement of David Wong Ken dated July 9, 2010). Second, NIBJ had direct and immediate access to the inner workings of WCC as they unfolded by virtue of NIBJ's appointed representative to WCC's board. NIBJ, through its director, would hear, first hand, the discussion of production and marketing strategies; participate in and actually be able to influence the decisions of WCC (see para. 34–37 of supplemental witness statement of David Wong Ken dated July 9, 2010). This circumstance, the theory goes, meant that NIBJ was in a fiduciary relationship with WCC and therefore ought to conduct itself in a manner that did not breach its fiduciary duties to WCC. The fiduciary duty [] said to be owed by NIBJ to WCC consisted of (a) not to have conflicting loyalties and (b) failing to bring to WCC's attention that the project was doomed to fail because it was based on an incorrect pricing strategy. NIBJ was said to be obliged to disclose (since it had that information) that WCC's project was not viable. This aspect of the fiduciary duty is said to have arisen from the moment NIBJ began the process of treating with WCC's first loan application. Added to this is the fact that by the time of WCC's first loan application NIBJ had already invested in CLCL [Clarendon Lime Company Limited] and held a directorship on CLCL's board. This meant that NIBJ now had conflicting loyalties to CLCL and WCC. These non-disclosures amounted to breaches of fiduciary duty.

The proposition has a knock-on effect. Since NIBJ was a public institution, the breach of fiduciary duty also amounted to the tort of misfeasance in public office because it occurred a in context where it was funding Mr Clarke's private investment in CLCL with public funds and did not ensure or find out or insist that Mr Clarke disclose his private interests to the Prime Minister and/or Cabinet of Jamaica, the Parliament or the people. The breach of fiduciary duty and the commission of the tort of misfeasance in public office were evidence of NIBJ's participation in a larger conspiracy to injure WCC in its business.

There were other developments which WCC says are relevant to its case theory. This relates to the non-disclosure of NIBJ's investment in CLCL. Even before WCC sought funding from NIBJ, NIBJ had also loaned money to CLCL, a rival of WCC. NIBJ made the loan to CLCL in an identical manner as that in relation to WCC – it took an equity position in CLCL. This it did in 1995, one year before WCC approached it for a loan. However, there was a qualitative difference between the two equity positions in the respective companies. It appears that NIBJ was an ordinary shareholder in CLCL whereas in WCC it was a preference shareholder with the right to a dividend rate of 26.5%. This meant that at no time was CLCL obliged to repay the money invested in it by NIBJ but WCC was under this obligation, albeit that the obligation was wrapped up in the preference shares. The commercial form of NIBJ's equity position was a disguise for giving Mr Clarke public funds which he would not be obliged to pay back in the event the project failed. In practical terms, the argument goes, Mr Clarke was getting public funds for free.

WCC made a second loan application to NIBJ in November 1997. It was approved in September 1998. WCC claims that this application was deliberately delayed by NIBJ in order to (a) facilitate CLCL taking active steps to secure its position in the quicklime market and (b) place a financial stranglehold on WCC in order to ensure its demise. The specific person accused of engineering this delay was Dr Lawrence. Thus when the second loan was eventually approved WCC was in such dire financial straits that not even the entrepreneurial genius, in combination or singly, of Mr. Gordon Stewart, Mr. George Soros, Mr. Carlos Slim, Mr. William Gates and the legendary Mr. Warren Buffet[t] could save it from collapse.

WCC alleges that Mr Clarke, while Minister of Agriculture and Mining (1995–1997), used his position to secure access to public funds from NIBJ, NDB [National Development Bank], CAP [Clarendon Alumina Production Limited] and JVF [Jamaica Venture Fund Limited] to further his private interest in Licojam [Limestone Corporation of Jamaica Limited] and CLCL at the expense of WCC. All these were said to be public sector entities except JVF which was a joint public/private sector company. It is further alleged that Dr. Vincent Lawrence used his position on the board of NIBJ to influence the delay in approving the second loan to WCC. It is also the theory that Dr. Lawrence used his influence over Jamalco's [JV between GoJ and Alcoa] board to persuade Jamalco to reject WCC as a potential long-term supplier of quicklime in favour of CLCL. These actions, WCC says, amount to misfeasance in public office on the part of NIBJ, Mr. Horace Clarke and Dr Vincent Lawrence. NIBJ committed the tort because it used public funds to further the private interest of Mr Clarke while delaying the second loan to WCC. Mr Clarke was concerned to develop his private economic interest at the expense of WCC while Dr Lawrence used his presence on the board of NIBJ and influence over Jamalco to ensure favourable outcomes for Mr Clarke.

As can be seen from this breathtaking picture outlined by the claimant, this is a conspiracy worthy of the pen of Robert Ludlum and John Le Carre, the great authors of spellbinding tales. Needless to say, to make good such allegations compelling evidence is required. These allegations are very serious and involve serious imputations on the integrity of all the defendants. It is now time to examine the law and the evidence in relation to each claim and defendant.

Held: Sykes, J

Mr Batts submitted that the conspiracy consisted of agreeing to build a lime plant to supply quicklime to the bauxite companies. This was said to be an agreement to do a lawful act (construct the quicklime plant) by unlawful means (misfeasance in public office and breach of fiduciary duty). The submission is that unlawful means were used. This conspiracy was said to have been formed in 1995. Since this court has concluded that NIBJ and Dr Lawrence did not commit the tort of misfeasance in public office then a conspiracy of the form alleged by WCC did not occur. However, in the event that the court is wrong on this it will consider the conspiracy allegation.

In the case of *Crofter Hand Woven Harris Tweed Company Ltd v Veitch and another* [1942] AC 435, the House of Lords held that in the civil tort of conspiracy to injure, the claimant must prove (a) the agreement; (b) the unlawful purpose and (c) damage. Unlike a criminal conspiracy, the tort requires more than just the agreement to effect an unlawful purpose because an agreement to injure, per se, does not cause harm. As Viscount Simons LC explained at pp 439–440:

> But the tort of conspiracy is constituted only if the agreed combination is carried into effect in a greater or less degree and damage to the plaintiff is thereby produced. It must be so, for, regarded as a civil wrong, conspiracy is one of those wrongs (like fraud or negligence) which sound in damage, and a mere agreement to injure, if it was never acted upon at all and never led to any result affecting the party complaining, could not produce damage to him.

As recently as 1991 the position was reaffirmed. In *Lonrho plc v Fayed and others* [1991] 3 All ER 303 Lord Bridge stated:

> . . . when conspirators intentionally injure the plaintiff and use unlawful means to do so, it is no defence for them to show that their primary purpose was to further or protect their own interests; it is sufficient to make their action tortious that the means used were unlawful.

From these cases, WCC must prove that acts done were in themselves unlawful where it is alleged that the conspiracy was to do a lawful act by unlawful means. The cases have also established that where unlawful means are used, if those means cause injury to claimant then it matters not whether there was a conspiracy. The reason is that no one has a right to use unlawful means to injure any one in their business. The evidence relied on to ground the conspiracy is the same as that used in the tort of misfeasance in public office and breach of fiduciary duty. From what has been said above this court has concluded that neither Dr Lawrence nor NIBJ was part of any conspiracy to injure WCC. In addition, there is no causal connection between the defendants' conduct and WCC's loss.

Deceit

In order to sustain an action of deceit, firstly, there must be proof of fraud, and nothing short of that will suffice. Secondly, fraud is proved when it is shown that a false representation has been made (1) knowingly, or (2) without belief in its truth, or (3) recklessly, carelessly, whether it be true or false. To prevent a false statement being fraudulent, there must always be an honest belief in its truth, for one who knowingly alleges that which is false obviously has no such honest belief. Third, if fraud be proved, the motive of the person guilty of it is immaterial. It does not matter that there was no intention to cheat or injure the person to whom the statement was made.

William Derry, J. C. Wakefield, M.M. Moore, J. Pethick, and S.J. Wilde v Sir Henry William Peek, Baronet (1889) LR 14 App Cas 337 HL (GB)

Facts: In February 1883 the appellants as directors of the company issued a prospectus containing the following paragraph:

> One great feature of this undertaking, to which considerable importance should be attached, is that, by the special Act of Parliament obtained, the company has the right to use steam or mechanical motive power, instead of horses, and it is fully expected that by means of this a considerable saving will result in the working expenses of the line as compared with other tramways worked by horses.

Soon after the issue of the prospectus the respondent, relying, as he alleged, upon the representations in this paragraph and believing that the company had an absolute right to use steam and other mechanical power, applied for and obtained shares in the company. The company proceeded to make tramways, but the Board of Trade refused to consent to the use of steam or mechanical power except on certain portions of the tramways. In the result the company was wound up, and the respondent in 1885 brought an action of deceit against the appellants claiming damages for the fraudulent misrepresentations of the defendants whereby the plaintiff was induced to take shares in the company. Appeal dismissed by the House of Lords.

Held: Lord Herschell
I think the authorities establish the following propositions: First, in order to sustain an action of deceit, there must be proof of fraud, and nothing short of that will suffice. Second, fraud is proved when it is shewn that a false representation has been made (1) knowingly, or (2) without belief in its truth, or (3) recklessly, careless [*sic*] whether it be true or false. Although I have treated the second and third as distinct cases, I think the third is but an instance of the second, for one who makes a statement under such circumstances can have no real belief in the truth of what he states. To prevent a false statement being fraudulent, there must, I think, always be an honest belief in its truth. And this probably covers the whole ground, for one who knowingly alleges that which is false, has obviously no such honest belief. Third, if fraud be proved, the motive of the person guilty of it is immaterial. It matters not that there was no intention to cheat or injure the person to whom the statement was made . . .

In my opinion making a false statement through want of care falls far short of, and is a very different thing from, fraud, and the same may be said of a false representation honestly believed though on insufficient grounds. Indeed Cotton LJ himself indicated, in the words I have already quoted, that he should not call it fraud. But the whole current of authorities, with which I have so long detained your Lordships, shews to my mind conclusively that fraud is essential to found an action of deceit, and that it cannot be maintained where the acts proved cannot properly be so termed . . . But for the reasons I have given I am unable to hold that anything less than fraud will render directors or any other persons liable to an action of deceit.

At the same time I desire to say distinctly that when a false statement has been made the questions whether there were reasonable grounds for believing it, and what were the means of knowledge in the possession of the person making it, are most weighty matters for consideration. The ground upon which an alleged belief was founded is a most important test of its reality. I can conceive many cases where the fact that an alleged belief was destitute of all reasonable foundation would suffice of itself to convince the Court that

> it was not really entertained, and that the representation was a fraudulent one. So, too, although means of knowledge are, as was pointed out by Lord Blackburn in *Brownlie v Campbell*, a very different thing from knowledge, if I thought that a person making a false statement had shut his eyes to the facts, or purposely abstained from inquiring into them, I should hold that honest belief was absent, and that he was just as fraudulent as if he had knowingly stated that which was false . . .
>
> The charge against the defendants is that they fraudulently represented that by the special Act of Parliament which the company had obtained they had a right to use steam or other mechanical power instead of horses. The test which I purpose employing is to inquire whether the defendants knowingly made a false statement in this respect, or whether, on the contrary, they honestly believed what they stated to be a true and fair representation of the facts . . . I agree with the Court below that the statement made did not accurately convey to the mind of a person reading it what the rights of the company were, but to judge whether it may nevertheless have been put forward without subjecting the defendants to the imputation of fraud, your Lordships must consider what were the circumstances . . . I conclude by saying that on the whole I have come to the conclusion that the statement, 'though in some respects inaccurate and not altogether free from imputation of carelessness, was a fair, honest and *bona fide* statement on the part of the defendants, and by no means exposes them to an action for deceit'.

In some cases, fraud (or more accurately, a fraudulent misrepresentation) is described as an element of the cause of action known as deceit; in other cases, the same elements are labelled collectively as the tort of fraudulent misrepresentation. Deceit and fraudulent misrepresentation have historically shared a close and interconnected relationship. In order for the deceit to be proved, very cogent evidence is required.

Althea Mitchell (Claimant) v Cheryl Stewart (Defendant) [2014] JMSC Civ 92 (JM)

Facts: The Claim brought by the Claimant at bar has its basis in fraud. In the particulars of fraud the Claimant pleads against the Defendant allegations of:

a) falsely taking the sum of US$9,000.00 from the Claimant and claimed to invest same for the Claimant;
b) falsely taking the sum of US$9,000.00 from the Claimant and refusing to return same despite the repeated requests of the Claimant;
c) taking the sum of US$9,000.00 from the Claimant and falsely pretending to invest same on behalf of the Claimant;
d) falsely pretending to be an investor when she was not so qualified or certified as an investor;
e) falsely claiming to be an investor and stating that her fee was two percent (2%) of the interest that would accrue on the investment of the Claimant's money;
f) fraudulently convincing the Claimant to give her the sum of US$9,000.00 when she fully well knew that she had no intention of returning it.

In answer to the above the Defendant refutes the allegations and denies the fraud. The Defendant avers that she was carrying out the instructions of the Claimant when she deposited the sums as described above into her Client account with Olint, an Investment Scheme and that since the deposit the said investment club fell into permanent delinquency thereby inflicting losses to its members.

Held: Morrison, J

The principle of law is that where fraud is intended to be charged it must be distinctly charged and its details specified. General allegations, however strong, are insufficient to amount to an averment of fraud of which any court ought to take notice: *Lawrence v Lord Norrey* (1890) 15 App Cas 221. However, a claim for fraud is really an action for deceit.

In *Derry v Peek* (1889) 14 App Cas 337, the directors of a tramway company issued a prospectus in which they stated that they had parliamentary powers to use steam in propelling their trams. In fact the grant of such powers was subject to the consent of the Board of Trade. The directors honestly but mistakenly believed the giving of this consent to be a merely formal matter; it was, however, refused. The company was wound up in consequence of the plaintiff who had bought shares in it on the faith of the prospectus, instituted an action for deceit against the directors.

The House of Lords, in reversing the decision of the Court of Appeal, gave judgment for the defendants, holding as it did that a false statement made carelessly and without reasonable ground for believing it to be true could not be fraud, though it may furnish evidence of it.

In the course of his judgment Lord Herschell delivered himself thus. 'First, in order to sustain an action on deceit, there must be proof of fraud, and nothing short of that will suffice. Secondly, fraud is proved when it is shown that a false representation has been made knowingly, or without belief in its truth, or (3) recklessly, careless[ly] whether it be true or false. To present a false statement being fraudulent, there must, I think, always be an honest belief in its truth.'

In *Bradford Building Society v Borders* [1941] 2 All ER 205, Lord Maugham set out five (5) criteria that a plaintiff must establish to prove an action for deceit:

a) there must be a representation of fact made by words or conduct;
b) the presentation must be made with the intention that it should be acted upon by the plaintiff, or by a class of persons which include the plaintiff, in the manner which resulted in damage to him;
c) it must be pro[v]ed that the plaintiff has acted upon the false statement;
d) it must be proved that the plaintiff suffered damage by so doing;
e) the presentation must be made with the knowledge that it is or may be false.

It must be willfully false, or at least made in the absence of any genuine belief that it is true.

In *Peek v Gurney* (1873) LR 6 HL 377 Lord Cairns said that there must be some active mis-statement of fact, or in all events, such a partial and fragmentary statement of fact, as that withholding of that which is not stated makes that which is stated absolutely false.

In the instant case, can it be said that the defendant made a false statement to the Claimant? The evidence adduced as adverted to earlier does not lend itself to an affirmative response. Even so, it has to be borne in mind that, though the standard of proof is on a balance of probabilities, in cases in which fraud is pleaded the authorities clearly indicate that what is required is very cogent evidence.

In *R (N) v Mental Health Review Tribunal (Northern Region)* [2005] EWCA Civ 1605 is a succinct statement of the application of the standard of proof[.] Although there is a single civil standard of proof on the balance of probabilities, it is flexible in its application. In particular, the more serious the allegation or [t]he more serious the consequences if the allegation is proved, the stronger must be the evidence before a court will find the allegation proved on the balance of probabilities. Thus the flexibility of the standard lies not in any adjustment to the degree of probability required for an allegation to be proved (such that a more serious allegation has to be proofed to a higher degree of probability), but in the strength or quality of the evidence that will in practice be required for an allegation to be proved on the balance of probabilities.

. . .

In distillation, what has to be considered, if relevant, are the inherent probabilities, in deciding where the where the truth lies. Accordingly, extreme and extra-ordinary allegations, such as asserting a conspiracy to pervert the course of Justice, involving attempts to murder and fraud, will not be taken seriously without cogent supporting evidence: *R (Sivasubramaniam) v Wandsworth County Court* [2003] 1 WLR 475. I now go on to apply the principles of law to the case at hand.

Where there is any conflict on the evidence between the parties I prefer the evidence of the Defendant to that of the Claimant mindful as I am that the halo of conscious virtue does not befit them both. Be that as it may I am to say that the impetus behind the Claimant's thrust to become a member of the *Olint* enterprise was opportune enrichment. She knew the risks associated with such a venture. Notwithstanding, she was not even daunted by the said risks or the fact that she could not on her own have attached membership to that dubious entity. Thus prepossessed, the Claimant was content to rely on the membership of the Defendant to that entity so as to be able to participate in the spoils of the venture. For the Claimant, her passion to gain entry into the venture[] made even haste seem slow.

Again, on principle, I am to say that I can find no cogent evidence that the Defendant falsely took and subsequently refused to return the sum of US$9,000.00 to the Claimant. I have come to this end on the basis that known to both parties, *Olint's* bank accounts were rendered inoperative by process of law shortly after the Claimant's manager's cheque was lodged therein the venture having been determined by the authorities to have been a bubble scheme. Surely, proof by assertion cannot be enough for the Claimant to say that she knows of persons similarly placed as the Defendant who were reimbursed by *Olint* up to 2008. Having regard to the standard and burden of proof much more was required.

I accept the evidence of the Defendant that she was not herself operating an investment scheme but was only trying to assist the Claimant to become a member of *Olint*.

Again, the standard and burden of proof that must be had to meet the allegation that the Defendant falsely pretended to be an investor, has failed to attain the mark and has in consequence not been discharged. For the reasons as have been advanced above judgment is entered in favour of the Defendant who is to have her costs agreed and if not then such costs are to be taxed.

Injurious/malicious falsehood

Injurious falsehood affords a remedy where the business or professional reputation of an individual is maliciously disparaged even though no aspersion is made against his personal character sufficient to give rise to a cause of action in defamation.

RBTT Merchant Bank Limited, RBTT Bank Limited, RBC Financial (Caribbean) Limited, (Claimants) v Reed Monza (Trinidad) Limited (In Receivership), James W. Sneddon Limited, Eugene Robert Gransaull (Defendants) (2012) CV2010–03699 (TT)

Facts: The essence of the Claimants' claim against the Defendants is that between June 2009 and June 2010 the latter published and/or threatened to publish defamatory material ('the publications') regarding the Claimants in Antigua, St. Lucia and Barbados. The Claimants alleged that the publications were likely to and/or calculated by the Defendants to damage their reputation and goodwill.

Held: Charles, J
In *Lonrho Plc. and Others v Fayed and Others (No. 5)* Dillon LJ held that a claimant in a civil action for conspiracy must prove actual pecuniary loss, though if he proves actual pecuniary loss the damages are at large, in the sense that they are not limited to a precise calculation of the amount of the actual pecuniary loss actually proved. Under this head, Counsel submitted that the Defendants circulated defamatory material throughout the Caribbean which questioned the integrity of their business operations and also accused them of dishonest practices. The evidence of the First and Third-named Defendants' conspiracy to defame the Claimants is contained in paragraph 18 of the Witness Statement of Darryl White, where he stated:

> This threat by the Defendants to continue its attack on the Claimants' reputation and business relationships with its competitors, clients and customers had the potential to negatively affect the Claimants' standing in the business community throughout the Caribbean region and in other jurisdictions in which the Claimants and their affiliates conducted business, thereby directly affecting the Claimants' ability to operate its business.

. . .

In *Ratcliffe v Evans*, Bowen LJ discussed the evidence to support such defamatory acts. He opined:

> . . . in an action for falsehood producing damage to a man's trade, which in its very nature is intended or reasonably likely to produce and which in the ordinary course of things does produce, a general loss of business, as distinct from loss of this and that known customer, evidence of that general decline of business is admissible.

The Claimants have not put forward actual evidence as that stated in *Ratcliffe v Evans* but Counsel asked the Court to consider the following in arriving at a determination:

i. The wide circulation of the adverse publications in the Caribbean through electronic media; and
ii. The prominence and considerable standing of the Claimants in the banking industry in the Caribbean in addition to the large clientele it hosts.

. . .

Again, I note that there has been no evidence on behalf of the Defendants and the Claimants have not proffered actual proof of damage. However, in *Exchange Telegraph Co. v Gregory*, a case which concerned inducement for breach of contract, the court held that where a breach occurs during the ordinary course of business, it must cause loss and it is unnecessary to demonstrate and prove particular items of loss as damages are at large. Lord Esher MR opined:

> To say that the damage must be such as can be measured – that you must show much how the wrongful act complained of would injure the person against whom it was done – is no answer . . . In such a case the jury may give any damages. It is not necessary to give proof of specific damage. The damages are at large.

In the circumstances, I am of the view that a nominal award should be given in the sum of $400,000.00 for conspiracy by unlawful means.

However, the courts are reluctant to support actions where the injurious falsehoods are mere puffs or the simple assertion as to the quality of a product in comparison with another.

Hubbuck & Sons, Limited v Wilkinson, Heywood & Clark, Limited [1899] 1 QB 86 CA (GB)

Facts: The plaintiffs had for many years carried on a large business in the export of white zinc to the East, particularly China and Japan. About April 1898 the defendants caused to be printed and published and issued in China and Japan, and continued the publication and issue of, a circular containing of the plaintiffs, and of them as such manufacturers and sellers of the said white zinc, and of them in the way of their business, the words following: 'Copy of a report of a trial of Bell Brand Genuine White Zinc' (meaning the white zinc manufactured and sold by the defendants) 'in comparison with Hubbucks' Patent White Zinc' (meaning the plaintiffs' said white zinc, and meaning that the defendants' white zinc was genuine, but that of the plaintiffs' was not genuine) 'by Fred and T. Thorne, builders and decorators, 266, Manchester Road, Cubitt Town, London, E. Paint-covering experiments.'

Held: Lindley, MR
The truth is that the defendants' circular when attentively read comes to no more than a statement that the defendants' white zinc is equal to, and, indeed, somewhat better, than the plaintiffs' . . . The fact that the defendants call their white zinc genuine, and contrast it with the plaintiffs' patent white zinc which is not called genuine, is relied upon by the plaintiffs as shewing that the circular is or may be fairly regarded as a defamatory libel on the plaintiffs – that is, a libel on them in the way of their trade. But when the whole circular is looked at, and it is found that the defendants state that for all practical purposes the two contrasted paints are in every respect equal, it is impossible to treat the circular as anything more than a disparagement of the white zinc paint made and sold by the plaintiffs . . .

We will now consider the circular in its other aspect, namely, as a disparagement of the plaintiffs' goods . . . The defendants in this case give the results of some experiments with the two sorts of paint, and in paragraph 5 of the statement of claim the plaintiffs say that the report of the experiments is untrue, and that the trials were not fairly made. But, supposing this to be the case, the result is not altered. Paragraph 5 merely states more particularly what has been already stated before in paragraph 3, where the general charge of falsehood is made. Even if each particular charge of falsehood is established, it will only come to this – that it is untrue that the defendants' paint is better than or equal to that of the plaintiffs, for saying which no action lies . . .

We regard this case as falling within the principle established by *Evans v Harlow, Young v Macrae* and *White v Mellin*. It is not necessary to consider how the case would have stood, if the defendants had not been rival traders simply puffing their own goods and comparing theirs with those of the plaintiffs. If the defendants had made untrue statements concerning the plaintiffs' goods beyond saying that they were inferior to, or, at all events, not better than, those of the defendants, or if the defendants were not rivals in trade and had no lawful excuse for what they said, it would not have been right summarily to strike out the statement of claim as shewing no reasonable cause of action. But the circular complained of is such as plainly to constitute no cause of action even if all the allegations in the statement of claim are true. Under these circumstances the appeal must be allowed . . . [J]udgment to be entered for the defendants.

Unlawful interference with trade

All interference with individual liberty of action in trading, if there is nothing more, is contrary to public policy and therefore void. That is the general rule. But there are exceptions: interference with individual liberty of action may be justified by the special circumstances of a particular case. It is a sufficient justification, and indeed it is the only justification, if the restriction is reasonable – reasonable, that is, in reference to the interests of the parties concerned and reasonable in reference to the interests of the public.

Natural Resources Conservation Authority v Seafood and Ting International Ltd; Natural Resources Conservation Authority v DYC Fishing Ltd (1999) 58 WIR 269 (JM)

Facts: The respondents, Seafood and Ting International Ltd and DYC Fishing Ltd, who processed conch for export, sought and obtained an order for an interim injunction from Courtenay Orr J with prohibitory and mandatory features. The mandatory feature ordered the Natural Resources Conservation Authority, the appellant, to grant the respondents permits for export. Both respondents processed conch for export. Before Jamaica's accession to the Convention on International Trade in Endangered Species of Wild Fauna and Flora (the convention) they processed and exported conch without let or hindrance, subject to a national quota being established. It was true that they obtained a licence from Jamaica Promotions Ltd (JAMPRO), but that was granted as a matter of course. In this instance the appellant had refused to grant the Convention in International Trade in Endangered Species (CITES) permit which is mandatory by international law if exported conch is marketed in countries which are signatories to the convention. There was a distinction between the respondents. Seafood did not receive any quota at all. DYC was discontented with the quantum allotted.

Held: Downer, JA
The evolving common law on this issue is illustrated by *Nagle v Feilden* [1966] 2 WLR 1027 and *Acrow (Automation) Ltd v Rex Chainbelt Inc* [1971] 3 All ER 1175. In *Nagle*, Lord Denning MR stated (at p 1031): 'The plaintiff is aggrieved by the refusal of a licence to her. So she has brought an action claiming a declaration that the practice of the stewards (in refusing a licence to any woman trainer) is void as against public policy, and also an injunction ordering the stewards to grant her a licence.' Then Lord Denning states the problem thus (at p 1032): 'By refusing or withdrawing a licence, the stewards can put a man out of business. This is a great power. If it is abused, can the courts give redress? That is the question.' Then the law was stated thus (at p 1033):

> The common law of England has for centuries recognised that a man has a right to work at his trade or profession without being unjustly excluded from it. He is not to be shut out from it at the whim of those having the governance of it. If they make a rule which enables them to reject his application arbitrarily or capriciously, not reasonably, that rule is bad. It is against public policy. The courts will not give effect to it . . . One of the principal functions of our courts is, whenever possible, to protect the individual from injustice and oppression. It is important, perhaps today more than ever, that we should not abdicate that function. The principle that courts will protect a man's right to work is well recognised in the stream of authority relating to contracts in restraint of trade . . . I take the principle of law to be that which I stated in *Torquay Hotel Co Ltd v Cousins* [1969] 1 All ER 522 at 530, [1969] 2 Ch 106 at 139, namely that, if one person, without just cause or excuse, deliberately interferes with the trade or business of another, and does so by unlawful means, that is by an act which he is not

> at liberty to commit, then he is acting unlawfully. He is liable in damages; and, in a proper case, an injunction can be granted against him.

. . . The respondents' contention was that the authorities suggest that, since they had a right to export conch without let or hindrance, then that position cannot be abridged without legislative intervention. In fact both sides would welcome legislation and the appellant has actually prepared a draft Bill. What is certain is that the convention cannot be administered so as unlawfully to interfere with the respondents' business interests. The livelihood of the respondents and others is dependent on the export of conch. So we are dealing with a matter of great public importance. Any regulation of the export trade in conch in the absence of legislation must facilitate the trade, not restrict or hinder it.

In this context it must be emphasised that the appellant has given the reason for refusing the permit to export and the essence of the respondents' case (with which I agree) is that the reasons are unlawful . . . That the export trade in conch is a matter of international concern and ought to be regulated in the interests of the environment is evident. That legislation is necessary to implement the provisions of the treaty as a constitutional imperative is well known. Yet this court was compelled to decide the important issues in this case on common law principles because of the failure of the executive to seek to incorporate the treaty provisions by legislation . . .

This appeal is dismissed and the mandatory injunction granted by Orr J has been extended at a hearing *inter partes*.

Inducement to breach of contract

If C has an existing contract with A and B is aware of it, and if B persuades or induces C to break the contract with resulting damage to A, this is, generally speaking, a tortious act for which B will be liable to A for the injury he has caused him. Malice is not an element of the tort of inducement to breach a contract but knowledge is. It does not matter whether the inducement is direct or indirect as long as there is knowledge of the act and outcome.

OBG v Allan [2008] 1 AC 1 (GB)

Facts: This appeal was combined with those of *Douglas v Hello! Ltd (No 3)* and *Mainstream Properties Ltd. v Young*. Lord Hoffman summarised the facts in his judgments as follows:

(a) In *OBG Ltd v Allan* [2005] QB 762 the defendants were receivers purportedly appointed under a floating charge which is admitted to have been invalid. Acting in good faith, they took control of the claimant company's assets and undertaking. The claimant says that this was not only a trespass to its land and a conversion of its chattels but also the tort of unlawful interference with its contractual relations. It claims that the defendants are liable in damages for the value of the assets and undertaking, including the value of the contractual claims, as at the date of their appointment. Alternatively, it says the defendants are liable for the same damages in conversion.

(b) In *Douglas v Hello! Ltd (No 3)* [2006] QB 125 the magazine 'OK!' contracted for the exclusive right to publish photographs of a celebrity wedding at which all other photography would be forbidden. The rival magazine 'Hello!' published photographs which it knew to have been surreptitiously taken by an unauthorised photographer pretending to be a waiter or guest. 'OK!' says that this was interference by unlawful means with its contractual or business relations or a breach of its equitable right to confidentiality in photographic images of the wedding.

(c) In *Mainstream Properties Ltd v Young* [2005] IRLR 964 two employees of a property company, in breach of their contracts, diverted a development opportunity to a joint venture in which they were interested. The defendant, knowing of their duties but wrongly thinking that they would not be in breach, facilitated the acquisition by providing finance. The company says that he is liable for the tort of wrongfully inducing breach of contract.

Held: (1) that the unified theory which treated causing loss by unlawful means as an extension of the tort of inducing a breach of contract was confusing and misleading and should be abandoned; and that, accordingly, inducing breach of contract and causing loss by unlawful means were two separate torts, each with its own conditions for liability;

(2) That inducing a breach of contract was a tort of accessory liability, and an intention to cause a breach of contract was a necessary and sufficient requirement for liability; that in order to be liable a person had to know that he was inducing a breach of contract and to intend to do so with knowledge of the consequences; that a conscious decision not to inquire into the existence of a fact could be treated as knowledge for the purposes of the tort; that a person who knowingly induced a breach of contract as a means to an end had the necessary intent even if he was not motivated by malice but had acted with the motive of securing an economic advantage for himself; that, however, a breach of contract which was neither an end in itself nor a means to an end but was merely a foreseeable consequence of a person's acts did not give rise to liability; and that there could be no secondary liability without primary liability, and therefore a person could not be liable for inducing a breach of contract unless there had in fact been a breach by the contracting party;

(3) That causing loss by unlawful means was a tort of primary liability, and acts against a third party counted as unlawful means only if they were actionable by that third party if he had suffered loss; that (per Lord Hoffmann, Lord Walker of Gestingthorpe, Baroness Hale of Richmond and Lord Brown of Eaton-under-Heywood) unlawful means consisted of acts intended to cause loss to the claimant by interfering with the freedom of a third party in a way which was unlawful as against that third party and which was intended to cause loss to the claimant, but did not include acts which might be unlawful against a third party but which did not affect his freedom to deal with the claimant;

(4) That in the first appeal, the only possible causes of action which could arise out of the alleged interference with contractual relations were the tort of procuring a breach of contract or the tort of causing loss by unlawful means; that none of the requirements of either of those torts could be established; that there had been no breach or non-performance of any contract, and therefore there was no wrong to which accessory liability for procuring a breach of contract could attach; that the receivers had acted in good faith and had neither employed unlawful means nor intended to cause any loss to the claimant; and that, accordingly, there was no primary liability for causing loss by unlawful means;

(5) Dismissing the first appeal, (Lord Nicholls of Birkenhead and Baroness Hale of Richmond dissenting) that strict liability for conversion applied only to an interest in chattels and not to choses in action; that it would be too drastic a reshaping of the law to extend the tort of conversion to apply also to choses in action and thereby impose strict liability for pure economic loss on receivers who had been appointed and had acted in good faith for conversion of the claimants' contracts; and that, accordingly, the claim against the receivers failed;

(6) Allowing the second appeal (Lord Nicholls of Birkenhead and Lord Walker of Gestingthorpe dissenting) that although information about the wedding generally was information that anyone was free to communicate, the photographic images of the wedding were not publicly available and were therefore confidential information; that there was no

conceptual reason why the obligation of confidence should not be imposed only in respect of the photographs if the third claimants were willing to pay for the right to be the only source of that particular form of information and did not mind that others were free to communicate other information about the wedding; that the photographs of the wedding constituted information of commercial value over which the first and second claimants had sufficient control to enable them to impose an obligation of confidence and there was no public policy reason why the law of confidence should not protect that obligation; that the third claimant, having bought the benefit of the obligation of confidence imposed by the first and second claimants on those present at the wedding, was entitled to protect the right to that benefit against any third party who intentionally destroyed it; that the duty of confidence imposed by the first and second claimants was binding upon the unauthorised photographer, and, by reason of the circumstances in which the first defendant had acquired the photographs, the duty of confidentiality had also been binding upon the first defendant when it had published the photographs to the detriment of the third claimants; that the fact that the third claimant had published its authorised photographs before the defendants had published the unauthorised photographs did not necessarily mean that the photographic images were by then in the public domain so that they could no longer be the subject of confidence; that whether information was in the public domain and whether there was still any point in enforcing the obligation of confidence thereafter depended on the nature of the information and the facts of the case; that the purpose of publishing the photographs had not merely been to convey the information that the first and second claimants had got married, but to convey the visual information of their wedding, and the transaction entered into between the claimants was that each picture would be treated as a separate piece of information which the third claimant would have the exclusive right to publish; that, therefore, publication of the authorised pictures had not put all the pictures in the public domain, and the duty of confidentiality continued in respect of any pictures of the wedding; and that, accordingly, the third claimants were entitled to damages against the first defendant for breach of confidence;

(7) That, in the second appeal (per Lord Hoffmann, Baroness Hale of Richmond and Lord Brown of Eaton-under-Heywood), although the defendants had made the third claimant's contractual rights less profitable than they would otherwise have been, they had done nothing to interfere with the first and second claimants' ability to deal with the third claimant or to perform their contractual obligations to the third claimant; that, however, the Court of Appeal had erred in holding that the defendants had no intention to cause loss to the third claimant and had only intended to maintain their own sales; that causing loss to the third claimant was the means whereby the defendants had intended to attain their desired end and the loss was not merely a foreseeable consequence of attaining that end; and that, accordingly, the defendants had the necessary intention to cause loss but they were not liable in tort because they had not interfered by unlawful means with the actions of the first and second claimants; and

(8) Dismissing the third appeal, that, on the judge's unchallenged findings, the sixth defendant had honestly believed that assisting the first and second defendants with the joint venture would not involve them in breaches of their contractual obligations; that the sixth defendant had not been indifferent as to whether there was a breach of contract or not, nor had he made a conscious decision not to inquire in case he discovered a disagreeable truth; and that, accordingly, he had not intended to cause a breach of contract nor had he caused loss by unlawful means.

In their decision, the House of Lords held that claims for interference with contractual relations could only be founded in one of two separate causes of action: procuring a breach of contract or unlawful interference. There are five requirements in the tort of inducing or procuring a breach of contract: 1) there must be a contract; 2) the contract must be breached; 3) the defendant's conduct must have procured or induced the breach; 4) the defendant must have known about the breached term or turned a blind eye to it; and 5) the defendant must have actually realised that the conduct procuring the breach would have that result. Thus, the liability of the person who induces the breach of contract – the defendant – is accessory in nature, and depends upon the contracting party committing the actionable breach of contract. In the tort of unlawful interference, the liability of the defendant is primary in nature, where such defendant has intentionally caused the claimant loss by unlawfully interfering with the interests of third parties. Hence, the House of Lords found that the administrative receivers in OBG were not liable under either tort, since there had been no breach or non-performance of the relevant contracts and so the administrative receivers were not accessorily liable. Similarly, the administrative receivers did not intentionally use any unlawful means to cause loss to the company.

Meretz Investments NV and another v ACP Ltd and others [2008] Ch 244 (GB)

Facts: The freeholder of Albert Court was Britel. Meretz was a sister company of Britel. Mr William Stern was London agent for both companies. The first defendant was ACP. FP, one of the mortgagees of the development lease, was also the parent of ACP. Mr and Mrs Olsson, third and fourth defendants in the action (but not parties to this appeal), were respectively the managing director of ACP and FP and his wife. Mr Tamimi was the purchaser of the development lease from FP. The problems in this case all stemmed from the funding of the project and the parties' contractual relationships. FP became interested in the commercial opportunity offered by the development, and it formed ACP as a special purpose vehicle for the purpose of entering into an agreement with Britel. Thus, ACP took the development lease pursuant to an agreement, called the preliminary agreement, dated 7 March 1996. Under this agreement Britel agreed to grant the development lease to ACP, when so requested by ACP, for a nominal sum of £1 and a nominal ground rent of £1 per annum. In due course ACP made that request and the development lease was granted on 4 November 1996.

The construction of the penthouses had, of course, to be financed. The plan was to develop the flats in phases and to use the proceeds of sale from one phase to finance the next one. So what had to be found was finance for the first phase. Clause 5.2 of the preliminary agreement provided that the development lease should be in such form as would enable ACP to execute a first legal mortgage, in favour of any commercial lender, to secure up to £1.5m. ACP only paid a nominal sum for the grant of the development lease. It was to take the risks involved in construction and the risk of obtaining and repaying the finance for the development. The reward for Britel was a share of the proceeds of sale. Under the preliminary agreement ACP agreed to make payments to Britel, called site payments, equivalent to 22.5 per cent of the net proceeds of sale of the penthouses up to £5.4m; Britel's profit share was capped at £1.215m. Britel was given the right to require a second charge to secure these site payments, and if a second charge were executed the parties were to enter into a deed of priority to regulate the priorities between the first and second charges. Clause 12 laid down a timetable for completion of the penthouses.

The obligation that ACP undertook was not an absolute obligation to develop the roofspace but an obligation to use all reasonable endeavours to do so within an agreed timetable. This allowed 54 months for completion of the works. But the timetable was itself subject to extension if circumstances occurred beyond ACP's control or if Britel agreed to give an extension. However, if ACP failed to fulfil its obligations, then by virtue of clause 12.4.2 Britel had the option to serve on ACP notice requiring ACP to grant it a development sublease of the undeveloped part of the demised property at a nominal premium of £1 and a nominal ground rent of £1 per annum. This was the leaseback option referred to above.

The obligation to use all reasonable endeavours to complete the works by the longstop date was subsequently breached so that Britel became entitled to exercise the option. Britel was entitled to exercise the leaseback option even if it had received its full entitlement to payment out of the proceeds of sale of the penthouses. It was, therefore, inserted to provide an incentive to ACP to complete the development within the agreed timetable. The freehold of Albert Court was charged to NUBBH to secure the sums due from Britel and (apparently) Mr Stern. NUBBH required Britel to obtain a guarantee from FP of the obligations of ACP to Britel under the preliminary agreement and the development lease. This was done by a guarantee, called the FP guarantee, also dated 7 March 1996. NUBBH also required ACP to charge the development lease to secure the sums due from it to Britel under the preliminary agreement.

By late 2001 the development had run into various construction problems. It was thought that the development was no longer profitable. ACP forecast a loss of £400,000. The directors of ACP and FP came to the view that they should use the FP charge 'to avoid a loss'. The idea was to appoint a receiver or exercise the power of sale under the FP charge so that the profits would go to FP and ACP. It was anticipated that on this basis there would be profits from the development. Meanwhile, Mr Tamimi emerged as the prospective purchaser of one of the penthouses, namely, penthouse A. The agreed price was £2.75m and the contract was signed on 8 January 2002. The contract gave Mr Tamimi 'step in rights' to take over the construction of penthouse A if ACP failed to complete it. Mr Tamimi agreed to advance money towards the building costs of penthouse A. In January and February 2002 he paid £140,000 and £280,000 respectively towards the purchase price of penthouse A, thus becoming financially committed to his purchase.

In April 2002 meetings took place between FP and Mr Tamimi. FP proposed that the development lease would be sold by it under its power of sale to a company controlled by Mr Tamimi for £1.15m, and that FP would reinvest the proceeds of sale in the development. On 27 May 2002, by order of Judge Seymour QC, Meretz obtained a judgment against ACP for £326,000 approximately, being sums due under the terms of the introduction agreement. ACP did not have the money to pay. Accordingly the proposed arrangements with Mr Tamimi were expanded to include a loan of the moneys needed to pay off the judgment. Mr Olsson informed Mr Tamimi that ACP could no longer complete his penthouse. Mr Tamimi's 'step in rights' to take over the construction of penthouse A were now triggered.

On 31 May 2002 ACP, FP and Mr Tamimi entered into an agreement called the wrap around agreement. This agreement provided for Mr Tamimi to finance the payment of the judgment. It also provided for the payment of the NUBBH charge over the development lease. It also provided for Mr Tamimi to purchase the development lease from FP when it took possession of the lease following the exercise of its power of sale. It further provided for Mr Tamimi to appoint FP as his agent to complete the development and to procure the sale of the penthouses. On 10 September 2002 Britel attempted to exercise the leaseback option but by then FP had exercised its power of sale and so ACP was unable to grant the development sublease required by clause 12.4.2 of the preliminary agreement. That event was the catalyst that led to the claims made in this litigation.

Held: Arden, LJ
The tort of inducing a breach of contract is committed when a person, with the requisite knowledge and intention (which I consider below), procures or persuades another person to breach his contract with a third party . . .

In *OBG Ltd v Allan* [2008] 1 AC 1, which was decided after the judge handed down his judgment in this case, the House of Lords considered the torts of inducing breach of contract and causing loss by unlawful means. Lord Hoffmann emphasised that a person is held liable for inducing breach of contract as an accessory to the liability of the contracting party . . . The tort of inducing breach of contract requires an intention to induce a breach of contract (*OBG Ltd v Allan*) and it follows from the findings of fact that there was no such intention.

. . .

(c) FP and Mr Tamimi did not by entering into the wrap around agreement induce any breach of contract by ACP. The breach was the pre-agreed consequence of FP's exercise of the power of sale . . .

To succeed in its claim for inducing breach of contract Britel must identify the breach of contract induced. There are pages of pleading on this point much of which is made irrelevant by the judge's decision against the claimants on points which are no longer in issue. As far as I can see, the only breaches of contract by ACP that are in issue are its failure to complete in accordance with the development timetable and its failure to perform its obligations under the leaseback option. The failure to complete in accordance with the development timetable was caused by other factors, such as lack of finance, not by the exercise of power of sale. Thus, Mr Boyle has relied on the failure to perform the leaseback option . . .

My conclusions on inducement are as follows. The concept of inducement was analysed in the *OBG* case by Lord Hoffmann and Lord Nicholls and I must test the parties' submissions on inducement by reference to their analysis. In the *OBG* case Lord Nicholls drew a distinction between inducing a breach of contract and preventing its performance. He held, at para 178:

> In inducement cases the very act of joining with the contracting party and inducing him to break his contract is sufficient to found liability as an accessory. In prevention cases the defendant does not join with the contracting party in a wrong (breach of contract) committed by the latter. There is no question of accessory liability. In prevention cases the defendant acts independently of the contracting party. The defendant's liability is a 'stand-alone' liability. Consistently with this, tortious liability does not arise in prevention cases, unless, as was the position in [*GWK Ltd v Dunlop Rubber Co Ltd* (1926) 42 TLR 376], the preventative means used were independently unlawful.

Lord Hoffmann did not use the distinction made by Lord Nicholls. However, as mentioned above, he too emphasised that the liability for inducing breach of contract was ancillary to that of the contracting party for breach of contract. Lord Hoffmann, at paras 34–8, discussed the distinction between direct and indirect interference with a contract. He was critical of this distinction and to illustrate the point he gave the following example:

> For example, in *Daily Mirror Newspapers Ltd v Gardner* [1968] 2 QB 762 the Federation of Retail Newsagents resolved to boycott the 'Daily Mirror' for a week to put pressure on the publishers to allow its members higher margins. The federation advised their members to stop buying the paper from wholesalers. The publishers claimed an injunction on the ground that the federation was procuring a breach of the wholesalers' running contracts with the publishers to take a given number of copies each day. Counsel for the federation (see the judgment

> of Lord Denning MR, at p 781) said that it was a case of indirect inducement because the federation 'did not exert directly any pressure or inducement on the wholesalers: but at most they only did it indirectly by recommending the retailers to give stop orders'. Lord Denning said it did not matter whether one procured a breach of contract 'by direct approach to the one who breaks the contract or by indirect influence on others'. There seems to me to be much sense in this observation, although whether it leads to the conclusion that the defendant should be liable in both cases or neither is another matter.

Lord Hoffmann considered whether the distinction meant no more than a direct communication between the defendant and the contract breaker as opposed to one through an agent. He continued:

> I cannot see why this should make a difference. If that is what the distinction between 'direct' and 'indirect' means, it conceals the real question which has to be asked in relation to *Lumley v Gye* (1853) 2 E & B 216: did the defendant's acts of encouragement, threat, persuasion and so forth have a sufficient causal connection with the breach by the contracting party to attract accessory liability? The court in *Lumley v Gye* made it clear that the principle upon which a person is liable for the act of another in breaking his contract is the same as that on which he is liable for the act of another in committing a tort. It follows, as I have said, that the relevant principles are to be found in cases such as *CBS Songs Ltd v Amstrad Consumer Electronics plc* [1988] AC 1013 and *Unilever plc v Chefaro Properties Ltd* [1994] FSR 135. By the test laid down in these cases, the Federation could not have incurred any liability. They were not encouraging or assisting the wholesalers in breaking their contracts. They were simply advising their members to exercise their own freedom to buy whatever newspapers they liked. The wholesalers had no right to the co-operation of the retailers in enabling them to perform their contracts. Liability could not depend upon the accident of whether the Federation had communicated (directly or through an intermediary) with the wholesalers. The distinction between direct and indirect interference was therefore irrelevant and misleading.

Lord Hoffmann accepted that facts giving rise to accessory liability for procuring a breach of contract might also give rise to primary liability for causing loss by unlawful means. He considered, however, that the two torts should be treated as separate. Similarly, Lord Nicholls considered that it was 'confusing and misleading' to treat prevention cases as part and parcel of the same tort as inducement cases. He held, at para 180:

> The rationale is not the same, nor are the ingredients. But the rationale and ingredients of liability in prevention cases are the same as those of the tort of interference with business by unlawful means. Prevention cases should be recognised for what they are: straightforward examples of the latter tort rather than as exemplifying a wider version of *Lumley v Gye* labelled 'interference with contractual relations'.

It is not suggested in the *OBG* case that there was any difference between the approach of Lord Nicholls and that of Lord Hoffmann to the question of inducement. They both regarded it as fundamental that liability for inducement was accessory to the liability of the party to the contract. Lord Brown of Eaton-under-Heywood expressly agreed with Lord Nicholls and Lord Hoffmann on matters where they were agreed and Lord Walker of Gestingthorpe and Baroness Hale of Richmond by implication agreed with them on those points. On the face of it the distinction drawn by Lord Nicholls as between prevention of performance and inducement would suggest that there was an inducement in this case. ACP was, as Mr Boyle points out, a party to the wrap around agreement and FP and ACP, as parent and subsidiary respectively, could not be said to act independently. However, in my judgment, it is necessary to look to the substance and not the form.

Although ACP was a party to the wrap around agreement, it had no role to play in FP's decision to enforce the charge or in its arrangements for the sale to Mr Tamimi. This was not, after all, the normal case where a contracting party is induced to commit a breach of contract. In the normal situation a contracting party has an option whether to perform his contract or to pay damages. Here the creation of the FP charge removed that choice once the power of sale became exercisable and had been exercised. In these circumstances the only course of action open to ACP was to pay compensation.

Thus the present case is not a persuasion case but a prevention case, as those terms are defined by Lord Nicholls. It therefore has to be shown that the preventative means used by FP were 'independently unlawful'. This cannot be done because FP was contractually entitled as against ACP and Britel to exercise its power of sale. (There is no evidence that the defendants caused any breach of ACP's obligation to pay damages.) I consider that Lord Hoffmann's test leads to the same answer. It is not enough to show that there was a relationship of parent and wholly owned subsidiary between ACP and FP or that ACP was a party to the wrap around agreement or to some of the negotiations which preceded it. It would have to be shown that FP's 'acts of encouragement, threat, persuasion and so forth have a sufficient causal connection with the breach by the contracting party to attract accessory liability'. But there is no evidence of any acts of encouragement or any conduct on the part of FP in the form of the wrap around agreement which had the effect of preventing ACP from delivering the development sublease when the leaseback option was exercised. The fact was that Britel had agreed to the creation of a contractual structure which gave FP a charge over the development lease and it was part and parcel of that structure that FP could take it out of ACP's power to deliver the development sublease. The die had been cast long before the wrap around agreement was thought of.

In the circumstances the instrumentality of FP, which exercised its power of sale and, as it were, lit the blue touch paper which caused the proprietary rights conferred by the leaseback option to be destroyed, did not in the circumstances constitute a sufficient causal connection to attract accessory liability. An analogy can be drawn between the inducement by exercising contractual rights as a secured creditor and the situation where, to enable it to obtain moneys to repay funds borrowed to purchase shares in the company, a secured creditor of a company enforces a pre-existing charge. In *MT Realisations Ltd v Digital Equipment Co Ltd* [2003] 2 BCLC 117 this court held that the company did not give 'financial assistance' contrary to section 151 of the Companies Act 1985 by allowing a secured creditor to exercise its secured rights because the secured creditor was entitled to exercise those rights by reason of a charge granted prior to that purchase. So, too, here ACP has not been induced by FP and Mr Tamimi to breach its contract with Britel. FP had a contractual right to exercise its power of sale as a secured creditor as against both Britel and ACP.

CONCURRENT LIABILITY IN TORT AND CONTRACT

The general rule is that where a given wrong *prima facie* supports an action in contract and in tort, the party may sue in either or both, subject to any limit the parties themselves have placed on that right by their contract. This limitation on the general rule of concurrency arises because it is always open to parties to limit or waive the duties which the common law would impose on them for negligence. The mere fact that the parties have dealt with a matter expressly in their contract does not mean that they intended to exclude the right to sue in tort. It all depends on how they have dealt with it. In so far as the tort duty is not contradicted by the contract, it remains intact and may be sued upon. Liability must be expressly limited to avoid an action in tort.

David Walcott (Appellant) v The Royal Bank of Trinidad and Tobago (Defendant) (2010) Civ App #158/2006 (TT)

Facts: The appellant contends that the defendant bank ('the Bank') was negligent when it refused to honour three cheques, issued by him and drawn on his current account, which were presented for payment on 28th December, 1995, 29th December, 1995 and 26th July, 1996 respectively. He alleges that the first two cheques were wrongfully dishonoured after the Bank failed to carry out the specific instructions he gave for the transfer of funds to his current account. The two cheques were issued on 23rd and 29th December, 1995 respectively. The appellant has claimed in negligence only, although his relationship with the Bank is essentially contractual. However, it is now well established that at common law, a remedy can exist concurrently in tort, in respect of a relationship which is governed primarily by contract. The foundation of that principle of law is the decision of the House of Lords in *Henderson v Merrett Syndicates Ltd* [1995] 2 AC 145 which was applied by the Court of Appeal in *Bank of Commerce (T&T) Ltd v David Lakhan*, Civ App 23 of 1991.

Held: Archie, CJ, Bereaux, Stollmeyer, JJA
The question which next arises is whether, having regard to the nature of its legal responsibilities, the Bank owed a duty of care in tort to the appellant in its provision of banking services to the appellant. There is no question that such a duty of care existed in contract and more specifically in the carrying out of payment instructions. See *Royal Products v Midland Bank* (supra). That such a duty may exist in tort independently of and concurrently with a contractual duty, was recognised and accepted by the Court of Appeal in *Bank of Commerce Trinidad and Tobago Ltd v David Lakhan* (unreported) applying *Henderson v Merritt.* In *Lakhan* the bank failed to remit payment of a life insurance premium to an insurance company, causing the policy to lapse. The premiums were payable monthly and the life assured had signed a 'standing order with the bank by which the bank undertook to remit to the insurer, the monthly premia on or before a particular date each month.' The bank admitted that it had misfiled the *'standing orders'* book which resulted in the failure to remit premiums for three consecutive months. The life assured died and the policy was found to have lapsed. The defendant thus instituted an action against the bank in both contract and tort for the loss of the lump sum payment due upon her death.

. . .

Hamel Smith J A went on to say at page 8, that as to the existence of concurrent remedies in tort and contract, in respect of an act governed primarily by contract:

> The decision of the House of Lords in *Henderson & ors v Merrett Syndicates Ltd & ors* [1994] 3 WLR 761 literally put the issue of concurrent liability to rest. Lord Goff, in delivering the lead judgment on behalf of the House, reviewed the law, paying tribute to Oliver J's analysis of the law (in *Midland Bank*) and held that it had been correctly decided. He founded liability squarely on the principle established in *Hedley Byrne* itself, from which it followed that 'an assumption of responsibility coupled with the concomitant reliance may give rise to a tortious duty of care irrespective of whether there is a contractual relationship between the parties, and in consequence, unless his contract precludes him from doing so, the plaintiff who has available to him concurrent remedies in contract and tort, may choose that remedy which appears to him to be the most advantageous.' The decision in *Henderson* is in keeping with the development of the law in other common law countries. As Lord Goff observed, 'not only did the decision in *Midland Bank* break the mould' but other common law countries began to follow the lead. The Irish Supreme Court, in *Finlay v Murtagh* (1979) IR 249, held that solicitors owed to their clients concurrent duties in tort and contract and in *Central Trust Co. v Rafuse* (1986) 31 DLR (4th) 481, Le Dain J., delivering the judgment on behalf of the Supreme Court of Canada, in a similar issue as in *Finlay*, said (at p 522):

> A concurrent or alternative liability in tort will not be admitted if its effect would be to permit the plaintiff to circumvent or escape a contractual exclusion or limitation of liability for the act or omission that would constitute the tort. Subject to this qualification, where concurrent liability in tort and contract exists, the plaintiff has the right to assert the cause of action that appears to be the most advantageous to him in respect of any particular legal consequence.

In the circumstances, the trial judge was right in holding that the claim of the respondent could be pursued in tort. The 'contract' between the parties under the standing order contained no express or implied restriction of limitation which would have precluded the respondent from enforcing the common law duty of care imposed on the bank to ensure that the premiums were paid on time . . . There is nothing in the contract with the bank when the order was given by the respondent and accepted by the bank that any action in tort is precluded. Rather, there is every good reason why the appellant should be held liable for breach of its plain common law duty. If the intention was that no other liability for failure to perform its part of the contractual bargain should arise at all, then it was a matter for the appellant to expressly limit its liability. In the absence of such provision, to deprive the respondent of a claim in tort could not be right.

. . .

As Hamel-Smith JA noted at page 10 of his judgment, the rationale behind the development of the law in *Henderson*, included permitting the litigant the benefit of a longer limitation period, as well as the benefit [of] other remedies and principles of law provided by the law of tort. In this regard, Lord Goff's dictum in *Henderson* at page 185E bears examination. He said:

> I think it is desirable to stress at this stage that the question of concurrent liability is by no means only of academic significance. Practical issues, which can be of great importance to the parties, are at stake. Foremost among these is perhaps the question of limitation of actions. If concurrent liability in tort is not recognised, a claimant may find his claim barred at a time when he is unaware of its existence. This must moreover be a real possibility in the case of claims against professional men, such as solicitors or architects, since the consequences of their negligence may well not come to light until long after the lapse of six years from the date when the relevant breach of contract occurred . . . Other practical problems arise, for example, from the absence of a right to contribution between negligent contract-breakers; from the rules as to remoteness of damage, which are less restricted in tort than they are in contract, and from the availability of the opportunity to obtain leave to serve proceedings out of the jurisdiction.

In view of the Court of Appeal's decision in *Bank of Commerce Trinidad and Tobago Ltd v David Lakhan* the question whether concurrent liability in tort can exist in respect of action which is primarily governed by contract, has been answered a definitive 'yes' . . . I would allow the appeal in part [for the 1995 claim]. The Bank will pay two thirds of the appellant's costs of this appeal and of the costs of the High Court.

CHAPTER 5

CRIMINALISING BUSINESS ACTIVITIES

It turns out "creative accounting" is a creative term for "white collar crime".

Reproduced with the permission of Stu's Views

The intersection of criminal law and commercial activities is an area of growing importance in the governance of modern society. While criminal law is not considered as a typical component of business law, the commission of crimes by persons, both natural and juridical, in the pursuit of commercial activities, requires examination in any contemporary exposition of the legal framework within which the business sector operates. It is hardly surprising that, in the business world, there are several activities that have attracted criminal sanction.

A crime is an act which the law, with appropriate penal sanctions, forbids. As prohibitions are not enacted in a vacuum, there is usually some evil or injurious or undesirable effect upon the public against which the law is directed. That effect may be in relation to social, economic or political interests where the legislature finds it necessary to suppress the evil or safeguard the interest threatened. A useful starting point is the definition of a crime but, in attempting a definition, what becomes apparent is the marked reticence by many writers to avoid such a task. One viewpoint is that the concept of what is a crime is better defined by examining the characteristics of a particular conduct rather than attempting a precise and all-embracing definition. It has been observed that criminal conduct generally contains elements of a public wrong and a moral wrong.[1] With regard to a public wrong, crimes are generally considered to be 'acts which have a particular harmful effect on the public and do more than interfere merely with private rights'.[2] The 'second characteristic of crimes which is usually emphasised is that they are acts which are morally wrong'.[3]

The consequence of an act or omission that contains the characteristics of being a public wrong and a moral wrong is the commission of a criminal offence. 'A criminal offence is a legal wrong for which the offender is liable to be prosecuted by or in the name of the State, and if found guilty liable to be punished.'[4] While breaches of contract or commission of torts may result in actions being taken by persons against the offending party, a criminal offence attracts the attention of the state which seeks to take action on behalf society in general. The American Law Institute's Model Penal Code provides a succinct analysis of the purpose of criminal law. As enunciated by Card, the purposes of criminal law are:

(a) To forbid and prevent conduct that unjustifiably and inexcusably inflicts or threatens substantial harm to individual or public interests.
(b) To subject to public control persons whose conduct indicates that they are disposed to commit crimes.
(c) To safeguard conduct that is without fault from condemnation as criminal.
(d) To give warning of the nature of conduct declared to be an offence.
(e) To differentiate on reasonable grounds between serious and minor offences.[5]

To be found liable for a criminal offence, there is the need generally for two requirements to be proven by the prosecutor beyond reasonable doubt, namely the *actus reus* and *mens rea*.

ACTUS REUS

Actus reus includes all the elements present in the definition of a crime except the mental state of the person accused of committing the crime.[6] One definition states that the:

> expression *actus reus* can be summarized as meaning an act (or sometimes an omission or other event) indicated in the definition of the offence charged together with:
>
> - any consequences of that act which are indicated by that definition; and
> - any surrounding circumstances (other than references to the *mens rea* required on the part of the defendant, or to any excuse).[7]

---

1 Ormerod, D, *Smith and Hogan: Criminal Law*, 2008, Oxford: Oxford University Press, p 10.
2 Ormerod, *Smith and Hogan*, p 10.
3 Ormerod, *Smith and Hogan*, p 12.
4 Card, R, *Card, Cross and Jones: Criminal Law*, 2008, Oxford: Oxford University Press, p 1.
5 Card, *Card, Cross and Jones*, p 4.
6 Ormerod, *Smith and Hogan*, p 45.
7 Card, *Card, Cross and Jones*, p 42.

An act or doing something is the dominant basis for ascribing criminal liability. It is often described as taking positive steps to engage in activities defined as criminal by society. The offence of dangerous driving, for example, requires an act of driving. Less commonly, criminal liability may be based on an omission which occurs when one fails to do something and that failure is considered to be criminal by society. Failing to file an income tax return, for instance, by the specified date or to report a traffic accident within a set time may result in criminal liability. Finally, a third manifestation of *actus reus* 'simply requires the occurrence of a specified event (or state of affairs) in which the defendant is involved, no act or omission on his part being required'.[8] Offences where a mere event attracts criminal liability are all statute-based, such as having in a public place any offensive weapon without lawful authority or reasonable excuse.

MENS REA

Mens rea is the other necessary component of criminal liability and it refers to the state of mind expressly or impliedly required by the definition of the offence that constitutes the crime.[9] There are many manifestations of this mental state of mind and these must be carefully explored in order to gain an insight into circumstances under which criminal liability can be attributed to persons, both natural and juridical.

Intention

> A person intends a consequence of his act (or omission) if he acted (or failed to act) with the aim or purpose of thereby bringing about that consequence. In addition, if a person foresees that a consequence is virtually certain to result from his conduct, although it is not his aim or purpose to achieve it, he can be found to have achieved that consequence. Sometimes the intention required by the definition of an offence relates not to a consequence of the defendant's conduct, but to something ulterior to it, which does not have to be brought about. Such intention is known as an 'ulterior intent'.[10]

R v Mohan [1976] QB 1 (GB)

Facts: A police officer on duty saw a motor car being driven by the appellant. The vehicle appeared to be exceeding the permitted speed limit. The officer stood in the path of the vehicle and signalled the appellant to stop. The vehicle slowed down but, when about ten yards away from the officer, accelerated hard and was driven straight at the officer who moved out of its way in order to avoid being knocked down.

The appellant was charged on three counts, one of which alleged that, on the day in question, having the charge of a motor vehicle, he had attempted, by wanton driving, to cause bodily harm to be done to the police officer. In relation to that charge the judge directed the jury that the Crown had to prove that the appellant had deliberately driven the vehicle wantonly and that he must have realised at the time that, unless he were to stop or there were some other intervening factor, such driving was likely to cause bodily harm or that he was reckless as to whether bodily harm was caused, but that it was not necessary

8 Card, *Card, Cross and Jones*, p 51.
9 Card, *Card, Cross and Jones*, p 76.
10 Card, *Card, Cross and Jones*, p 77.

to prove an intention actually to cause bodily harm. The appellant was convicted on that count and appealed.

Held: James, LJ
The first question we have to answer is: what is the meaning of 'intention' when that word is used to describe the *mens rea* in attempt? It is to be distinguished from 'motive' in the sense of an emotion leading to action: it has never been suggested that such a meaning is appropriate to 'intention' in this context. It is equally clear that the word means what is often referred to as 'specific intent' and can be defined as 'a decision to bring about a certain consequence' or as the 'aim'. In *R v Hyam* [1975] AC 55, 74, Lord Hailsham of St Marylebone cited with approval the judicial interpretation of 'intention' or 'intent' applied by Asquith LJ in *Cunliffe v Goodman* [1950] 2 KB 237, 253:

> An 'intention' to my mind connotes a state of affairs which the party 'intending' – I will call him X – does more than merely contemplate: it connotes a state of affairs which, on the contrary, he decides, so far as in him lies, to bring about, and which, in point of possibility, he has a reasonable prospect of being able to bring about, by his own act of volition.

If that interpretation of 'intent' is adopted as the meaning of *mens rea* in the offence of attempt, it is not wide enough to justify the direction in the present case. The direction, taken as a whole, can be supported as accurate only if the necessary *mens rea* includes not only specific intent but also the state of mind of one who realises that, if his conduct continues, the likely consequence is the commission of the complete offence and who continues his conduct in that realisation, or the state of mind of one who, knowing that continuation of his conduct is likely to result in the commission of the complete offence, is reckless as to whether or not that is the result . . .

We do not find in the speeches of their Lordships in *Reg. v Hyam* anything which binds us to hold that *mens rea* in the offence of attempt is proved by establishing beyond reasonable doubt that the accused knew or correctly foresaw that the consequences of his act unless interrupted would 'as a high degree of probability', or would be 'likely' to, be the commission of the complete offence. Nor do we find authority in that case for the proposition that a reckless state of mind is sufficient to constitute the *mens rea* in the offence of attempt. Appeal upheld.

There are other manifestations of the *mens rea* based on intention and, although not exact subsections, these apply more or less in a similar manner and include states of mind, such as "wilfully", "deliberately", and "knowingly".

Recklessness

Recklessness is another important type of *mens rea*. The first requirement to establish recklessness is the need for the prosecution to show that a defendant took an unjustifiable risk. It is with respect to the second requirement that the law has been shrouded in controversy, that is, the knowledge of the existence of the risk.[11] The dominant test was known as *Cunningham*[12] recklessness, named after a decision that enunciated the principle that recklessness constitutes

11 Ormerod, *Smith and Hogan*, p 108.
12 *R v Cunningham* [1957] 2 All ER 412 (GB).

a subjective form of *mens rea* as it focuses on the defendant's own perception of the existence of a risk:

> A person may be reckless as to a consequence or a circumstance. A person is reckless as to a consequence if he is aware of a risk that it will occur, and as to a circumstance if he is aware of a risk that it exists or will exist, and in either case, in the circumstances known to him, it is unreasonable to take the risk.[13]

There was a brief time in the 1980s and 1990s when an attempt was made to create an objective definition of recklessness known as *Caldwell* recklessness[14] but this has in recent times been largely rejected.[15]

Foster (Trevor) and Williams (Cedric) v R (2007) 70 WIR 60 (PC) (BB)

Facts: Ruby Grecia, otherwise Kellman, the grandmother of the appellant Foster, lived in a house at Cambridge, St Joseph, which was also occupied by the appellant's father Denzil Grecia, his uncle Winston Grecia and the appellant himself. The house, which was some 30 feet by 22 feet, was of wooden construction with a galvanised roof. It had three bedrooms, one of which was occupied by the appellant. Ruby Grecia was aged about 83 years at the time of her death and had limited mobility, being able to move around only with the assistance of another person.

On the evening of 6 November 1988 a fire broke out in the house, which was burned down. Ruby and Winston Grecia were burned to death in the fire. It was not in dispute that the fire had been caused by the actions of the appellant in his bedroom, but the issue in the trial was the nature and intent of those actions. The Crown case was that he deliberately set the house on fire, with the intention of causing death or grievous bodily harm to his father and uncle. The appellant's case, on the other hand, was that the fire was accidentally caused when he spilled kerosene in the course of attempting to top up an oil lamp.

Held: Lord Carswell (delivering the reasons of the Board)
Mr Blake submitted that the judge should have directed the jury that if they found that the victim's death was (or may have been) caused recklessly, in the sense of a grossly negligent act without subjective appreciation by the appellant of the risk of fatal consequences, then they should return a verdict of manslaughter. He argued that the judge should have posed three factual possibilities:

(a) intentional causing of death, which would also include subjective recklessness, viz actual foresight of the risk of death, coupled with indifference as to that consequence;
(b) accidental causing of death, connoting absence of any intention to cause it or appreciation of the risk of death; and
(c) recklessness without subjective foresight of the risk of fatal consequences.

The first would lead to a verdict of murder, the second to acquittal and the third to a verdict of manslaughter. Counsel advanced the proposition that to convict the appellant of felony/murder the prosecution must prove either that he deliberately intended to endanger

13 Card, *Card, Cross and Jones*, p 91.
14 *Commissioner of Metropolitan Police v Caldwell* [1982] AC 341 (GB).
15 *R v G* [2003] 1 AC 1034 (GB).

life or was subjectively aware of the danger to life and proceeded to set fire to the house indifferent to that danger . . .

The Crown case was that the appellant deliberately set fire to the house and that he either had the intention of causing death or grievous bodily harm to some at least of the occupants or took the risk of its being burnt down with occupants inside, with knowledge that that risk existed. The defence case made at trial in the appellant's evidence was that it was a pure accident, which did not leave him liable to a criminal sanction.

If the defence of accident was rejected, the case was entirely clear. Setting the house on fire was obviously dangerous to life and likely in itself to cause death. As the appellant was aware that there were people in the house, he must when he started the fire have foreseen that danger to them, especially to an old lady with limited mobility. There was no room on the facts for an obvious alternative to murder which would suggest itself to the mind of any ordinarily knowledgeable and alert criminal judge (*R v Coutts* [2006] UKHL 39, [2006] 1 WLR 2154 at p 2167, para [23], per Lord Bingham of Cornhill). In these circumstances the possibility did not exist of a version of the facts which might have called for a direction on the lines advocated on behalf of the appellant.

Negligence

'A person is negligent if his conduct in relation to a risk of which a reasonable person would have been aware, falls below the standard which would be expected of a reasonable person in the light of that risk.'[16] As eloquently stated in *Smith and Hogan*, 'Recklessness is the conscious taking of an unjustifiable risk, negligence is the inadvertent taking of an unjustifiable risk.'[17]

Brown (Uriah) v R (2005) 66 WIR 238 (PC) (JM)

Facts: On 4 March 2000 a serious traffic accident involving several vehicles occurred on the road between Montego Bay and St Ann's Bay, Jamaica. A police car being driven in the direction of St Ann's Bay by the appellant, a serving police officer, with another officer (Sgt Christie) as passenger, came into collision with a Nissan car travelling in the opposite direction. The collision also involved a Ford Ranger pickup truck driven by Michael McKennon, which was travelling in the same direction as the appellant's car. Both the Nissan and the police car, which was in close contact with it after the collision, caught fire. The two occupants of the Nissan, Mark Williams and Gregory Vassell, were killed, the appellant was seriously injured and his passenger, Sgt Christie, also sustained injuries. The appellant was indicted on two counts of manslaughter.

Held: Lord Carswell
Such was the state of the law when the House of Lords returned to the topic of involuntary manslaughter in *R v Adomako* [1995] 1 AC 171, in which a charge of manslaughter was based on an allegation of gross negligence on the part of an anaesthetist. Their lordships accepted the correctness of the submission of the appellant's counsel that 'the law in this

16 Card, *Card, Cross and Jones*, p 100.
17 Ormerod, *Smith and Hogan*, p 116.

area should have the characteristics of clarity, certainty, intellectual coherence and general applicability and acceptability'. The Court of Appeal had adopted the 'gross negligence' test, without reference to that of recklessness, as sufficient for all cases of involuntary manslaughter, except those of motor manslaughter. The House of Lords set out, however, to frame a definition which would serve as a universal test for directing juries in all cases of this type, including those concerned with motor manslaughter. Lord Mackay of Clashfern LC, with whose opinion the other members agreed, reasserted the authority of *R v Bateman* (1925) 19 Cr App Rep 8 and *Andrews v Director of Public Prosecutions* [1937] AC 576, describing the latter decision as the most authoritative statement of the present law. He went on to state (at p 187):

> On this basis in my opinion the ordinary principles of the law of negligence apply to ascertain whether or not the defendant has been in breach of a duty of care towards the victim who has died. If such breach of duty is established the next question is whether that breach of duty caused the death of the victim. If so, the jury must go on to consider whether that breach of duty should be characterised as gross negligence and therefore as a crime. This will depend on the seriousness of the breach of duty committed by the defendant in all the circumstances in which the defendant was placed when it occurred. The jury will have to consider whether the extent to which the defendant's conduct departed from the proper standard of care incumbent upon him, involving as it must have done a risk of death to the patient, was such that it should be judged criminal.

It is true that to a certain extent this involves an element of circularity, but in this branch of the law I do not believe that is fatal to its being correct as a test of how far conduct must depart from accepted standards to be characterised as criminal. This is necessarily a question of degree and an attempt to specify that degree more closely is I think likely to achieve only a spurious precision. The essence of the matter which is supremely a jury question is whether having regard to the risk of death involved, the conduct of the defendant was so bad in all the circumstances as to amount in their judgment to a criminal act or omission . . .

Notwithstanding the importance of achieving clarity, simplicity and consistency in manslaughter directions, the decision in *R v Adomako* cannot be applied as a test in jurisdictions where causing death by reckless driving is a possible alternative offence . . . In jurisdictions, such as Jamaica, where the statutory offence of causing death by reckless driving continues to coexist along with the common law crime of manslaughter, it is in their lordships' view important that juries should ordinarily be made aware of the existence of the lesser offence . . . Their lordships will humbly advise Her Majesty that the appeal should be allowed.

DEFENCES

There are many defences to prevent responsibility for conduct that has been classified as criminal. This book will not review all these defences but will address two common areas where the issue of the appropriateness of claimed defences arises.

Mistake as to facts

An honest mistake as to facts may provide a defence against criminal liability.

Williams (Hubert) v The State (1995) 48 WIR 328 (TT)

Facts: The applicant was a senior police officer. The incident occurred shortly after midnight on 31 December (Old Year's day) and a few minutes into the dawn of the New Year (New Year's Day). It is common ground that for the purpose of ushering in the New Year the head of the family, Alfred Boodoosingh, had arranged a function at his home at La Pastora Road in Santa Cruz at which a host of his relatives and a few friends, including the deceased (his brother-in-law) and the applicant and his wife, were invitees and were in attendance. Much feasting, merriment and imbibing of alcohol were taking place. As the Old Year was coming to its end and with the New Year on the horizon, there was agreement that the participants should all leave the upstairs portion of the building, where they were celebrating, and proceed to the grounds outside the building to gather there and continue the celebration into the New Year. This they all did. The lighting in this area was not good, more particularly so (as emphasised by both attorneys for the applicant and the state) since it was then late into the night.

As the New Year arrived, there was gay abandon and revelry among the crowd, and pleasantries were exchanged. And during all this, there were numerous loud explosions of bamboo and of fire crackers outside the premises and in the surrounding neighbourhood. There was also the loud bursting of fire crackers on the premises itself. These are features which are common and customary in the life of Trinidad and Tobago on this night and at about this time. As a matter of fact, so gay was the merriment that in the course of it a child of a member of the family exploded a fire cracker the sparks from which latched on to her dress and caught it afire. Happily, aid was rushed to her and the fire was put out. It was, no doubt, the portent of a most tragic event that was to follow.

During all these exchanges of pleasantries, merriment, loud explosions and commotion Alfred Boodoosingh, unknown to the other celebrants, went back to his house, fetched his licensed firearm, which was quite 'tiny', and rejoined the group. In the midst of all this spirit of camaraderie, he fired off his firearm and passed it to the deceased who did likewise; and later it was passed on to the applicant with the invitation to do the same. No one told the applicant that what was being passed to him was a loaded firearm. On receiving the firearm the applicant, who was by that time some distance away from the deceased and who at the time was not standing erect but was in a swaying motion, obliged. The deceased then fell to the ground. Except for Alfred Boodoosingh, of course, everybody felt that this act on the part of the deceased was all fun, for he himself was displaying that sort of mood and was known to be in the habit of indulging in jocular behaviour regularly. It was only after Calina Boodoosingh, the wife of Alfred Boodoosingh, having approached the deceased and realised his condition, raised an alarm, that those present realised what was the matter. Pandemonium then reigned. In the case of the applicant, he immediately expressed surprise and concern and thereafter rebuked Alfred Boodoosingh. The deceased was rushed to hospital accompanied by Alfred Boodoosingh, his son (Neil Boodoosingh) and the applicant but succumbed to his death.

Held: Bernard, CJ

That if the applicant was labouring under a mistake of fact as to the material circumstances when he committed the alleged offence, he was to be judged according to his mistaken view of the facts (a subjective test), regardless of whether his mistake was reasonable or unreasonable (viewed objectively); the reasonableness (or otherwise) of the accused's belief was only material to the issue whether he in fact held that belief. The firearm, which

Alfred Boodoosingh had fetched from his room, unknown to the company, and which he and the deceased fired off during all these noises and revelry, was 'tiny'. When the applicant, on invitation, did likewise and the deceased fell to the ground, everyone felt that this was all a case of play-acting. As soon as the truth was appreciated, the applicant expressed surprise at first, followed later by expressions of indignation at Alfred Boodoosingh's thoughtlessness. At the first opportunity, he raised the point about his belief. This found support from the firearms experts themselves, one of whom was a prosecution witness. To say that despite all of these compelling circumstances, gross recklessness ought to be found nonetheless on the flimsy premise that he was a man trained in musketry, would not only bestow upon the applicant the gift of infallibility, as we said, but indeed take the onerous burden of proof of guilt into the realm of absurdity.

Having regard to all the circumstances of this case, we are satisfied that no reasonable jury properly directed would convict the applicant. In the result, we decline to order a retrial and we set the applicant free.

Ignorance of the law

The idea of ignorance of the law being a defence against criminal liability is one that has been rejected. It has been frequently asserted that a purported defence of ignorance of the law is wholly unacceptable and has no place in the jurisprudence of criminal law.

Pouderoyen Village Council v Singh; Pouderoyen Village Council v Samuels, Jahoor, Deonaraine And Others (1961) 3 WIR 178 (GY)

Facts: The respondents were ratepayers of the Village District of P. The appellants, the Village Council of P, prior to levying a rate, by their chairman published a notice calling upon owners of houses in the district 'to call at the Village Office on Monday, 4 January 1960, between the hours of 8 am and 11 am so as to receive Schedules which after filling should be handed to the appraisers at the Village Office on Monday, 18 January 1960, between 8 am and 11 am.' The notice was posted up about 7.30 am on 4 January 1960, and at that hour many of the villagers had already left for work and would not return until later in the day. In an action seeking a declaration that the appraisements made were null and void and an injunction restraining the appellants from recovering the taxes, the judge held that the notice was bad because a reasonable time in which to obtain their forms from the Village Office had not been given to ratepayers, and granted the declaration and injunction.

Held: Wylie, J (COA)
The respondent, as I understand the argument, contends, however, that one or other of these requirements must be read into that section because a proprietor will lose his right of appeal if he does not supply the approved particulars and there is no provision elsewhere for these particulars to be brought to the notice of proprietors. That state of the law, as I understand his contention, means that the legislature must be presumed to have intended to impose an obligation to bring these particulars to the notice of proprietors and that, as the particulars are provided for only in s 97(1) when dealing with this notice, the intention of the legislature must have been to cast that obligation on the local authority and to require the latter to fulfil it either by including the particulars in the notice or by providing for a reasonable opportunity in the notice to obtain these particulars. The fallacy in that reasoning lies in the assumption that the legislature must have intended to impose an obligation on someone to bring the approved particulars to the notice of proprietors.

> All that can be conclusively presumed from this state of the law is that the legislature must have intended that a proprietor must be able to obtain the necessary information. If he can obtain it, he can protect his right of appeal. Ignorance of the law is no excuse and therefore it must be assumed that a proprietor will be aware of the state of the law and that, when a notice is published pursuant to s 97(1), he will be aware of his legal position as set out in s 101(3) . . . Section 97 of the Ordinance did not require the Village Council to specify in the notice a time and place at which proprietors could obtain forms containing the particulars and the notice complied with the provisions of the section. Appeal allowed.

CORPORATE CRIMINAL LIABILITY

The general rule is that a corporation (such as an incorporated company) may be criminally liable in the same manner as a natural person. Corporate criminal liability arises in three main ways.

Vicarious liability

Vicarious liability is the mechanism by which the court places blame on a person for the acts of another.[18] This position must be understood in the context that in criminal law a person is not vicariously liable for the acts of another which he has not aided, abetted, counselled or procured.[19] However, it is recognised that in some instances an employer can be liable for the offence of another although he has not aided, abetted, counselled or procured the commission of the offence (such as cases of public nuisances or criminal libel).[20] In criminal law, retail companies are often held to be vicariously liable for acts of employees committed during the sale process.

> *Anderton v Rodgers* [1981] Crim LR 404, DC (GB)
>
> **Facts:** Non-members of a social club, which was a members' club registered under the Licensing Act 1964 section 40, were found to have purchased intoxicating liquor from the bar staff. The respondents were the committee of the club and were charged with selling intoxicating liquor contrary to section 160 of the 1964 Act. It was agreed that the bar staff were the committee's servants and that none of the committee members had connived at, aided or abetted or been accessories to the illegal sales.
>
> **Held:** Allowing the prosecutor's appeal and remitting to the magistrates with a direction to convict the respondents, that section 160 was an absolute offence; once it was admitted that the bar staff were the committee's servants, the committee members were *ipso facto* guilty under s 160, bearing in mind the objects of the section as set out in *Williamson v Norris* [1899] 1 QB 7; the fact that a servant contravened a specific order in committing the offence was no defence for those who gave the order.

Individual liability for breach of a statutory duty

There are criminal offences committed in the name of a corporation that can be attributed to individuals. A model of individual responsibility has been adapted by the common law to

18 Ormerod, *Smith and Hogan*, p 258.
19 Card, *Card, Cross and Jones*, p 798.
20 Card, *Card, Cross and Jones*, p 798.

corporations by breaking them down, metaphorically, into their underlying human components to see if there was an individual within the company who had committed the *actus reus* of a crime with the appropriate *mens rea.*

R v Patterson 2002 NSPC 14 (CA)

Facts: The Canada Customs and Revenue Agency charged Mark Ramsay Patterson, the accused, that he did, at or near Halifax, in the County of Halifax, Province of Nova Scotia between 1 May 1997 and 30 September 1997 commit several breaches of the Excise Tax Act. The accused, pursuant to Criminal Code ss 655 and 795 admitted the following facts:

(a) That the taxpayer was an officer and director of the numbered company, 3007299 Nova Scotia Limited, an incorporated company registered in Nova Scotia, hereafter referred to as the company and referred to in Exhibits 374, 286 and 287 of Volume II.
(b) That the company dealt with Darren Throop and his numbered company, 3006970 Nova Scotia Limited, an incorporated company also registered in Nova Scotia and referred to in Exhibits 269, 270, and 271 of Volume II, and also dealt with Dale Guiney and his numbered company, 3008894 Nova Scotia Limited, an incorporated company also registered in Nova Scotia.
(c) That Darren Throop and Dale Guiney through their said numbered companies applied for input tax credits pursuant to the Excise Tax Act amounting to CAN$189,135.98 over the time period and sought to receive CAN$99,713.88 in tax refunds over the time period pursuant to the Excise Tax Act, RSC 1985, chapter E-15.

The said tax refunds were based on the alleged purchase of 40 used vehicles from the company. The said used vehicles were never in the possession of the company during the time period and were never sold to Darren Throop and/or his numbered company, or to Dale Guiney and/or his numbered company. The said used vehicles were also never shipped to Yukon Auto Sales, a registered company incorporated in the province of Quebec and owned and operated by Robert Arena of Montreal, Quebec, hereinafter referred to as Yukon Auto. The bills of lading of Classy Carriers, Exhibits 186 to 210 inclusive, were all fraudulent. Classy Carriers never transported the said used vehicles as listed in Exhibits 36 to 132, and 156 to 180 to Yukon Auto. As a result of the non-existent used vehicles, no valid purchase and/or sale agreements or transactions took place; and therefore, no one was entitled to input tax credits or tax refunds pursuant to the Excise Tax Act as applied for by Darren Throop, Dale Guiney or their said numbered companies as referred to in Exhibits 1 to 5, Volume I, and Exhibits 283–4 of Volume II inclusive. The company never remitted any tax purportedly collected as referred to in Exhibits 36–42, Volume I, and Exhibits 278, 282, Volume II inclusive. Exhibits 1–5, Volume I and Exhibits 278, 282–4, Volume II inclusive, are false and deceptive statements pursuant to the said Excise Tax Act.

Held: Williams, J
I concluded that the accused, along with others, put into place a scheme. It required the active participation of at least three corporate entities, two in Nova Scotia, where we pay Harmonised Sales Tax and one in Quebec, where they do not combine Goods and Services Tax and Provincial Sales Tax. It also required the involvement of individuals who were familiar with the buying and selling of vehicles. Therefore, understanding the means of communicating the scheme is important as the principals who created the companies are different legal personalities to the companies themselves. However, the principals are

the means by which the will or purposes of the companies are communicated or expressed. In theory, it is a question of the act of the company versus the acts of the principals. This aspect can however be resolved in looking at the role of the principals and in particular, as here, the role and function of the accused.

In my view, on the evidence that I accept, he acted as the fulcrum between the Nova Scotia companies and the Quebec company. It was through him that all the corporate entities found fulfilment of the common goal. Without him or his co-operation, the Quebec company could not fulfil its role in carrying out its part of the common enterprise and the Nova Scotia companies, in particular the numbered company 3007299 Nova Scotia Limited, could not function or actualise their designed functions and roles. Further, I think that the purpose for the creation of the triad of companies never could have evolved separate and apart from the active participation and co-operation of the principals in the scheme.

Thus, it seems to me that the accused actions became fused or assumed in the activities of the numbered company, 3007299 Nova Scotia Limited. Although he is an individual separate and apart from the company, he voluntarily and willingly participated in its activities and vicariously in that of the other companies. His actions were contingent upon or depended upon the activities of the triad of companies. In his co-ordinated activity with the activity of the principals of the participating companies he benefited from the common enterprise. His personal undeclared incomes, his offshore banking account and his lifestyle manifested this. Because a corporation is an abstraction with no mind of its own, humans who become its directing mind must direct its activities and will. Thus, frequently, the state of mind of the human individual is the state of mind of the corporation. Therefore, on that premise, I think that it makes no difference whether the accused, as here, is an individual or the company itself if it can be shown that he is united in his activities with that of the company that he directs. Here, I think that he, so to speak, because of his conduct, as found, became an embodiment of the company. In short, he assumed his company's personality and is therefore, in practical terms, the company and, as such, the company's purposes are manifested or realised through him. Consequently, as his company is part of the triad of companies created, as I have found, for a common purpose, he knowingly participated and helped in the furtherance of that common fraudulent scheme.

Woodhouse v Walsall Metropolitan Borough Council [1994] Env LR 30 QBD (GB)

Facts: The appellant was employed as General Manager, Special Waste Division. He was head-hunted by the company for his knowledge and expertise in the field. The site at Minworth was the only waste disposal site to employ a general manager, that site being the largest and most significant waste disposal site of the company. He had peripheral responsibilities to two other sites, that is Renfrew and Cardiff, of a technical and developmental nature, his main responsibilities being towards the Minworth site. The appellant was responsible to the Director of Special Waste Disposal. The director prepared a monthly report for the board from information imparted by the appellant. At the relevant time approximately 40 people were employed at the site. The management team included the appellant, a site manager and two supervisors. The appellant was in a position to formulate and issue instructions to the site manager and supervisors. He had the authority to inspect the site. The appellant had no authority to hire employees. He had authority to spend money on behalf of the company with the permission of his director. The site manager reported to the appellant that he had a right to question the appellant's decision on commercial or legal aspects. The appellant was informed of the annual budget which detailed how he was expected to spend money. The appellant had stated in interview that he had authority to speak on behalf of the company.

As to the commission of the alleged offence, Minworth includes an area used as a vehicle park. Between 4 and 30 April 1991 CEL used a trailer parked on the area as a vehicle park for storing controlled waste. That was an offence under section 3(1)(b) [which prohibited unlicensed disposal of waste], of which CEL was convicted by Sutton Coldfield Magistrates on a plea of guilty on 12 October 1992. Additionally, a prosecution was brought against Mr Woodhouse personally under section 87(1) on the basis that he was a manager. He was convicted on 28 October 1992. The sole ground of challenge to that conviction was that Mr Woodhouse was not a manager and therefore not a person who could be convicted under section 87(1). Looking at the articles of association of CEL, they provided that the business of CEL should be managed by the directors. It appeared that in practice CG was managed as a group. There was a Group Board and an Executive Management Committee. All this was to be discovered from the documents. Mr Woodhouse reported to Mr Hynes, Special Waste Director, who was one of the directors of CEL and was a member of the Group Executive Management Committee, which Mr Woodhouse was not.

The basic contention on behalf of the appellant was that the words 'Director, manager, secretary, or other similar officer of the body corporate' in section 87(1), and similar provisions in other penal statutes, refer to those persons who by the memorandum and articles of association, or as a result of action taken by the directors or by the company in general meeting pursuant to the articles, are entrusted with the exercise of the powers of the company.

Held: McCowan, LJ
I have said that a board of directors can delegate part of their functions of management so as to make their delegate an embodiment of the company within the sphere of the delegation . . . The questions posed for the opinion of the High Court were these:

(1) Whether, in the light of the facts we found we were right in law in the case of information laid against Mr Michael Woodhouse to find that Mr M Woodhouse was a manager within the meaning of section 87(1) of the *Control of Pollution Act* 1974.
(2) Whether there was any evidence to support the finding that Mr Michael Woodhouse was a manager within the said subsection.

I would give the answer 'no' to both those questions. It follows that I would allow the appeal.

Liability on the basis of the 'directing mind' principle

In *mens rea* offences, if the court finds the officer or managerial level employee to be a vital organ of the company and virtually its directing mind in the sphere of duty assigned him so that his actions and intent are deemed the action and intent of the company itself, the company can be held criminally liable even where the criminal act was performed not wholly for the benefit of the company. The individual must, however, have been acting within the scope of the area of the work assigned to him. In the case of fraud, where the benefit accrues only to the manager employee and is not intended to be for the benefit of the company, the corporate entity may be able to escape liability.

Presidential Security Services of Australia Pty Ltd v Brilley [2008] NSWCA 204 (AU)

Facts: At about 4.00 am on 23 June 2003 the plaintiff broke into and entered the Earlwood Bardwell Park Sports Club. He was in the company of three others. They intended to steal cash from the club's gambling room. At the time, David Arthur Bingle, a security guard, was in the club. He was the managing director and sole employee of the appellant. Mr Bingle was guarding the premises in the course of his employment with the appellant. Shortly after the plaintiff entered the club, Mr Bingle fired a Magnum revolver at him and wounded him. Mr Bingle then fired at the plaintiff's accomplices, who fled. The Magnum carried six bullets. Mr Bingle fired several shots. He did not know how many. Mr Bingle attempted to eject the spent cartridges and fumbled in his pockets for bullets. While he was doing this, the plaintiff ran out of the club and jumped into a car that he and his accomplices had parked in the parking area. As the car drove away, Mr Bingle fired a shot at it and then a further shot that caused the rear window of the vehicle to shatter. Mr Bingle admitted only the latter shot. The car then drove away from the scene.

The plaintiff claimed damages for personal injuries from the appellant (and not Mr Bingle personally). He relied on two causes of action, namely, negligence, and/or alternatively 'assault and/or battery . . . on the part of the appellant through its servants, agents and/or sub-contractors'. O'Toole DCJ dismissed the plaintiff's claim in negligence and that cause of action played no part in this appeal. Her Honour, however, upheld the cause of action based on assault and battery and awarded the plaintiff damages amounting in total to AU$185,267. The appellant appealed against her Honour's judgment.

Held: Ipp, JA

There are two classes of criminal offence that a company cannot commit. The first class arises by virtue of a company's status as an unnatural or artificial person. For example, a company cannot commit suicide or bigamy. The second class arises by virtue of the company's inability to be punished. Thus, a company cannot commit a crime where the only punishment is a term of imprisonment . . . The fact that a company is capable of committing a crime and may be indicted for an offence does not, however, mean that the inherent characteristics of an artificial person are not relevant to whether a company may be found guilty of certain offences, particularly those offences of which *mens rea* is an element. Generally speaking, once a company is capable of committing a particular offence, it may be found guilty of that offence on one of two bases, namely, on the grounds of vicarious responsibility or on the basis that the person who committed the *actus reus* and had the requisite *mens rea* was the directing mind and embodiment of the company in the *Tesco Supermarkets Ltd v Nattrass* [1972] AC 153 sense. Whether the company may be found guilty on one or other of these bases depends on the legislation applicable, the nature of the offence in question, and the status and position within the company of the person who performs the acts said to constitute the offence.

Generally, a company will not be found guilty, on the basis of vicarious liability for a criminal offence having *mens rea* as an element. This is traceable to at least the eighteenth century. In *Huggins* (1730) 2 Stra 883, Raymond CJ stated at 885: 'It is a point not to be disputed but that in a criminal case the principal is not answerable for the act of his deputy, as he is in civil cases; they must each answer for their own acts, and stand or fall by their own behaviour.' As Lord Morris and Lord Diplock explained in *Tesco Supermarkets Ltd v Nattrass*, the rejection of vicarious liability in the criminal context is based upon a refusal to attach criminal liability to a person absent a guilty mind. Lord Morris said, (at 179):

'In general, criminal liability only results from personal fault. We do not punish people in criminal courts for the misdeeds of others. The principle of *respondeat superior* is applicable in our civil courts but not generally in our criminal courts.' Lord Diplock said, (at 199):

> To constitute a criminal offence, a physical act done by any person must generally be done by him in some reprehensible state of mind. Save in cases of strict liability where a criminal statute, exceptionally, makes the doing of an act a crime irrespective of the state of mind in which it is done, criminal law regards a person as responsible for his own crimes only. It does not recognise the liability of a principal for the criminal acts of his agent: because it does not ascribe to him his agent's state of mind. *Qui peccat per alium peccat per se* is not a maxim of criminal law.

I reiterate that, absent a statutory provision to the contrary, vicarious liability has been rejected as a means of establishing *mens rea* in crimes requiring proof of that element (as otherwise criminal guilt could be found without the offender possessing the necessary intent).

The situation is different, however, where *mens rea* does not form part of the offence. Parliament may create offences of strict or absolute liability, and it has long been accepted that, in such a case, the application of vicarious liability principles is not inhibited . . . Assault is not an offence of strict or absolute liability. Furthermore, there is nothing in ss 59 or 61 of the Crimes Act that indicates that the requisite *mens rea* for the establishment of those offences can be derived vicariously from a servant or agent of a corporation. It follows that the appellant in this case could not be vicariously criminally liable for an assault committed by Mr Bingle in the course of his employment.

The issue whether the appellant was criminally liable for assault because Mr Bingle was its directing mind and physical embodiment was not raised in the pleadings, nor was it dealt with in her Honour's reasons. It was, however, the subject of the parties' written submissions and in my view it must be considered in this appeal. It is an obvious issue and it is of fundamental importance. It was common ground that Mr Bingle was the managing director and sole employee of the appellant. He referred in evidence to the appellant as 'my company'. On the recognised tests, Mr Bingle was the directing mind and embodiment of the appellant . . . Once it is accepted that Mr Bingle was the directing mind and embodiment of the appellant, his conduct and his state of mind were capable of being attributed to the appellant, provided of course that his relevant acts were performed on the appellant's behalf. I have mentioned that the appellant admitted in the pleadings that it was vicariously liable for the acts of Mr Bringle on the morning in question. I think inherent in that admission are the further admissions that Mr Bingle's acts were performed in the interests of the appellant, were its acts, and Mr Bingle performed those acts when acting as the directing mind and embodiment of the appellant. Accordingly I would accept that the primary judge correctly attributed Mr Bingle's conduct and state of mind during each of the three episodes on 23 June 2003 to the appellant . . .

In my opinion, the problems I have identified with her Honour's factual findings are so material that they cannot stand . . . The appeal is upheld.

Canadian Dredge & Dock Co. v The Queen [1985] 1 SCR 662 (CA)

Facts: Four corporate appellants appealed their convictions under ss 338(1) and 423(1)(d) of the Criminal Code. The several counts in the indictment related to contracts between certain public authorities and the accused where the bids were alleged to have been tendered on a collusive basis, with the low bidders including in their costs compensation to be paid to the 'high bidders' or 'non-bidders'. Each company had a manager who conducted the business of the company relating to the submission of bids for tender. Corporate criminal liability was denied by the appellants, notwithstanding the position of these managers because these managers allegedly (1) were acting in fraud of the appellant-employers, (2) were acting throughout for their own benefit, or (3) were acting contrary to instructions and hence outside of the scope of their employment with the appellants. Several companies also challenged the existence of any theory of corporate criminal liability for *mens rea* offences.

Held: Estey, J (delivering the judgment of the Court)
The position of the corporation in criminal law must first be examined. Inasmuch as all criminal and quasi-criminal offences are creatures of statute the amenability of the corporation to prosecution necessarily depends in part upon the terminology employed in the statute . . .

At common law a corporate entity could not generally be convicted of criminal offence. Corporate criminal immunity stemmed from the abhorrence of the common law for vicarious liability in criminal law, and from the doctrine of *ultra vires*, which regarded criminal activities by corporate agents as beyond their authority and beyond corporate capacity. At the other extreme in the spectrum of criminal offences there are certain crimes which cannot in any real sense be committed by a corporation as a principal, such as perjury and bigamy, whatever the doctrine of corporate criminal liability may be. As a corporation may only act through agents, there are basically only three approaches whereby criminal intent could be said to reside or not reside in the corporate entity:

(i) a total vicarious liability for the conduct of any of its agents whatever their level of employment or responsibility so long as they are acting within the scope of their employment;
(ii) no criminal liability unless the criminal acts in question have been committed on the direction or at the request, express or clearly implied, of the corporation as expressed through its board of directors;
(iii) a median rule whereby the criminal conduct, including the state of mind, of employees and agents of the corporation is attributed to the corporation so as to render the corporation criminally liable so long as the employee or agent in question is of such a position in the organisation and activity of the corporation that he or she represents its de facto directing mind, will, centre, brain area or ego so that the corporation is identified with the act of that individual.

There is said to be on this theory no responsibility through vicarious liability or any other form of agency, but rather a liability arising in criminal law by reason of the single identity wherein is combined the legal entity and the natural person; in short, a primary liability. This rule stands in the middle of the range or spectrum. It is but a legal fiction invented for pragmatic reasons.

The position of the corporation in criminal law has been under examination by courts and lawmakers for centuries . . . I apprehend that, according to the authorities that my Lord has cited, his knowledge and intention must be imputed to the company. See also *R v I.C.R. Haulage, Ltd.* [1944] KB 551 to the same effect. These general principles found application in the courts of this country in a series of cases. In *R v Fane Robinson Ltd.* [1941] 3 DLR 409, the Court of Appeal of Alberta set aside an acquittal of two companies where two of its directors and officers conspired with another to defraud an insurance company by inflating the charges made by the defendant company to the insurance company for automobile repairs. Ford JA, for the Court, found, at p 415, that the two officers were the acting and directing will of [the accused corporation] generally and in particular in respect of the subject matter of the offences with which it is charged, that their culpable intention (*mens rea*) and their illegal act (*actus reus*) were the intention and the act of the company and that conspiracy to defraud and obtaining money by false pretences are offences which a corporation is capable of committing. In so doing the Court followed the United Kingdom authorities, including *Lennard's, supra*, and found the company criminally liable stating, at p 410: 'if the act complained of can be treated as that of the company, the corporation is criminally responsible for all such acts as it is capable of committing and for which the prescribed punishment is one which it can be made to endure' . . .

The transition from virtual corporate immunity from criminal liability to virtual equality with humans in like circumstances under the criminal law is traced in greater detail by Jessup J, as he then was, in *R v J.J. Beamish Construction Co., supra*. Three years later Schroeder JA, of the Court of Appeal of Ontario, in *R v St. Lawrence Corp., supra*, at pp 315–21, again reviewed this transition. In the end Schroeder JA, at p 320, adopted the same statement of the governing principle as Jessup J had in *Beamish, supra*, although the earlier case is not cited:

> While in cases other than criminal libel, criminal contempt of court, public nuisance and statutory offences of strict liability criminal liability is not attached to a corporation for the criminal acts of its servants or agents upon the doctrine of *respondeat superior*, nevertheless, if the agent falls within a category which entitles the court to hold that he is a vital organ of the body corporate and virtually its directing mind and will in the sphere of duty and responsibility assigned to him so that his action and intent are the very action and intent of the company itself, then his conduct is sufficient to render the company indictable by reason thereof.

. . . This rule of law was seen as a result of the removal of the officer or managerial level employee from the general class of inferior servants or agents for whose acts the corporate employer continued (as in the case of the human employer) to be immune from vicarious liability in criminal law. This result is generally referred to as the 'identification' theory. It produces the element of *mens rea* in the corporate entity, otherwise absent from the legal entity but present in the natural person, the directing mind. This establishes the identity between the directing mind and the corporation which results in the corporation being found guilty for the act of the natural person, the employee . . .

The Court in *St. Lawrence, supra*, in describing the elements of the delegation theory, concluded by adding that attribution to the corporation occurred only so long as the directing will was acting in the scope of his employment. The expression comes from the law of tort and agency and from master and servant law. It is not apt in relation to the identification theory. It smacks of vicarious liability and it invites the defence that criminal actions must prima facie be beyond the scope of an employee's duty and authority. The learned trial judge, in directing the jury, expressed it more accurately: 'so long as he was acting within the scope of the area of the work assigned to him'. In *Tesco, supra*, at p 171, Lord Reid employed the phrase acting within the scope of delegation of the corporation's business. The essence of the test is that the identity of the directing mind and the company coincide so long as the actions of the former are performed by the manager within the sector of corporation operation assigned to him by the corporation . . . Glanville Williams, in *Textbook of Criminal Law* (1978), states, at p 947: 'the director or other controlling officer will almost always be a co-perpetrator of or accessory in the offence.' . . . In *St. Lawrence, supra*, and other authorities, a corporation may, by this means, have more than one directing mind . . . The corporation which set the directing mind in position to do the wrong will suffer an economic penalty.

While it is true that this penalty will feed through to the stockholders, who may well be totally innocent as in the case of a large public company, it may be seen as a risk or cost associated with the privilege of operating through the corporate vehicle. In the case of personal corporations, the imposition of a criminal penalty on the corporation may be an additional penalty imposed upon the 'personal' corporate stockholder but such a result would be an acceptable part of the sentencing process as it simply reflects the economic identification, as well as the legal identification, present in such a corporation. In the case of a public corporation, the economic identification factor is absent, and in a theoretical sense there is an additional penalty for the same act which must be justified in some way other than that suggested above. This is the inevitable result of the pragmatic adoption of the attribution of the acts of its delegates to the delegating corporation in order to bring that corporation within the system of criminal justice.

Whether the route taken be the doctrine of *respondeat superior* or identification, the result is the same. The corporation in reality has three elements: the legal entity, the personal shareholder (a natural person directly or indirectly), and the employee. Once the process is set in motion, the criminal penalty will extend directly or indirectly to all three which is quite unlike the situation of a natural proprietor where only two of these elements are present. All this, in my view, while not entirely logical, is a tolerable result for a community where reality dictates corporate criminal accountability in certain circumstances . . .

I turn to the submission by the appellants that the identification theory cannot import into the criminal law a brand of vicarious liability under any of the authorities where the wrongful acts of the directing mind were done in fraud on the employer, for the benefit of the employee, or contrary to the instructions issued by the employer . . . Where the directing mind conceives and designs a plan and then executes it whereby the corporation is intentionally defrauded, and when this is the substantial part of the regular activities of the directing mind in his office, then it is unrealistic in the extreme to consider that the manager is the directing mind of the corporation. His entire energies are, in such a case, directed to the destruction of the undertaking of the corporation. When he crosses that line he ceases to be the directing mind and the doctrine of identification ceases to operate.

The same reasoning and terminology can be applied to the concept of benefits. Where the criminal act is totally in fraud of the corporate employer and where the act is intended to and does result in benefit exclusively to the employee-manager, the employee-directing mind, from the outset of the design and execution of the criminal plan, ceases to be a directing mind of the corporation and consequently his acts could not be attributed to the corporation under the identification doctrine. This might be true as well on the American approach through *respondeat superior*. Whether this is so or not, in my view the identification doctrine only operates where the Crown demonstrates that the action taken by the directing mind (a) was within the field of operation assigned to him; (b) was not totally in fraud of the corporation; and (c) was by design or result partly for the benefit of the company . . .

There is no evidence, however, that the directing minds in these affairs acted wholly for their own benefit, nor did any of them act wholly in fraud of their employer in the sense of designing and executing a scheme to deprive their respective employer corporations of any and all dredging business or benefit therefrom. Here the voluminous evidence paints a clear picture of a design conceived by a group of conspiratorial directing minds which was not aimed at the destruction of the respective corporate employers but rather was calculated to ensure their existence at a level of profits sustained by fraudulently enhanced prices for the work and services of the corporations . . .

There can be no complete rationalisation of corporate criminal liability in the criminal law whether the attempt be made under the banner of vicarious liability or the identification theory or otherwise. The corporation does not have, in the human sense of the term, a mind capable of reaching the state identified in criminal law as *mens rea*. The criminal law does not recognise in *mens rea* offences criminal liability in the proprietor employer for the unlawful actions of the proprietor's employees save in the case of authorisation, express or implied. A corporation, however, is found liable in some countries, as we have seen, on vicarious liability, and in other jurisdictions on the basis of the identification theory. Both doctrines are the product of judicial necessity brought on by the realities of the modern community . . . The identification theory, however, loses its basis in rationality when it is applied to condemn a corporation under the criminal law for the conduct of its manager when that manager is acting not in any real sense as its directing mind but rather as its arch enemy . . .

In my view, the very pragmatic origins of the identification rule militate against its extension to the situation which would have existed here had one or more of the directing minds acted entirely for his own benefit and directed his principal efforts to defrauding the company. Where the corporation benefited or was intended to be benefited from the fraudulent and criminal activities of the directing mind, the *rationale* of the identification rule holds. Where the delegate of the corporation has turned against his principal, the *rationale* fades away . . . The appeals should be dismissed.

Tesco Supermarkets Ltd. v Nattrass [1971] AC 153 (GB)

Facts: The appellants owned a large number of supermarkets in which they sold a wide variety of goods. The goods were put out for sale on shelves or stands, each article being marked with the price at which it was offered for sale. The customer selected the articles he wanted, took them to the cashier, and paid the price. From time to time the appellants, apparently by way of advertisement, sold 'flash packs' at prices lower than the normal price. In September 1969 they were selling Radiant washing powder in this way. The normal price was 3s 11d but these packs were marked and sold at 2s 11d. Posters were displayed in the shops drawing attention to this reduction in price. These prices were displayed in the appellants' shop at Northwich on 26 September.

Mr Coane, an old-age pensioner, saw this and went to buy a pack. He could only find packs marked 3s 11d. He took one to the cashier who told him that there were none in stock for sale at 2s 11d. He paid 3s 11d and complained to an inspector of weights and measures. This resulted in a prosecution under the Trade Descriptions Act 1968 and the appellants were fined £25 and costs.

Held: Lord Reid

In some of these cases the employer charged with the offence was a limited company. But in others the employer was an individual and still it was held that he, though personally entirely blameless, could not rely on these provisions if the fault which led to the commission of the offence was the fault of a servant in failing to carry out his duty to instruct or supervise his subordinates. Where a limited company is the employer difficult questions do arise in a wide variety of circumstances in deciding which of its officers or servants is to be identified with the company so that his guilt is the guilt of the company.

I must start by considering the nature of the personality which by a fiction the law attributes to a corporation. A living person has a mind which can have knowledge or intention or be negligent and he has hands to carry out his intentions. A corporation has none of these: it must act through living persons, though not always one or the same person. Then the person who acts is not speaking or acting for the company. He is acting as the company and his mind which directs his acts is the mind of the company. There is no question of the company being vicariously liable. He is not acting as a servant, representative, agent or delegate. He is an embodiment of the company or, one could say, he hears and speaks through the persona of the company, within his appropriate sphere, and his mind is the mind of the company. If it is a guilty mind then that guilt is the guilt of the company. It must be a question of law whether, once the facts have been ascertained, a person in doing particular things is to be regarded as the company or merely as the company's servant or agent. In that case any liability of the company can only be a statutory or vicarious liability . . .

In some cases the phrase alter ego has been used. I think it is misleading. When dealing with a company the word alter is I think misleading. The person who speaks and acts as the company is not alter. He is identified with the company and when dealing with an individual no other individual can be his alter ego. The other individual can be a servant, agent, delegate or representative but I know of neither principle nor authority which warrants the confusion (in the literal or original sense) of two separate individuals . . .

I think that the true view is that the judge must direct the jury that if they find certain facts proved then as a matter of law they must find that the criminal act of the officer, servant or agent including his state of mind, intention, knowledge or belief is the act of the company. I have already dealt with the considerations to be applied in deciding when such a person can and when he cannot be identified with the company. I do not see how the nature of the charge can make any difference. If the guilty man was in law identifiable with the company then whether his offence was serious or venial his act was the act of the company but if he was not so identifiable then no act of his, serious or otherwise, was the act of the company itself . . . It is sometimes argued – it was argued in the present case – that making an employer criminally responsible, even when he has done all that he could to prevent an offence, affords some additional protection to the public because this will induce him to do more. But if he has done all he can how can he do more? . . .

I have said that a board of directors can delegate part of their functions of management so as to make their delegate an embodiment of the company within the sphere of the delegation. But here the board never delegated any part of their functions. They set up a chain of command through regional and district supervisors, but they remained in control. The shop managers had to obey their general directions and also take orders from their superiors. The acts or omissions of shop managers were not acts of the company itself. In my judgment the appellants established the statutory defence. I would therefore allow this appeal.

Held: Lord Diplock

In my view, therefore, the question: what natural persons are to be treated in law as being the company for the purpose of acts done in the course of its business, including the taking of precautions and the exercise of due diligence to avoid the commission of a criminal offence, is to be found by identifying those natural persons who by the memorandum and articles of association or as a result of action taken by the directors, or by the company in general meeting pursuant to the articles, are entrusted with the exercise of the powers of the company . . .

My Lords, there may be criminal statutes which upon their true construction ascribe to a corporation criminal responsibility for the acts of servants and agents who would be excluded by the test that I have stated to be appropriate in determining whether a corporation has itself committed a criminal offence. The Trade Descriptions Act 1968, however, so far from containing anything which compels one to reject that test, recognises, by section 20, the distinction between 'any director, manager, secretary or other similar officer of a body corporate' and other persons who are merely its servants or agents. Section 20 (1) provides as follows:

> Where an offence under this Act which has been committed by a body corporate is proved to have been committed with the consent and connivance of, or to be attributable to any neglect on the part of, any director, manager, secretary or other similar officer of the body corporate, or any person who was purporting to act in any such capacity, he as well as the body corporate shall be guilty of that offence and shall be liable to be proceeded against and punished accordingly.

The natural persons described in this subsection correspond with those who under the memorandum and articles of association of a company exercise the powers of the company itself. From this it follows that if any of them is guilty of neglect in the exercise of those powers such neglect is that of the company itself . . .

Any legal duty, whether arising at common law or imposed by statute, may generally be performed by the person upon whom it is imposed through the agency of some other person. But if it is not performed, the person upon whom the duty is imposed is liable for its non-performance. It is irrelevant that he instructed a servant or agent to perform it on his behalf, if that servant or agent failed to do so. All that is relevant is that the duty was not performed. When the duty is imposed upon a person by statute and non-performance is made a criminal offence without any requirement of *mens rea* this is what is meant by an offence of 'strict liability'. The fallacy lies in the next step of the argument. Where Parliament in creating an offence of 'strict liability' has also provided that it shall be a defence if the person upon whom the duty is imposed proves that *he* exercised all due diligence to avoid a breach of the duty, the clear intention of Parliament is to mitigate the injustice, which may be involved in an offence of strict liability, of subjecting to punishment a careful and conscientious person who is in no way morally to blame. To exercise due diligence to prevent something being done is to take all reasonable steps to prevent it. It may be a reasonable step for an employer to instruct a superior servant to supervise the activities of inferior servants whose physical acts may in the absence of supervision result in that being done which it is sought to prevent. This is not to delegate the employer's duty to exercise all due diligence; it is to perform it. To treat the duty of an employer to exercise due diligence as unperformed unless due diligence was also exercised by all his servants to whom he had reasonably given all proper instructions and upon whom he could reasonably rely to carry them out, would be to render the defence of due diligence nugatory and so thwart the clear intention of Parliament in providing it. For, *pace R. C. Hammett Ltd. v London County Council*, 97 JP 105, there is no logical distinction to be drawn between diligence in supervising and diligence in acting, if the defaults of servants are to be treated in law as the defaults of their employer.

My Lords, the Divisional Court was, I think, right in treating the instant case as governed by the decision in *Series v Poole* [1969] 1 QB 676. But that case was, in my view, wrongly decided and the proposition of law for which *R. C. Hammett Ltd. v London County Council* has been treated as an authority is also erroneous, although the actual decision in that case to dismiss the appeal could have been justified on quite different grounds. I would allow this appeal.

CRIMINAL LIABILITY FOR ACTS IN PURSUANCE OF COMMERCIAL ACTIVITIES

Criminal liability has been ascribed to those engaged in commercial activities where legislatures genuinely determine that their actions ought to be suppressed in the public interest through the use of criminal sanctions. Some of the main areas include public welfare and consumer protection, occupational health and safety, the environment, the economy, money laundering and the internet.

R v Hinchey [1996] 3 SCR 1128 (CA)

Facts: The appellant Morgan Hinchey was employed as a district engineer by the Department of Transportation for the Province of Newfoundland. Beothuck Crushing and Paving Limited was a construction company engaged in the construction of roads for the Province and various municipalities. During the summer and autumn of 1984, James Wall, the General Manager and one of the owners of Beothuck, placed Barbara Hinchey, the wife of the appellant, on the payroll of the company as a standby flag person. Barbara Hinchey was never asked to do any work by Beothuck yet she received payments from the company in the amount of some CAN$7,400. Beothuck also provided Barbara Hinchey with a record of employment confirming that she had been employed for 20 weeks as a flag person from 30 July 1984 to 14 December 1984, thereby qualifying for unemployment insurance benefits.

The appellant, as district engineer of the Department of Transportation, had a great deal of experience in the construction industry. He was in charge of overseeing the construction of roads for the Province and municipal authorities within the Province. In that position he frequently dealt with James Wall acting on behalf of Beothuck which was principally engaged in road construction work. The appellant had the authority to direct, suspend and generally supervise the work done by Beothuck. The appellant and his wife were charged with two counts of fraud (counts 1 and 3) and the appellant with a breach of s 121(1)(c) of the Criminal Code (count 2).

Held: The judgment of La Forest, L'Heureux-Dubé, Gonthier and McLachlin, JJ was delivered by L'Heureux-Dubé, J

Protecting the integrity of government is crucial to the proper functioning of a democratic system. Criminal law has a historic and well-established role in helping to preserve that integrity . . . Canadian courts have repeatedly recognised that s 121(1)(c) exists to preserve both the integrity of the public service and the appearance of integrity of the public service. The government's business must be free from any suggestion of 'under-the-table' rewards or benefits made to those who conduct business on behalf of the government by those who stand to gain from those dealings . . . That integrity is compromised not only by bribery and corruption in their crassest forms, but by other insidious arrangements whereby a government employee profits from his or her position or employment by way of a private benefit or advantage received from a person having dealings with the government. Such advantages or benefits can create the appearance of impropriety and suggest that the loyalty of the employee has been divided between his or her government employer and the private benefactor . . .

[T]he question of the proper scope of the criminal law has been oft considered by both academics and jurists. *Mewett & Manning on Criminal Law* (3rd edn 1994), at pp 16–17, have set out the issue in the following way: How does one determine what acts ought to be subject to criminal sanctions? Some acts, such as a breach of contract or negligent behaviour, may cause untold damage and yet not be criminally punishable while others, such as the theft of a piece of garbage or a minor assault, may cause little or no damage and yet be subject to criminal sanctions. In fact, the harm caused, while one element to be considered, is only one element. Indeed, in some crimes such as conspiracy or attempt, no harm at all may actually materialise . . . Criminal law is premised on the belief that there are some acts that ought to be prevented and on the belief that a criminal process is the best way to achieve this . . . [T]he essence of criminal law is its public nature. A crime is, in fact, not a wrong against the actual person harmed, if there is one – the victim as he may be called (although it may also and coincidentally be a civil wrong against him) – but a wrong against the community as a whole. The prevention – or lessening, since total prevention is not possible – of crime cannot be left to an individual's choice but is the responsibility of any member of the community and, in particular, those who represent the state – the police or the prosecuting authorities. Given this public nature, it is fitting that parliament has consistently played the major role in defining exactly what type of conduct can be considered criminal in nature . . .

A very helpful definition of criminal law can be found in the *Reference re Validity of Section 5(a) of the Dairy Industry Act (Margarine Reference)* [1949] SCR 1. In that case Rand J stated at p 49: 'A crime is an act which the law, with appropriate penal sanctions, forbids; but as prohibitions are not enacted in a vacuum, we can properly look for some evil or injurious or undesirable effect upon the public against which the law is directed. That effect may be in relation to social, economic or political interests; and the legislature has had in mind to suppress the evil or to safeguard the interest threatened.' Lord Atkin expresses the underlined portion, part of a larger quotation by him in a Privy Council decision on the validity of the Combines Investigation Act, RSC 1927, c. 26: '. . . if parliament genuinely determines that commercial activities which can be so described are to be suppressed in the public interest, their Lordships see no reason why parliament should not make them crimes.'

SENTENCING CORPORATIONS

Sanctions for corporations are evaluative and declaratory not merely of the wrongdoing, but of the benefits and desirability of appropriate conduct. In a real sense, corporate sanction may be an inheritance, not a response, to the present or even predecessor corporation's malefaction. Moreover, mechanical application of pre-determined sanctions based upon the technical finding of an offence may be appropriate for certain types of regulatory offences if graded sensibly, but such a process can also resemble licensing or taxation, thus submerging essentials of the punitive message. It follows that, for serious corporate offences, the sentencing process must be designed and carried out with close attention to the particular offence (in its conduct, circumstances and consequences), and the particular statutory framework, and the particular corporate offender. Whereas the sentencing of human beings directly impinges upon the offender, the potential spread of the sanction for corporate offenders makes it necessary for the court to be as clear and precise as possible. If one appreciates this difficulty with corporate sentencing, one can see that some of the principles, concepts and factors included within sentencing policy for individuals do not carry over to sentencing corporations in the same way, if at all.[21]

21 Per Watson, J in *R v General Scrap Iron & Metals Ltd* [2003] ABQB 22 (CA) paras 31–3.

R v General Scrap Iron & Metals Ltd [2003] ABQB 22 (CA)

Facts: The appellant challenged the sentence disposition made by a provincial court judge in relation to its conviction for a count of failure to ensure 'as was reasonably practicable the health and safety of a worker' under s 2(1)(a) of the Occupational Health and Safety Act. The sentence disposition was a fine of CAN$100,000.00, supplemented by a 15 per cent surcharge under the Victims of Crime Act, for a total cost to the appellant of CAN$115,000.00. The count related to the death of a worker on 22 February 2000, at the appellant's scrap yard location at 11915–156 Street, Edmonton. The unfortunate employee, Wlodzimierz Kochanowski, died as a result of a very heavy bale of scrap tech wire falling upon him from a four-high stack of such bales, while he was working nearby the stack. The appellant was also found guilty by the trial judge on a count of 'failure to take all reasonable steps to ensure that such materials were contained or restrained to eliminate the potential danger' related to 'a potential danger of dislodgment, or movement of materials, to wit: bales of wire' under s 67 of the relevant regulation.

Held: Watson, J

Except to the extent that officers, managers or directors of corporations can be implicated in the prosecution as parties to the offences, the sanctioning of corporations themselves has the challenge that, often, the entity being sanctioned is not the entity being spoken to by the sentence disposition. The operating mind[s] of corporations are human beings, but those individuals may not be the same on the date of the offence as on the date of sanction. The configuration of the ownership and management of corporations may change fairly easily . . .

It follows that the communicative aspect of sentencing – which is a vital feature of principles of denunciation and deterrence – is somewhat to speak beyond the corporation itself and to its past, present and future participants, and to those who might participate in similar corporate activity in future. Unless human beings who do or may participate in the sanction receive the applicable message, the sanctioning of corporations would have a reduced long-term effect. It is therefore vital that the recipients of the message carried by the sanction be able to not only understand and appreciate the justness of the sanction, but also that the sanction and sanctioning process persuades those persons to participate in the effort to ensure corporate good conduct and to enhance the well-being of the public. The mere enactment of public welfare offences applicable to corporations cannot achieve the goals of so doing without the voluntary participation and indeed commitment of corporate managers and employees to those goals and the processes designed to achieve them. Accordingly, sanctions for corporations are evaluative and declaratory not merely of the wrongdoing, but of the benefits and desirability of appropriate conduct. In a real sense, corporate sanction may be an inheritance, not a response to the present or even predecessor corporation's malefaction . . .

I conclude, then, that the appropriate approach for sentencing corporations should be to evaluate three aspects of the matter:

(1) the conduct, circumstances and consequences of the offence,

(2) the terms and aims of the relevant enactment or regulation, considered in the larger context of comparable regulation and legitimate corporate functioning in the relevant areas, and

(3) the participation, character and attitude of the corporation offender, considered in the larger context of corporations engaged in relevant industrial or business activity as to aspect (1), in a process which identifies the aggravating and mitigating factors so as to allow rational comparison between cases, and to allow for reasonable expression of why one set of aspects deserves a more or less severe sanction than another . . .

What follows is not intended to be an exhaustive list of matters to consider, nor is it intended to be any sort of mandate. What is offered here is mainly intended to suggest an analytical approach. The court could consider:

(1) the conduct, circumstances and consequences of the offence, noting, for example:

(a) *What were the specific facts which constituted the offence, and what aggravating and mitigating factors related to those specific facts.* The court could consider whether the occurrence of those facts were isolated, or occasional, or regular, or programmatic. The court could consider whether the facts were the product of corporate planning, corporate recklessness, corporate inattention, or corporate incompetence. The court could consider the involvement of particular employees or agents of the corporation, including perhaps the persons who might have become victims of what occurred, and the degree of control of and responsibility for such persons that the corporation can realistically be said to have had.

(b) *What were the surrounding circumstances of the offence, and aggravating and mitigating factors related to those circumstances.* The court could consider issues like the risk of collateral damage as well as the particular harm, and whether it was predictable. The court could consider the relationship between the proscribed conduct and the functioning of the corporation, having regard to such issues as profitability, and also the relationship between the proscribed conduct and the functioning of the relevant industry. The court could consider whether there was flagrance, or whether there was effort to suppress public awareness, or whether the events were unintended incidents occurring unfortunately in an otherwise ordinary and reasonable course of activity. The court could consider the degree to which the activity is regulated or superintended by state agents. The court could consider whether the corporation was in compliance with delegated supervisory duties, or with requirements for reporting to state agents connected with such activity.

(c) *What were the consequences of the offence, and aggravating and mitigating factors related to those circumstances.* The court could consider who were the victims or what damages were caused. The court could consider the *nexus* between the damages and the offence. The court could consider the degree of contribution by the corporation to the offence and through that to the damages. The court could consider if the damages were irreparable, or were reparable only in part, or were reparable fully, or were purely economic and compensable. The court could consider if the corporation had maintained a compensatory capacity for unforeseen damage. The court could consider if the corporation profited or could be expected to profit from the conduct, and if any such profit might be thought to outweigh the hazards of the conduct, noting level of risk of successful prosecution as well as sanction.

(2) the terms and aims of the relevant enactment or regulation, considered in the larger context of comparable regulation and legitimate corporate functioning in the relevant areas, noting, for example:

(a) *What is the extent of state regulatory involvement.* The court could note if the corporate activity was or is highly regulated or loosely regulated, or largely delegated to the private sector. The court could note the wording and implications of the applicable statute and regulations. The court could note the objectives of the applicable statute and regulations. The court could note whether the applicable statute and regulations relate to economic matters, general industrial regulation, occupational health and safety, the environment, or what have you. The court could note the association of the applicable statute or regulation with any larger schemes of public welfare or governmental purposes.

(b) *What are the relevant terms of sanction.* The court could note any maximum or minimum penalties, whether they have changed over time, and what related sanction capacities there might be. The court could consider whether the offence as designed was intended to be closer to absolute liability or closer to *mens rea* on the scale of responsibility. The court could consider whether the legislature or parliament intended that the sanctions mostly be routinised and regular and predictable, or whether the legislature or parliament intended for a wide discretion on the part of the court. The court could consider the nature and location of the offence and the sanctions in any overall architecture of offences and sanctions.

(c) *What would be the consequences of sanction.* The court could note what the effect might be on the corporation or on innocent third parties arising from the sanction that might be imposed upon the corporation. The court could consider options to more focus the sanction on those responsible for the offence. The court could consider combining of sanctions, or emphasising sanctions which compensate or benefit those adversely affected by the offence. The court could note what would be the effect of alternative sanctions on the efficacy or viability of the regulatory or statutory scheme as a whole.

(3) the participation, character and attitude of the corporation offender, considered in the larger context of corporations engaged in relevant industrial or business activity as to aspect (1), noting, for example:

(a) *What was the state of mind of the corporation at the relevant time.* The court could consider whether the offence was the consequence of rogue activity by an individual or individuals inadequately supervised by the corporation, or was the consequence of a corporate culture which turned a blind eye to such activity, or was it the consequence of a corporate culture which encouraged such activity, or was the consequence of planned activity by the operating minds of the corporation. The court could consider if the corporation had a single operating mind, or many, or what sort of managing or directorial levels of responsibility there were.

(b) *What was and is the physical structure of the corporation.* The court could consider the size of the corporation, its position in the relevant industry, its market share, its profitability, its practices generally. The court could consider the nature of management and other features of corporate operations. The court could consider how long the corporation had been in business, whether its managers, directors and employees have had continuity. The court could consider the relative significance of the corporation in the community generally.

(c) *What was and is the attitude and prior conduct of the corporation generally.* The court could consider the extent of corporate good conduct, such as attempts to comply with the law, or to foment safety or good business practices generally, and so on prior to as well as after the offence. The court could consider prior examples of wilful misconduct, or recklessness, or carelessness, or obduracy, or incompetence. The court could consider whether the corporation is, can be, or already has been rehabilitated or reoriented. The court could consider remorse, voluntary efforts to make amends or compensate, and so on.

(d) *What message is intended for and can be given to others.* This would include messages for the public generally, or for corporate leaders and participants in the same or related fields of endeavour . . .

In the result, it is my judgment that the trial judge reached a reasonable conclusion of fact, principle, factor, and fitness as to sentence.

CHAPTER 6

THE LAW OF AGENCY

Reproduced with the permission of Stu's Views

WHAT IS AGENCY?

The law of agency is particularly important to allow for the smooth flow of commercial transactions, some of which require specialised knowledge. It would be near impossible to expect a single person to carry out all his business single-handedly. For this reason, principals employ the services of agents to act on their behalf to enter into contracts or dispose of their property. These actions are traditionally considered to encompass the law of agency. One author correctly notes, however, that agency should not be so strictly construed as agents are sometimes delegated the legal powers of the principal without performing either of these two tasks.[1] One case in point is the real estate agent who, assuming the legal power of the principal, may show a property but not necessarily have the authority to dispose of it or enter into a contract for that purpose.

Agency is, of necessity and inherently, a legal relationship between the principal (P), the agent (A) and one or more third parties (T). This relationship is governed by three main factors, it is argued: consent of both P and A, the authority of A to affect P's legal position and P's control of A's action.[2] There are, of course, instances when A acts without the consent of P but

1 See Djieufack, R, 'The Nature of Agency Relationship under the OHADA Uniform Act on General Commercial Law and Common Law: A Comparative Study', 2004, Post-Graduate Thesis, University of Dschang, p 15.

2 Per Sexton, JA in *Canada v Glengarry Bingo Assn.* (1999–0305) FCA A-502–95 at para 32.

his actions are still held to be legal. This occurs under peculiar circumstances, for example, in cases of emergency, such as those where P's property or interests are in imminent danger and immediate action must be taken to safeguard them; or where, after the fact, P approves of or ratifies the action taken. Similarly, while A may have the authority to act and bind P, he may exceed his authority; nevertheless, his actions may still be deemed to be of legal effect. One particular instance, *inter alia*, is when the action carried out is considered by P to be in excess of the authority given but, in general and actual practice, is deemed to be an acknowledged function of an agent in such circumstances.

According to *Bowstead*, agency is 'the fiduciary relationship which exists between two persons, one of whom expressly or impliedly consents that the other should so act as to affect his relations with third parties, and the other of whom similarly consents so to act or so acts on his behalf'.[3] It should be noted that while consent is certainly an important aspect of agency, it happens that actions can take place without it, as in the examples in the previous paragraph. Moreover, when a case is to be determined by a court of law, while it must take into account the facts, it ultimately decides the issue of agency as a question of law:

> [W]hile agency must derive from consent, the consent need not necessarily be to the relationship of principal and agency itself (indeed the existence of it may be denied) but may be to a state of facts on which the law imposes the consequences which results from Agency. It is consensual not contractual.[4]

Gloria Wilson (Appellant/Opposer) v Wigvon Cadogan and Selby Renetta Ross (Respondents/Petitioners) (2010) Appeal No. 3 of 2008 (GY)

Facts: This appeal is against an award of title by prescription in favour of the Respondents by the Commissioner of Title sitting in the Land Court . . . The subject matter of this appeal is described as 'Area "Z" being a portion of Lot numbered 20 Beau Voisin, Canal No. 1, West Bank Demarara' . . . In summary they contended that:

a) From 1966 they occupied and exercised possession and dominion over the said land.
b) They have since that time been cultivating it with sugar cane and cash crops.
c) They have *now* completely occupied the said land.
d) They by *themselves* have beneficially occupied the land.
e) Their occupation has been undisturbed and they have been in continuous possession.
f) For over 38 years they have exercised all acts of ownership upon the said land to the exclusion of all other persons.

Held: Roy, Cummings-Edwards, JJA; Singh, Chancellor (Ag)
However, the learned Commissioner went further. He had earlier misconstrued and resultingly misled himself about the nature of the Petitioner[s'] case. In a brief outline of the Petitioner[s'] case in his written decision, he noted that 'the Petitioners by themselves *and through their agents* claim to have been in occupation of the aforesaid farm land from 1966 . . .'. This was a startling statement coming from the Court. Nowhere in their Petition did the Petitioners claim occupation 'through their agents'. The Petition makes absolutely no

3 *Bowstead and Reynolds on Agency*, §1–001 quoted in Markesinis, B and Munday, R, *An Outline of the Law of Agency*, 1998, London: Butterworths, p 5.
4 Per Lord Wilberforce in *Branwhite v Worcester Works Finance Ltd* [1969] 1 AC 522 at 587.

reference to the acts of agents. The use of the pronouns '*I*' and '*we*' in the evidence of Wigvon Cadogan was referable to the alleged acts of herself and her sister . . .

It appears that the learned Commissioner was influenced by the evidence of Wigvon Cadogan that 'my brother cultivated the land for *me* and sold the cane to Guysuco' to support the course he adopted of a finding that the Petitioners had proved their case by showing that they were in possession through their agents . . .

It permits of no dispute that if a person takes control of land as an agent, the agent's possession is thereby regarded as the possession of the principal. In *Williams v Pott* (1871) L R 12 Eq. 149 at page 154, Lord Romilly, M R explained: 'the possession of the agent is the possession of the principal'. To have found that the Petitioners had possession through their agents, those agents had to be identified and there should have been evidence of the creation of the agency. The learned authors of *Bowstead & Reynolds on Agency* (18th ed. at para- 1–001) define an agency as 'the fiduciary relationship which exists between two persons one of whom expressly or impliedly manifests assent that the other should act on his behalf so as to affect his relations with third parties, and the other of whom similarly manifests assent so to act or so acts pursuant to the manifestation'. The only bit of evidence which came close to the hint of an agency is the evidence of Wigvon, who referring to Walter Helwig said that 'he marketed cane for us'. Given the definition cited above, the evidence of the existence of an agency was absent or, at the barest minimum, woefully inadequate.

AUTHORITY OF AN AGENT

Express actual authority

P may explicitly state to A the authority he may exercise when conducting transactions on P's behalf. This may be reduced in writing in the form of a contract and courts will determine A's authority on the basis of the true construction of the words of appointment. Where A's appointment is oral, courts will make determinations on the basis of evidence presented. In some cases, an agency arrangement can be purely consensual – the agency relationship is generally inherently consensual – as opposed to contractual. One example of this is the power of attorney which creates a consensual, but often non-contractual, agency.[5] The attorney in fact makes no promise to act, nor does the power granted necessarily provide for his payment or compensation; yet, he agrees to act. The main difference between contractual and consensual agency, therefore, is the presence or absence of consideration and the fact that, where a contract is involved, there is a legal obligation on the part of A to perform his duties with a reciprocal obligation on the part of P to remunerate A.[6]

While courts will be prepared to make a determination that A's actions bind P on the basis of a contract, express actual authority may be determined on the basis of either form (contractual or consensual). The scope of the agency agreement is ascertained by applying ordinary principles of construction of contracts, including offer and acceptance, consideration, intention to create a legal relationship, any proper implications from the express words used, the usages of the trade, or the course of business between the parties.[7]

5 Emerson, R, *Business Law*, 2003, Hauppauge, NY: Barron's Educational Series, Inc, p 278.

6 See Markesinis, B, and Munday, R, *An Outline of the Law of Agency*, 1998, London: Butterworths, p 18. Nevertheless, A still has rights against P where A performs a task gratuitously.

7 See Markesinis and Munday, *An Outline of the Law of Agency*, p 19.

Marubeni Hong Kong and South China Limited v Ministry of Finance of Mongolia [2004] EWHC 472 (Comm) (GB)

Facts: The claim was brought by a Hong Kong company (MHK) that carried on business as an import/export and general trading company. It was a wholly owned subsidiary of Marubeni Corporation (Marubeni) a Japanese company with its principal place of business in Japan. The defendant was the Mongolian Government acting through its Ministry of Finance (MMOF). The claim was made on a letter dated 11 May 1996 (the MMOF Letter or the guarantee), which was addressed to MHK and signed by the Minister of Finance at the time, Mr Byambajav.

On about 29 March 1996, MHK entered into a Deferred Payment Sales Contract (the DPS 1 Contract) with Buyan Holding Company Limited (Buyan), a Mongolian company. Pursuant to the DPS 1 Contract Buyan agreed to buy and the claimant agreed to sell machinery, equipment and materials for a cashmere processing plant. The purchase price was US$18,811,670. The first instalment of the price was to be paid within 60 days of the signature of the DPS 1 Contract, and the remaining amount was to be paid in 12 equal semi-annual instalments. The first of these was due on 19 October 1998. Pursuant to Article 7 of the DPS contract Buyan arranged the provision of a guarantee.

It was common ground that the putative proper law of this contract was English law. The defendant said that Mr Byambajav did not have authority to bind the defendant, and that the guarantee had not subsequently been adopted or ratified by the Mongolian Government. The claimant said that the MMOF Letter was issued on behalf of the defendant with express actual authority, alternatively that Mr Byambajav had usual authority or the defendant held him out as having apparent/ostensible authority, or the defendant ratified the MMOF Letter. The claimant said that on a true construction of the MMOF Letter, the defendant undertook a primary liability (joint and/or several) to the claimant. The defendant said that on a true construction of the MMOF Letter it had not undertaken a primary liability. The defendant said that it was discharged from liability under the guarantee. The claimant disputed this.

Held: Creswell, J

If approval did not have to be in a particular form, [did] Mr Byambajav [have] 'Government approval' (or permission) to issue the MMOF Letter, such approval (or permission) being given either at the meeting of the Mongolian Cabinet on 27 March 1996 or at its meeting on 3 April 1996? For the reasons set out above, I do not consider that approval had to be in a particular form. Mr Byambajav had government approval or permission to issue the MMOF Letter. Such approval/permission was given at the meeting of the Mongolian Cabinet on 27 March and/or 3 April 1996, as evidenced in the minutes of the meeting on 3 April 1996. I have carefully considered all the evidence and materials before the court and the submissions of the parties. The defendant has not persuaded me on a balance of probability that I should find that the disputed minute did not accurately record the decision arrived at, at one or both of the relevant meetings. It follows that I find that the MMOF Letter was issued on behalf of the defendant with express actual authority, provided that it is correctly characterised as a guarantee. The minute of the Cabinet Meeting on 3 April 1996 did not authorise the Minister of Finance to undertake (on behalf of the defendant) a primary liability (joint and/or several). It referred expressly to 'guarantees'.

Extent of agent's actual authority

GENERAL AGENCIES

An agency agreement may cover any range of actions that P may authorise A to undertake. A general agency is an unusual commercial relationship as it delegates to A the authority to perform any and all tasks in relation to the subject matter of the agency. A general power of attorney may allow for unfettered actions on the part of A. Nevertheless, if the courts determine an abuse of such power of attorney, A will be held liable to P.

Marie Egger v Herbert Egger (2004) Civ App 17 of 2002 (LC)

Facts: The appellant Marie Egger, a wealthy alcoholic, and the respondent Herbert Egger, also wealthy following the death of his previous wife, were married on 9 June 1982 in Eschenbach, Switzerland. She sold her house in Switzerland and he received the net proceeds of the sale. The wife was at the time 55 years old and the husband was 57. They had each been married three times before. A mere two weeks after the marriage, Mrs Egger signed a power of attorney empowering her new husband to perform legal acts of any kind on her behalf, and on 8 September 1982, Mrs Egger signed a general power of attorney giving her new husband, whom she had met only some three months before the marriage, complete control over all her property, movable as well as immovable. The respondent purchased two pieces of land under this authority. He then induced the appellant to execute another general power of attorney on his behalf on 3 July 1984 and purchased more land that very day. Between his arrival in St Lucia in January 1984, 18 months after their marriage, and May 1989, some two years before their divorce, the husband had acquired five separate properties in St Lucia on his own behalf as purchaser and under the authority of the power of attorney, totalling some 3.95 acres at Cap Estate, for which he had paid a total of EC$525,206, and from any interest in which the wife, who *prima facie* was entitled to a half share interest by virtue of the community of property law of St Lucia, had been excluded either by her own direct act or by the act of the husband under authority of the power of attorney which she had executed in his favour. A third power of attorney was executed in April 1991 authorising him to handle all her affairs after he discovered that Mrs Egger's son visited St Lucia to manage her affairs; he also procured from her a general withdrawal of any power of attorney she may have granted to her son.

On 11 July 1991 the marriage was dissolved, and on 27 September 1995 the wife filed a writ seeking various declarations and orders, including declarations that she was induced to sign a power of attorney in favour of the husband by undue influence exerted by him. She also sought a declaration that her signature to the deeds of sale respecting three properties in St Lucia, in which she admitted that the said properties were the separate property of the husband, was procured by the undue influence of the husband, as was her signature to a power of attorney by virtue of which he signed, purportedly on her behalf, admissions on two further deeds conveying land to her husband solely. She sought a declaration that the said properties were the properties of the wife solely or alternatively were the joint properties of the husband and the wife; and that the husband held the said properties in trust for the wife. She sought an order that the husband execute all necessary documents to transfer title to the said properties to the wife solely, or alternatively a half-share interest therein; an injunction restraining the husband from transferring, selling or otherwise dealing with the said properties; and an account of all dealings with the said properties.

Held: Alleyne, Saunders, JJA; Rawlins, JA (Ag)
The wife asserts that she trusted and had all confidence in her husband, and that he breached that trust and confidence by unduly influencing her to represent in the deeds of sale to which she appended her signature that the immovable properties described therein were purchased with his separate funds and were his sole property, and in respect of the deeds which he signed on her behalf under authority of the power of attorney, that this was done without her consent and in breach of his duty as her attorney . . .

Mr Egger in his evidence said that he used his own money to buy the property in St Lucia, and that he put it in his sole name because he did not want her children to inherit any part of his property. He claimed that his wife agreed. He said he was given the power of attorney 'to buy the land and the land was to be bought in my name and she had agree(d) to that. Power of attorney was used to sign on deeds that she had no interest before.' Despite being pressed in cross-examination, Mr Egger failed to produce any documents, tax returns, bank statements, evidence of the value of his inheritance from his third wife, his alleged stock market trading, or any other evidence to verify that he had the resources to finance the purchases of these properties. He provided no documentary or independent evidence as to how or when the money came into St Lucia, or from what source or sources . . .

An analysis of the totality of the evidence, in my view, leads inexorably to the inescapable inference that from shortly after they met and at least until 1991, the appellant placed complete trust and confidence in the respondent in relation to the management of her financial affairs (indeed of all her affairs). The appellant was evidently a very vulnerable person. Contrary to what the learned trial judge held, it seems to me that, as in the case of *Bank of Montreal v Stuart*, the evidence taken as a whole gives rise to the unavoidable inference that the husband's influence over her was 'deep-rooted' and 'lasting' . . .

In all the circumstances, and for the reasons given above, I would allow the appeal, discharge the order of the learned trial judge, and enter judgment for the appellant for:

(1) A declaration that the appellant was induced to sign the power of attorney appointing the respondent as her attorney, and the deeds of sale, admitting that the respondent acquired the five properties . . . by the undue influence of the respondent.
(2) A declaration that the said immovable properties which were conveyed to the respondent solely are the joint property of the appellant and the respondent.
(3) A declaration that the respondent holds and has held the said properties together with the building erected thereon as trustee for and on behalf of himself and the appellant.
(4) An order that the respondent do execute all such documents and do all such acts and things as may be necessary to transfer to the appellant her half share interest in the said properties.
(5) An injunction restraining the respondent, whether by himself his servants or agents or howsoever otherwise from transferring, selling, leasing, donating, hypothecating, assigning or in any way dealing with the said immovable properties otherwise than as herein directed
(6) Costs in the Court below in the sum of [EC]$72,760, and of the appeal in the sum of [EC]$48,506, based on a value of the claim taken as [EC]$525,206, the amount paid for the properties in dispute.

SPECIFIC AGENCY

Conversely, a power of attorney may specify the actions A may undertake; his authority will be limited to the purpose for which it was given.[8] A may be appointed to conduct a specific transaction or to act in a specific manner. Where A has been mandated to act in a specific manner and he acts outside the scope of such instructions, a person relying on A and aware that he holds a limited agency will not be able to recover from P as A would have violated the terms of his specific agency. Where T is not aware of the limited agency and acts to his detriment, he may be able to recover from P or A depending on the facts surrounding the case.

Lloyd Michael Pommells Claimant v EW Lewis Investments & Finance Ltd Defendant [2013] JMCC Comm 10 (JM)

Facts: The claimant is the owner of property which overlooks the Constant Spring Golf Course. The said property was registered at Volume 1438 Folio 155 of the Register Book of Titles. In or about the year 2009, he and Plantation Development Company Ltd. (Plantation) entered into a contract whereby he sold the said property to Plantation for its conversion into 18 apartments for the affluent. The consideration was both monetary and an apartment. The development was appropriately named 'Front Nine' because of its proximity to the golf course. Unfortunately it is now at the 'front line' of a legal battle. In furtherance of the agreement between the parties, the claimant gave the title to the said property which was registered at Volume 1438 Folio 155 to Mrs. Jennifer Messado, the Attorney-at-Law who represented them (claimant and Plantation). She was also given a Power of Attorney for the purpose of facilitating 'the continuation and completion of Front Line.' In order to facilitate the development, 18 splinter titles were obtained in the name of the claimant and the original title which was registered at Volume1438 Folio 155 was cancelled. The parties agreed that the duplicate certificates of title would remain the property of the claimant until the completion of the development at which point he would transfer the titles to the purchasers. The attorney, however, handed over the said titles to the defendant without the permission and knowledge of the claimant hence the claim for the delivery up of the six titles, which the defendant has its in possession, and for damages *inter alia.*

Held: Sinclair-James, J

Is The Claimant Bound By The Representations By Its Attorney To The Defendant?

The Law

Mr. Nigel Jones submits that the claimant is not bound by any representation made by Mrs. Messado that she was authorized to pledge his titles. He relies on the English case of *Overbrooke Estates Ltd. v Glencombe Properties Ltd.* [1974] 1 WLR 1335. Brightman J in *Overbrooke Estates* said:

> An agent, as between himself and a third party, has such authority as is actually conferred on him by his principal, or such authority as has ostensibly been conferred on him because of the manner or circumstances in which he has been held out as an agent . . .
>
> . . .

8 Markesinis and Munday, *An Outline of the Law of Agency*, p 19.

> Was there representation made by the claimant or conduct by him which could be construed as conferring on the attorney the authority to pledge the title or to deal with the titles without restraint? The evidence regarding the scope of the attorney's authority is contained in the Power of Attorney. The said Power of Attorney limits the attorney's authority to the sale and development of the property . . . There is no dispute between the claimant and the attorney that indeed the attorney's authority was so confined. It is significant that the splinter titles were all issued in the claimant's name. This supports his contention that he never intended to relinquish control over his property until the development was concluded and he duly received consideration . . . The Power of Attorney specifically confined Plantation and the attorney's authority to the construction of the development at 54 Norbrook Drive, not to any other development or for any other reason.

Implied actual authority

According to *Bowstead*, 'An agent has implied authority to do whatever is necessary for, or ordinarily incidental to, the effective execution of his express authority in the usual way.'[9] This is especially so when it can be inferred from the conduct of the parties involved and the circumstances of the case.

> *Crown Corke de Guatemala SA (Claimant) v Carlo Products Limited (1st Defendant), Carlys Dahlia Hughes (Executrix of the Estate of David Henry Hughes, Deceased) (2nd Defendant)* (2009) Claim No. CLC – 324 of 1999 (JM)
>
> **Facts:** The claim against Carlo Products is for the sum of US $418, 215.23 for goods sold and delivered by Crown Corke to Carlo Products at the request of David Henry Hughes 'Mr Hughes', the managing director of Carlo Products while acting in his capacity as agent of Carlo products . . . Crown Corke [claims] that Mr Hughes fraudulently represented that he was acting on behalf of Carlo Products when he ordered the goods in question and claims for breach of warranty of authority on the part of Mr Hughes.
>
> **Held:** Mangatal, J
> The general rule is that when an agent acts within the scope of his actual authority, the principal is bound by contracts made by the agent on his behalf . . . Actual authority can either be express or implied. Express authority is that which arises from the express words used. Implied authority is inferred from the conduct of the parties and the circumstances of a case. In *Hely-Hutchinson v Brayhead* [1967] 3 All ER 98, a decision of the English Court of Appeal, Lord Denning MR defines express and implied authority at page 102, paragraph A as follows:
>
> > It is express when it is given by express words, such as when a board of directors pass a resolution which authorises two of their number to sign cheques. It is implied when it is inferred from the conduct of the parties and the circumstances of the case, such as when the board of directors appoint one of their number to be managing director. They thereby impliedly authorise him to do all such things as fall within the usual scope of that office.

9 *Bowstead and Reynolds on Agency*, Art. 27 quoted in *Donsland Ltd v Nicholas Van Hoogstraten, Barnhill Investments Ltd, Selective Management Ltd* [2002] EWCA Civ 253 (GB).

Implied authority may itself be broken down into four types: incidental authority, usual authority, customary authority and authority derived from the circumstances of the case . . . At paragraph 31–042 of *Chitty*, usual authority is discussed as follows:

> Agents authorised to conduct particular trades or businesses normally have implied authority to do whatever is usually done by persons occupying such positions . . .

It is common ground that Mr Hughes was the managing director of Carlo Products. Thus it does appear to me that although Mr Hughes is not here to state anything about his actual authority, the evidence when looked at overall, supports Crown Corke's position that they did not contract with OG Smith regarding goods, and in so doing, on a balance of probabilities, demonstrates that Mr Hughes had actual authority by means of implied authority . . . In my judgment, it appears that Mr Hughes had implied authority in the form of usual authority as managing director to enter into the contract with Crown Corke for the supply of the subject goods . . . I find some support for my reasoning in the judgment of Lord Pearson in *Hely-Hutchinson* at page 107 I to 108 B where, although the judge at first instance had found that there was ostensible authority, Lord Pearson indicated that the Court of Appeal was not precluded[] and[,] indeed went on to find, that there was also actual authority. He referred to, and concurred with Diplock LJ's comment in the *Freeman* case that actual authority and ostensible authority are not only not mutually exclusive, they generally co-exist and coincide. Lord Pearson states:

> On the first question I agree that on the learned judge's finding of fact, which are not disputed, there is proof that Mr Richards had actual authority to make contracts on behalf of Brayhead. The points to which I attach most importance in coming to this conclusion are these. Mr Richards, while acting as de facto managing director and chief executive and entering into large transactions on behalf of the company, would sometimes merely report the transactions and not seek prior authority or subsequent confirmation by the board, and the board acquiesced in the course of dealing . . .

In my judgment, it was plainly within the ordinary and usual powers of a managing director in transacting the company's affairs for him to enter into the contracts which he did on behalf of Carlo Products in respect of Carlo Products main business which involved obtaining aerosol cans to fill with Carlo Products' products.

Apparent/ostensible authority

Apparent authority, or ostensible authority or agency by estoppel as it is variably called, has often been confused with the notion of implied actual authority. Although they may often coincide, coexist and overlap, they are very clearly distinguishable. Apparent authority is not really authority at all. It gives rise to the 'appearance of authority' whether there is in fact authority or not.[10] In determining whether apparent authority existed, the courts will examine P's actions, as the onus to circumscribe A's actions and representations to T lies with P. The behaviour of P in relation to the actions of A may give rise to agency by estoppel. In such a case, P will be prevented by the courts from denying an agency relationship existed even where it did not exist or where A acted dishonestly, especially where T relied on A's representation to his detriment. According to Markesinis and Munday, there are four categories of cases under which this may fall:[11]

10 Markesinis and Munday, *An Outline of the Law of Agency*, p 37.

11 Markesinis and Munday, *An Outline of the Law of Agency*, pp 37–8.

(1) Cases in which a person allows another to appear as if he were his agent, whereas in fact he is not.
(2) Cases where P allows A to give the impression that he has more authority than he actually has.
(3) Cases where P allows A to continue to appear as his agent whereas in fact the agency relationship between them has been terminated.
(4) Cases in which P limits A's actual implied authority but fails to inform T, who deals with him, of A's limited authority.

Even though A may have had neither authority nor consent to represent or bind P, P is held liable 'on grounds of public policy, business efficacy, or equity'.[12]

There are three elements that give rise to apparent authority or agency by estoppel: (i) representation (usually by P or lawfully authorised A to T, or by P creating an 'apparent' authority of an A by conduct), (ii) reliance by T on the representation and (iii) alteration of T's position resulting from such reliance. In commonly encountered cases, the ostensible authority is general in character, arising when P has placed A in a position which in the outside world is generally regarded as carrying authority to enter into transactions of the kind in question. Ostensible general authority may also arise where A has had a course of dealing with a particular contractor and P has acquiesced in this course of dealing and has honoured transactions arising out of it.

Rembert Thomas Claimant v 1. Quarry Products Limited 2. Kernie Emmanuel Defendants (2011) Claim No. SLUHCV 2009/0693 (LC)

Facts: In this matter the claimant Rembert Thomas based his claim on the fact that he had to do remedial work on a floor slab because the Second Named defendant Kernie Emmanuel completed a floor slab with hand mixed concrete rather than readymixed concrete. Rembert Thomas had contracted with the First Named defendant Quarry Products Limited, a company which supplied concrete, to supply ready-mixed concrete for the floor slab and the company had not performed this contract but returned the funds tendered for the said contract to Kernie Emmanuel without his knowledge. One of the issues that arise in this case is whether Kernie Emmanuel was the agent or apparent agent of the claimant with respect to all matters related to the work site and pouring the concrete.

Held: Belle, J
The legal concept of agency is defined as the relationship which arises whenever one person (the agent) acts on behalf of another person (the principal) and has power to affect the principal's legal position with regard to a third party. See *Dowrick* (1954) 17 MLR 24. It is also said that the two most important functions of an agent are (a) making contracts on his principal's behalf and (b) disposition of the property. A more modern definition contained in the eighteenth edition of *Bowstead & Reynolds on Agency* para. 1–0003, page 2 is as follows:

> The word 'agency', to a common lawyer, refers in general to a branch of the law under which one person, the agent, may directly affect the legal relations of another person, the principal, as regards yet other persons, called third parties, by acts which the agent is said to have the principal's authority to perform on his behalf and which when done are in some respects treated as the principal's acts. These acts are probably thought of as most likely to occur in connection with the formation and discharge of contracts and in disposition of property, but the same idea appears, sometimes in modified form, in many other parts of the law.

12 Markesinis and Munday, *An Outline of the Law of Agency*, p 39.

Ms. John Counsel for Mr Thomas argued that the matter turns on the issue of ostensible agency. She relied on the reference to Lord Diplock's dictum in *Freeman & Lockyer v Buckhurst Park Properties (Mangal) Ltd* [1964] 2 QB 480.

> An 'apparent' or 'ostensible' authority . . . is a legal relationship between the principal and the contractor created by a representation, made by the principal to the contractor, intended to be and in fact acted upon by the contractor, that the agent has authority to enter on behalf of the principal into a contract of a kind within the scope of the 'apparent' authority, so as to render the principal liable to perform any obligations imposed upon him by such contract. To the relationship so created the agent is a stranger. He need not be (although he generally is) aware of the existence of the representation but he must not purport to make the agreement as principal himself. The representation, when acted upon by the contractor by entering into a contract with the agent, operates as an estoppel, preventing the principal from asserting that he is not bound by the contract. It is irrelevant whether the agent had actual authority to enter into the contract.

Freeman & Lockyer was applied in the ECSC Court of Appeal decision of *Village Cay Marina Limited v John Acland et al* [1996] ECLR 161, page 168 where Floissac CJ stated after quoting another passage from *Freeman & Lockyer*:

> The doctrine is further explained in *Armagos Ltd v Mundogas, SA* (1986) 2 All ER 385. There Lord Keith (delivering the judgment of the House) said [at] pp. 389 & 390 'Ostensible authority comes about where the principal, by words or conduct, has represented that the agent has the requisite actual authority, and the party dealing with the agent has entered into a contract with him in reliance on that representation. The principal in these circumstances is estopped from denying that actual authority existed. In the commonly encountered case, the ostensible authority is general in character, arising when the principal has placed the agent in a position which in the outside world is generally regarded as carrying authority to enter into transactions of the kind in question.

The submission is further supported by *Chitty on Contract[s]*, 26th Edition, para. 2530:

> The basis of the doctrine of apparent authority is that the third party is entitled to assume that an agent has such authority as he appears to have or would normally have, whether or not the principal has in fact granted such authority.

. . . The issue of an agent's apparent authority is not new to the law. Cases older than *Freeman & Lockyer v Buckhurst* laid down the prerequisites for the application of the principle. For example [i]n *Rama Corporation v Proved Tin and General Investments Ltd.* [1952] 2 Q.B. 147, 149–150 Slade J held,

> Ostensible or apparent authority which negatives the existence of actual authority is merely a form of estoppel and a party cannot call in aid an estoppel unless three ingredients are present (1) representation, (2) a reliance on that representation and (3) an alteration of his position resulting from such reliance.

In confirming the legal doctrine of estoppel based on the representation, Lord Halsbury stated:

> But the doctrine that a person shall not be permitted to represent or permit to be represented a state of facts at one time and afterwards, when such representation has induced another person to change his position, seek to shew that such his representation was erroneous is a doctrine too well established now to be shaken, and whether it is called 'estoppel' or not the principle is perfectly intelligible.

It has been argued that the company aught to have inquired with Mr. Thomas whether he had terminated the contract and authorised the tendering of the cheque to Mr. Emmanuel. But unlike the situation in *Colonial Bank v Cady*, in the case at Bar Mr. Emmanuel was integrally connected to both Mr Thomas and the pouring of the concrete for the floor slab. Those facts, plus the fact that the rain had prevented the company from delivering the ready-mixed concrete, made Kernie Emmanuel's act less suspicious than that of the brokers in *Colonial Bank* case. Furthermore I believe Mr. Liburd of Quarry Products when he says that Mr. Thomas told him that Mr. Emmanuel was in charge of the project in his absence. His assertion is supported by the witness Mr. Benoit. Even if Emmanuel's authority was restricted to the laying of the slab, the point is that no distinction was made in the communication as to the authority for the laying of the slab, and the authority for paying the cost of mixing the cement and laying the slab. Although Mr. Thomas never said that Emmanuel had authority to deal with financial matters, he never asserted that Emmanuel did not have such authority.

It is therefore entirely plausible that this was an honest mistake by the company in presuming that Kernie Emmanuel had authority to ask for the refund and proceed to complete the slab-laying project by some other means.

Persaud and Another v Neal and Massy Enterprises Limited (2001) 63 WIR 122 (GY)

Facts: Between March 1989 and October 1992 a company (Neal and Massy) manufactured batteries and (under an agreement) exported them to Guyana where the defendants (Persaud and Another) sold them. When the company sought payment from the defendants for goods sold and delivered, the defendants sought to recover their promotional expenses (in respect of which they claimed that an agreement had been reached between themselves and an agent acting on behalf of the company) and also a sum in respect of the loss of goodwill in the products.

Held: Kennerd, C

I must state that the issues which, in my view, arise for determination are these:

(1) Was a contract entered into between Steve Sogrim and the defendant, Roopnarine Persaud, for the payment of promotional expenses?

(2) If so, was there a representation by the company that Sogrim had authority to enter, on behalf of the company, into a contract of the kind sought to be enforced, and which representation was made to the defendants so that the company would be bound thereby? . . .

In relation to the second issue, *Freeman & Lockyer (a firm) v Buckhurst Park Properties (Mangal) Ltd.* [1964] 1 All ER 630 is very instructive. In that case Lord Diplock stated (at p 646):

> If the foregoing analysis of the relevant law is correct, it can be summarised by stating four conditions which must be fulfilled *to entitle a contractor to enforce against a company a contract entered into on behalf of a company by an agent who had no actual authority to do so. It must be shown*:
>
> (a) that a representation that the agent had authority to enter on behalf of the company into a contract of the kind sought to be enforced was made to the contractor;
>
> (b) that such representation was made by a person or persons who had 'actual' authority to manage the business of the company either generally or in respect of those matters to which the contract relates;

(c) that he, the contractor, was induced by such representation to enter into the contract, i.e. that he had in fact relied on it; and,

(d) that under its memorandum or articles of association the company was not deprived of the capacity either to enter into a contract of the kind sought to be enforced or to delegate authority to enter into a contract of that kind to the agent (see also *Hely-Hutchinson v Brayhead Ltd* [1968] 1 QB 549, *Charlesworth and Morse: Company Law* by Geoffrey Morse (15th Edn) 111, and *Panorama Developments (Guildford) Ltd v Fidelis Furnishing Fabrics Ltd* [1971] 2 QB 711, where the secretary had apparent authority to hire motor cars on behalf of the company).

In *Freeman's* case the facts were: 'The articles of a company formed to purchase and resell an estate empowered the directors to appoint one of their body managing director. K, a director was never appointed managing director but, *to the knowledge of the board he acted as such.* On behalf of the company he instructed architects to do certain works in connection with the estate:

> *Held*, the company was bound by the contract and was liable for the architects' fees. K had apparent authority because he had been held out by the board as managing director and, therefore, as having authority to do what a managing director would usually be authorised to do on behalf of the company and this act was within the usual authority of a managing director. Accordingly, the plaintiffs could assume that he had been properly appointed.

In *Bowstead on Agency* (12th edn, 1959) it is stated at p 10 under the heading 'Agency by Estoppel: Holding out':

> Where any person, by words or conduct represents or permits it to be represented that another person has authority to act on his behalf, he is bound by the acts of such other person with respect to anyone dealing with him as an agent on the faith of such representation, to the same extent as if such other person had authority which he was so represented to have. Ostensible or apparent authority is merely a form of estoppel, indeed it has been termed agency by estoppel, and you cannot call in aid an estoppel unless you have three ingredients: (1) a representation, (2) a reliance on the representation, and (3) an alteration of your position resulting from such reliance (see *Rama Corporation v Proved Tin* [1952] 2 QB 147, at 149–150, and *Midland Bank v Reckitt* [1933] AC 1).

For agency by estoppel, see also *Cheshire, Fifoot & Furmston's Law of Contract* (13th edn) 485, 486. Lord Cranworth said in *Pole v Leask* (1861) 33 LJ Ch 155 at 161, 162:

> No-one can become the agent of another person except by the will of that person. His will may be manifested in writing, or orally or simply by placing another in a situation in which according to the ordinary rules of law, or perhaps it would be more correct to say, according to the ordinary usages of mankind, that other is understood to represent and act for the person who has so placed him . . . This proposition, however, is not at variance with the doctrine that where one has so acted as from his conduct to lead another to believe that he has appointed someone to act as his agent, and knows that that other person is about to act on that belief, then, unless he interposes, he will in general be estopped from disputing the agency, though in fact no agency really existed . . . Another proposition to be kept constantly in view is, that the burden of proof is on the person dealing with anyone as an agent, through whom he seeks to charge another as principal. *He must show that the agency did exist, and that the agent had the authority he assumed to exercise, or otherwise that the principal is estopped from disputing it.*

Before examining the evidence to see whether or not there was a concluded contract to pay for promotional expenses, I wish to deal with the submission made by Mr Juman-Yassin for the defendants to the effect that, the company not having responded to the proposals (exhibit G) submitted to it by the defendants, it must be assumed that the company, by acquiescence, had accepted the terms of the proposal. It is clear law that, before a contract can come into being, there must be both an offer and acceptance together with consideration, and the evidence concerning these must be clear and unequivocal (see *Ram Singh v Bacchus* (1996) 54 WIR 246 and *Heyman v Darwins Ltd* [1942] 1 All ER 337). In the latter case Viscount Simon LC said (at p 341): 'It takes two to form a contract – offer on the one side and acceptance of the offer on the other side.' Exhibit G was addressed to Sogrim, and according to his evidence: '*It was never approved by the board of directors. There was no discussion on it at board level.*' In the circumstances, and having regard to the law on the matter, I cannot say that the company had acquiesced in the terms of exhibit G and, therefore, there was no acceptance of the terms of the proposal since as Sogrim testified 'there was no discussion on it [exhibit G] at board level'.

I will now examine the evidence led at the trial in order to determine whether or not there was in fact a concluded contract. Raphyl Williams, finance director of the company stated (*inter alia*), 'My company got a proposal from the defendant in *1991–1992* requesting certain other arrangements, but we did not entertain the proposal' . . . In re-examination, the witness Sogrim stated (*inter alia*), 'The terms of proposal by Persaud in exhibit G were never put to the board of directors. The company would have had to ratify it.' . . . From the totality of the evidence led at the trial I am unable to find that there was a concluded contract, orally or otherwise, for the payment of promotional expenses . . . It is quite clear that the first two conditions laid down in *Freeman's* case have not been satisfied, that is to say:

(1) there was no representation that the agent Steve Sogrim had authority to enter on behalf of the company into a contract of the kind sought to be enforced [and] made to the defendants, nor
(2) that such representation was made by a person (or persons) who had 'actual authority' to manage the business of the company either generally or in respect of those matters to which the contract relates.

As we all know a company usually acts through a 'responsible officer' (see *Royal British Bank v Turquand* (1856) 119 ER 100). In this case there is no evidence that any 'responsible officer' of the company had represented to the defendants that Steve Sogrim had authority to enter into an agreement with the defendants to pay for promotional costs. The representation, if made, was made by Steve Sogrim, unknown to the company as the trial judge had rightly found.

Usual authority

Usual authority may be considered a subset of implied authority. The case of usual authority, however, refers more specifically to agents who practise a particular trade, business or profession and are normally authorised to do everything which is usually or ordinarily done in such a trade, business or profession.[13] For courts to accept that A was exercising usual authority, the practice must be one that is clearly established, so well-known that it is taken for granted by those who conduct that type of business as an implied term, and it must be reasonable.[14] Moreover, the practice must be consistent with the express authority and instructions conferred on A.

13 Markesinis and Munday, *An Outline of the Law of Agency*, p 30.
14 Markesinis and Munday, *An Outline of the Law of Agency*, pp 31–2.

Watteau v Fenwick [1893] 1 QB 346 (GB)

Facts: Humble had carried on business at a beerhouse called the Victoria Hotel, at Stockton-on-Tees, which business he had transferred to the defendants, a firm of brewers, some years before this action. After the transfer of the business, Humble remained as defendants' manager; but the licence was always taken out in Humble's name, and his name was painted over the door. Under the terms of the agreement made between Humble and the defendants, the former had no authority to buy any goods for the business except bottled ales and mineral waters; all other goods required were to be supplied by the defendants themselves. The action was brought to recover the price of goods delivered at the Victoria Hotel over some years, for which it was admitted that the plaintiff gave credit to Humble only: they consisted of cigars, Bovril, and other articles. The learned judge allowed the claim for the cigars and Bovril only, and gave judgment for the plaintiff for £22 12s 6d. The defendants appealed.

Held: Wills, J
The learned county court judge held that the defendants were liable. I am of opinion that he was right. There seems to be less of direct authority on the subject than one would expect. But I think that the Lord Chief Justice during the argument laid down the correct principle, viz, once it is established that the defendant was the real principal, the ordinary doctrine as to principal and agent applies – that the principal is liable for all the acts of the agent which are within the authority usually confided to an agent of that character, notwithstanding limitations, as between the principal and the agent, put upon that authority. It is said that it is only so where there has been a holding-out of authority – which cannot be said of a case where the person supplying the goods knew nothing of the existence of a principal. But I do not think so. Otherwise, in every case of undisclosed principal, or at least in every case where the fact of there being a principal was undisclosed, the secret limitation of authority would prevail and defeat the action of the person dealing with the agent and then discovering that he was an agent and had a principal . . . In my opinion this appeal ought to be dismissed with costs.

Dr P Samuels v Lakeland Farms Limited [2003] JMCA 8 (31 July 2003) (JM)[15]

Held: Forte, P
Did Mr Murphy have authority to enter into an agreement with the appellant for the payment of a lesser sum than was the normal fee, in return for veterinary services being offered by the appellant? . . . The question arises however, whether the mere fact that Mr Murphy was the farm manager was sufficient for the appellant to conclude that he (Mr Murphy) had the authority to enter into this special contract. Was the company thereby representing to the appellant that Mr Murphy as farm manager could enter on its behalf into this special contract?

The answer to the question must depend on whether entering into the agreement was within the ambit of the occupation of a farm manager. It is only then that the company could be said to have made representations that Mr Murphy had the authority in question. The evidence, however, was to the contrary. Apart from the evidence of Mr Lake, the farm manager who succeeded Mr Murphy, Elizabeth Ann Miller testified that it is not within the ambit of a farm manager in that particular industry to vary or set the rates to be charged. This witness

15 See facts in Chapter 2.

who had been engaged as farm manager in Jamaica and in England for over 30 years testified that at no time would she discuss fees with the owner of the horses as the fees were set. She would give the owner a schedule of the fees. It was consequently not proved that the agreement entered into with the respondent was within the ambit of the occupation of Mr Murphy.

As a result it cannot be concluded that the respondent company, per Mr Richard Lake, made any representation to the appellant that Mr Murphy had any such authority. Indeed the only representation that Mr Murphy had such an authority came from Mr Murphy himself and 'a representation made by the agent as to his authority cannot of itself create apparent authority:' (See *Chitty on Contracts* 28th edition Volume 2 at paragraph 32–057).

It was advanced also that the learned judge did not deal with this question in her judgment. Mr Henry for the respondent, while conceding this fact, referred to the finding of the learned judge that the appellant did not do any work on the farm. This of course relates to the purported contract contended for by the appellant where he stated in evidence: 'It was explained to me that [JM]$100 was below the farm rate at the time. The reason was as stated because of the reciprocal arrangement that I would make myself available to do work on the farm at all times on request.' Mr Henry therefore maintained that since a material aspect of the 'reciprocal arrangement' was not established, then effect could not be given to the other part which required the [JM]$100 per day rate. It appears however that the learned judge did give some consideration to the question when she said in her judgment:

> The defendant had an obligation to pay the rates agreed from time to time and whatever 'special' arrangements he might have had with Mr David Murphy (and these are questionable as there is no evidence that Mr Murphy had authority or approval to make such arrangement) would have ended when Mr Murphy ceased to be farm manager of Lakeland Farms and the normal going rates would apply.

I would conclude that there was no evidence that Mr Murphy had either actual or ostensible authority and consequently the issue must be resolved in favour of the respondent.

See also *Crown Corke de Guatemala SA (Claimant) v Carlo Products Limited (1st Defendant), Carlys Dahlia Hughes (Executrix of the Estate of David Henry Hughes, Deceased) (2nd Defendant)* (2009) Claim No. CLC – 324 of 1999 (JM) above.

AGENCY OF NECESSITY

Agency relationships usually derive from consent between P and A, or as seen in the case of ostensible authority, from representation by P to T. In any event, courts will determine an agency relationship as an issue of law. Nevertheless, there is the 'category of agency where the relationship arises by operation of law'.[16] This is different from other instances of agency as it arises in cases of emergency where the parties have neither agreed to create an agency relationship nor has there been any representation to any T dealing with these parties that one is acting as agent for the other. The doctrine of agency of necessity is most commonly applied to shipping cases and bestows upon the master of a vessel the power to deal with his vessel and her cargo outside the ordinary scope of his authority.[17]

16 Markesinis and Munday, *An Outline of the Law of Agency*, p 51.
17 Markesinis and Munday, *An Outline of the Law of Agency*, p 35.

As Markesinis and Munday state:

> the law imposes an agency of necessity in a limited number of situations where a party (the 'agent'), confronted with an emergency which poses such an imminent threat to the property or other interests of another person that there is no opportunity to seek the latter's prior authority or instructions, acts for that person without his authority in order to preserve or protect that property or those interests.[18]

This has been further refined to state that while communications have been made, instructions were nevertheless not received. One can, of course, argue that, in this new era of advanced communications technologies, seeking instructions or authority should not be an issue.

There are four conditions which must be met to create an agency of necessity:

(1) A must be able to show that he was unable to obtain instructions from P.
(2) A must satisfy the court that he acted in a *bona fide* manner in the interests of P.
(3) A's actions must have been reasonable and prudent in the circumstances.
(4) There must have been some necessity or emergency to compel A to so act.

China Pacific SA v Food Corporation of India [1982] AC 939 (GB)

Facts: The *Winson*, a bulk carrier owned by a one-ship Panamanian company (the shipowner) was chartered by the Food Corporation of India (the cargo owner) to carry a full cargo of wheat from United States Gulf ports to ports in India under a voyage charterparty in the Baltimore Berth Grain Charter form with numerous special conditions. The cargo owner was a nationalised enterprise possessing separate legal personality which the Government of India used for purchasing imports of foodstuffs needed for that country. The cargo was loaded in December 1974 and on 21 January 1975, in the course of the voyage to India, the *Winson* stranded on the North Danger reef in the South China Sea. China Pacific SA (the salvors), who were professional salvors, were quickly on the scene and on the following day a salvage agreement with the salvors in Lloyd's open form was entered into on behalf of the shipowner and the cargo owner.

In the course of carrying out the salvage services to both the shipowner and the cargo owner that the salvors by that agreement had undertaken with each separately to use their best endeavours to render, it was necessary to lighten the stranded vessel by offloading part of the cargo into barges provided by the salvors and carrying it to a place of safety. This was done, and some 15,429 tonnes of wheat were offloaded and carried to Manila which, it was not disputed, was a proper place of safety. The carriage was in six separate parcels which arrived in Manila at various dates between 10 February and 20 April 1975.

The salvage operations at the site of the stranding were temporarily suspended on 15 April 1975, owing to fighting in the vicinity having broken out between the forces of North Vietnam and South Vietnam. It is not disputed that it never became practicable thereafter to resume the salvage operations and on 20 May 1975, the salvors gave formal notice of termination of their salvage services. The *Winson*, with the remainder of the cargo of wheat still on board her, eventually became a total loss. Upon arrival of each parcel of salvaged wheat at Manila, where the salvors had no storage premises of their own, it became necessary for it to be stored in suitable accommodation under cover, if it were not

18 Markesinis and Munday, *An Outline of the Law of Agency*, p 51.

to deteriorate rapidly from exposure to the elements during the period before a decision as to what was to be done with it was reached by whoever at the time that such decision was in fact made was legally entitled to require its removal from the accommodation in which it was stored. The salvors arranged for the storage of the salvaged wheat as to part in a vessel, the *Maori*, lying in Manila Harbour, and as to the remainder in a bonded warehouse ashore. In doing so they incurred expenses for stevedoring and charter hire of the *Maori* and warehouse charges ashore and the stored wheat was held to their order by those in whose vessel and warehouse it was stored (the depositaries). These expenses, which the salvors became personally liable to pay under the contracts that they made as principals with the depositaries, continued to be incurred by them until the cargo owner had completed taking possession of the salved wheat – which it did not do until 5 August 1975.

It was not disputed that storage under cover of the salvaged wheat upon its arrival at Manila was necessary to prevent its rapid deterioration; nor was it disputed that the storage obtained by the salvors at Manila was reasonably suited for that purpose or that the charges paid for it by the salvors to the depositaries were also reasonable. The cargo owner accepted liability for and paid the expenses incurred by the salvors for the storage of the wheat in Manila after the date on which the shipowner gave notice to the cargo owner on 24 April 1975 that he had abandoned the chartered voyage. By that date it was obvious that the completion of the carriage of the cargo in the *Winson* to its destination under the charterparty, even if it were to become physically possible (which, in the event, it did not), would involve such long delay as would frustrate the adventure for which the charterparty provided. Assuming that this stranding was caused by an excepted peril (as to which there may have been doubt), the shipowner had in law an option either to abandon the chartered voyage or to on-carry the salvaged wheat from Manila to its contractual destination in other bottoms. By giving formal notice of abandonment of the voyage the shipowner was divested of this latter option and it was undisputed that the contract voyage terminated on 24 April 1975.

For some reason, which is not clear, the cargo owner paid the expenses incurred by the salvors for the storage of the wheat in Manila from 15 April instead of 24 April, from which later date alone it acknowledged that it was under any legal liability to do so; but, so far as concerns any issue that your Lordships have to determine in this appeal, the relevant period for which the cargo owner disclaims liability to reimburse the salvors for the expenses that they incurred in providing covered storage for the salvaged wheat is from 10 February, when the first barge-load of salvaged wheat arrived in Manila Harbour, until 24 April 1975, when, upon receipt by the cargo owner of the shipowner's notice of abandonment, the contract voyage terminated. The action was brought by the salvors against the cargo owner to obtain reimbursement of the expenses incurred by them during this period and the amount at stake is agreed at $110,982. The main propositions on which the cargo owner's case was based were:

(1) that, since by virtue of the contract of carriage created by the charterparty the immediate right to possession as between shipowner and cargo owner vested in the shipowner for so long as that contract of carriage had not been terminated by performance or otherwise, it was the shipowner and not the cargo owner to whom the salvors were under a duty to deliver each separate parcel of the cargo upon its arrival at Manila (subject to the provision to the Committee of Lloyd's of security for salvage remuneration if this were demanded by the salvors); and

(2) that, accordingly, it was the shipowner, and not the cargo owner, who was liable to reimburse the salvors for any expenses reasonably incurred by them in preserving the cargo from deterioration during the period while the contract of carriage remained unterminated, if they were entitled to be reimbursed by anyone at all.

Held: Lord Diplock
My Lords, it is not suggested that there is any direct authority on the question of law that is posed in this appeal. In my opinion the answer is to be found by applying to the unusual circumstances of the instant case well-known and basic principles of the common law of salvage, of bailment and of lien. In part (1) of the cargo owner's main propositions, the statement about the contractual rights *as between shipowner and cargo owner* to possession of the cargo so long as the contract of affreightment remained afoot is unexceptionable; to use a convenient Americanism, it is hornbook law for which no citation of authority is needed. But it does not in my view follow that as between salvors and shipowner or as between salvor and cargo owner it was to the former and not to the latter or to their order that the salvors would have been under a legal obligation to deliver up possession of the salved wheat upon its arrival in Manila Harbour if such delivery had been demanded . . .

Part (2) of the cargo owner's main propositions is predicated on the correctness of part (1). The Court of Appeal regarded the crucial question in the case as being whether part (1) was correct in law. If it were correct (as they held it was), they regarded part (2) as doing no more than state a necessary legal consequence of part (1). For my part, however, even if, contrary to my own view, part (1) of the main propositions were correct, I would not accept that it followed that part (2) also was correct. A person who holds possession of goods as sub-bailee of an original direct bailee of the owner of goods also owes some duty of care towards the owner: *Morris v CW Martin & Sons Ltd* [1966] 1 QB 716.

My Lords, with modern methods of communication and the presence of professional salvors within rapid reach of most parts of the principal maritime trade routes of the world, nearly all salvage of merchant ships and their cargoes nowadays is undertaken under a salvage contract in Lloyd's open form. The contract is one for the rendering of services; the services to be rendered are of the legal nature of salvage and this imports into the contractual relationship between the parties to the contract by necessary implication a number of mutual rights and obligations attaching to salvage of vessels and their cargo under common law, except in so far as such rights and obligations are inconsistent with express terms of the contract . . .

The legal nature of the relationship between the master and the owner of the cargo aboard the vessel in signing the agreement on the latter's behalf is often though not invariably an agency of necessity. It arises only when salvage services by a third party are necessary for the preservation of the cargo. Whether one person is entitled to act as agent of necessity for another person is relevant to the question whether circumstances exist which in law have the effect of conferring on him authority to create contractual rights and obligations between that other person and a third party that are directly enforceable by each against the other. It would, I think, be an aid to clarity of legal thinking if the use of the expression 'agent of necessity' were confined to contexts in which this was the question to be determined and not extended, as it often is, to cases where the only relevant question is whether a person who without obtaining instructions from the owner of goods incurs expense in taking steps that are reasonably necessary for their preservation is in law entitled to recover from the owner of the goods the reasonable expenses incurred by him in taking those steps. Its use in this wider sense may, I think, have led to some confusion in the instant case, since where reimbursement is the only relevant question all of those conditions that must be fulfilled in order to entitle one person to act on behalf of another in creating direct contractual relationships between that other person and a third party may not necessarily apply . . .

It is, of course, true that in English law a mere stranger cannot compel an owner of goods to pay for a benefit bestowed upon him against his will; but this latter principle does not apply where there is a pre-existing legal relationship between the owner of the goods and the bestower of the benefit, such as that of bailor and bailee, which imposes upon the bestower of the benefit a legal duty of care in respect of the preservation of the goods that is owed by him to their owner . . . My Lords, it may be that this would have been so if the question in the instant case had been whether the depositaries could have sued the cargo owner directly for their contractual storage charges on the ground that the cargo owner was party as principal to the contracts of storage made on its behalf by the salvors as its agents of necessity; for English law is economical in recognising situations that give rise to agency of necessity. In my view, inability to communicate with the owner of the goods is not a condition precedent to the bailee's own right to reimbursement of his expenses. The bailor's failure to give any instructions when apprised of the situation is sufficient. So, on the cargo owner's main propositions of law in this appeal, I think it fails.

Bisnath Boodram v The Bank of Nova Scotia Trinidad and Tobago and Leelawatie Boodram (1990) HCA S-1301 and S-1438 of 1986 (TT)

Facts: The plaintiff Bisnath Boodram was involved in a vehicular accident in 1973 and suffered permanent brain damage. In 1975 Leelawatie Boodram, the wife of the plaintiff, gave instructions for the action to be brought on behalf of the said Bisnath Boodram. When the defendant received monies from the solicitors of the plaintiff as damages, she deposited TT$50,000 in a fixed deposit with a son, claiming that such monies were reimbursement for legal expenses and so on, with a further TT$18,000.00 being deposited into an account with another son. The defendant argued *inter alia*, that she did nothing wrong as all along she acted as an agent of necessity for the plaintiff and was reimbursing her expenses.

Held: Permanand, J
Bowstead on Agency 12th edn. The following is stated: 'An authority of necessity is conferred by law in certain cases where a person is faced with an emergency in which the property or interests of another are in imminent jeopardy and it becomes necessary in order to preserve property or interests to act before the owner's instructions can be obtained. The law assumes the consent of the owner to the creation of the relationship of principal and agent or to the extension of an existing authority to the act done in the emergency' . . .

From the above it can be seen that agency of necessity arises only under urgent necessity and to protect the interests of the other, and from the facts before this Court, the defendant deposited the cheque . . . made payable to Bisnath Boodram on 28 February 1986 at the bank and it was not until 12 March 1986 that she withdrew nine thousand dollars . . . in cash and transferred fifty thousand dollars . . . to a fixed deposit . . . in her name and that of . . . another son. Accordingly, I find that on a balance of probability there is no evidence before this Court that there was, and that the defendant became an agent of necessity or that her husband was unable to act for himself at the time when the moneys were deposited as the Assistant Manager testified that Bisnath Boodram attended at the bank in March 1986 and spoke with him. There are conditions which entitle an agent to exceed his authority, namely:

(1) that he could not communicate with his principal;
(2) that the course he took was necessary in the sense that it was in the circumstances the only reasonable and prudent course to take; and
(3) he acted bona fide in the interests of the party concerned.

Again, the conditions do not apply to the situation before this court . . . Judgment for the plaintiff.

RATIFICATION OF ACTS DONE WITHOUT AUTHORITY

The doctrine of ratification comes into effect when A acts without authority or exceeds his existing authority and P, *after the fact*, sanctions A's acts through formal approval or recognition of the act. Ratification may even occur through P's silence and inaction after having been apprised of A's actions and not having taken any action to repudiate A's behaviour, correct the situation or inform T of A's want of authority. This is especially so, as with cases dealing with ostensible authority, if T relied on this representation and acted to his detriment. Inaction due to ignorance of A's actions, however, does not amount to ratification. Ratification in cases of inaction and silence will be determined on the facts surrounding the case.

According to Markesinis and Munday, the person on whose behalf the acts were purportedly done may, *ex post facto*, decide to ratify them.[19] In so doing, P adopts A's acts as if he had in fact previously authorised them and an agency relationship then comes into existence. Ratification of A's act also means that P and T become liable to each other in the event of legal action; A cannot be held liable for exceeding his authority; and P is liable to provide reasonable remuneration to or indemnity for loss sustained by A. Conversely, where A's actions are not ratified by P, A becomes liable to T whether he acted in good faith or fraudulently.

> To constitute a valid ratification three conditions must be satisfied: first, the agent whose act is sought to be ratified must have purported to act for the principal; secondly, at the time the act was done the agent must have had a competent principal; and, thirdly, at the time of the ratification the principal must be legally capable of doing the act himself. Mere acquiescence or inactivity on the part of the principal can be sufficient to establish ratification, depending on the facts of the case.[20]

It must be noted that ratification relates only to past acts and does not provide A with authority to undertake future acts.[21]

New Falmouth Resort Limited v International Hotels Jamaica Limited [2013] UKPC 11 (GB)

Facts: This appeal concerns the right to possession of 4¾ acres of land known as Lot 3A adjacent to the Starfish Hotel in the parish of Trelawny in Jamaica. The appellant, New Falmouth Resorts Ltd, seeks possession of the land from the respondent, International Hotels Jamaica Ltd, and claims damages for its wrongful use and occupation. On 20th February 2009 Hibbert J sitting in the Supreme Court of Justice of Jamaica in Civil Division held that the appellant's claims must fail and judgment was accordingly entered in favour of the respondent with costs. On 15th April 2011 the Jamaican Court of Appeal dismissed the appellant's appeal with costs but later on 23rd January 2012 granted final leave to appeal to Her Majesty in Council.

The issue in the appeal

It was as long ago as 17th February 1982 that the appellant agreed to sell Lot 3A to National Hotels and Properties Ltd ('NHP') for $184,000 payable by way of a deposit of $62,000 with the balance to be paid on completion which was fixed for 31st March 1982. A remarkable feature of the case is that completion has still not taken place. This agreement was

19 Markesinis and Munday, *An Outline of the Law of Agency*, p 65.
20 Per Lord Wright, *Firth v Staines* [1897] 2 QB 70 at 75 (GB).
21 Markesinis and Munday, *An Outline of the Law of Agency*, p 77.

signed on the appellant's behalf by John H. Phelan III, ('John'). The central issues which arise on the appeal are whether John was authorised to sign on the company's behalf, alternatively whether the company ratified the agreement on 21st June 1982 at a properly constituted meeting of the board of directors.

Held: Neuberger, Walker, Mance, Sumption, LLJ, Sir Ward
At the crucial meeting of the Board on June 21st 1982 the sale of the land to National Hotels and Properties came up for discussion and Mr Chen, attorney-at-law, who was representing the Phelan family confirmed that there was a sale agreement signed by John. The minutes of the meeting record:

> The meeting at three to one voted to approve the following resolution moved and seconded by Messrs David and Frank Phelan respectively.

Resolved

> That the sale agreement dated February 17th, 1982 and presented at this meeting be approved and that the authority vested in John Phelan by the board of directors to act for and on behalf of the board in such transaction be endorsed . . .

In conclusion on this issue, there is a document recording Frank's election in 1970, there are a number of subsequent formal documents recording him as a director (see paras 20, 27 and 28 above), he was competent to continue as a director, there is no resolution declining to re-elect him, he behaved as if he were a director, and the only reason for doubting whether he was a director in 1982, the absence of a document formally recording his re-election, is explicable by the very limited and patchy nature of the company's record-keeping. In those circumstances the proper conclusion to be drawn, at any rate on the unusual facts of this case, is that Frank had not ceased to be a director before the end of 1982. In those circumstances there is nothing to suggest that Frank ceased to be a director. If he was in post on June 21, 1982, then the resolution approving the sale agreement was properly passed by a majority of at least 2–1 and no casting vote was needed to carry the resolution. The Court of Appeal was, therefore, correct to decide that 'the acts of an agent on behalf of the principal outside his actual authority may be adopted and ratified' and that 'if there is ratification, it has retrospective effect, i.e. it renders the transaction with the company binding on it from the time it was entered into by the agent.' There was a clear ratification of the contract for the sale of Lot 3A to NHP which cures any original want of authority for John to have entered into it as he did. The sale is valid. The respondent is entitled to possession of the land and the appellant's claims were rightly dismissed. For that reason the Board will humbly advise Her Majesty to dismiss the appeal with costs.

Ramsay v Walker [1962] 4 WIR 539 (JM)

Facts: This was an appeal by the defendant from the judgment of the Resident Magistrate for the parish of Westmoreland awarding the plaintiff damages for cattle trespass. The respondent's case was that he had a cultivation on a parcel of land at Mountain Spring, Summerfield, in the parish of Westmoreland, which formed part of a much larger parcel of land belonging to the appellant, and which the respondent had rented in March 1961 from one Gladstone Brown, the appellant's headman. On 18 July 1961 the appellant's cows entered the respondent's cultivation and damaged it.

The appellant's defence was, substantially, that Gladstone Brown was not her headman and had no authority to rent her land to the respondent and, that in any event, the entry of the cows into the respondent's cultivation was due to the fact that the respondent had cut, damaged and destroyed the appellant's fence. As regards the relationship between the appellant and Gladstone Brown, the Resident Magistrate found as follows:

(1) that the appellant had acted in such a manner as to lead others to believe that Gladstone Brown had the authority of a headman of the property;
(2) that as headman, it was within the scope of his ostensible authority to rent lands;
(3) that he did rent lands to the respondent on which the respondent had his cultivation.

The Resident Magistrate also rejected the appellant's allegations that the entry of the cows into the respondent's cultivation was due to the respondent having cut, damaged or destroyed the appellant's fence.

Held: Waddington, J
[W]hether or not Gladstone Brown had any express or implied authority to rent the land, it seems to us clear from the evidence that the appellant, after becoming aware of the respondent's cultivation and having been told that Gladstone Brown had rented the land to the respondent, took no steps to repudiate what Gladstone Brown had purported to do and to remove the respondent from the land. Indeed, it appears from the evidence that the chief concern of the appellant was the fact that Brown had given the respondent that particular piece of land and that the respondent was planting his crops too close to the appellant's cultivation. It appears to us that the appellant had acquiesced in the respondent having his cultivation on the land, provided he did not cultivate too near to her cultivation. This in our view would amount to a ratification of what Brown had done . . . It was not disputed that it was the appellant's cows which damaged the respondent's crops, nor was the amount of the damage contested. For these reasons the appeal must be dismissed.

DUTIES OF THE AGENT TO THE PRINCIPAL

Acting in good faith is the very foundation of the relationship between P and A. In addition, there are a number of strict obligations imposed upon A in his relationship with P. A is expected to look after P's interests and act dutifully and in good faith. When A is performing a task on behalf of P, as a general principle, A must carry out such task on behalf of and for the benefit of P as the relationship between the parties is akin to that of a fiduciary relationship. This means that, at the very least, A must act in good faith to protect and serve the best interests of P, and to avoid a conflict of interest or duty. It is expected that a commercial agent will adhere to the following fiduciary duties:

(a) the duty not to delegate his office (unless this is agreed to by P or is a usual practice in the particular trade of A);
(b) the duty not to put himself in a situation where his duties as agent conflict with his own interests (unless he fully discloses his interests to P and P approves);
(c) the duty not to accept bribes or secret commissions from T (otherwise A will be held criminally liable and liable to P to forfeit any monies so received in excess of the remuneration agreed to by P: T will also be liable);
(d) the duty not to take advantage of his position in order to gain benefits for himself (such as deposit P's monies into A's account to accrue interest for himself or use for his own purposes information or knowledge acquired for use by P to make a profit);

(e) the duty to hand over to P money which he holds to his use, and to account to P (any monies or property held by A for P are deemed to be held in trust for P).[22]

These strict fiduciary duties necessarily require A to:

(a) comply with reasonable instructions given by his principal;
(b) act with skill and care;
(c) make proper efforts to negotiate and, where appropriate, conclude the transactions he is instructed to take care of; and
(d) communicate to P all the necessary information available to him.

Winston Padmore Claimant v James Morgan First Defendant, Roderick A. Thomas Second Defendant, Yacoob Ali Third Defendant (2009) CV2006–277 (TT)

Facts: This was an action for recovery of a debt as well as for damages for breach of the contract of agency. In 2003, the Claimant and the Defendants had been shareholders in two companies, that is to say Trinidad and Tobago Stocks and Shares Ltd (TTSSL) and Equities and Investments Ltd (E&I Ltd). In 2004, the shareholdings of the parties were sold to the AIC Financial Group Ltd (the AIC). The Claimant alleged that, while acting as agent for the Defendants he advanced specified sums to the AIC. He seeks reimbursement of such sums. The Defendants have relied on the contention that there was no relationship of agent and principal existing between the Claimant and the Defendants. They have argued further that the Claimant had breached his fiduciary duties as agent by placing himself in a position where his fiduciary duties were in conflict with other interests. On the 30th day of July 2009, I dismissed the Claim mainly on the finding that the Claimant acted in breach of his fiduciary duties.

Held: Dean-Armorer, J

Duty not to have a conflicting interest
An agent will not be allowed to put his duty in conflict with his interest, and therefore he must not enter into any transaction likely to produce that result, unless he has first made to his principal the fullest disclosure of the exact nature of his interest and the principal has assented. *Chitty* frames the duty as follows:

> A more general principle . . . is that as a fiduciary, an agent must not, without first obtaining the informed consent of his principal, put himself in a position where his duty to his principal conflicts, or may conflict with his own interests or the interests of the principal. Any benefit or gain made in circumstances where a conflict or a significant possibility of conflict existed must be accounted for to the principal. . . .

This is a very important duty and is very strictly applied by the Courts.

An agent who acts in conflict with his fiduciary duty is not entitled to recover monies due and owing to him. See *Bowstead on Agency* (17th 2001) Ed. Article 65:

> An agent is not entitled to reimbursement of expenses incurred by him. . . . in consequence of his own negligence, default . . . or breach of duty . . .

Negligence and Breach of Fiduciary Duty
Every agent, including a gratuitous agent[,] is responsible to his principal for any loss occasioned by his want of proper care, skill or diligence, in the carrying out of his undertaking.

22 See Markesinis and Munday, *An Outline of the Law of Agency*, pp 98–115.

No absolute standard can be laid down as to what constitutes proper care, skill or diligence, and each case must be judged by its own circumstances. An agent who acts gratuitously is only bound to use such skill as he has, except where he has represented himself as possessing skill in which case the amount of skill required is such as may reasonably be expected under the circumstances. The care and diligence required are such as persons ordinarily use in their own affairs. However, a higher standard is exacted where an agent acts for reward. In that case, the care, skill or diligence required is not merely that which the agent in fact possesses, but such as is reasonably necessary for the due performance of his undertaking. He must show at least such diligence in conducting his principal's business as the principal would reasonably have been able to display if the principal had undertaken the business himself.

By his Witness Statement filed herein on the 2nd April 2007, the Claimant testified as follows:

> I recognised the contractual obligation of the Defendants and took the decision as Agent to defray it in order to complete the transaction expecting of course the Defendants to honour their obligation to me as their Agent . . .

Nowhere in his Witness Statement did the Claimant take the further step of deposing that he in fact made the payment. The Court observes the use of the words, 'I . . . took the decision as Agent to defray it . . .' There was no evidence that he acted on his decision and actually defrayed the alleged debt.

Moreover, the Claimant has produced no documentary proof of payment. I accept that the absence of proof was not put to the Claimant in cross-examination. However, in determining issues of fact the Court is required to have regard to contemporaneous documents. No contemporaneous document was adduced to support the allegation that the Claimant in fact incurred the debt as alleged. In my view, the Claimant as the party who carries the burden of proof has failed to provide any proof whatsoever of payment and on this ground the Claim must fail.

The Defendants have contended further that they never authorised the Claimant to act on their behalf. They argued instead that the companies TTSSL and E&I Ltd. had been constituted their agents for the purpose of the sale of their shares. For the purpose of resolving this issue the First Defendant falls into a different category from the Second and Third. Warm, cordial letters passed between the Claimant and the First Defendant. In particular the faxed letter by the First Defendant on the 4th May 2004 suggested strongly that the First Defendant saw the Claimant as conducting the sale on his behalf. In respect of the Second and Third Defendants, the Claimant admitted that documents sent to the First Defendant were never sent to the Second and Third Defendants. There is no dispute that they forwarded their share certificates as recommended at the Directors meeting on the 4th day of March 2004. This was, however, pursuant not to the recommendation of the Claimant but that of the Board. Accordingly, the Second and Third Defendants are entitled to rely on the express provision of the Articles of Continuance that by providing notice of the shareholders' desire to transfer shares, the company is constituted agent for the sale of the shares. (*See Item 5 of the Articles of Continuance*). In my view however, it is of little consequence whether the Company or the Claimant had acted as agent for the sale of the shares. The Court will therefore assume that the Claimant was the authorised agent and then consider on that basis whether the Defendants are liable.

Assuming that the Claimant acted as agent, the conjoint effect of the letter of the 1st April 2004, and the First Defendant's fax note of the 7th April 2004 was to authorise the Claimant to sell at a minimum price of $12.00 per share. There was no authority given to the Claimant to bind the Defendants by the terms and warranties of the '*Padmore Agreement*'. I agree with the submission of Learned Senior Counsel for the Claimant that the agent is invested to do what is necessary to achieve what he was authorised to do. However, it seems that it would have been reasonable for the agent to bring the terms of the '*Padmore Agreement*' to his principals to obtain their further authority. This the Claimant admitted was never done. Accordingly, it is my view and I hold that in concluding the '*Padmore Agreement*' the Claimant acted outside of his authority and the Defendants are not bound thereby.

Assuming that I am wrong in so concluding, it is my view that the Claimant acted negligently as agent in executing the "*Padmore Agreement*". The Claimant made the following admissions:

- He never warned the Defendants of warranties which bound them as in "*Padmore Agreement*".
- The Claimant took no legal advice before concluding the "*Padmore Agreement*".

Accordingly, I agree with learned Counsel for the First Defendant that the Claimant's negligent breach of duty disentitles him to recover any sums claimed.

Even beyond his negligence however, is the fact that the Claimant as agent placed himself in a position where his duty as agent conflicted with his duty to the AIC. It is undisputed that following the execution of the '*Padmore Agreement*', the Claimant immediately accepted an offer by the AIC to act as a consultant for a period of three (3) months at a monthly fee of thirty thousand dollars ($30,000.00).

Accordingly, when the Claimant negotiated with Mr. Prescod of the AIC on the 21st May 2004, the Claimant as someone whose services were engaged by the AIC, negotiated on behalf of the shareholders. Moreover, in the course of those negotiations, one of the adjusted items was the Managing Director/s bonus of seventy four thousand dollars ($74,000.00) which would ultimately redound to the Claimant[']s enrichment.

The Claimant therefore placed himself in a position of conflict in two ways:

- by his engagement to the AIC
- negotiating a result from which he stood to benefit personally.

In my view, the existence of the conflict between his duties to the Defendants and his duty to the AIC and together with the likelihood of his personal gains[] have the ultimate effect of negating any entitlement that the Claimant may otherwise have had. Accordingly, I dismissed the claim.

While A is not required to inform P of every piece of information pertinent to the discharge of his agency, A has a duty to exercise reasonable care when executing his agency to make immediately known to P all significant information coming to his knowledge which might influence P's instructions.

Kelly v Cooper and Another [1992] 41 WIR 80 (BM)

Facts: Mr Kelly was at all material times the beneficial owner of 'Caliban', a house in Tucker's Town in Bermuda, which was built on an oblong-shaped area of land measuring

2.85 acres fronting on to the ocean. Adjacent to Caliban to the west, but separated by a small ravine which prevented direct access from one property to the other, was a house 'Vertigo' built on a similar shaped area of land measuring 2.742 acres also fronting on to the ocean. Vertigo belonged to a Mr Brant. Although direct access between the two properties was not possible because of the ravine, both properties fronted on to the same beach which, although public, was not much used by outsiders. Access from one property to the other was possible along that beach or along the road.

Since about 1979, Mr Kelly had been keen to sell Caliban and had employed a number of estate agents for that purpose, including apparently Coopers. By a letter dated 7 March 1983 Mr Kelly formally appointed Coopers as agents to sell Caliban at a price of BM$3.5 million or such sum as Mr Kelly might agree to accept, Coopers to be paid a commission of 5 per cent of the selling price. Up to 1985 Caliban attracted limited interest and no offers acceptable to Mr Kelly had been made.

At a date which is not identified in the evidence Coopers were also instructed by Mr Brant as agents to sell Vertigo. Both Caliban and Vertigo were available for sale to those who did not have Bermudan status (that is to expatriates) with the consent of the Governor, but in practice the Governor did not permit an expatriate to purchase more than one property. In April 1985 an American, Mr H Ross Perot arrived on the Islands and approached Coopers with a view to purchasing property. Coopers had previously encountered Mr Perot in 1983 when they had sought to negotiate a letting of Caliban to Mr Perot, but the negotiations had broken down. On 19 April 1985 Coopers took Mr Perot to view both Caliban and Vertigo. On 20 April Mr Perot made an offer of BM$2 million for Vertigo. On the same day he told Coopers that he was interested in making an offer for Caliban and asked Margot Cooper to sound out what would be Mr Kelly's response to an offer in the range of BM$2 to BM$2.5 million gross, that is Mr Kelly to bear the agent's commission. Margot Cooper passed on to Mr Kelly this indication of interest by Mr Perot. Mr Kelly responded by saying he was interested in selling at BM$2.5 million but would prefer that sum to be net of commission. Margot Cooper told Mr Perot of Mr Kelly's response. On 22 April Mr Brant accepted Mr Perot's offer of BM$2 million for Vertigo. On the same day Mr Perot made an offer of BM$2.5 million gross for Caliban. On 23 April Helen Cooper took a letter to Mr Kelly containing particulars of this offer by Mr Perot for Caliban. On that occasion, Mr Kelly asked her if she thought that Mr Perot would increase the offer: she told him that her feeling was that he would not, but that certainly there was nothing to prevent Mr Kelly from making a counter-offer. At no time did Coopers tell Mr Kelly of Mr Perot's proposed purchase of Vertigo, and it was this fact which gave rise to this litigation.

Contracts for the sale of Vertigo were exchanged on 14 May 1985 and completed on 16 August. Contracts for the sale of Caliban were exchanged on 17 June 1985 and completion took place on 13 November. The purchaser of Caliban was expressed to be Mr Perot's son, Mr Perot junior; at one stage during the negotiation of the contract it was suggested that Mr Perot's daughters would be the purchasers. After completion, Mr Kelly discovered that Mr Perot and his family had bought both Caliban and Vertigo. He took the view that his agents, Coopers, should have told him of the Perots' interest in both properties, being material information relating to his sale of Caliban. He refused to pay the commission of BM$125,000 due to Coopers and proceedings were started by Coopers for its recovery.

Held: Lord Browne-Wilkinson

Quite apart from this evidence, it is self-evident that, if a purchaser is interested in buying two adjoining properties, there is a special market in which the purchaser may, but not necessarily will, pay over the ordinary price to achieve his objective. Their Lordships therefore consider that Mr Perot's interest in buying both the properties was a material factor which could have influenced the negotiations for the price at which Caliban was sold.

Was there any contractual duty on Coopers to disclose this material fact to Mr Kelly? The judge started from the proposition in *Bowstead on Agency* (15th edn) page 147: 'An agent is, in general, under a duty to keep his principal informed about matters which are his concern.' He then sought to reconcile this proposition with the fact that Coopers were also agents for Mr Brant and it was in the course of that agency, not whilst acting as agents for Mr Kelly, that Coopers had learned that Mr Perot was interested in buying Vertigo. Since, as has throughout been common ground, Coopers were not at liberty to divulge to others' information acquired as agents for Mr Brant, Coopers could not tell Mr Kelly the true position without breaching their duty to Mr Brant. As their Lordships understand the judgment, the trial judge found this reconciliation primarily in the decision of Donaldson J in *North and South Trust Co v Berkeley* [1971] 1 WLR 470. He regarded that case as deciding that an agent for principal A who has chosen to act for another principal B on whose behalf he acquires information cannot be forced to divulge such information to principal A but can be held liable in damages to principal A for breach of duty.

In the view of the Board the resolution of this case depends upon two fundamental propositions: first, agency is a contract made between principal and agent; second, like every other contract, the rights and duties of the principal and agent are dependent upon the terms of the contract between them whether express or implied. It is not possible to say that all agents owe the same duties to their principals: it is always necessary to have regard to the express or implied terms of the contract.

This fact is fully recognised in the introduction to Chapter 5 of *Bowstead* (pages 137, 138): the rest of the chapter, including the proposition on which the judge relied, deals with the duties which will arise from the terms normally found in a contract of agency. In a case where a principal instructs as selling agent for his property or goods a person who to his knowledge acts and intends to act for other principals selling property or goods of the same description, the terms to be implied into such agency contract must differ from those to be implied where an agent is not carrying on such general agency business. In the case of an estate agent, it is its business to act for numerous principals: where properties are of a similar description, there will be a conflict of interest between the principals, each of whom will be concerned to attract potential purchasers to his property rather than that of another. Yet, despite this conflict of interest, estate agents must be free to act for several competing principals otherwise they would be unable to perform their function.

Yet it is normally said that it is a breach of an agent's duty to act for competing principals. In the course of acting for each of their principals, estate agents will acquire information confidential to that principal. It cannot be sensibly suggested that an estate agent is contractually bound to disclose to any one of his principals information which is confidential to another of his principals. The position as to confidentiality is even clearer in the case of stock brokers who cannot be contractually bound to disclose to their private clients inside information disclosed to the brokers in confidence by a company for which they also act. Accordingly, in such cases there must be an implied term of the contract with such an agent that he is entitled to act for other principals selling competing properties and to keep confidential the information obtained from each of his principals. Similar considerations apply to the fiduciary duties of agents. The existence and scope of these duties depends upon the terms on which they are acting. In *New Zealand Netherlands Society 'Oranje' Inc v*

Kuys [1973] 1 WLR 1126 at page 1129 Lord Wilberforce, in giving the judgment of this Board, said:

> The obligation not to profit from a position of trust, or, as it is sometimes relevant to put, not to allow a conflict to arise between duty and interest, is one of strictness. The strength and indeed the severity of the rule has recently been emphasised by the House of Lords: *Phipps v Boardman* [1967] 2 AC 46. It retains its vigour in all jurisdictions where the principles of equity are applied. Naturally it has different applications in different contexts. It applies, in principle, whether the case is one of a trust, express or implied, of partnership, of directorship of a limited company, of principal and agent, or master and servant, but the precise scope of it must be moulded according to the nature of the relationship. As Lord Upjohn said in *Phipps v Boardman* (at page 123): 'Rules of equity have to be applied to such a great diversity of circumstances that they can be stated only in the most general terms and applied with particular attention to the exact circumstances of each case'.

In *Hospital Products International Pty Ltd. v US Surgical Corporation* (1984) 58 ALJR 587 at page 608, Mason J in the High Court of Australia said this:

> That contractual and fiduciary relationships may coexist between the same parties has never been doubted. Indeed, the existence of a basic contractual relationship has in many situations provided a foundation for the erection of a fiduciary relationship. In these situations it is the contractual foundation which is all important because it is the contract that regulates the basic rights and liabilities of the parties. The fiduciary relationship, if it is to exist at all, must accommodate itself to the terms of the contract so that it is consistent with, and conforms to, them. The fiduciary relationship cannot be superimposed upon the contract in such a way as to alter the operation which the contract was intended to have according to its true construction.

Thus, in the present case, the scope of the fiduciary duties owed by Coopers to Mr Kelly (and in particular the alleged duty not to put themselves in a position where their duty and their interest conflicted) are to be defined by the terms of the contract of agency. Applying those considerations to the present case, their Lordships are of the view that since Mr Kelly was well aware that Coopers would be acting also for other vendors of comparable properties and, in so doing, would receive confidential information from those other vendors, the agency contract between Mr Kelly and Coopers cannot have included either (a) a term requiring Coopers to disclose such confidential information to Mr Kelly, or (b) a term precluding Coopers acting for rival vendors, or (c) a term precluding Coopers from seeking to earn commission on the sale of the property of a rival vendor. Their Lordships are therefore of opinion that Coopers committed no breach of duty, whether contractual or fiduciary, by failing to reveal to Mr Kelly Mr Perot's interest in buying Vertigo, since such information was confidential to Mr Brant. Nor did the fact that Coopers had a direct financial interest in securing a sale of Vertigo constitute a breach of fiduciary duty since the contract of agency envisaged that they might have such a conflict of interest . . .

As to Coopers' claim for commission, even if a breach of fiduciary duty by Coopers had been proved, they would not thereby have lost their right to commission unless they had acted dishonestly. In *Keppel v Wheeler* the agents admitted an honest breach of fiduciary duty by mistake and yet were entitled to their commission. In the present case Mr Kelly did not allege, nor did the judge find, any bad faith by Coopers. Even on the view the judge took, therefore, there was no ground for depriving Coopers of their commission.

PRINCIPAL'S DUTIES TO THE AGENT; AGENT'S RIGHTS AGAINST THE PRINCIPAL

P's duties to A seem to be much less onerous than those owed by A to P (see previous section). Nevertheless, it is expected that P will act in good faith in his relations with A. P must in particular:

- provide A with the necessary documents relating to the goods concerned;
- obtain for A the information necessary for the performance of the agency contract and, in particular, notify A within a reasonable period once he anticipates that the volume of commercial transactions will be significantly lower than that which A could normally have expected;
- inform A within a reasonable period of his acceptance, refusal, and any non-execution of a commercial transaction which A has procured for P;
- pay to A fees and commission.

Related to the last point, A possesses specific, though fairly limited, rights against P. The most important right A possesses against P is the right to be remunerated according to the terms of the contract, whether they be express or implied.[23] Where A works for a commission, this will also form part of the contract. In cases of agency by necessity where there is no agency contract or where A acts outside the scope of his authority and this is not ratified by P, however, A has no entitlement to commission. Moreover, where the contract states that A will only be entitled to commission once he performs certain acts or brings about a specified result, if he fails to meet these requirements, he will not be entitled to receive commission.

Furthermore, entitlement to commission requires A not only to complete his task but to show that 'his services were the effective cause in bringing about that particular result'.[24] He must have been the actual 'agent' of causation in bringing successful closure to the transaction, that is, to cause P (vendor) and T (purchaser) to enter into a binding contract. If A was not in fact the effective cause, perhaps because there was some interruption between finding a purchaser and the point of sale (such as termination of his services and the employment of another agent who then caused the parties to enter into a contract), then A will not be deemed to have been the effective cause of the transaction. In another instance, A may have introduced a tenant to P and therefore will be entitled to a finder's fee; nevertheless, if the tenant eventually becomes a purchaser through no causation of A, A has no grounds for expecting a commission.

As noted, commission is only due when P and T enter into a binding contract. This is further circumscribed by the fact that T (purchaser), introduced by A, must be willing and able to complete the purchase.[25] This principle has emerged as a safeguard to P. The courts will interpret such terms strictly and have held that where T makes an offer 'subject to contract', T is not actually willing to purchase. Only where an unconditional offer of purchase is made will T be deemed to be willing to purchase. Entering into a contract is, of course, evidence of such willingness.

Apart from his ability to claim remuneration from P under their contract, albeit under very particular circumstances, A also has the right to be reimbursed by P for all expenses and

23 Markesinis and Munday, *An Outline of the Law of Agency*, pp 115–18.
24 Markesinis and Munday, *An Outline of the Law of Agency*, p 119. See also pp 119–22.
25 Markesinis and Munday, *An Outline of the Law of Agency*, p 129.

indemnified against all losses and liabilities incurred by him while acting within the scope of his authority.[26] The inverse also applies: A is not entitled to reimbursement or indemnification when he acts outside the scope of his authority.

One specific issue that may arise is whether P is under any obligation not to prevent A from earning his commission. Markesinis and Munday state that A may only sue P for damages to compensate him for having been deprived of an opportunity to earn commission if an express term of the contract imposes such a duty on P to do so or if such a term must be implied to give the contract business efficacy.[27] In the case of a real estate agent, the contract is usually unilateral and requires no action on the part of A. He will receive his commission on the sale of the property,[28] or where he has introduced a willing and able purchaser at the time of the deposit. The time of his payment will turn on the construction of the contract. P reserves the right, however, to withdraw from a sale agreement without incurring any liability to A before any agreement has been signed. This does not mean that A cannot successfully sue P for damages on account of P preventing him from earning a commission but it will depend on a true construction of the contract. Where the only reason the contract is not performed is that P was either unwilling or unable to perform it, the courts will generally not permit P to dishonour the contract with T so as to deprive A of the remuneration due to him under the agency contract. In such cases, the courts will imply a term that P will not fail to perform his contract with T so as to deprive A of the remuneration due to him. Where A has not discharged all his obligations under the agreement, however, he may not be entitled to commission.

Where A has a claim against P, the law accords to A a lien on the goods and chattels of P in respect of all claims arising out of his employment as agent to facilitate his recovery of expenses properly owed.[29] A lien entitles A to retain possession of P's property until P has satisfied the legitimate claims of A. In no way does this confer upon A title to P's property to treat with as he wishes: it merely entitles him to keep it in his possession until P meets his legal obligations. This right to acquire a lien on P's goods is as heavily circumscribed as his right to claim commission. Unless the contract expressly or impliedly excludes A's right to a lien, A must be able to prove that he lawfully came into possession of P's goods in his capacity as agent. To exercise the lien, the goods must be in A's physical or constructive possession. Once the lien is applicable to P's goods and chattels, it offers A a broad measure of security as the lien will continue to be valid even if P becomes insolvent or bankrupt or T acquires title or rights in the goods. A loses the lien automatically, obviously, when P fulfils his obligations to A. A may also lose the lien if he waives his rights voluntarily or acts in a manner inconsistent with the lien's existence, such as allowing P free access to his property. Additionally, if A gives up possession of the goods or chattels to which the lien adheres, the lien will be lost.

Fazal v Annamanthadoo (1991) 48 WIR 150 (GY)

Facts: The respondent was a property agent and the appellant the owner by transport of certain lands, which were stated to comprise 500 acres, situated at Plantation Friends on the east bank of the Berbice River. On 5 May 1982 the appellant signed a written authorisation to the respondent empowering him to sell the lands and, in pursuance thereof, to enter into an agreement of purchase and sale. The sale price was stated to be GY$200,000

26 Markesinis and Munday, *An Outline of the Law of Agency*, p 130.
27 Markesinis and Munday, *An Outline of the Law of Agency*, p 122.
28 Markesinis and Munday, *An Outline of the Law of Agency*, pp 126–30.
29 Markesinis and Munday, *An Outline of the Law of Agency*, pp 134–9.

and the conditions under which the agreement was to be effected were also set out in the document which included the payment of a commission on the sale. On 30 August 1983 the respondent entered into a contract of purchase and sale with A (in his capacity as agent of B) for the required consideration of GY$200,000 and received a cheque representing 10 per cent of the purchase price. The contract of purchase and sale was prepared at the office of Mr Bacchus, attorney at law, who the appellant had told the respondent was his legal adviser, and Mr Bacchus signed as a witness. In addition to the first four terms that were authorised to be included in the contract, it also included a guarantee to the purchaser of a title free from all encumbrances and required that the transport be passed within four months of the date of the contract, which period was stated to be the essence of the contract.

On the next day the respondent went to the appellant at his business premises in Strand, New Amsterdam. There he gave him a copy of the agreement and the cheque. After reading the agreement, the appellant threw both documents on the floor saying that he had no intention of selling the property to A as he had robbed him. The respondent then spoke to Mr Bacchus, who sent a letter to the appellant in which he enclosed the agreement and the cheque. The appellant responded by letter written by Mr Hardyal, attorney at law, which rejected the respondent's authority to sell the property. This resulted in the respondent issuing proceedings for breach of contract claiming the commission of 4 per cent of the purchase price, or GY$8,000. The breach complained of was the refusal of the appellant without any reasonable cause to take steps to bring the binding contract between himself, through the respondent as his agent, and the purchaser to fruition by embarking upon the necessary legal procedures.

Held: George, C
Here is a vendor who, according to the trial judge, 'within a very short time of the agreement of the sale . . . expressed a settled intention that he would not complete the sale to the purchaser', a conclusion which was no doubt influenced by the respondent's evidence of the appellant's reaction when he read the contract and realised who was the purchaser, viz that he was not selling to A as he had robbed him. It is well known that in all but a very few instances a purchaser hardly has the whole of the purchase price for the property available at the time that he enters into a binding agreement of sale. Invariably, it is only after he has signed the contract that he commences efforts to obtain some portion, large or small in order to make up the full purchase price; and this is done either by means of a mortgage or some other financial transaction. Therefore, in general, the important date for a determination of a purchaser's ability to pay is the date when transport ought to be passed. In this regard, it is worthy of note that in *Rightside Properties Ltd. v Gray* [1974] 2 All ER 1169 a similar conclusion was reached. That was a case of vendor and purchaser in which one of the issues was whether there was an obligation on the part of the purchaser to prove his ability to complete despite a renunciation by the vendor. Walton J said (at page 1183):

> Of course, in the present case the repudiation was not accepted at once: Rightside [the purchasers] kept the contract open. Equally, however, there was at all times until, and there was persisted in during the trial, a wrongful repudiation. It appears to me that in consequence Rightside was never at any time under any obligation to show that it was 'able' to perform its part of the contract. 'Ability' in this connection, means arranging the finances, which under modern conditions, could be done either by arranging a mortgage or a sub-sale, and doubtless there are other methods as well. But they all involve some form of preparation on the part of the person raising the finance; and it appears to me *pessimi exempli* if the vendor was in a position to say: 'Because you were not on a particular day ready with your finance, you cannot claim damages against me. True it is that it would have been perfectly useless for

> you to make the preparations because I told you I was not going to complete, but I can now huff you for having failed to carry out this perfectly useless exercise.' This is the morality of a game, not of a serious legal contest.

If, however, it was the purchaser who had resiled from his contract then it goes without saying that the agent could not properly claim to be entitled to his commission because he would not then have found a purchaser who was ready willing and able to buy the property (see for example *Peter Long & Partners v Burns* [1956] 3 All ER 207). But by a parity of reasons if the vendor is in breach by refusing to proceed with the sale he cannot be allowed to invoke his own default as a defence to an action for breach of his obligation to his agent. In *Luxor (Eastbourne) Ltd. v Cooper* [1941] 1 All ER 33 Lord Russell of Killowen was at pains to point out that commission contracts possessed no special features to distinguish them from other contracts. He said (at page 43):

> (1) Commission contracts are subject to no peculiar rules or principles of their own. The law which governs them is the law which governs all contracts and all questions of agency.
> (2) No general rule can be laid down by which rights of the agent or liabilities of the principal under commission contracts are to be determined. In each case, these must depend upon the exact terms of the contract in question, and upon the true construction of those terms.
> (3) Contracts by which owners of property, desiring to dispose of it put it in the hands of agents on commission are not . . . contracts of employment in the ordinary meaning of those words. No obligation is imposed on the agent to do anything.

And as regards the vendor's liability to his property agent in the event that he desired to renege on the agreement entered into Lord Russell had this to say (at page 44):

> The position will no doubt be different if the matter had proceeded to the stage of a binding contract having been made between the principal and the agent's client. In that case it can be said with truth that a 'purchaser' had been introduced by the agent. In other words, the event has happened upon the occurrence of which a right to the promised commission has become vested in the agent. From that moment, no act or omission by the principal can deprive the agent of that vested interest.

. . . In my opinion, however, when a vendor instructs an agent to sell his property without more, and gives him a copy of the transport, two representations must necessarily be implied. The first is that the property that is to be sold is that described in the transport, and the second is that it is to be sold free from the registered encumbrance of any mortgage that may be annotated thereon . . . It is my opinion that, by giving the agent a copy of his transport which was devoid of any annotation of either of the two contracts, the appellant must be deemed to have represented to the respondent that what he was offering for sale was all the property that was described in the title deed . . . If it turns out that it was not within his power to sell the whole, because he was otherwise contractually obligated in respect of some portion of it, he could not take advantage of his own failure to represent the true position to the agent as a lawful reason for depriving him of his commission, after he has introduced or (as the case may be) entered into a contract of purchase and sale with a purchaser who is ready, willing and able to buy the whole of the property . . . For the above reasons I would dismiss the appeal.

Wayne Camps (Claimant) v Angela Attong (Defendant) (2010) CV2007–00840 (TT)

Facts: The Defendant to this action is an estate agent. She agreed to find a buyer in respect of property owned by the Claimant. The Defendant in fact procured a purchaser who entered into a binding agreement for sale. Upon signing the agreement for sale, the Claimant paid the Defendant the agreed commission. Subsequently however, the purchaser was unable to complete the sale. The Claimant forfeited the purchaser's deposit and asked the Defendant to relist the property for sale. After having waited in vain for several months for the Defendant to find a suitable purchaser, the Claimant instituted these proceedings to recover the $300,000.00 which he had paid to the Defendant as commission. In this judgment, the Court considered the terms of agreements between estate agents and property owners. In particular, the Court considered when and in what circumstances the estate agent's commission became due and payable.

Held: Dean-Armorer, J

1. The law in respect of the entitlement of estate agents to commission is set out in *Chitty on Contracts* (28th ed.), Vol. 2, page 79, paragraph 32–140:

> First, when an agent claims that he has earned the right to commission, the test is whether upon the proper interpretation of the contract between the principal and the agent the event has happened upon which commission is to be paid. Secondly, there are no special principles of construction applicable to commission contracts with estate agents. Thirdly, contracts under which a principal is bound to pay commission for an introduction which does not result in a sale must be expressed in clear language.

Luxor (Eastbourne) Limited v Cooper

This was a decision of the House of Lords in which the Plaintiff, Cooper[,] sued the two Appellants for commission allegedly due to him for introduction of purchasers to properties held by the companies. Cooper alleged that he produced ready and willing purchasers who were prepared to buy on terms that the companies were prepared to sell. The sale never took place. Cooper claimed damages equivalent to his commission, on the ground that the Appellants had an implied term of contract that they would do nothing to prevent Cooper from earning his commission. The majority of their Lordships ruled against Cooper and held that there was no implied term as suggested on his behalf. In *Luxor (Eastbourne) Limited v Cooper*, Lord Russell of Killowen considered whether there was an implied term that the vendor would do nothing to prevent the agent from earning his commission. Lord Russell of Killowen had this to say:

> I can find no safe ground on which to base the introduction of any such implied term. Implied terms, as we all know, can only be justified under the compulsion of some necessity. No such compulsion or necessity exists in the case under consideration. The agent is promised a commission if he introduces a purchaser at a specified or minimum price. The owner is desirous of selling. The chances are largely in favour of the deal going through, if a purchaser is introduced. The agent takes the risk in the hope of a substantial remuneration for comparatively small exertion . . . The position will no doubt be different if the matter has proceeded to the stage of a binding contract having been made between the principal and the agent's client. In that case it can be said with truth that a 'purchaser' has been introduced by the agent; in other words the event has happened upon the occurrence of which a right to the promised commission has become vested in the agent.

Learned Counsel, Ms. Greene relied on the statement of Lord Russell in support of her proposition that the agent's commission becomes due and payable when the vendor and the purchaser enter into a binding contract.

Mc Callum v Hicks

Both parties referred to the decision in *Mc Callum v Hicks*, in which the Defendant orally instructed the Plaintiff 'to find someone to buy my house'. Nothing was said at the time about the commission. The Defendant signed a provisional agreement, subject to contract. The Defendant withdrew his instructions from the Plaintiff who then commenced proceedings. The Court of Appeal held that the words '. . .*find someone to buy*' were equivalent to '*find a purchaser* . . .' and the Plaintiff was not entitled to commission for he had not introduced a person who had actually completed the contract or entered into a binding enforceable contract. Bucknill LJ, in holding that the trial Judge had placed an incorrect construction on the agreed words, said:

> . . . where the vendor is a poor man . . . he would naturally pay the commission out of the purchase price, which he will not receive until a formal and binding contract has been made.

Denning LJ had this to say at page 274:

> When an ordinary house-owner goes to a house agent and asks him to 'find a purchaser,' that means that the agent is to find a person who will actually complete the purchase of the house, it being understood that the agent's commission is to be paid out of the purchase price. That is the common understanding of men in these matters. If the sale is not complete, the agent gets no commission unless he has procured an actual, binding and enforceable contract for purchase.

Denning LJ then made the following ruling, which was relied upon by Learned Counsel, Ms. Greene:

> Once the purchaser and vendor have signed and exchanged a contract the agent has earned his commission because if the purchaser does not complete the vendor can recover the amount of the commission by way of damages.

Denning LJ then referred to the words of Lord Romer in *Luxor (Eastbourne) Limited v Cooper* and quoted the learned law Lord as saying: 'Where an owner of property employs an agent to find a purchaser, that must mean at least a person who enters a binding contract to purchase.' The pronouncements in *Mc Callum v Hicks*, in my view, provide authority for the proposition that the estate agent ordinarily becomes entitled to her commission when the vendor and purchaser have entered into a valid binding agreement.

Dennis Reed Ltd v Goody

In this matter the identical panel of Court of Appeal judges considered the meaning of the words:

> I hereby instruct you to find a person ready, able and willing to purchase the above property . . . Upon your introducing such a person I will pay you commission.

The Plaintiffs introduced a potential purchaser who signed an agreement, subject to the vendor agreeing to indemnify against road charges. The Defendant took time to seek legal advice. During the delay, the potential purchaser withdrew his offer. The Court of Appeal held that the agent was not entitled to a commission since the proposed purchaser withdrew before a binding contract had been made. In the course of his decision, Denning LJ said at page 284:

> So many cases have now come before the courts on claims by house agents to commission that the document cannot, I think, be interpreted in vacuo. It must be interpreted in the light of the general law on the subject . . .

Denning LJ then proceeded to set out the general law on the subject as follows:

> When a house owner puts his house into the hands of an estate agent, the ordinary understanding is that the agent is only to receive a commission if he succeeds in effecting a sale; but if not, he is entitled to nothing . . .

Denning LJ said later in his judgment that no particular words were required to create the relationship. Denning LJ then said:

> The common understanding of men is . . . that the agent's commission is payable out of the purchase price. The service rendered by the agent may be merely an introduction. He is entitled to commission if his introduction is the efficient cause in bringing about a sale . . . But that does not mean that commission is payable at the moment of introduction: it but is only payable on completion of the sale.

Denning LJ then doubted his pronouncement in *Mc Callum v Hicks* by stating:

> This has led some people to suppose that commission is payable as soon as a contract is signed. . . . But this is not correct.

Denning LJ then specified:

> . . . if the vendor could show that the purchaser would not in any event have been able or willing to complete, he would not be liable to commission. When it is not the vendor, but the purchaser, who withdraws, the case is entirely different; for even though a binding contract has been made, nevertheless, if the purchaser is unable or unwilling to complete, the agent is not entitled to his commission . . . The vendor is not bound to bring an action for specific performance or for damages simply to enable the agent to get commission; but if he does get his money, he will probably be liable to pay the commission out of it.

Copeland v Wedlock

Learned Counsel, Ms. Greene relied on the Canadian decision of *Copeland v Wedlock*, where the law was stated as follows:

> . . . if a person occupying the position of the plaintiffs is authorized to find a purchaser for property at a price named, and does find a purchaser satisfactory to his principal, and procures a binding contract to be entered into, he is entitled to his commission, although the sale does not go through owning to the default of the buyer.
>
> . . .

Having considered the evidence in this matter, on a balance of probabilities, it has been established that the Claimant commissioned the Defendant by way of an oral agreement *'to sell his property'* situate at School Street, Carenage. It was agreed that the price should not be less th[a]n $6 million and that the Defendant's commission would be 5% of the purchase price. The Defendant procured a purchaser R.C.D. Systems and Processes Ltd. following which the Claimant and the purchaser entered into a binding agreement for sale of the property. On the date of signing the Agreement for Sale, the Claimant paid to the Defendant $300,000.00 representing 5% of the agreed purchase price. The purchaser was never able to complete the agreement. The Claimant forfeited the deposit and asked the Defendant to re-list the property for sale. The Claimant over a period of one year was not able to find a purchaser at the required sale price. Having regard to the foregoing facts, the Court considered whether the Defendant as estate agent was entitled to receive her commission upon introducing a purchaser or upon the formation of a binding agreement for sale between the Claimant and a purchaser. The Court also considered whether no commission became due and payable until the sale is completed. The law governing estate agent's agreements is set out in *Bowstead and Reynolds on Agency* 18th ed:

> Where an agent is entitled to his remuneration upon the happening of a future event, his entitlement does not arise until that event has occurred. *The event upon which the agent's entitlement... arises is to be ascertained from the terms of the agency contract*... (Emphasis mine).

It therefore falls to this Court to discern what was the event, as agreed between the parties when the Defendant became entitled to her remuneration. Textbooks and authorities have been consistent however in emphasising that what obtains depends on what was agreed between the parties. Denning LJ, as he then was, referred to the 'common understanding of men.' The common understanding may vary from agreement to agreement and what is relevant is what was actually agreed between the parties in question. In support of this proposition, the Court relies on the statement in *Bowstead and Reynolds on Agency* that the event upon which the agent's entitlement arises is to be ascertained from the terms of the agency contract. The Court must therefore consider what were the terms which obtained between the Claimant and the Defendant and in particular what was the event which entitled the Defendant to her commission. In the course of cross-examination, the Claimant agreed with Learned Counsel, Ms. Greene that once he entered a binding agreement and received a deposit, the agent's commission would be due and payable. Such was the Claimant's understanding of his obligation. The Claimant also admitted in cross-examination that he received the deposit on 5th August, 2005 and that having received the deposit, he paid the Defendant her commission.

The Court considered whether, in the face of such a candid admission on the part of the Claimant, it could be contended by him that the agreed event was not the signing of a binding agreement for sale, but the actual completion of such an agreement. The admission of the Claimant must be seen as well in the light of his actions in actually paying the commission upon the signing of the agreement for sale. In my view, the Claimant's action in paying the Defendant's commission upon the signing of the agreement for sale constituted a tacit acknowledgement that the signing of the agreement was the agreed event when the commission became payable. Accordingly it is my view and I hold that, having regard to the evidence before this Court, it was agreed between the parties that the critical event was the date upon which the procured purchaser entered a binding agreement for sale. It follows that the commission was paid when it was due under the agreement and that the Defendant is not liable to refund same. The Claim is accordingly dismissed.

Palace Amusement Company Ltd (1921) v CD Alexander Company Realty Ltd (2005) SC Civ App No. 34/2003 (JM)

Facts: The substance of the appellant's complaint as contained in its grounds was that the learned trial judge was incorrect to find that the introduction of the Odeon complex to the appellant by the respondent's agent was the 'effective' cause of the sale and therefore the respondent was entitled to the commission of 5 per cent because the first introduction had evaporated. In addition, it was unreasonable to find that Ravers Ltd was not paid a commission.

Held: Harrison, J
The authors of *Bowstead and Reynolds on Agency*, 16th edition (1996) at paragraph 7–029 page 301, referring to the commission payable to an estate agent said:

> Apart from the general principle that in the absence of other indications the agent must be the effective cause of the transaction taking place, no clear principles can be easily derived from the many cases on this topic. The agent will normally be entitled to his commission if he causes a person to negotiate with his principal and contract, no substantial break in the negotiations having taken place. It appears that the agent does not have to complete or even take part in the negotiations.

The test is what action of the agent brought about the sale.

The authors, in discussing the test, recognised that it has been variously described as 'an effective cause' or 'the effective cause', and observed at paragraph 7–029 at page 300: 'There is doubt as to whether the rule is more helpfully formulated by requiring that the agent's act be "the effective cause".'

Mrs M ColeSmith, J, found on page 106 of the record: 'From the minutes, Exhibit 7, and the date of the contract exhibit 1, it is quite evident that the first introduction had evaporated and the meeting that Georgia Stewart had with Major Brown was the "effective" or "efficient" cause of the sale.' In *Chasen Ryder & Co. v Hedges* [1993] 8 EG 119 the Court of Appeal (England) allowed an appeal by the defendant vendor who had paid a commission to a second firm of estate agents instead of the plaintiff. The plaintiff had introduced a purchaser who had made no offer nor effected a purchase. The second firm of estate agents had contacted the same purchaser some 11 months later and a purchase of the property was completed. Staughton, LJ, at page 120 said:

> The burden is on the plaintiff to show that his introduction in any case was the effective cause of the purchase. If, however, he shows that he was the first to introduce the purchaser, and that a purchase followed, and if no other facts are established, then it may well be that the judge will infer that the plaintiff was the effective cause. It can therefore be said that the evidential burden in such a case passes to the defendant whether the other agent or the vendor, to prove more facts which displace that inference. But, even in such a case, I do not think that the further facts which the defendant then has to prove must be such as to show that interest aroused by the first introduction has evaporated, that is to say, entirely disappeared. It will be a matter for consideration in each case as to how far the defendant has to go before he has displaced an inference which might arise from the mere fact of the introduction followed by the purchase.

The court did not endorse the dictum of Forbes, J in *John D Wood v Dantata* [1987] 2 EGLR 23 that an agent who did a second introduction to a purchaser, in order to be entitled to his commission, had necessarily to prove that the interest of the purchaser in respect of the first introduction had evaporated, making the second introduction the effective cause of the purchase. Each case has to be decided on its own particular circumstances.

The issue frequently arising is which of the two tests should be employed, namely, 'an effective cause' or 'the effective cause' of the purchase, in determining the commission payable, where competing claims exist. In *Burchell v Gowrie* [1910] AC 614, their Lordships in the Privy Council held that an appellant agent was entitled to his commission on the sale of property, although it had been sold behind his back on different terms, because he had brought the vendor company in relation to the actual purchaser. The test was that the agent's introduction was 'an efficient cause' of the sale. The Board held (*per* Lord Atkinson), at page 624:

> There was no dispute about the law applicable to the first question (whether the acts of the agent was an 'efficient' cause of the sale). It was admitted that, in the words of Erle CJ in *Green v Bartlett*, 'if the relation of buyer and seller is really brought about by the act of the agent, he is entitled to commission although the actual sale has not been effected by him.' Or in the words of the later authorities, the plaintiff must shew that some act of his was the

> *causa causans* of the sale (*Tribe v Taylor* (1876), 1 CPD 505, 510) or was an efficient cause of the sale (*Millar v Radford* (1903) 19 Times LR 575)

and further on page 624 continuing on page 625:

> On this question of fact there was, their Lordships think, ample evidence to sustain the conclusion at which the referee presumably arrived, namely, that the appellant's acts were an effective cause of the sale which actually took place. In their Lordships' view, it was the right conclusion, and the finding to that effect ought not, they think, to be disturbed.

The later authorities prefer the term 'an effective cause' instead of 'efficient cause'. The Court of Appeal, in *Brian Cooper & Co. v Fairview Estates (Investments) Co.* [1987] 1 EGLR 18, was not prepared to imply in all commission agreements, a term that the agent is 'an effective' cause of the transaction. Woolf, LJ (as he then was) was of the view that: 'It could create problems where there are two or more effective causes, each of which could be the subject of a claim for commission.'

'The effective cause' test is a more decisive test referable to the direct consequences which brought about the sale. It is, however, a more onerous test than 'an effective cause' of the sale. The latter test recognises the existence of one or more effective causes. There can exist in a transaction other events which could have influenced the sale and be effectively labelled as 'effective causes'. The test 'the effective cause' is akin to an absolute state of affairs. 'An effective cause' countenances the variables that can occur culminating in the ultimate purchase. On the state of the authorities, the test 'an effective cause' as preferred in *Burchell v Gowrie, supra*, should be followed, unless the particular circumstances otherwise so mandate.

In the instant case, the initial introduction of the property by the appellant in 1998, to the Transport Authority produced no sale. Consequently, the appellant approached the respondent in May 1999, and signed a listing agreement . . . The appellant is not claiming that it was its own introduction that brought about the sale . . . There is no evidence of any activity nor interaction with the purchaser, the Government of Jamaica, Transport Authority, by any of the said named estate agents other than the respondent. The only effective introduction to the said property since 1999 was therefore the respondent. The learned trial judge quite correctly found:

> I reject the evidence of Mr Graham that he paid Ravers Limited 3% commission and I find that his answer to the Court contradicts his answer to question five in the interrogatories. There is no documentary evidence to show that 3% was paid to Ravers Limited and I find it strange.

There is no evidence of any contractual agreement nor any interaction nor activity between Ravers Ltd and the Transport Authority to cause a commission to be payable to the former. Certainly, in the interrogatories, signed by Charles Douglas Graham on 17 October 2001, he said that: 'The commission was payable and none has been paid to anyone as a result of the 1998 introduction.' The only introduction in 1998 was by the appellant who was not 'claiming a commission'. No such commission could be payable to Ravers Ltd. The evidence of the said Charles Douglas Graham to the Court, namely: 'After the meeting on 12 August 1998 some months later I contracted Ravers Limited', is imprecise and misleading. Ravers Ltd, on the interrogatories, was contracted in the year 2000. His further evidence to the Court that: 'I heard from the Financial Officer of the Ministry as a result of discussions that had taken place between Ravers and themselves' is hearsay and inadmissible. The respondent was the direct cause that brought about the purchase of the Odeon Complex by the Transport Authority and therefore was properly entitled to its commission, as the learned trial judge found. Its action was, in the circumstances of this case, the effective cause of the ultimate purchase. This appeal ought to be dismissed with costs to the respondent.

Leona Francis (Claimant) v Daven Joseph (Defendant)[,] (2013) Claim No. ANUHCV2011/0573 (AG)

Facts: The Claimant, Leona Francis (Ms Francis)[,] claims that the Defendant Daven Joseph owes her the sum of $19,250.00 being a commission arising out of Daven Joseph's sale of his property registered as Registration Section West Central Block 11, 2192 B Parcel 406. Ms Francis claims that Daven Joseph breached his oral agreement with her, whereby it was agreed that she would seek a purchaser for Daven Joseph's property, and that if she found a purchaser who eventually purchased the property, she would be entitled to a commission of 5% of the purchase price. Ms Francis alleges that pursuant to the oral agreement, she subsequently caused a commissioner's fee agreement to be prepared, but Daven Joseph refused to sign it, and has failed to pay her the commission due to her. Ms Francis alleges that by reason of Daven Joseph's failure to pay the commission due and owing, she has suffered loss and damage. By way of Defence, Daven Joseph denied entering into any agreement with Ms Francis as alleged. However, he admitted that he informed Ms Francis about his intention to sell the property. He also admitted that Ms Francis introduced him to Lerry Joseph, a potential purchaser of the property. Further, he admitted that he had not paid any commission to Ms Francis, because he told her that he would not pay her a commission, and that if she required a commission, it should be paid by the purchaser and/or added to the sale price. He denied that Ms Francis has suffered any loss and/or damage and puts her to strict proof thereof. Ms Francis replied. She maintained that there was such an agreement as alleged by her.

Held: Lanns, J (Ag)
The first requirement for the formation of a contract is that the parties must have reached agreement. A valid contract requires an agreement; an intention to create legal relations, and consideration. The onus of proof is on Ms Francis to prove that an agreement existed for finding someone interested in purchasing Daven Joseph's property, and eventually purchasing it and for the payment of a commission. Ms Francis says there was an agreement for providing a purchaser for the property and for the payment of a 5% commission. Daven Joseph says there was no such agreement. The court is called upon to decide on a balance of probabilities if there was an agreement between the parties to pay a 5% commission for providing a purchaser for the said property. Ms Francis is in the business of selling houses for commission. Daven Joseph knew that. He knew Ms Francis for over five years. They had discussions pertaining to real estate matters before. She said that she had a discussion with Daven Joseph about the sale of his property at Paynters. Her case is that there was an oral agreement as to the payment of a commission once she found a purchaser who eventually purchased the property. Daven Joseph does not deny he had a conversation with Ms Francis about his willingness to sell the property and payment of a commission. This is evident in paragraph 3 of his Defence where he avers '. . . The Defendant told the Claimant that if she required a commission, the said commission should be paid by the purchaser and/or added to the sale price['].

I do not accept Daven Joseph's evidence that at all times Ms Francis was aware that he would not be paying her a commission. I find that at all times he knew she was a realtor seeking a purchaser for his property on a commission basis. Nor do I accept his oral testimony that he never gave Ms Francis any authority to sell the property. I do not believe

Daven Joseph when he said that he told Ms Francis from the onset that he would not be paying her a commission because she was neither his broker nor his agent. Lerry Joseph in a telling remark said 'I was not aware from the onset that Ms Francis was not acting for Daven Joseph. Only when the deal closed, I realized there were some discrepancies as to what transpired between them.' In the circumstances, I have no hesitation in finding that there was an oral agreement between Ms Francis and Daven Joseph for finding a purchaser for Daven Joseph's property. I also find, based on the evidence, that there was an oral agreement for the payment of a 5% commission once the prospective purchaser identified by Ms Francis eventually bought the property.

. . .

As to the issue of time when the sale was effected, the court is not at all persuaded by the evidence proffered. Furthermore, no evidence was led before me that time was of the essence, or as to when time expired for the sale of the property. Lord Russel of Killowe[]n, in the case, *Luxor (Eastbourne) v Cooper*, one of the leading cases on commission contracts remarked:

> Commission contracts are subject to no peculiar rules or principles of their own . . . In each case the rights of the agent or the liability of the principal must depend on the exact terms of the contract in question.

Guided by the case of *Luxor*, I therefore find that no weight should be attached to time when the sale was effected because the contract did not stipulate a time limit for the sale of the property. In my view, the condition precedent to the commission was the introduction of Lerry Joseph to Daven Joseph. When Lerry Joseph bought the property it triggered the commission. The court accepts the evidence of Ms Francis that Daven Joseph told her that he was asking $365,000.00 for the property, and that she told him about the commission and that he said it was OK with him. I believe her when she said that they agreed that the property would be sold for $385[,]000. This included her 5% commission. I believe her when she said that Daven Joseph and Lerry Joseph surreptitiously kept her out of the negotiations after Daven decided to lend Lerry the deposit funds. I believe her when she said that the second agreement came about when she communicated with Daven Joseph's attorney requesting the deletion of the deposit from the original agreement, so as [t]o facilitate the bank's request . . . On the totality of the evidence, I find that Ms Francis is entitled to her 5% commission on the sale price.

Martin Devaux (Claimant) v (1) Theresa Goddard (2) Mark Goddard (3) Roebuck Properties (St. Lucia) Ltd. Defendants (2010) Claim No. SLUHCV2008/0405 (LC)

Facts: Issues arising include: Whether on interpretation of the Second Agreement, the Claimant can be deemed to have 'found a potential purchaser', namely, Roebuck Properties (St. Lucia) Ltd. Whether on interpretation of the Second Agreement the Claimant is entitled to the sum of US$485,000.00.

Held: Wilkinson, J
In *Chitty on Contracts* it is states:

> 2607 Right to remuneration. It is the duty of the principal to pay his agent a commission or other remuneration agreed upon. When there is an express term as to the payment of remuneration, the right to payment and the amount will depend on that term. Thus if the contract provides that the amount of remuneration is left to the discretion of the principal, the court cannot determine the basis and rate of commission, since to do so would be making a new

agreement between the parties and transferring to the court the discretion vested in the principal. There is an implied agreement to pay remuneration whenever a person is employed to act as an agent under circumstances which raise the presumption that he would to the knowledge of the principal have expected to be paid. The amount of the payment and the conditions on which it is payable will depend on the circumstances. If there is a custom or usage of the particular trade regulating the payment or remuneration, there is a presumption, in the absence of any express agreement to the contrary, that the parties contracted for the payment of the remuneration in accordance with this custom or usage. But if there is no proof of such custom and no express agreement, then a reasonable remuneration is payable. In estimating what is a reasonable remuneration, evidence of the bargaining between the parties is admissible as showing the value put upon the agent's services by the parties . . .

2608 Commission. The remuneration of the agent frequently takes the form of a commission being a percentage of the value of the transaction the agent is to bring about for the principal. In such cases the agent does not become entitled to his commission until the event has occurred upon which his entitlement arises. What this event is must be ascertained from the terms of the agency contract. In most cases where the agent is engaged to find a third party to enter into a contract with the principal there will be little difficulty because the event will occur when the principal and the third party enter into the contract which the agent was engaged to bring about. The agent's task is then successfully completed.

2609 Estate agents. There is a great many cases concerning the commission payable to such agents. They turn on the words used in the particular agreement. The difficulties have arisen because estate agents have frequently considered that their task is completed and that they should therefore be entitled to commission when they introduce to their principal (the potential vendor) a person who shows a real interest in buying. This stage is normally reached when the potential purchaser makes an offer 'subject to contract,' or 'subject to survey' or subject to some other condition. But in law such an offer, even if accepted, does not create a contract between the potential vendor and the potential purchaser. The contract is not made, according to normal conveyancing practice, until the parties exchange contracts. There is a third stage to the transaction, completion, at which the vendor hands the title deeds to the purchaser in exchange for the purchase price. The agent is engaged to bring about a sale, but he generally wants his commission before sale, i.e. at the 'subject to contract' stage. He is free to stipulate whatever event he wishes in his agency contract, but it is the 'common understanding of men that the agent's commission is payable out of the purchase price,' and it requires clear and unequivocal words to entitle the agent to commission if no sale is made. In all cases however the question is whether the event upon which it is stipulated that commission is due has taken place.

2610 Commission on the introduction of a purchaser. At one time it was frequent for estate agents to stipulate for their commission on some such event as 'the introduction of a purchaser', or on 'finding a purchaser' or 'finding someone to buy.' In one case commission was payable 'in the event of business resulting[']. ' Whenever the event is referable to a contract ultimately taking place, commission is not earned until the contract has been made. Thus, if the agent introduces a person who makes an offer 'subject to contract' which is accepted, he does not become entitled to commission, because such transaction is not in law a contract at all. The agent's entitlement cannot, in such a case, arise until the parties have entered into a contract of sale. For example, if the event is the introduction or finding of a 'purchaser,' the person introduced or found is not a 'purchaser' until he actually purchases by entering into a contract. Moreover, if the person introduced withdraws after contract but before completion, whether rightfully or wrongfully vis-à-vis the vendor, the agent is no longer entitled to commission because *ex hypothesi* the person he introduced was not a 'purchaser' since he never purchased. But is seems that if the vendor wrongfully (vis-à-vis) the purchaser withdraws, the agent's entitlement to commission may not be lost though this must depend on the precise words used and his right may sometimes be one for damages for breach of an implied term.

In *George Trollope & Sons v Martyn Brothers* the real estate agent, plaintiff found a purchaser for the defendants' property, and the defendants agreed in the exchange of communication between themselves and the plaintiff to complete the sale 'subject to contract'. The defendants were to pay commission based on the usual scale of commission. The defendant refused to execute the contract for sale. The plaintiff filed a claim for their agreed commission or in the alternative damages for breach of an implied term that the defendant[s] would do nothing to prevent the plaintiff from earning their commission. It was held that although in an agreement 'subject to contract,' the matter, as between vendor and purchaser, must be deemed to remain in negotiation until contracts are exchanged, there must, as between the plaintiffs and the defendants, be implied a term that if the purchaser introduced by the plaintiffs was ready and able to complete the contract, the defendants would not by refusing to complete prevent the plaintiffs from earning their commission, and as the defendant[s] had, without just excuse, refused to complete, they were liable to the plaintiffs in damages, the proper measure of which in the circumstances was the amount of commission the plaintiffs would have earned had the transaction been completed . . .

The language of the Second Agreement is to my mind very precise. The Claimant in drawing the Second Agreement knew exactly what he wanted to achieve. What he wanted to achieve in short was full control so as to ensure he obtained the maximum amount of commission possible on the sale, and without any issue arising to his payment. He being resident at Saint Lucia and being in the business of selling real estate, would I believe, have been the most knowledgeable amongst the parties about the kind of prices per square foot that land in[] and around Saint Lucia could attract. He therefore burden himself with not only finding the 'Potential Purchaser' with whom the he undertook to negotiate the price, but he also burdened himself to pay all sums due on the sale including vendor's tax, pay the Defendants $2,500,000.00 from the sale price, and thereafter he was to retain the balance of monies from the sale price as his commission.

The Claimant having assigned these burdens to himself in the Second Agreement, it seems to me that in order to earn his commission the Claimant must release himself of each, and every one of the burdens which he assigned unto himself before he can earn any commission. He was clearly required to do more than find a potential purchaser. Further on reading the Second Agreement, it clearly anticipated that the sale monies would be the monies out of which the Claimant would be paid. His admission under cross-examination, and to which I have referred prior, that it was correct that part of his responsibility to finalize the sale for US$2,985,000.00 clearly shows that he knew he had to do more tha[n] find a potential purchaser.

On the evidence it is clear that the Claimant was in control of negotiating the sale price, and out of those negotiations he delivered to the Defendants an agreement for sale for the sum of US$2,985,000.00. The Defendants duly executed the agreement for sale, and returned it to him for execution by Roebuck Properties (St. Lucia) Ltd. It is a fact that this agreement for sale was never executed by Roebuck Properties (St. Lucia) Ltd. This being the case, the Claimant was never able to relinquish the burdens which he had placed on himself so as to earn as his commission of 'all sums remaining after the payment of US$2,500,000.00'. As I observed earlier, the agreement for sale was delivered to the Defendants approximately six months before Mr. Neal Sweeney's email of 1 May 2007, requesting that it be issued. As stated in *Chitty* paragraph 2609 'it requires clear and unequivocal words to entitle the agent to commission if no sale is made by his efforts'. Support is also found at *Chitty*'s paragraph 2610, no commission arises until the parties have entered an agreement for sale . . . I therefore find that the Claimant's claim must fail because he never relinquished the burdens which he placed upon himself. He was duty bound to not only find the potential purchaser, but also carry out his burdens to earn his commission.

CHAPTER 7

INTERNET LAW AND BUSINESS[1]

Reproduced with the permission of Stu's Views

> [T]he explosion of Electronic Commerce on the Internet [is] creating huge opportunities for businesses, governments, industries and entire countries to transform themselves. At the same time, these developments have resulted in new threats – the same businesses, governments, industries and countries now face the risk of being marginalised if they do not respond to the changes taking place around them. . . . the pace with which developments take place in the new networked world means that even if the right actions are identified and execution begun, those who move too slowly will be overtaken by others who can make the commitment to move at Internet speed.[2]

This statement was issued 16 years ago but remains true as the use and evolution of the internet continue to grow by leaps and bounds. Highlighted here is the speed with which technological

---

1 All the cases in this chapter are drawn from various US jurisdictions. While the geographical focus of this book remains the Commonwealth Caribbean, the authors have found that the law relating to the internet is very well developed in the United States and took the decision to use US case law here. It should be noted that the European Union also has its own laws dealing with the internet, but they are considerably different in approach to the ones that apply in the United States. On EU law concerning the internet, see Rustad, M, *Global Internet Law in a Nutshell*, 2013, St Paul, MN: West. It should further be noted that this chapter is certainly not exhaustive on the topic of internet law, but is meant to be introductory.

2 Report of the National Electronic Commerce Policy Committee, 'Preparing Trinidad and Tobago for Doing Business in the Internetworked Global Digital Economy', 1999, Port of Spain: Government of Trinidad and Tobago, p 6, [accessed 9 January 2015]. Available at: http://unpan1.un.org/intradoc/groups/public/documents/caricad/unpan008535.pdf.

developments take place and the fact that e-commerce has become an integral part of general commerce. To support this, e-commerce sales in the United States over the last four quarters (3rd Qtr 2014–4th Qtr 2013) amounted to some US$294bn, representing a total of 6.3 per cent of total retail sales for the same period.[3] In the United Kingdom, figures for 2013 indicate that internet sales by UK businesses amounted to £557bn, reflecting a total of 20 per cent of total business turnover for the United Kingdom.[4]

Such figures indicate a definite shift in the way global commerce occurs and:

> is forcing the legal infrastructure of commerce to change in order to keep up with technology. Around the world nations are building the legal infrastructure to succeed in the global digital economy. Worldwide, revisions in laws regarding online privacy, electronic contracting, digital signatures, and consumer protection have been enacted in order to provide the essential 'e-confidence' needed for electronic commerce to prosper.[5]

The increasing use of the internet to conduct trade, communicate and find information illustrates its growing popularity, but this use has brought with it inherent legal difficulties. Contracting over the internet and issues arising out of online contracts, such as jurisdiction, choice of forum, choice of law and taxation, are important in understanding the evolution of internet law as it relates to business activities.

CONTRACTING IN THE DIGITAL MARKETPLACE

Conducting commercial transactions online has become commonplace; this is certainly evidenced by the high level of commercial activity taking place online, as noted above. One of the early issues that arose was that of contract formation. It has since been agreed that the enforceability of internet contracts is governed by the well-established legal principles which apply to traditional written contracts.[6] As with traditional contracts, to form an enforceable contract online, there must be a 'meeting of the minds' of the parties to the contract and an intention to contract, supported by some consideration.

Nonetheless, the issue of the signature created some difficulty such that the US Congress passed the Electronic Signatures in Global and National Commerce Act (E-SIGN Act) in 2000.[7] Globally, so problematic became the issue of online contracting that the United Nations adopted a Convention on the Use of Electronic Communications in International Contracts[8] which

---

3 US Census Bureau, Department of Commerce, 'Quarterly Retail E-Commerce Sales, 3rd Quarter 2014', 9 January 2015. Available at: http://www.census.gov/.

4 UK Office for National Statistics [online], 'E-Commerce and ICT Activity 2013', 28 November 2014, [accessed 9 January 2015]. Available at: http://www.ons.gov.uk/.

5 Kunkel, RG [online], 'Recent Developments in Shrinkwrap, Clickwrap and Browsewrap Licenses in the United States', (2002) *Murdoch University Electronic Journal of Law* 9(3). Available at: http://www.murdoch.edu.au/elaw/issues/v9n3/kunkel93.html.

6 See Frieden, J [online], 'FAQ: Is an Internet Contract Enforceable?', *E-Commerce Law*, posted 11 May 2009, [accessed 9 January 2015]. Available at: http://ecommercelaw.typepad.com/ecommerce_law/2009/05/faq-is-an-internet-contract-enforceable.html#more.

7 Craig, B, *Cyberlaw: The Law of the Internet and Information Technology*, 2013, Pearson Education Inc., p. 72. There are other pieces of legislation that address the same matter as well.

8 See United Nations General Assembly Resolution, A/RES/60/21, 9 December 2005. The adoption rate has been, admittedly, poor; the Convention has only 18 signatories and six parties since its entry into force on 1 March 2013. See United Nations Commission on International Trade Law [online], 'Status: United Nations Convention on the Use of Electronic Communications in International Contracts (New York, 2005)', 2015, [accessed 9 January 2015]. Available at: http://www.uncitral.org/uncitral/en/uncitral_texts/electronic_commerce/2005Convention_status.html.

provides for legal recognition of electronic contracts which need not be in any particular form.[9] Nevertheless, while a written contract necessarily has a formal or handwritten signature of the parties involved, one difficulty with online contracts is determining what constitutes an online signature. It has, however, come to be accepted that:

> electronic signatures include: a name typed at the end of an e-mail message by the sender; a digitized image of a handwritten signature that is attached to an electronic document (sometimes created via a biometrics-based technology called signature dynamics); a secret code or PIN (such as that used with ATM cards and credit cards) to identify the sender to the recipient; a code or 'handle' that the sender of a message uses to identify himself; a unique biometrics-based identifier, such as a fingerprint or a retinal scan; and a digital signature (created through the use of public key cryptography). Digital signature is simply a term for one technology-specific type of electronic signature. It involves the use of public key cryptography to 'sign' a message, and is perhaps the one type of electronic signature that has generated the most business and technical efforts, as well as legislative response . . . Thus, while handwritten signatures in most cases serve merely to indicate the signer's intent, signatures in an electronic environment typically serve three critical purposes for the parties engaged in an e-commerce transaction – i.e., to identify the sender, to indicate the sender's intent (e.g., to be bound by the terms of a contract), and to ensure the integrity of the document signed.[10]

While this particular notion of the electronic signature can be said to apply to parties who are actively negotiating via email, the typical online contract tends to take the form of an agreement *without* a signature, where the terms of the contract are non-negotiable and consent may or may not be given by the user. These characteristics of online contracting present inherent difficulties for businesses trying to enforce unreasonable terms and conditions on users or for users who could be reasonably expected, depending on the circumstances of the case, to have taken the time to read and understand the contract before continuing to use the website or download software. Such internet contracts generally fall into one of three categories: shrink-wrap, click-wrap and browse-wrap agreements.

Shrink-wrap agreements

Shrink-wrap agreements are usually found printed on the back of, or included inside (notice of this may be provided on the outside), computer software packaging. By breaking the cellophane shrink-wrap packaging, the purchaser or user agrees to be bound by the terms of the agreement.[11] As applied to software applications, the typical software licence includes a conspicuous notice of agreement, title retention in the seller, restrictions on transfer and modification, prohibition of reverse engineering and limited copying provisions. Applied generally to a broad range of contracts in e-commerce, common features of the shrink-wrap agreement may include an arbitration clause, a forum selection clause, and disclaimer of warranties and limitation of remedies. Despite any individual variances, the shrink-wrap agreement is uniformly used to dictate the sellers' terms to the purchaser.[12] This unilateral agreement is inherently controversial, as the user is denied any notice of the terms and conditions to which he blindly agrees. This is especially so if the agreement is inside the box and requires the user to break the seal – which is deemed to indicate automatic consent by the purchaser – before he

9 See Articles 8 and 9 of the Convention.

10 Smedinghoff, TJ and Bro, RH, 'Moving With Change: Electronic Signature Legislation as a Vehicle for Advancing E-commerce', (1999) *The John Marshall Journal of Computer and Information Law*, 17(3): 723.

11 Darrell, K, *Issues in Internet Law: Society, Technology, and the Law*, 2008, Boca Raton, FL: Amber Book Company, p 325.

12 Kunkel, 'Recent Developments in Shrinkwrap, Clickwrap and Browsewrap Licenses in the United States'.

is able to actually read the terms and conditions contained therein. This is what is known as a layered or rolling contract, or 'cash now, terms later', where a customer will manifest assent to different terms at different points in time.[13] Examples of this may be found with the terms of service agreements provided by social media networks which may reserve the right to unilaterally change terms of use or service. In a landmark appeal case in the United States, however, it was held that a shrink-wrap agreement was valid where the user is provided with '[n]otice on the outside, terms on the inside, and a right to return the software for a refund if the terms are unacceptable (a right that the license expressly extends)'.[14] Where the user does not return the product, it is generally understood that he has assented to the terms of the vendor.

> *M.A. Mortenson Co. v Timberline Software Corp., et al.* Docket No. 67796–4 (Wash, 2000)
>
> **Facts:** Mortenson was a nationwide construction contractor with its corporate headquarters in Minnesota. Since at least 1990 Mortenson had used Timberline's Bid Analysis software to assist with its preparation of bids. Mortenson had used Medallion, an earlier version of Bid Analysis, at its Minnesota headquarters and its regional offices. In early 1993 Mortenson installed a new computer network operating system at its Bellevue office and contacted Mark Reich (Reich), president of Softworks, to reinstall Medallion. Reich discovered, however, that the Medallion software was incompatible with Mortenson's new operating system. Reich informed Mortenson that Precision, a newer version of Bid Analysis, was compatible with its new operating system. Mortenson wanted multiple copies of the new software for its offices, including copies for its corporate headquarters in Minnesota and its north-west regional office in Bellevue. Reich informed Mortenson he would place an order with Timberline and would deliver eight copies of the Precision software to the Bellevue office, after which Mortenson could distribute the copies among its offices. After Reich provided Mortenson with a price quote, Mortenson issued a purchase order dated 12 July 1993, confirming the agreed-upon purchase price, set-up fee, delivery charges and sales tax for eight copies of the software.
>
> All Timberline software was distributed to its users under licence. Both Medallion and Precision Bid Analysis were licensed Timberline products. In the case of the Mortenson shipment, the full text of Timberline's licence agreement was set forth on the outside of each diskette pouch and the inside cover of the instruction manuals. The first screen that appears each time the program is used also references the licence and states, '[t]his software is licensed for exclusive use by: Timberline Use Only.' Further, a license to use the protection device was wrapped around each of the devices shipped to Mortenson. The following warning preceded the terms of the licence agreement:
>
>> CAREFULLY READ THE FOLLOWING TERMS AND CONDITIONS BEFORE USING THE PROGRAMS. USE OF THE PROGRAMS INDICATES YOUR ACKNOWLEDGEMENT THAT YOU HAVE READ THIS LICENSE, UNDERSTAND IT, AND AGREE TO BE BOUND BY ITS TERMS AND CONDITIONS. IF YOU DO NOT AGREE TO THESE TERMS AND CONDITIONS, PROMPTLY RETURN THE PROGRAMS AND USER MANUALS TO THE PLACE OF PURCHASE AND YOUR PURCHASE PRICE WILL BE REFUNDED. YOU AGREE THAT YOUR USE OF THE

---

13 Rustad, *Global Internet Law*, p. 102.

14 *ProCD Incorporated v Matthew Zeidenberg and Silken Mountain Web Services Inc.* 86 F.3d 1447 (7th Cir. 1996), No. 96–1139.

PROGRAM ACKNOWLEDGES THAT YOU HAVE READ THIS LICENSE, UNDERSTAND IT, AND AGREE TO BE BOUND BY ITS TERMS AND CONDITIONS.

Reich claims when he arrived at Mortenson's Bellevue office he noticed the software had been opened and had been placed on a desk, along with a manual and a protection device.

In December 1993 Mortenson utilised the Precision Bid Analysis software to prepare a bid for a project at Harborview Medical Center in Seattle. On the day of the bid, the software allegedly malfunctioned multiple times and gave the following message: 'Abort: Cannot find alternate.' Mortenson received this message 19 times that day. Nevertheless, Mortenson submitted a bid generated by the software. After Mortenson was awarded the Harborview Medical Center project, it learned its bid was approximately US$1.95 million lower than intended. Mortenson filed an action in King County Superior Court against Timberline and Softworks alleging breach of express and implied warranties. Timberline moved for summary judgment of dismissal in July 1997, arguing the limitation on consequential damages in the licensing agreement barred Mortenson's recovery. Mortenson countered that its entire contract with Timberline consisted of the purchase order and it never saw or agreed to the provisions in the licensing agreement.

Held: Johnson, J

Although no Washington case specifically addresses the type of contract formation at issue in this case, a series of recent cases from other jurisdictions have analysed shrinkwrap licenses under analogous statutes. See *Brower v Gateway 2000, Inc.* 246 AD2d 246, 250–51, 676 NYS2d 569 (1998); *Hill v Gateway 2000, Inc.* 105 F3d 1147 (7th Cir.), cert. denied, 522 US 808 (1997); *ProCD, Inc. v Zeidenberg* 86 F.3d 1447 (7th Cir. 1996). In *ProCD,* which involved a retail purchase of software, the Seventh Circuit held software shrinkwrap licence agreements are a valid form of contracting under Wisconsin's version of UCC section 2–204, and such agreements are enforceable unless objectionable under general contract law such as the law of unconscionability. *ProCD,* 86 F.3d at 1449–52. The court stated, '[n]otice on the outside, terms on the inside, and a right to return the software for a refund if the terms are unacceptable (a right that the license expressly extends), may be a means of doing business valuable to buyers and sellers alike.' *ProCD,* 86 F.3d at 1451. In *Hill,* the customer ordered a computer over the telephone and received the computer in the mail, accompanied by a list of terms to govern if the customer did not return the product within 30 days. *Hill,* 105 F.3d at 1148. Relying in part on *ProCD,* the court held the terms of the 'accept-or-return' agreement were effective, stating, '[c]ompetent adults are bound by such documents, read or unread'. *Hill,* 105 F.3d at 1149. Elaborating on its holding in *ProCD,* the court continued:

> The question in *ProCD* was not whether terms were added to a contract after its formation, but how and when the contract was formed – in particular, whether a vendor may propose that a contract of sale be formed, not in the store (or over the phone) with the payment of money or a general 'send me the product', but after the customer has had a chance to inspect both the item and the terms. *ProCD* answers 'yes', for merchants and consumers alike. (*Hill,* 105 F.3d at 1150.)

Interpreting the same licensing agreement at issue in *Hill,* the New York Supreme Court, Appellate Division concluded shrinkwrap licence terms delivered following a mail order purchase were not proposed additions to the contract, but part of the original agreement between the parties. *Brower,* 246 AD2d at 250–51. The court held UCC section 2–207 did not apply because the contract was not formed until after the period to return the merchandise. *Brower,* 246 AD2d at 250.

We find the approach of the *ProCD, Hill* and *Brower* courts persuasive and adopt it to guide our analysis under RCW 62A.2–204. We conclude because RCW 62A.2–204 allows a contract to be formed 'in any manner sufficient to show agreement . . . even though the moment of its making is undetermined', it allows the formation of 'layered contracts' similar to those envisioned by *ProCD, Hill,* and *Brower*. See *ProCD*, 86 F.3d at 1452–3 (holding shrinkwrap licence agreement was a valid form of contracting under UCC section 2–204). We, therefore, hold under RCW 62A.2–204 the terms of the licence were part of the contract between Mortenson and Timberline, and Mortenson's use of the software constituted its assent to the agreement, including the licence terms. The terms of Timberline's licence were either set forth explicitly or referenced in numerous locations. The terms were included within the shrinkwrap packaging of each copy of Precision Bid Analysis; they were present in the manuals accompanying the software; they were included with the protection devices for the software, without which the software could not be used.

Click-wrap agreements

Users of commercial websites or purchasers of electronic hardware, such as a digital camera, requiring the use of software packages often are required to agree to terms and conditions before accessing the services of, or downloading content from, the website or installing the software. In some cases, the software is pre-installed on a computer but requires the user's agreement to become usable. Upon downloading, installation or first use of the application, the terms and conditions of the licence opens up in a scrollable window requiring the user or purchaser to scroll down to read them. The user is asked to click either 'I agree' or 'I do not agree'. If the user does not agree, the process is terminated.[15] Where the user clicks on the button indicating his agreement, it is assumed that he has read the terms and conditions and understands them as they were available to be read. Agreements entered into in this fashion are referred to as 'click-wrap' agreements because the user typically indicates his agreement to the terms and conditions by clicking a button or hyperlink marked 'I agree'.[16]

While click-wrap agreements are generally held to be binding once the terms and conditions are available to be read, nevertheless, a click-wrap agreement may be held to be invalid where it is unreasonable or would contravene public policy. This was so in one particular case where the terms and conditions were excessively lengthy and available to be read on 91 computer screens which, even if printed on paper, could cause the reader to fall into a 'trance of lethargy and inattentiveness'.[17] Moreover, the website recognised that the length of the terms and conditions would likely deter a prospective user from agreeing to use it and featured two 'OK, I Agree' buttons before the user would have had the opportunity to become familiar with the terms and conditions and offered him the choice of signing up first and then reading the terms of service afterwards. In a 2009 case, it was held unreasonable for a website to include as part of its click-wrap agreement that it reserves the right to unilaterally change, without notice or notification to its users, its terms and conditions to be effective immediately upon posting the changes.[18] The user must be given the opportunity to review the change and either accept

15 Kunkel, 'Recent Developments in Shrinkwrap, Clickwrap and Browsewrap Licenses in the United States'.

16 See Frieden, 'FAQ: Is an Internet Contract Enforceable?'.

17 See judgment of Samuels, J in *Russell Scarcella v America Online Inc.* 2004 NY Slip Op 51021(U); 4 Misc 3d 1024 A (NY Civ Ct 2004).

18 See *Cathryn Harris v Blockbuster Inc.* No. 3:09-cv-217-M (15 April 2009).

or reject it. Posting revisions online does not constitute adequate notice. As stated in *Douglas v Talk America* with similar facts, 'Parties to a contract have no obligation to check the terms on a periodic basis to learn whether they have been changed by the other side. Indeed, a party can't unilaterally change the terms of a contract; it must obtain the other party's consent before doing so.'[19] In early 2014, Microsoft took cue from this and gave all their users several months' notice that it was going to update its privacy policy and made it available for review. Continued use after the implementation of the new policy indicated users' assent to it; anyone not in agreement with the policy would have had to stop using the services or close their accounts.[20]

One author has identified six strategies that will make it likely that a court will find a particular click-wrap agreement valid and enforceable:[21]

- Review. The user must have the opportunity to review all terms of the click-wrap agreement, bar unreasonable and hidden ones.
- Form and Content. The terms of the agreement must be clearly displayed, concise and not contradict any other terms on the website or other marketing materials.
- Affirmative Assent. The agreement must provide an 'I Agree' or 'I Consent' button to be clicked before access to the information is made. The end of the agreement should clearly indicate that clicking on this button will cause the parties to enter into a binding and enforceable contract.
- Opportunity to Correct Errors. The most reasonable adaptation of this rule is the provision of a confirmation screen where the user is given the opportunity to correct errors or confirm the validity of the submitted information.
- Rejection of Terms. Should the user not agree to the terms and conditions of use, he should have equal opportunity to decline, as he would to assent, by clicking on an 'I Do Not Agree' or 'I Do Not Consent' button, which would terminate the process immediately and prohibit the user from accessing the information.
- Records. The user should have the option of printing the agreement for future reference.

Cathryn Harris v Blockbuster Inc. No. 3:09-cv-217-M (15 April 2009)

Facts: This case arose out of alleged violations of the Video Privacy Protection Act by defendant Blockbuster Inc. (Blockbuster). Blockbuster operates a service called Blockbuster Online, which allows customers to rent movies through the internet. Blockbuster entered into an agreement with Facebook (the Blockbuster contract) which caused Blockbuster's customers' movie rental choices to be disseminated on the customers' Facebook accounts through Facebook's 'Beacon' program. In short, when a customer rented a video from Blockbuster Online, the Beacon program would transmit the customer's choice to Facebook, which would then broadcast the choice to the customer's Facebook friends. The plaintiff claimed that this arrangement violated the Video Privacy Protection Act, 18 USC § 2710, which prohibits a videotape service provider from disclosing personally identifiable information about a customer unless given informed, written consent at the time the disclosure is sought. The Act provides for liquidated damages of US$2,500 for each violation.

19 *Joe Douglas v Talk America Inc.* No. 06–75424 (9th Cir. 2007).

20 See Hachman, M [online], 'Microsoft's updated privacy policy makes it clear it's not selling ads against your words', *PC World*, 11 June 2014 [accessed 14 January 2015]. Available from http://www.pcworld.com/article/2362130/microsofts-updated-privacy-policy-makes-it-clear-its-not-selling-ads-against-your-words.html.

21 Trout, B, *A Legal Arsenal for Online Business*, 2007, New York: World Audience Inc., pp 83–4.

Blockbuster attempted to invoke an arbitration provision in its 'Terms and Conditions', which included a paragraph governing 'Dispute Resolution' that states, in pertinent part: '[a]ll claims, disputes or controversies . . . will be referred to and determined by binding arbitration.' It further purportedly waives the right of its users to commence any class action. As a precondition to joining Blockbuster Online, customers were required to click on a box certifying that they had read and agreed to the Terms and Conditions. On 30 August 2008, before the case was transferred to this Court, the defendant moved to enforce the arbitration provision. The plaintiffs argued that the arbitration provision is unenforceable, principally for two reasons: (1) it is illusory; and (2) it is unconscionable.

Held: Lynn, J
Legal Standard. In Texas a contract must be supported by consideration, and if it is not, it is illusory and cannot be enforced. In *Morrison v Amway Corp.*, the Fifth Circuit analysed a very similar arbitration provision to that in the subject Terms and Conditions and held it to be illusory. In *Morrison*, [the] defendant, a seller of household products marketed through a chain of distributors, was sued by its distributors for a variety of torts, including racketeering and defamation. The defendant sought to enforce an arbitration provision in which each distributor agreed:

> [T]o conduct [his or her] business according to the Amway Code of Ethics and Rules of Conduct, as they are amended and published from time to time in official Amway literature . . . I agree I will give notice in writing of any claim or dispute arising out of or relating to my Amway distributorship, or the Amway Sales and Marketing Plan or Rules of Conduct to the other party or parties . . . I agree to submit any remaining claim or dispute arising out of or relating to any Amway distributorship, the Amway Sales and Marketing Plan, or the Amway Rules of Conduct . . . to binding arbitration in accordance with the Amway Arbitration rules, which are set forth in the Amway Business Compendium.

The *Morrison* court held that the provision was illusory because:

> [t]here is no express exemption of the arbitration provisions from Amway's ability to unilaterally modify all rules, and the only express limitation on that unilateral right is published notice. While it is inferable that an amendment thus unilaterally made by Amway to the arbitration provision would not become effective until published, there is nothing to suggest that once published the amendment would be inapplicable to disputes arising, or arising out of events occurring, *before* such publication . . .

Analysis. The basis for the plaintiffs' claim that the arbitration provision is illusory is that Blockbuster reserves the right to modify the Terms and Conditions, including the section that contains the arbitration provision, 'at its sole discretion' and 'at any time', and such modifications will be effective immediately upon being posted on the site. Under the heading "Changes to Terms and Conditions", the contract states:

> Blockbuster may at any time, and at its sole discretion, modify these Terms and Conditions of Use, including without limitation the Privacy Policy, with or without notice. Such modifications will be effective immediately upon posting. You agree to review these Terms and Conditions of Use periodically and your continued use of this Site following such modifications will indicate your acceptance of these modified Terms and Conditions of Use. If you do not agree to any modification of these Terms and Conditions of Use, you must immediately stop using this Site.

The Court concludes that the Blockbuster arbitration provision is illusory for the same reasons as that in *Morrison*. Here, as in *Morrison*, there is nothing in the Terms and

> Conditions that prevents Blockbuster from unilaterally changing any part of the contract other than providing that such changes will not take effect until posted on the website. There are likewise no '*Halliburton* type savings clauses', as there is 'nothing to suggest that once published the amendment would be inapplicable to disputes arising, or arising out of events occurring, before such publication'. The Fifth Circuit in *Morrison* noted the lack of an 'express exemption' of the ability to unilaterally modify all rules, which the Blockbuster agreement also does not contain. The Blockbuster contract only states that modifications 'will be effective immediately upon posting', and the natural reading of that clause does not limit application of the modifications to earlier disputes . . . For these reasons, the Court concludes that the arbitration provision of the Blockbuster contract is illusory and unenforceable.

Browse-wrap agreements

Browse-wrap agreements initially presented peculiar difficulties for businesses attempting to have policies, contracts or terms and conditions upheld in court. Unlike click-wrap agreements, a browse-wrap agreement is not available on the screen for review, but the website may provide notice of where to find it. Reading the agreement is optional as it requires the user to click on a hyperlink, where he will find the terms and conditions; moreover, the user is not required to accept the terms as a condition precedent to continue browsing the website. There need not be any other manifestation of affirmative action indicating agreement by the user.[22] It is these characteristics that made browse-wrap agreements much more susceptible to challenge by users: on the grounds of lack of reasonable notice and *bona fide* assent to the browse-wrap terms.[23] Nevertheless, where the user habitually takes advantage of the services offered on the website, he may be deemed to have had notice of the terms and conditions and to have assented to them.[24]

Moreover, in *Hines v Overstock*, a 2009 decision, it was held that, 'Unlike a clickwrap agreement, a browsewrap agreement does not require the user to manifest assent to the terms and conditions expressly . . . [a] party instead gives his assent simply by using the website'.[25] This, however, must be accompanied by 'actual or constructive notice'[26] prior to use of the site. According to the court, 'Hines . . . lacked notice of the Terms and Conditions because the website did not prompt her to review the Terms and Conditions and because the link to the Terms and Conditions was not prominently displayed so as to provide reasonable notice . . .'. Consequently, she had neither actual nor constructive notice of the Terms and Conditions. The terms of use link must be conspicuous and repeatedly brought to the attention of the user for the court to enforce a browsewrap agreement. Ideally, the website would also prompt the user to demonstrate assent.

---

22 See Frieden, 'FAQ: Is an Internet Contract Enforceable?'.
23 Kunkel, 'Recent Developments in Shrinkwrap, Clickwrap and Browsewrap Licenses in the United States'.
24 See *Register.com v Verio, Inc.* Docket No. 00–9596 (2nd Cir. 2004).
25 *Hines v Overstock.com Inc.*, 668 F. Supp. 2d 362 (EDNY 2009).
26 In law, 'constructive notice' refers to the fact that persons are expected to have knowledge of an issue simply because it is in the public domain. Here, it refers to the user's presumed knowledge of the terms and conditions.

Nguyen v Barnes & Noble Inc., No 12–56628 DC No 8:12-cv-00812-JST-RNB (9th Cir. 2014)

Facts: Barnes & Noble, Inc. ('Barnes & Noble') appeals the district court's denial of its motion to compel arbitration against Kevin Khoa Nguyen ('Nguyen') pursuant to the arbitration agreement contained in its website's Terms of Use. In order to resolve the issue of arbitrability, we must address whether Nguyen, by merely using Barnes & Noble's website, agreed to be bound by the Terms of Use, even though Nguyen was never prompted to assent to the Terms of Use and never in fact read them. We agree with the district court that Barnes & Noble did not provide reasonable notice of its Terms of Use, and that Nguyen therefore did not unambiguously manifest assent to the arbitration provision contained therein.

Held: Noonan, Wardlaw, District Judges; Silver, Senior District Judge
'While new commerce on the Internet has exposed courts to many new situations, it has not fundamentally changed the principles of contract.' *Register.com, Inc. v Verio, Inc.*, 356 F3d 393, 403 (2d Cir. 2004). One such principle is the requirement that '[m]utual manifestation of assent, whether by written or spoken word or by conduct, is the touchstone of contract.' *Specht v Netscape Commc'ns Corp.*, 306 F3d 17, 29 (2d Cir. 2002) (applying California law).

Contracts formed on the Internet come primarily in two flavors: 'clickwrap' (or 'click-through') agreements, in which website users are required to click on an 'I agree' box after being presented with a list of terms and conditions of use; and 'browsewrap' agreements, where a website's terms and conditions of use are generally posted on the website via a hyperlink at the bottom of the screen. *See Register.com*, 356 F3d at 428–30. Barnes & Noble's Terms of Use fall in the latter category.

'Unlike a clickwrap agreement, a browsewrap agreement does not require the user to manifest assent to the terms and conditions expressly . . . [a] party instead gives his assent simply by using the website.' *Hines v Overstock.com, Inc.*, 668 F Supp 2d 362, 366–67 (EDNY 2009) (citation and quotation marks omitted) (alteration in original). Indeed, 'in a pure-form browsewrap agreement, "the website will contain a notice that – by merely using the services of, obtaining information from, or initiating applications within the website – the user is agreeing to and is bound by the site's terms of service."' *Fteja v Facebook, Inc.*, 841 F Supp 2d 829, 837 (SDNY 2012) (quoting *United States v Drew*, 259 FRD 449, 462 n.22 (CD Cal 2009)). Thus, 'by visiting the website – something that the user has already done – the user agrees to the Terms of Use not listed on the site itself but available only by clicking a hyperlink.' *Id.* 'The defining feature of browsewrap agreements is that the user can continue to use the website or its services without visiting the page hosting the browsewrap agreement or even knowing that such a webpage exists.' *Be In, Inc. v Google Inc.*, No. 12-CV-03373-LHK, 2013 WL 5568706, at *6 (N.D. Cal. Oct. 9, 2013). 'Because no affirmative action is required by the website user to agree to the terms of a contract other than his or her use of the website, the determination of the validity of the browsewrap contract depends on whether the user has actual or constructive knowledge of a website's terms and conditions.' *Van Tassell v United Mktg. Grp., LLC*, 795 F Supp 2d 770, 790 (N.D. Ill. 2011) (citing *Sw. Airlines Co. v BoardFirst, LLC*, No. 06-CV-0891-B, 2007 WL 4823761, at *4 (N.D. Tex. Sept. 12, 2007)); *see also* Mark A. Lemley, *Terms of Use*, 91 Minn. L. Rev. 459, 477 (2006) ('Courts may be willing to overlook the utter absence of assent only when there are reasons to believe that the [website user] is aware of the [website owner's] terms.').

Were there any evidence in the record that Nguyen had actual notice of the Terms of Use or was required to affirmatively acknowledge the Terms of Use before completing his online purchase, the outcome of this case might be different. Indeed, courts have consistently enforced browsewrap agreements where the user had actual notice of the agreement. *See, e.g* , *Register.com*, 356 F3d at 401–04 (finding likelihood of success on the merits in a breach of browsewrap claim where the defendant 'admitted that . . . it was fully aware of the terms' of the offer); *Sw. Airlines Co.*, 2007 WL 4823761, at *4–6 (finding proper contract formation where defendant continued its breach after being notified of the terms in a cease and desist letter); *Ticketmaster Corp. v Tickets.com, Inc.*, No. CV-997654, 2003 WL 21406289, at *2 (CD Cal. Mar. 7, 2003) (denying defendants' summary judgment motion on browsewrap contract claim where defendants continued breaching contract after receiving letter quoting the browsewrap contract terms). Courts have also been more willing to find the requisite notice for constructive assent where the browsewrap agreement resembles a clickwrap agreement – that is, where the user is required to affirmatively acknowledge the agreement before proceeding with use of the website. *See, e.g.*, *Zaltz v JDATE*, 952 F Supp 2d 439, 451–52 (E.D.N.Y. 2013) (enforcing forum selection clause where prospective members had to check box confirming that they both read and agreed to the website's Terms and Conditions of Service to obtain account); *Fteja*, 841 F Supp 2d at 838–40 (enforcing forum selection clause in website's terms of service where a notice below the 'Sign Up' button stated, 'By clicking Sign Up, you are indicating that you have read and agree to the Terms of Service,' and user had clicked 'Sign Up').

But where, as here, there is no evidence that the website user had actual knowledge of the agreement, the validity of the browsewrap agreement turns on whether the website puts a reasonably prudent user on inquiry notice of the terms of the contract. *Specht*, 306 F3d at 30–31; *see also In re Zappos.com, Inc. Customer Data Sec. Breach Litig.*, 893 F Supp 2d 1058, 1064 (D Nev 2012). Whether a user has inquiry notice of a browsewrap agreement, in turn, depends on the design and content of the website and the agreement's webpage. *Google*, 2013 WL 5568406, at *6. Where the link to a website's terms of use is buried at the bottom of the page or tucked away in obscure corners of the website where users are unlikely to see it, courts have refused to enforce the browsewrap agreement. *See, e.g.*, *Specht*, 306 F3d at 23 (refusing to enforce terms of use that 'would have become visible to plaintiffs only if they had scrolled down to the next screen'); *In re Zappos.com*, 893 F Supp 2d at 1064 ('The Terms of Use is inconspicuous, buried in the middle to bottom of every Zappos.com webpage among many other links, and the website never directs a user to the Terms of Use.'); *Van Tassell*, 795 F Supp 2d 792–93 (refusing to enforce arbitration clause in browsewrap agreement that was only noticeable after a 'multi-step process' of clicking through non-obvious links); *Hines*, 668 F Supp 2d at 367 (plaintiff 'could not even see the link to [the terms and conditions] without scrolling down to the bottom of the screen – an action that was not required to effectuate her purchase'). On the other hand, where the website contains an explicit textual notice that continued use will act as a manifestation of the user's intent to be bound, courts have been more amenable to enforcing browsewrap agreements. *See, e.g.*, *Cairo, Inc. v Crossmedia Servs., Inc.*, No. 04–04825, 2005 WL 756610, at *2, *4–5 (ND Cal. Apr. 1, 2005) (enforcing forum selection clause in website's terms of use where every page on the website had a textual notice that read: 'By continuing past this page and/or using this site, you agree to abide by the Terms of Use for this site, which prohibit commercial use of any information on this site'). *But see Pollstar v Gigmania, Ltd.*, 170 F Supp 2d 974, 981 (ED Cal. 2000) (refusing to enforce browsewrap agreement where textual notice appeared in small gray print against a gray background). In short, the conspicuousness and placement of the 'Terms of Use' hyperlink, other notices given to users of the terms of use, and the website's general design all contribute to whether a reasonably prudent user would have inquiry notice of a browsewrap agreement.

Barnes & Noble argues that the placement of the 'Terms of Use' hyperlink in the bottom left-hand corner of every page on the Barnes & Noble website, and its close proximity to the buttons a user must click on to complete an online purchase, is enough to place a reasonably prudent user on constructive notice. It is true that the location of the hyperlink on Barnes & Noble's website distinguishes this case from *Specht*, the leading authority on the enforceability of browsewrap terms under New York law. There, the Second Circuit refused to enforce an arbitration provision in a website's licensing terms where the hyperlink to the terms was located at the bottom of the page, hidden below the 'Download' button that users had to click to initiate the software download. *See Specht*, 306 F3d at 30. Then-Second Circuit Judge Sotomayor, writing for the panel, held that 'a reference to the existence of license terms on a submerged screen is not sufficient to place consumers on inquiry or constructive notice of those terms.' *Id.* at 32. By contrast, here the 'Terms of Use' link appears either directly below the relevant button a user must click on to proceed in the checkout process or just a few inches away. On some pages, the content of the webpage is compact enough that a user can view the link without scrolling. On the remaining pages, the hyperlink is close enough to the 'Proceed with Checkout' button that a user would have to bring the link within his field of vision in order to complete his order.

But the proximity or conspicuousness of the hyperlink alone is not enough to give rise to constructive notice, and Barnes & Noble directs us to no case law that supports this proposition. The most analogous case the court was able to locate is *PDC Labs., Inc. v Hach Co.*, an unpublished district court order cited by neither party. No. 09–1110, 2009 WL 2605270 (C.D. Ill. Aug. 25, 2009). There, the 'Terms [and Conditions of Sale] were hyperlinked on three separate pages of the online . . . order process in underlined, blue, contrasting text.' *Id.* at *3. The court held that '[t]his contrasting text is sufficient to be considered conspicuous,' thereby placing a reasonable user on notice that the terms applied. *Id.* It also observed, however, that the terms' conspicuousness was reinforced by the language of the final checkout screen, which read, 'STEP 4 of 4: *Review terms*, add any comments, and submit order,' and was followed by a hyperlink to the Terms. *Id.* (emphasis added).

As in *PDC*, the checkout screens here contained 'Terms of Use' hyperlinks in underlined, color-contrasting text. But *PDC* is dissimilar in that the final screen on that website contained the phrase 'Review terms.' *PDC Labs*, 2009 WL 2605270, at *3. This admonition makes *PDC* distinguishable, despite the court's explanation that the blue contrasting hyperlinks were sufficiently conspicuous on their own. That the *PDC* decision couched its holding in terms of procedural unconscionability rather than contract formation further distinguishes it from our case. *See id.*

In light of the lack of controlling authority on point, and in keeping with courts' traditional reluctance to enforce browsewrap agreements against individual consumers, we therefore hold that where a website makes its terms of use available via a conspicuous hyperlink on every page of the website but otherwise provides no notice to users nor prompts them to take any affirmative action to demonstrate assent, even close proximity of the hyperlink to relevant buttons users must click on – without more – is insufficient to give rise to constructive notice. While failure to read a contract before agreeing to its terms does not relieve a party of its obligations under the contract, *Gillman v Chase Manhattan Bank, N.A.*, 73 NY 2d 1, 11 (1988), the onus must be on website owners to put users on notice of the terms to which they wish to bind consumers. Given the breadth of the range of technological savvy of online purchasers, consumers cannot be expected to ferret out hyperlinks to terms and conditions to which they have no reason to suspect they will be bound.

Barnes & Noble's argument that Nguyen's familiarity with other websites governed by similar browsewrap terms, including his personal website <www.kevinkhoa.com>, gives rise to an inference of constructive notice is also of no moment. Whether Nguyen has experience with the browsewrap agreements found on other websites such as Facebook,

LinkedIn, MySpace, or Twitter, has no bearing on whether he had constructive notice of Barnes & Noble's Terms of Use. There is nothing in the record to suggest that those browsewrap terms are enforceable by or against Nguyen, much less why they should give rise to constructive notice of Barnes & Noble's browsewrap terms . . . We hold that Nguyen had insufficient notice of Barnes & Noble's Terms of Use, and thus did not enter into an agreement with Barnes & Noble to arbitrate his claims.

ISSUES ARISING OUT OF INTERNET CONTRACTS

Jurisdiction

Many cases brought before the courts on account of online transactions gone sour see one party attempt to have it dismissed on the basis of lack of jurisdiction. Jurisdiction looks very simply at the power of a court to hear a matter and issue a decision. A party to a proceeding may claim to be from another country or not even engaged in any commercial activities in the country where it is before the judicial system. In this way, e-commerce presents an interesting challenge when a court must determine whether it may exercise jurisdiction over the parties (*in personam* jurisdiction), over the case (subject matter jurisdiction), or over a thing, such as a domain name (*in rem* jurisdiction).[27]

There are several factors that are taken into account by courts in determining whether they may exercise jurisdiction in a particular case. US courts look at whether the defendant 'purposely availed' himself or itself of the forum state by deliberately establishing ties with that state.[28] From this emerged the three-pronged test which is now used to determine whether the exercise of specific personal jurisdiction over a non-resident defendant is appropriate:

(1) the defendant must have sufficient 'minimum contacts' with the forum state (or otherwise purposefully have availed himself of the privileges of conducting activities in the forum),
(2) the claim asserted against the defendant must arise out of those contacts, and
(3) the exercise of jurisdiction must be reasonable.[29]

The 'minimum contacts' test, also referred to as 'substantial or continuous and systematic contacts test', includes determining whether the defendant maintains a deliberate 'presence' in the forum state, such as an agent or an office, and whether the defendant engages in active solicitation toward and participation in the state's markets, that is, the economic reality of the defendant's activities in the state.[30] This is, nevertheless, circumscribed by 'the reach of each state's "long-arm" statute[31], as that reach is limited by constitutional standards of due process and fair play'.[32] As explained by the judicial panel in *Pebble Beach Co. v Caddy*:[33]

---

27 See Darrell, *Issues in Internet Law*, pp 9–10.

28 See Darrell, *Issues in Internet Law*, p 11.

29 Quoted in *Zippo Mfg. Co. v Zippo Dot Com, Inc.* 952 F.Supp 1119 (WD Pa 1997).

30 See *Gator.com Corp., v LL Bean, Inc.* 341 F.3d 1072 (9th Cir. 2003) *Rehearing en Banc Granted*, 366 F.3d 789 (9th Cir. 2004). See also *Amazon.com LLC and Amazon Services LLC v New York State Department of Taxation and Finance and The State of New York* No. 60124708 (New York Sup Ct 2008).

31 A 'Long-arm Statute' provides for jurisdiction over a non-resident defendant who has had some contact with the jurisdiction in which the petition is filed. Craig, *Cyberlaw*, p. 5.

32 Radin, M, 'Retooling Contract for the Digital Era'. In N Imparato (ed), *Public Policy and the Internet: Privacy, Taxes, and Contract*, 2000, Stanford, CA: Hoover Institution Press, p 143.

33 No. 04–15577 D.C. No. CV-03–04550-PJH, 453 F.3d 1151 (9th Cir. 2006). Briefed below.

> The exercise of Rule 4(k)(2) as a federal long-arm statute requires the plaintiff to prove three factors. First, the claim against the defendant must arise under federal law . . . Second, the defendant must not be subject to the personal jurisdiction of any state court of general jurisdiction . . . Third, the federal court's exercise of personal jurisdiction must comport with due process.

Personal jurisdiction related to internet transactions will be determined based on the level of interactivity permitted by the website.[34] This concept of the sliding scale of interactivity was introduced in *Zippo Manufacturing Co. v Zippo Dot Com, Inc.*, 952 F. Supp 1119 (WD Pa.1997). Rustad notes that passive websites that only post information will not give rise to personal jurisdiction while operation of an interactive, commercial website will often suffice to do so.[35] *Chloé v Queen Bee of Beverly Hill, LLC* 616 F.3d 158 established that a single commercial transaction can suffice to give rise to personal jurisdiction under statute, especially where an interactive website is used which purposefully directs its activities toward the forum state.[36]

Chloé v Queen Bee of Beverly Hill, LLC 616 F.3d 158 (2010)

Facts: Chloé, which refers both to a division of Delaware corporation Richemont North America, Inc. ('Chloé NA') headquartered in New York and the French corporation ('Chloé SA') headquartered in Paris, is a fashion company that sells women's clothing and accessories. Chloé SA is the owner of a trademark registration for the word mark CHLOÉ for handbags. Chloé NA is the exclusive U.S. licensee of the CHLOÉ trademark for all Chloé branded goods. In 2005, Chloé was selling leather handbags for approximately $1,600 in Chloé's boutiques and as the suggested retail price for its wholesale accounts. Defendants sold counterfeit copies of this handbag on their website (www.queenbeebeverlyhills.com) for $1,200, plus shipping. Defendant Queen Bee of Beverly Hills, LLC ('Queen Bee'), is an Alabama LLC. Defendants Rebecca Rushing ('Rushing') and Simone Ubaldelli ('Ubaldelli') were the principals and operators of Queen Bee. The company maintained showrooms in and shipped goods from Beverly Hills, California, and Huntsville, Alabama. Defendants maintained two websites with nearly identical URLs, and both sites directed users to the same content.

The sites advertised 'trunk shows' across the country, offered to sell handbags purportedly manufactured by various name-brand designers-including Chloé-and offered to ship bags anywhere in the continental United States and to select locations worldwide. Specifically, the website permitted a customer viewing the handbags to 'Click here . . . to purchase this item.' It then provided both a telephone number customers could call to make credit card payments and an interface through which customers could pay for their orders online through PayPal.

In November 2006, a complaint was filed and Ubaldelli moved to dismiss the case against him on the basis that the court lacked personal jurisdiction over him. This case is an appeal from the District Court judge's ruling in favour of Ubaldelli.

Held: Raggi, Hall, Circuit Judges; Carman, J.

II. Discussion

This case involves an update to our jurisprudence on personal jurisdiction in the age of internet commerce. We hold that on the basis of the facts contained in the record

34 See Rustad, *Global Internet Law in a Nutshell.*

35 Rustad, *Global Internet Law in a Nutshell*, p. 61

36 Case briefed below.

and given the posture of this case on appeal, the single act of an out-of-state defendant employee shipping an item into New York, combined with his employer's extensive business activity involving New York, gives rise to personal jurisdiction over the employee. We arrive at our conclusion by first considering Ubaldelli's single act and Queen Bee's business activity and then imputing that activity to Ubaldelli. We next discuss the application of New York's long-arm statute and conclude with the application of the Constitution's Due Process Clause.

A. *Sale and Shipment of Counterfeit Chloé Handbag into New York*

. . . Based on the evidence in the record and reasonable inferences drawn therefrom, and keeping in mind how we must review the record at this stage of the litigation, we hold that the evidence supports the conclusion that Ubaldelli either physically shipped or was responsible for the shipment of the counterfeit handbag from California to New York.

B. *Queen Bee's Contacts with New York*

Having identified the single act of an out-of-state defendant employee shipping an item into New York, we next review the record as it relates to Queen Bee's contacts with New York. In this regard, we note that both New York's long-arm statute and the Due Process Clause require that Queen Bee's contacts with New York have some connection to Chloé's trademark infringement claim. *See Helicopteros*, 466 U.S. at 414, 104 S.Ct. 1868 (noting that specific jurisdiction is proper '[w]hen a controversy is related to or 'arises out of' a defendant's contacts with the forum'); *Chaiken v VV Publ'g Corp.*, 119 F.3d 1018, 1028 (2d Cir 1997) (same); *Kreutter*, 527 N.Y.S.2d 195, 522 NE 2d at 43 (requiring 'substantial relationship' between single act transaction 'and the claim asserted' under NY CPLR § 302(a)(1)); *McGowan v Smith*, 52 NY 2d 268, 437 NYS 2d 643, 419 NE 2d 321, 323 (1981) (requiring 'some articulable nexus between the business transacted and the cause of action sued upon') . . .

We think the district court's characterization of Defendants' non-Chloé sales as constituting purposeful availment of New York only for '*some* business activity,' but not for 'the purpose of selling Chloé handbags-the only activity upon which Plaintiffs' complaint is based,' *id.*, too narrowly construes the nexus requirement, which merely requires the cause of action to 'relate to' defendant's minimum contacts with the forum . . . In fact, Queen Bee, through its website, offered Chloé handbags-including the counterfeit handbag sent to plaintiff's investigator for sale to New York consumers, itself a possible trademark violation. *See* 15 U.S.C. § 1114(1). It further sold other designer merchandise to New York consumers. Thus, these additional contacts show that the shipment of a counterfeit Chloé bag was not, as the district court thought, a 'one-off transaction,' *Chloé II*, 630 FSupp 2d at 354, but rather a part of a larger business plan purposefully directed at New York consumers.

Accordingly, we conclude that the relevant minimum contacts between Queen Bee and New York include the more than fifty sales of designer handbags into New York and are not limited to the narrow subset of one sale that involved a Chloé handbag shipped to Plaintiffs-Appellants' New York law firm.

D. *New York's Long-arm Statute*

Having established Ubaldelli's single act of shipping an item into New York and his employer's extensive business activity involving New York-activity which may be imputed to Ubaldelli – we next turn to the law of personal jurisdiction. As laid out above, in order for a federal court sitting in New York to assert jurisdiction over Ubaldelli, a California resident, Chloé must satisfy the requirements of both New York's long-arm statute and the Due Process Clause of the United States Constitution. On appeal, Chloé asserts that jurisdiction over Ubaldelli was proper under NY CPLR § 302(a)(1) and (a)(3) because Ubaldelli transacted business within the state and committed a tortious act causing injury in the state. Because we conclude that Ubaldelli transacted business within the state under section 302(a)(1), we need not reach the question of whether a New York court could properly exercise jurisdiction under section 302(a)(3).

Section 302(a)(1) states that 'a court may exercise personal jurisdiction over any non-domiciliary . . . who in person or through an agent . . . transacts any business within the state or contracts anywhere to supply goods or services in the state.' As we observed in *Best Van Lines*, 'New York decisions . . . at least in their rhetoric, tend to conflate the long-arm statutory and constitutional analyses by focusing on the constitutional standard: whether the defendant's conduct constitutes "purposeful availment."' *Best Van Lines*, 490 F3d at 247 (brackets omitted). Thus, a defendant need not be physically present in New York to transact business there within the meaning of the first clause of section 302(a)(1) . . . Further, the second clause of section 302(a)(1) provides for jurisdiction where the defendant has only 'minimal contacts' with New York but contracts to deliver goods or services to the state . . .

Accordingly, courts have explained that section 302 'is a "single act statute" and proof of one transaction in New York is sufficient to invoke jurisdiction, even though the defendant never enters New York, so long as the defendant's activities here were purposeful and there is a substantial relationship between the transaction and the claim asserted.' *Kreutter*, 527 NYS 2d 195, 522 NE 2d at 43; *see also Grand River*, 425 F3d at 166. Applying this standard, district courts in this circuit have concluded that the 'single act' of selling counterfeit goods into New York satisfies the long-arm statute under section 302(a)(1). In *Baron Philippe de Rothschild, S.A. v Paramount Distillers, Inc.*, 923 FSupp 433 (S.D.N.Y.1996), the district court ruled that since the defendants admitted shipping goods into New York that allegedly infringed a trademark, the 'shipments were purposeful and substantially related to plaintiffs' claim of trademark infringement,' and section 302(a)(1) was therefore satisfied. *Id.* at 436.

In *Mattel, Inc. v Adventure Apparel*, No. 00 CIV 4085, 2001 WL 286728 (SDNY Mar 22, 2001), a trademark infringement case, the district court ruled that when an investigator for Mattel (located in New York) ordered an item from defendant Adventure Apparel's website (an Arizona company with its website hosted by a separate California company), [t]his activity not only involved the exchange of payment and shipping information but, moreover, was a commercial transaction that was actually consummated on line. These activities were sufficient to bring Adventure into the category of a defendant 'transact[ing] any business,' via the internet, in New York within the meaning of NY CPLR § 302(a)(1). Under this reasoning, Ubaldelli's single act of shipping a counterfeit Chloé bag might well be sufficient, by itself, to subject him to the jurisdiction of a New York court under section 302(a)(1). We need not, however, decide that question because, in this case, Queen Bee also operated a highly interactive website offering such bags for sale to New York consumers, *see Best Van Lines*, 490 F3d at 252 (holding that website's interactivity 'may be useful' for analyzing personal jurisdiction 'insofar as it helps to decide whether the defendant "transacts any business" in New York'); *Vandermark v Jotomo Corp.*, 42 AD3d 931, 839 NYS2d 670, 671 (NYAppDiv2007) (holding that website may confer personal jurisdiction where it 'has significant commercial elements, which typically are found to constitute the transaction of business'), and engaged in fifty-two other transactions where merchandise was shipped to New York.

Viewed in their totality, these contacts sufficiently demonstrate Ubaldelli's purposeful availment of the benefits of transacting business in New York . . . Accordingly, jurisdiction under section 302(a)(1) is proper because Defendants transacted business within the State of New York.

E. *The Due Process Clause*

There are two components to the due process analysis undertaken to determine whether Ubaldelli is subject to the court's jurisdiction for commercial activity involving the State of New York: (1) the minimum contacts inquiry and (2) the reasonableness inquiry . . .

1. *Minimum contacts*

We conclude that assertion of personal jurisdiction over Ubaldelli comports with due process for the same reasons that it satisfies New York's long-arm statute. Namely, by offering bags for sale to New York consumers on the Queen Bee website and by selling bags-including at least one counterfeit Chloé bag-to New York consumers, Ubaldelli has 'purposefully avail[ed] [him]self of the privilege of conducting activities within the forum State, thus invoking the benefits and protections of its laws.' *Burger King*, 471 US at 475, 105 SCt 2174 (internal quotation marks omitted). In other words, jurisdiction is appropriate in New York because Queen Bee has developed and served a market for its products there. *See, e.g., World-Wide Volkswagen Corp. v Woodson*, 444 US 286, 297, 100 SCt 559, 62 LEd2d 490 (1980). In actually sending items to New York, there can be no doubt that Ubaldelli's conduct was 'purposefully directed toward the forum State.' *Asahi*, 480 US at 112, 107 S.Ct. 1026 (emphasis in original). As Chloé correctly asserts, that Queen Bee's business attempted to serve a nationwide market does not diminish any purposeful contacts with Queen Bee's New York consumers. *See Kernan v Kurz-Hastings, Inc.*, 175 F.3d 236, 243 (2d Cir.1999) (upholding personal jurisdiction where ' "exclusive sales rights" agreement, which contemplates that Kurz-Hastings will sell Navitas's machines in North America and throughout the world, serves as evidence of Navitas's attempt to serve the New York market, albeit indirectly').

Relying on *Travelers Health Association v Virginia*, 339 US 643, 70 SCt 927, 94 LEd 1154 (1950), *McGee v International Life Insurance Co.*, 355 US 220, 78 SCt 199, 2 LEd2d 223 (1957), and *Burger King*, the district court concluded that Chloé could not demonstrate the requisite purposeful availment because Ubaldelli did not develop a continuing relationship with any particular New York consumer. *Chloé II*, 630 FSupp2d at 354. Summarizing the various ways a defendant might have 'purposefully directed' his conduct at residents of the forum state, the Supreme Court has noted that 'parties who reach out beyond one state and create continuing relationships and obligations with citizens of another state are subject to regulation and sanctions in the other State for the consequences of their activities.' *Burger King*, 471 US at 472–73, 105 SCt 2174 (internal quotation marks omitted). But, while it may be sufficient to provide a basis for asserting jurisdiction, a continuing relationship is not necessary for conduct to be purposefully directed at the forum. Rather, as the Supreme Court observed, a court could assert jurisdiction over a corporation that, like Queen Bee, 'delivers its products into the stream of commerce with the expectation that they will be purchased by consumers in the forum State and those products subsequently injure forum consumers.' *Id.* at 473, 105 SCt 2174 (internal quotation marks omitted) (quoting *World-Wide Volkswagen*, 444 US at 297–98, 100 SCt 559). And, similarly, 'a publisher who distributes magazines in a distant State may fairly be held accountable in that forum for damages resulting there from an allegedly defamatory story.' *Id.* . . . This case is more akin to these latter circumstances where personal jurisdiction has been upheld even in the absence of a continuing relationship. Unlike *McGee*, for example, where the record indicated that 'respondent has never solicited or done any insurance business in California apart from the policy involved,' *McGee*, 355 US at 222, 78 SCt 199, Queen Bee has shipped numerous items into New York. It therefore does not offend due process to require Ubaldelli to answer in New York for the consumer confusion allegedly caused there through his purposeful direction of bags into the state.

Chloé also submits that jurisdiction is proper under *Calder v Jones*, because trademark infringement is a tort and its effects are felt in New York where Chloé is located and consumers might be deceived. Because we have concluded that Ubaldelli has purposefully availed himself of the benefits of the New York forum, we need not decide whether Ubaldelli's act of shipping a counterfeit Chloé bag represented conduct 'expressly aimed at' New York under the *Calder* effects test . . . Accordingly, we conclude that Ubaldelli has sufficient contacts with New York to satisfy the 'minimum contacts' inquiry of the Due Process Clause.

2. *Reasonableness*

Even where an out-of-state defendant purposefully avails himself of the forum state, plaintiffs must still demonstrate that the exercise of jurisdiction does not 'offend traditional notions of fair play and substantial justice' and is thus reasonable under the Due Process Clause. *Asahi*, 480 US at 113, 107 SCt 1026 (internal quotation marks omitted). The Supreme Court has set forth five factors that must be considered when determining the reasonableness of a particular exercise of jurisdiction: A court must consider [1] the burden on the defendant, [2] the interests of the forum State, and [3] the plaintiff's interest in obtaining relief. It must also weigh in its determination [4] the interstate judicial system's interest in obtaining the most efficient resolution of controversies; and [5] the shared interest of the several States in furthering fundamental substantive social policies. *Id.*; *see also Metro. Life*, 84 F3d 560, 568. The district court analyzed these factors in a footnote in *Chloé II* and concluded that the five factors favored Ubaldelli. *Chloé II*, 630 FSupp2d at 354 n. 2. We disagree.

With regard to the first factor, we acknowledge that there will be some burden on Ubaldelli if he must travel to New York for trial. The inconvenience, however, cuts both ways since all of Chloé's witnesses would have to travel to California if the case were brought there. *Cf. Bank Brussels*, 305 F3d at 129–30 ('Even if forcing the defendant to litigate in a forum relatively distant from its home base were found to be a burden, the argument would provide defendant only weak support, if any, because the conveniences of modern communication and transportation ease what would have been a serious burden only a few decades ago.' (internal quotation marks omitted)). The second factor favors New York as the forum state since a state frequently has a 'manifest interest in providing effective means of redress for its residents.' *Burger King*, 471 US at 483, 105 SCt 2174 (internal quotation marks omitted). The third factor necessarily favors Chloé since Chloé N.A.'s headquarters are in New York and some of its witnesses are located there. The final two factors are neutral.

In light of our holding that Chloé 'has made a threshold showing of minimum contacts at the first stage of the inquiry,' *Metro. Life*, 84 F3d at 568, Ubaldelli's generalized complaints of inconvenience arising from having to defend himself from suit in New York do not add up to 'a compelling case that the presence of some other considerations would render jurisdiction unreasonable.' *id.* (quoting *Burger King*, 471 US at 477, 105 SCt 2174). Consequently, we hold that asserting jurisdiction over Ubaldelli comports with 'traditional notions of fair play and substantial justice,' *see Int'l Shoe*, 326 US at 316, 66 SCt 154, such that it satisfies the reasonableness inquiry of the Due Process Clause.

III. Conclusion

We hold that on the basis of the record before us at this stage of the litigation, Chloé has satisfied its burden to show that this Court has personal jurisdiction over Ubaldelli based on the totality of his contacts with the forum state of New York. We hold that those contacts permit the exercise of personal jurisdiction under NY CPLR § 302(a)(1), and satisfy both the minimum contacts test and the reasonableness test of the Due Process Clause. Accordingly, we VACATE the judgment of the district court and REMAND for further proceedings consistent with this opinion.

Forum selection clause and venue

Many online contracts contain a forum selection clause. This is a contractual provision in which the parties establish the place (such as the country, state or type of court) for specified litigation between them.[37] They may be classified into two types: non-exclusive or exclusive. The former refers to 'an agreement to litigate in the agreed forum or fora', the latter to 'an agreement to litigate *only* in a forum or fora'.[38] This clause addresses the specific venue in which the matter is to be heard. 'Venue' here refers to the specific court that will determine the matter,[39] such as the Supreme Court, Port of Spain as opposed to the Magistrate's Court, for example.

Whether the court will enforce the terms of a forum selection clause depends on the reasonableness of it and whether there was sufficient notice of the clause prior to entering the contract.[40] In cases where applying the clause will present an undue inconvenience, the doctrine of *forum non conveniens* will be applied by the court.

Forum non conveniens is a Latin term meaning a 'forum which is not convenient'. This doctrine is employed when the court chosen by the plaintiff is inconvenient for witnesses or poses an undue hardship on the defendants. The hardship may arise from such factors as travel distance to the courthouse or presence of witnesses and evidence in another state, such as frequently occurs in internet disputes that reach the courts. The defendant must petition the court for an order transferring the case to a more convenient court. A court may use its discretion in declining to exercise jurisdiction over a matter because of the inconvenience of the forum or on the basis of public policy. In exercising its discretion to do so, however, the court will only dismiss the case if there is another forum available to the plaintiff.[41] In addition, the court reviews the private and public interests involved before making a determination.

There are four main reasons that a court will consider in determining whether to set aside a forum selection clause:[42]

(1) Enforcement would be unreasonable and unjust;
(2) The clause is invalid because of fraud or overreaching, such that a trial in the contractual forum would be so gravely difficult and inconvenient that the challenging party would, for all practical purposes, be deprived of his or her day in court;
(3) Enforcement would contravene a strong public policy of the forum in which suit is brought, whether declared by statute or by judicial decision; and
(4) The fundamental unfairness of the chosen law will deprive the plaintiff of a remedy.

37 Craig, *Cyberlaw*, p. 9.
38 Sorenson, M, 'Enforcement of Forum-Selection Clauses in Federal Court after *Atlantic Marine*', (2014) *Fordham Law Review* 82(5): 2521 at 2528.
39 Craig, *Cyberlaw*, p. 9.
40 Craig, *Cyberlaw*, p. 9
41 US Legal Definitions [online], '*Forum Non Conveniens* Law and Legal Definition', 2015, [accessed 17 January 2015]. Available at: http://definitions.uslegal.com/f/forum-non-conveniens/.
42 See *Russell Scarcella v America Online Inc.* 2004 NY Slip Op 51021(U); 4 Misc 3d 1024 A (NY Civ Ct 2004).

The Canadian courts have also identified certain factors to be considered in determining the issue of *forum non conveniens* and these are as follows:

(i) the location where the contract in dispute was signed or where the loss or damage occurred;
(ii) the applicable law of the contract;
(iii) the location in which the majority of witnesses reside and the convenience or inconvenience posed to them;
(iv) the location of key witnesses;
(v) the location where the bulk of the evidence will come from;
(vi) the jurisdiction in which the factual matters or cause of action arose;
(vii) the residence or place of business of the parties;
(viii) juridical disadvantage to the defendant or juridical advantage to the plaintiff;
(ix) costs of conducting litigation in the jurisdiction;
(x) difficulty in proving foreign law, where applicable.[43]

Tricome v eBay, No. 09–2492 (ED Pa, 2009)

Facts: EBay, Inc. ('Defendant') operates an online marketplace on which 'users' – *i.e.*, individuals who register to use eBay's services – may list items they wish to sell and through which buyers may purchase items from third-party sellers. In order to buy or sell on eBay, individuals must first register. As part of the registration process, a potential user must complete a registration form and electronically submit the form to eBay. In order to activate the registration process, the potential user must read and agree to eBay's User Agreement, which contains the terms and conditions pertaining to the relationship between the user and eBay. The potential user must accept the User Agreement by affirmatively checking a box that states 'I accept the User Agreement and Privacy Policy,' and then clicking on a button to continue with the registration process. Users who do not check the box stating 'I accept the User Agreement and Privacy Policy' are not permitted to complete the registration process. The eBay User Agreement contains a provision (the 'Forum Selection Clause') that specifically requires that disputes between eBay and its users be resolved through a court action filed in Santa Clara County, California. See User Agr., Resolution of Disputes.

In 2006, Domenic Tricome ('Plaintiff') was the owner/operator of www.supplement market.com, an online store which allowed customers to purchase various types of vitamins and supplements . . . In conjunction with Plaintiff's own website, Plaintiff also listed items from his store for auction on eBay's website, www.ebay.com . . . When Plaintiff registered with eBay, he explicitly followed the registration procedures by clicking the box stating 'I accept the User Agreement and Privacy Policy.' Had Plaintiff not clicked that box, he would not have been allowed to register.

Held: Jones, II, J

II. Discussion

A. Forum Selection Clause

A forum selection clause is *prima facie* valid 'and should be enforced unless enforcement is shown by the resisting party to be unreasonable under the circumstances.' *Applied Card*

43 See judgment of Binder, J in *Swimwear Etc. v Raymark Xpert Business Systems Inc.* 2006 ABQB 82.

Systems, Inc. v Winthrop Resources Corp., No. Civ. A. 03–4104, 2003 WL 22351950, *2 (ED Pa. Sept. 23, 2003) (citing *The Bremen v Zapata Off-Shore Co.*, 407 US 1, 10 (1972)) . . . Where the forum selection clause is valid, the plaintiff 'bear[s] the burden of demonstrating why [he] should not be bound by the [parties'] contractual choice of forum.' *Id.* Plaintiff argues that the Forum Selection Clause contained in the User Agreement should not be enforced because the User Agreement is a standard form contract which is procedurally and/or substantively unconscionable.

. . . Agreeing to the User Agreement, and thus all of its terms, was not necessary for Plaintiff; instead, Plaintiff did so merely to increase his business opportunities (and thus, his profits). Plaintiff had the opportunity to carefully read the User Agreement and reject the terms contained therein. However, he accepted the User Agreement. Moreover, eBay did not engage in high pressure tactics or put external pressure on Plaintiff to accept the User Agreement – it simply made the opportunity available to the general public. Here, Plaintiff – an experienced businessman – sought out eBay's services, chose to become a registered user of eBay, and by doing so acknowledged that he had read and agreed to the terms of the User Agreement, including the Forum Selection Clause. Moreover, the same rationale applies here as in *Carnival Cruise Lines* [finding the non-negotiable forum selection clause to be acceptable because the cruise line had a special interest in limiting fora as it could be subject to suit in many locales] – eBay has similar concerns as *Carnival* because its users are located across the US and the world – so the Forum Selection Clause has a legitimate basis.

Plaintiff also maintains that the Forum Selection Clause is substantively unconscionable because it was 'one-sided and non-negotiable' and that Plaintiff had 'no meaningful choice but to accept.' For substantive unconscionability, courts look for overly harsh or one-sided results that are so 'unreasonably favorable to the drafter,' *Grant*, 2009 WL 1845231, at *7, that they 'shock the conscience,' *Feldman*, 513 F Supp 2d at 242. See also *Pentecostal Temple Church v Streaming Faith, LLC*, 2008 WL 4279842, at *5 (WD Pa Sept. 16, 2008) (same). The Court concludes that the Forum Selection Clause is not substantively unconscionable because it is not so unduly one-sided so as to shock the conscience. EBay operates around the world and it not shocking for it to want to focus its legal defense in a particular forum rather than have to litigate in potentially hundreds or thousands of other jurisdictions. The Court agrees with eBay that the Forum Selection Clause also conserves litigant and judicial resources by dispelling confusion over where suits are to be brought; this is not a 'shocking' motive or result. Moreover, once again, it is clear that Plaintiff certainly had a meaningful choice not to accept – he sought to use eBay merely to augment an existing business. There is simply nothing unique about the Forum Selection Clause that shocks the conscience.

B. Transfer of Venue

Third Circuit precedent leaves no doubt that 'dismissal is a permissible means of enforcing a forum selection clause that allows suit to be filed in another federal forum.' *Applied Card Systems, Inc.*, 2003 WL 22351950, at *1 (citing *Salovaara v Jackson Nat'l Life Ins. Co.*, 55 F.3d 289 (3d Cir. 2001)). The Third Circuit has noted, however, that, as a general matter, it makes better sense when the parties have agreed upon a not-unreasonable forum selection clause that points to another federal venue, to transfer rather than dismiss. *Salovaara*, 246 F.3d at 299. 28 USC § 1404(a) is the appropriate statutory provision for transfer of an action when jurisdiction is proper in both the original and the requested forum. *Jumara*, 55 F.3d at 878. Section 1404(a) provides 'For the convenience of the parties and witnesses, in the interest of justice, a district court may transfer any civil action to any other district or division where it might have been brought.' Beyond sole reliance on this statutory authority, the Third Circuit has enumerated additional private and public interests that the court may consider in deciding whether to grant a motion to transfer. The private interests include: plaintiff's forum preference as manifested in the original choice; the defendant's preference; whether the claim arose elsewhere; the convenience of the parties as indicated by their relative physical and financial condition; the convenience of the witnesses – but only to the extent that the witnesses may actually be unavailable for trial in one of the fora; and the location of the books and records. *Applied Card Systems, Inc.*, 2003 WL 22351950, at *2 (citing *Jumara*, 55 F3d at 879–80). The public interests include: the enforceability of the judgment; practical considerations that could make the trial easy, expeditious, or inexpensive; the relative administrative difficulty in the two fora resulting from court congestion; the local interest in deciding local controversies at home; and the familiarity of the trial judge with the applicable state law in diversity cases. *Id.* Importantly, however, while the court must balance these factors, the 'presence of a forum selection clause . . . will be a significant factor that figures centrally in the district court's calculus,' *id.* (citing *Stewart Org., Inc.*, 487 US at 30), and should be given 'substantial consideration,' *Jumara*, 55 F3d at 880. Accordingly, the Court begins its balancing with the fact that the valid Forum Selection Clause is a central and significant factor that weighs in favor of transfer.

Weighing the 1404(a) factors in light of the Forum Selection Clause, the Court finds that transfer to the US District Court for the Northern District of California, San Jose Division is appropriate in this case. The plain language of the Forum Selection Clause encompasses this action within its scope and suggests that venue in California is mandatory. As discussed, *supra*, Plaintiff does not contend that the Forum Selection Clause was procured through fraud or overreaching. In fact, the User Agreement was a freely negotiated contracted entered into by a sophisticated business and a sophisticated businessman and thus expresses a mutual preference for California venue.

Although it may be challenging, the Court is not convinced that litigating this dispute in California would be prohibitively difficult for Plaintiff. Inconvenience or additional expense is not the test of unreasonableness 'since it may be assumed that the plaintiff received under the contract consideration for these things . . .' *Cent. Contracting Co. v Maryland Casualty Co.*, 367 F2d 341, 344 (3d Cir 1966) (citation omitted). The Court finds that Plaintiff's limitations are not so gravely difficult as to preclude him from participating in the litigation of the instant dispute. Plaintiff's local attorney may represent him *pro hac vice* in California at the same rates, thus relieving Plaintiff from the requirement of hiring a California lawyer. Moreover, eBay has represented on the record that it will make physical accommodations for Plaintiff, such as telephonic or video appearances and the scheduling of depositions near Plaintiff's home in Pennsylvania. Additionally, Plaintiff's presence is not even required (electronically or otherwise) at every court conference and/or argument (or even the majority thereof).

Furthermore, the Court finds that the Northern District of California would provide a more convenient forum for this action. Most of the eBay's employees and records are located in California. Moreover, the local courts have a strong interest in resolving this matter, given that eBay, a California corporation with its principal place of business in California, utilizes the same User Agreement in its business dealing with every individual who is registered (*i.e.*, permitted) to use eBay's services. Finally, a California district judge would be more familiar with the law governing plaintiff's supplemental state law claims.

III. Conclusion

The Court finds that the User Agreement, including the Forum Selection Clause, is valid, because it is not procedurally or substantively unconscionable. The Court concludes that transfer of venue is more desirable than dismissal. The Court concludes that transfer to California would not be so gravely difficult or inconvenient as to deny Plaintiff his day in court. Weighing the appropriate factors and the parties' Forum Selection Clause, the Court finds that this action should be transferred to the Northern District of California, San Jose Division.

Choice of law

A choice of law provision is a contractual term which designates the jurisdiction of any state or country whose law will govern any disputes that arises between the parties.[44] Choice of law clauses are usually included as part of the terms of use of a website, but without the express agreement of the parties involved, this may be held to be inapplicable. It would appear that in the absence of agreement in internet disputes, the law of the state (United States) in which enforcement is sought would govern. Similarly, in international disputes, it would appear that the law of the jurisdiction where the injury has occurred would govern. Nevertheless, in *Yahoo!, Inc. v La Ligue Contre Le Racisme et L'Antisémitisme*,[45] the dissenting judgment of the US 9th Circuit court indicated that a French Court's orders to censor speech by a US entity outside of France should not be enforceable under the laws of the United States, as it would have violated the First Amendment of the US Constitution.

Apart from constitutional matters, there are instances where courts will not enforce a choice of law provision, such as where it contravenes public policy.

Fiser v Dell Computer Corp., No. 30,424 (SC NM, 2008)[46]

Facts: Plaintiff Robert Fiser purchased a computer from Defendant via the company's website. He subsequently filed a putative class action lawsuit contending that Defendant systematically misrepresents the memory size of its computers. He alleges violations of the New Mexico Unfair Practices Act (UPA), NMSA 1978, Sections 57–12–1 to-26 (1967, as amended through 2003), the New Mexico False Advertising Act, NMSA 1978, Sections 57–15–1 to-10 (1965), the New Mexico Uniform Commercial Code (UCC), NMSA 1978, Sections 55–1–101 to-12–111 (1961, as amended), and common law concepts of breach of contract, breach of warranty, misrepresentation, violations of the covenants of good faith and fair dealing, bad faith, and unjust enrichment.

Central to the issue presented is the scant amount of damages alleged: Plaintiff estimates that Defendant's alleged misrepresentation results in a monetary loss to its customers of just ten to twenty dollars per computer.

. . . Defendant argued that, pursuant to the 'terms and conditions' on its website at the time of the purchase, Plaintiff is required to individually arbitrate his claims and is precluded from proceeding on a classwide basis either in litigation or arbitration. The 'terms and conditions' included an arbitration clause mandating that 'any claim, dispute, or controversy against Dell [was subject to] binding arbitration administered by the National Arbitration Forum (NAF).' The terms also included a clause (hereinafter referred to as the class action ban) which directed that the arbitration was 'limited solely to the dispute or controversy between [Plaintiff] and Dell.' Finally, the 'terms and conditions' contained a choice-of-law

44 See Rustad, *Cyberlaw*, p. 8.

45 433 F.3d 1199 (9th Cir. 2006).

46 Available from http://caselaw.findlaw.com/nm-supreme-court/1327124.html.

provision declaring Texas law to be controlling. Although the parties disagree over whether Plaintiff assented to Defendant's 'terms and conditions,' we do not reach that issue. We assume without deciding, for the purpose of our analysis, that he assented to the terms.

Held: Chávez, CJ, Serna, Maes, Bosson, and Daniels, JJ.

II. Discussion

A. Application of Texas Law Would Violate New Mexico Public Policy

1. New Mexico Respects Choice-of-Law Provisions Unless Application of the Chosen Law Would Contravene New Mexico Public Policy

The threshold question in determining the validity of the class action ban is which state's law must be applied to this potentially multi-state class action that was filed in New Mexico by a New Mexico resident against a defendant that maintains its principal place of business in Texas for damages relating to a contract that contains a choice-of-law clause directing that Texas law be applied.

New Mexico respects party autonomy; the law to be applied to a particular dispute may be chosen by the parties through a contractual choice-of-law provision . . . However, when application of the law chosen by the parties offends New Mexico public policy, our courts may decline to enforce the choice-of-law provision and apply New Mexico law instead . . . New Mexico courts will not give effect to another state's laws where those laws would 'violate some fundamental principle of justice.' *Reagan v McGee Drilling Corp.*, 1997-NMCA-014, ¶9, 123 NM 68, 933 P2d 867 (quoted authority omitted).

Application of Texas law to the instant matter would likely require enforcing the class action ban . . . Unless enforcement of the class action ban would run afoul of fundamental New Mexico public policy, our conflict of law rules counsel respecting the choice-of-law provision and applying Texas law.

2. It is Fundamental New Mexico Policy that Consumers Have a Viable Mechanism for Dispute Resolution, No Matter the Size of the Claim

New Mexico policy strongly supports the resolution of consumer claims, regardless of the amount of damages alleged. That policy is demonstrated by several of our statutes. For example, the New Mexico legislature enacted the UPA, which is unequivocal: '[u]nfair or deceptive trade practices and unconscionable trade practices in the conduct of any trade or commerce are unlawful.' Section 57–12–3. The UPA was clearly drafted to include a remedy for small claims: a party need not show any monetary damage to be entitled to an injunction, Section 57–12–10(A), and '[a]ny person who suffers any loss of money [may] recover actual damages or the sum of one hundred dollars ($100), whichever is greater.' Section 57–12–10(B).

The fundamental New Mexico policy of providing consumers a mechanism for dispute resolution is also seen in the False Advertising Act, which specifically empowers private individuals to bring rights of action in the name of the state and for 'all others similarly situated.' Section 57–15–5.

Yet another example of New Mexico's fundamental public policy in ensuring that consumers have an opportunity to redress their harm is the Consumer Protection Division of the Attorney General's Office, which is charged with protecting New Mexico citizens from unfair and deceptive trade practices. In this effort, the Consumer Protection Division is authorized and funded to investigate suspicious business activities, informally resolve the complaints of dissatisfied consumers, educate citizens about their consumer rights, and file lawsuits on behalf of the public.

3. The Class Action Device is Critical to Enforcement of Consumer Rights in New Mexico

The opportunity to seek class relief is of particular importance to the enforcement of consumer rights because it provides a mechanism for the spreading of costs. The class action device allows claimants with individually small claims the opportunity for relief that would otherwise be economically infeasible because they may collectively share the otherwise prohibitive costs of bringing and maintaining the claim. See, e.g., 1 Alba Conte & Herbert B. Newberg, *Newberg on Class Actions* § 1.6, at 26 (4th ed. 2002). 'In many cases, the availability of class action relief is a *sine qua non* to permit the adequate vindication of consumer rights.' *State ex rel. Dunlap v Berger*, 211 WVa 549, 567 SE.2d 265, 278 (2002). 'The class action is one of the few legal remedies the small claimant has against those who command the status quo.' *Eisen v Carlisle & Jacquelin*, 417 US 156, 186, 94 SCt 2140, 40 LEd.2d 732 (1974) (Douglas, J, dissenting in part).

The opportunity for class relief and its importance to consumer rights is enshrined in the fundamental policy of New Mexico and evidenced by our statutory scheme. See, e.g., Rule 1–023 NMRA (setting forth the rules of civil procedure governing class actions). Notably, the UPA specifically references class actions as a private remedy available under the act. Section 57–12–10(E). Further, the New Mexico Uniform Arbitration Act declares that arbitration clauses that require consumers to decline participation in class actions are unenforceable and voidable . . .

In New Mexico, we recognize that the class action was devised for 'vindication of the rights of groups of people who individually would be without effective strength to bring their opponents into court at all.' *Romero v Philip Morris, Inc.*, 2005-NMCA-035, ¶ 36, 137 NM 229, 109 P3d 768 (quoted authority omitted). A purpose of the class action is to conserve party resources. *Id.* As the United States Supreme Court recognized, [t]he policy at the very core of the class action mechanism is to overcome the problem that small recoveries do not provide the incentive for any individual to bring a solo action prosecuting his or her rights. A class action solves this problem by aggregating the relatively paltry potential recoveries into something worth someone's (usually an attorney's) labor. *Amchem Prods., Inc. v Windsor*, 521 US 591, 617, 117 SCt 2231, 138 LEd2d 689 (1997) (quoted authority omitted).

'Where it is not economically feasible to obtain relief within the traditional framework of a multiplicity of small individual suits for damages, aggrieved persons may be without any effective redress unless they may employ the class-action device.' *Deposit Guar. Nat'l Bank, Jackson, Miss. v Roper*, 445 US 326, 339, 100 SCt 1166, 63 LEd.2d 427 (1980). The Federal Rules Advisory Committee recognized the critical nature of the class action to individuals with small claims when it directed that one of the grounds on which class certification may be appropriate is where 'the amounts at stake for individuals [are] so small that separate suits would be impracticable.' FedRCivP 23(b)(3), advisory committee note (1966 amendment).

Thus, beyond merely a procedural tool, the class action functions as a gatekeeper to relief when the cost of bringing a single claim is greater than the damages alleged. When viewed in this light, a contractual provision that purports to ban class actions for small claims implicates not just the opportunity for a class action but the more fundamental right to a meaningful remedy for one's claims. This Court has recognized that the right of access to the courts is part of the right to petition for redress of grievances guaranteed by both the United States and New Mexico constitutions. *Jiron v Mahlab*, 99 NM 425, 426, 659 P2d 311, 312 (1983); see also US Const. amends. I, XIV; N.M. const., art. II, §18. While the class action ban may or may not rise to the level of a constitutional violation, a prohibition on class relief where there is no meaningful alternative for redress of injury certainly does not provide for effective vindication of rights . . .

In view of the fact that Plaintiff's alleged damages are just ten to twenty dollars, by attempting to prevent him from seeking class relief, Defendant has essentially foreclosed the possibility that Plaintiff may obtain any relief. Thus, we conclude that Defendant's prohibition on class action relief, when applied to small claims plaintiffs, is contrary to New Mexico's fundamental public policy to provide a forum for relief for small consumer claims. The words of the California Supreme Court are apropos:

By imposing this clause on its customers, [Defendant] has essentially granted itself a license to push the boundaries of good business practices to their furthest limits, fully aware that relatively few, if any, customers will seek legal remedies, and that any remedies obtained will only pertain to that single customer without collateral estoppel effect. The potential for millions of customers to be without an effective method of redress cannot be ignored. *Discover Bank v Super.* Ct, 36 Cal. 4th 148, 30 Cal.Rptr.3d 76, 113 P.3d 1100, 1108 (2005).

. . . For all of the foregoing reasons, New Mexico's fundamental public policy requires that consumers with small claims have a mechanism for dispute resolution via the class action. Therefore, application of Texas law, that would allow the class action ban, is contrary to New Mexico public policy. See *AutoNation*, 105 SW3d at 199–201. Accordingly, we invoke the public policy exception and apply New Mexico law rather than Texas law to analyze the validity of the class action ban.

Taxation

Taxation on e-commerce presents special difficulties, as internet transactions do not defer to state or country borders or jurisdictions. Currently, in the United States, there are two main taxes that may be applied to consumers: sales and use. "A use tax is the companion to a sales tax – in general, the sales tax is imposed on the sale of goods and services within the state's borders, while the use tax is imposed on purchases made by the state's residents from out-of-state (remote) sellers. The purpose of the use tax is to dissuade residents from purchasing goods and services from out-of-state merchants in order to avoid the sales tax."[47] While online sellers located in a particular state must collect sales tax on in-state sales, states currently cannot compel out-of-state sellers to collect tax on sales to state residents.[48] Consequently, use taxes tend to go uncollected. Collecting these taxes would be administratively burdensome given that there are over 9600 taxing districts in the United States.[49] A great deal of monitoring will be

47 Lunder, E and Pettit, C [online], '"Amazon Laws" and Taxation of Internet Sales', *CRS Report* R42629, November 2014. Available at: https://www.fas.org/sgp/crs/misc/R42629.pdf.

48 Einav, L, Knoepfle, D, Levin, J and Sundaresan, N [online], 'Sales Taxes and Internet Commerce' (2014) *American Economic Review* 104(1): 1–26. Available at http://web.stanford.edu/~jdlevin/Papers/SalesTaxes.pdf.

49 Dolmetsch, C [online], 'Amazon, Overstock Lose Challenge to NY Web Sales Tax', *Bloomberg.com*, 2013. Available at: http://www.bloomberg.com/news/2013–03–28/amazon-overstock-lose-challenge-to-n-y-web-sales-tax.html. In order to standardise and simplify tax collection and administration in the United States, particularly for retailers operating in multiple states such as Amazon, a Streamlined Sales Tax Project was initiated in 2002. To date, however, only 24 of the 44 participating states have enacted the necessary legislation. See Streamlined Sales Tax Governing Board, Inc [online], 'About Us: Frequently Asked Questions', 2011 [accessed 17 January 2015]. Available at: http://www.streamlinedsalestax.org/.

required to ensure that the tax is correctly collected.[50] A further clarification to this approach was provided in 1992: the US Supreme Court exempted out-of-state retailers from collecting sales tax in out-of-state transactions, that is, where they sold goods to residents of a state where the retailer had no physical presence, such as a store, office or warehouse.[51] Although *Quill* dealt with a mail order company, this decision now applies to internet transactions as well.[52]

The application of taxation requires that a nexus, as evidenced by a physical presence in the state where the sale took place, be established for the purposes of paying taxes there. Internet retailers generally do not collect taxes for online transactions; however, in two 2008 judgments involving Amazon.com and Overstock.com, it was established that, under a then implemented tax amendment, out-of-state online retailers are required to collect New York State sales tax if they use independent contractors or other New York residents to solicit sales in excess of US$10,000 from New York residents, as this creates a physical and substantial nexus to the state. In 2008, Amazon.com took the decision to collect the tax, whereas Overstock.com decided to drop its New York affiliates.

Amazon.com LLC and Amazon Services LLC v New York State Department of Taxation and Finance and The State of New York No. 60124708 (New York Sup Ct 2008)

Facts: Since 1995 Amazon has been operating a retail internet business. Its goods are sold online and shipped to buyers worldwide, including to New York. Amazon does not own property in New York or maintain any New York offices. None of its employees work or reside in New York. Amazon created an 'Associated Program', which allows participants (Associates) to maintain links to Amazon.com on their own websites and compensates them by paying 'a percentage of the proceeds of the sale'. Amazon also offers incentives to Associates that 'directly refer' customers to its Amazon Prime program through website links, paying them a '[US]$12 bounty' for each new enrollee. Prospective Associates must apply to join the program. Assuming that Amazon accepts the application, the parties enter into an Operating Agreement, which makes clear that the 'Relationship of [the] Parties' is that of 'independent contractors'. Associates are granted 'a revocable, non-exclusive, worldwide, royalty-free license . . . solely for purposes of facilitating referrals from [their sites] to the Amazon Site' . . . Amazon has hundreds of thousands of Associates. Thousands 'of them have provided Amazon with addresses in New York'. Sales to New York customers originating from New York-based Associate referrals constitute less than 1.5 per cent of Amazon's New York sales. Without disclosing the dollar amount of those sales, Amazon simply acknowledges that its 'Associates Program generates more tha[n] [US]$10,000 per year in sales to customers located in New York' . . . A 2008 amendment to New York's Tax law now requires collection of New York taxes from New Yorkers by out-of-state sellers that contractually agree to pay commissions to New York residents for referring potential customers to them, provided that more than US$10,000 was generated from such New York referrals during the preceding four quarterly periods. In the law, the

50 See McLure Jr, C, 'The Taxation of Electronic Commerce: Background and Proposal'. In N Imparato (ed), *Public Policy and the Internet: Privacy, Taxes, and Contract*, 2000, Stanford, CA: Hoover Institution Press, p 63.

51 *Quill Corp. v North Dakota* 504 US 298 (1992).

52 Lager, H [online], 'The "Amazon Tax" Upheld in New York, Enabling State Taxation of Web Sales: *Amazon.com LLC v New York State Dept. of Taxation and Finance*', 8 April 2009, [accessed 17 January 2015]. Available at: http://www.lawupdates.com/commentary/the_amazon_tax_upheld_in_new_york_enabling_state_taxation_of_web_sales/.

definition of 'vendor' is: 'A person who solicits business either: (1) by employees, independent contractors, agents or other representatives . . .'

Once the Commission-Agreement Provision was enacted, Amazon began collecting taxes from its New York customers under protest. On 25 April 2008, Amazon commenced this action, alleging that the Commission-Agreement Provision 'violates the Commerce Clause of the United States Constitution, both facially and as applied to Amazon, because it imposes tax collection obligations on out-of-state entities who have no substantial nexus with New York'. Amazon also contended that the provision violates Federal and State constitutions' Due Process Clauses, both facially and as applied, because 'it effectively creates an irrebuttable presumption of "solicitation" and is overly broad and vague'. Amazon further maintained that the enactment violates the Constitutions' Equal Protection Clauses because it intentionally targets Amazon.

Held: Bransten, J
A state may require an entity engaged in interstate commerce to collect taxes on its behalf provided the 'tax is applied to an activity with a substantial nexus with the taxing State, is fairly apportioned, does not discriminate against interstate commerce, and is fairly related to the services provided by the State' (*Complete Auto Transit, Inc. v Brady* 430 US 274, 279 [1977]). To establish a 'substantial nexus' with the taxing state, 'physical presence of the vendor is required [however] it need not be substantial. Rather, it must be 'demonstrably more tha[n] a "slightest presence".' And it may be manifested by . . . economic activities in the taxing State performed by the vendor's personnel or on its behalf' (*Matter of Orvis Co. v Tax Appeals Tribunal*, 86 NY2d 165, 178 [1995]). As Amazon acknowledges, physical presence 'can be actual or imputed based on the in-state solicitation of sales by an employee, agent, or independent contractor or the retailer on its behalf' (Amazon's Memorandum of Law at 14). In *Scripto v Carson*, 362 US 207, 209 (1960), for example, the United States Supreme Court held that a state could require tax collection by an out-of-state company that had contracts with 10 in-state residents – deemed 'independent contractor[s]' – who solicited orders for products on its behalf. The agreement with the contractors provided that they were to be paid commission and salespeople sent orders out of state for fulfilment (*id.*; see also *Standard Pressed Steel Co. v Washington Department of Revenue*, 419 US 560, 561 [1975] [sufficient nexus based on single employee who resided in-state and consulted with customer therein]); *Felt & Tarrant MFG. Co. v Gallagher*, 306 US 62, 64 [1939] [collection mandated based on presence of two general agents contractually granted the right to solicit in-state orders who were to be paid by commission]; *Matter of Orvis Co.*, 86 NY 2d at 165 [in-state activity sufficient based on employee visits to solicit business]). In contrast, if the *only* connection with the state is solicitation from out of state – through catalogues, flyers, advertisements in national periodicals or telephone calls – and delivery of merchandise to customers by common carrier or use of mail, there is an insufficient nexus for taxation purposes (see *Quill Corp v North Dakota*, 504 US 298 [1992]; *National Bellas Hess, Inc. v Department of Revenue*, 386 US 753 [1967]). So long as there is a 'substantial nexus' with the taxing state, the taxes that must be collected need not derive from the seller's in-state activity (*National Geographic Society v California Board of Equalization*, 430 US 551, 560 [1977] [non-profit society required to collect taxes from California mail-order customers based on maintenance of two offices in California from which advertising was solicited for its monthly magazine]) . . . In the end, the Commission-Agreement Provision does not broadly tax any and all internet sales to New York consumers. It requires a substantial nexus between an out-of-state seller and New York through a contract to pay commissions for referrals with a New York resident along with realisation of more than [US]$10,000 of revenue from New York sales earned through the arrangement. The neutral statute simply

obligates out-of-state sellers to shoulder their fair share of the tax-collection burden when using New Yorkers to earn profit from other New Yorkers.

While the decision was appealed in 2013, the 2008 decision was upheld by a majority. The dissenting judge, however, did not feel that there was any substantial nexus created.

Overstock.com, Inc., Appellant, v New York State Department of Taxation and Finance, et al., Respondents. No. 33 and Amazon.com, LLC, et al., Appellants, v New York State Department of Taxation and Finance, et al., Respondents. No. 34 (NY Ct App, 2013)

Held: Lippman, Chief Judge, Graffeo, Read and Pigott, JJ.
The Internet tax is constitutional on its face . . . Subsequent to *Quill*, we further explained that, although an in-state physical presence is necessary, it 'need not be substantial. Rather, it must be demonstrably more than a "slightest presence"' (*Orvis*, 86 NY2d at 178, quoting *National Geographic Soc. v California Bd. of Equalization*, 430 US 551, 556 [1977]). The presence requirement will be satisfied if economic activities are performed in New York by the seller's employees or on its behalf (see *Orvis*, 86 NY2d at 178).

Essentially, through these types of affiliation agreements, a vendor is deemed to have established an in-state sales force.

Viewed in this manner the statute plainly satisfies the substantial nexus requirement. Active, in-state solicitation that produces a significant amount of revenue qualifies as 'demonstrably more than a 'slightest presence'' under *Orvis*.

Indeed, an entity 'that is engaged in continuous and widespread solicitation of business within a State . . . clearly has fair warning that [its] activity may subject [it] to the jurisdiction of a foreign sovereign,' even in the absence of physical presence (*Quill*, 504 US at 308 [internal quotation marks and citation omitted]). In this respect, we believe that a brigade of affiliated websites compensated by commission are [*sic*] the equivalent of 'a deluge of catalogs' and 'a phalanx of drummers' (*Quill*, 504 US at 308).

Here, the fact proved is that the resident is compensated for referrals that result in purchases. The fact presumed is that at least some of those residents will actively solicit other New Yorkers in order to increase their referrals and, consequently, their compensation. It is plainly rational to presume that, given the direct correlation between referrals and compensation, it is likely that residents will seek to increase their referrals by soliciting customers. More specifically, it is not unreasonable to presume that affiliated website owners residing in New York State will reach out to their New York friends, relatives and other local individuals in order to accomplish this purpose. As noted above, the record contains examples of this type of solicitation by schools and certain other organizations . . .

Accordingly, in both cases, the judgment appealed from and the order of the Appellate Division brought up for review should be affirmed, with costs.

Dissent: Smith, J
Our task here is to decide whether certain New York based websites – Overstock's 'Affiliates' and Amazon's 'Associates' – are the equivalent of sales agents, soliciting business for Overstock and Amazon, or are only media in which Overstock and Amazon advertise their products. I think they are the latter. The Overstock and Amazon links that appear on websites owned by New York proprietors serve essentially the same function as advertising that a more traditional out-of-state retailer might place in local newspapers. The websites

are not soliciting customers for Overstock and Amazon in the fashion of a local sales agent. Of course the website owners solicit business for themselves; they encourage people to visit their websites, just as a newspaper owner would seek to boost circulation. But there is no basis for inferring that they are actively soliciting for the out-of-state retailers . . .

To infer, from an agreement to put a link on a website and to compensate the website owner in proportion to the resulting sales, that the website owner is actively soliciting business for the seller 'is so strained as not to have a reasonable relation to the circumstances of life as we know them' (*Tot v United States*, 319 US at 468).

BIBLIOGRAPHY

Books, Chapters

Ashurst, *Interpretation of Contracts under English Law*, 2012, London: Ashurst.

Card, R, *Card, Cross and Jones: Criminal Law*, 2008, Oxford: Oxford University Press.

Chkhikvadze, VM (ed), *The Soviet State and the Law*, trans. Y Sdobnikov, 2000, Honolulu, HI: University Press of the Pacific.

Craig, B, *Cyberlaw: The Law of the Internet and Information Technology*, 2013, New York, NY: Pearson Education Inc.

Darrell, K, *Issues in Internet Law: Society, Technology, and the Law*, 2008, Boca Raton, FL: Amber Book Company.

Deakin, S, Johnston, A and Markesinis, B, *Markesinis and Deakin's Tort Law*, 2007, Oxford: Oxford University Press.

De Smith, S and Brazier, R, *Constitutional and Administrative Law*, 1998, London: Penguin Books.

Emerson, R, *Business Law*, 2003, Hauppauge, NY: Barron's Educational Series, Inc.

Furmston, M, *Cheshire, Fifoot & Furmston's Law of Contract*, 2001, London: Butterworths.

Glendon, M *et al*, *Comparative Legal Traditions in a Nutshell*, 1999, St Paul, MN: West Group.

Markesinis, B and Munday, R, *An Outline of the Law of Agency*, 1998, London: Butterworths.

McGraw, B, 'Introduction: Church and State in Context'. In A Duncan and S Jones (eds), *Church-State Issues in America Today: Religion and Government*, 2007, Santa Barbara, CA: Praeger Publishers.

McKendrick, E, *Contract Law: Text, Cases and Materials*, 2008, Oxford: Oxford University Press.

McLure Jr, C, 'The Taxation of Electronic Commerce: Background and Proposal'. In N Imparato (ed), *Public Policy and the Internet: Privacy, Taxes, and Contract*, 2000, Stanford, CA: Hoover Institution Press.

Merryman, J, *The Civil Law Tradition: An Introduction to the Legal Systems of Western Europe and Latin America*, 1985, Stanford, CA: Stanford University Press.

Mumisa, M, *Islamic Law: Theory and Interpretation*, 2002, Beltsville, MD: Amana Publications.

Murphy, J, *Street on Torts*, 2012, Oxford: Oxford University Press.

Ormerod, D, *Smith and Hogan: Criminal Law*, 2008, Oxford: Oxford University Press.

Radin, M, 'Retooling Contract for the Digital Era'. In N Imparato (ed), *Public Policy and the Internet: Privacy, Taxes, and Contract*, 2000, Stanford, CA: Hoover Institution Press.

Rogers, WVH, *Winfield and Jolowicz on Tort*, 2002, London: Sweet & Maxwell.

Rustad, M, *Global Internet Law in a Nutshell*, 2013, St Paul, MN: West.

Ryan, S, *The Judiciary and Governance in the Caribbean*, 2001, St. Augustine, Trinidad: Sir Arthur Lewis Institute of Social and Economic Studies, UWI.

Salzedo, S *et al*, *Briefcase on Contract Law*, 2004, London: Cavendish Publishing.

Sinha, SP, *What is Law?: The Differing Theories of Jurisprudence*, 1989, New York, NY: Paragon House.

Slapper, G and Kelly, D, *The English Legal System*, 2000, London: Cavendish Publishing Limited.

Steele, J, *Tort Law: Text, Cases and Materials*, 2007, Oxford: Oxford University Press.

The Common Law Library, *Chitty on Contracts: Volume 1, General Principles*, 1999, London: Sweet & Maxwell.

Trout, B, *A Legal Arsenal for Online Business*, 2007, New York, NY: World Audience Inc.

Wheare, KC, *Modern Constitutions*, 1966, London: Oxford University Press.

Wolf-Phillips, L, *Constitutions of Modern States*, 1967, London: Pall Mall.
Zander, M, *The Law-Making Process*, 1999, London: Butterworths.
Zemer, M, *Evolving Halakhah: A Progressive Approach to Traditional Jewish Law*, 1999, Woodstock, VT: Jewish Lights Publishing.
Zweigert, K and Kötz, H, *An Introduction to Comparative Law*, trans. T Weir, 1998, Oxford: Oxford University Press.

Journal Articles

Einav, L, Knoepfle, D, Levin, J and Sundaresan, N, [online], 'Sales Taxes and Internet Commerce', (2014) *American Economic Review* 104(1): 1–26. Available at http://web.stanford.edu/~jdlevin/Papers/SalesTaxes.pdf.
Kunkel, R, [online], 'Recent Developments in Shrinkwrap, Clickwrap and Browsewrap Licenses in the United States', (2002) *Murdoch University Electronic Journal of Law* 9(3). Available at: http://www.murdoch.edu.au/elaw/issues/v9n3/kunkel93.html.
Lo, CW-H, 'Socialist Legal Theory in Deng Xiao-Ping's China' (1997), 11 *Columbia Journal of Asian Law* 469.
Smedinghoff, TJ, and Bro, RH, 'Moving With Change: Electronic Signature Legislation as a Vehicle for Advancing E-commerce', (1999) *The John Marshall Journal of Computer and Information Law*, 17(3), 723.
Sorenson, M, 'Enforcement of Forum-Selection Clauses in Federal Court after *Atlantic Marine*', (2014) *Fordham Law Review*, 82(5): 2521. Available at: http://ir.lawnet.fordham.edu/flr/vol82/iss5/18.
Zeller, B, 'Good Faith – Is it a Contractual Obligation?', (2003) *Bond Law Review* 15(2): 215–39. Available at: http://epublications.bond.edu.au/cgi/viewcontent.cgi?article=1268&context=blr.

Online News

Cross, R and Harris, J, *Precedent in English Law*, 1991, Oxford: Oxford University Press.
Elsing, S, and Townsend, JM, 'Bridging the Common Law Civil Law Divide in Arbitration', (2002) *Arbitration International* 18(1): 4.
Frieden, J, [online], 'Common Issues Facing E-Commerce Businesses', E-Commerce Law, posted 31 May 2006, [accessed 29 June 2009]. Available at: http://ecommercelaw.typepad.com/ecommerce_law/keyword_advertising.
Garrison, L and Cain, R, [online], 'E Commerce Tax Policy Project', UMKC Bloch School of Business and Public Administration, 2008, [accessed 26 June 2009]. Available at: http://www.bloch.umkc.edu/ecommerce/domestic.html.
Goode, R, *Commercial Law*, 1995, London: Penguin Books.
Grusd, B, [online], 'Contracting Beyond Copyright: *ProCD, Inc. v Zeidenberg*', (1997) *Harvard Journal of Law and Technology*, 10(2): 353–67. Available at: http://jolt.law.harvard.edu/articles/pdf/v10/10HarvJLTech353.pdf.
Hawkins, J, [online], 'ProCD, Inc. v Zeidenberg: Enforceability of Shrinkwrap Licenses Under the Copyright Act', (1997) *Richmond Journal of Law and Technology* 3(6). Available at: http://law.richmond.edu/jolt/v3i1/hawkins.html.
Legal Information Institute, [online], 'International Law: An Overview', [accessed 7 December 2009]. Available at: http://www.law.cornell.edu/topics/international.html.
López Rodríguez, AM, [online], 'Lex Mercatoria', 2002, [accessed 7 December 2009]. Available at: http://www.rettid.dk/artikler/20020046.pdf.

Marks, C, 'Not What, but When is an Offer? Rehabilitating the Rolling Contract', (2013) *Connecticut Law Review*, 46(1): 73.
Michaelson, J, 'The A-Z of ADR: Your need to know guide to ADR', (24 January 2003) *New Law Journal* 153 (7064): 105.
Schaefer, E, [online], 'Understanding Trademark Infringement and Google Keyword Advertising', [accessed 29 June 2009]. Available at: http://ezinearticles.com/?Understanding-Trademark-Infringement-and-Google-Keyword-Advertising&id=2189733.
Shearer, I, *Starke's International Law*, 1994, London: Butterworths.
Swamber, K, [online], 'Court orders boss to pay injured co-worker: Welder electrocuted . . .', *Trinidad Express*, 15 June 2009. Available at: http://www.trinidadexpress.com/index.pl/article?id=161490918.
TechTerms.com, [online], 'Meta Tag', 2009, [accessed 29 June 2009]. Available at: http://www.techterms.com/definition/metatag.
Whincup, M, *Contract Law and Practice: The English System and Continental Comparisons*, 1996, The Hague: Kluwer Law International.

Online Resources

Articlesbase, [online], 'The Need for the Intention to Create Legal Relations in Contract Law', posted 8 April 2008, [accessed 21 January 2015]. Available at: http://www.articlesbase.com/law-articles/the-need-for-intention-to-create-legal-relations-in-contract-law-381745.html.
Blackwell, [online], 'Ratio Decidendi', 2004 [accessed 30 December 2014]. Available at: http://www.blackwellreference.com/public/tocnode?id=g9781405106795_chunk_g978140510679519_ss1-11.
Bridge, J, 'Values, Principles and Standards in the Public Law of the United Kingdom'. Delivered at Newcastle Law School Staff Seminar, 23 May 2000.
BusinessDictionary.com, [online], 'Unilateral Contract', 2009, [accessed 27 August 2009]. Available at: http://www.businessdictionary.com/definition/unilateral-contract.html.
Call, J, [online], 'The Halakhah and its Role in Modern Israeli Law', [accessed 27 May 2003]. Available at: http://www.law2.byu.edu/lwb/papers/Call-Halakhah_FINAL.PDF [link no longer active; copy available with the author].
Colleg Gwent, [online], 'Statutory Interpretation: Purposive Approach' [PPT Presentation], [accessed 05 January 2015]. Available at: http://learn.coleggwent.ac.uk/mod/resource/view.php?id=144939.
Dolmetsch, C, [online], 'Amazon, Overstock Lose Challenge to NY Web Sales Tax', *Bloomberg.com*, 2013. Available at: http://www.bloomberg.com/news/2013-03-28/amazon-overstock-lose-challenge-to-n-y-web-sales-tax.html.
Dube, B and Magagula, A, [online], 'The Law and Legal Research in Swaziland', *Hauser Global Law School Program, New York University School of Law*, September / October 2007, [accessed 30 December 2014]. Available at: http://www.nyulawglobal.org/globalex/swaziland.htm#_Swazi_National_Courts.
Factmonster, [online], 'Equity', [Columbia University Press, 2000], [accessed 30 December 2014]. Available at: http://www.factmonster.com/ce6/society/A0817541.html.
Farlex, [online], 'The Free Dictionary: Equity', 2009, [accessed 30 December 2014]. Available at: http://legal-dictionary.thefreedictionary.com/equity.
Frieden, J, [online], 'FAQ: Is an Internet Contract Enforceable?', *E-Commerce Law* posted 11 May 2009, [accessed 5 June 2009]. Available at: http://ecommercelaw.typepad.com/ecommerce_law/2009/05/faq-is-an-internet-contract-enforceable.html#more.

Hachman, M, [online], 'Microsoft's updated privacy policy makes it clear it's not selling ads against your words', *PC World*, 11 June 2014, [accessed 14 January 2015]. Available from http://www.pcworld.com/article/2362130/microsofts-updated-privacy-policy-makes-it-clear-its-not-selling-ads-against-your-words.html

Hussain, D, [online], 'Notes on Statutory Interpretations', 2009, [accessed 5 January 2015]. Available at http://home.loxfordlaw.co.uk/unit1/notes-on-statutory-interpretations.

Kreling, P, [online], 'In Praise of Common Law and Equity and Against Statute Law', 1991, London: Libertarian Alliance, [accessed 30 December 2014]. Available at: http://www.libertarian.co.uk/lapubs/legan/legan013.pdf.

Kuruk, P, [online], 'Customary Water Laws and Practices: Nigeria' (n.d.), pp 7–8, [accessed 30 December 2014]. Available at: http://www.fao.org/fileadmin/templates/legal/docs/CaseStudy_Nigeria.pdf.

Lager, H, [online], 'The "Amazon Tax" Upheld in New York, Enabling State Taxation of Web Sales: *Amazon.com LLC v New York State Dept. of Taxation and Finance*', 8 April 2009, [accessed 17 January 2015]. Available at: http://www.lawupdates.com/commentary/the_amazon_tax_upheld_in_new_york_enabling_state_taxation_of_web_sales/.

Law.com Dictionary, [online], 'Contract', n.d., [accessed 25 January 2015]. Available at: http://dictionary.law.com/Default.aspx?selected=337.

Legal Information Institute, [online], 'Equity: An Overview', [accessed 30 December 2014]. Available at: http://www.law.cornell.edu/topics/equity.html.

Lunder, E and Pettit, C, [online], '"Amazon Laws" and Taxation of Internet Sales', *CRS Report* R42629, November 2014. Available at: https://www.fas.org/sgp/crs/misc/R42629.pdf.

National Electronic Commerce Policy Committee, 'Preparing Trinidad and Tobago for Doing Business in the Internetworked Global Digital Economy', 1999, Port of Spain: Government of Trinidad and Tobago, [accessed 9 January 2015]. Available at: http://unpan1.un.org/intradoc/groups/public/documents/caricad/unpan008535.pdf.

Patil, VH, [online], 'General Rules of Statutory Interpretation', *I.T. Review*, July 2001, p 5 [accessed 7 December 2009] [link no longer active; copy available with the author].

Rich, T, [online], 'Halakhah: Jewish Law', [accessed 30 December 2014]. Available at: http://www.jewfaq.org/halakhah.htm.

Streamlined Sales Tax Governing Board, Inc, [online], 'About Us: Frequently Asked Questions', 2011, [accessed 17 January 2015]. Available at: http://www.streamlinedsalestax.org/.

UK Office for National Statistics, [online], 'E-Commerce and ICT Activity 2013', 28 November 2014, [accessed 9 January 2015]. Available at: http://www.ons.gov.uk/.

United Nations Commission on International Trade Law, [online], 'Status: United Nations Convention on the Use of Electronic Communications in International Contracts (New York, 2005)', 2015, [accessed 9 January 2015]. Available at: http://www.uncitral.org/uncitral/en/uncitral_texts/electronic_commerce/2005Convention_status.html.

US Census Bureau, Department of Commerce, 'Quarterly Retail E-Commerce Sales, 3rd Quarter 2014', 9 January 2015. Available at: http://www.census.gov/.

US Legal Definitions, [online] '*Forum Non Conveniens* Law and Legal Definition', 2015, [accessed 17 January 2015]. Available at: http://definitions.uslegal.com/f/forum-non-conveniens/.

Other Resources

Djieufack, R, 'The Nature of Agency Relationship under the OHADA Uniform Act on General Commercial Law and Common Law: A Comparative Study', 2004, Post-Graduate Thesis, University of Dschang.

United Nations General Assembly Resolution, A/RES/60/21, 9 December 2005.

INDEX

acceptance 73–85; conduct, by 83–5; definition 73–5; email, by 78–9; facsimile transmission, by 79–80; post, by 75–6; telegram, by 75–6; telephone, by 80–3; telex, by 76–8; video conference, by 80–3
agency 374–416; agent's rights against principal 403–16; commission 404; duties of agent to principal 396–402 *see also* duties of agent to principal; nature of 374–5; principal's duties to agent 403–16; ratification of acts done without authority 394–6; fiduciary duties 396–7; negligence of principal / breach of fiduciary duty of principal 397–402; extent 378–81; general agencies 378–9; specific agency 380–1
authority of agent 376–89; apparent authority 382–7; express actual authority 376–81; implied actual authority 381–2; agency of necessity 389–93; ostensible authority 382–7; usual 387–9

Bingham, Lord 45
books of authority 19–20
breach of contract 224–36; damages 224–9; remedies 224–36

capacity to contract 149–60; drunkards 156–8; legal ability 149–60; mentally ill 158–60; minors 150–6; taking advantage 160–74; unconscionability 164–7; undue influence 160–4; unequal bargaining power 167–9; duress 169–74
case law 12–19; advantages 19; disadvantages 19
Certainty of contract 89
China: legal reform 6
civil codes 4
civil law 4
codifying legislation 11
colonialism 5
common law 5
common law jurisdictions: subjects of law 9–20; books of authority; case law; constitution, equity, legislation, statutory interpretation
conditions 140–3
consideration 94–111; bargain 96–7; compromise 99–104; duty under contract in favour of third party 110–11;duty under law 109–10; forbearance 99–104; meaning 94–5; nature of 97–8; past 104–7; performance of duty as, performance of duty under existing contract 107–9
constitutions 9
contract 36–148; acceptance *see* acceptance; battle of the forms 93–4; breach *see* breach of contract; capacity *see* capacity; certainty of contract 89–91; concurrent liability in tort 345–7; conditions *see* conditions; counter offers 91–2; consideration 94–111; duress 169–74; exemption clauses 145–8; factual results 36–7; frustration *see* frustration; illegal *see* illegal contracts; intention to create legal relations 85–9; interpretation 40–5; invitation to treat 49–70; meaning of contract 36; misrepresentation *see* misrepresentation; mistake *see* mistake; privity 221–4 *see also* breach of contract; offer 45–9; contrary to public policy *see* public policy; restraint of trade *see* restraint of trade; tenders 52–70; terms 111–48 *see also* terms of contract; terms and conditions 37–40; to commit crime 220–1; unconscionability 164–7; undue influence 160–4; unequal bargaining power 167–9; unilateral 70–3; warranties *see* warranties
contractual interpretation 40–5; context 40–5
contributory negligence 264–6
corporate criminal liability 357–68; 'directing mind' principle 360–8; individual liability: breach of statutory duty 357–60; vicarious liability 303–9, 357, *actus reus*, *mens rea*, liability of corporations; sentencing corporations 370–3
counter-offers 91–4; battle of the forms 92–4;
Court of Appeal 17
courts; hierarchy 16–18
creative accounting 348
crime: contract to commit 220–1; meaning 348–9
criminal law: commercial activities, and 348; intention 350–1; *actus reus* 349–50; defences; illegal contracts 207–21; *mens rea* 350–4; recklessness 351–3; negligence 353–4; sentencing corporations 370–3; breach of statutory duty: individual liability 357–60
criminal liability: acts in pursuance of commercial activities 369–70
criminal offence: meaning 349
custom: certainty 127–8; continuity 128; immemorial 126–7; reasonable 127
customary law 8

damages for breach of contract 224–9, 248–64; economic loss 251–6; injured feelings

256–7; liquidated 232–4; mitigating losses 226–9; nervous shock 257–64; remoteness 225–6, 248–51; specific performance 234–6; underlying principle 224–5; *quantum meruit* principle; penalty clauses;
deceit 330–5
defences 354–7; criminal liability and; mistake as to facts 354–6; ignorance of law 356–7
Dicey, AV 2
digital marketplace 418–29
Director of Public Prosecutions 33–4

e-commerce: taxation, and 442–6
E-SIGN Act 418–19
electronic signature 419
employers' liability 293–303; safe place and system of work 300–2; *volenti non fit injuria* 302–3
equity 20
executive: role of 33–4
express terms 113–15

fraud 330–5
fraudulent misrepresentation , see also deceit
frustration 201–7; contemporary formulation 202–7; early developments 201–2; self-induced

global commerce: internet, and 418

High Court 17
House of Lords 16

immemorial custom 125–9
implied terms 118–40; business efficacy 131–7; combined business efficacy/officious bystander test; custom and usage 124–8; law, implied by 137–40; legal incidents of particular class or kind of contract 129–31; officious bystander 134–7
injured feelings 256–7
injurious falsehood 334–6 see also malicious falsehood
intention to create legal relations 85–9; commercial agreements 85–7; domestic agreements 87–9; letter of intent 85; subject to contract 85
internet 417–46; evolution 417–18; jurisdiction 429–35; use 417–18; browse-wrap agreements 425–9; choice of law 439–42; click-wrap agreements 422–5; shrink-wrap agreements 419–22; jurisdiction: internet contracts 429–35; minimum contacts test 429; *forum non conveniens* 435; forum selection 435–9; venue 435–9; taxation: e-commerce, and 442–6; software licence 419–22
invitation to treat 49–70; advertisements 50–2; tenders *see* tenders
Islamic law, *Shari'ah* 6–7

Judaic law, *Halakhah*, 7–8
judges: stated role of 2
Judicial and Legal Services Commission 34–5
Judicial Committee of Privy Council 18
judicial independence 34–5

legal traditions or families 3–9; see civil law, common law, socialist law, religious law, customary law, mixed legal system
legislation 10–11; drafting 10–11; legislative process 10; parameters 10–11; types 11
Locke, John 33

malicious falsehood 334–6 see also injurious falsehood
mere puffs
misrepresentation 187–201; ambiguity 193–5; damage 198; false statement of fact 187; inducement 195–7; knowledge of representee 198–201; materiality 192–3; opinion not honestly held 188; reliance 197–8; statement of opinion 188
mistake 174–87; mutual 176–83; unilateral 183–7
mixed legal system 8–9
Montesquieu 33

necessaries: meaning 150–3
negligence 238–78, criminal 353–4
negligent misstatement/misrepresentation 278–85; liability 282, 284–5; negligent action 284; reasonable reliance 284; special relationship 283; untrue, inaccurate or misleading representation 283–4; *Hedley Byrne* principle
nervous shock 257–64
nuisance 310–12; sensible material damage 311; substantial interference with enjoyment of land 311; Rule in *Rylands v Fletcher see* Rule in *Rylands v Fletcher*

obiter dictum 15–16
occupiers' liability 286–94; unusual danger 288–9
offer 45–9

parliamentary sovereignty 33
passing off 317–22; different products 319–23; discerning consumer 324–5; locality-based

action 323–4; similar products/business 317–19
Patel, VH 21
penalty clauses 232–4
precedent 12–14
Private Acts 11
privity of contract 221–4; reform 223–4
product liability 267–78; defective products 268–72; intermediate examination 273–5; sale 272–3; negligence 275–8; range of defendants 268; ultimate customer 272
Public Acts 11
public policy 218–20, contracts contrary to

quantum meruit 229–32

ratio decidendi 14–15
Raz, Joseph 3
religious law 6–8
restraint of trade 208–18; exceeding product area of business 211–12; excessive geographical width 215–16; protecting an excessively wide range of products or services 213–15; restraining use of specialist skills 212–13; unreasonable period of restraint 216–18
rule of law 1–3
Rule in Rylands v Fletcher 312–17; non-natural use of land 313–16

Sale of Goods Act
separation of powers 33–5
Sinha, SP: law, on 1
socialist law 5–6
stare decisis 12–14
statutory interpretation 20–32; golden rule 23–6; literal rule 21–3; mischief rule 26–30; narrow meaning 23–4; purposive approach 30–2; wide meaning 24–6

Talmud 7
tenders 52–70; bid shopping 64–7; contract A and contract B 57–60; duty to act fairly 62–4; the privilege clause 60–2; request for proposals 55–7; substantial compliance 67–70
terms of contract 111–48; express 113–15; implied 118–40 *see also* implied terms; incorporation by express reference 116–18; exemption clauses 145–8; warranties; conditions
Thompson, EP 3
tort 237–347; causation 243–8; concurrent liability in contract and 345–7; damages 248–64 (remoteness; foreseeability of damage; recovery of pure economic losses); definition 237–8; duty, concept of 238–40; neighbour principle 238–9; standard of care 240–3;
Trinidad and Tobago: constitution 9; parliament 10

Unfair Contract Terms Act 145
unilateral contracts 70–3
unlawful interference with trade 337–8; conspiracy 325–30; inducement to breach of contract 338–45
United Kingdom: constitutional and administrative law 2
usul al-fiqh 6

volenti non fit injuria 302–3

warranties 143–5
white collar crime 143–5

For Product Safety Concerns and Information please contact our EU representative GPSR@taylorandfrancis.com
Taylor & Francis Verlag GmbH, Kaufingerstraße 24, 80331 München, Germany

www.ingramcontent.com/pod-product-compliance
Ingram Content Group UK Ltd.
Pitfield, Milton Keynes, MK11 3LW, UK
UKHW022006180926
475701UK00003B/222

* 9 7 8 1 1 3 8 0 2 4 2 6 7 *